LANGOSH AND PEPPI : FUGITIVE DAYS

VERONICA POST

FIRST EDITION

PRINTED AND BOUND IN CANADA BY THE
PROLIFIC GROUP

LIBRARY AND ARCHIVES CANADA CATALOGUING
IN PUBLICATION

TITLE : LANGOSH AND PEPPI : FUGITIVE DAYS / BY
VERONICA POST
OTHER TITLES : LANGOSH AND PEPPI
NAMES : POST, VERONICA , 1984 - AUTHOR
IDENTIFIERS : CANADIANA 20190223537
ISBN 9781772620443 (SOFTCOVER)
SUBJECTS : LCGFT : GRAPHIC NOVELS
CLASSIFICATION : LCC PN6733.P67 L36
2020 | DDC 741.5/971 - dc23

CONUNDRUM PRESS
WOLFVILLE , N.S , CANADA
WWW.CONUNDRUMPRESS.COM

DISTRIBUTED IN CANADA BY LITDISTCO
DISTRIBUTED IN US BY CONSORTIUM
DISTRIBUTED IN UK AND INTERNATIONAL BY INGRAM

CONUNDRUM PRESS ACKNOWLEDGES THE
FINANCIAL SUPPORT OF THE GOVERNMENT
OF CANADA THROUGH THE DEPARTMENT
OF CANADIAN HERITAGE , THE CANADA COUNCIL
FOR THE ARTS , THE PROVENCE OF NOVA SCOTIA
THROUGH THE CREATIVE INDUSTRIES FUND
AND ARTS NS

NOVA SCOTIA

Arts NOVA SCOTIA NOUVELLE-ÉCOSSE

Canada Council for the Arts
Conseil des Arts du Canada

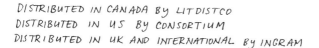

THIS BOOK IS DEDICATED TO

BOBBY
AND
ANNA

THIS BOOK IS A FICTIONALIZED MASH-UP OF MY DIARIES FROM 2012-2015 AND THUS IS NOT MEANT AS AN ACCURATE HISTORICAL ACCOUNT OF THINGS EXACTLY AS THEY WERE, OR ARE.

THE CHARACTERS AND THE HUNGARIAN VILLAGE OF "FÁK" ARE FICTIONAL, BUT ALL THE EVENTS ARE BASED ON REAL LIFE EXPERIENCES.

I HOPE YOU ENJOY THIS BOOK.

CHAPTER ONE

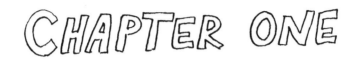

BUDAPEST, 2015

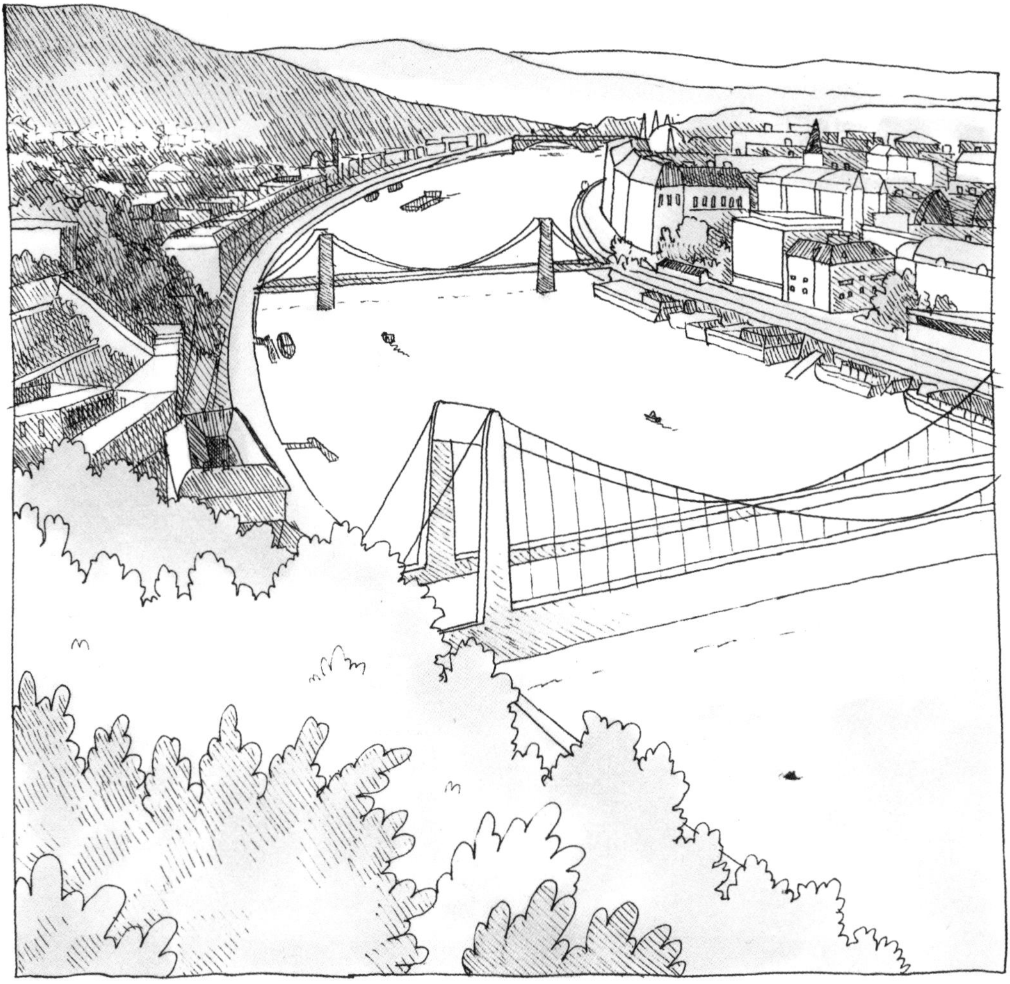

THIS IS THE STORY OF HOW I LIVED AS A FUGITIVE FROM JUSTICE. I FLED JAILTIME IN CANADA FOR A STRING OF PETTY OFFENCES SIX YEARS AGO AND ENDED UP IN HUNGARY. IT'S EASY TO LIVE CHEAP AND KEEP MY PASSPORT STAMPED. I BOP DOWN TO THE SERBIAN BORDER EVERY 3 MONTHS AND THEY DON'T EVEN BAT AN EYE. CANADIAN PASSPORT? AUTOMATIC STAMP. BUDAPEST WAS NEVER MY PLAN, BUT ONCE I GOT HERE, I HAD A "FEELING"...

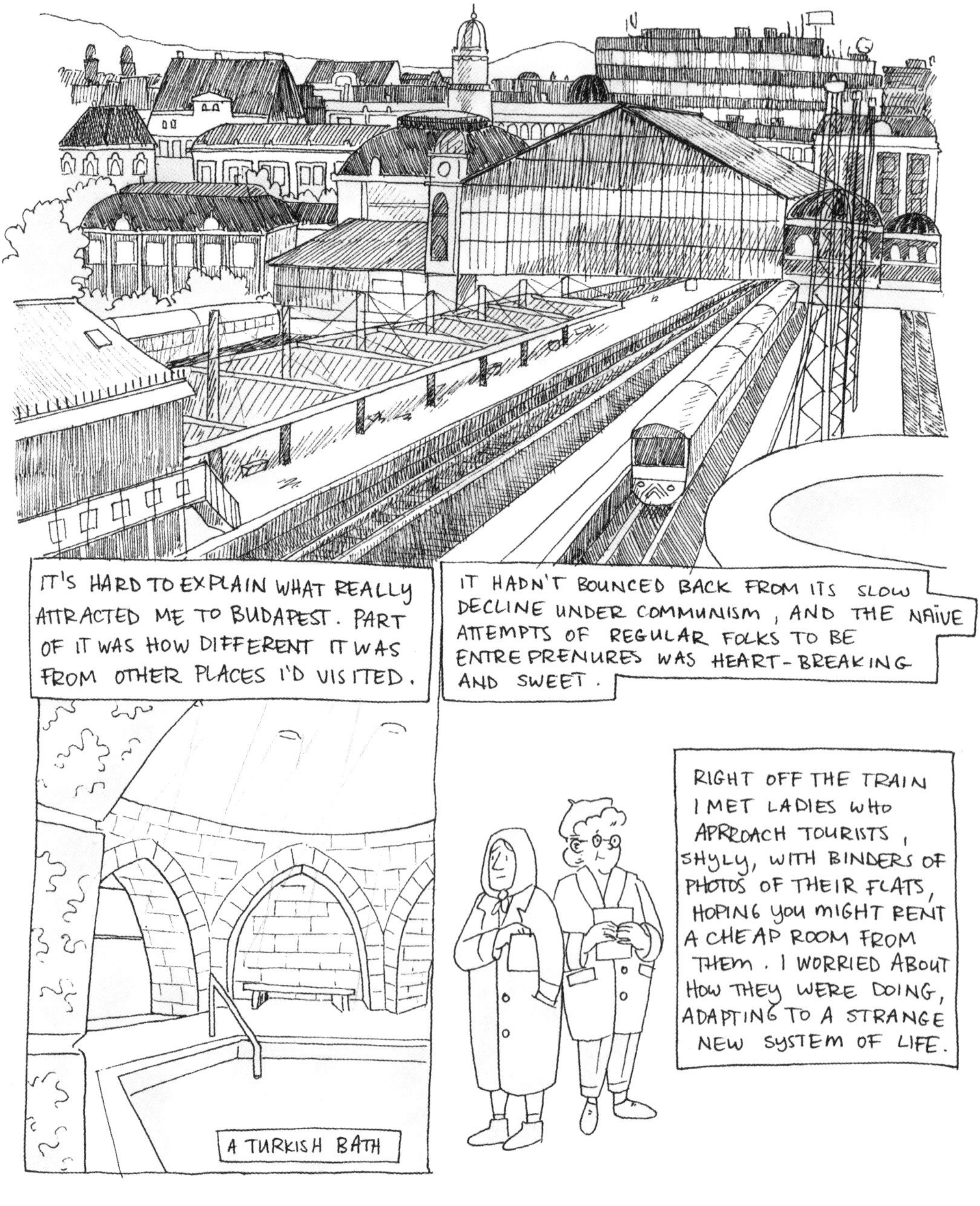
IT'S HARD TO EXPLAIN WHAT REALLY ATTRACTED ME TO BUDAPEST. PART OF IT WAS HOW DIFFERENT IT WAS FROM OTHER PLACES I'D VISITED.
IT HADN'T BOUNCED BACK FROM ITS SLOW DECLINE UNDER COMMUNISM, AND THE NAÏVE ATTEMPTS OF REGULAR FOLKS TO BE ENTREPRENURES WAS HEART-BREAKING AND SWEET.
A TURKISH BATH
RIGHT OFF THE TRAIN I MET LADIES WHO APPROACH TOURISTS, SHYLY, WITH BINDERS OF PHOTOS OF THEIR FLATS, HOPING YOU MIGHT RENT A CHEAP ROOM FROM THEM. I WORRIED ABOUT HOW THEY WERE DOING, ADAPTING TO A STRANGE NEW SYSTEM OF LIFE.

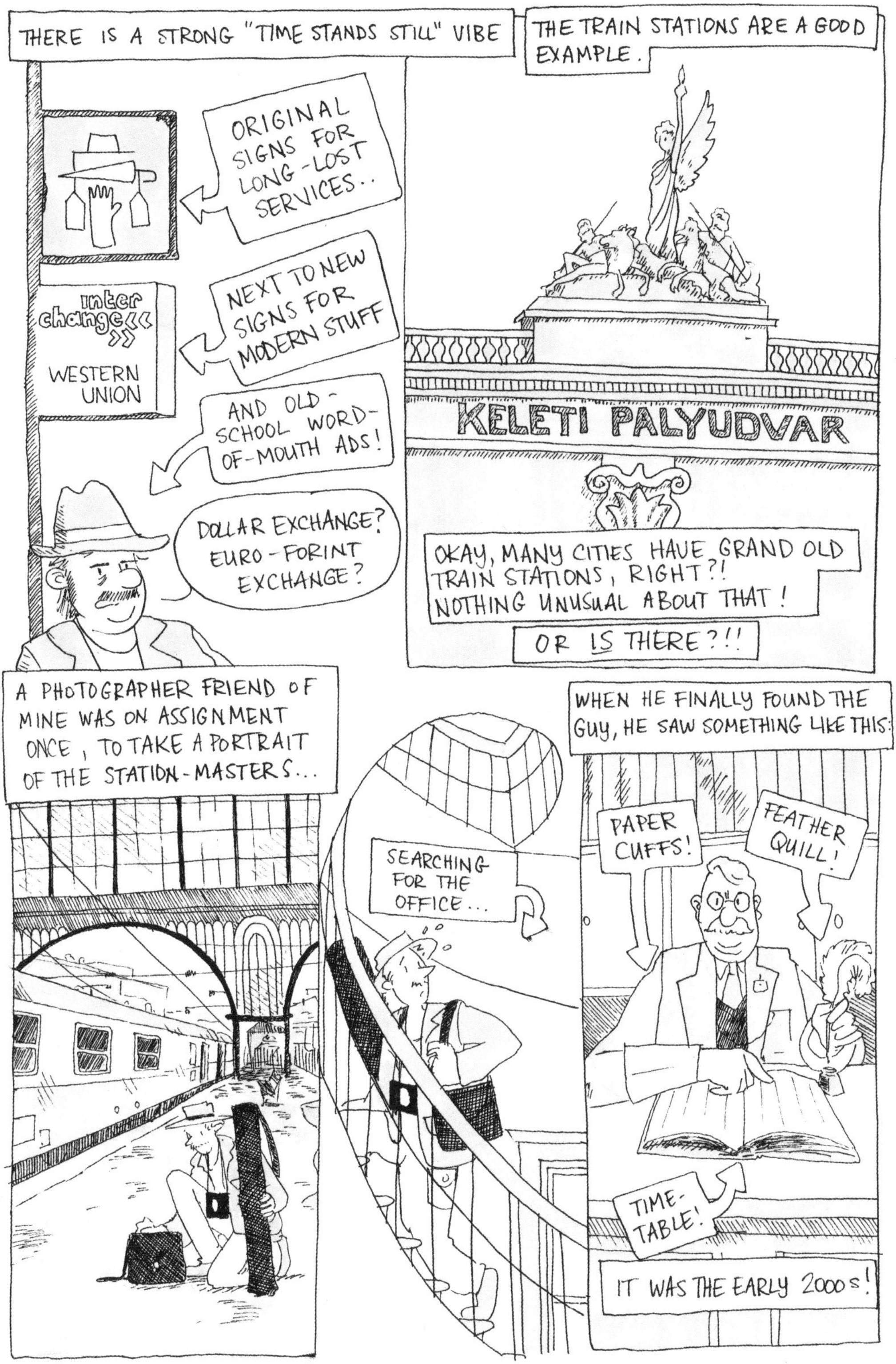
THERE IS A STRONG "TIME STANDS STILL" VIBE
ORIGINAL SIGNS FOR LONG-LOST SERVICES...
inter change
WESTERN UNION
NEXT TO NEW SIGNS FOR MODERN STUFF
AND OLD-SCHOOL WORD-OF-MOUTH ADS!
DOLLAR EXCHANGE? EURO-FORINT EXCHANGE?
THE TRAIN STATIONS ARE A GOOD EXAMPLE.
KELETI PALYUDVAR
OKAY, MANY CITIES HAVE GRAND OLD TRAIN STATIONS, RIGHT?! NOTHING UNUSUAL ABOUT THAT!
OR IS THERE?!!
A PHOTOGRAPHER FRIEND OF MINE WAS ON ASSIGNMENT ONCE, TO TAKE A PORTRAIT OF THE STATION-MASTERS...
SEARCHING FOR THE OFFICE...
WHEN HE FINALLY FOUND THE GUY, HE SAW SOMETHING LIKE THIS:
PAPER CUFFS!
FEATHER QUILL!
TIME-TABLE!
IT WAS THE EARLY 2000s!

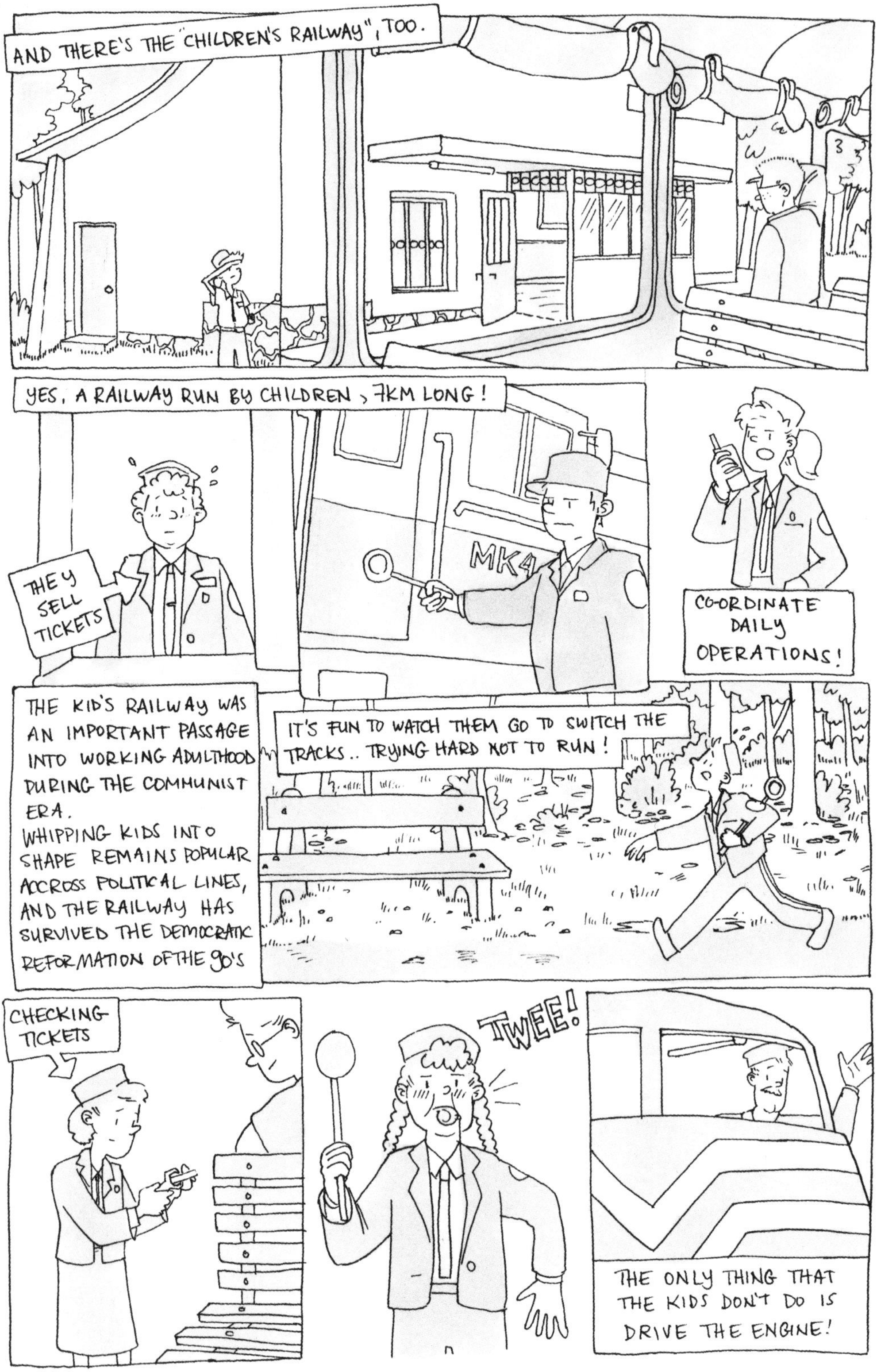
AND THERE'S THE "CHILDREN'S RAILWAY", TOO.
YES, A RAILWAY RUN BY CHILDREN, 7KM LONG!
THEY SELL TICKETS
MK4
CO-ORDINATE DAILY OPERATIONS!
THE KID'S RAILWAY WAS AN IMPORTANT PASSAGE INTO WORKING ADULTHOOD DURING THE COMMUNIST ERA.
WHIPPING KIDS INTO SHAPE REMAINS POPULAR ACCROSS POLITICAL LINES, AND THE RAILWAY HAS SURVIVED THE DEMOCRATIC REFORMATION OF THE 90'S
IT'S FUN TO WATCH THEM GO TO SWITCH THE TRACKS.. TRYING HARD NOT TO RUN!
CHECKING TICKETS
TWEE!
THE ONLY THING THAT THE KIDS DON'T DO IS DRIVE THE ENGINE!

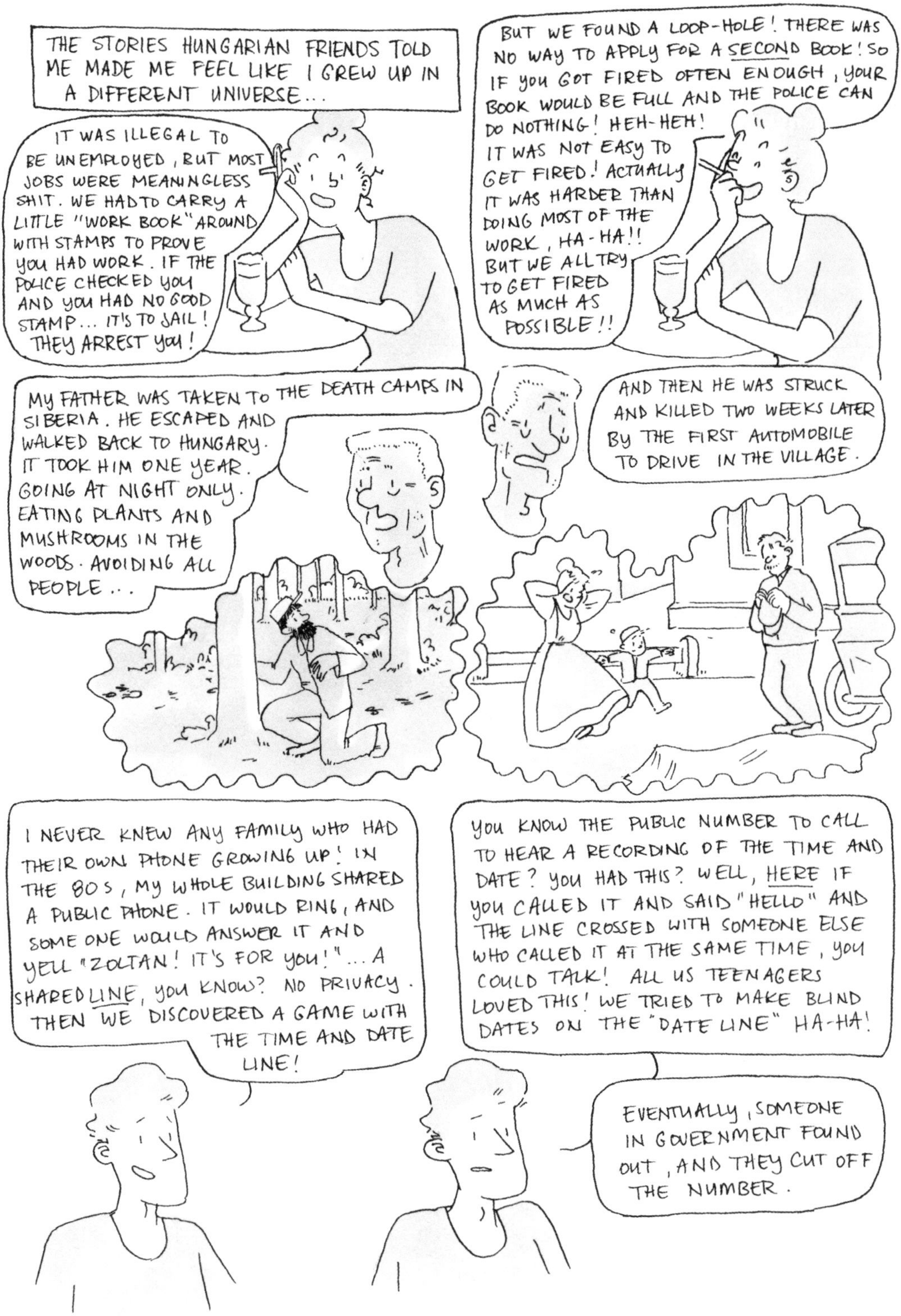

THE STORIES HUNGARIAN FRIENDS TOLD ME MADE ME FEEL LIKE I GREW UP IN A DIFFERENT UNIVERSE...
IT WAS ILLEGAL TO BE UNEMPLOYED, BUT MOST JOBS WERE MEANINGLESS SHIT. WE HAD TO CARRY A LITTLE "WORK BOOK" AROUND WITH STAMPS TO PROVE YOU HAD WORK. IF THE POLICE CHECKED YOU AND YOU HAD NO GOOD STAMP... IT'S TO JAIL! THEY ARREST YOU!
BUT WE FOUND A LOOP-HOLE! THERE WAS NO WAY TO APPLY FOR A SECOND BOOK! SO IF YOU GOT FIRED OFTEN ENOUGH, YOUR BOOK WOULD BE FULL AND THE POLICE CAN DO NOTHING! HEH-HEH!
IT WAS NOT EASY TO GET FIRED! ACTUALLY IT WAS HARDER THAN DOING MOST OF THE WORK, HA-HA!! BUT WE ALL TRY TO GET FIRED AS MUCH AS POSSIBLE!!
MY FATHER WAS TAKEN TO THE DEATH CAMPS IN SIBERIA. HE ESCAPED AND WALKED BACK TO HUNGARY. IT TOOK HIM ONE YEAR. GOING AT NIGHT ONLY. EATING PLANTS AND MUSHROOMS IN THE WOODS. AVOIDING ALL PEOPLE...
AND THEN HE WAS STRUCK AND KILLED TWO WEEKS LATER BY THE FIRST AUTOMOBILE TO DRIVE IN THE VILLAGE.
I NEVER KNEW ANY FAMILY WHO HAD THEIR OWN PHONE GROWING UP! IN THE 80S, MY WHOLE BUILDING SHARED A PUBLIC PHONE. IT WOULD RING, AND SOME ONE WOULD ANSWER IT AND YELL "ZOLTAN! IT'S FOR YOU!"... A SHARED LINE, YOU KNOW? NO PRIVACY. THEN WE DISCOVERED A GAME WITH THE TIME AND DATE LINE!
YOU KNOW THE PUBLIC NUMBER TO CALL TO HEAR A RECORDING OF THE TIME AND DATE? YOU HAD THIS? WELL, HERE IF YOU CALLED IT AND SAID "HELLO" AND THE LINE CROSSED WITH SOMEONE ELSE WHO CALLED IT AT THE SAME TIME, YOU COULD TALK! ALL US TEENAGERS LOVED THIS! WE TRIED TO MAKE BLIND DATES ON THE "DATE LINE" HA-HA!
EVENTUALLY, SOMEONE IN GOVERNMENT FOUND OUT, AND THEY CUT OFF THE NUMBER.

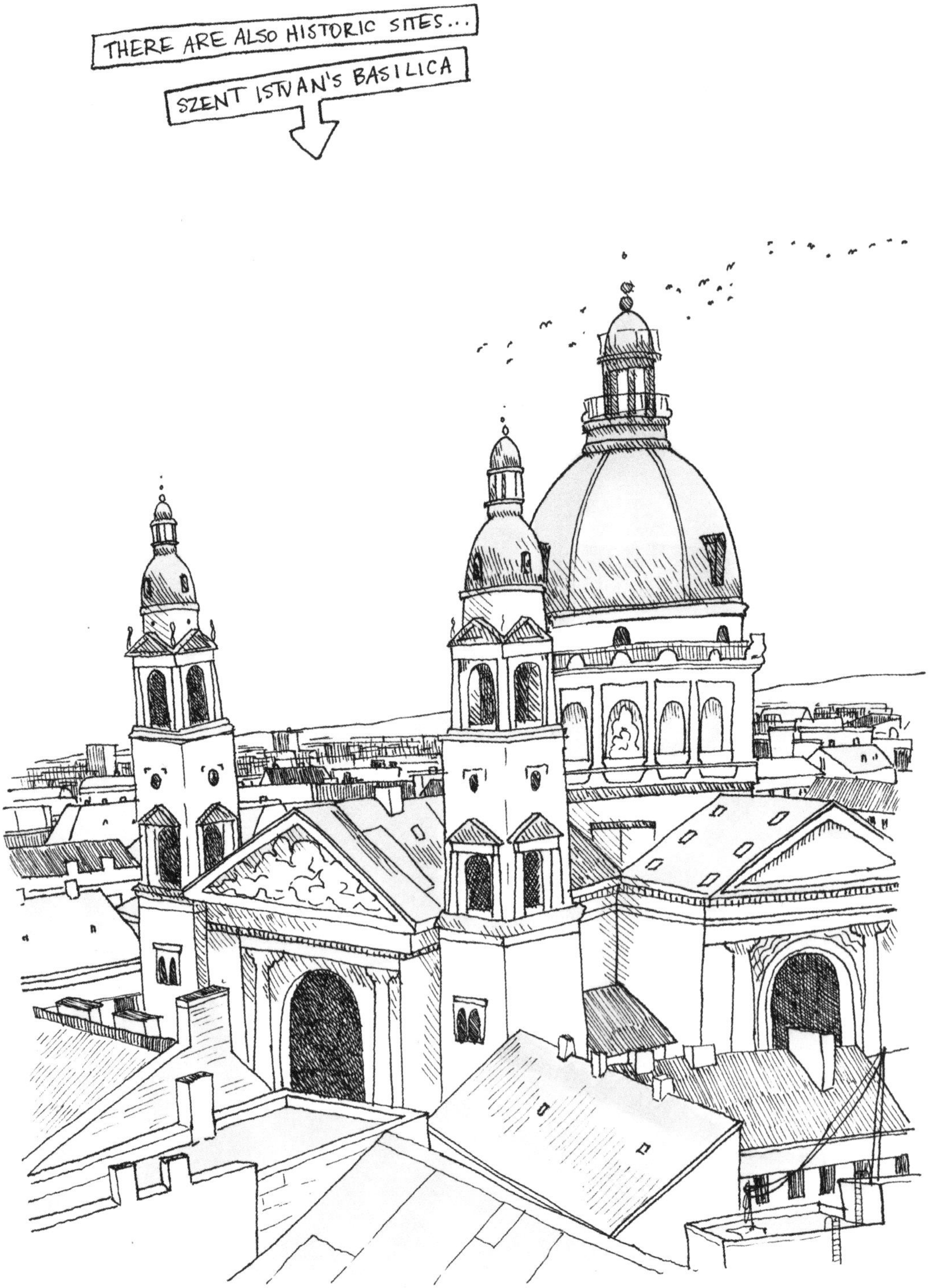
THERE ARE ALSO HISTORIC SITES...
SZENT ISTVAN'S BASILICA

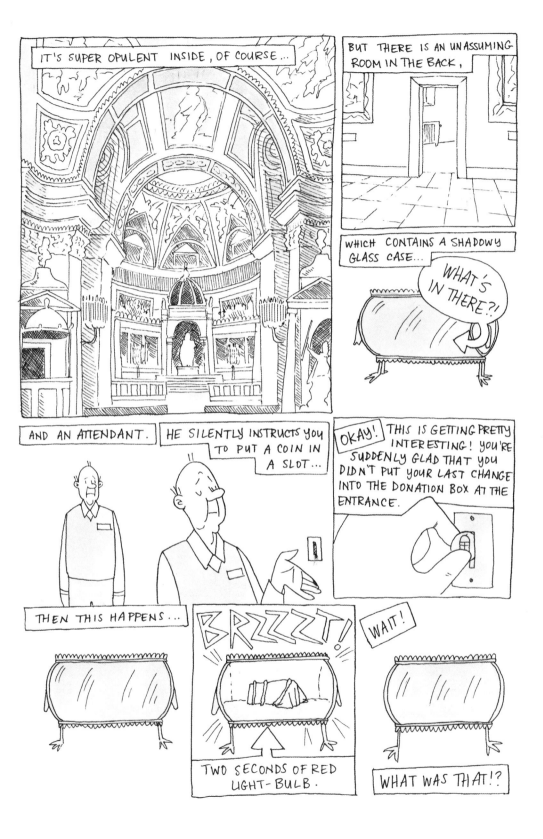

IT'S SUPER OPULENT INSIDE, OF COURSE...

BUT THERE IS AN UNASSUMING ROOM IN THE BACK,

WHICH CONTAINS A SHADOWY GLASS CASE...

WHAT'S IN THERE?!

AND AN ATTENDANT.

HE SILENTLY INSTRUCTS YOU TO PUT A COIN IN A SLOT...

OKAY! THIS IS GETTING PRETTY INTERESTING! YOU'RE SUDDENLY GLAD THAT YOU DIDN'T PUT YOUR LAST CHANGE INTO THE DONATION BOX AT THE ENTRANCE.

THEN THIS HAPPENS...

BRZZZT!

TWO SECONDS OF RED LIGHT-BULB.

WAIT!

WHAT WAS THAT!?

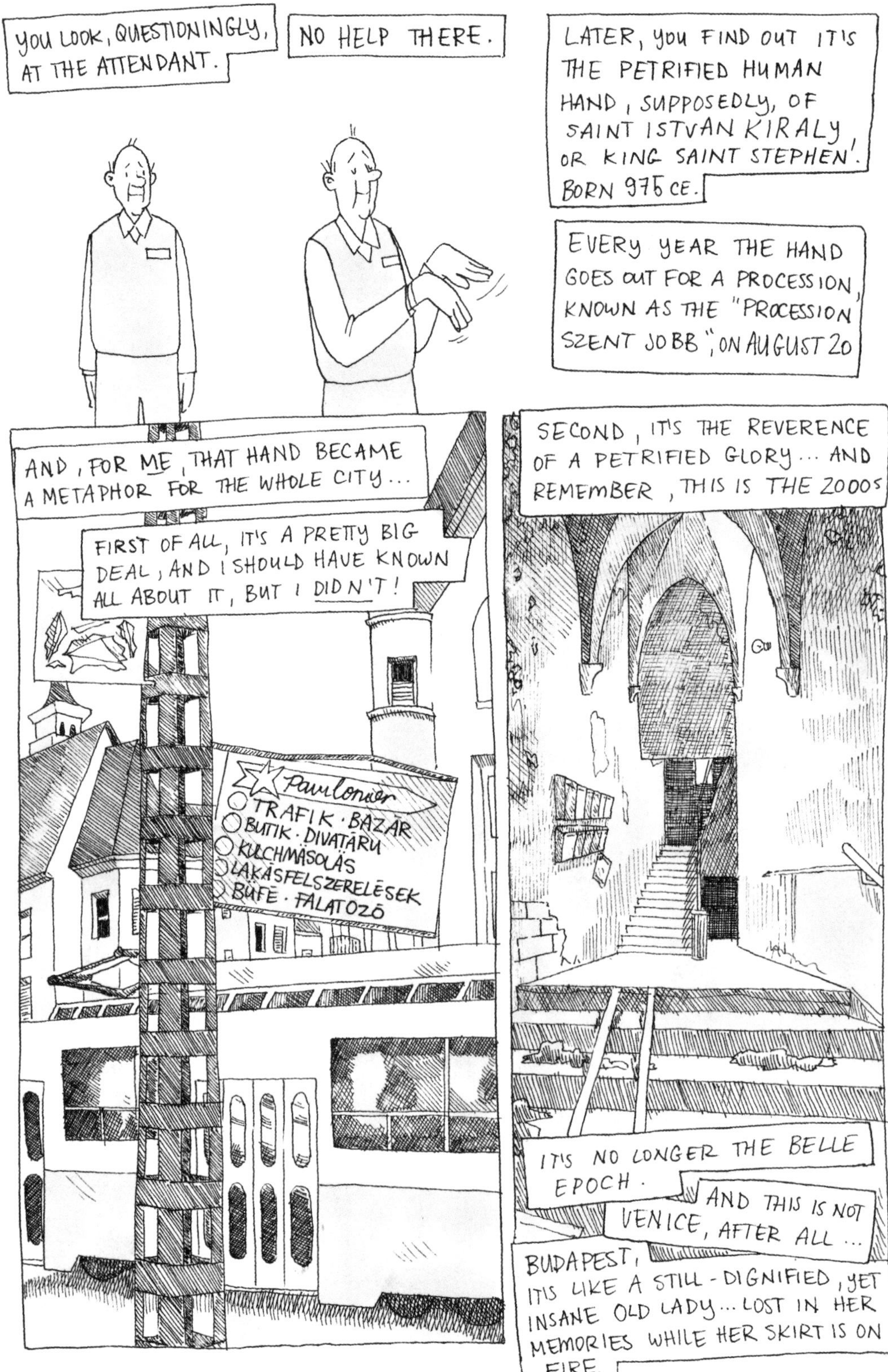
YOU LOOK, QUESTIONINGLY, AT THE ATTENDANT.
NO HELP THERE.
LATER, YOU FIND OUT IT'S THE PETRIFIED HUMAN HAND, SUPPOSEDLY, OF SAINT ISTVAN KIRALY, OR 'KING SAINT STEPHEN'. BORN 975 CE.
EVERY YEAR THE HAND GOES OUT FOR A PROCESSION, KNOWN AS THE "PROCESSION SZENT JOBB", ON AUGUST 20
AND, FOR ME, THAT HAND BECAME A METAPHOR FOR THE WHOLE CITY...
FIRST OF ALL, IT'S A PRETTY BIG DEAL, AND I SHOULD HAVE KNOWN ALL ABOUT IT, BUT I DIDN'T!
TRAFIK · BAZÁR
BUTIK · DIVATÁRU
KULCHMÁSOLÁS
LAKÁSFELSZERELÉSEK
BÜFÉ · FALATOZÓ
SECOND, IT'S THE REVERENCE OF A PETRIFIED GLORY... AND REMEMBER, THIS IS THE 2000s
IT'S NO LONGER THE BELLE EPOCH.
AND THIS IS NOT VENICE, AFTER ALL...
BUDAPEST, IT'S LIKE A STILL-DIGNIFIED, YET INSANE OLD LADY... LOST IN HER MEMORIES WHILE HER SKIRT IS ON FIRE.

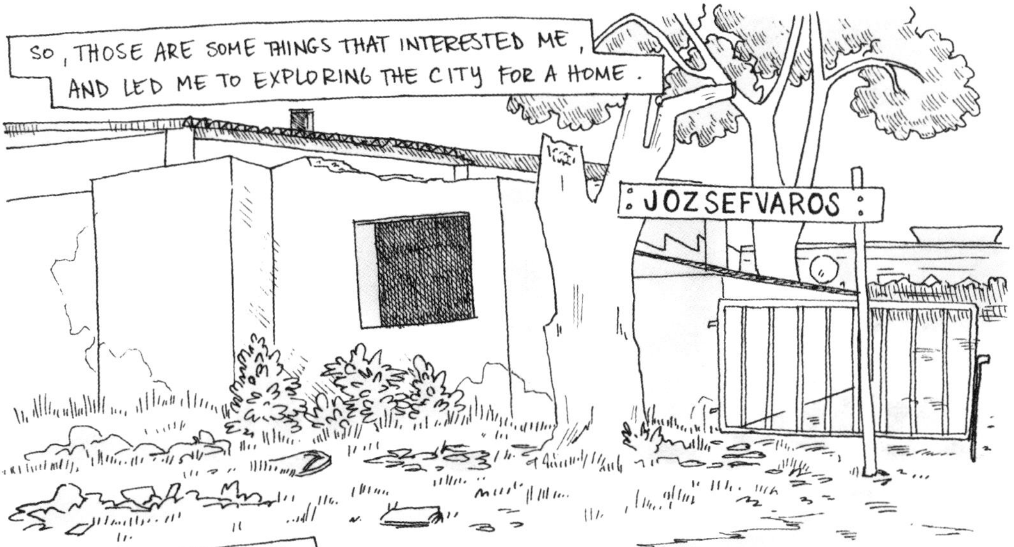
SO, THOSE ARE SOME THINGS THAT INTERESTED ME, AND LED ME TO EXPLORING THE CITY FOR A HOME.
JOZSEFVAROS

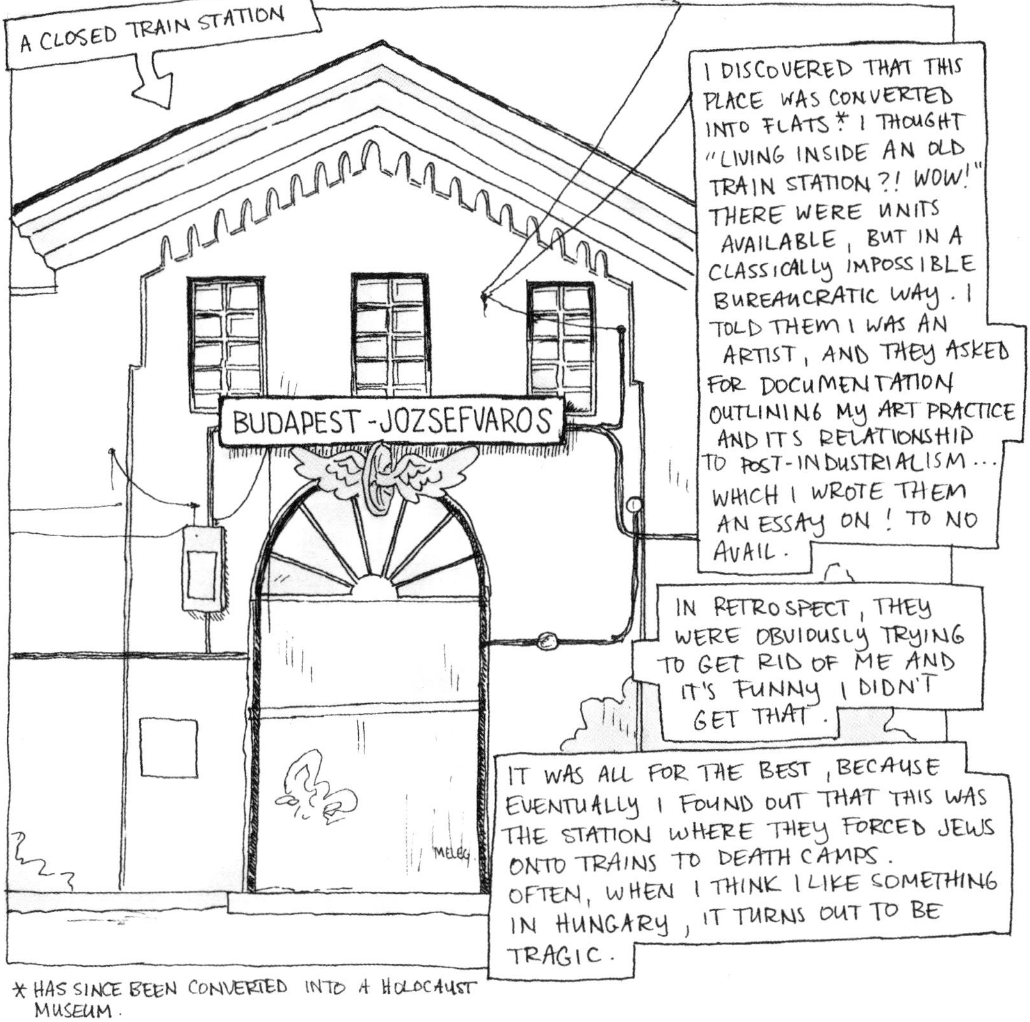
A CLOSED TRAIN STATION
BUDAPEST-JOZSEFVAROS
I DISCOVERED THAT THIS PLACE WAS CONVERTED INTO FLATS.* I THOUGHT "LIVING INSIDE AN OLD TRAIN STATION?! WOW!" THERE WERE UNITS AVAILABLE, BUT IN A CLASSICALLY IMPOSSIBLE BUREAUCRATIC WAY. I TOLD THEM I WAS AN ARTIST, AND THEY ASKED FOR DOCUMENTATION OUTLINING MY ART PRACTICE AND ITS RELATIONSHIP TO POST-INDUSTRIALISM... WHICH I WROTE THEM AN ESSAY ON! TO NO AVAIL.
IN RETROSPECT, THEY WERE OBVIOUSLY TRYING TO GET RID OF ME AND IT'S FUNNY I DIDN'T GET THAT.
IT WAS ALL FOR THE BEST, BECAUSE EVENTUALLY I FOUND OUT THAT THIS WAS THE STATION WHERE THEY FORCED JEWS ONTO TRAINS TO DEATH CAMPS. OFTEN, WHEN I THINK I LIKE SOMETHING IN HUNGARY, IT TURNS OUT TO BE TRAGIC.
MELEG

* HAS SINCE BEEN CONVERTED INTO A HOLOCAUST MUSEUM.

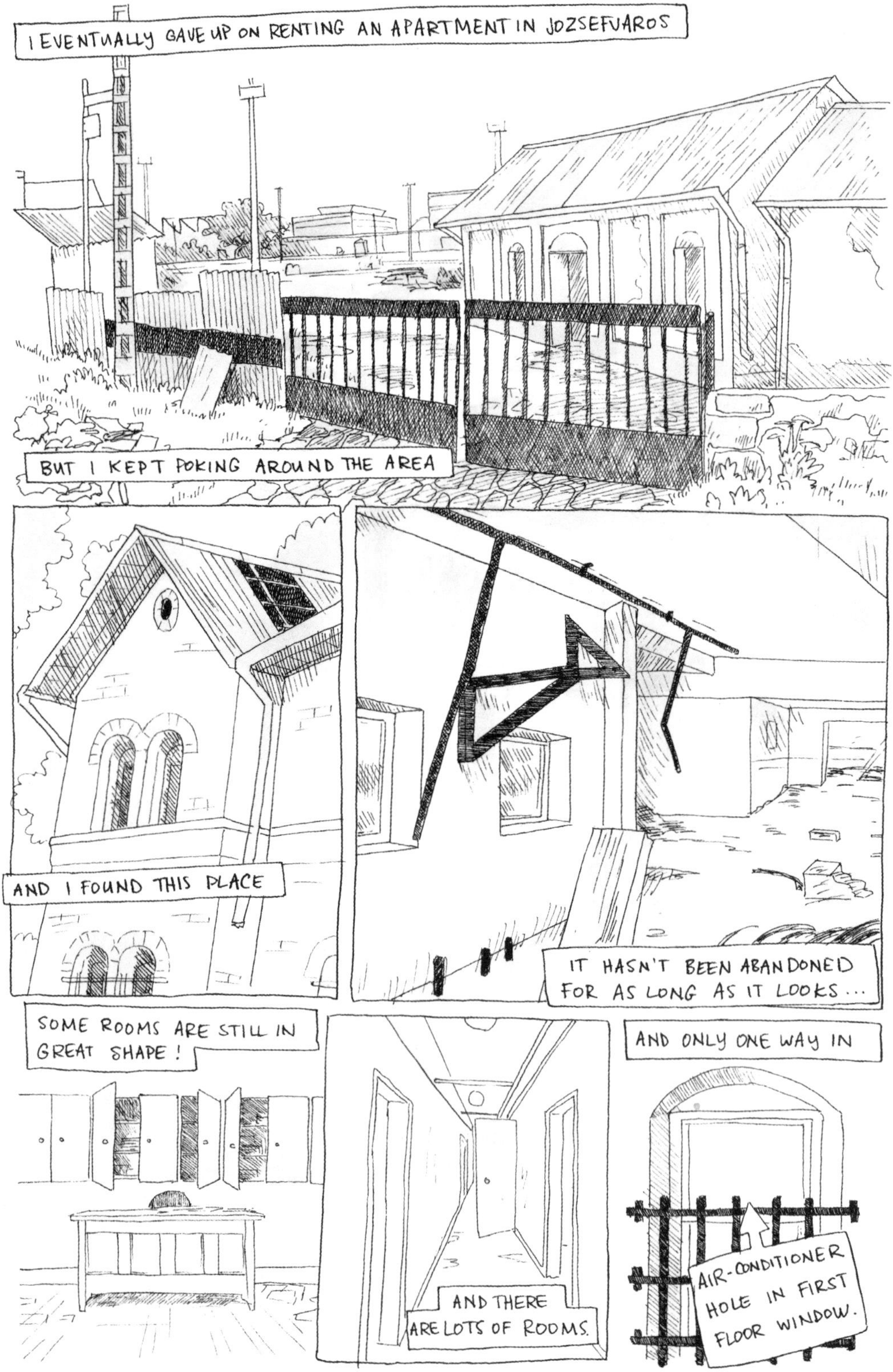
I EVENTUALLY GAVE UP ON RENTING AN APARTMENT IN JOZSEFVAROS
BUT I KEPT POKING AROUND THE AREA
AND I FOUND THIS PLACE
IT HASN'T BEEN ABANDONED FOR AS LONG AS IT LOOKS...
SOME ROOMS ARE STILL IN GREAT SHAPE!
AND THERE ARE LOTS OF ROOMS.
AND ONLY ONE WAY IN
AIR-CONDITIONER HOLE IN FIRST FLOOR WINDOW.

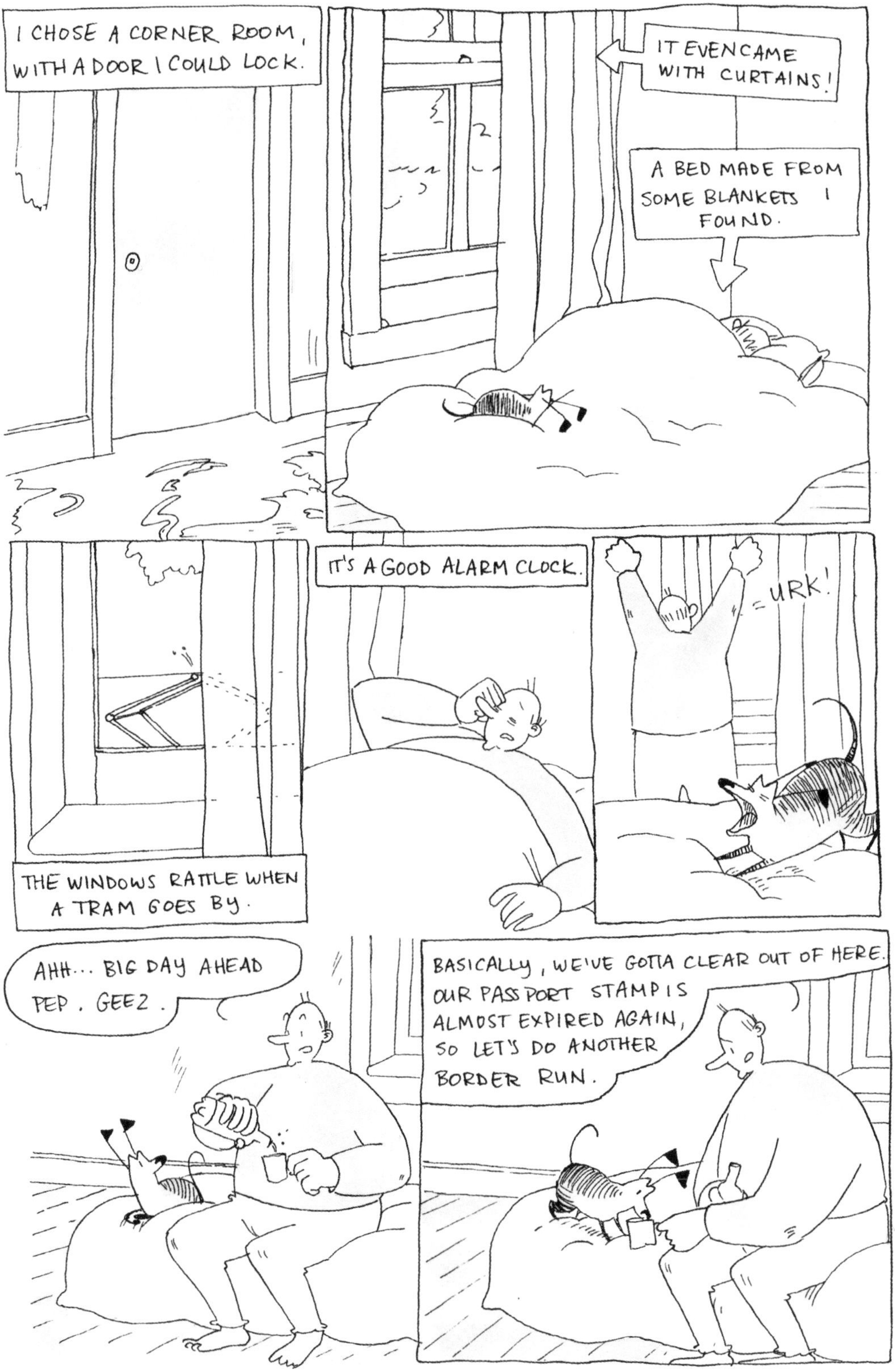
I CHOSE A CORNER ROOM, WITH A DOOR I COULD LOCK.
IT EVEN CAME WITH CURTAINS!
A BED MADE FROM SOME BLANKETS I FOUND.
THE WINDOWS RATTLE WHEN A TRAM GOES BY.
IT'S A GOOD ALARM CLOCK.
URK!
AHH... BIG DAY AHEAD PEP. GEEZ.
BASICALLY, WE'VE GOTTA CLEAR OUT OF HERE. OUR PASSPORT STAMP IS ALMOST EXPIRED AGAIN, SO LET'S DO ANOTHER BORDER RUN.

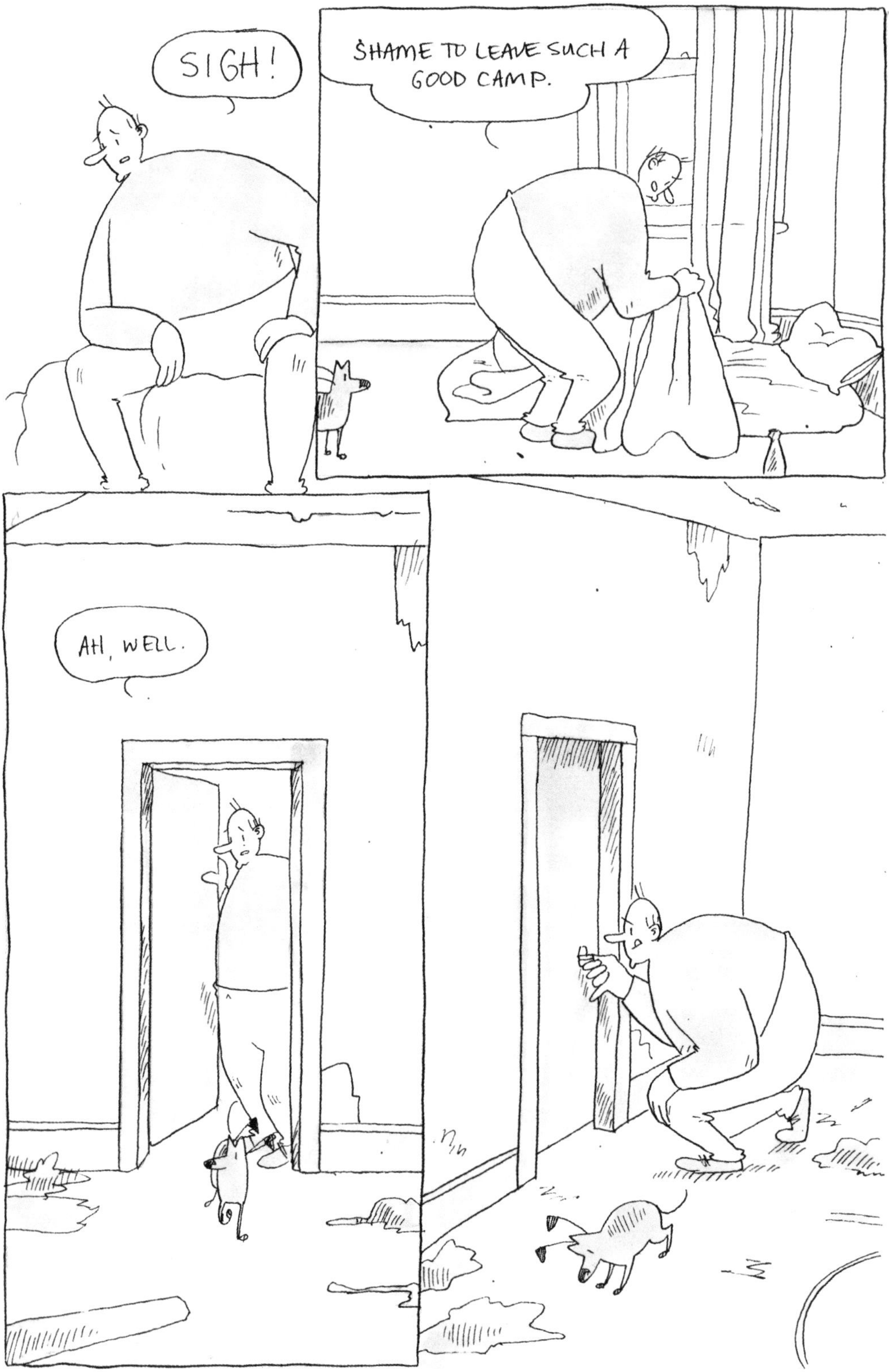
SIGH!
SHAME TO LEAVE SUCH A GOOD CAMP.
AH, WELL.

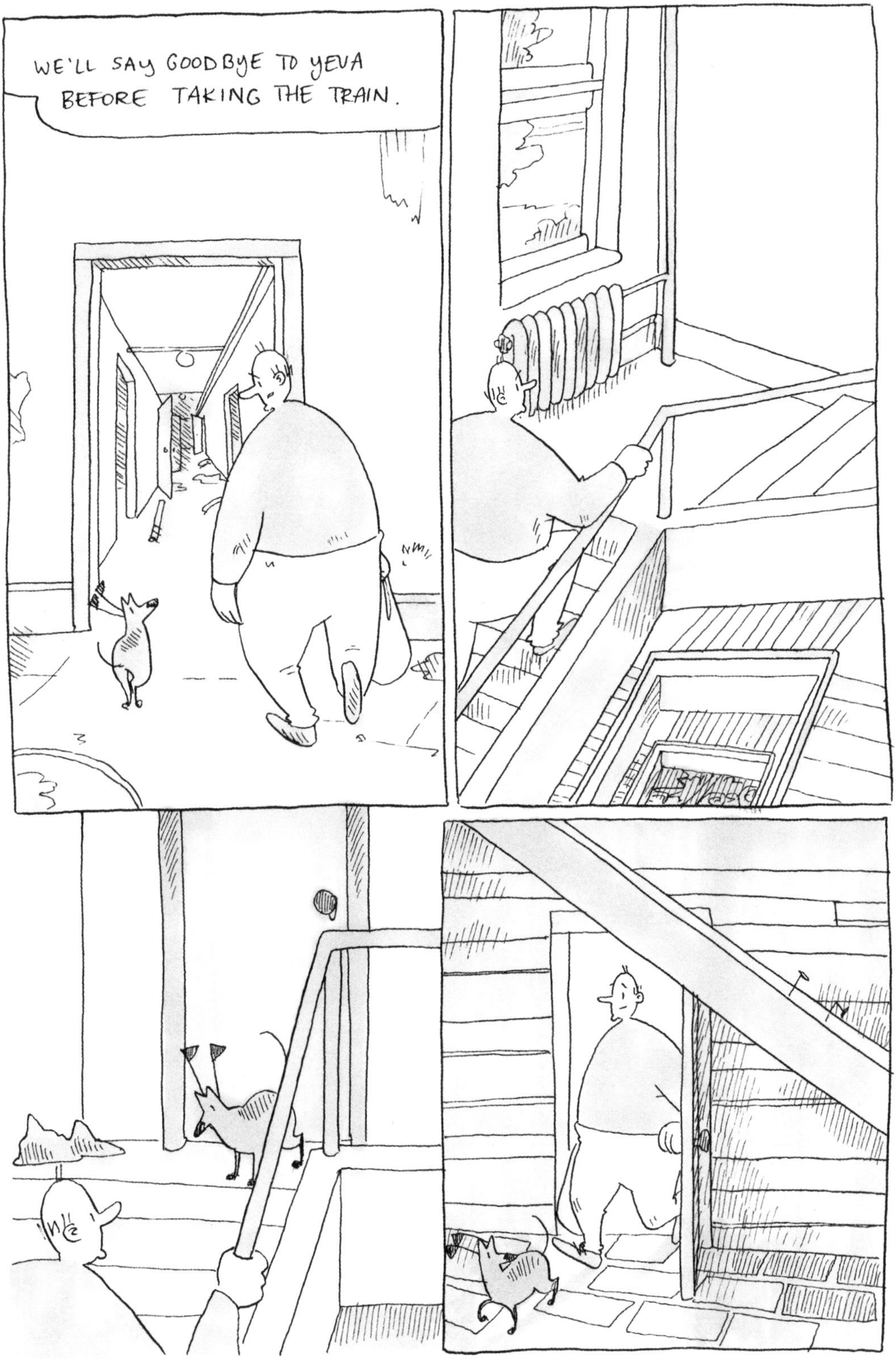
WE'LL SAY GOODBYE TO YEVA BEFORE TAKING THE TRAIN.

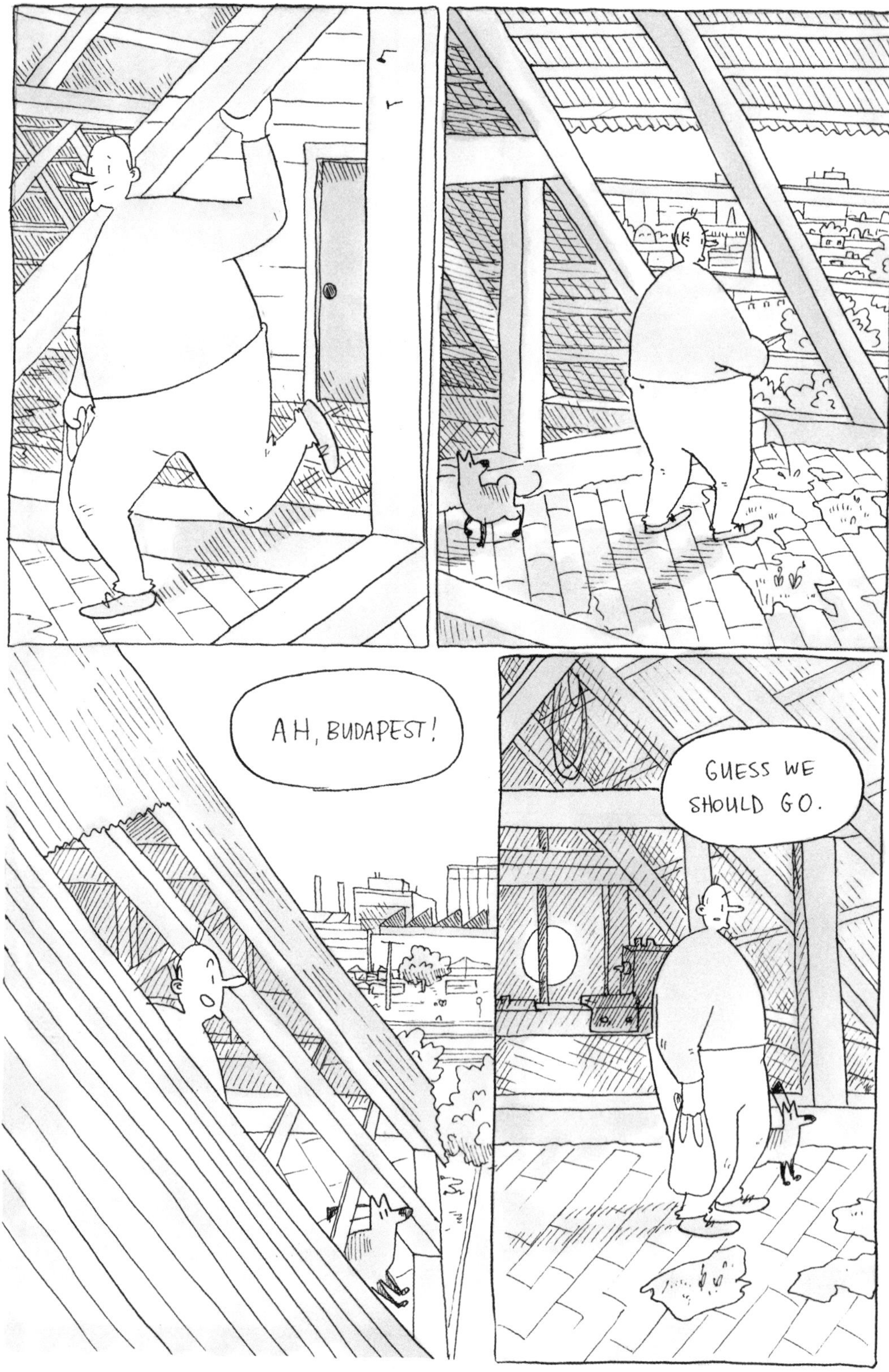
AH, BUDAPEST!
GUESS WE SHOULD GO.

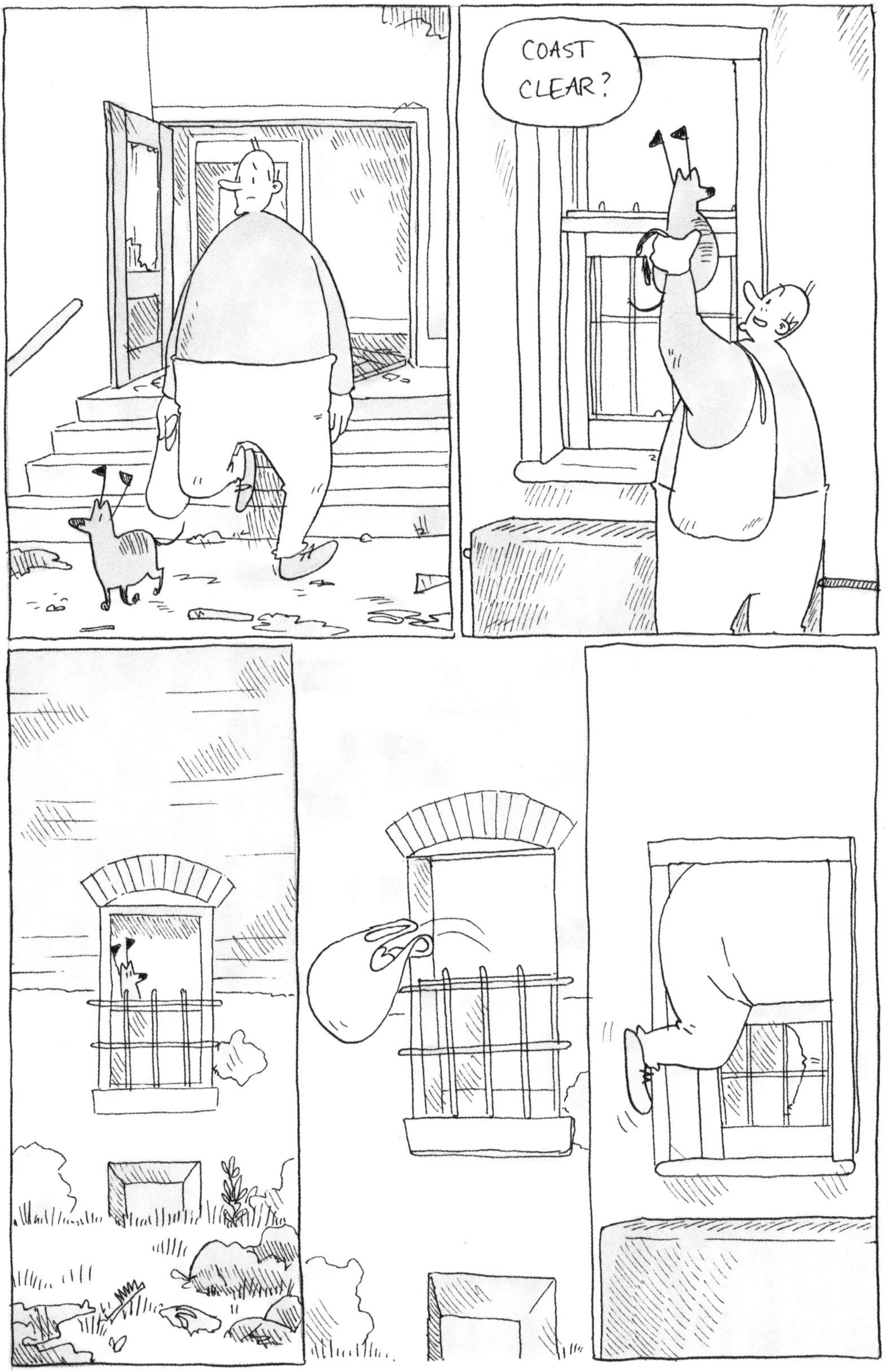
COAST CLEAR?

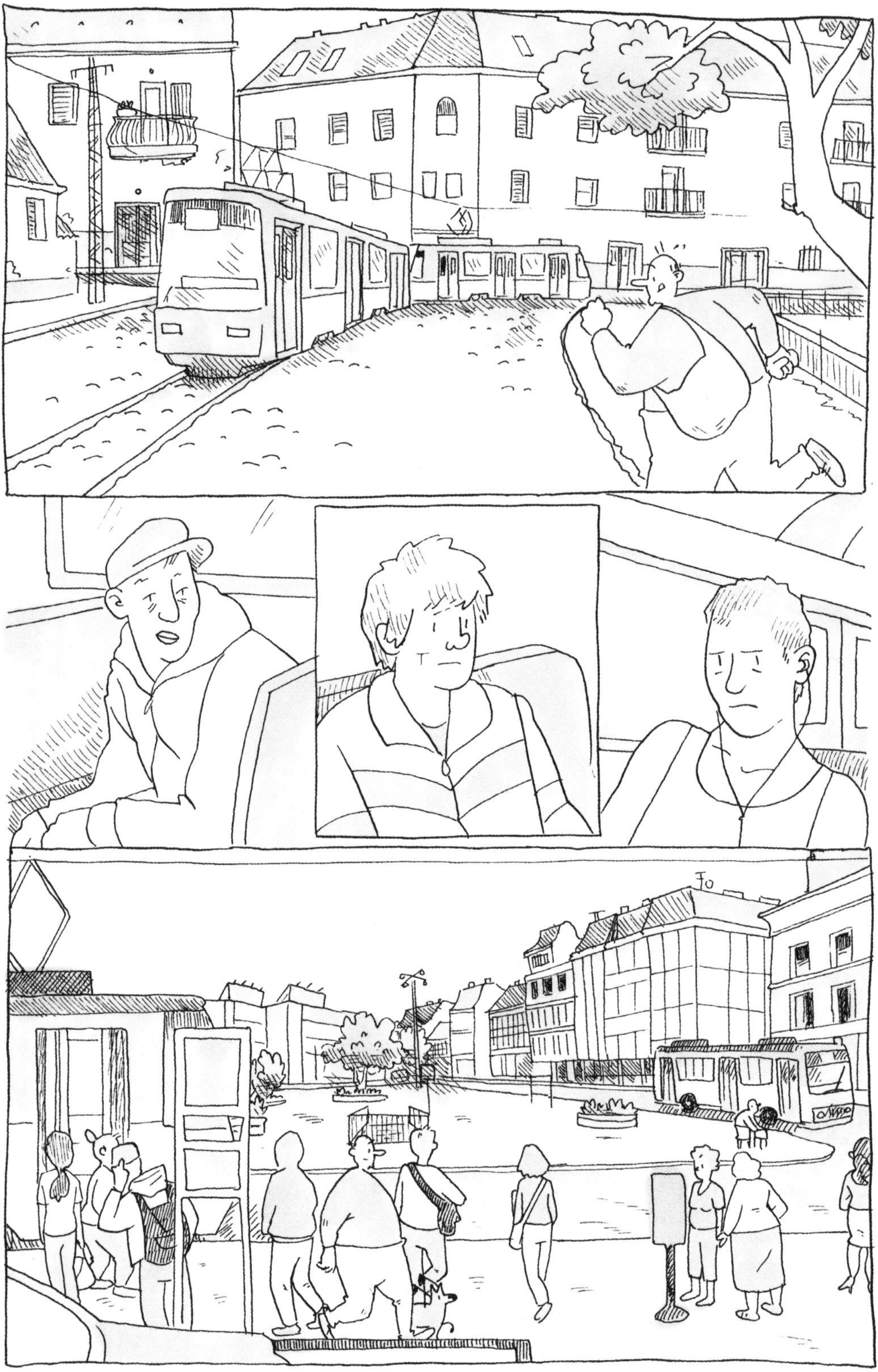

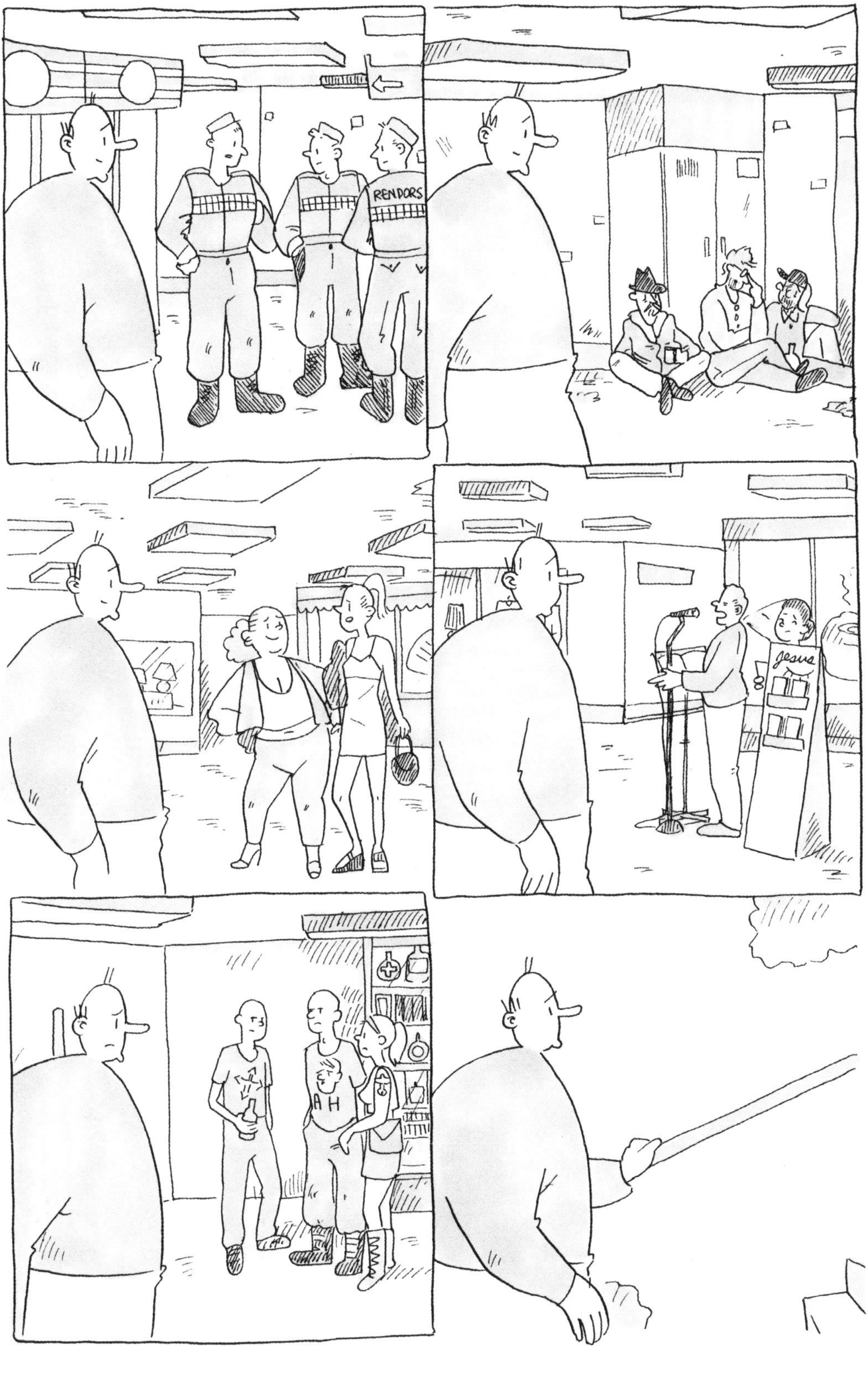
RENDORS
Jesus
AH

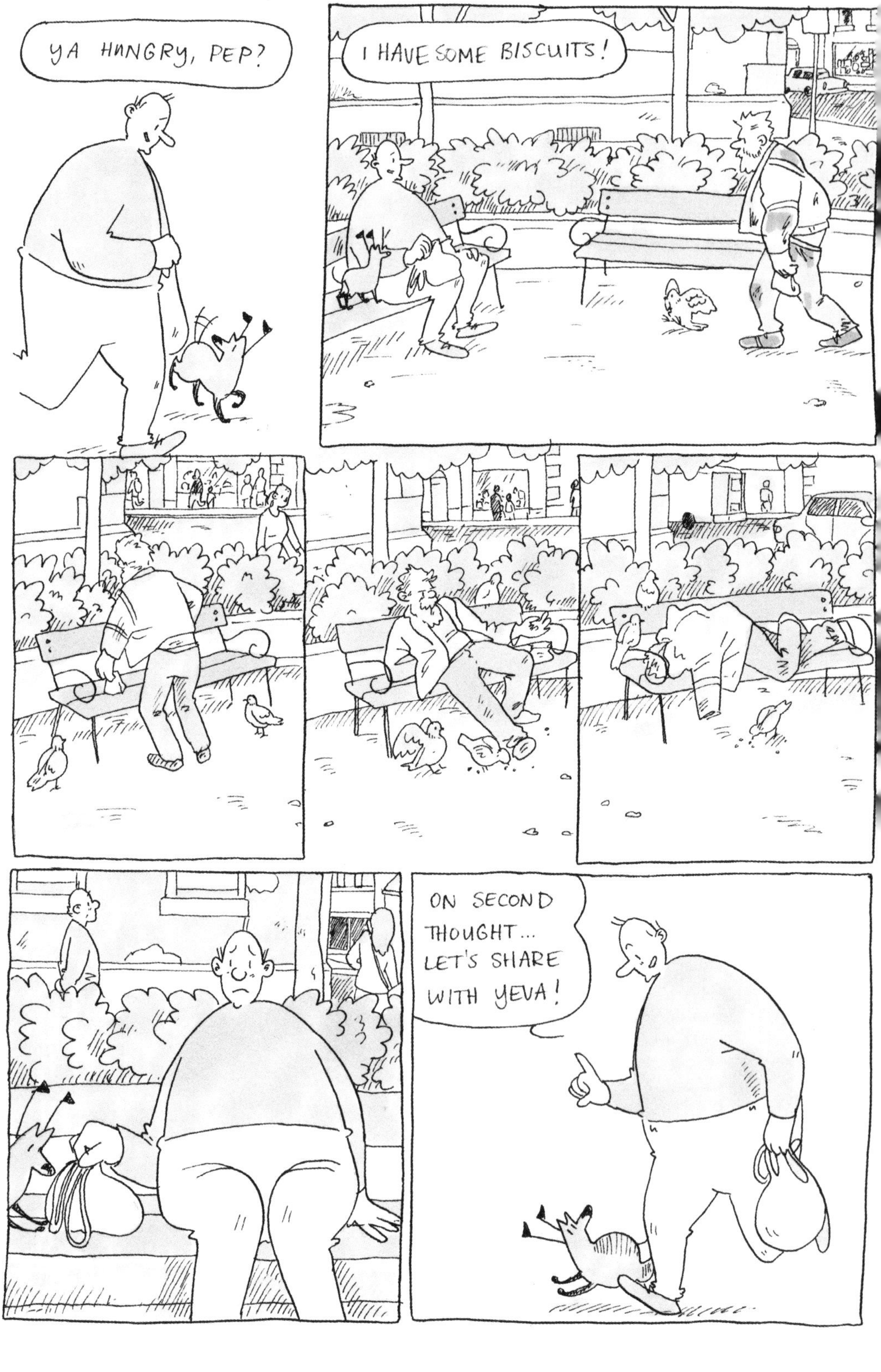
YA HUNGRY, PEP?
I HAVE SOME BISCUITS!
ON SECOND THOUGHT... LET'S SHARE WITH YEVA!

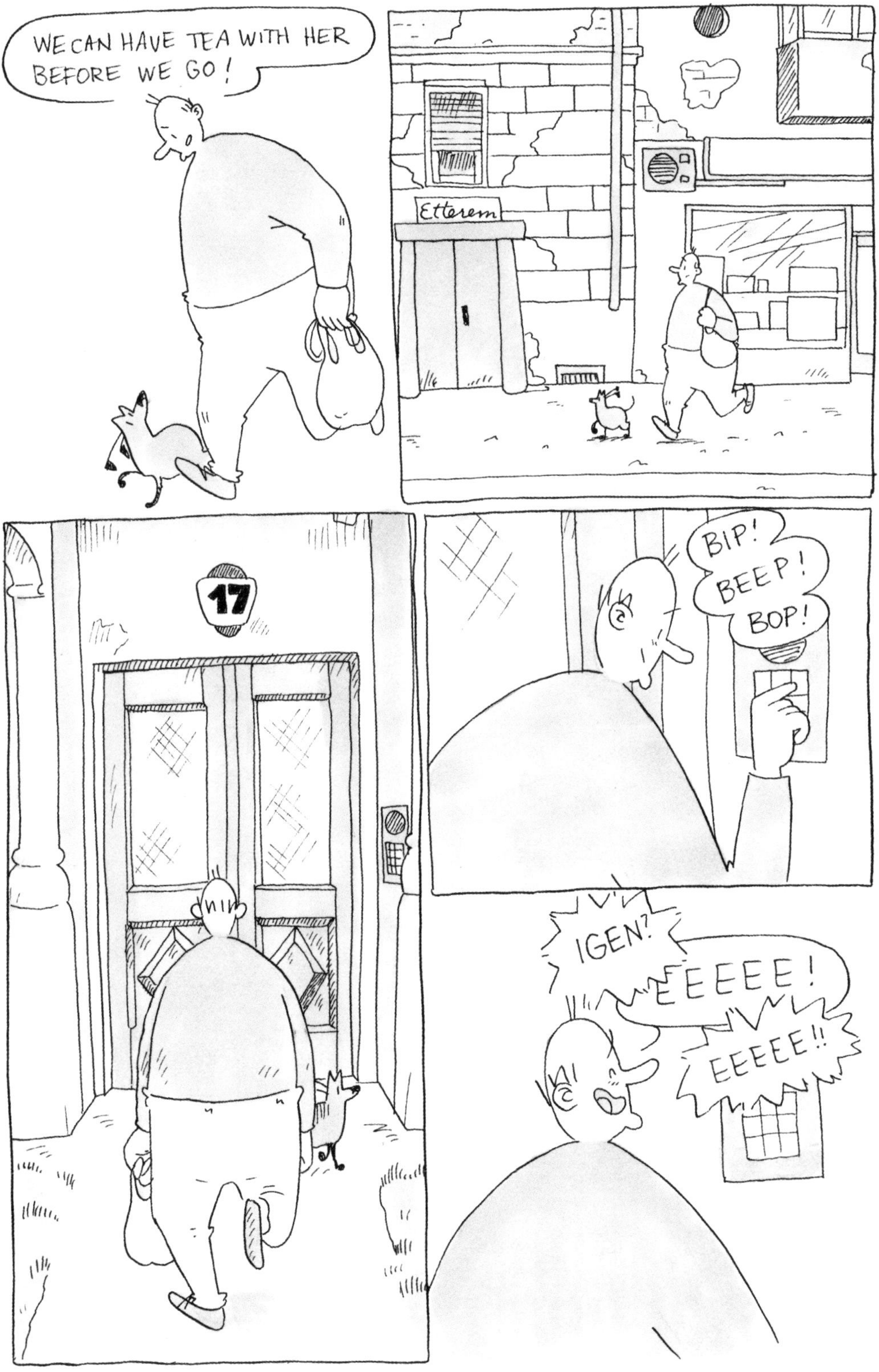
WE CAN HAVE TEA WITH HER BEFORE WE GO!
Etterem
17
BIP!
BEEP!
BOP!
IGEN?
EEEEE!
EEEEE!!

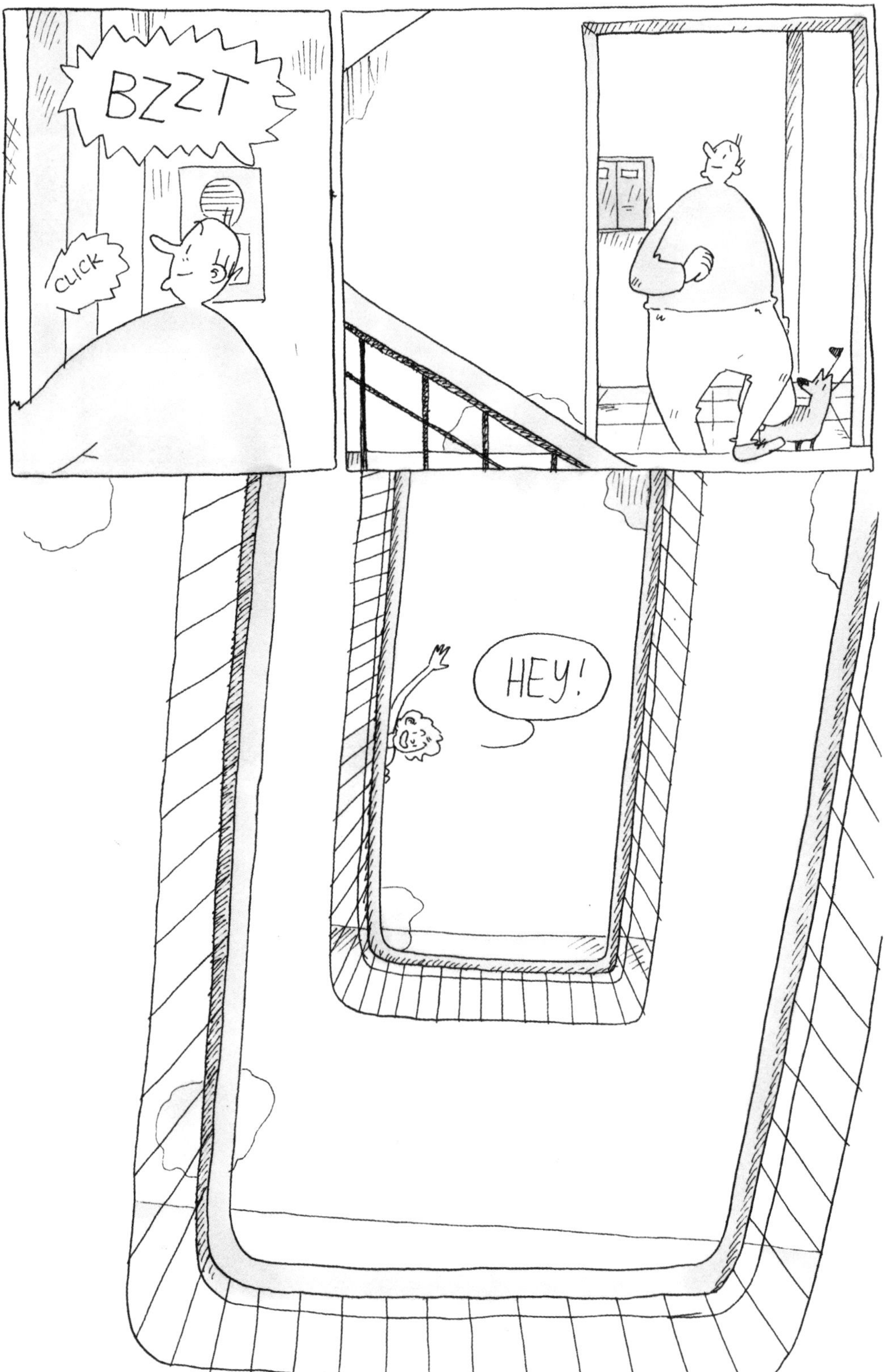
BZZT
CLICK
HEY!

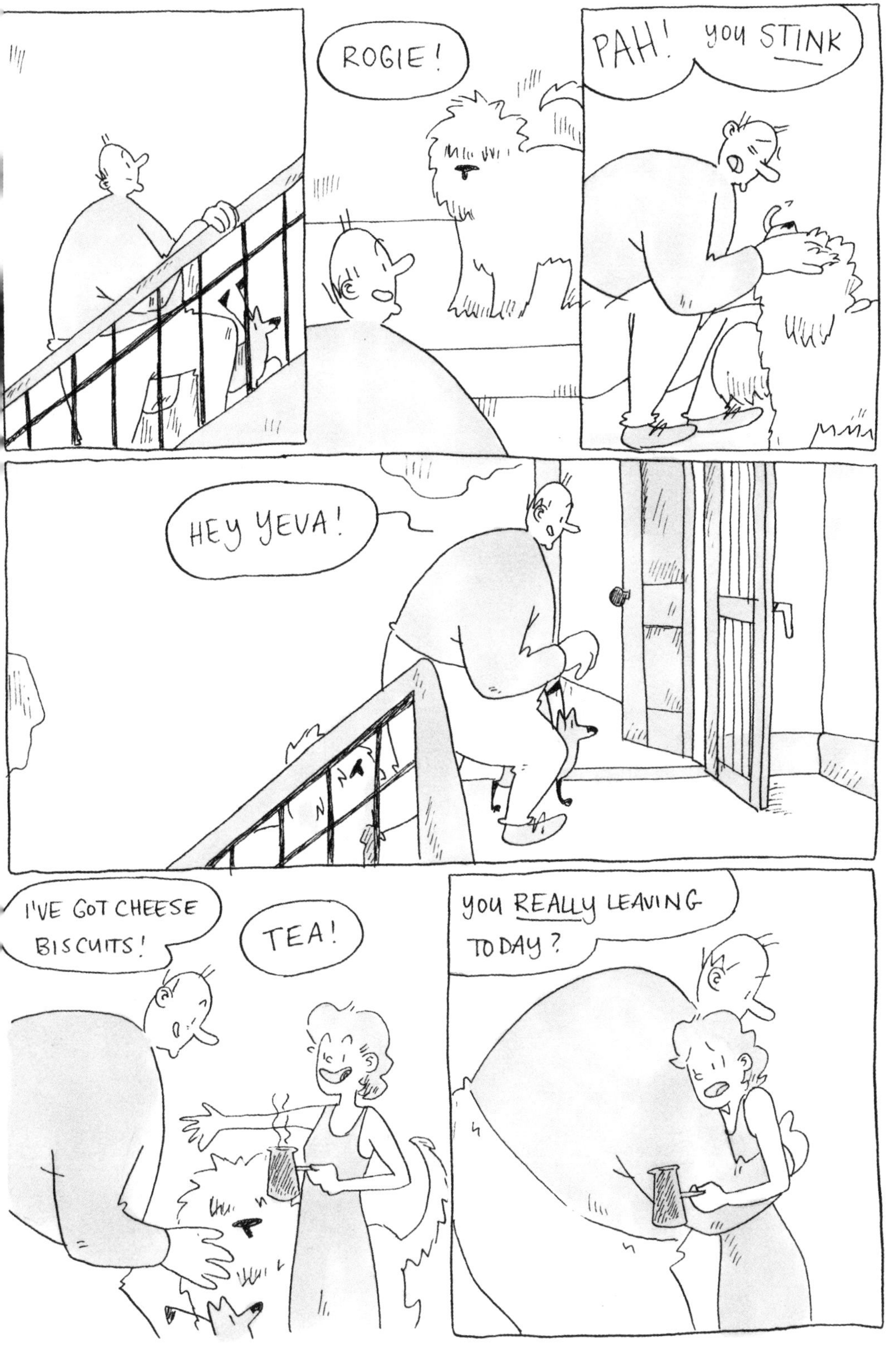
ROGIE!
PAH! you STINK
HEY YEVA!
I'VE GOT CHEESE BISCUITS!
TEA!
you REALLY LEAVING TODAY?

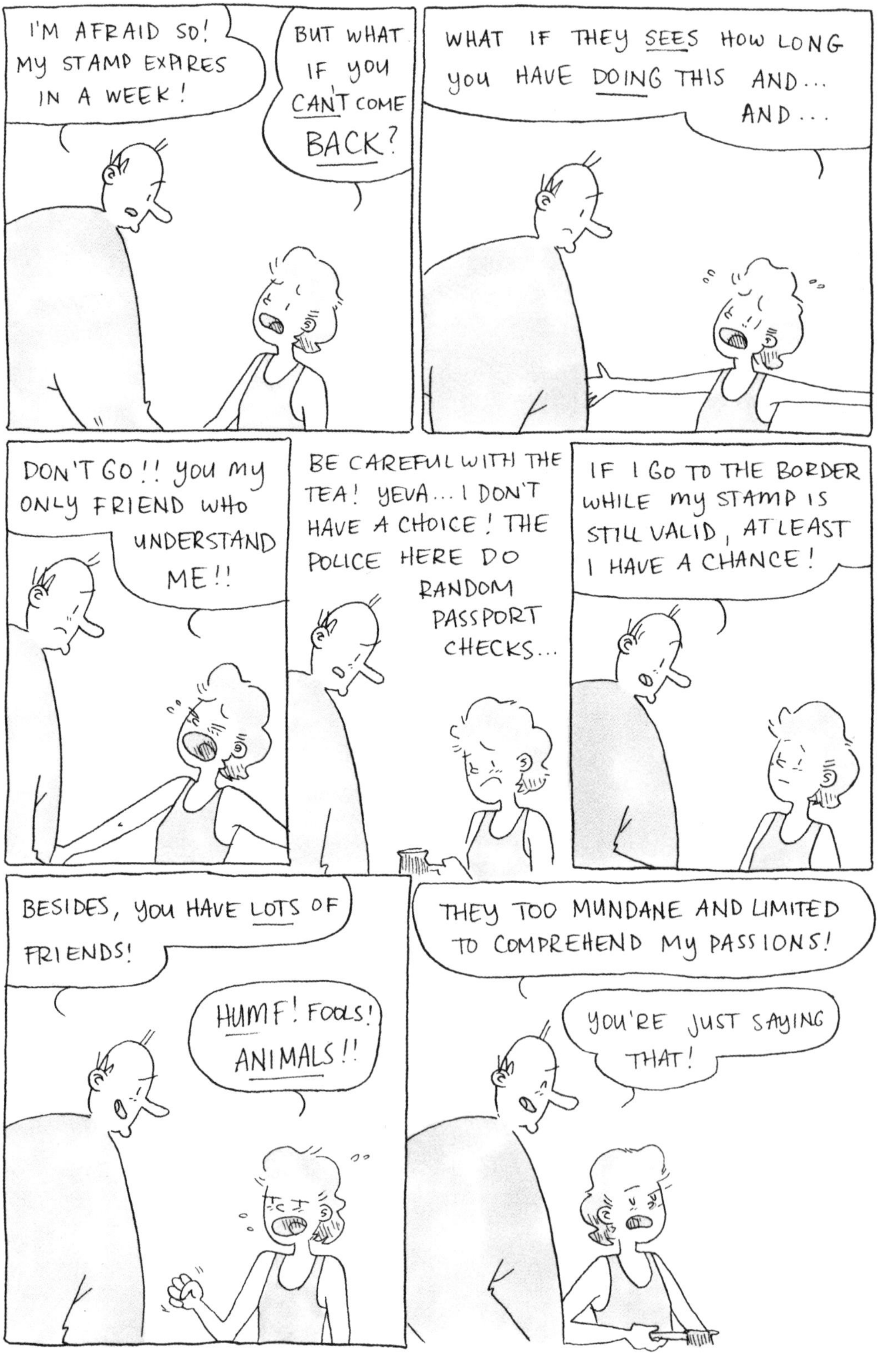
I'M AFRAID SO! MY STAMP EXPIRES IN A WEEK!
BUT WHAT IF YOU CAN'T COME BACK?
WHAT IF THEY SEES HOW LONG YOU HAVE DOING THIS AND... AND...
DON'T GO!! YOU MY ONLY FRIEND WHO UNDERSTAND ME!!
BE CAREFUL WITH THE TEA! YEVA... I DON'T HAVE A CHOICE! THE POLICE HERE DO RANDOM PASSPORT CHECKS...
IF I GO TO THE BORDER WHILE MY STAMP IS STILL VALID, AT LEAST I HAVE A CHANCE!
BESIDES, YOU HAVE LOTS OF FRIENDS!
HUMF! FOOLS! ANIMALS!!
THEY TOO MUNDANE AND LIMITED TO COMPREHEND MY PASSIONS!
YOU'RE JUST SAYING THAT!

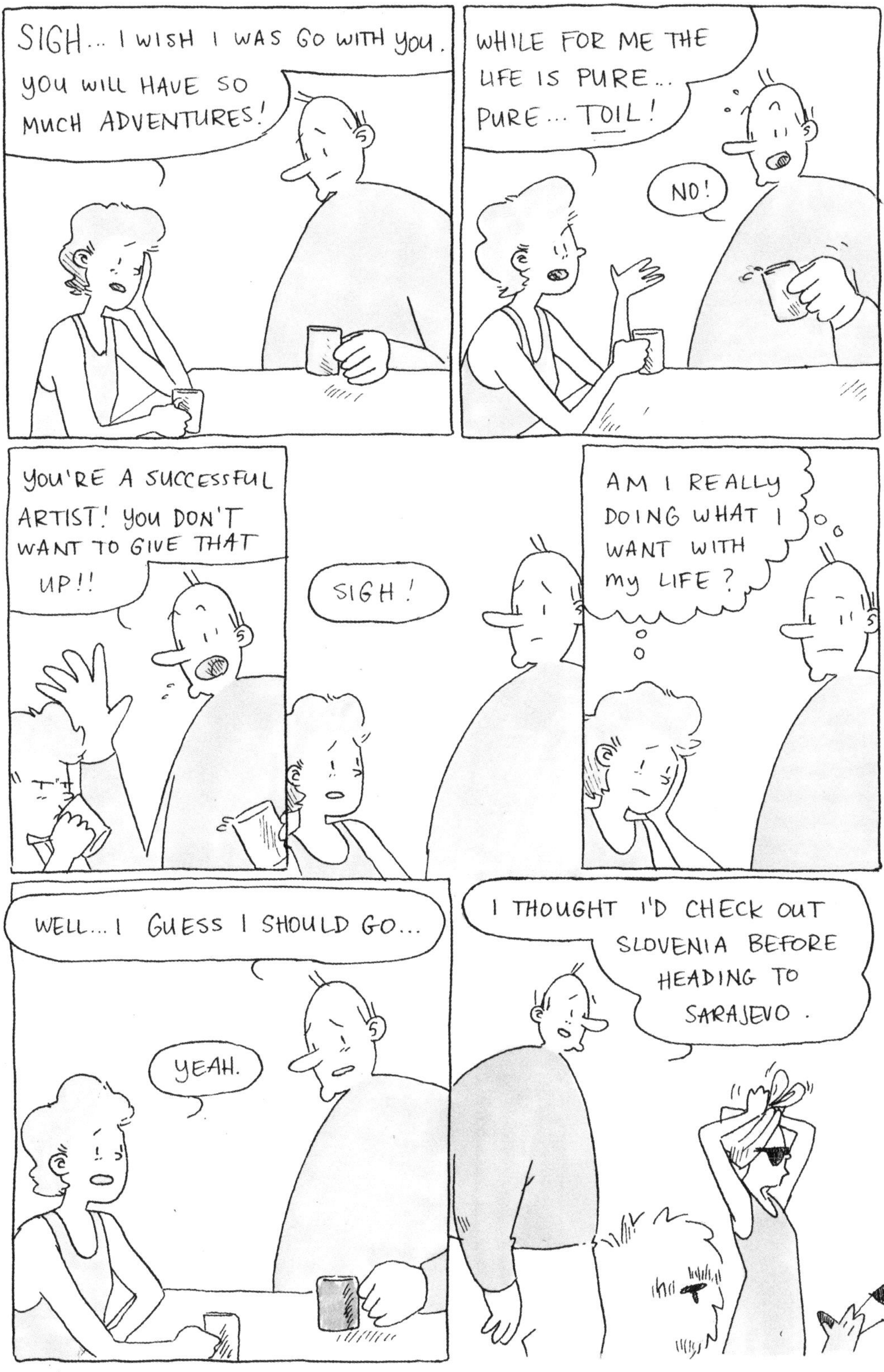
SIGH... I WISH I WAS GO WITH YOU. YOU WILL HAVE SO MUCH ADVENTURES!
WHILE FOR ME THE LIFE IS PURE... PURE... TOIL!
NO!
YOU'RE A SUCCESSFUL ARTIST! YOU DON'T WANT TO GIVE THAT UP!!
SIGH!
AM I REALLY DOING WHAT I WANT WITH MY LIFE?
WELL... I GUESS I SHOULD GO...
YEAH.
I THOUGHT I'D CHECK OUT SLOVENIA BEFORE HEADING TO SARAJEVO.

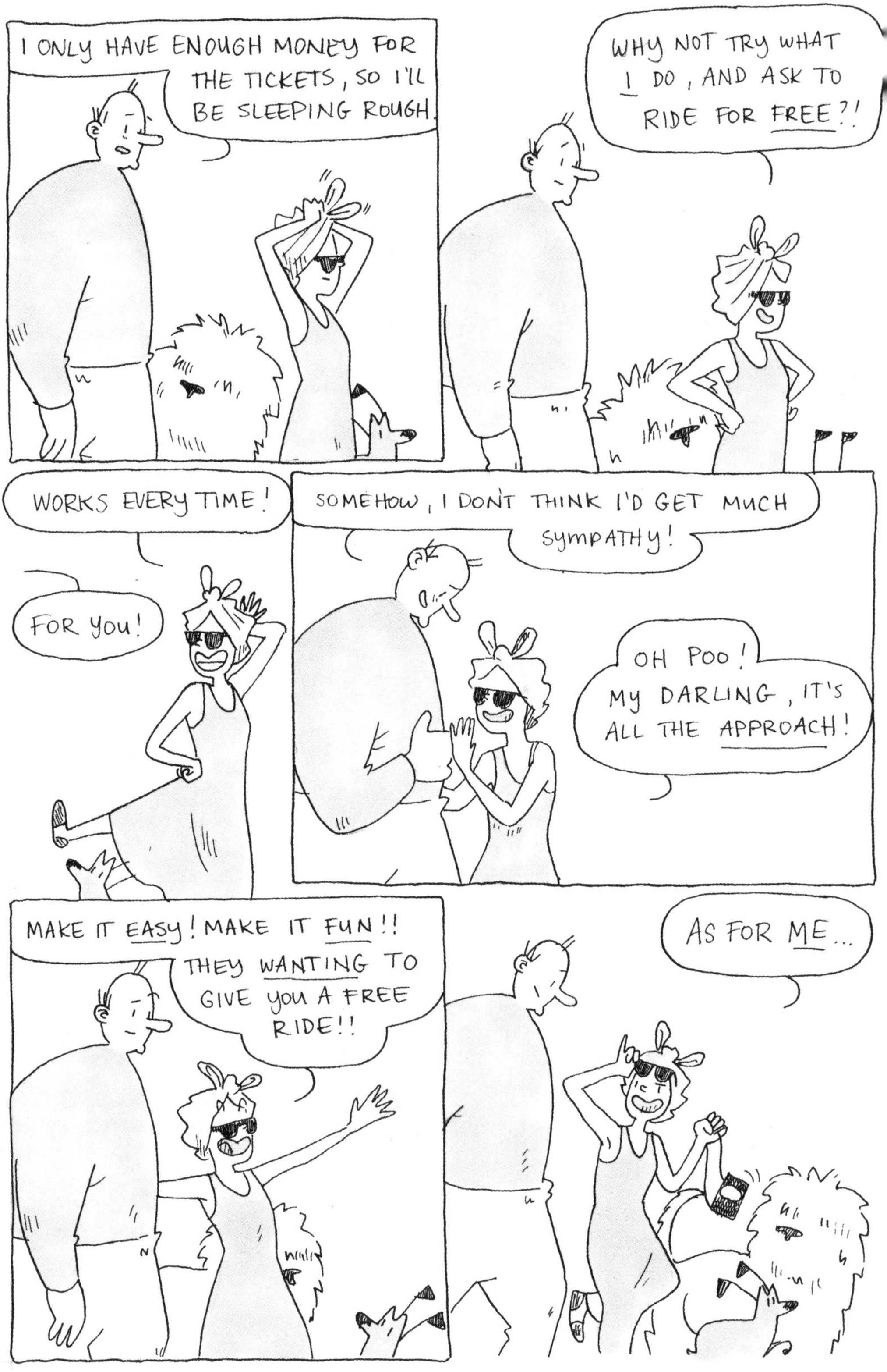
I ONLY HAVE ENOUGH MONEY FOR THE TICKETS, SO I'LL BE SLEEPING ROUGH
WHY NOT TRY WHAT I DO, AND ASK TO RIDE FOR FREE?!
WORKS EVERY TIME!
FOR YOU!
SOMEHOW, I DON'T THINK I'D GET MUCH SYMPATHY!
OH POO! MY DARLING, IT'S ALL THE APPROACH!
MAKE IT EASY! MAKE IT FUN!!
THEY WANTING TO GIVE YOU A FREE RIDE!!
AS FOR ME...

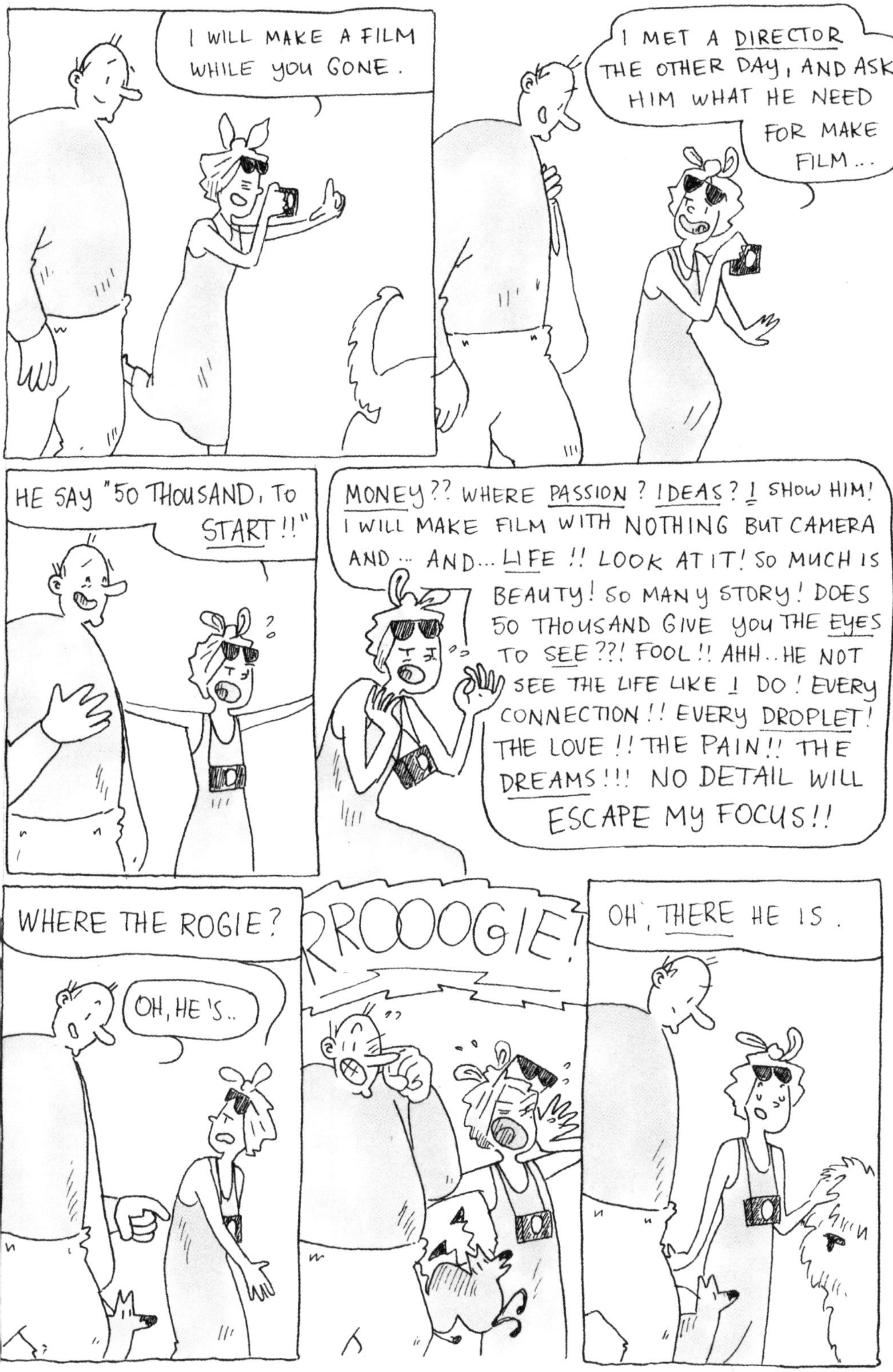
I WILL MAKE A FILM WHILE YOU GONE.
I MET A DIRECTOR THE OTHER DAY, AND ASK HIM WHAT HE NEED FOR MAKE FILM...
HE SAY "50 THOUSAND, TO START!!"
MONEY?? WHERE PASSION? IDEAS? I SHOW HIM! I WILL MAKE FILM WITH NOTHING BUT CAMERA AND... AND... LIFE!! LOOK AT IT! SO MUCH IS BEAUTY! SO MANY STORY! DOES 50 THOUSAND GIVE YOU THE EYES TO SEE??! FOOL!! AHH.. HE NOT SEE THE LIFE LIKE I DO! EVERY CONNECTION!! EVERY DROPLET! THE LOVE!! THE PAIN!! THE DREAMS!!! NO DETAIL WILL ESCAPE MY FOCUS!!
WHERE THE ROGIE?
OH, HE'S..
RROOOOGIE!
OH, THERE HE IS.

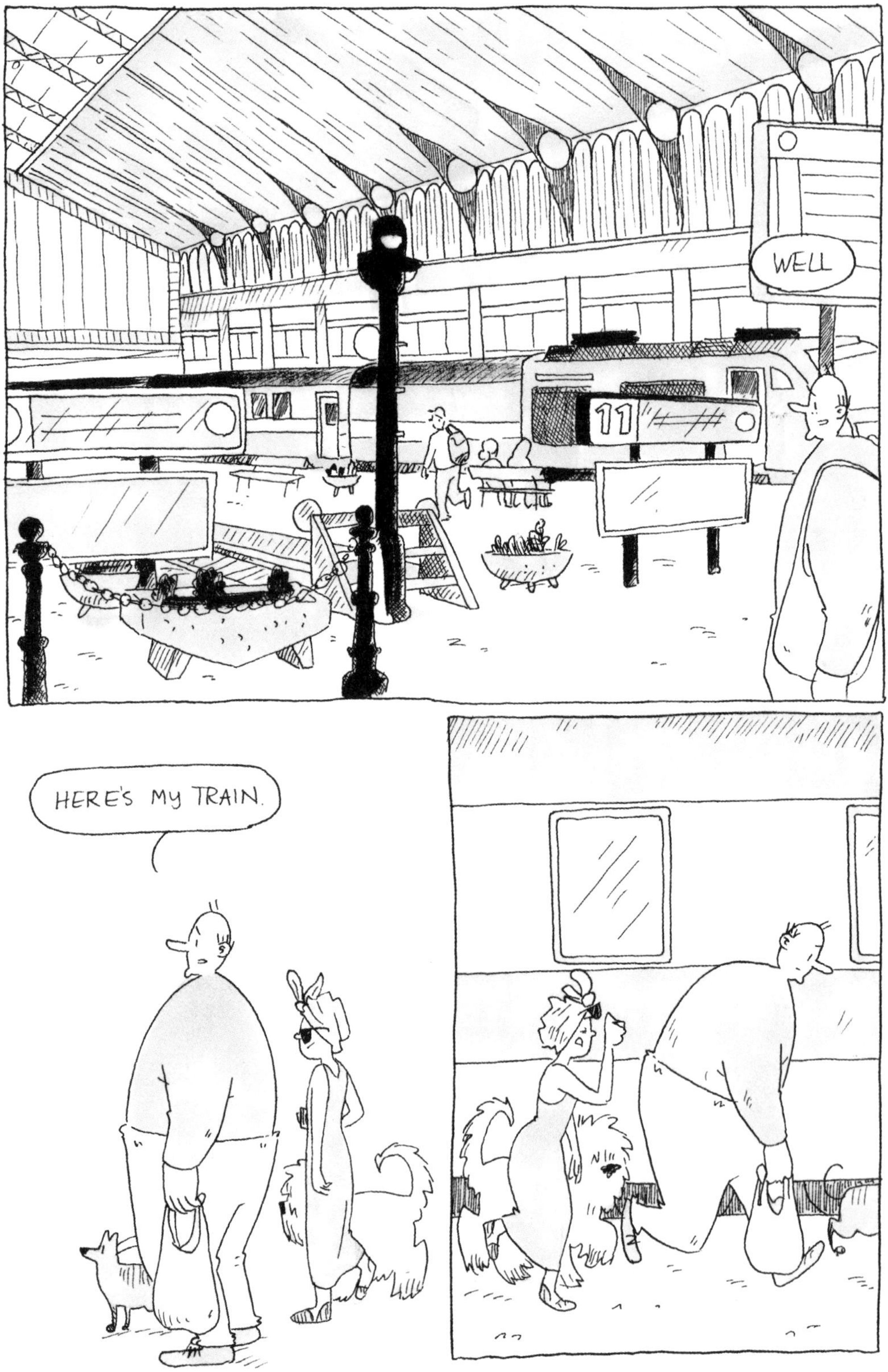
WELL
11
HERE'S MY TRAIN.

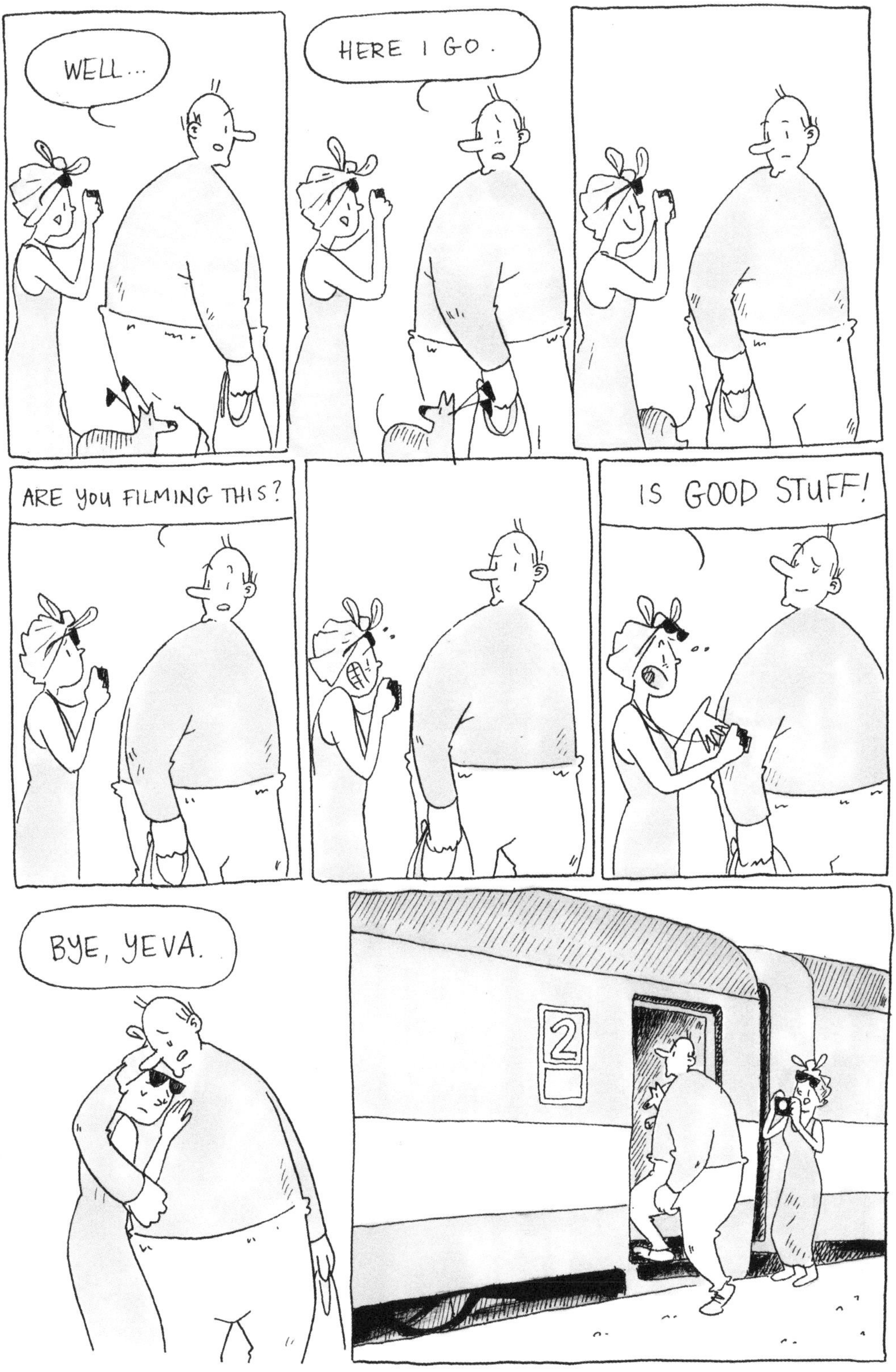
WELL...
HERE I GO.
ARE YOU FILMING THIS?
IS GOOD STUFF!
BYE, YEVA.
2

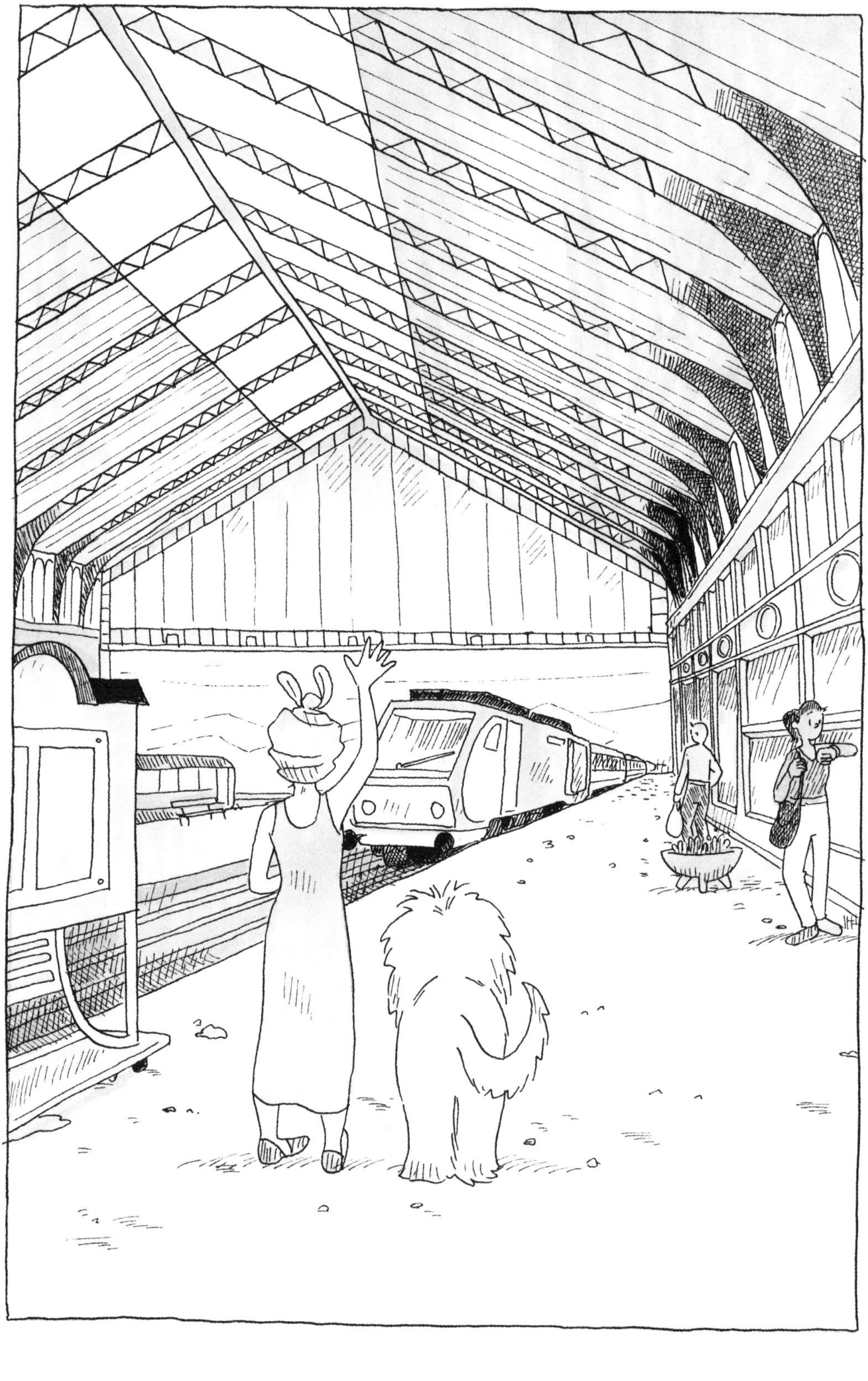

CHAPTER TWO

THE ADVENTURE

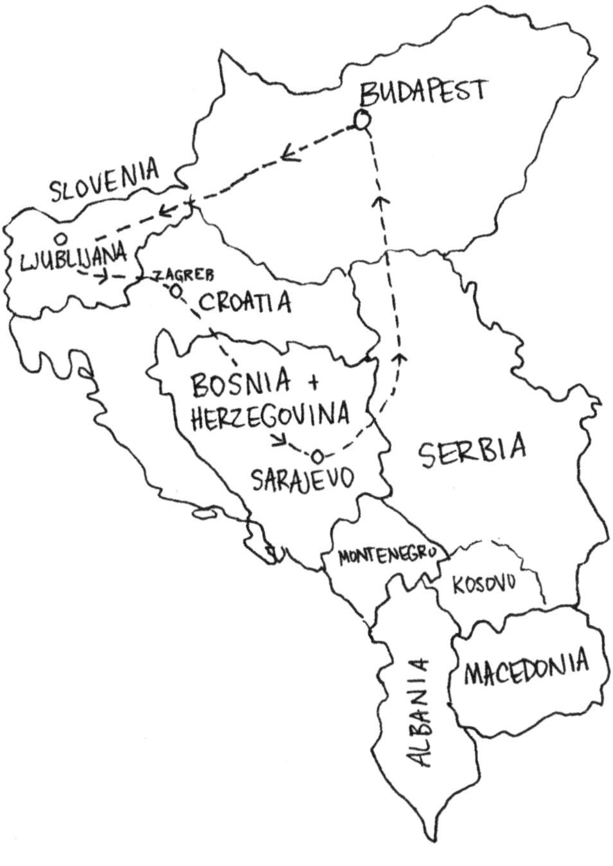

BUDAPEST
SLOVENIA
LJUBLJANA
ZAGREB
CROATIA
BOSNIA +
HERZEGOVINA
SARAJEVO
SERBIA
MONTENEGRO
KOSOVO
ALBANIA
MACEDONIA

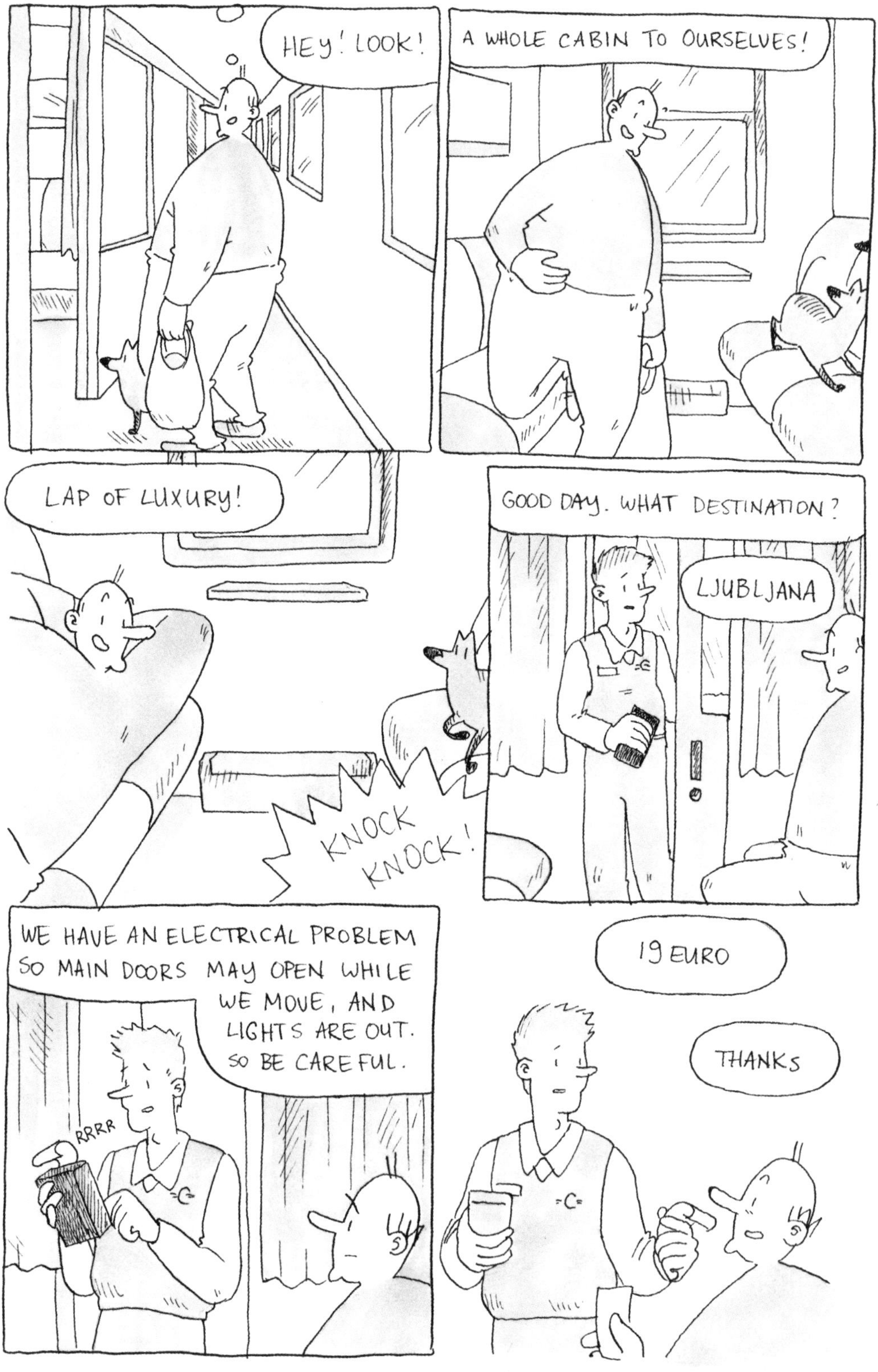

HEY! LOOK!
A WHOLE CABIN TO OURSELVES!
LAP OF LUXURY!
KNOCK KNOCK!
GOOD DAY. WHAT DESTINATION?
LJUBLJANA
WE HAVE AN ELECTRICAL PROBLEM SO MAIN DOORS MAY OPEN WHILE WE MOVE, AND LIGHTS ARE OUT. SO BE CAREFUL.
RRRR
19 EURO
THANKS

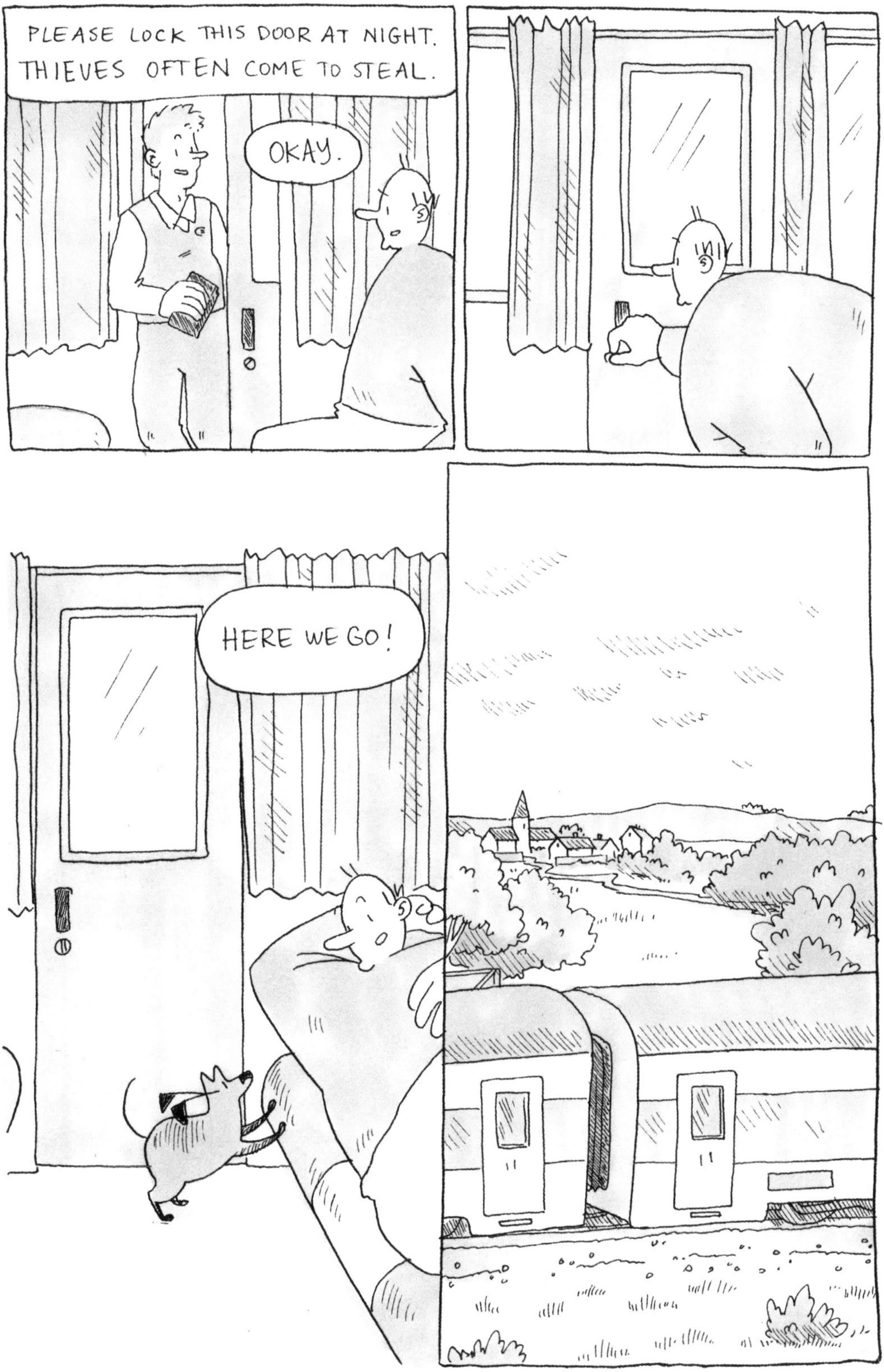
PLEASE LOCK THIS DOOR AT NIGHT. THIEVES OFTEN COME TO STEAL.
OKAY.
HERE WE GO!

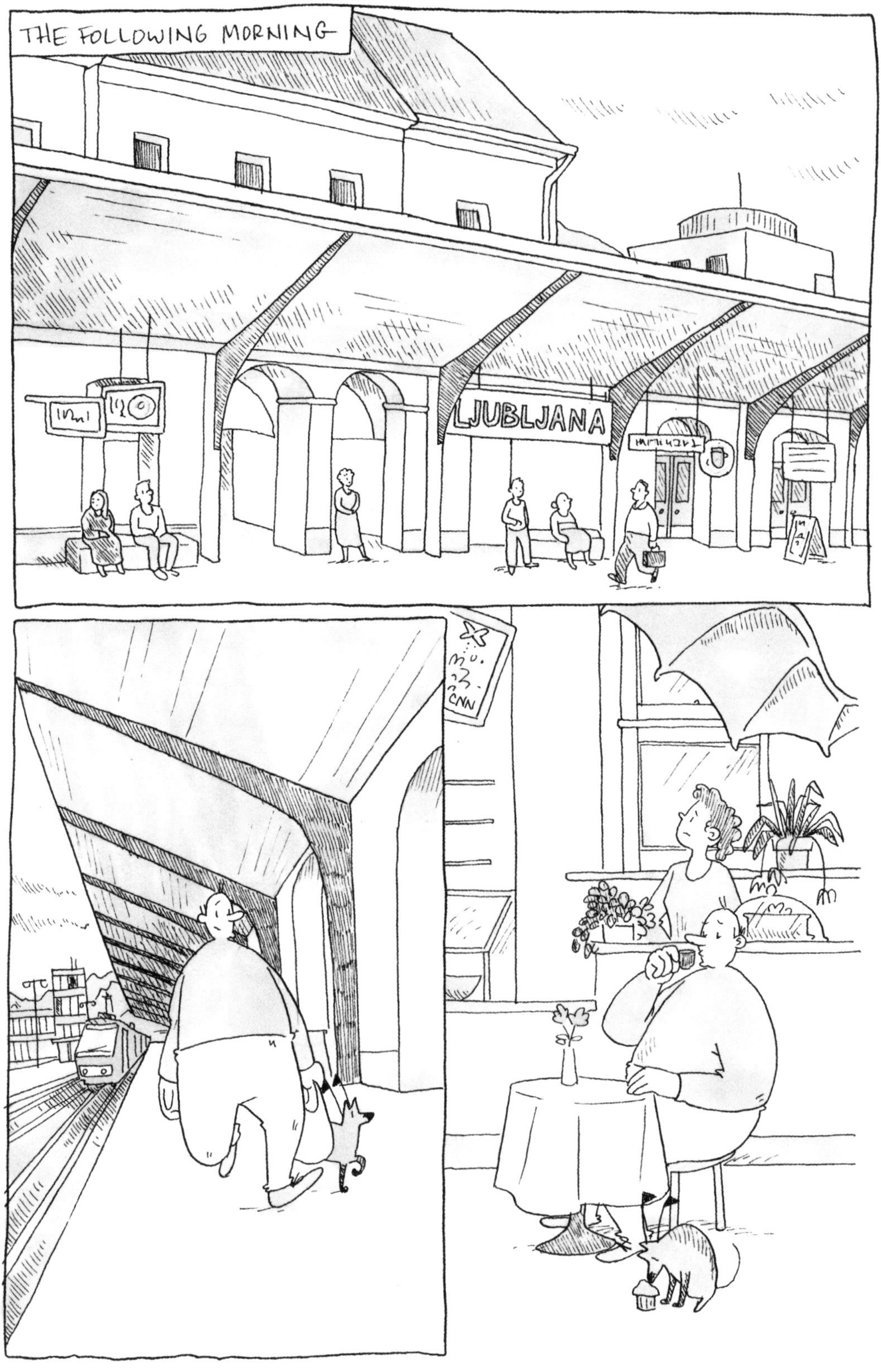
THE FOLLOWING MORNING
LJUBLJANA
CNN

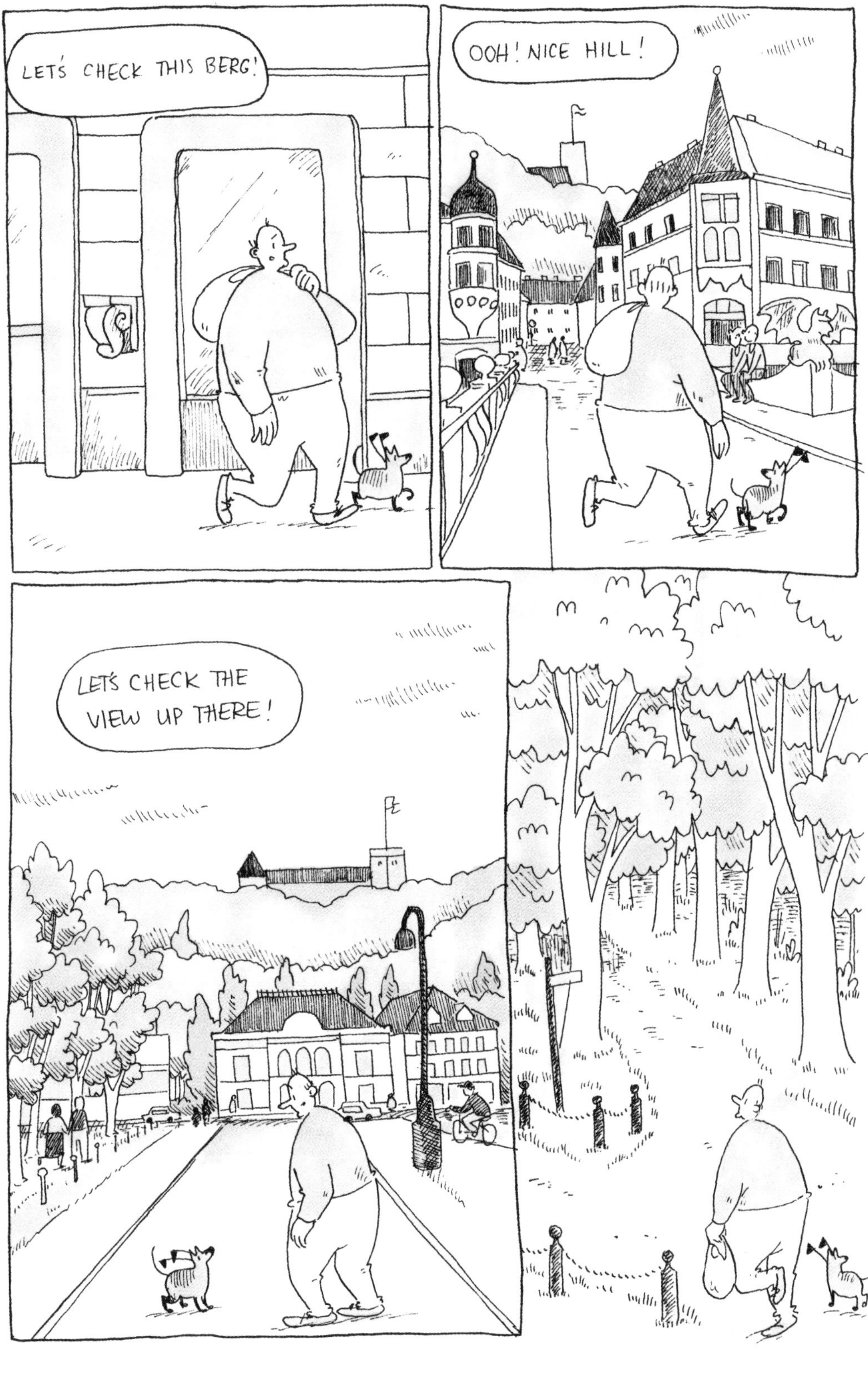
LET'S CHECK THIS BERG!
OOH! NICE HILL!
LET'S CHECK THE VIEW UP THERE!

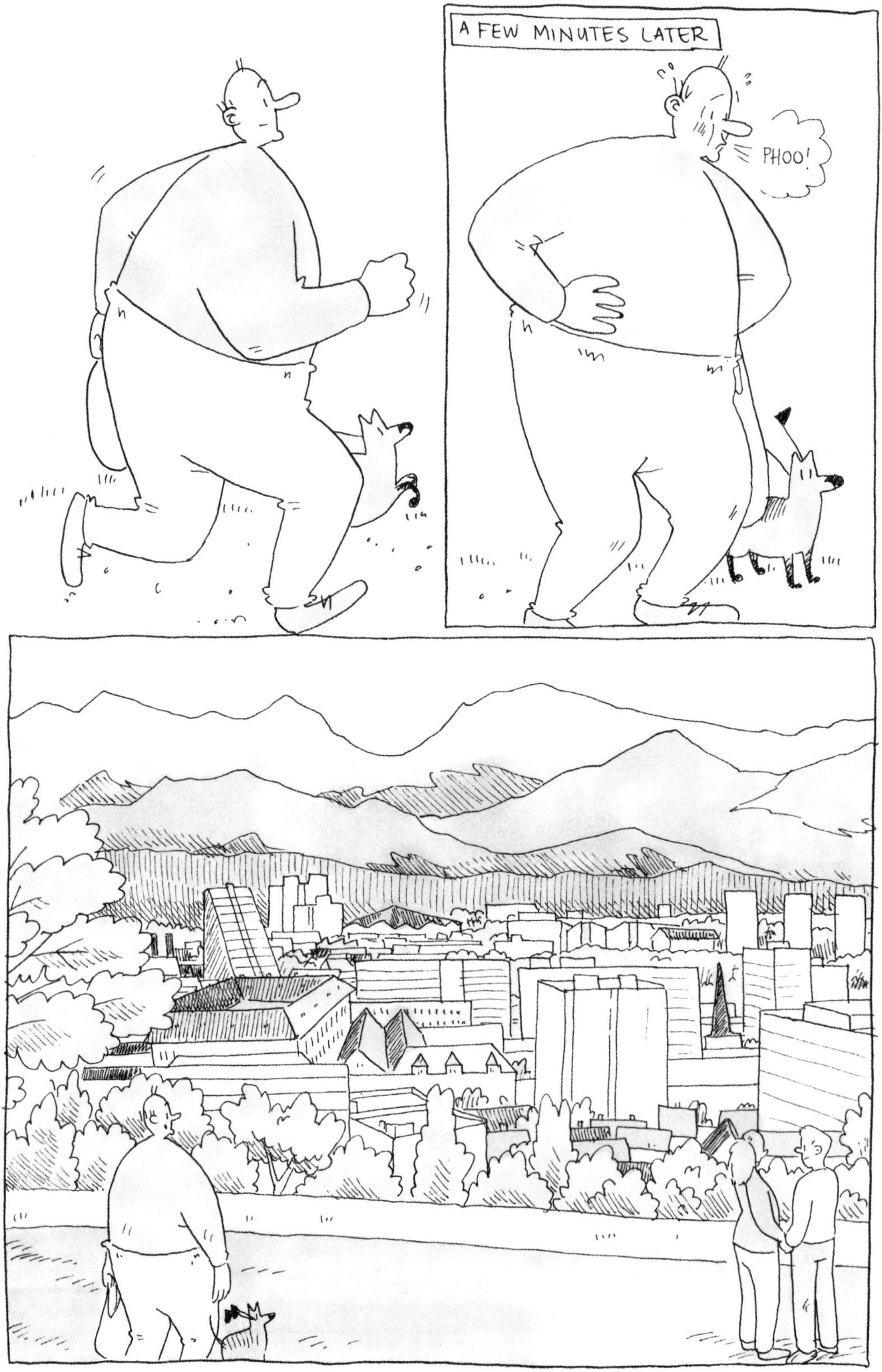
A FEW MINUTES LATER
PHOO!

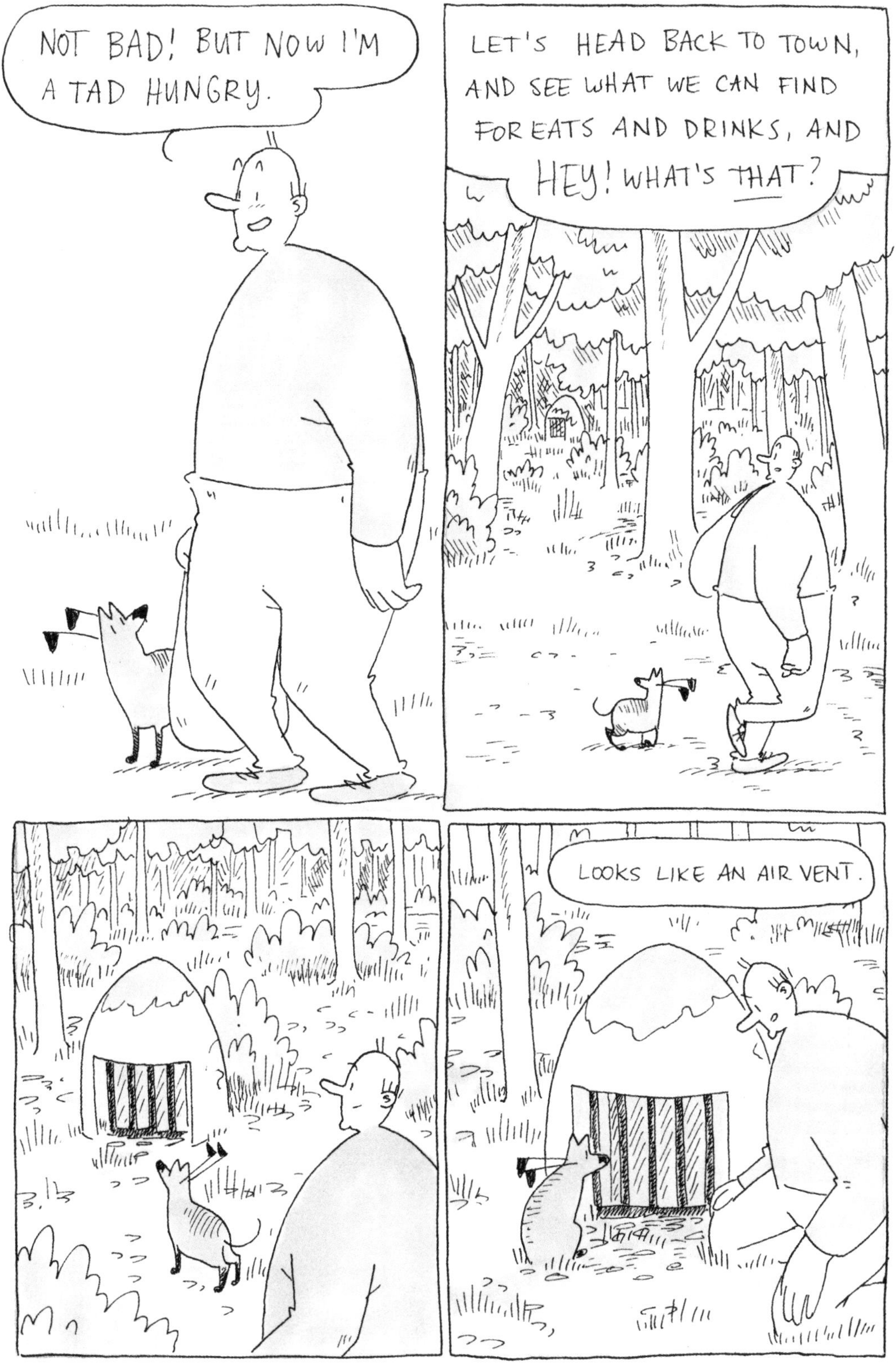
NOT BAD! BUT NOW I'M A TAD HUNGRY.
LET'S HEAD BACK TO TOWN, AND SEE WHAT WE CAN FIND FOR EATS AND DRINKS, AND HEY! WHAT'S THAT?
LOOKS LIKE AN AIR VENT.

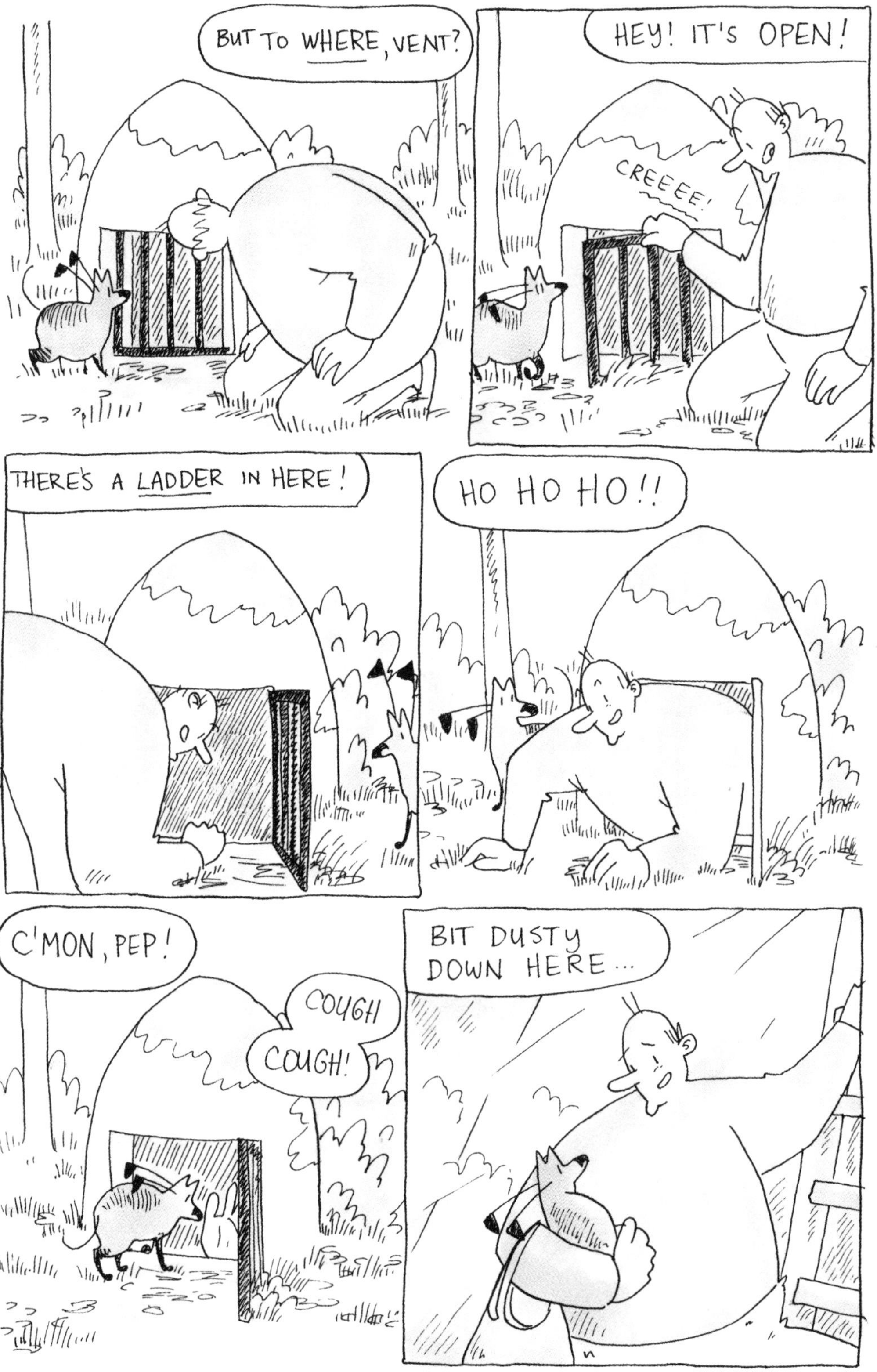
BUT TO WHERE, VENT?
HEY! IT'S OPEN!
CREEEE!
THERE'S A LADDER IN HERE!
HO HO HO!!
C'MON, PEP!
COUGH
COUGH!
BIT DUSTY
DOWN HERE...

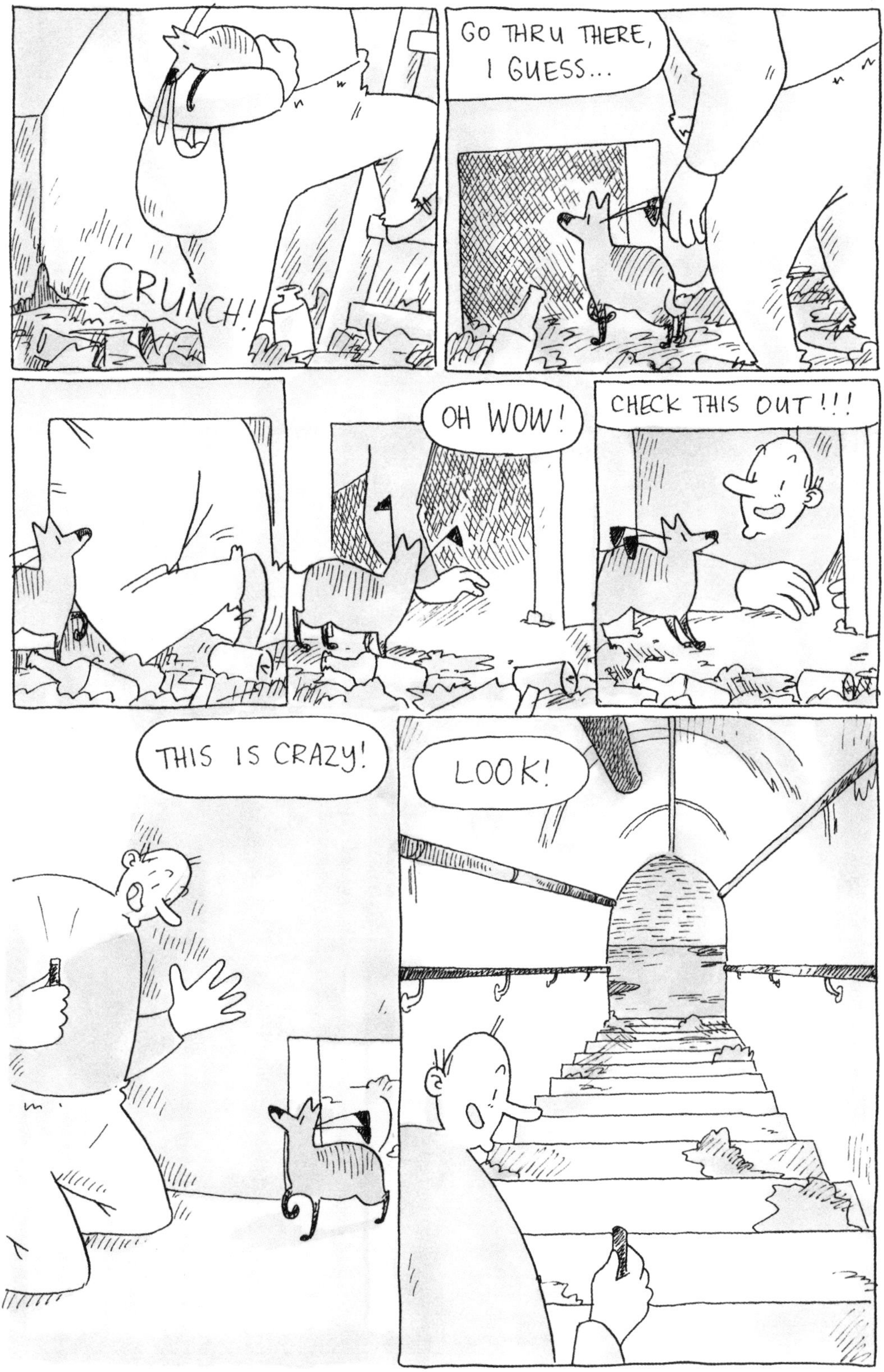
CRUNCH!
GO THRU THERE, I GUESS...
OH WOW!
CHECK THIS OUT!!!
THIS IS CRAZY!
LOOK!

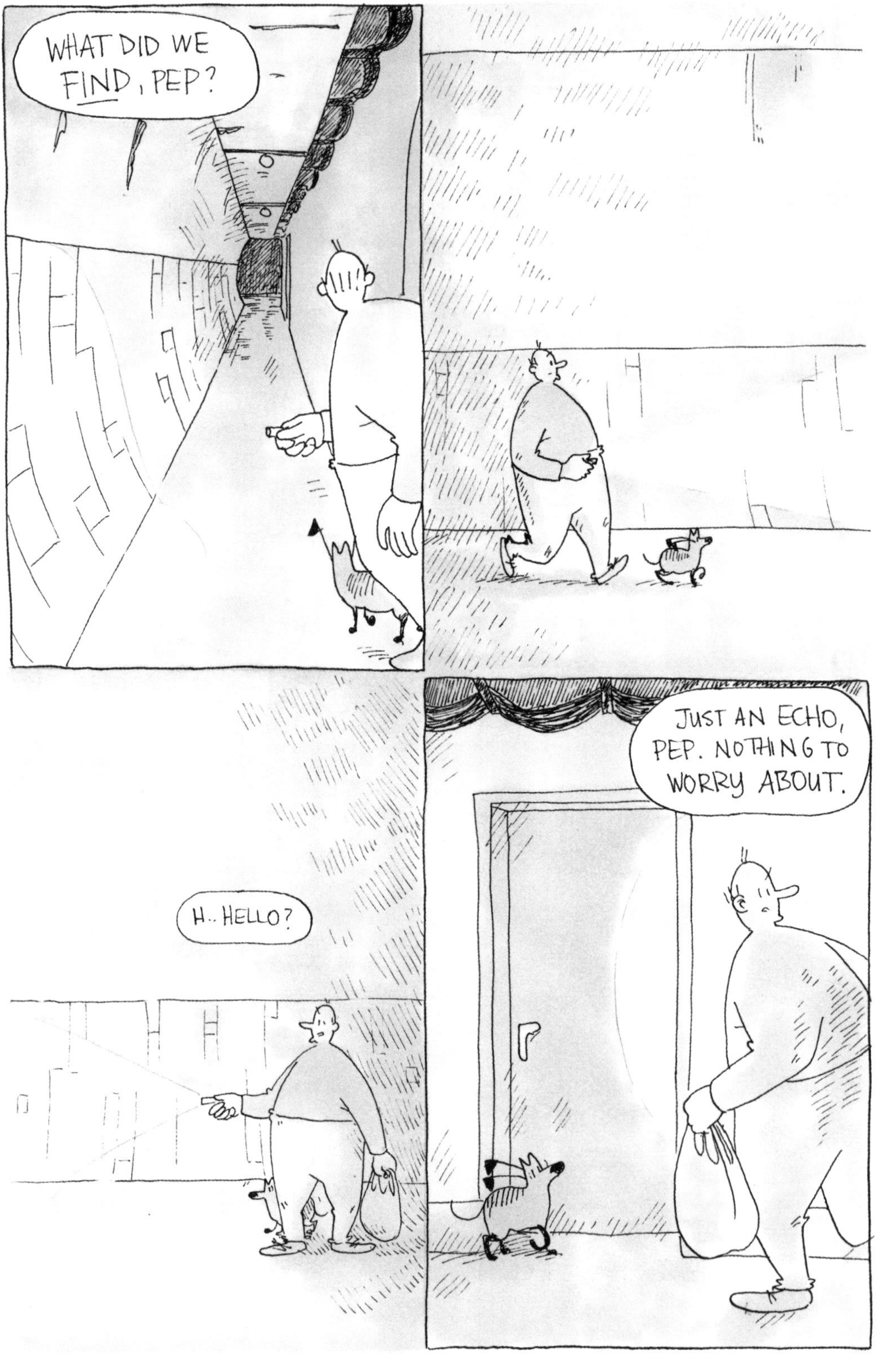
WHAT DID WE FIND, PEP?
H.. HELLO?
JUST AN ECHO, PEP. NOTHING TO WORRY ABOUT.

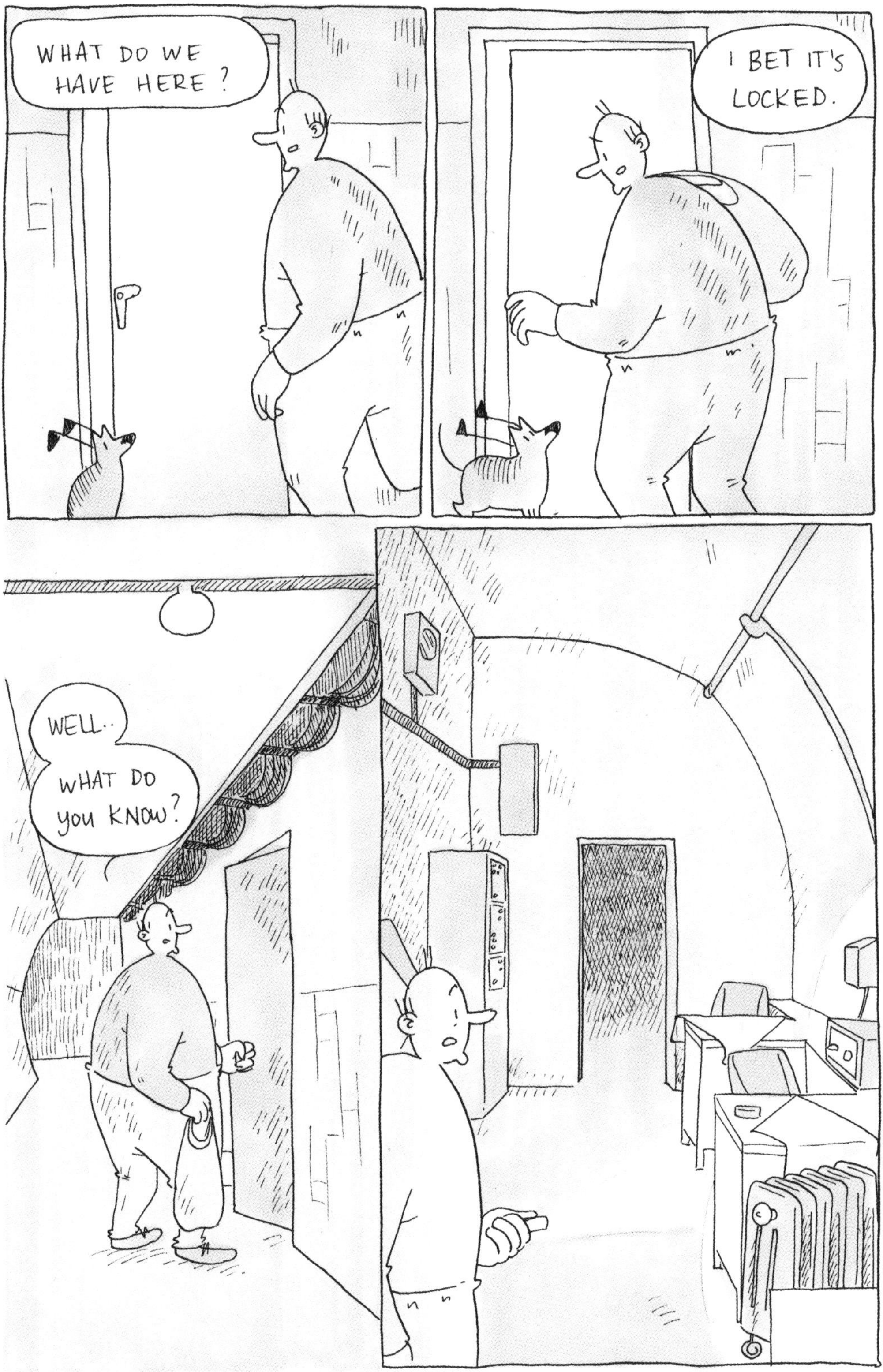
WHAT DO WE HAVE HERE?
I BET IT'S LOCKED.
WELL..
WHAT DO YOU KNOW?

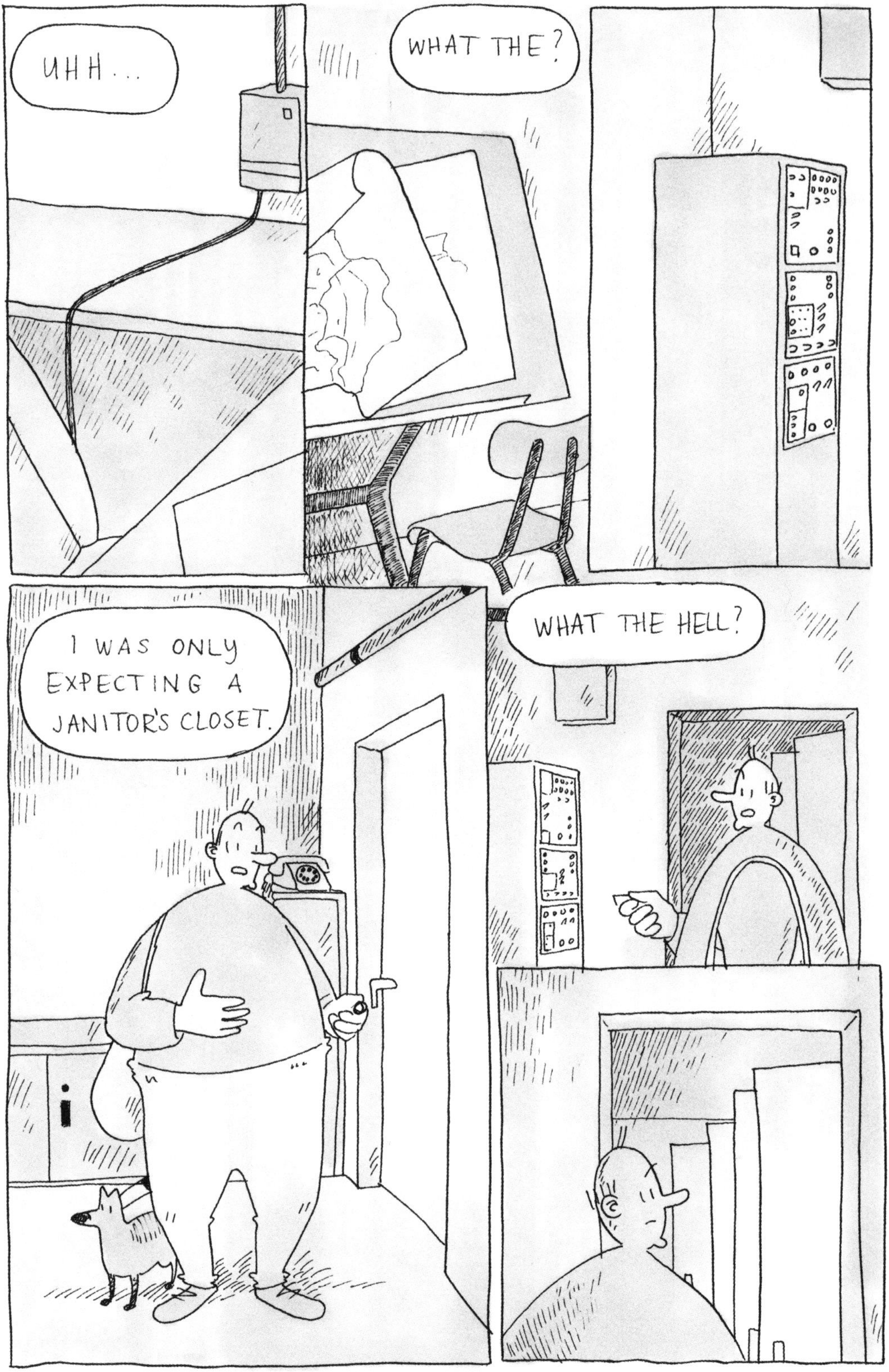
UHH...
WHAT THE?
I WAS ONLY EXPECTING A JANITOR'S CLOSET.
WHAT THE HELL?

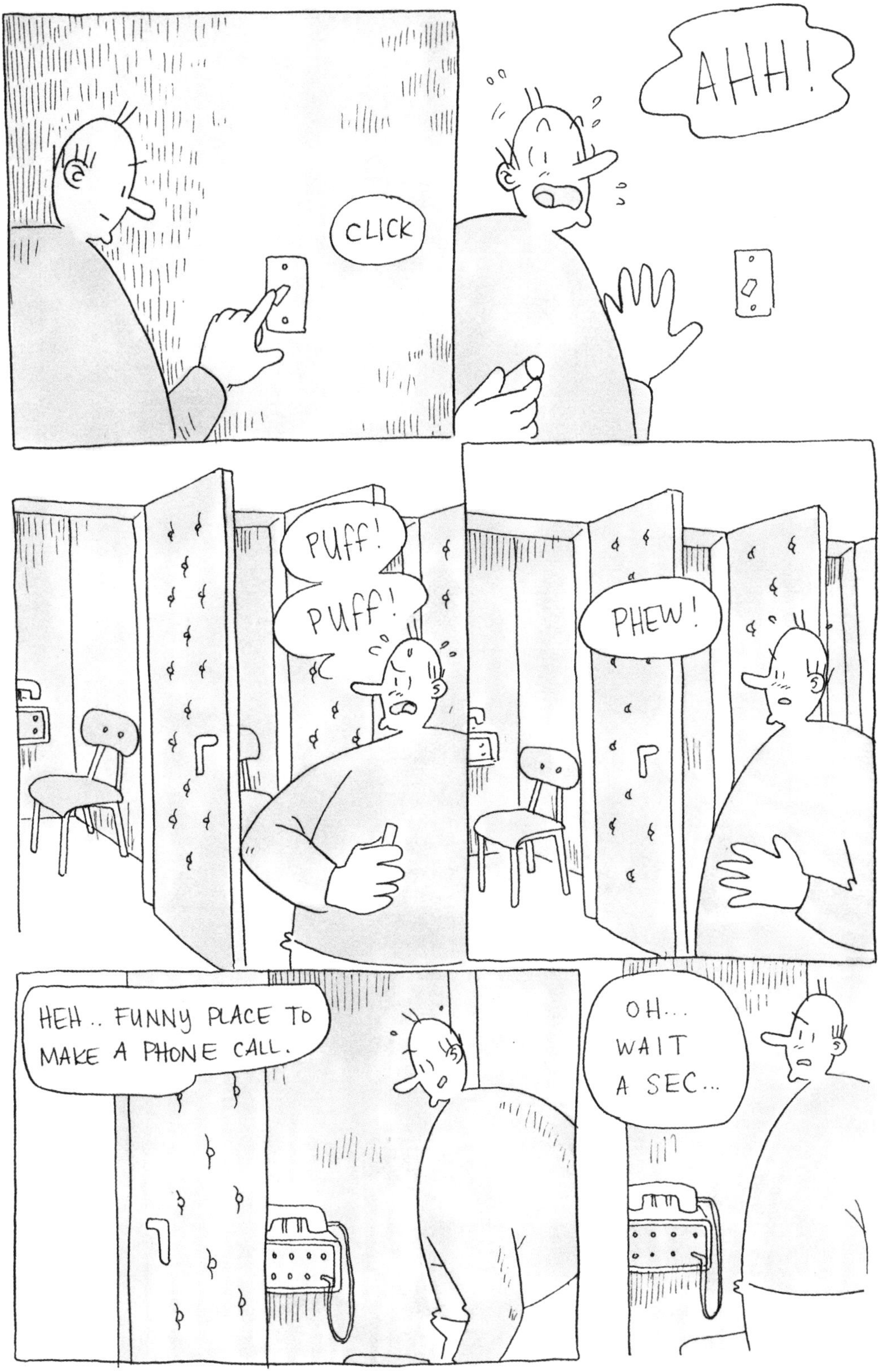
CLICK
AHH!
PUFF!
PUFF!
PHEW!
HEH.. FUNNY PLACE TO MAKE A PHONE CALL.
OH... WAIT A SEC...

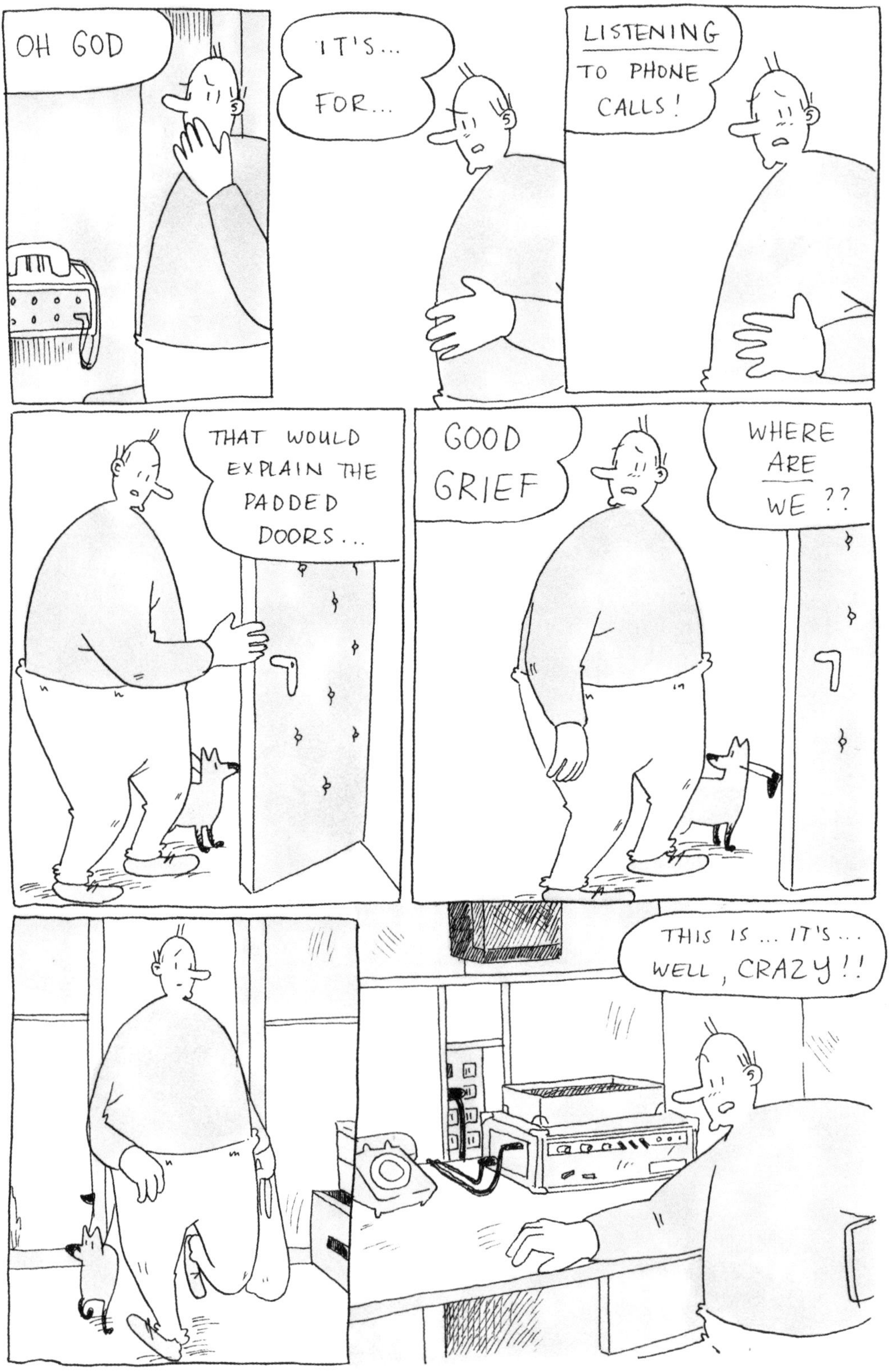
OH GOD
IT'S... FOR...
LISTENING TO PHONE CALLS!
THAT WOULD EXPLAIN THE PADDED DOORS...
GOOD GRIEF
WHERE ARE WE ??
THIS IS ... IT'S... WELL, CRAZY!!

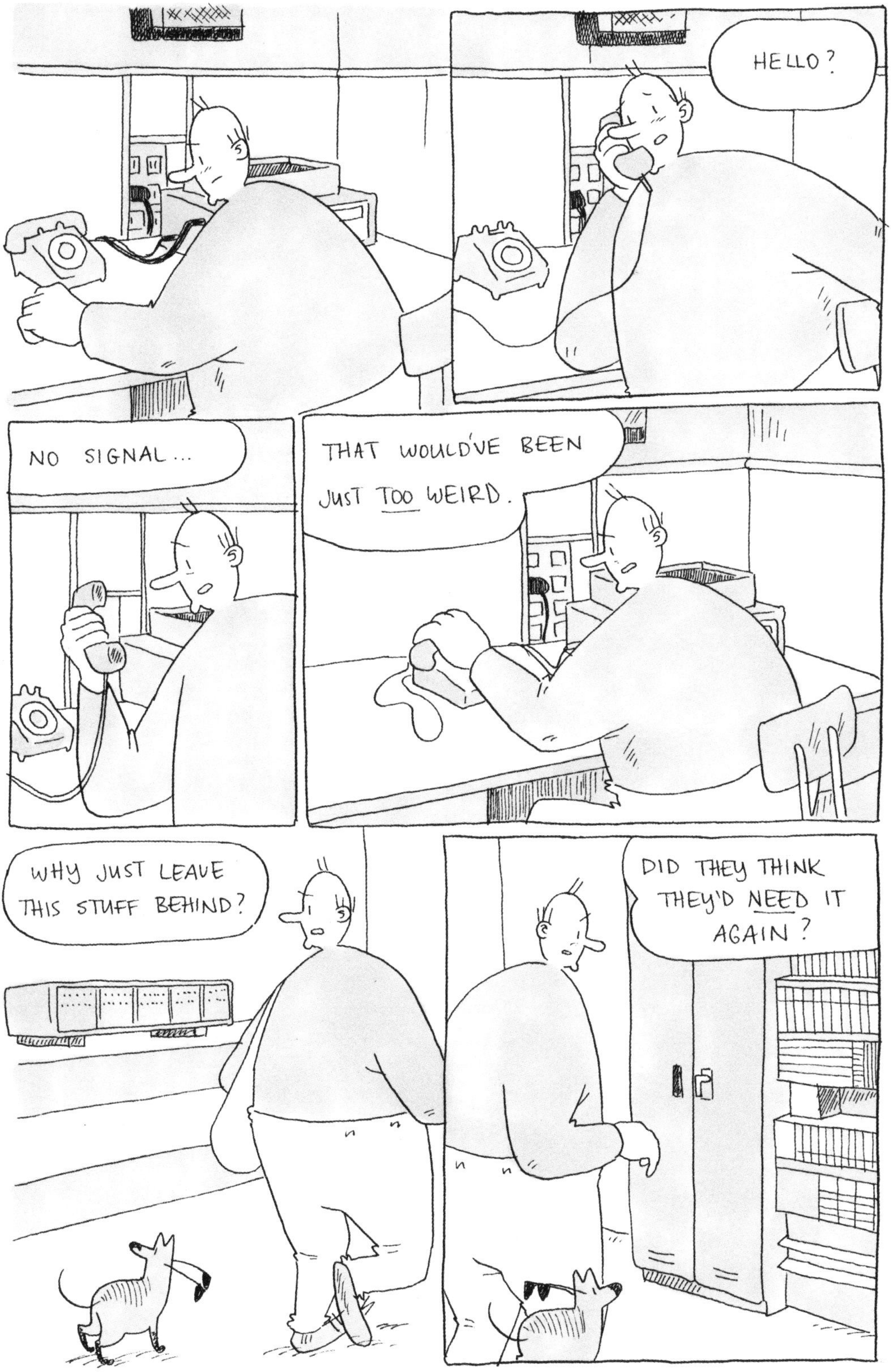
HELLO?
NO SIGNAL...
THAT WOULD'VE BEEN JUST TOO WEIRD.
WHY JUST LEAVE THIS STUFF BEHIND?
DID THEY THINK THEY'D NEED IT AGAIN?

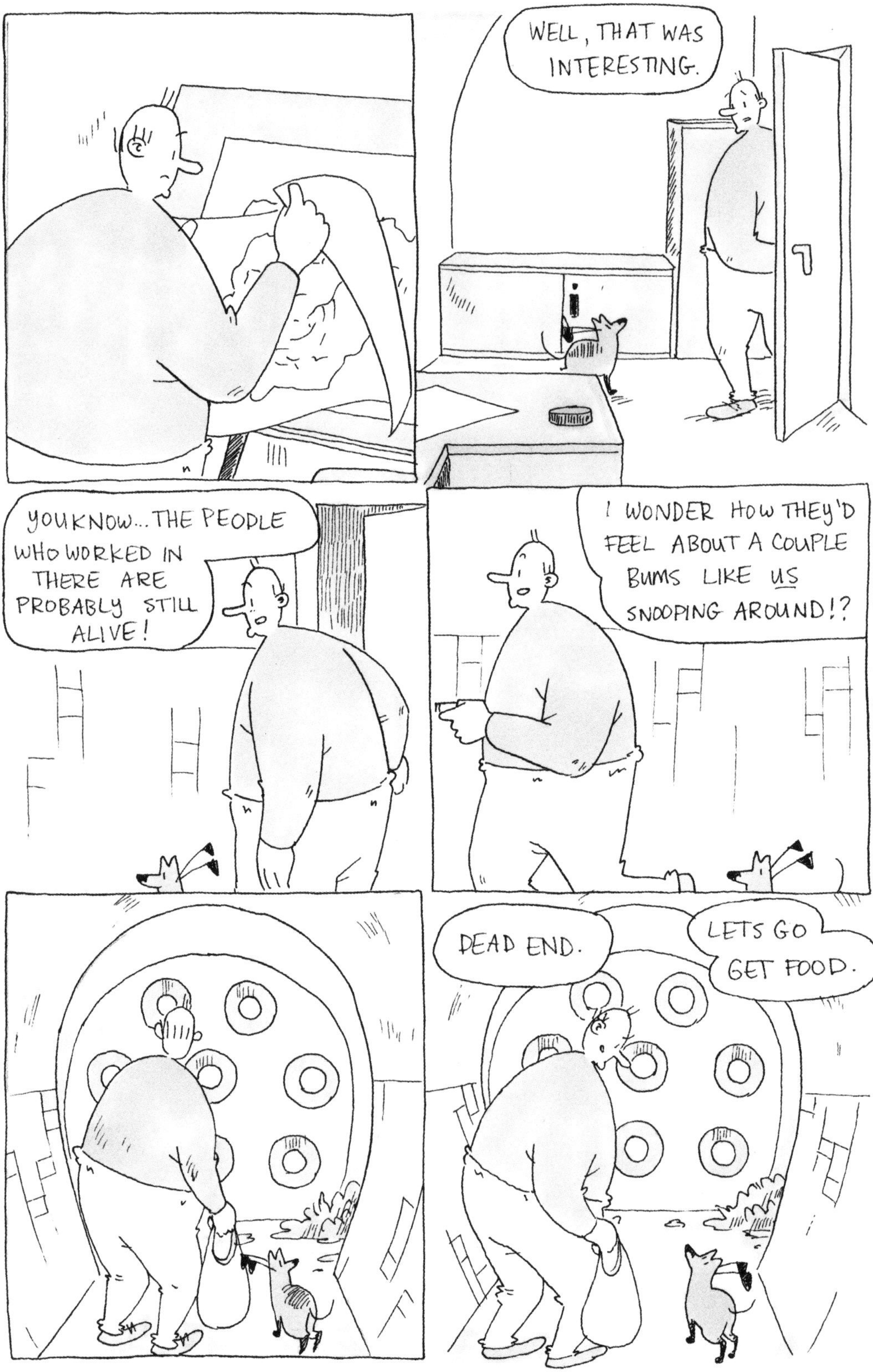
WELL, THAT WAS INTERESTING.
YOU KNOW... THE PEOPLE WHO WORKED IN THERE ARE PROBABLY STILL ALIVE!
I WONDER HOW THEY'D FEEL ABOUT A COUPLE BUMS LIKE US SNOOPING AROUND!?
DEAD END.
LETS GO GET FOOD.

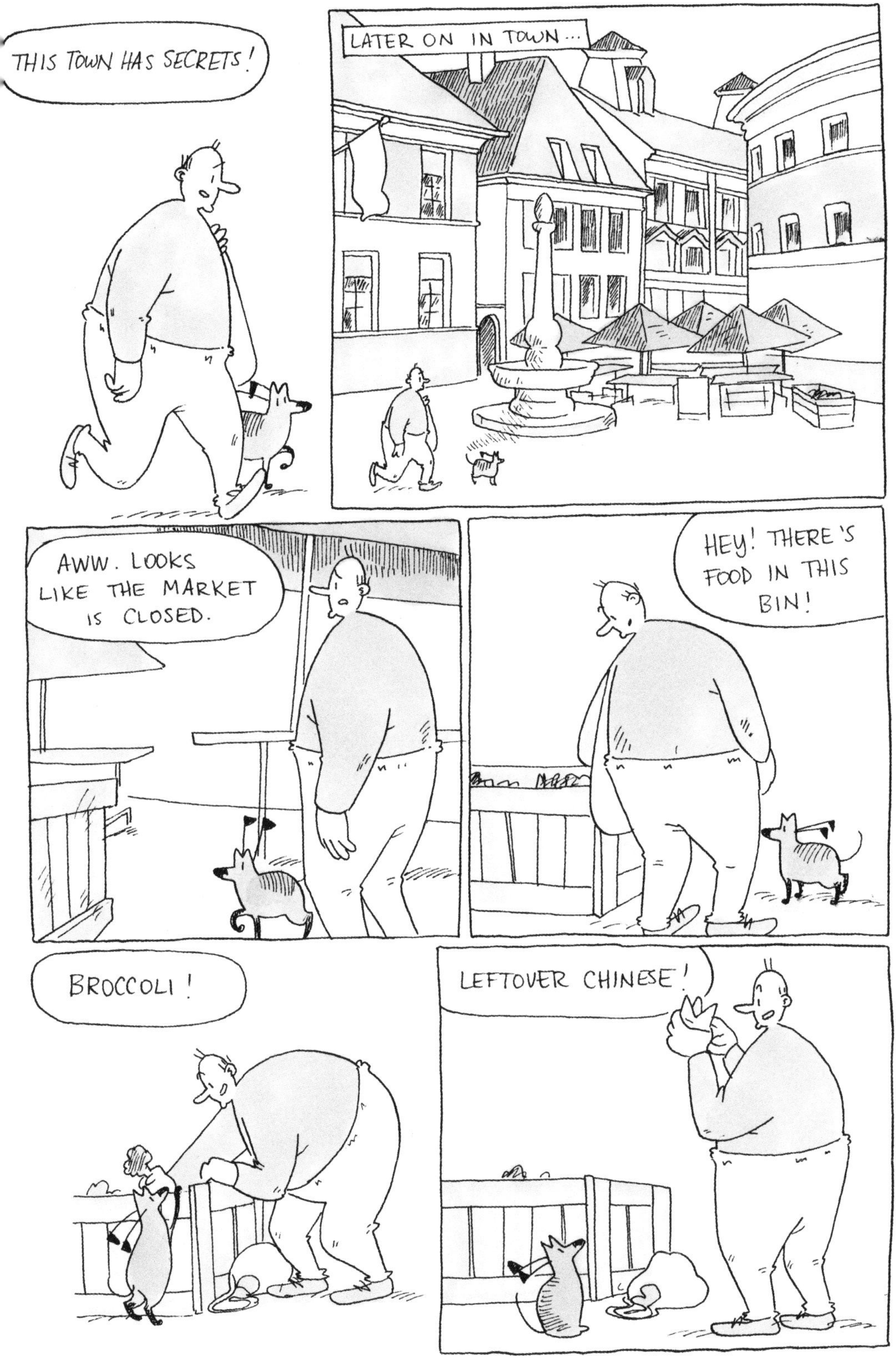
THIS TOWN HAS SECRETS!
LATER ON IN TOWN...
AWW. LOOKS LIKE THE MARKET IS CLOSED.
HEY! THERE'S FOOD IN THIS BIN!
BROCCOLI!
LEFTOVER CHINESE!

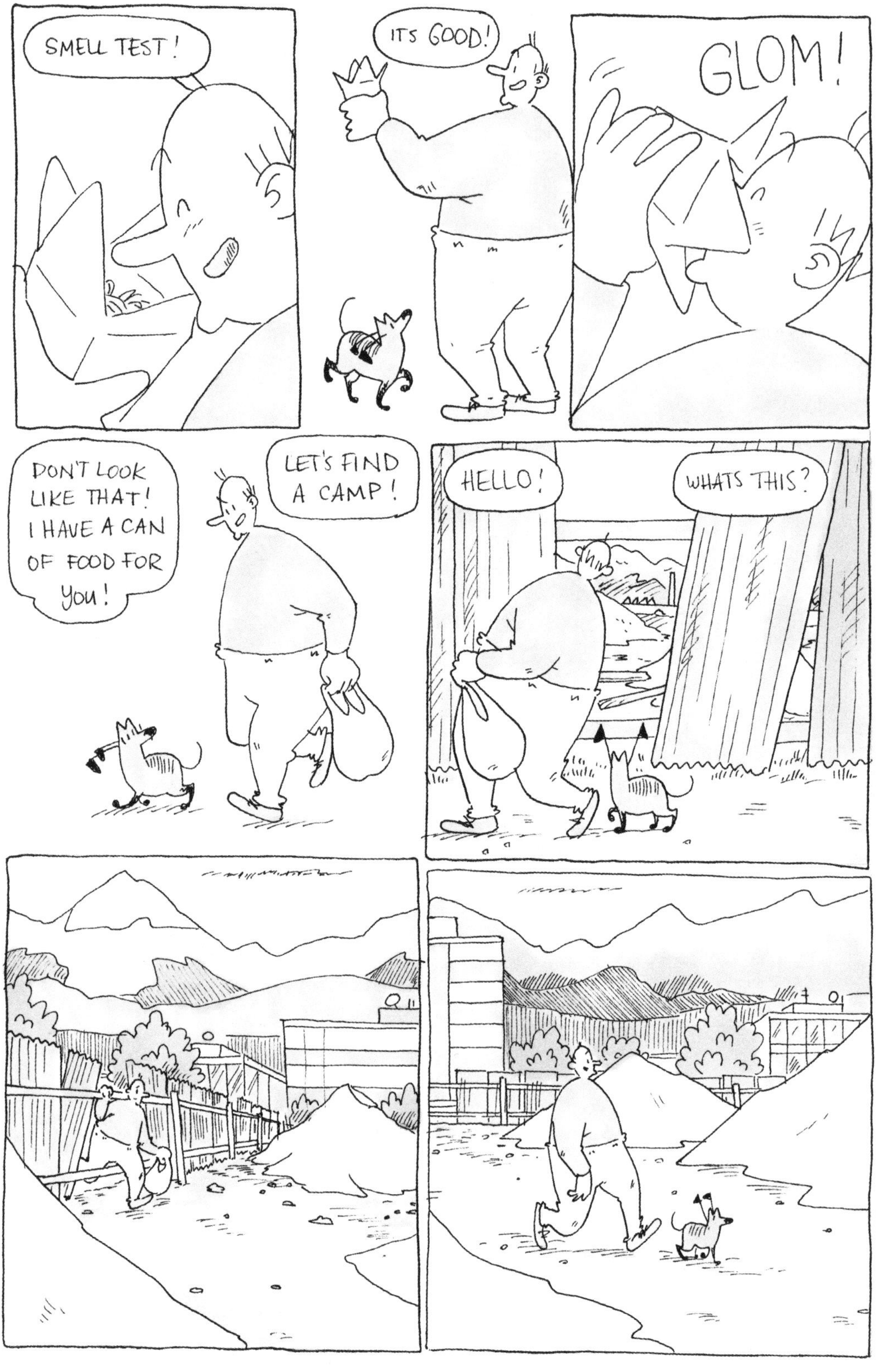
SMELL TEST!
ITS GOOD!
GLOM!
DON'T LOOK LIKE THAT! I HAVE A CAN OF FOOD FOR YOU!
LET'S FIND A CAMP!
HELLO!
WHATS THIS?

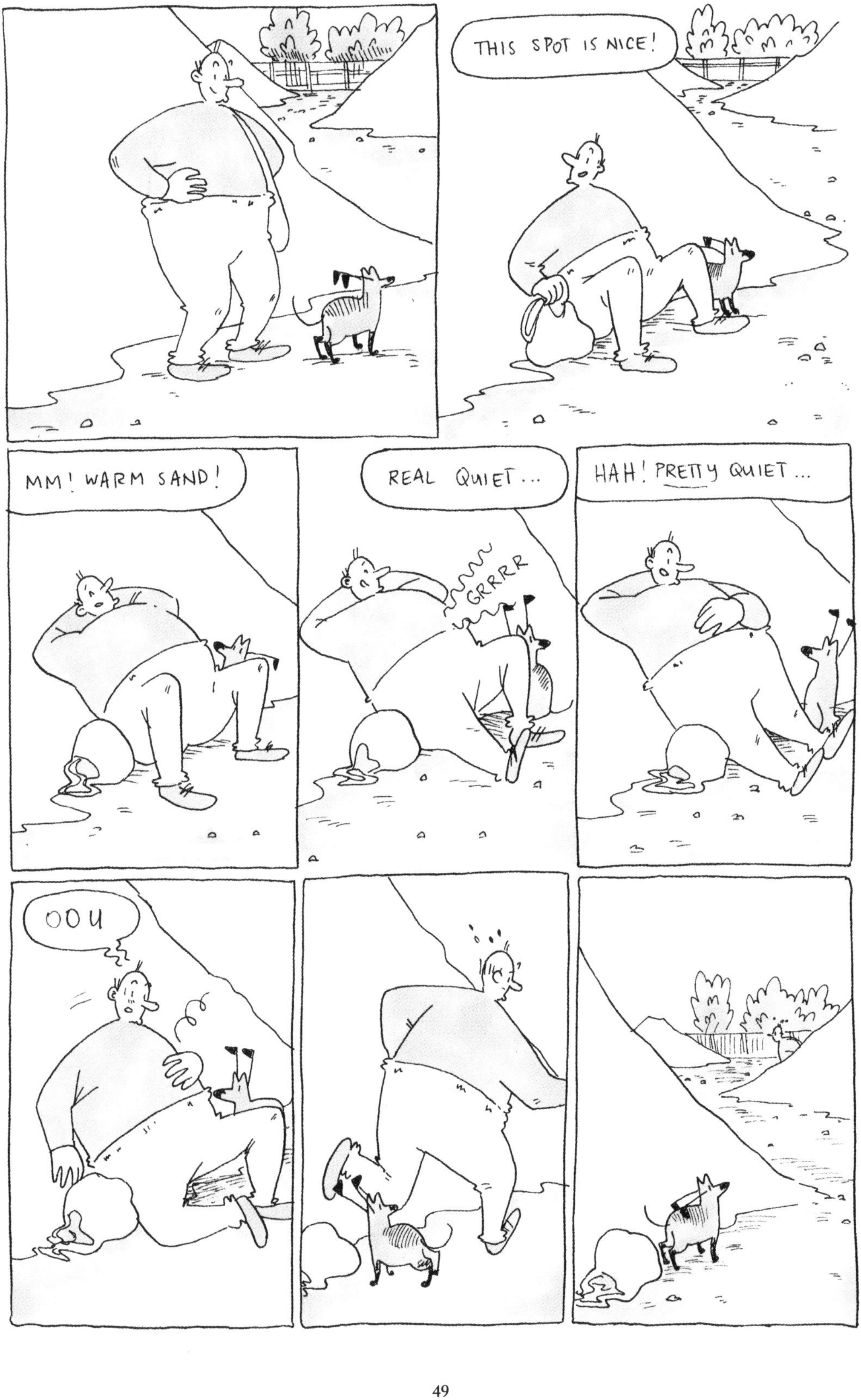
THIS SPOT IS NICE!
MM! WARM SAND!
REAL QUIET...
GRRRR
HAH! PRETTY QUIET...
OOU

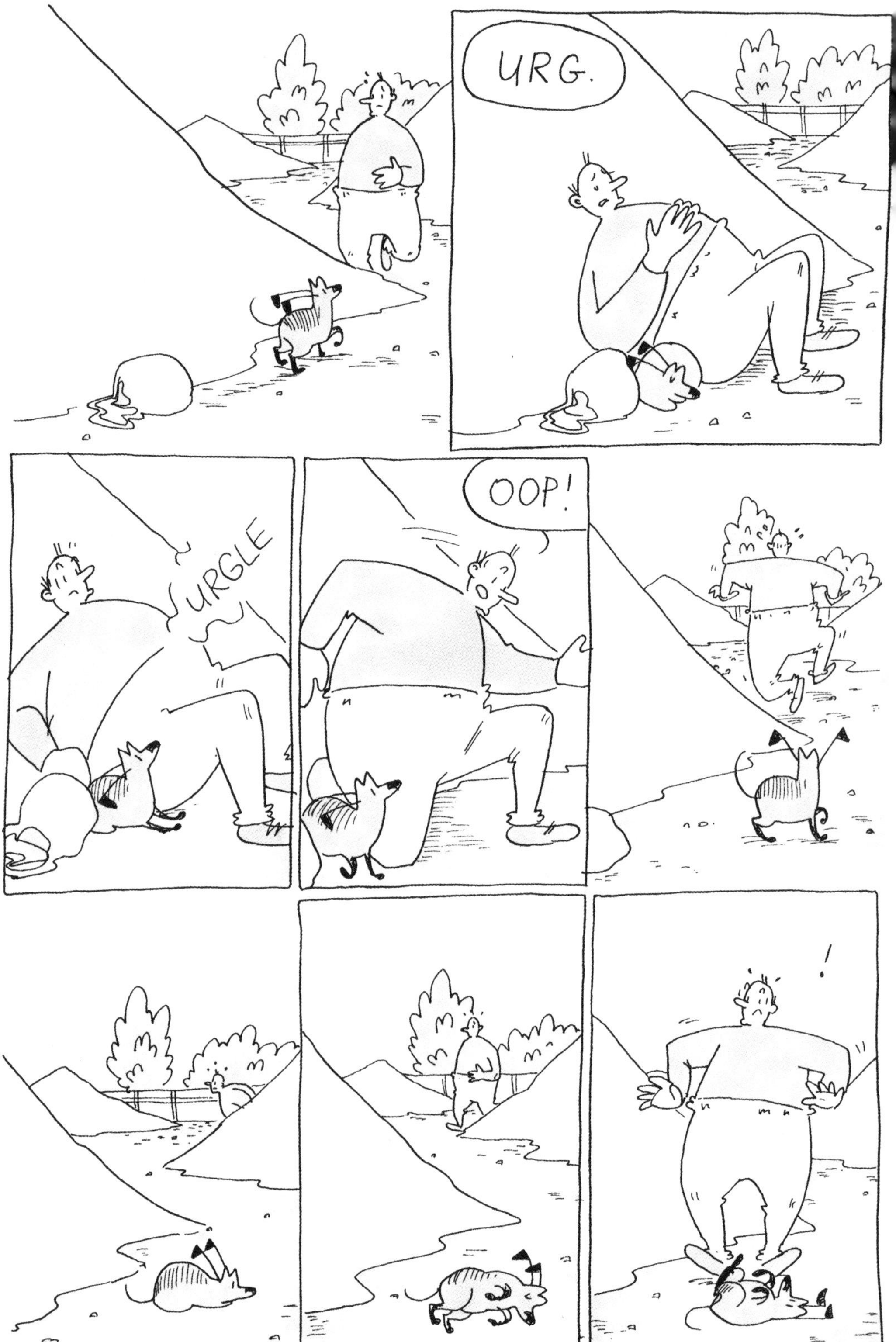
URG.
URGLE
OOP!
!

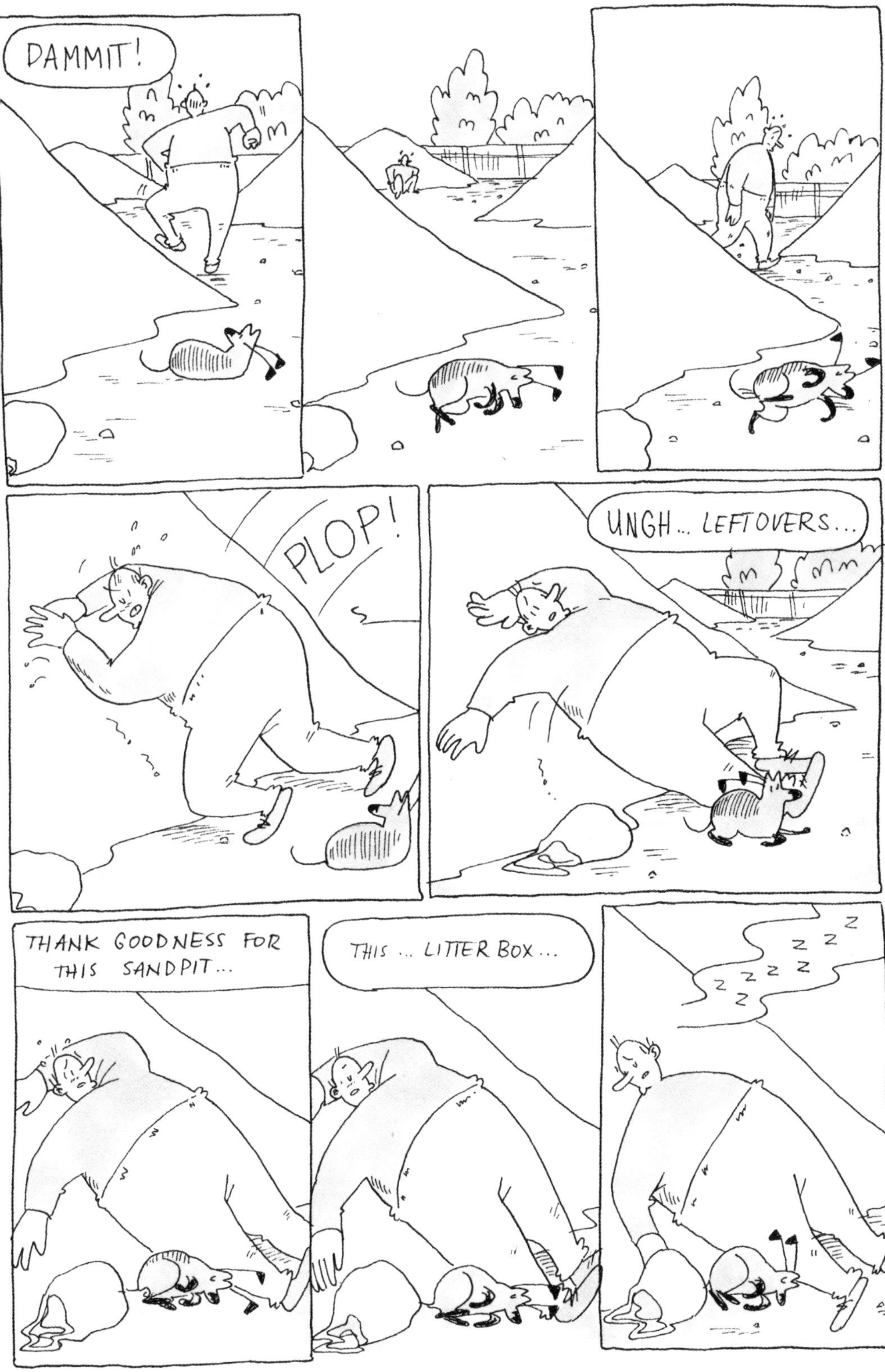
DAMMIT!
PLOP!
UNGH... LEFTOVERS...
THANK GOODNESS FOR THIS SANDPIT...
THIS ... LITTER BOX ...
Z Z Z Z Z Z Z Z Z Z

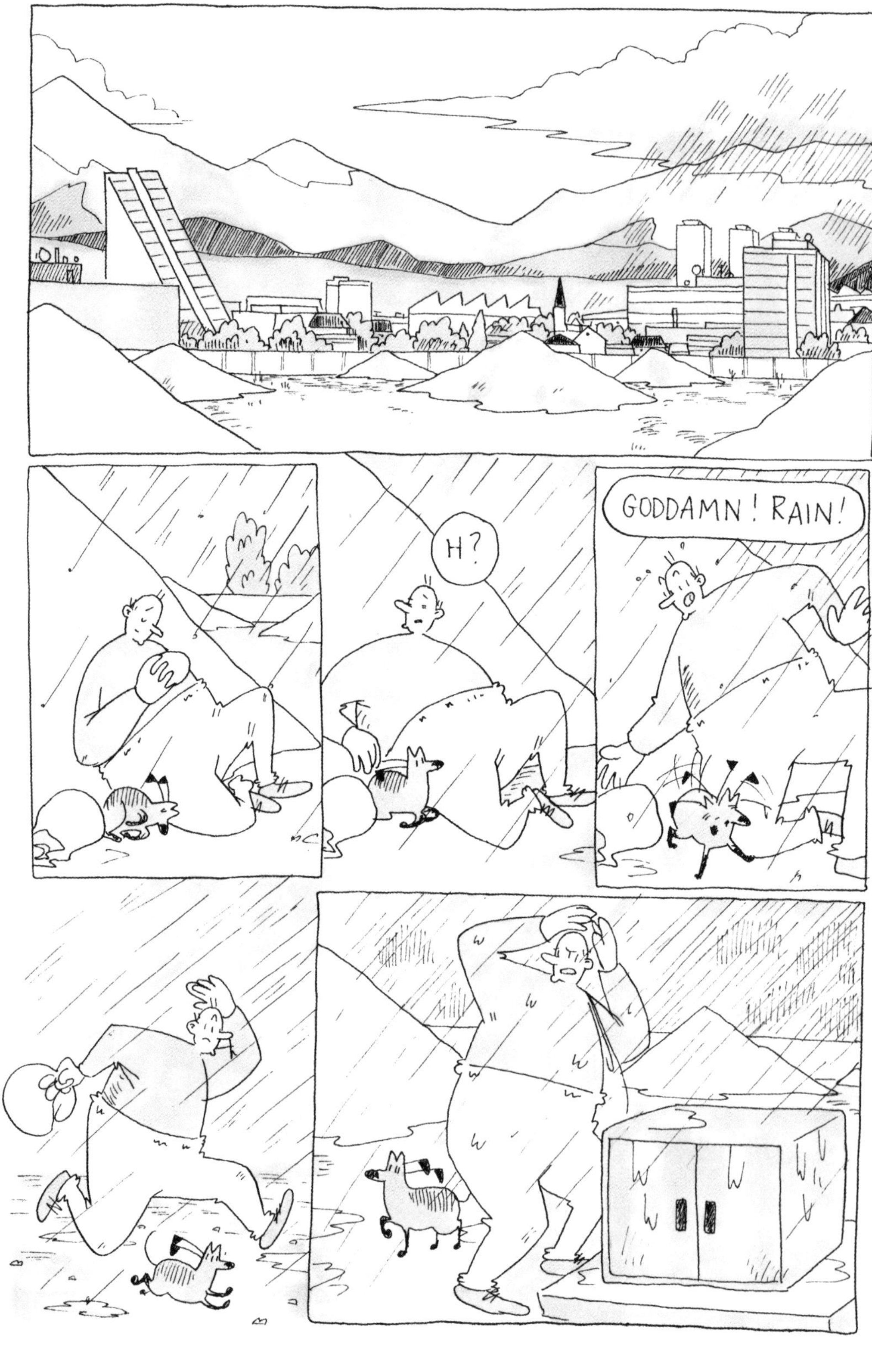
H?
GODDAMN! RAIN!

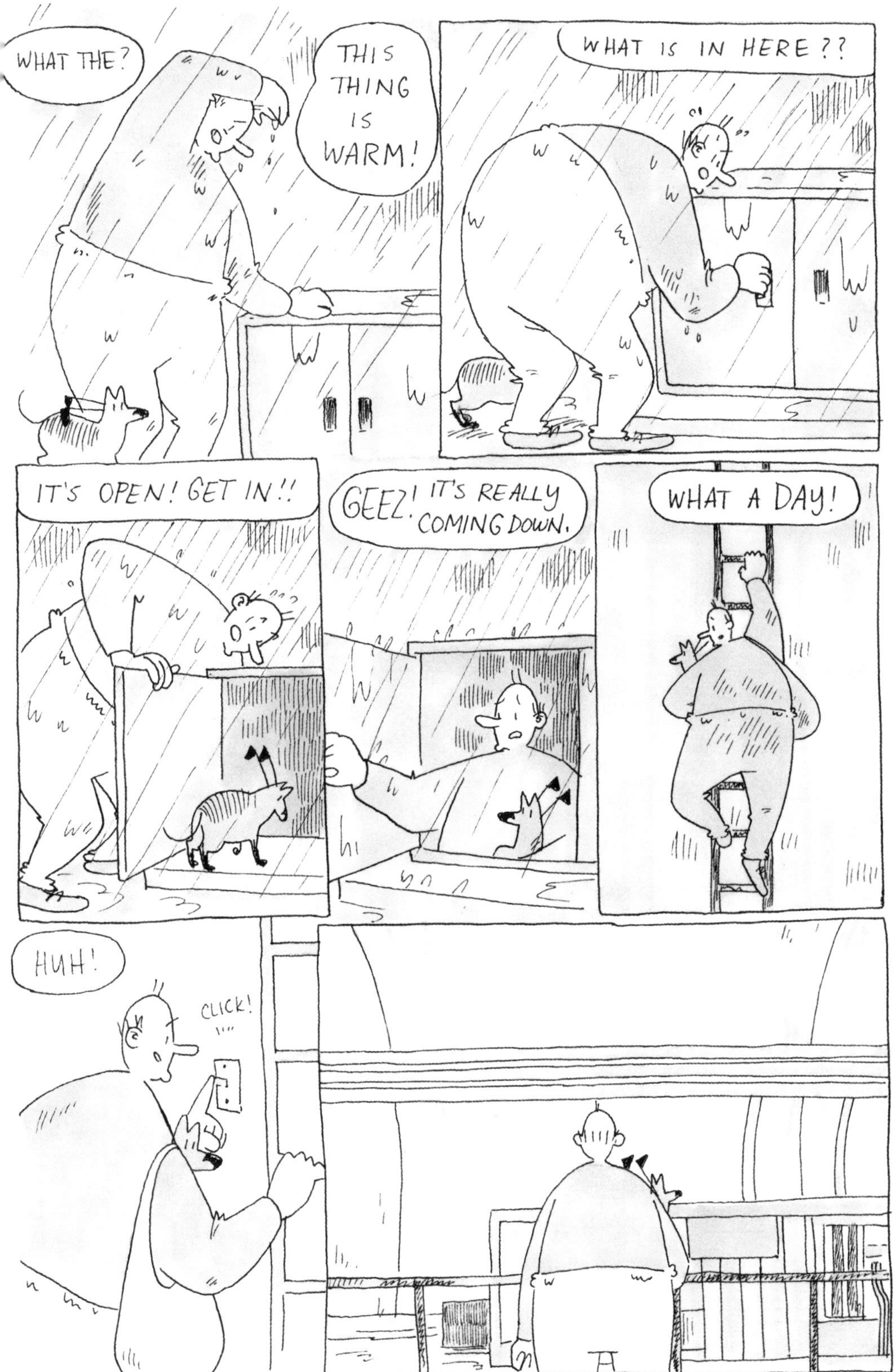
WHAT THE?
THIS THING IS WARM!
WHAT IS IN HERE??
IT'S OPEN! GET IN!!
GEEZ! IT'S REALLY COMING DOWN.
WHAT A DAY!
HUH!
CLICK!

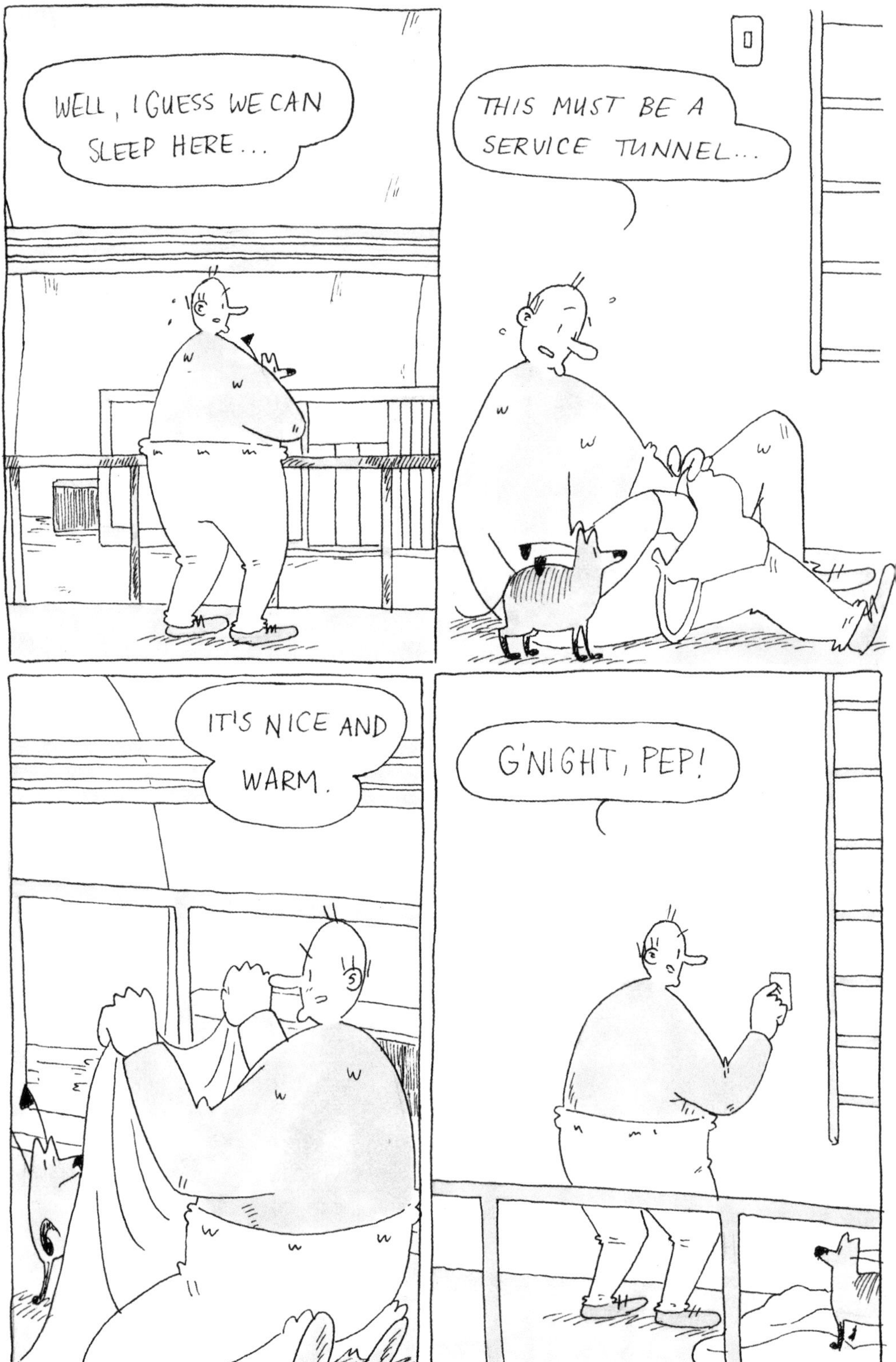
WELL, I GUESS WE CAN SLEEP HERE...
THIS MUST BE A SERVICE TUNNEL...
IT'S NICE AND WARM.
G'NIGHT, PEP!

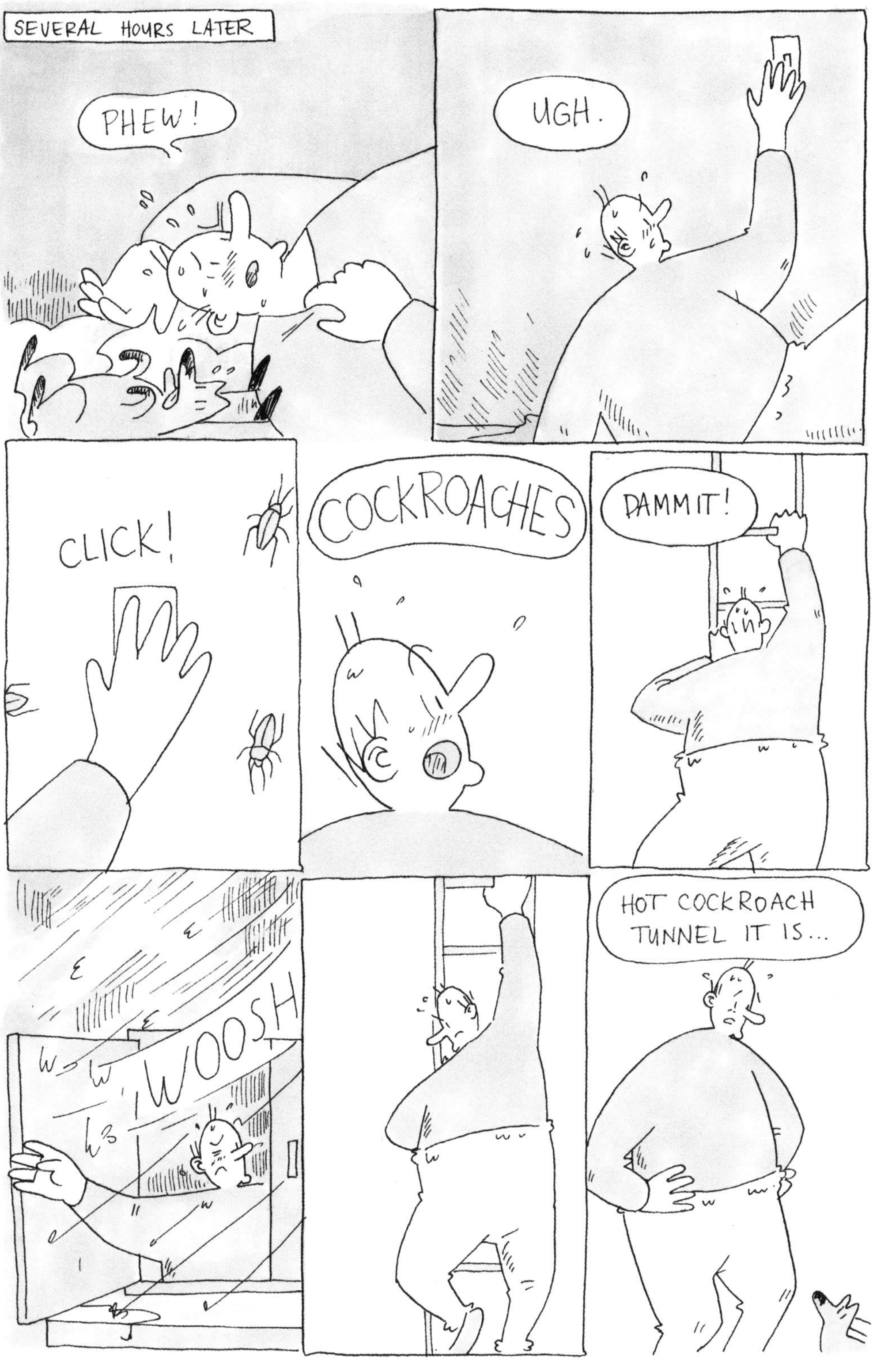
SEVERAL HOURS LATER
PHEW!
UGH.
CLICK!
COCKROACHES
DAMMIT!
WOOSH
HOT COCKROACH TUNNEL IT IS...

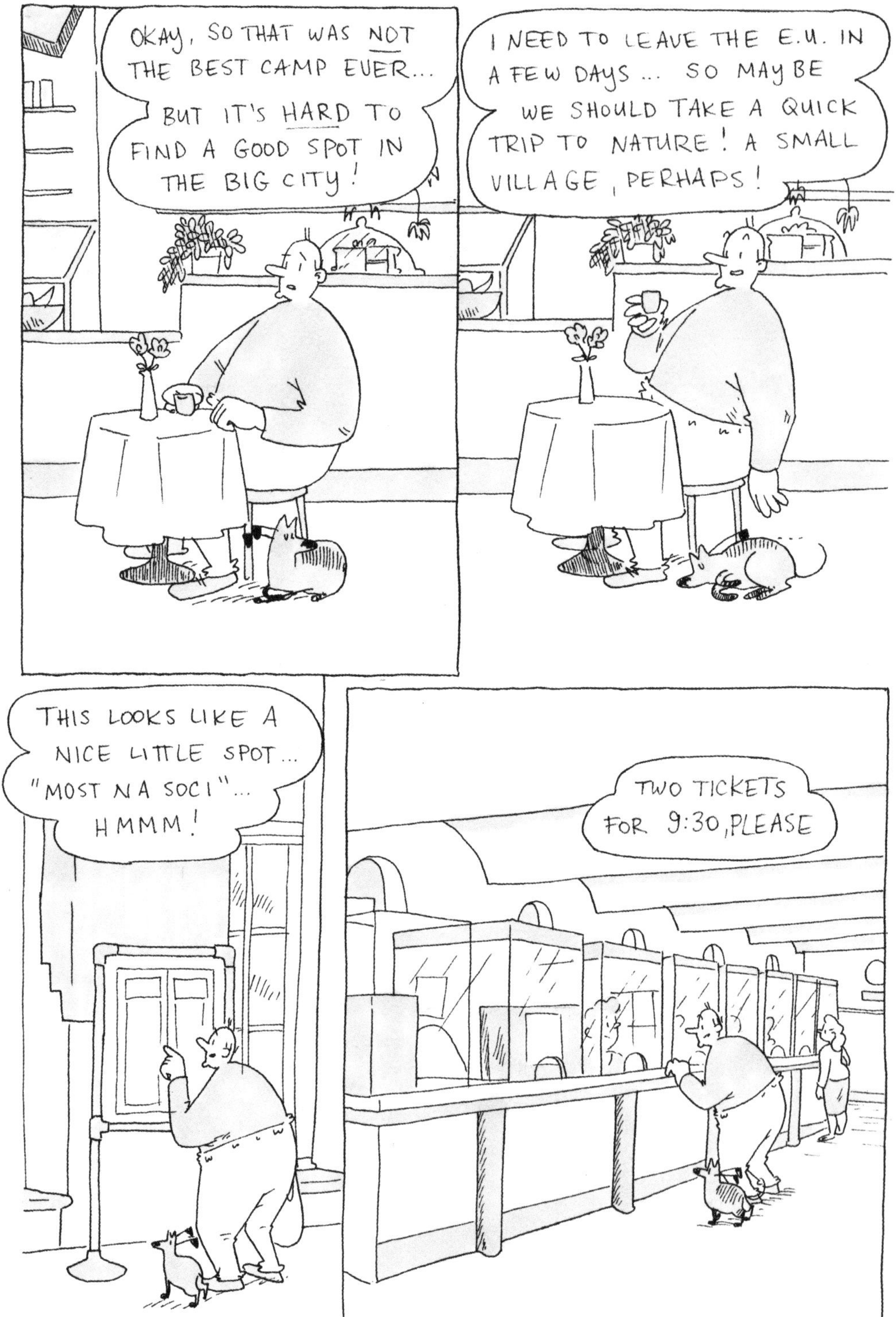
OKAY, SO THAT WAS NOT THE BEST CAMP EVER...
BUT IT'S HARD TO FIND A GOOD SPOT IN THE BIG CITY!
I NEED TO LEAVE THE E.U. IN A FEW DAYS... SO MAYBE WE SHOULD TAKE A QUICK TRIP TO NATURE! A SMALL VILLAGE, PERHAPS!
THIS LOOKS LIKE A NICE LITTLE SPOT... "MOST NA SOCI"... HMMM!
TWO TICKETS FOR 9:30, PLEASE

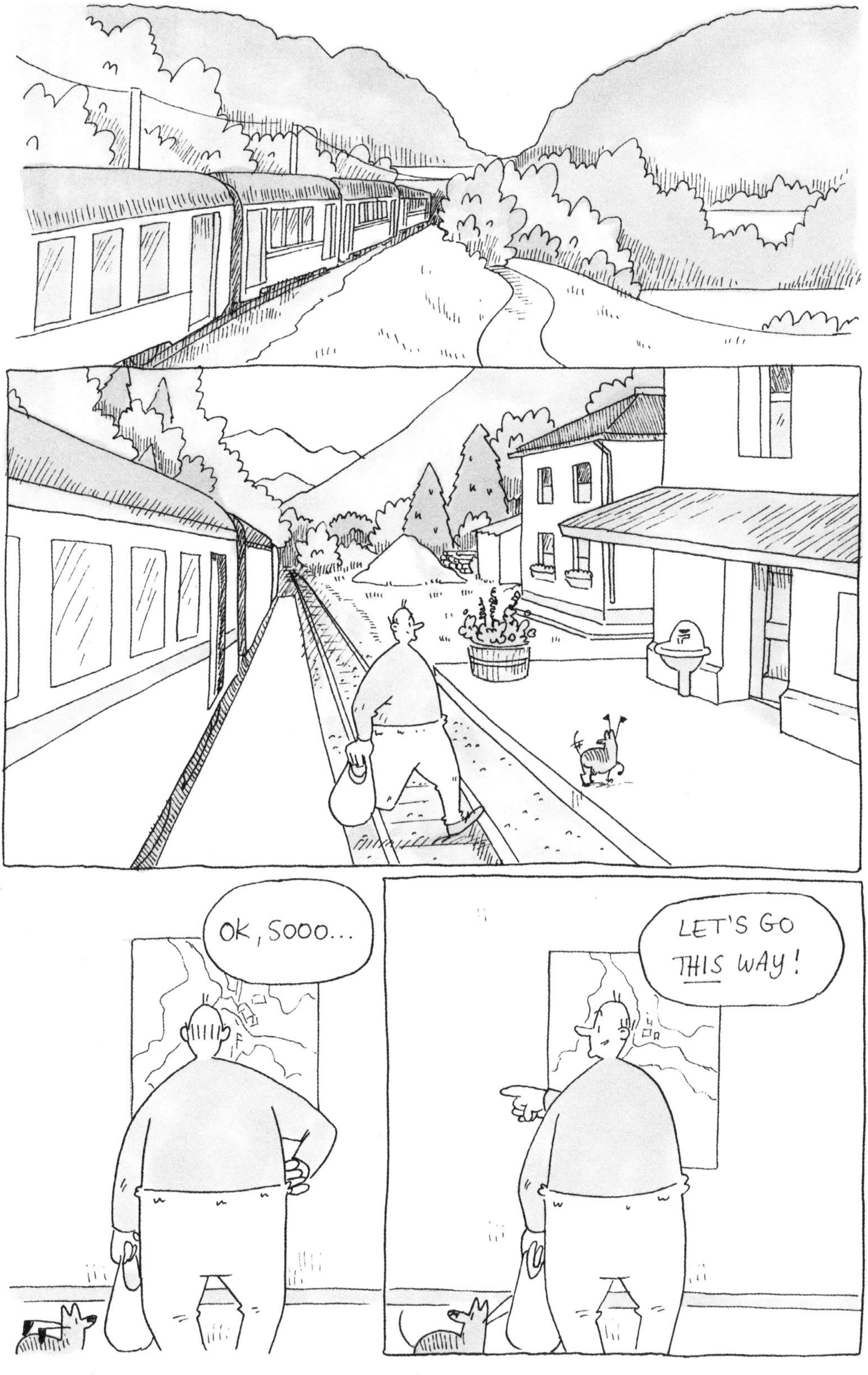
OK, SOOO...
LET'S GO THIS WAY!

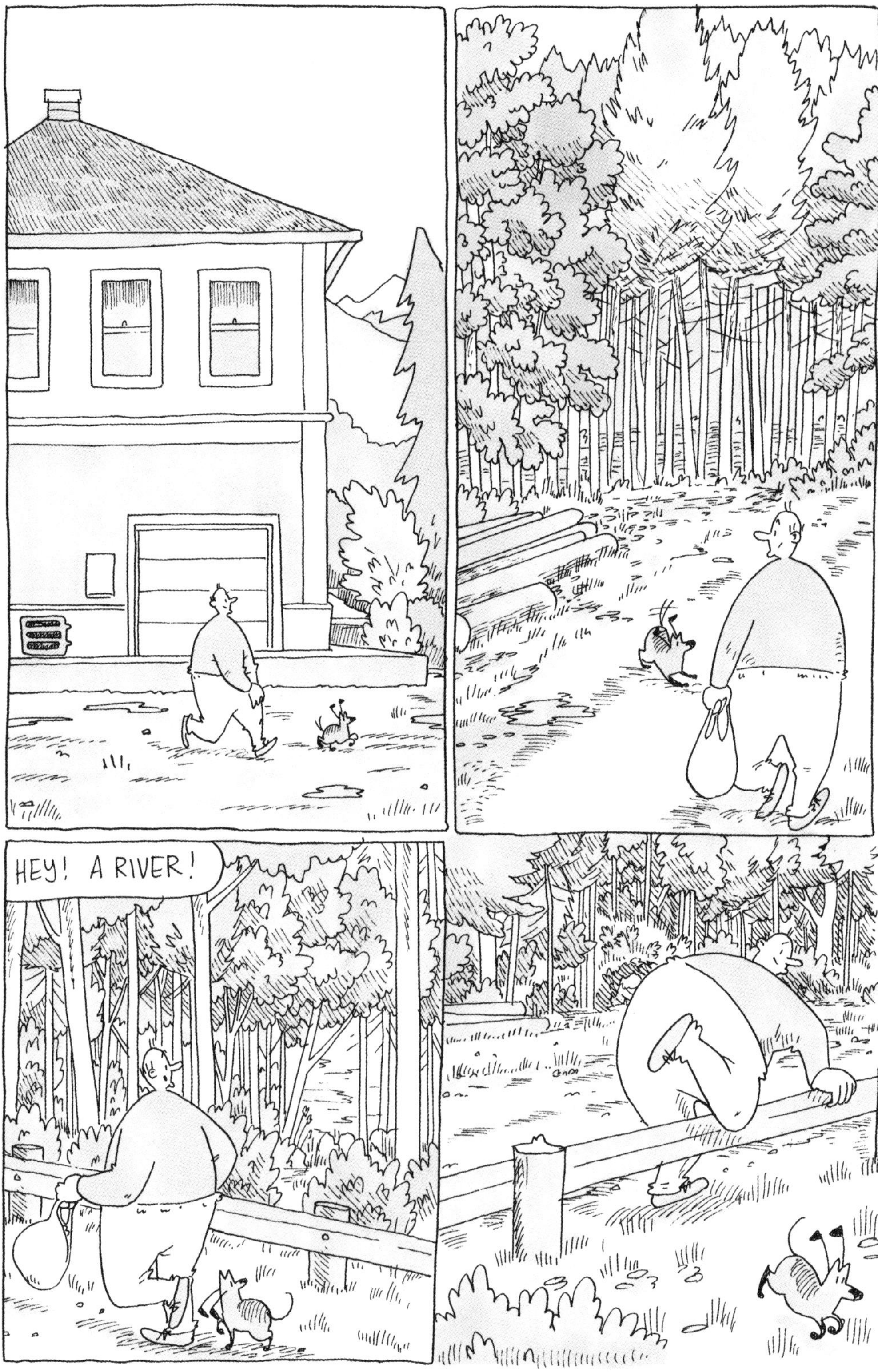
HEY! A RIVER!

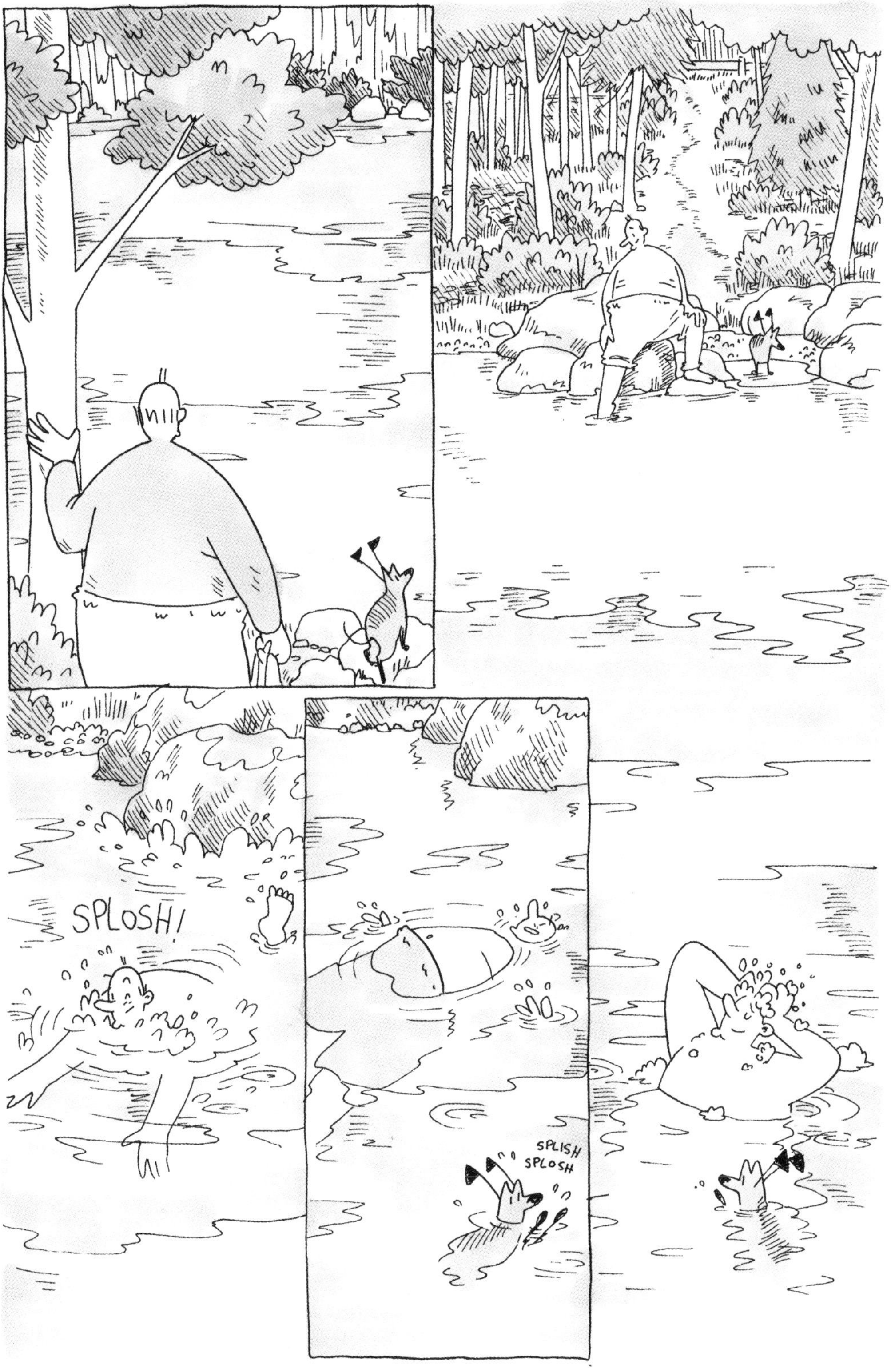
SPLOSH!
SPLISH
SPLOSH

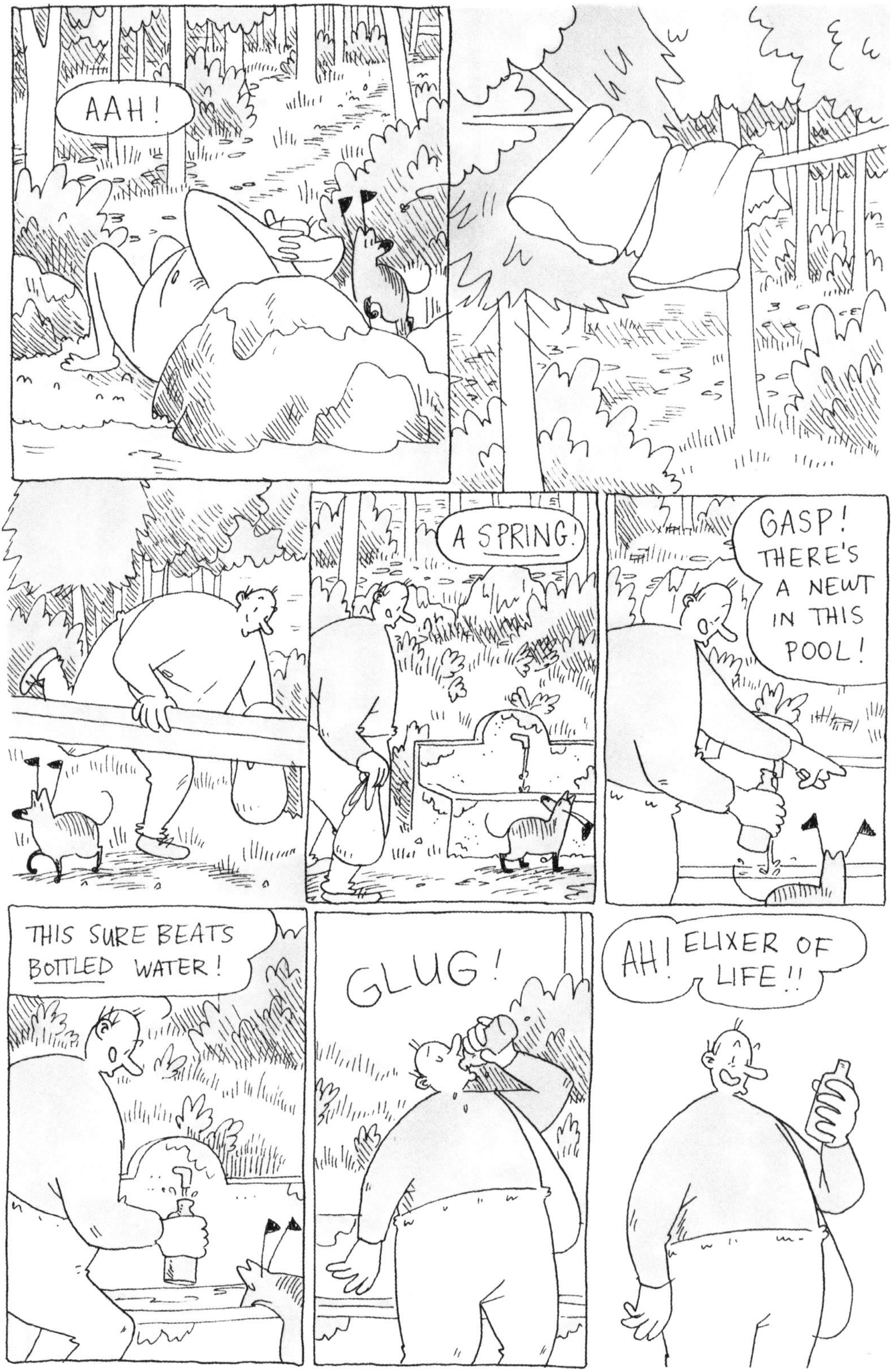
AAH!
A SPRING!
GASP! THERE'S A NEWT IN THIS POOL!
THIS SURE BEATS BOTTLED WATER!
GLUG!
AH! ELIXER OF LIFE!!

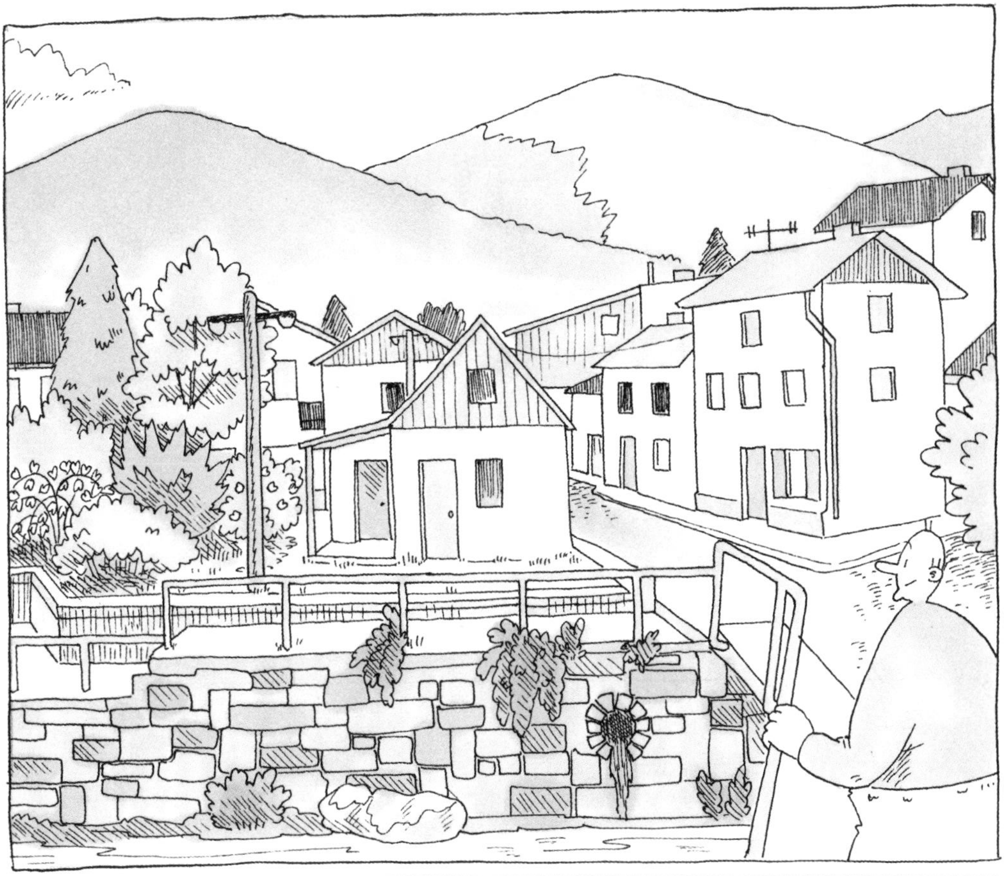

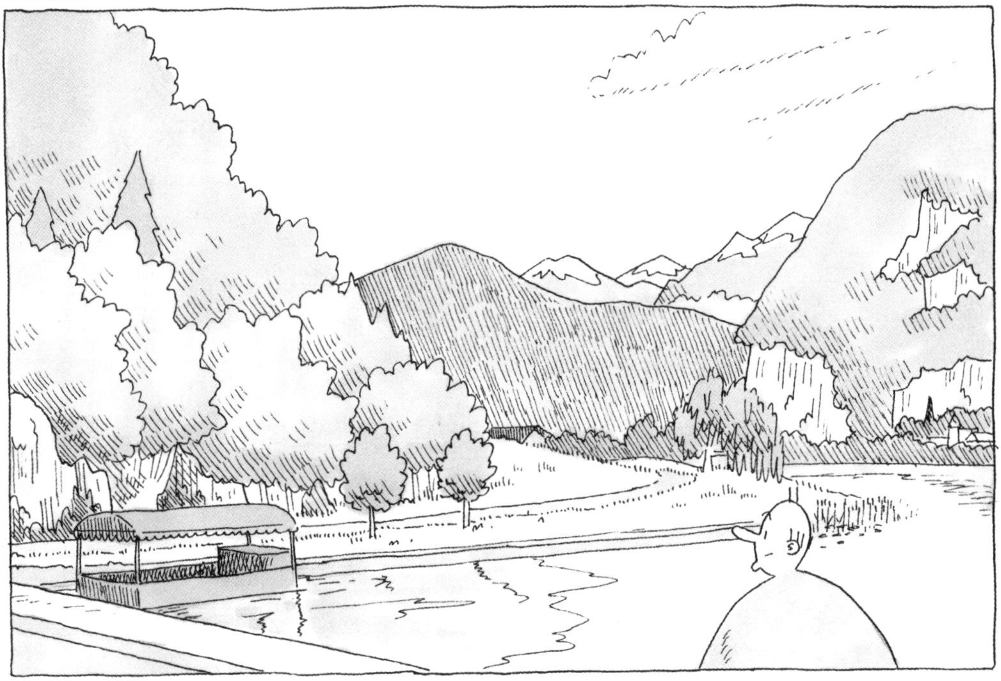

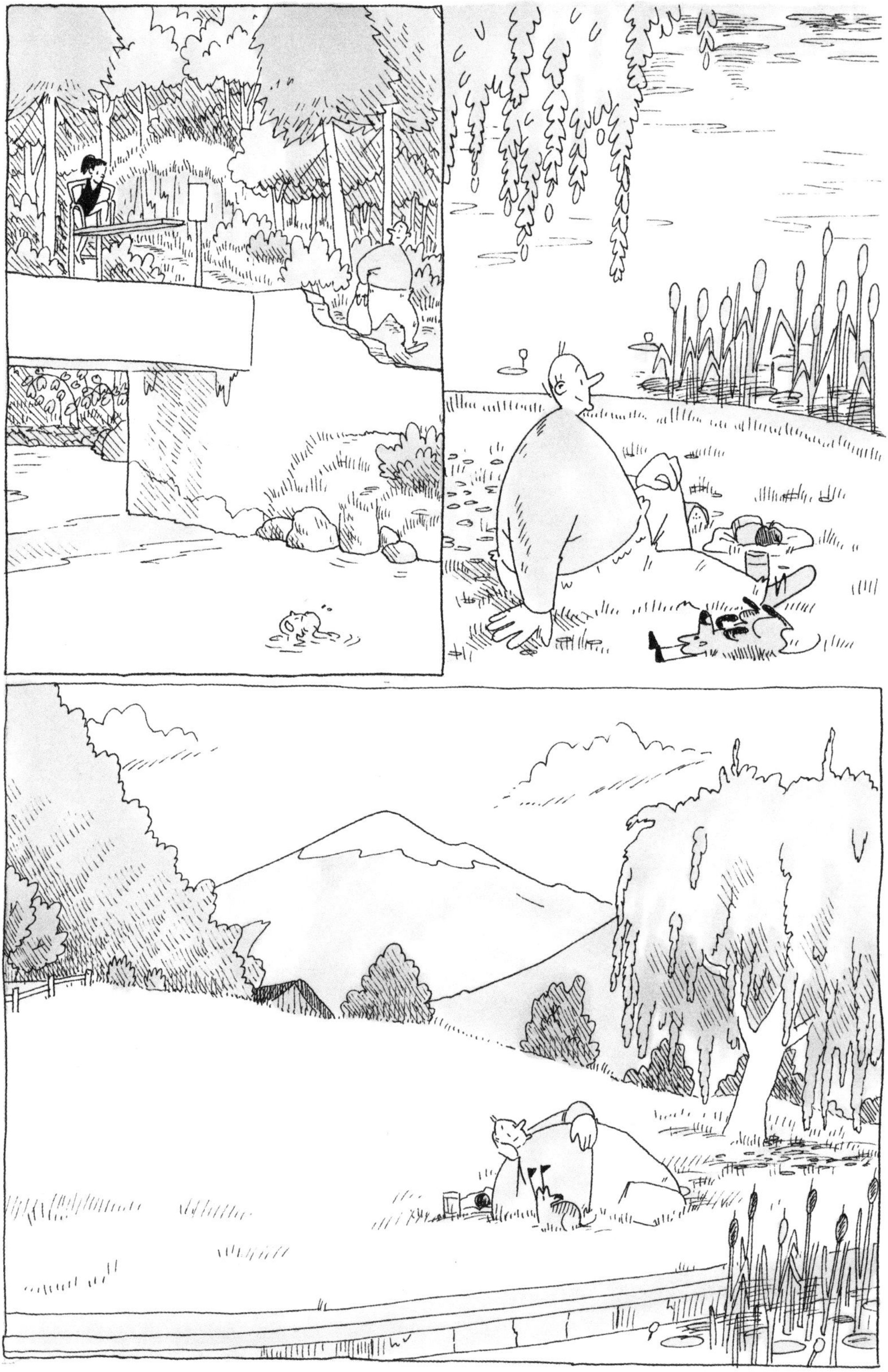

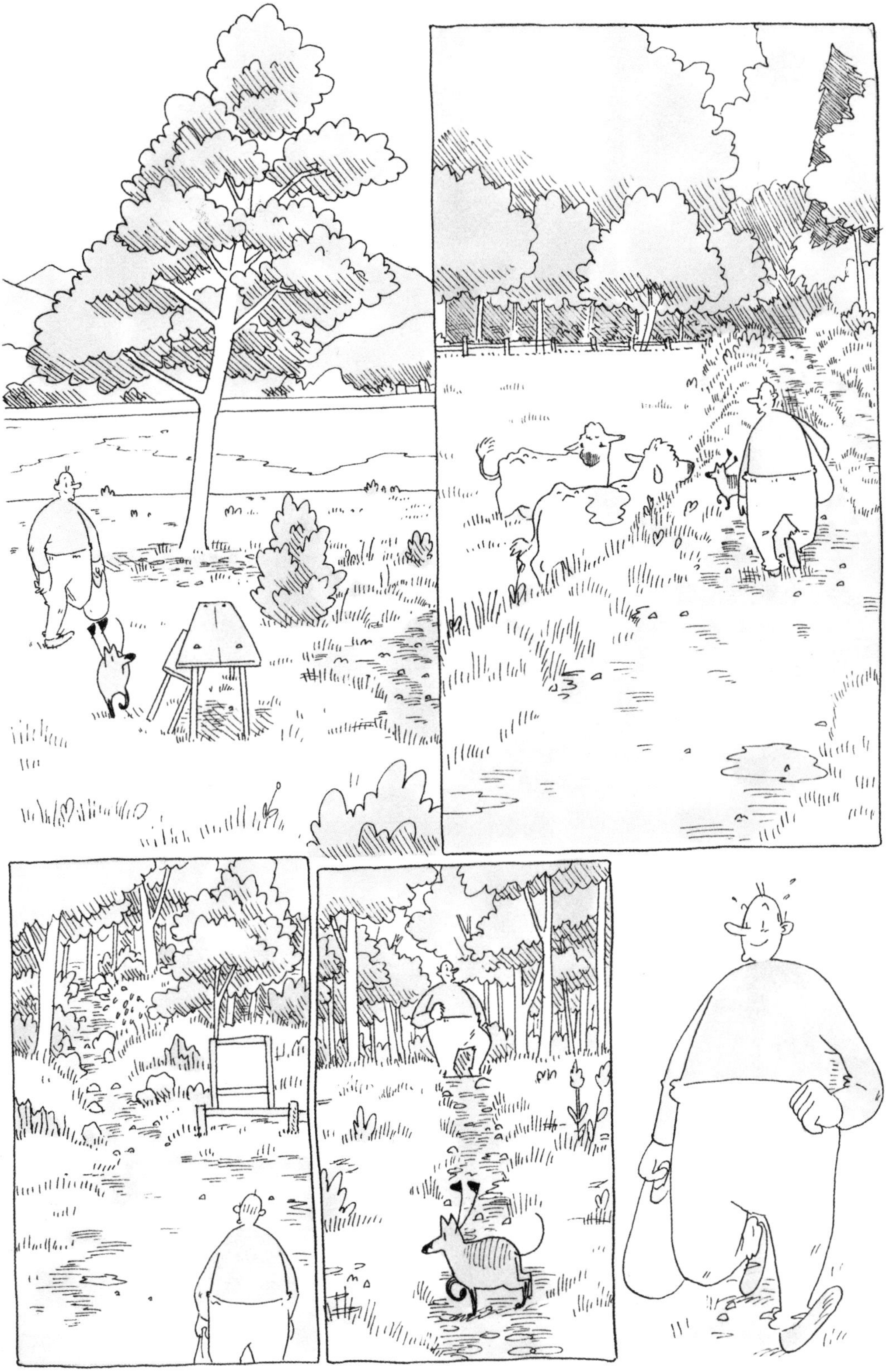

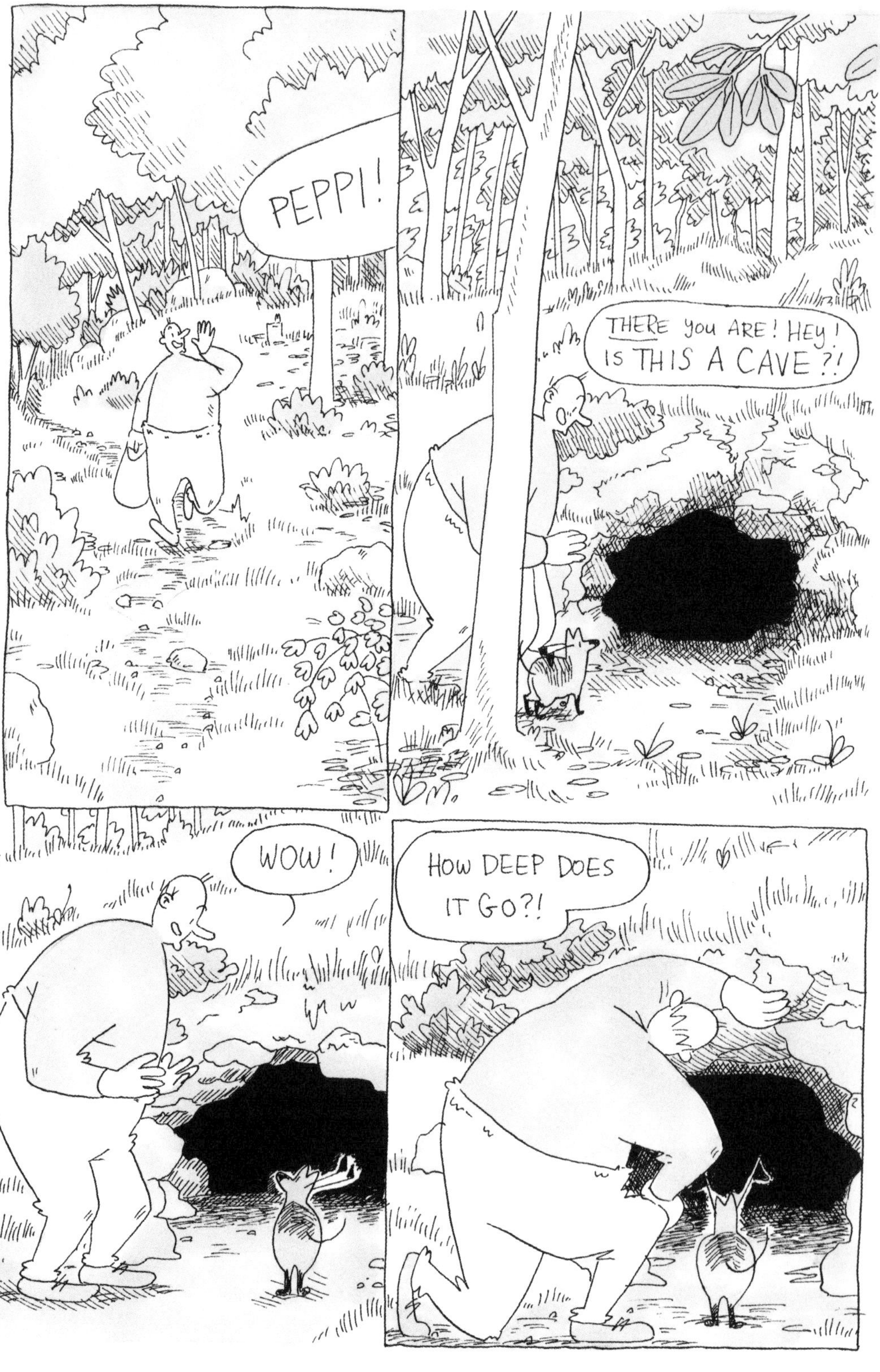
PEPPI!
THERE you ARE! HEY! IS THIS A CAVE?!
WOW!
HOW DEEP DOES IT GO?!

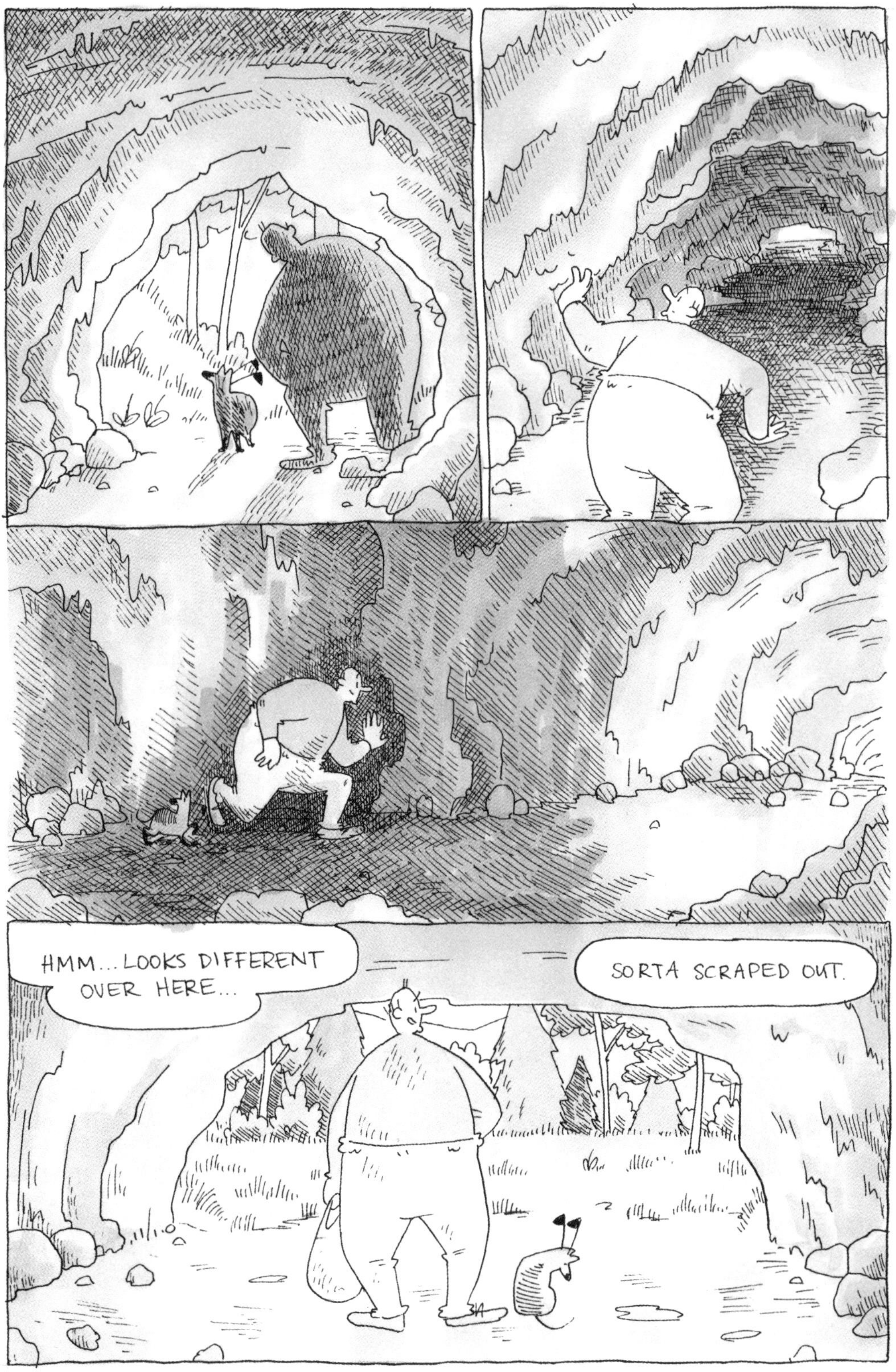
HMM... LOOKS DIFFERENT OVER HERE...
SORTA SCRAPED OUT.

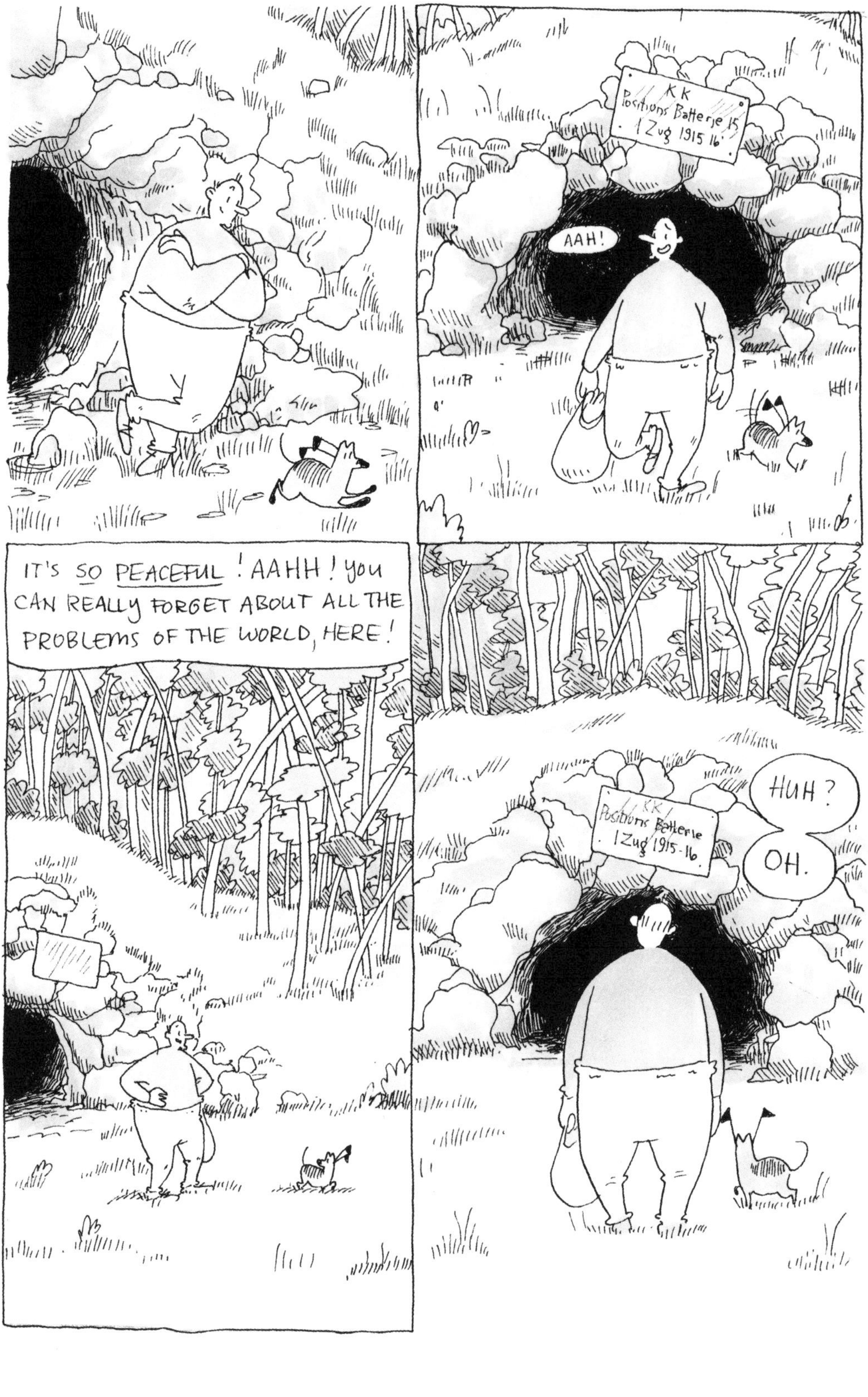
K K
Positions Batterie 15
1 Zug 1915-16
AAH!
IT'S SO PEACEFUL! AAHH! YOU CAN REALLY FORGET ABOUT ALL THE PROBLEMS OF THE WORLD, HERE!
K K
Positions Batterie
1 Zug 1915-16
HUH?
OH.

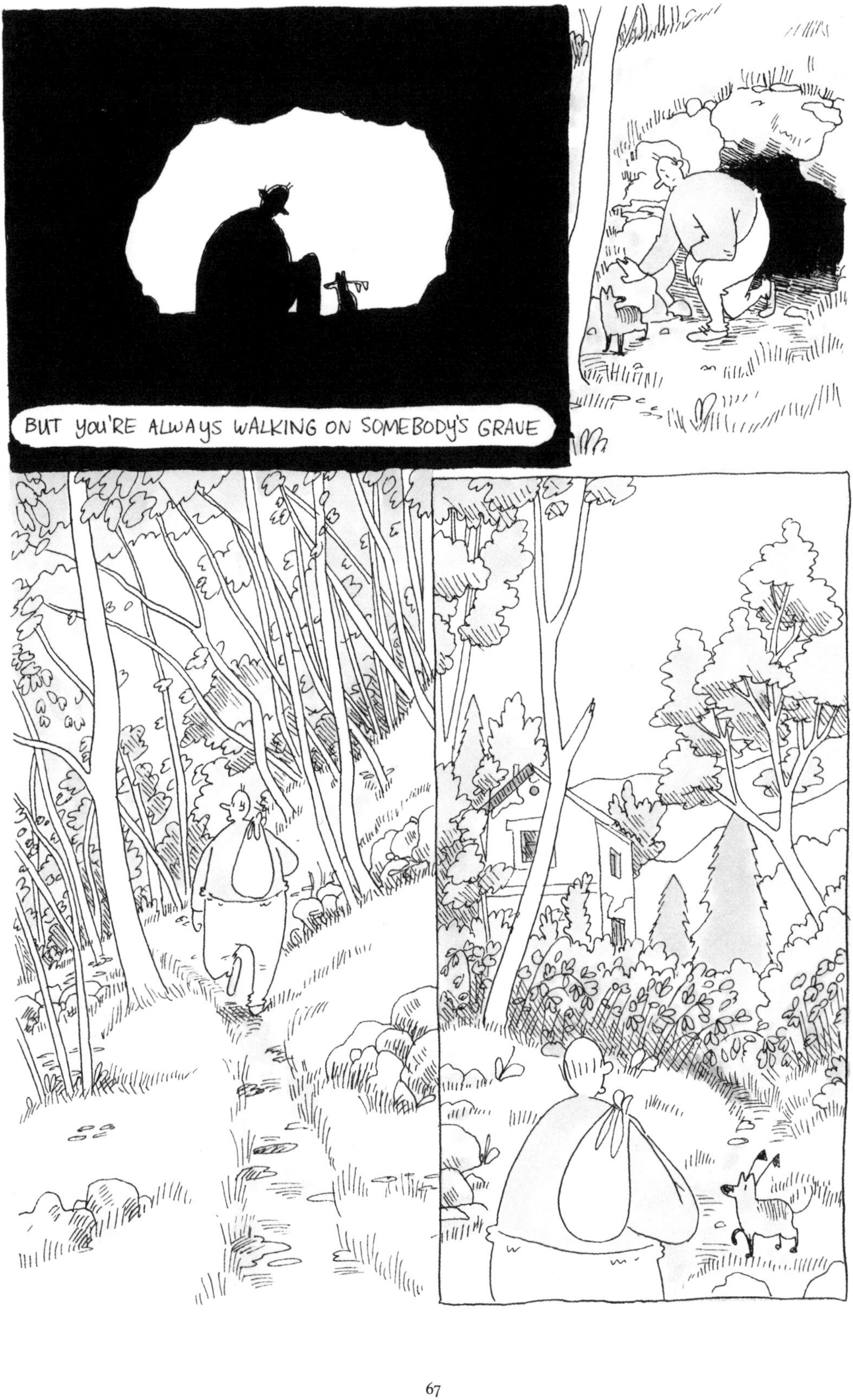
BUT YOU'RE ALWAYS WALKING ON SOMEBODY'S GRAVE

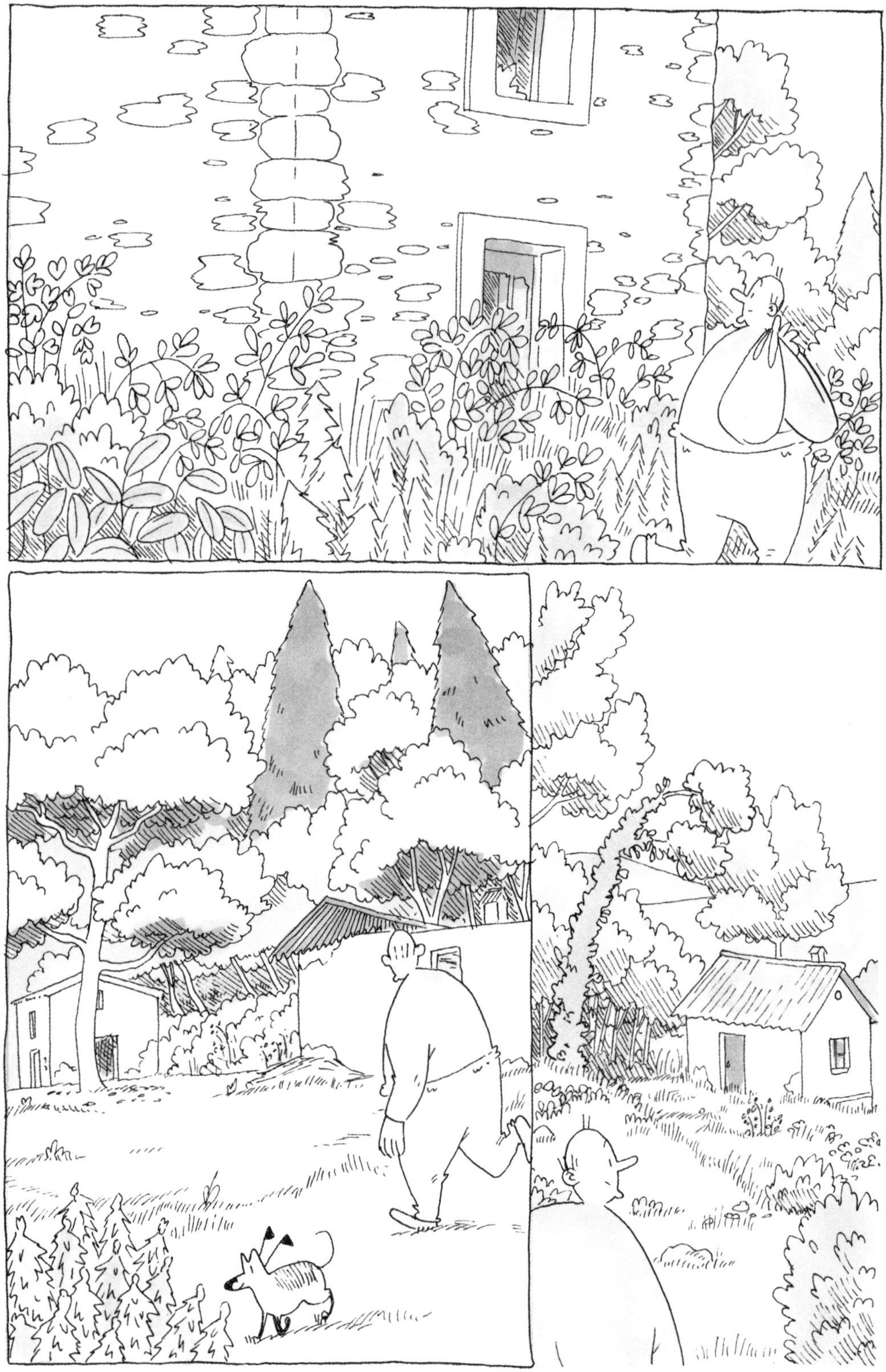

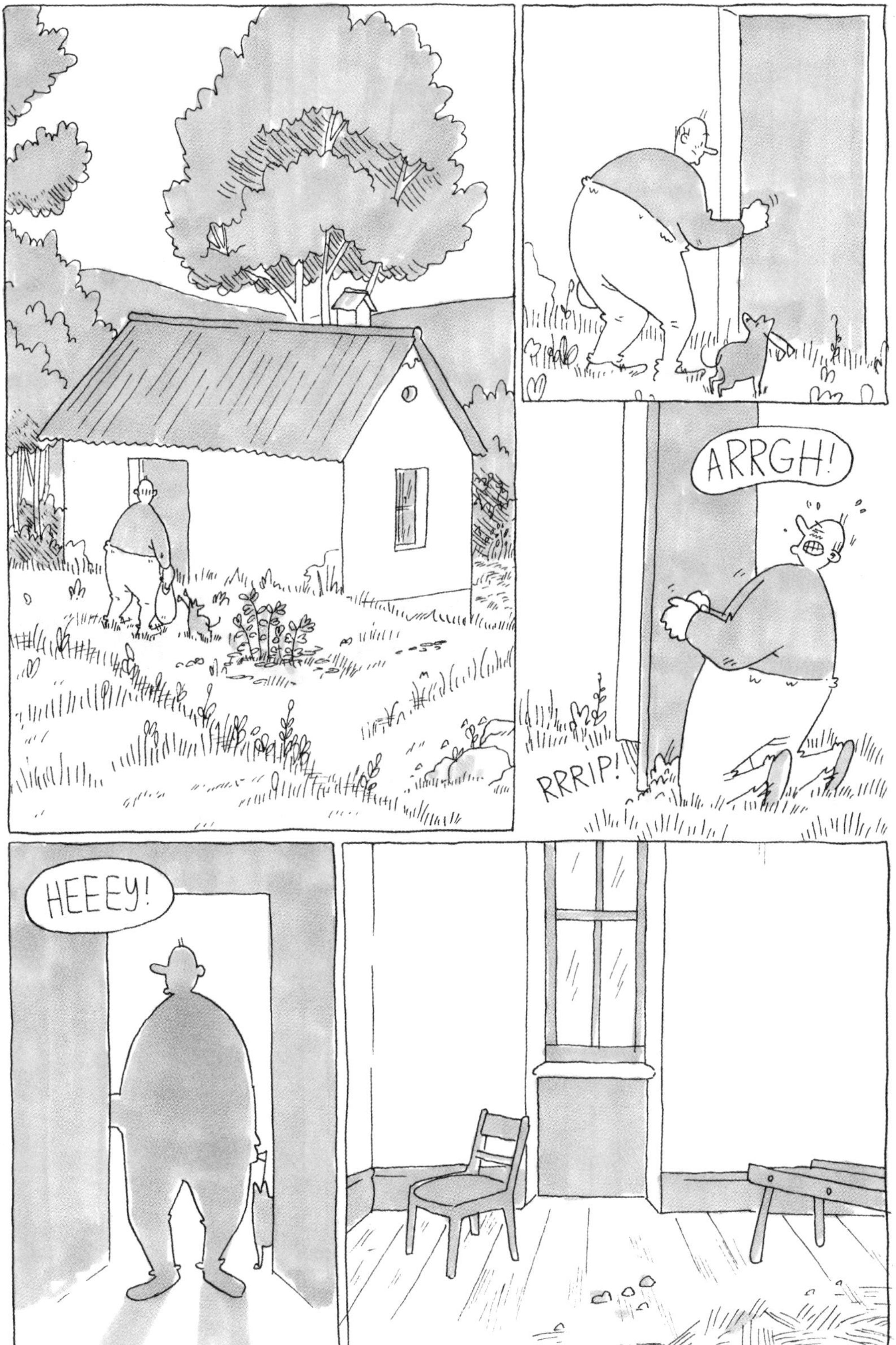
ARRGH!
RRRIP!
HEEEY!

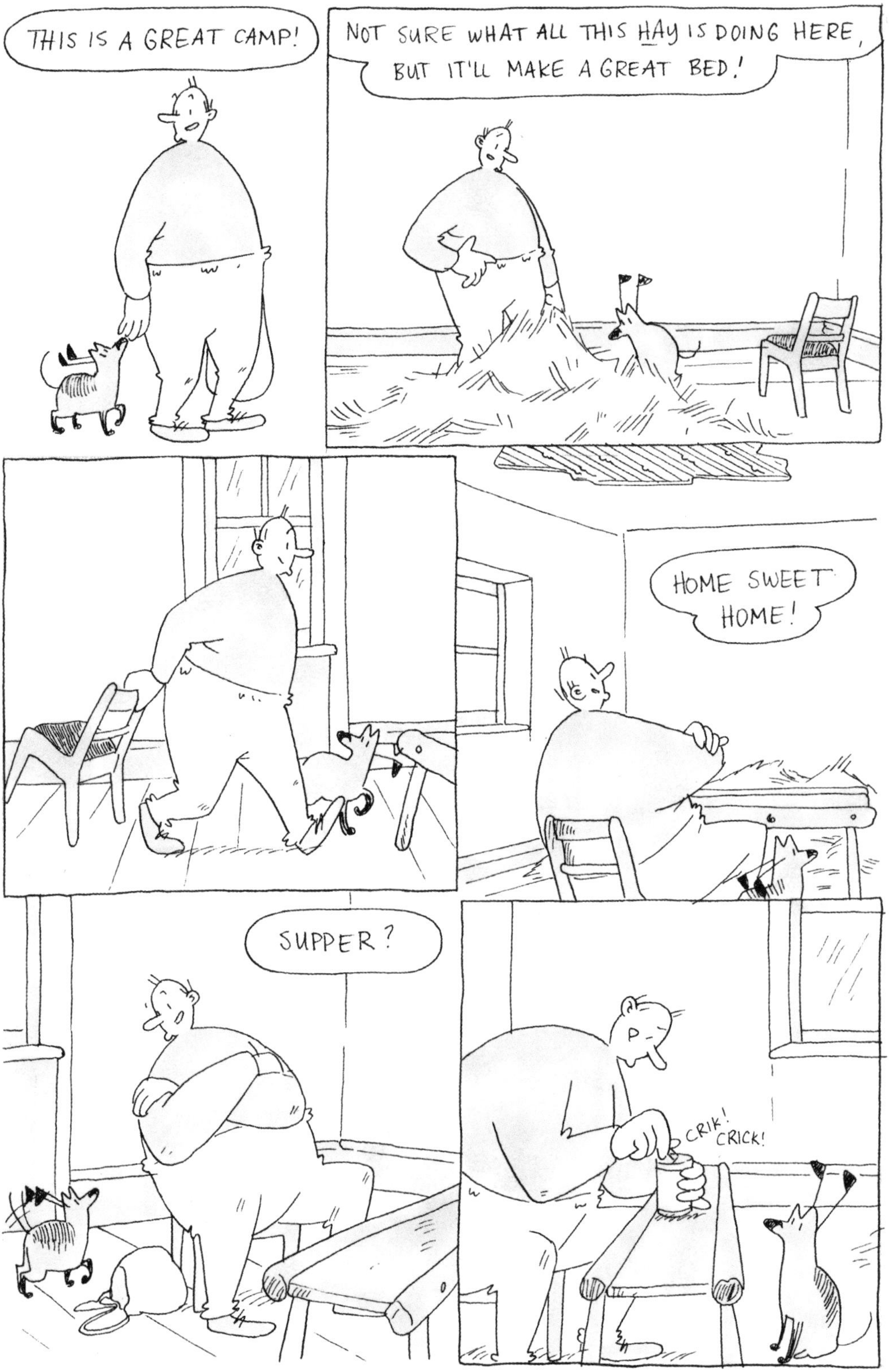
THIS IS A GREAT CAMP!
NOT SURE WHAT ALL THIS HAY IS DOING HERE, BUT IT'LL MAKE A GREAT BED!
HOME SWEET HOME!
SUPPER?
CRIK!
CRICK!

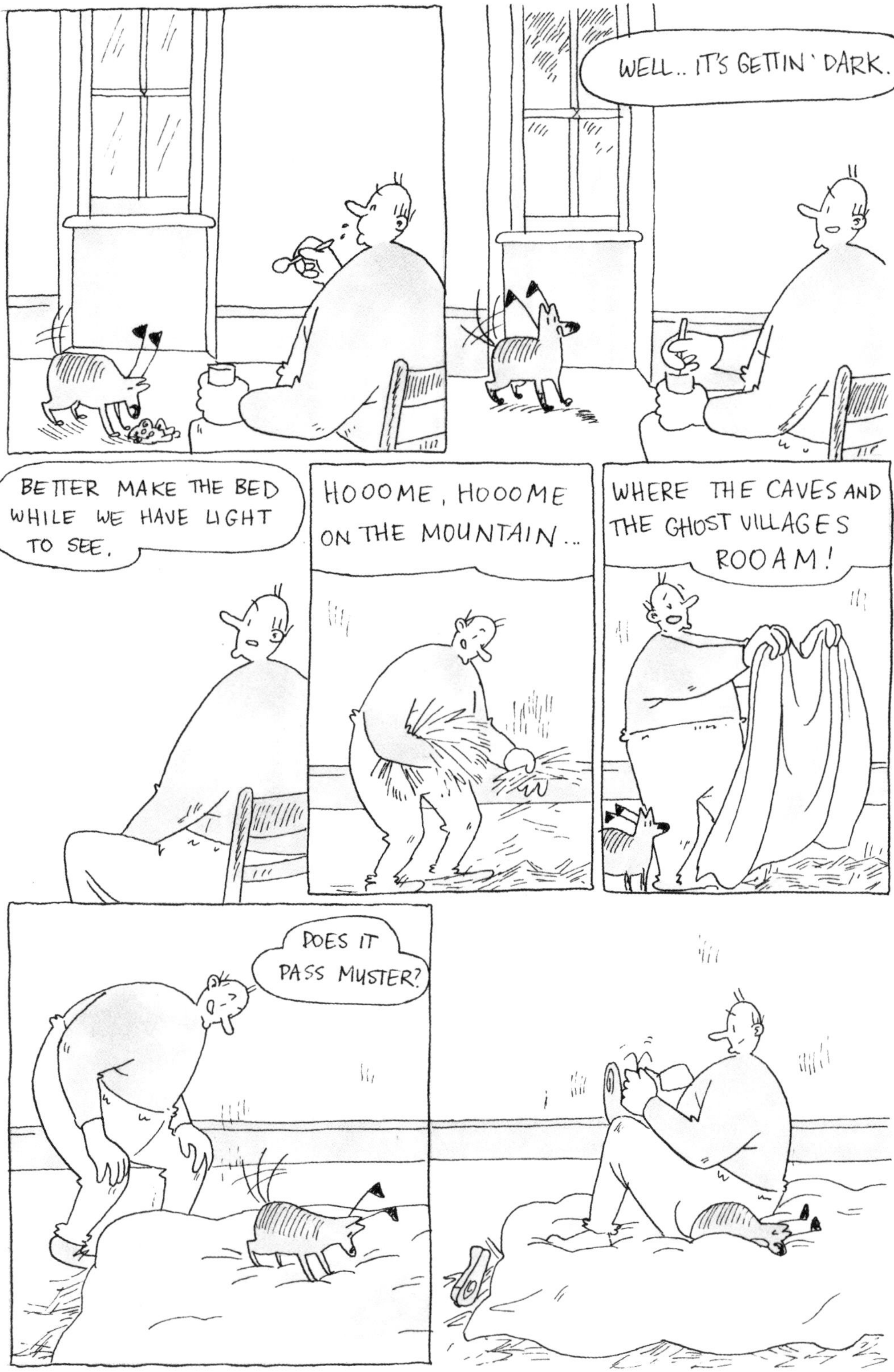
WELL.. IT'S GETTIN' DARK.
BETTER MAKE THE BED WHILE WE HAVE LIGHT TO SEE.
HOOOME, HOOOME ON THE MOUNTAIN...
WHERE THE CAVES AND THE GHOST VILLAGES ROOAM!
DOES IT PASS MUSTER?

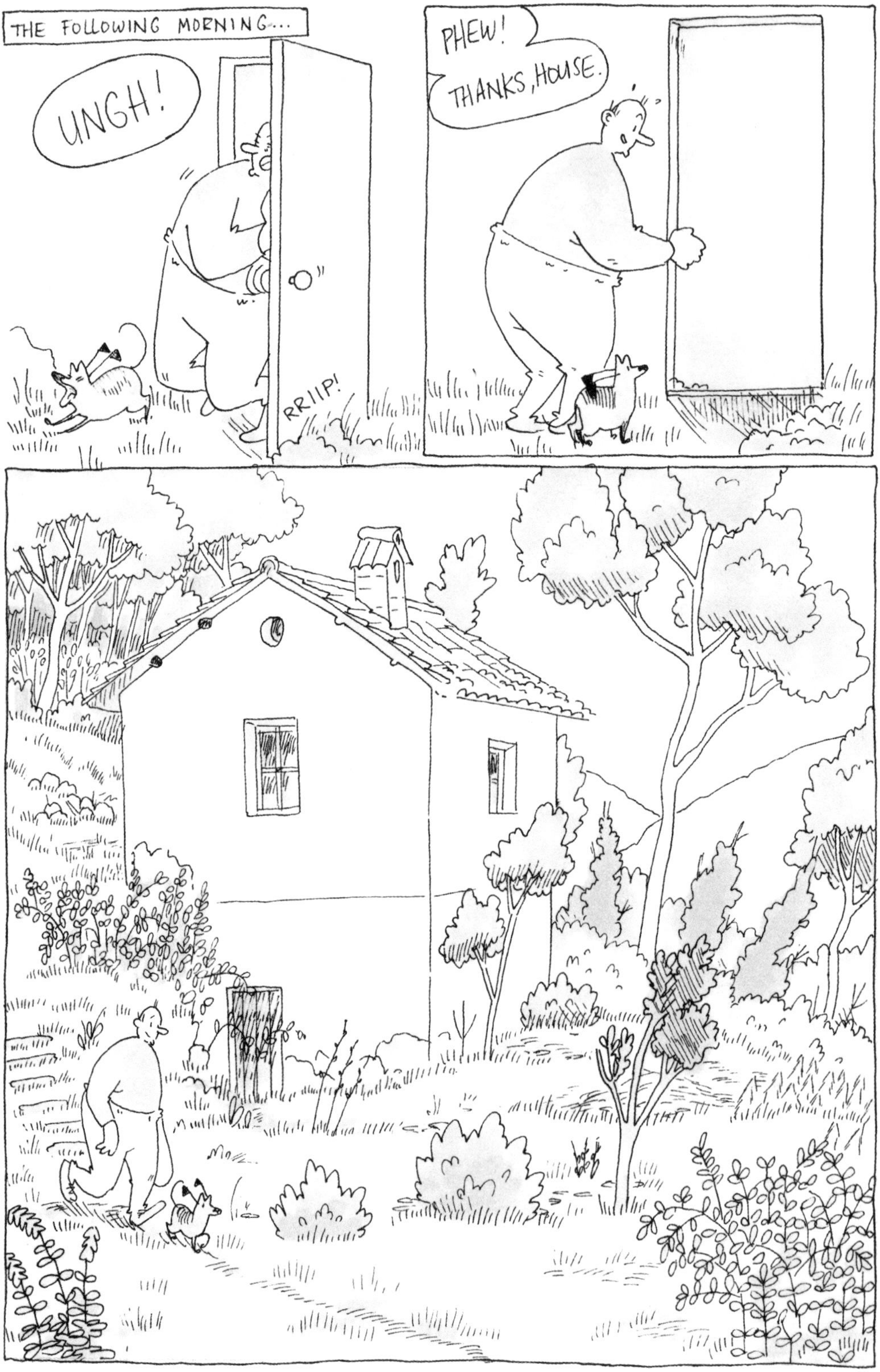
THE FOLLOWING MORNING...
UNGH!
RRIIP!
PHEW!
THANKS, HOUSE.

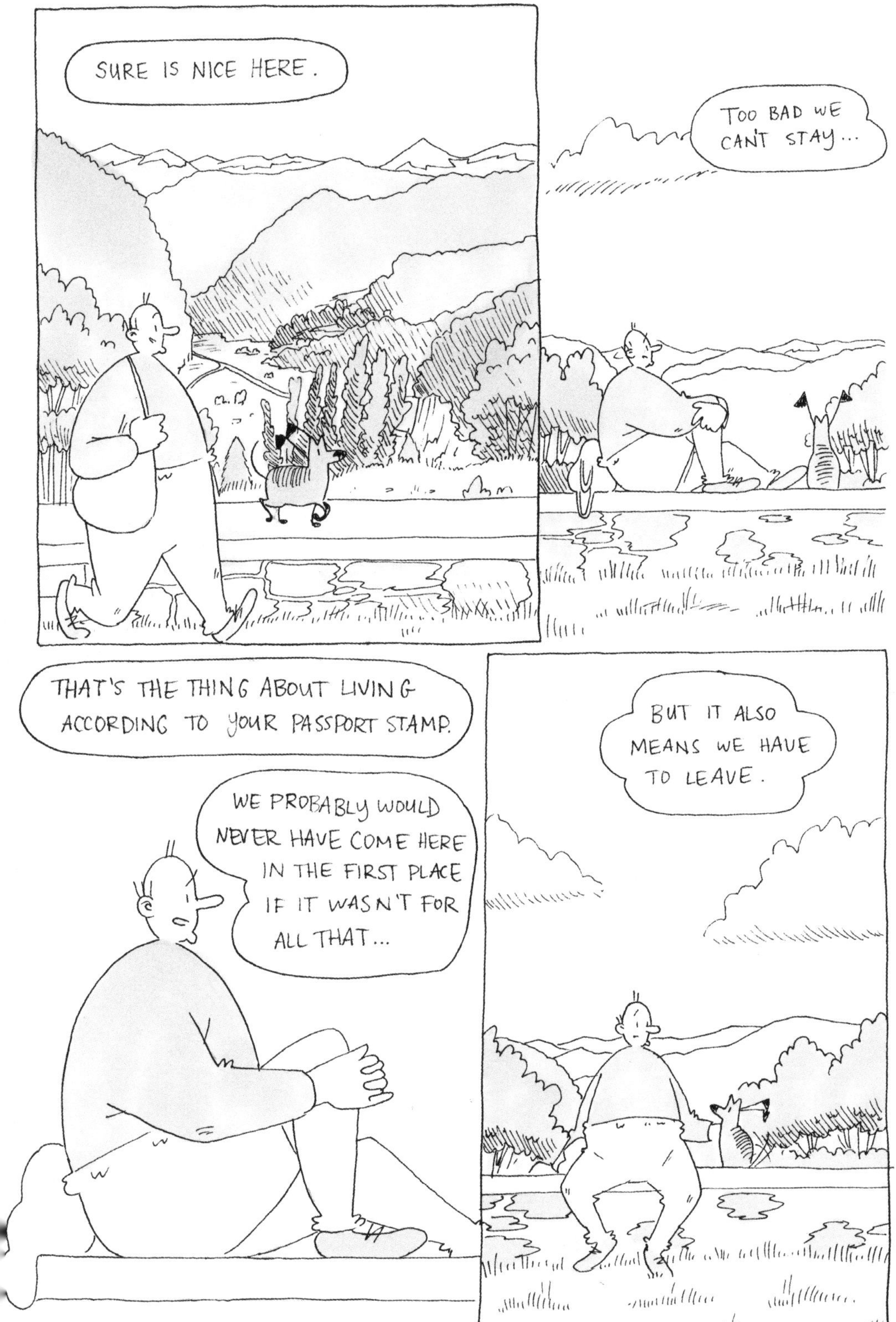
SURE IS NICE HERE.
TOO BAD WE CAN'T STAY...
THAT'S THE THING ABOUT LIVING ACCORDING TO YOUR PASSPORT STAMP.
WE PROBABLY WOULD NEVER HAVE COME HERE IN THE FIRST PLACE IF IT WASN'T FOR ALL THAT...
BUT IT ALSO MEANS WE HAVE TO LEAVE.

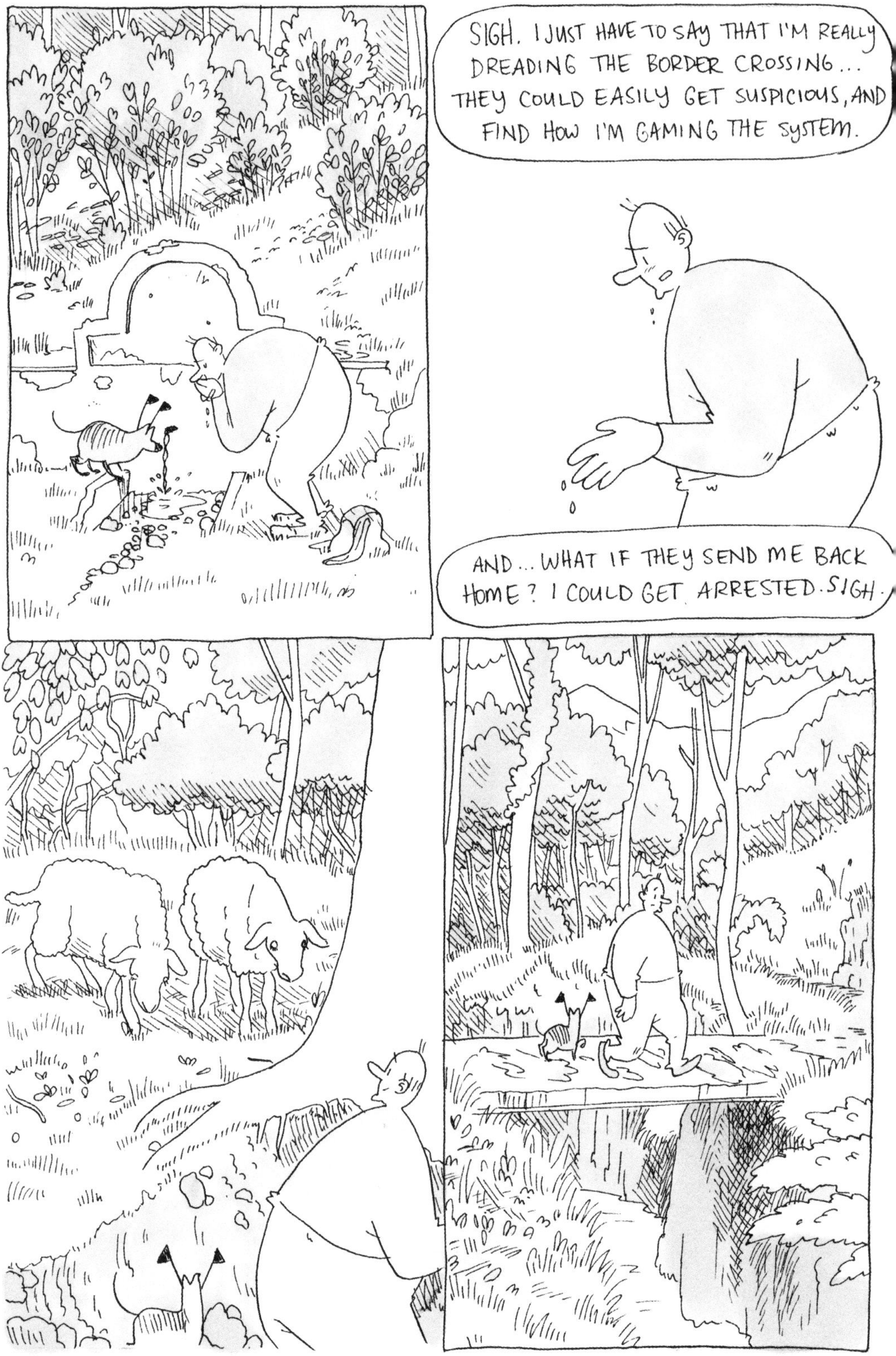
SIGH. I JUST HAVE TO SAY THAT I'M REALLY DREADING THE BORDER CROSSING... THEY COULD EASILY GET SUSPICIOUS, AND FIND HOW I'M GAMING THE SYSTEM.
AND... WHAT IF THEY SEND ME BACK HOME? I COULD GET ARRESTED. SIGH.

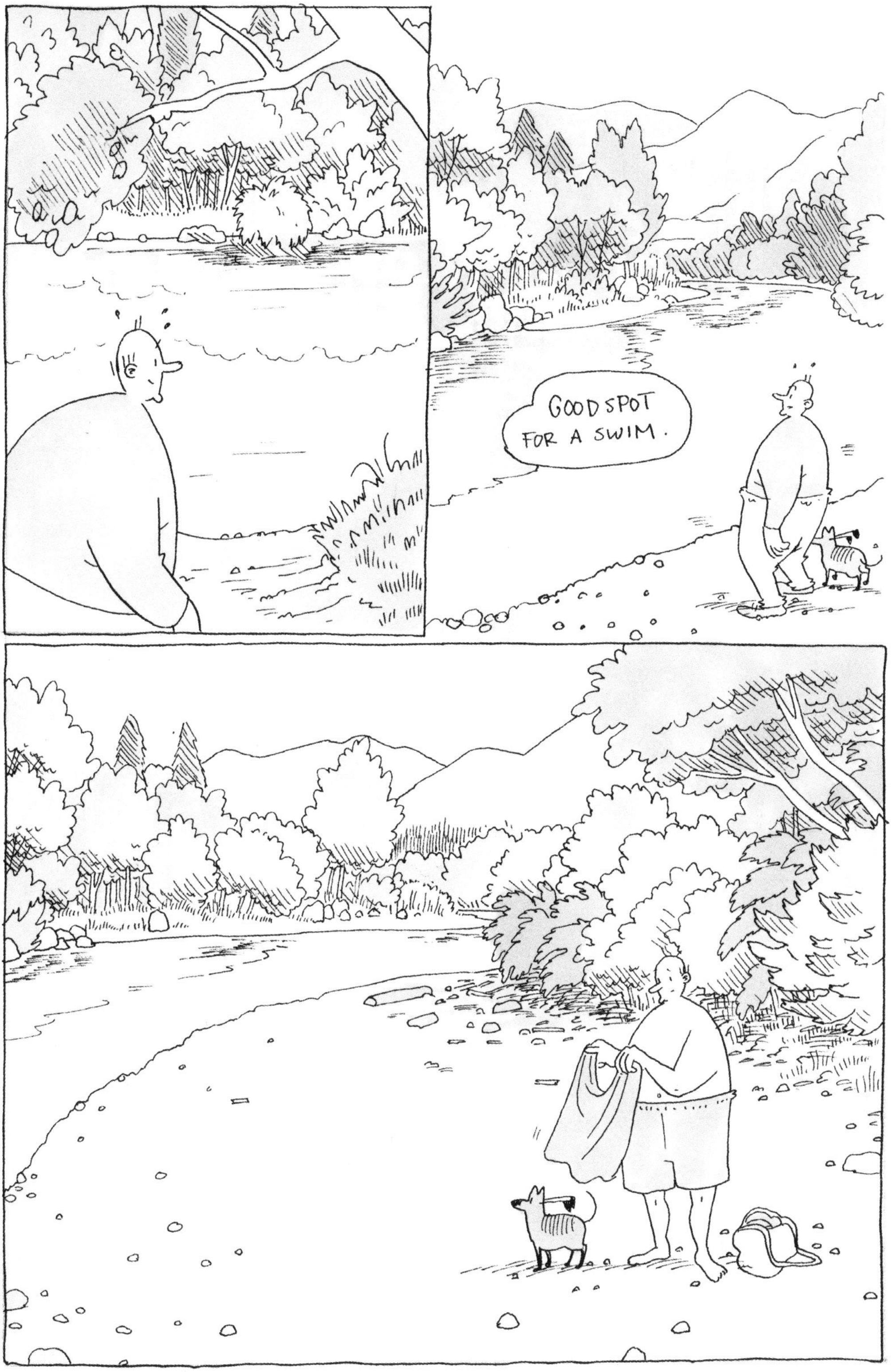
GOOD SPOT
FOR A SWIM.

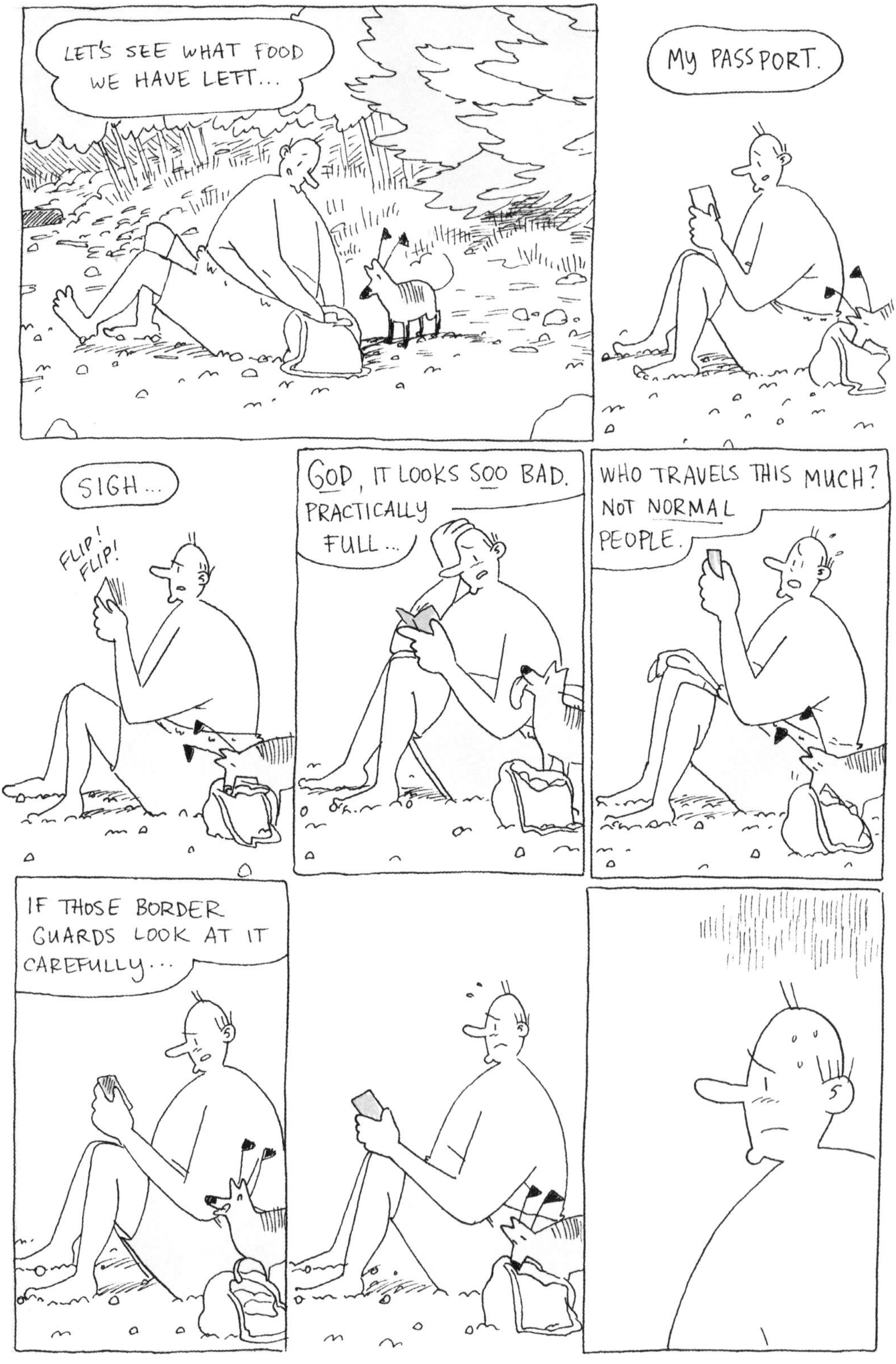
LET'S SEE WHAT FOOD WE HAVE LEFT...
MY PASSPORT.
SIGH...
FLIP! FLIP!
GOD, IT LOOKS SOO BAD. PRACTICALLY FULL...
WHO TRAVELS THIS MUCH? NOT NORMAL PEOPLE.
IF THOSE BORDER GUARDS LOOK AT IT CAREFULLY...

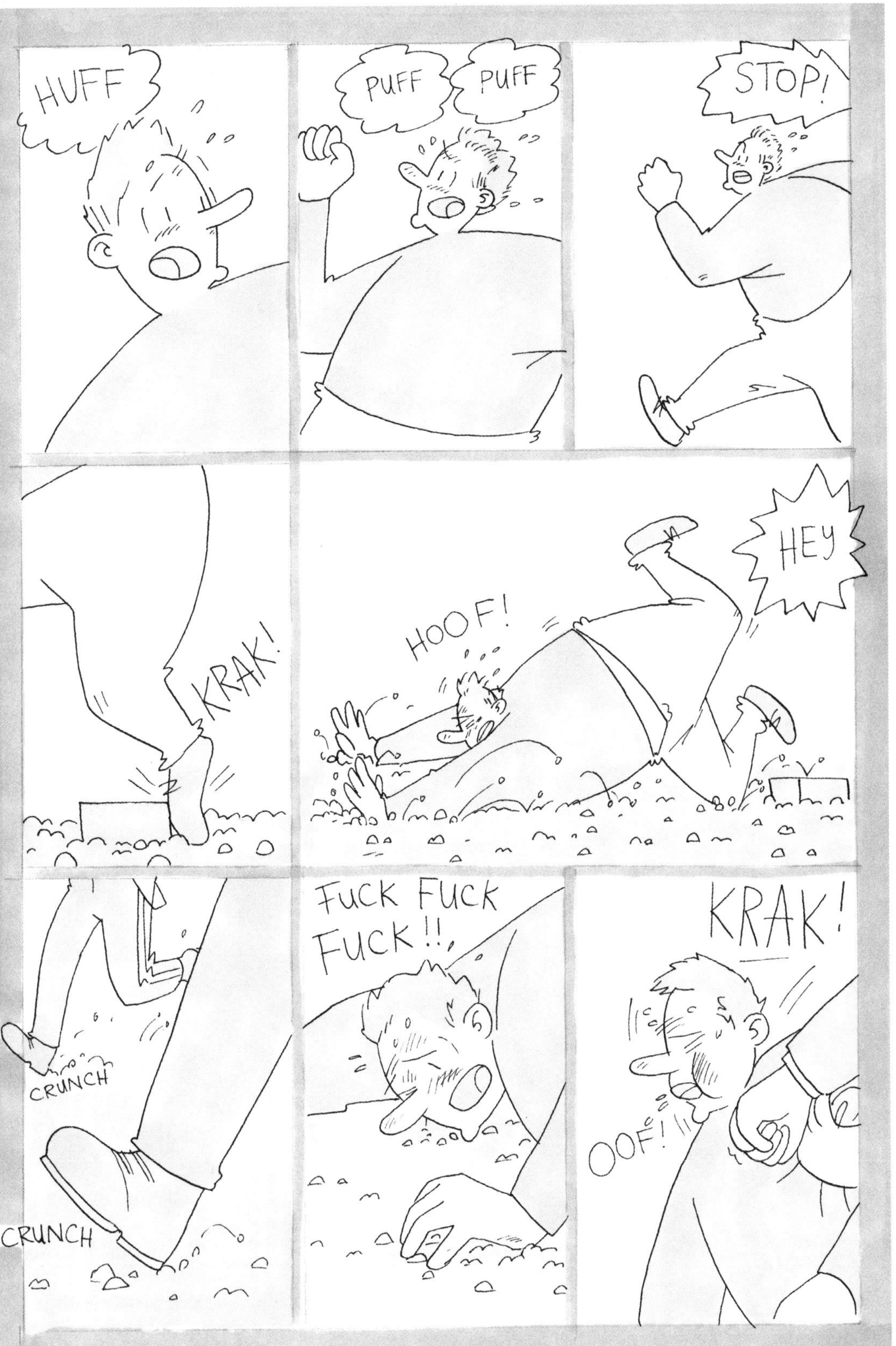
HUFF
PUFF
PUFF
STOP!
KRAK!
HOOF!
HEY
CRUNCH
CRUNCH
FUCK FUCK
FUCK!!
KRAK!
OOF!

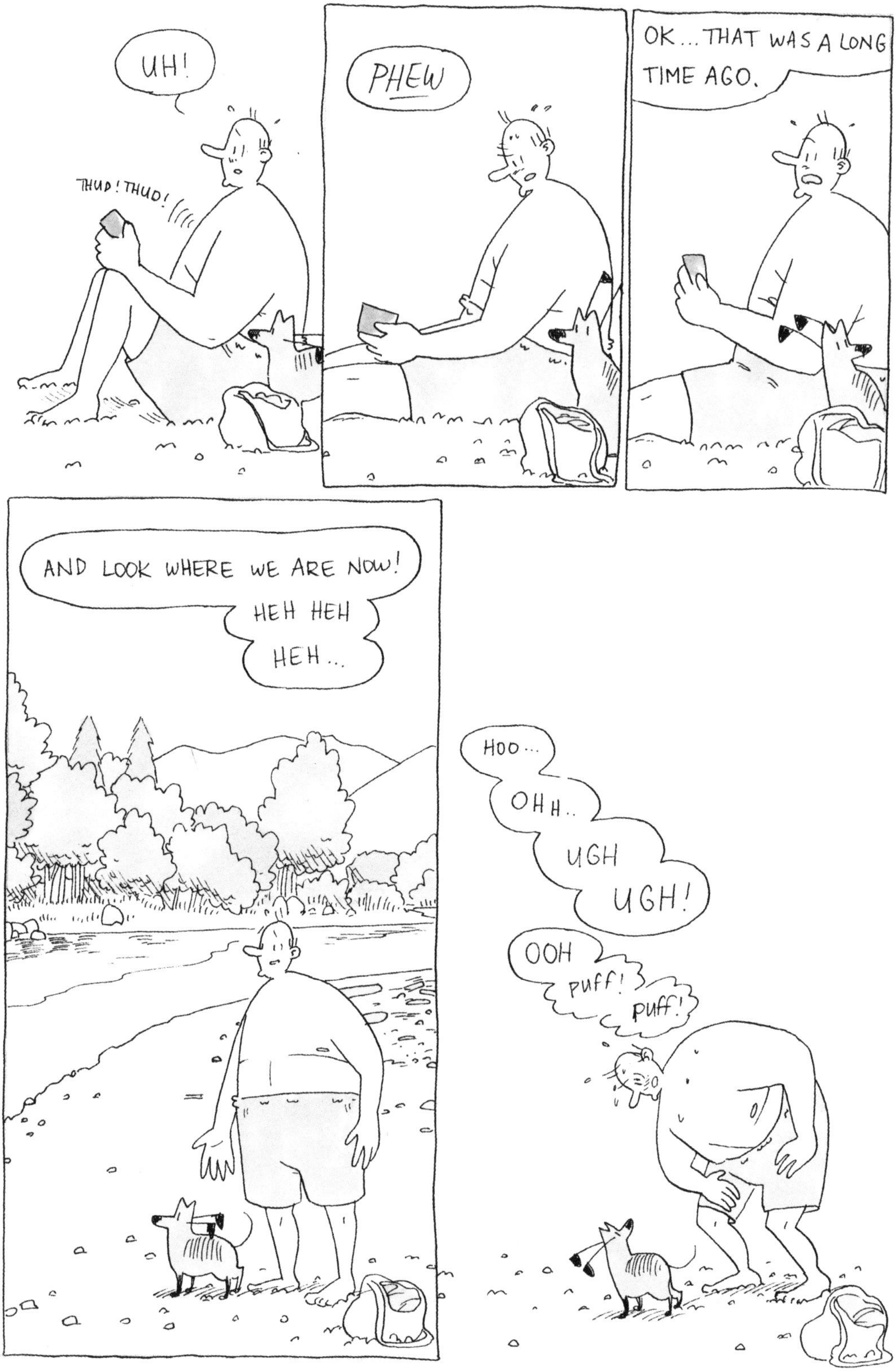
UH!
THUD! THUD!
PHEW
OK... THAT WAS A LONG TIME AGO.
AND LOOK WHERE WE ARE NOW!
HEH HEH
HEH...
HOO...
OHH..
UGH
UGH!
OOH
puff!
puff!

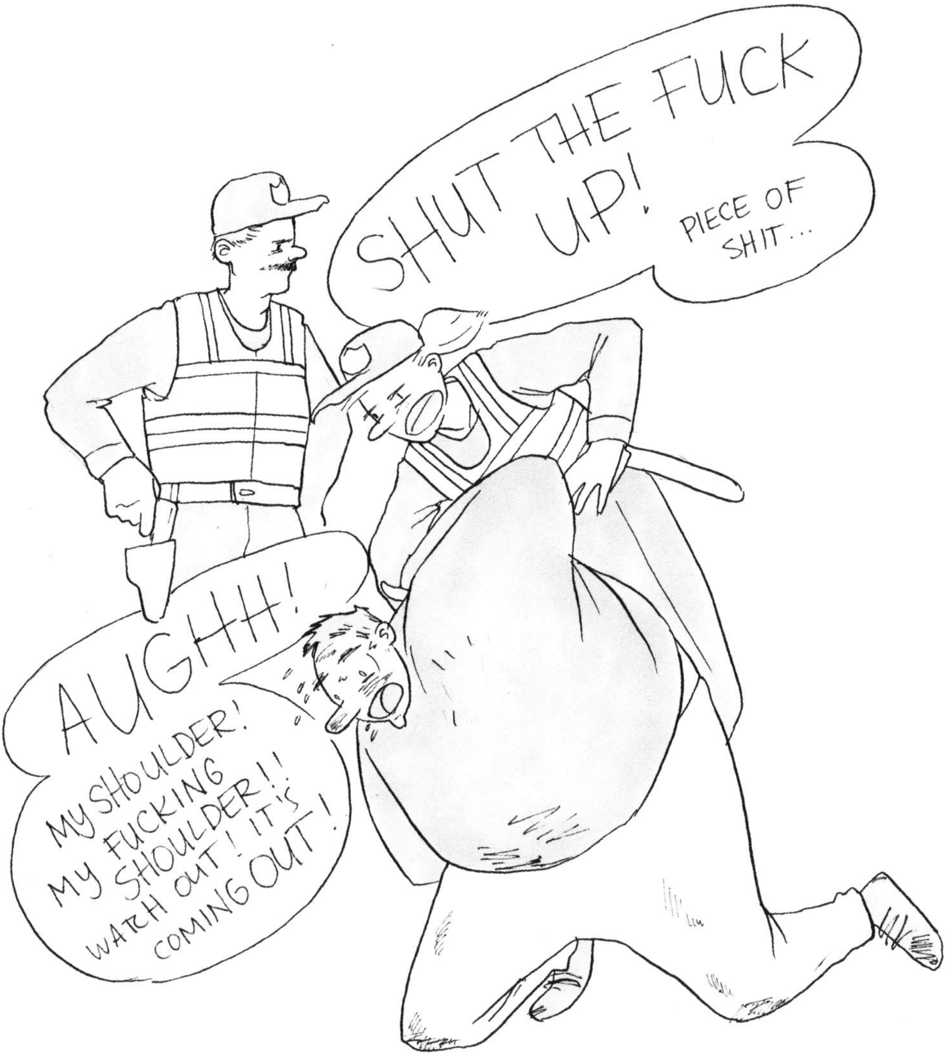
SHUT THE FUCK UP! PIECE OF SHIT...
AUGHH! MY SHOULDER! MY FUCKING SHOULDER!! WATCH OUT! IT'S COMING OUT!

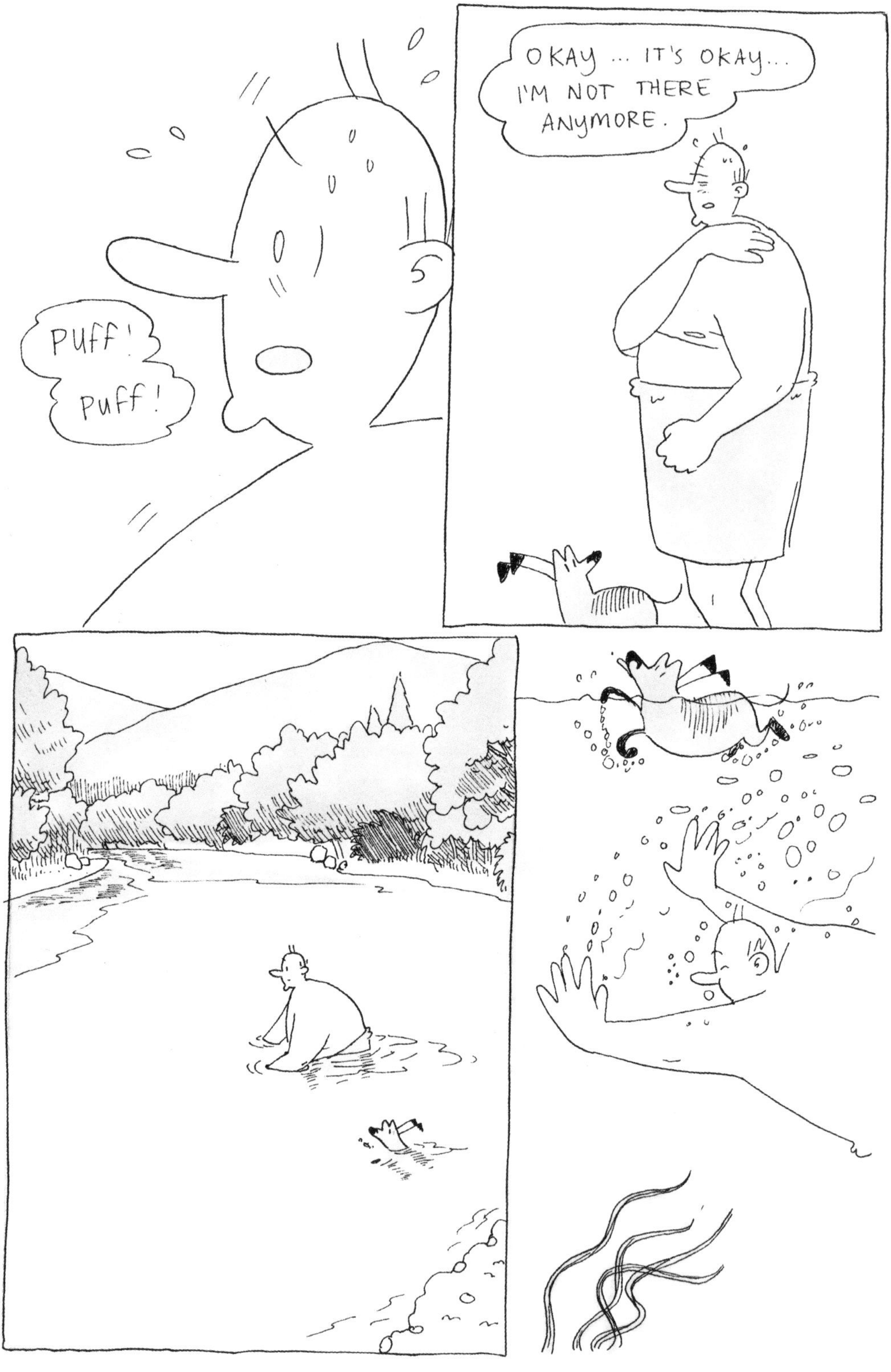
PUFF!
PUFF!
OKAY ... IT'S OKAY...
I'M NOT THERE
ANYMORE.

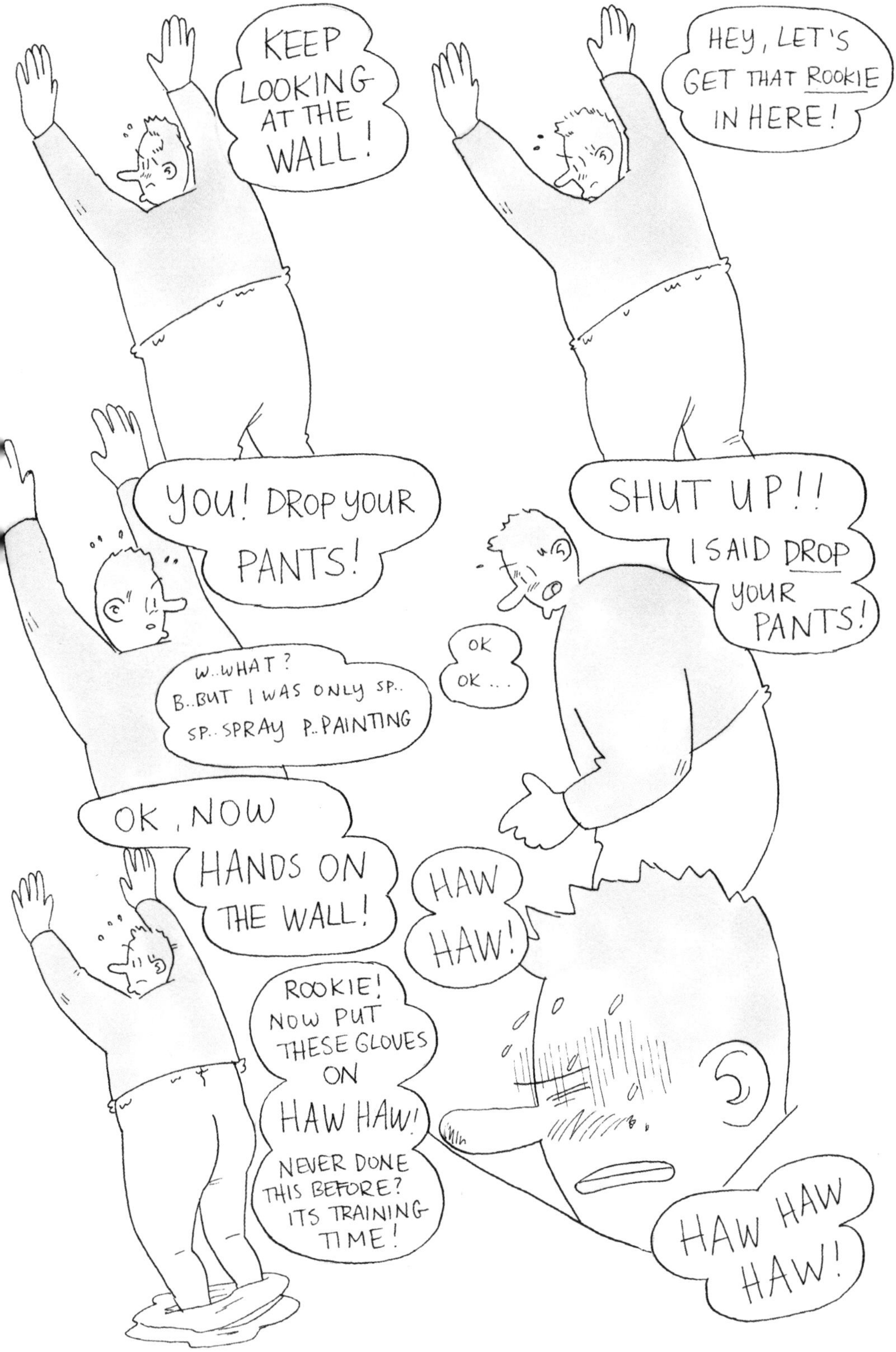
KEEP LOOKING AT THE WALL!
HEY, LET'S GET THAT ROOKIE IN HERE!
YOU! DROP YOUR PANTS!
W..WHAT? B..BUT I WAS ONLY SP.. SP..SPRAY P..PAINTING
SHUT UP!! I SAID DROP YOUR PANTS!
OK OK...
OK, NOW HANDS ON THE WALL!
HAW HAW!
ROOKIE! NOW PUT THESE GLOVES ON
HAW HAW!
NEVER DONE THIS BEFORE? ITS TRAINING TIME!
HAW HAW HAW!

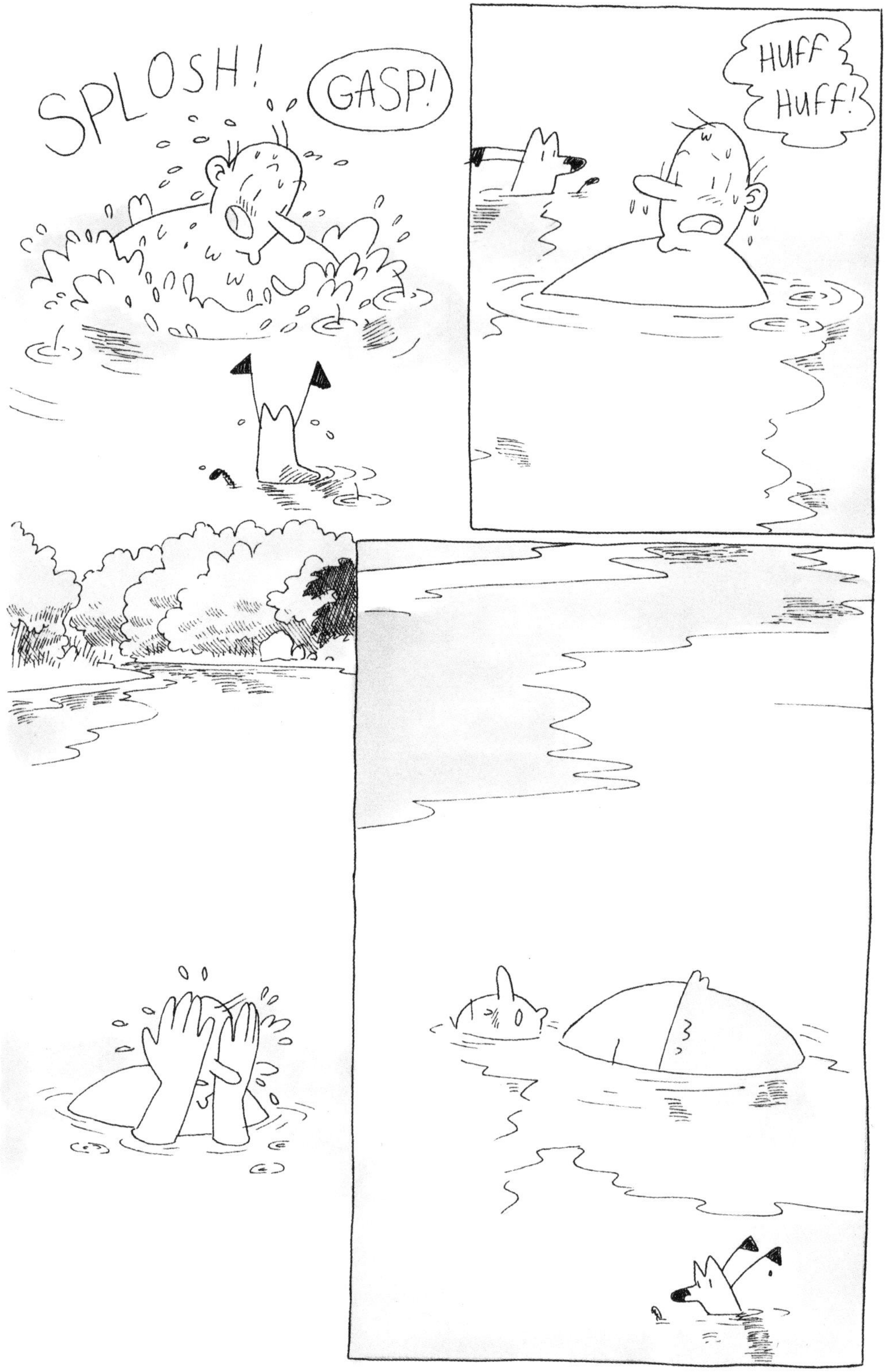
SPLOSH!
GASP!
HUFF HUFF!

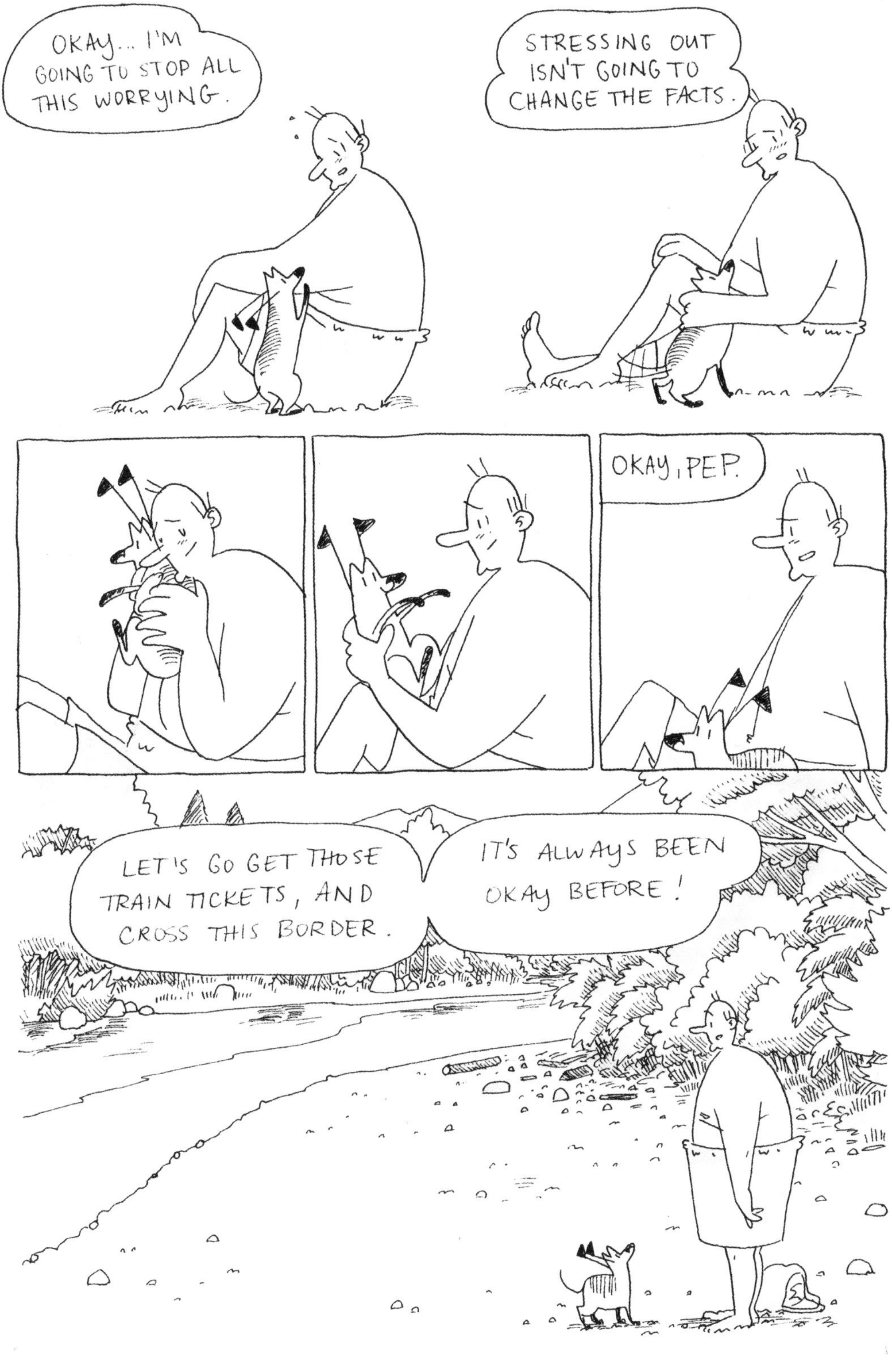
OKAY... I'M GOING TO STOP ALL THIS WORRYING.
STRESSING OUT ISN'T GOING TO CHANGE THE FACTS.
OKAY, PEP.
LET'S GO GET THOSE TRAIN TICKETS, AND CROSS THIS BORDER.
IT'S ALWAYS BEEN OKAY BEFORE!

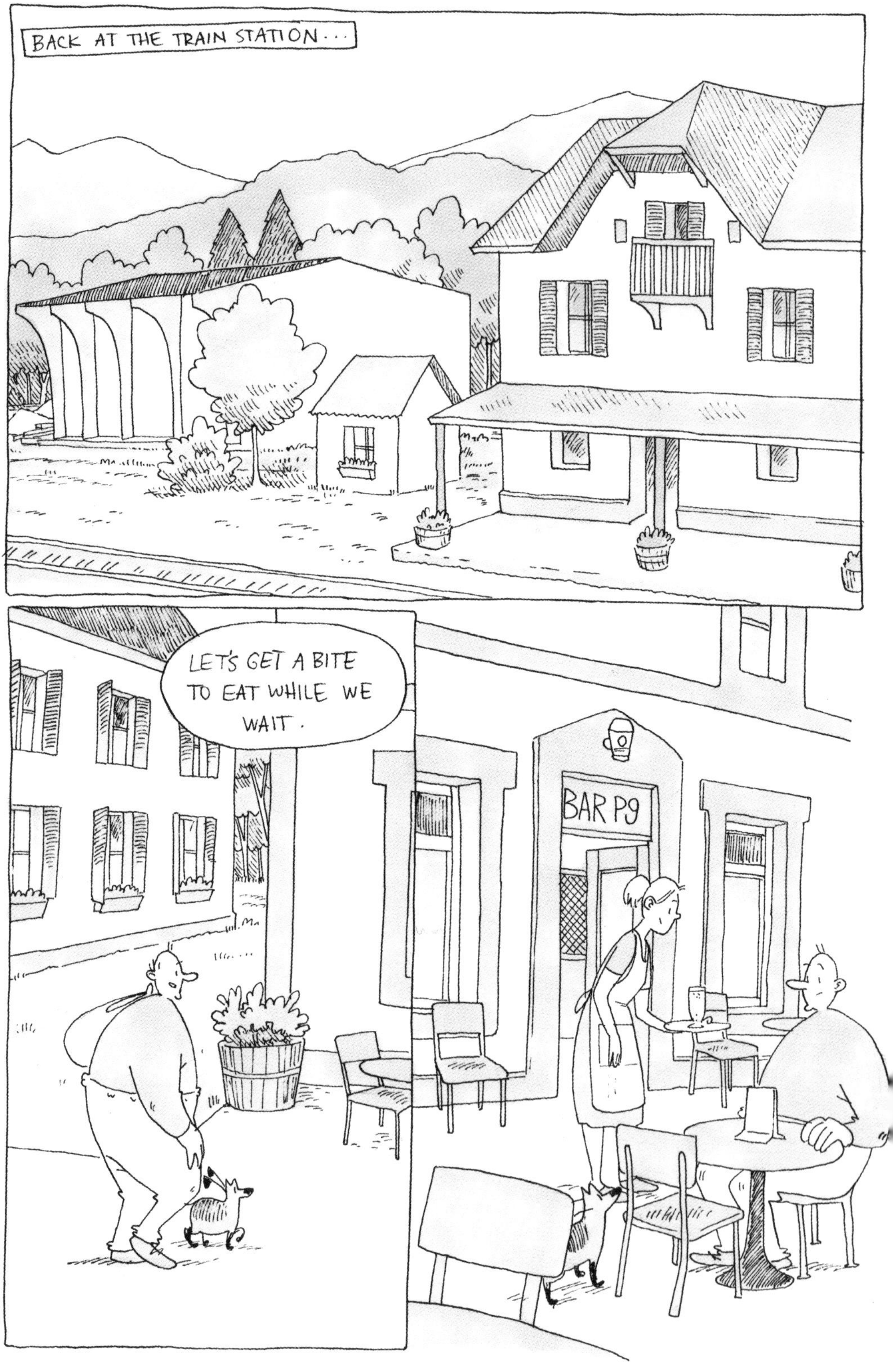
BACK AT THE TRAIN STATION...
LET'S GET A BITE TO EAT WHILE WE WAIT.
BAR P9

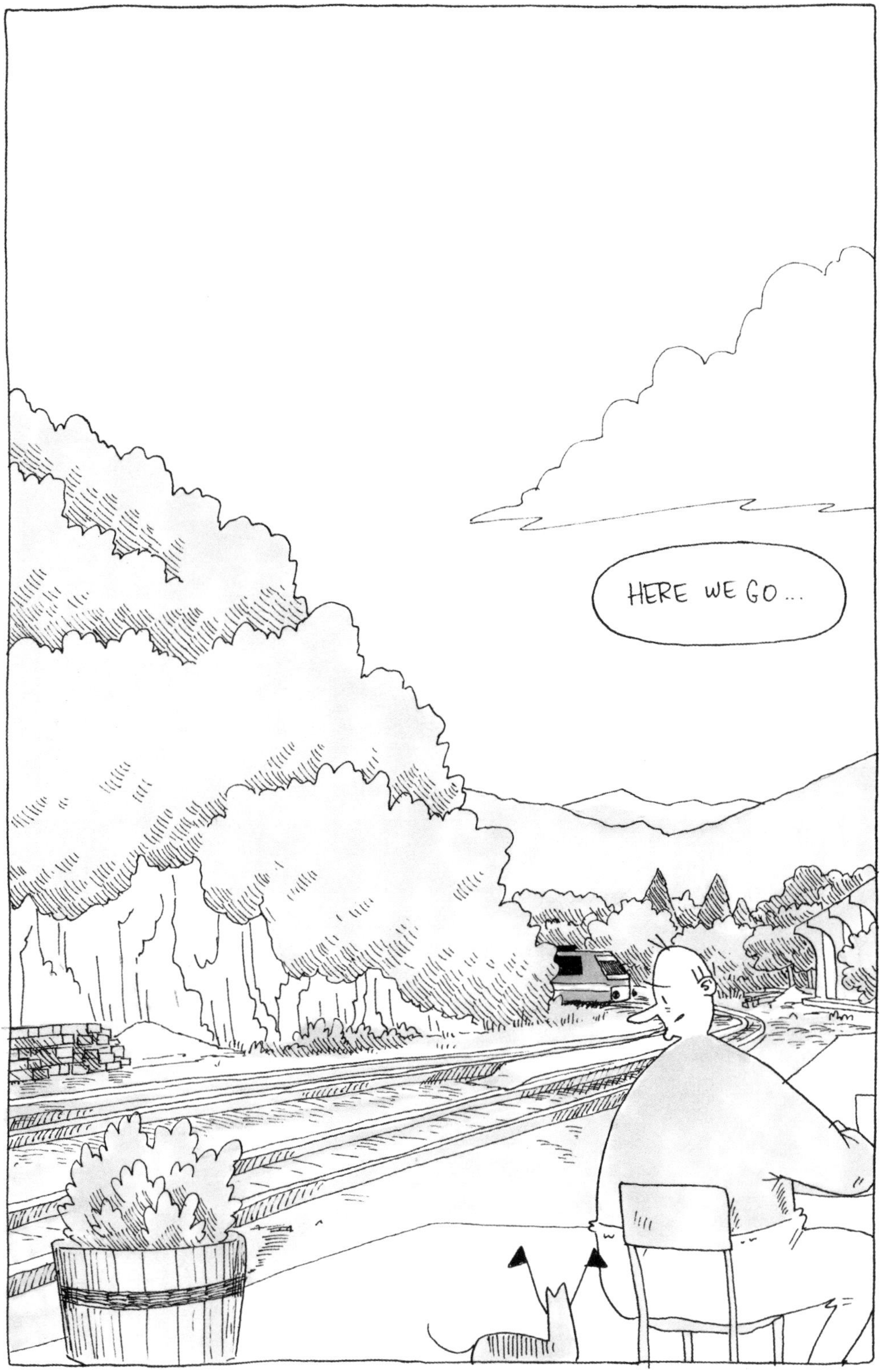
HERE WE GO...

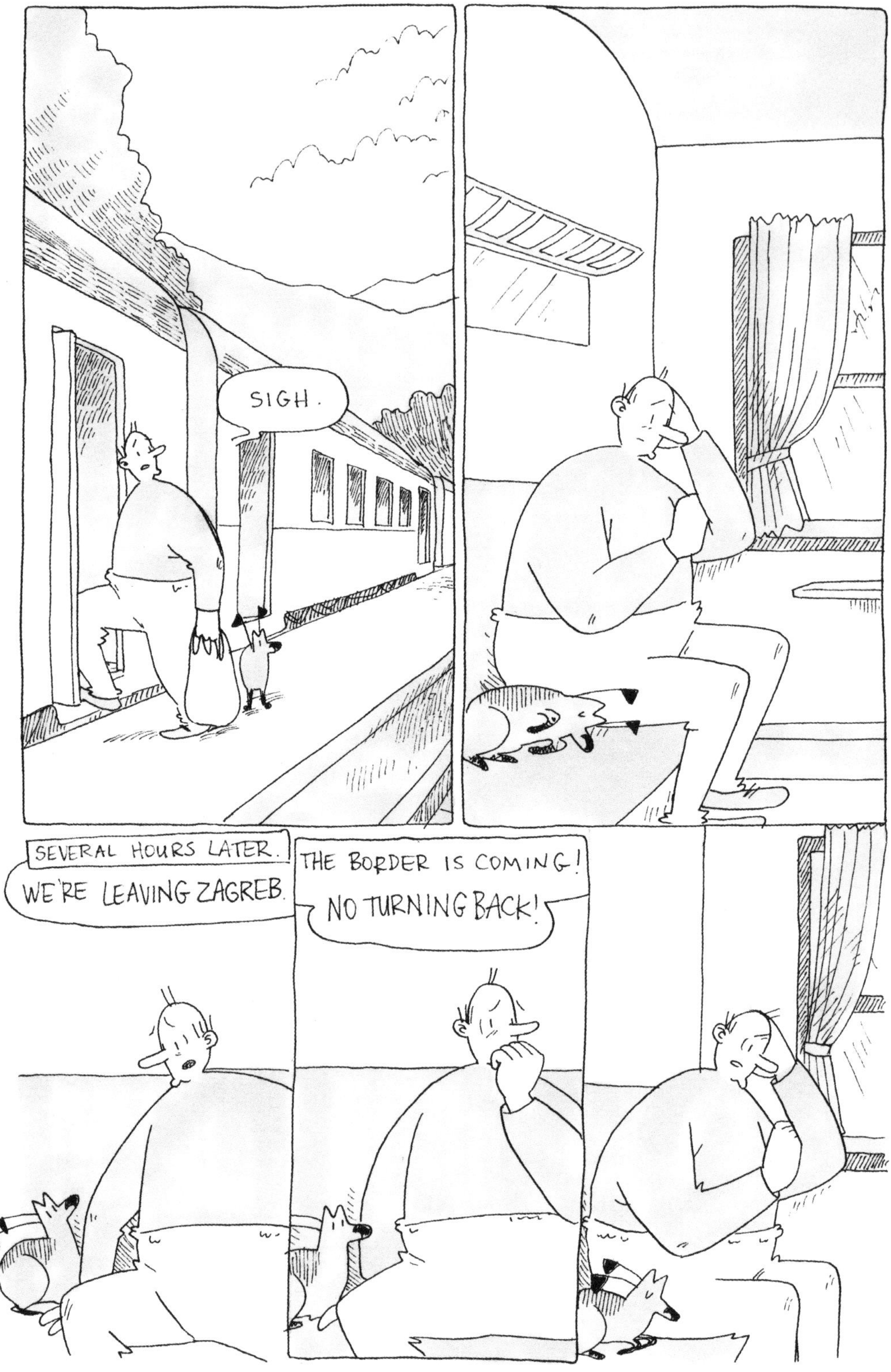
SIGH.
SEVERAL HOURS LATER.
WE'RE LEAVING ZAGREB.
THE BORDER IS COMING!
NO TURNING BACK!

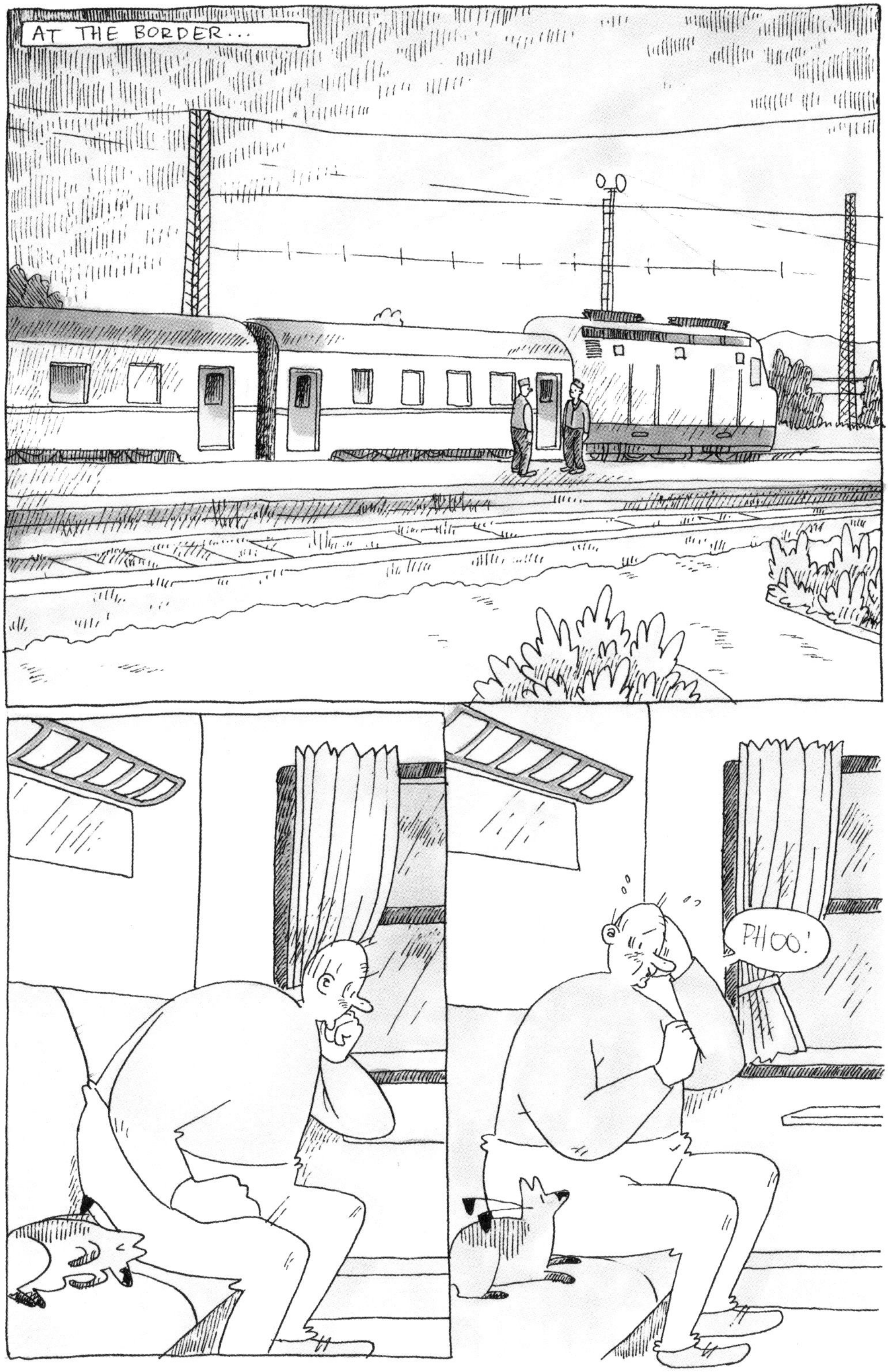
AT THE BORDER...
PHOO!

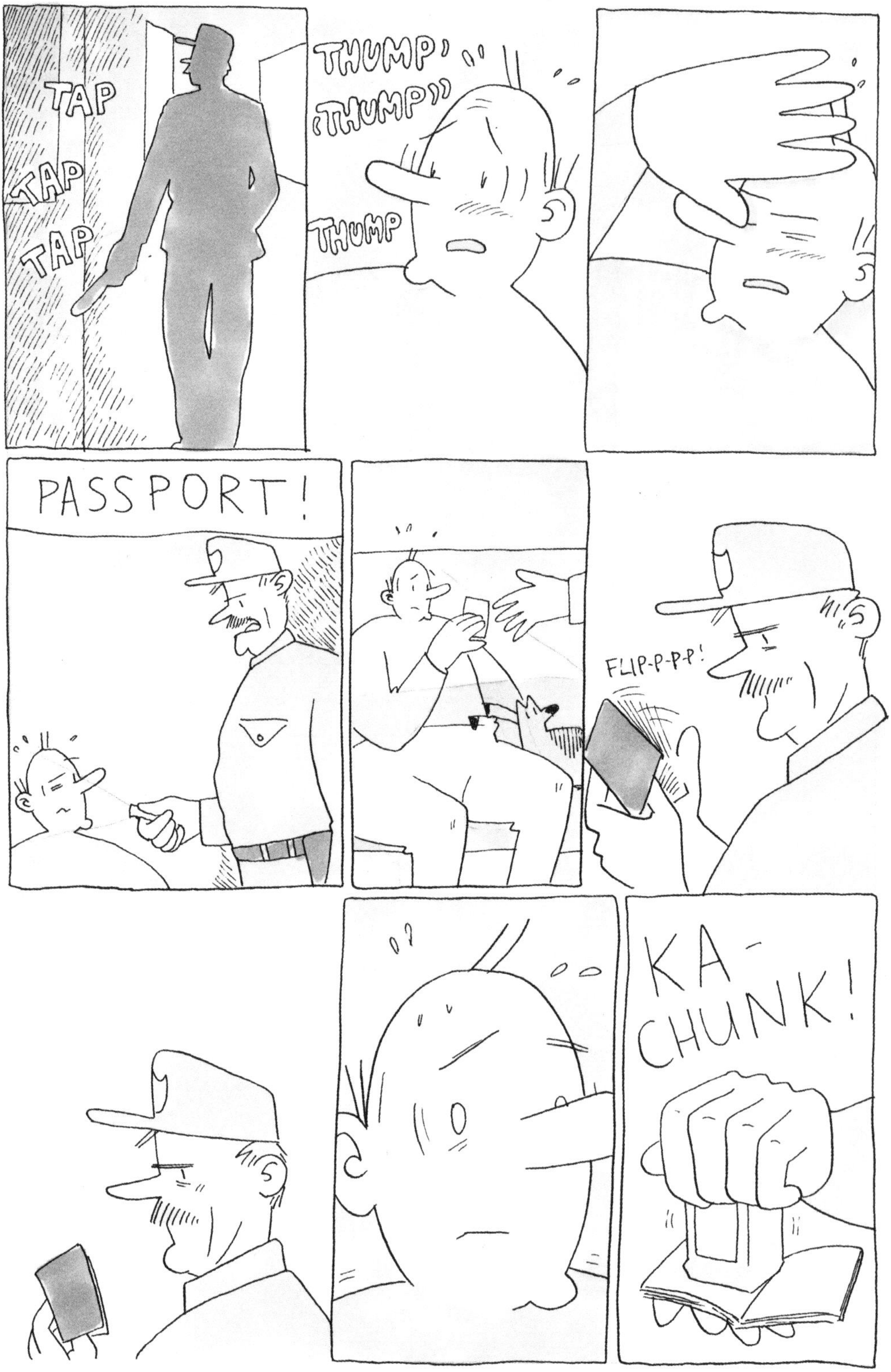
TAP
TAP
TAP
THUMP
THUMP
THUMP
PASSPORT!
FLIP-P-P-P!
KA-
CHUNK!

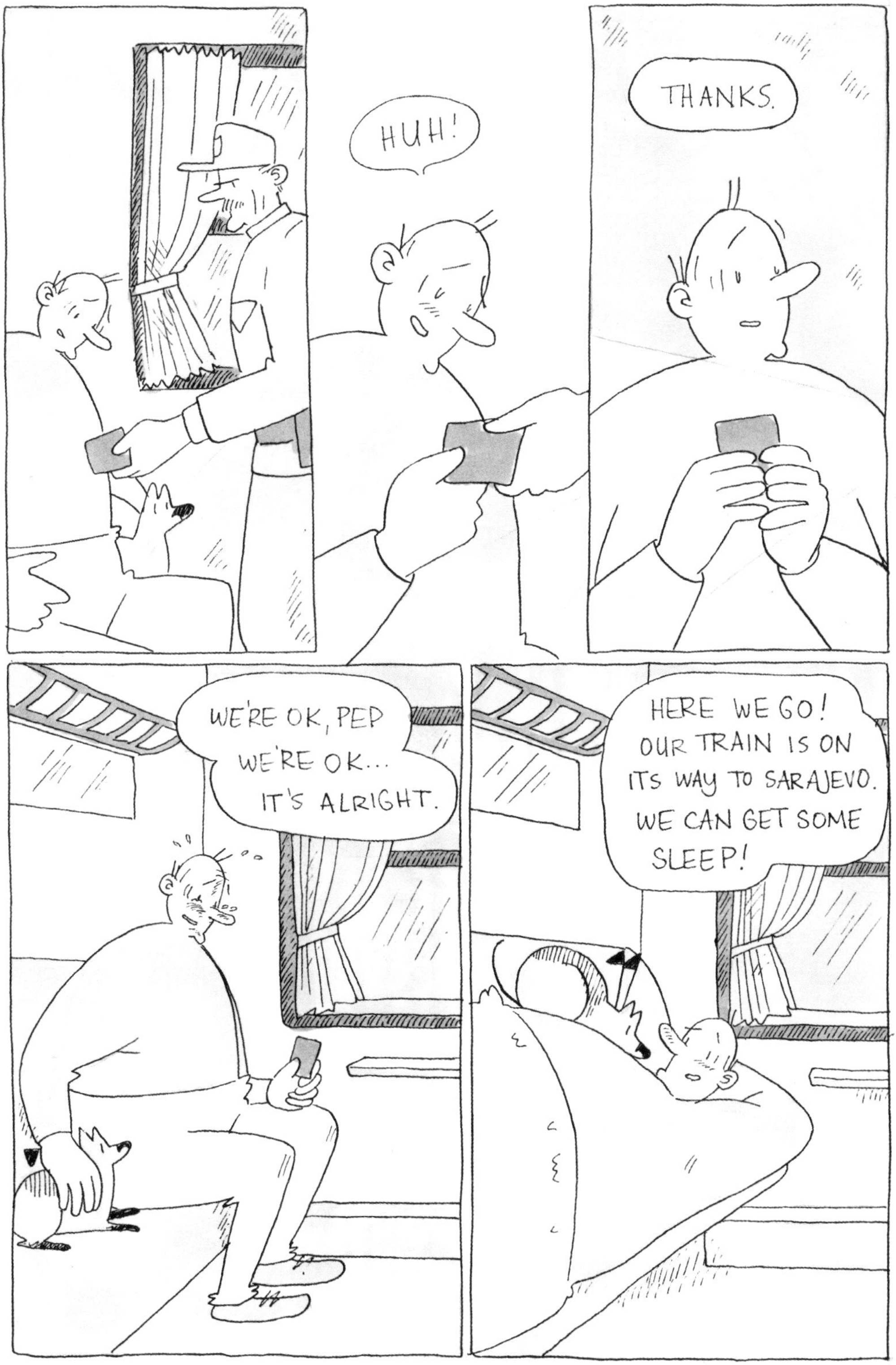
HUH!
THANKS.
WE'RE OK, PEP
WE'RE OK...
IT'S ALRIGHT.
HERE WE GO!
OUR TRAIN IS ON
ITS WAY TO SARAJEVO.
WE CAN GET SOME
SLEEP!

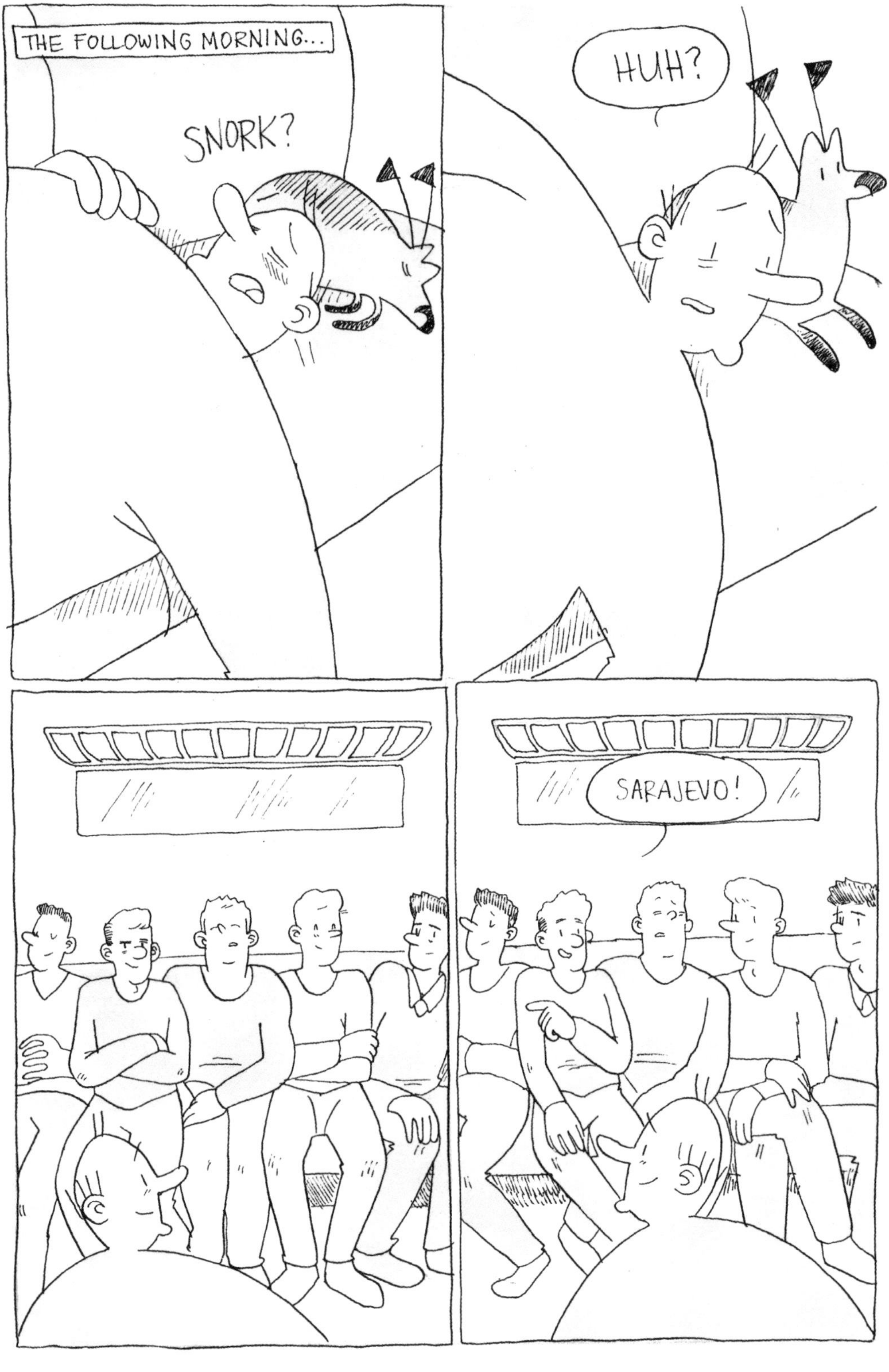
THE FOLLOWING MORNING...
SNORK?
HUH?
SARAJEVO!

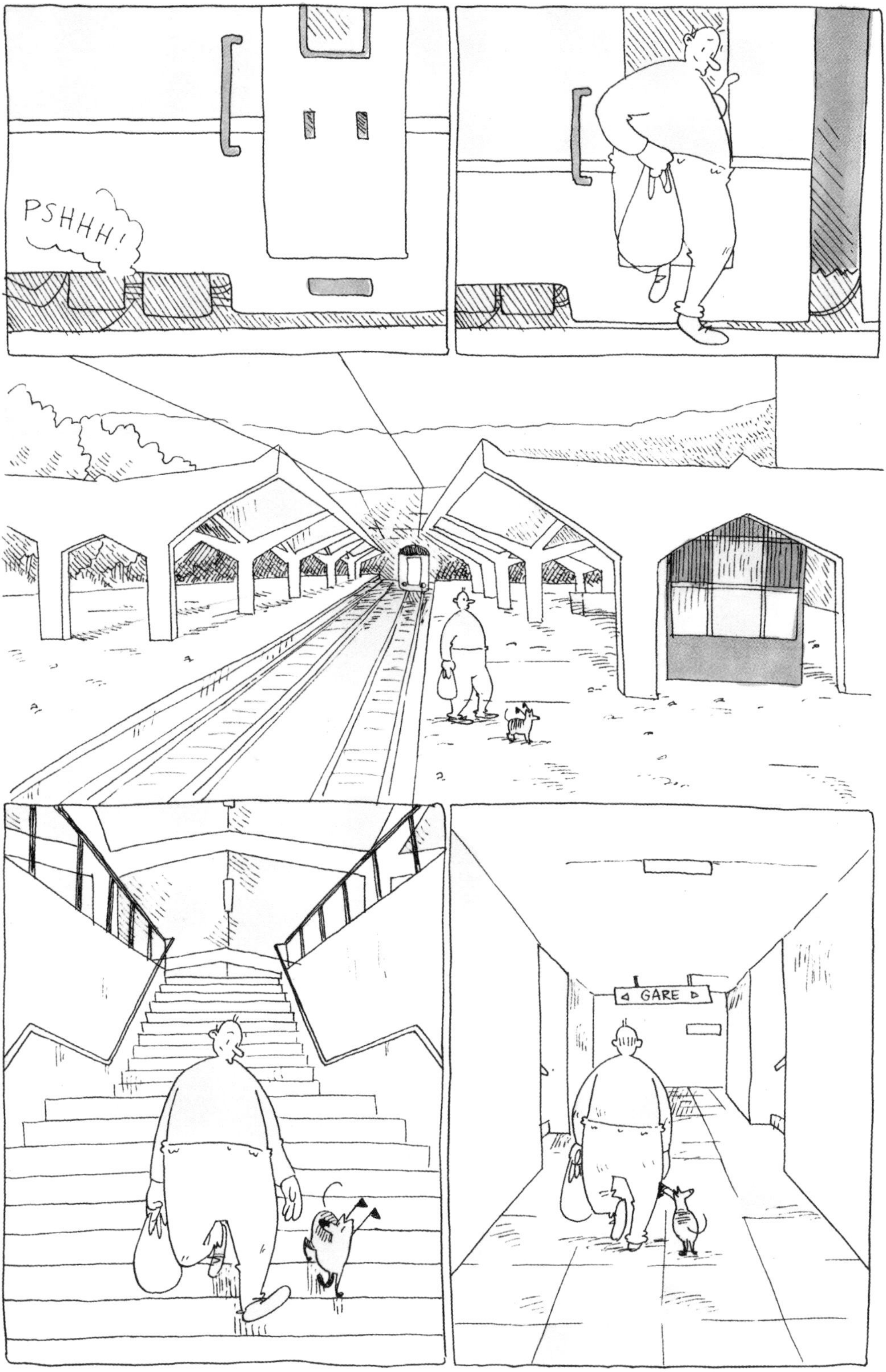
PSHHH!
GARE

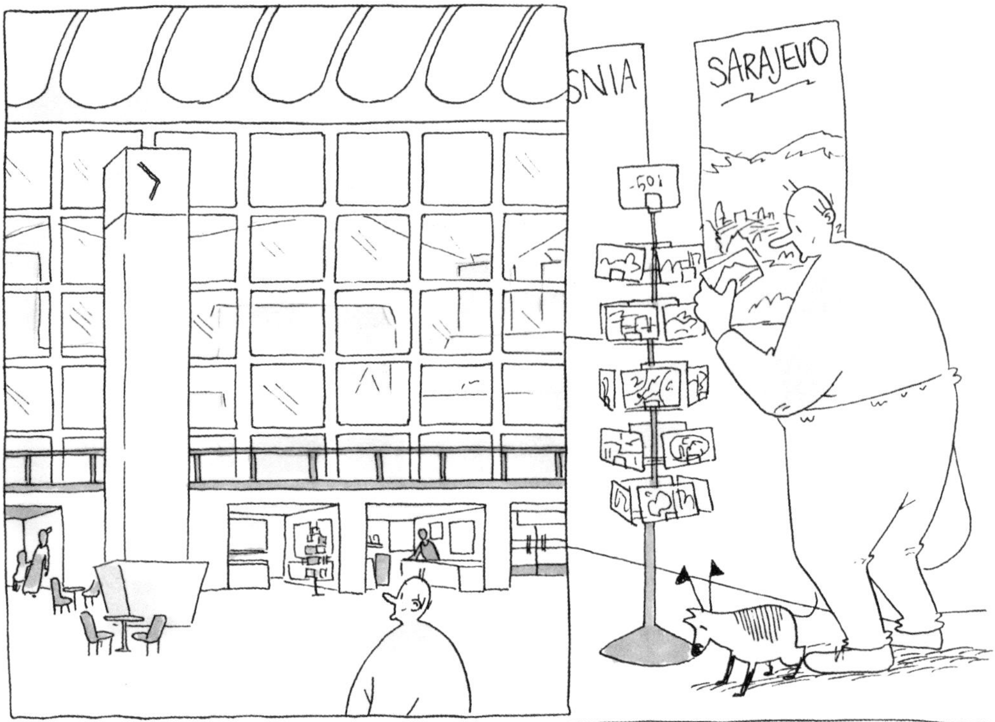
SNIA
SARAJEVO

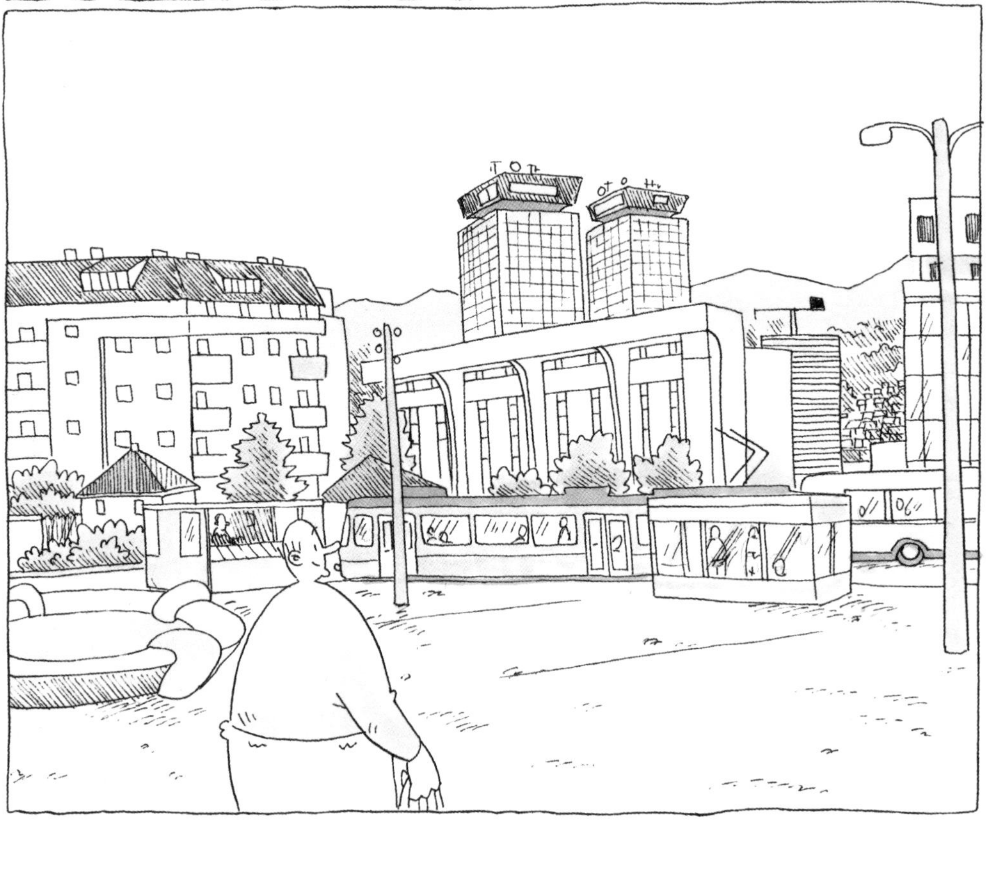

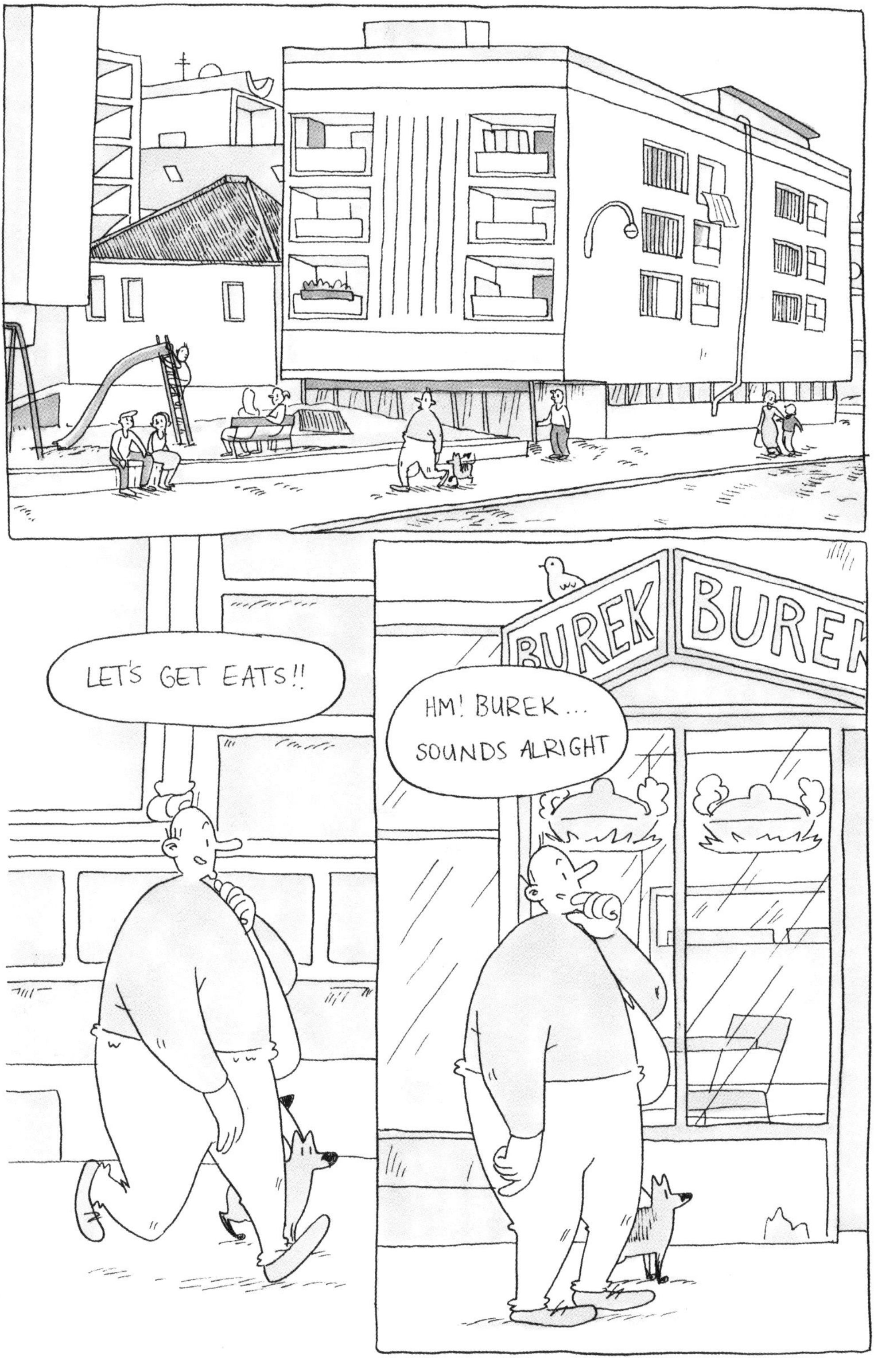
LET'S GET EATS!!
BUREK BUREK
HM! BUREK...
SOUNDS ALRIGHT

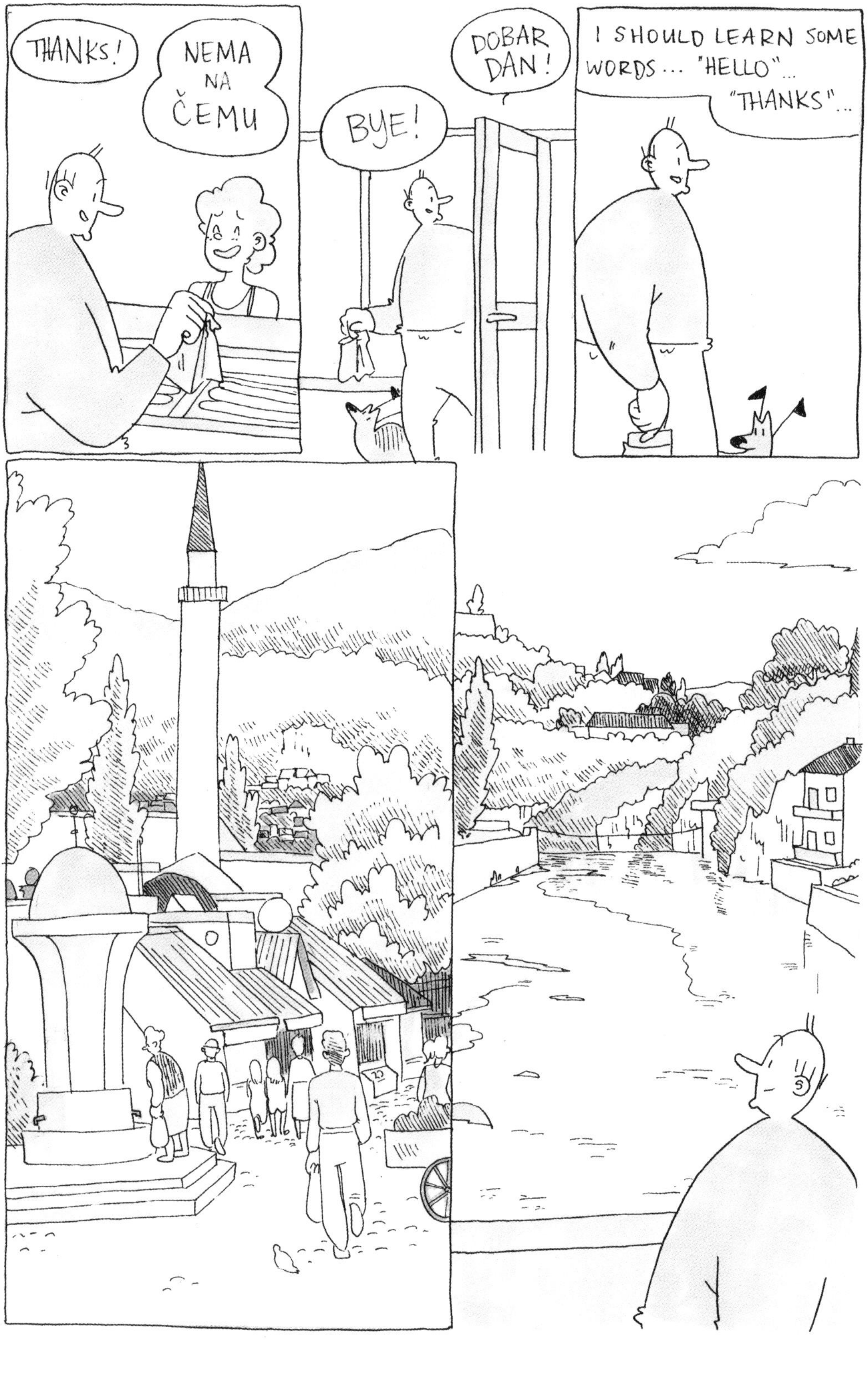
THANKS!
NEMA NA ČEMU
BYE!
DOBAR DAN!
I SHOULD LEARN SOME WORDS... "HELLO"... "THANKS"...

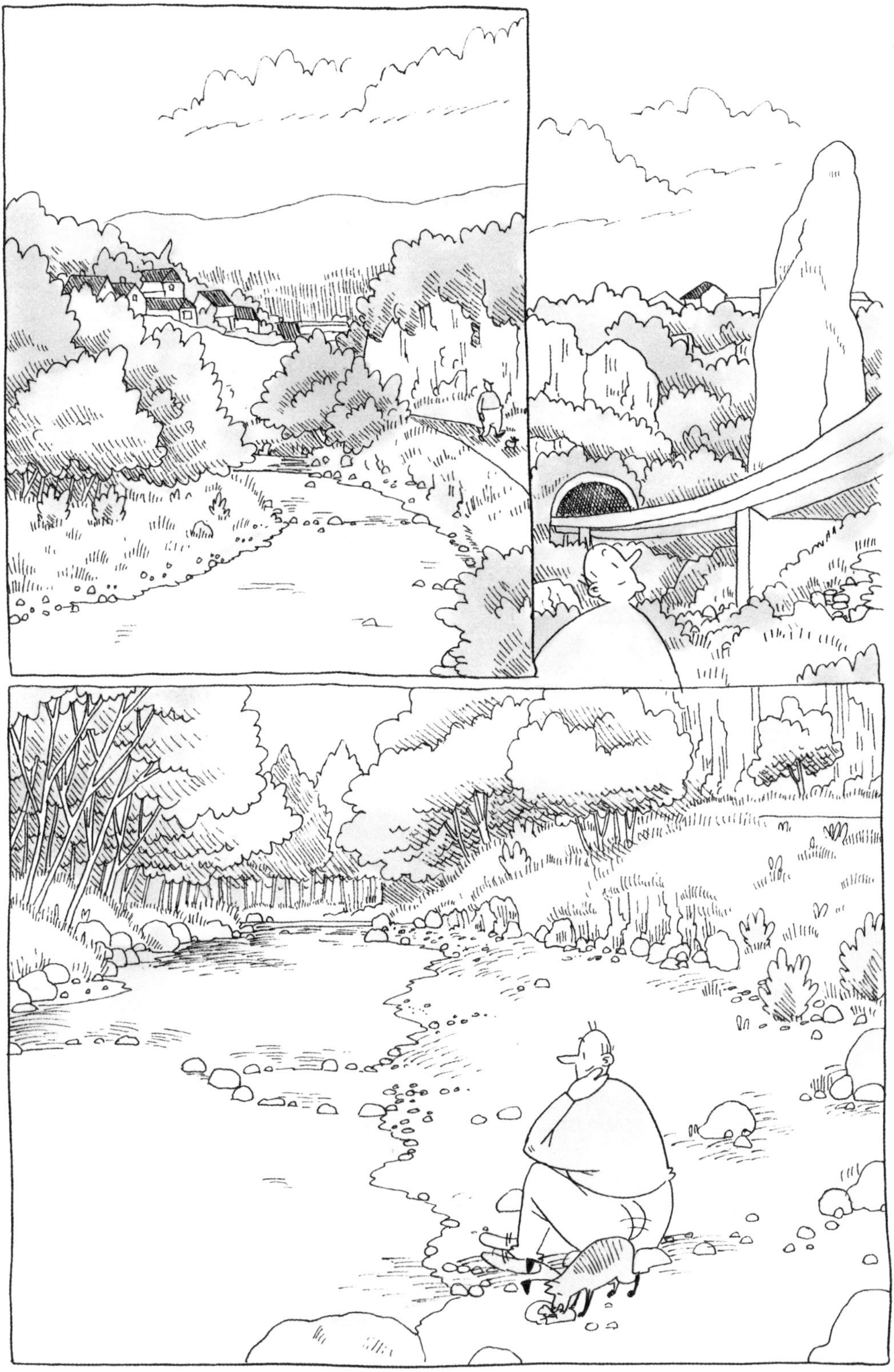

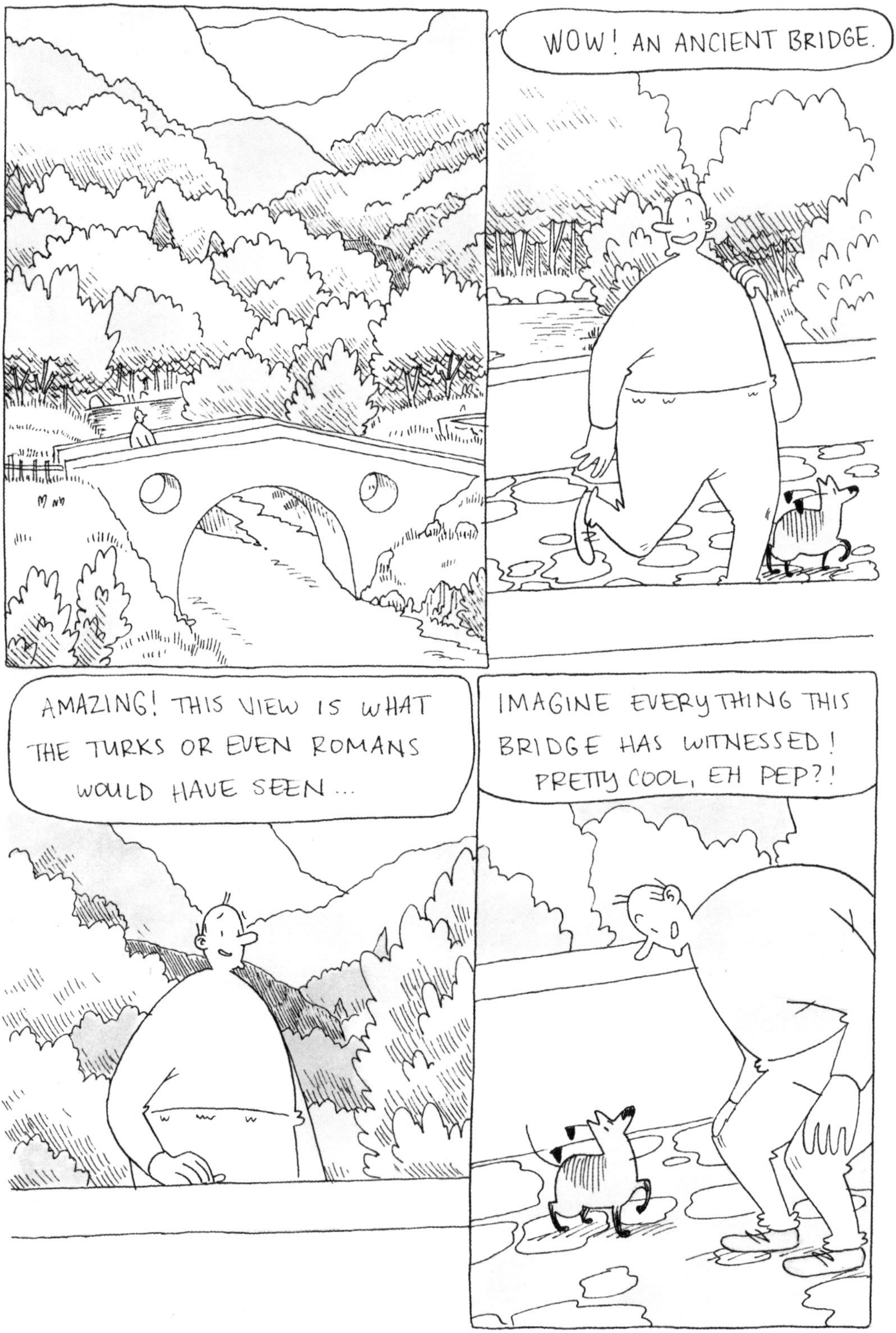
WOW! AN ANCIENT BRIDGE.
AMAZING! THIS VIEW IS WHAT THE TURKS OR EVEN ROMANS WOULD HAVE SEEN...
IMAGINE EVERYTHING THIS BRIDGE HAS WITNESSED! PRETTY COOL, EH PEP?!

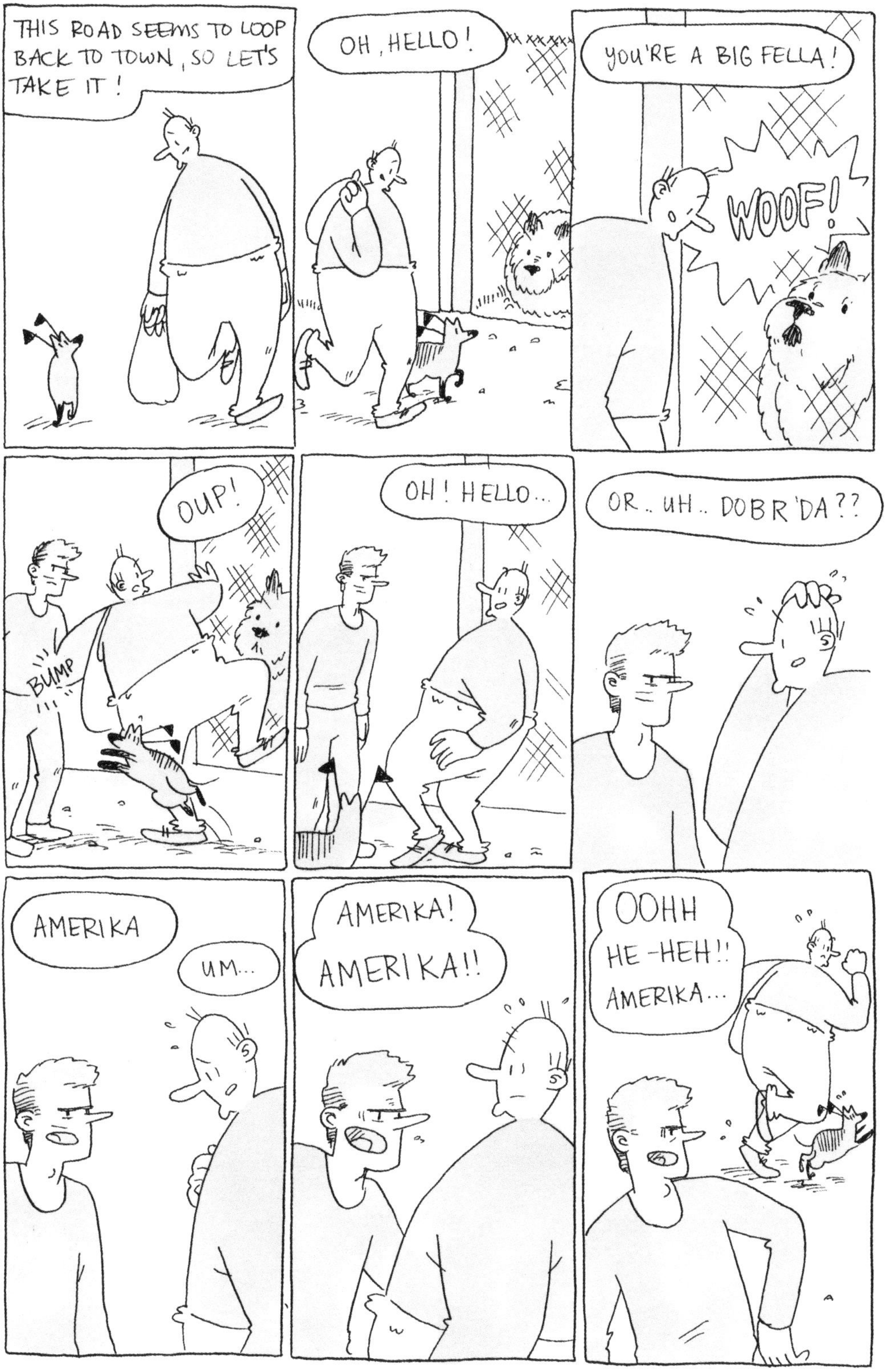
THIS ROAD SEEMS TO LOOP BACK TO TOWN, SO LET'S TAKE IT!
OH, HELLO!
YOU'RE A BIG FELLA!
WOOF!
OUP!
BUMP
OH! HELLO...
OR.. UH.. DOBR'DA??
AMERIKA
UM...
AMERIKA!
AMERIKA!!
OOHH
HE-HEH!!
AMERIKA...

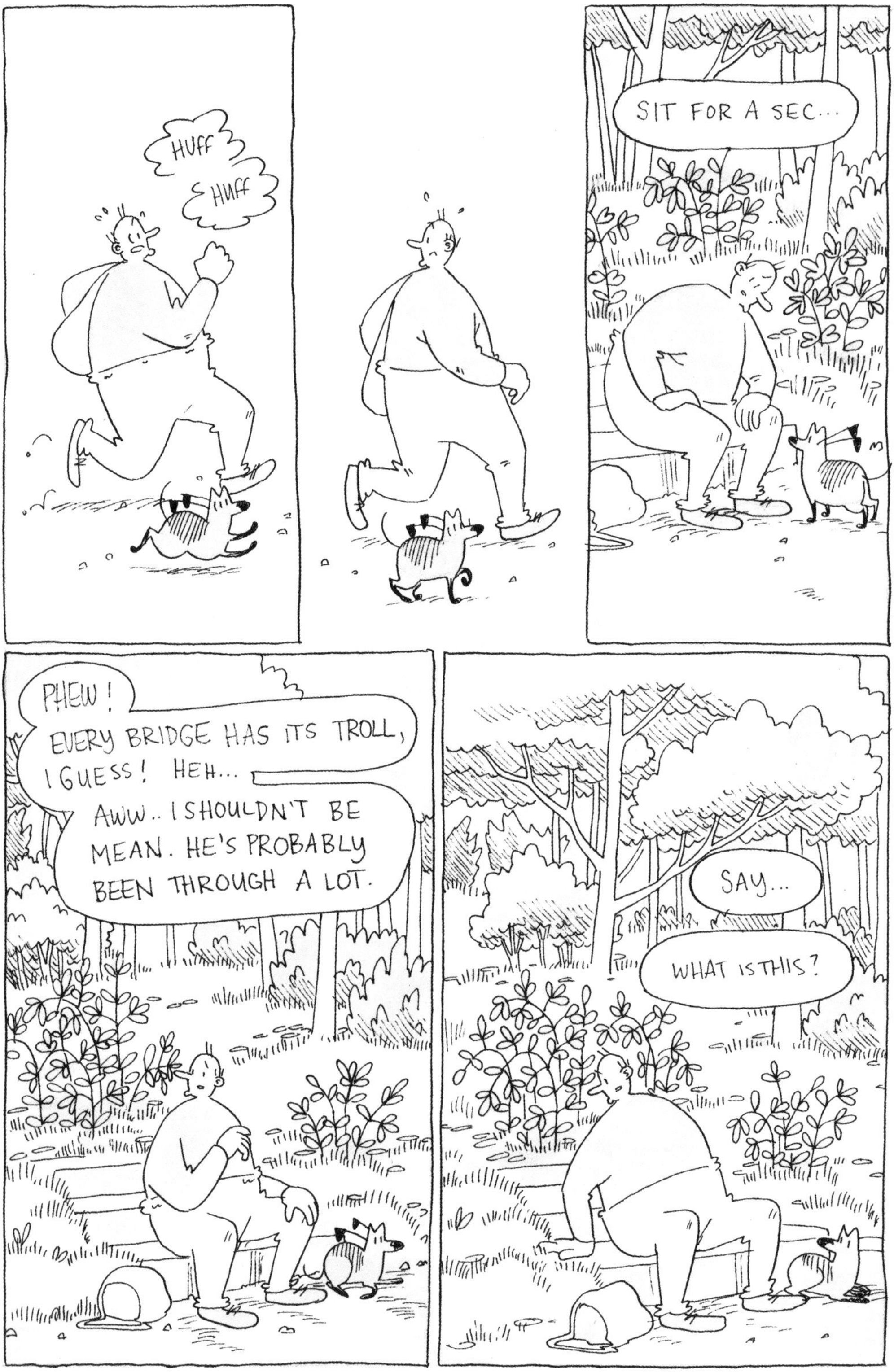
HUFF
HUFF
SIT FOR A SEC...
PHEW!
EVERY BRIDGE HAS ITS TROLL, I GUESS! HEH...
AWW.. I SHOULDN'T BE MEAN. HE'S PROBABLY BEEN THROUGH A LOT.
SAY...
WHAT IS THIS?

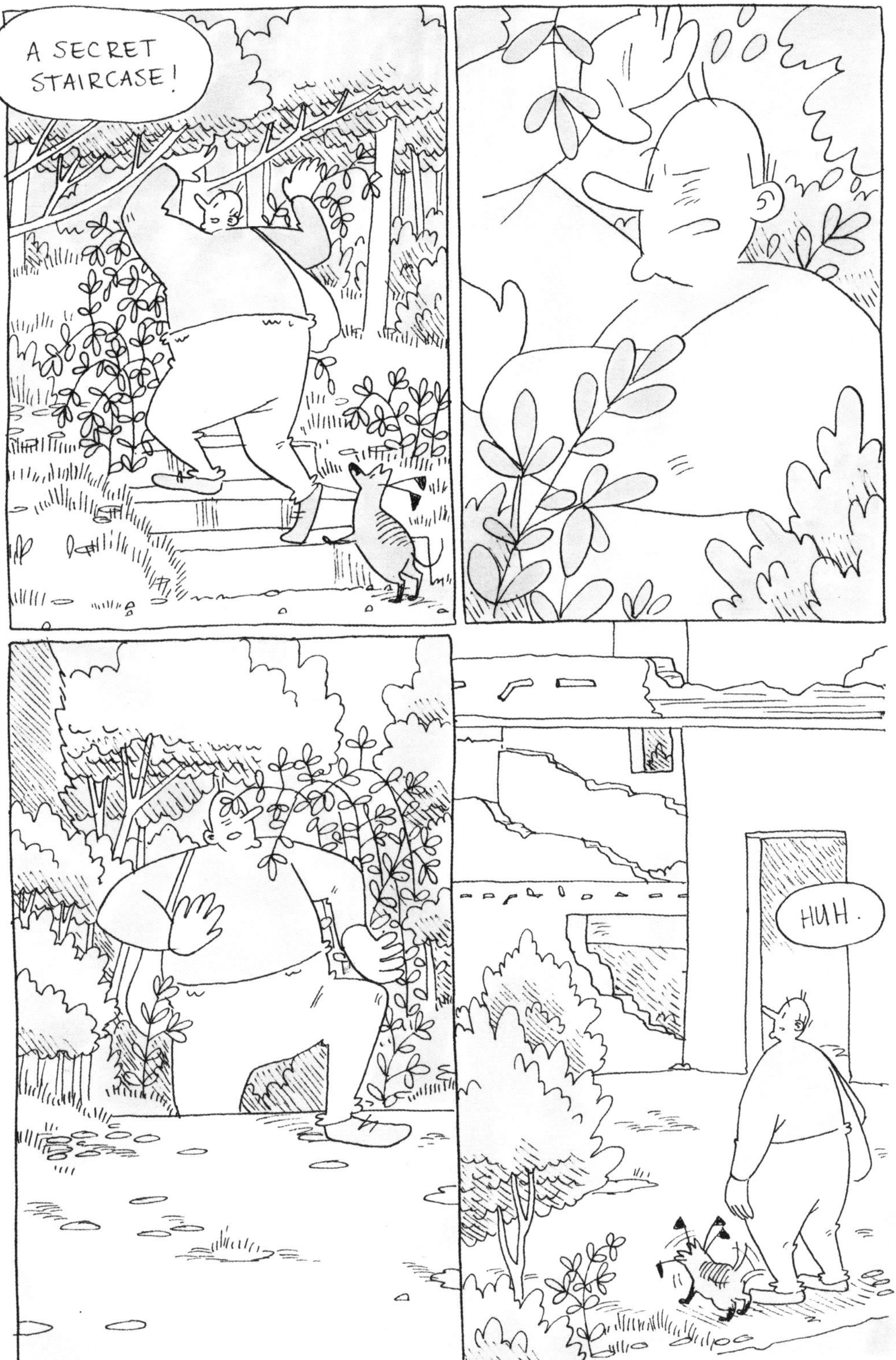
A SECRET STAIRCASE!
HUH.

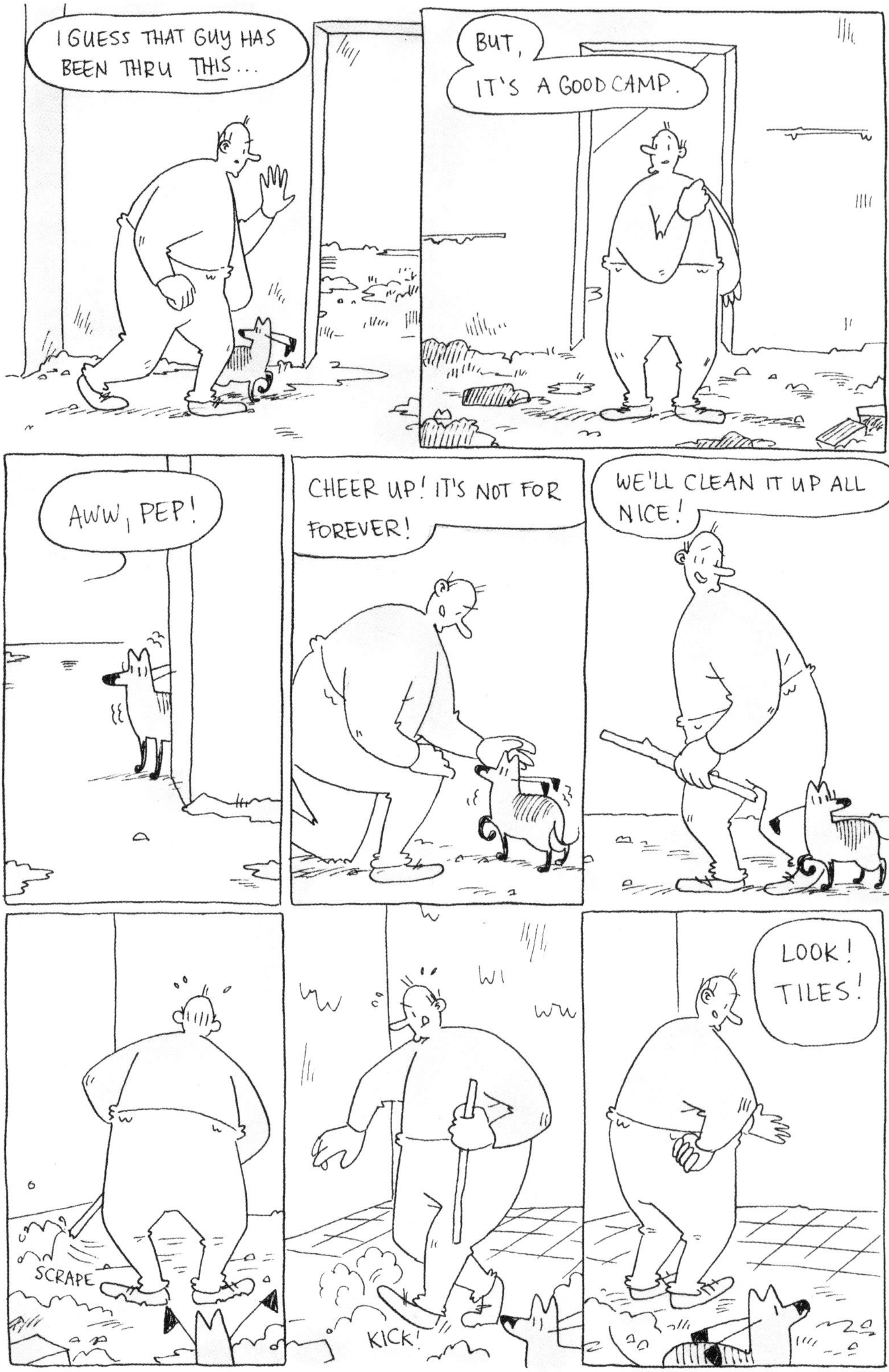
I GUESS THAT GUY HAS BEEN THRU THIS...
BUT,
IT'S A GOOD CAMP.
AWW, PEP!
CHEER UP! IT'S NOT FOR FOREVER!
WE'LL CLEAN IT UP ALL NICE!
SCRAPE
KICK!
LOOK! TILES!

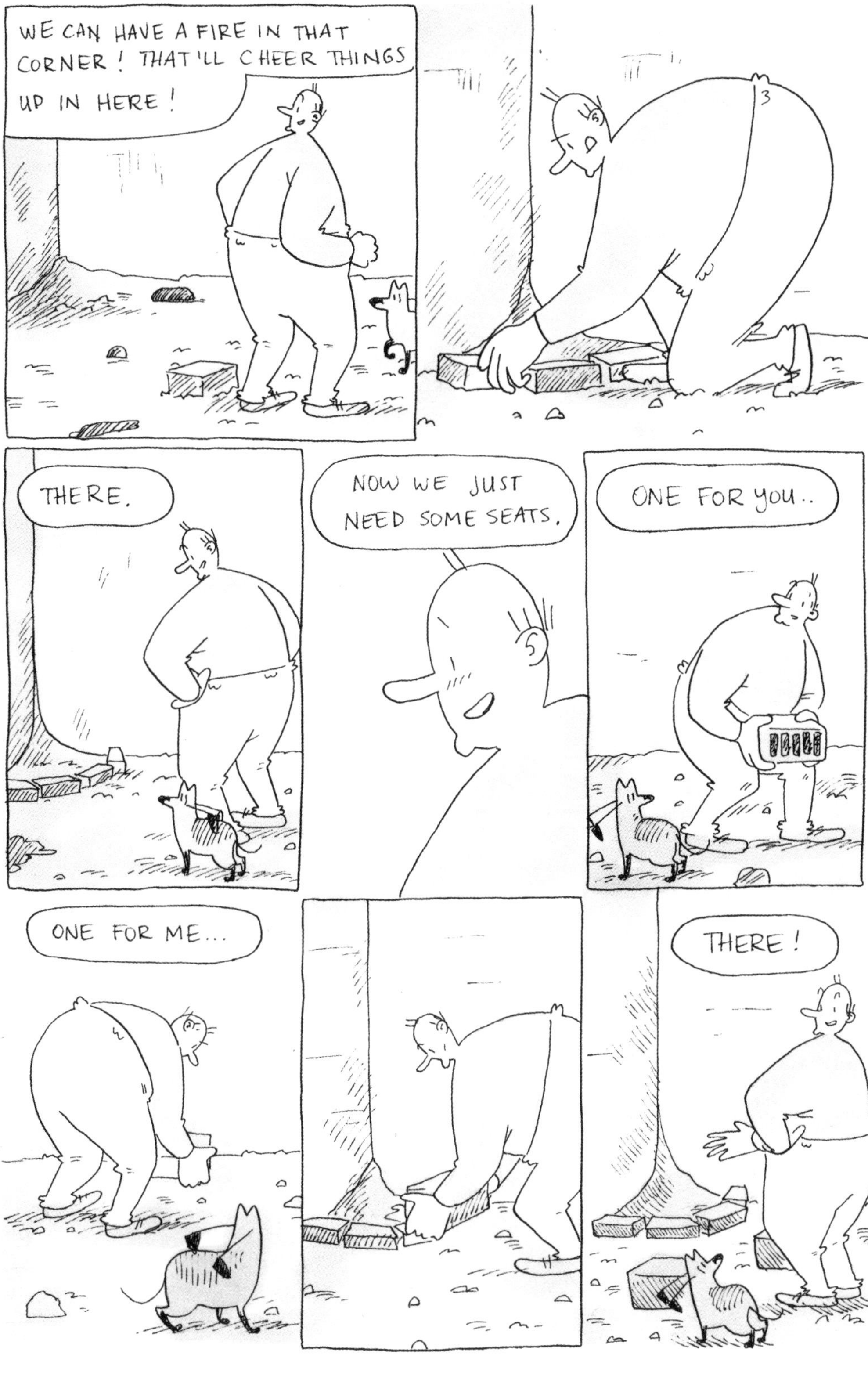
WE CAN HAVE A FIRE IN THAT CORNER! THAT'LL CHEER THINGS UP IN HERE!
THERE.
NOW WE JUST NEED SOME SEATS.
ONE FOR YOU..
ONE FOR ME...
THERE!

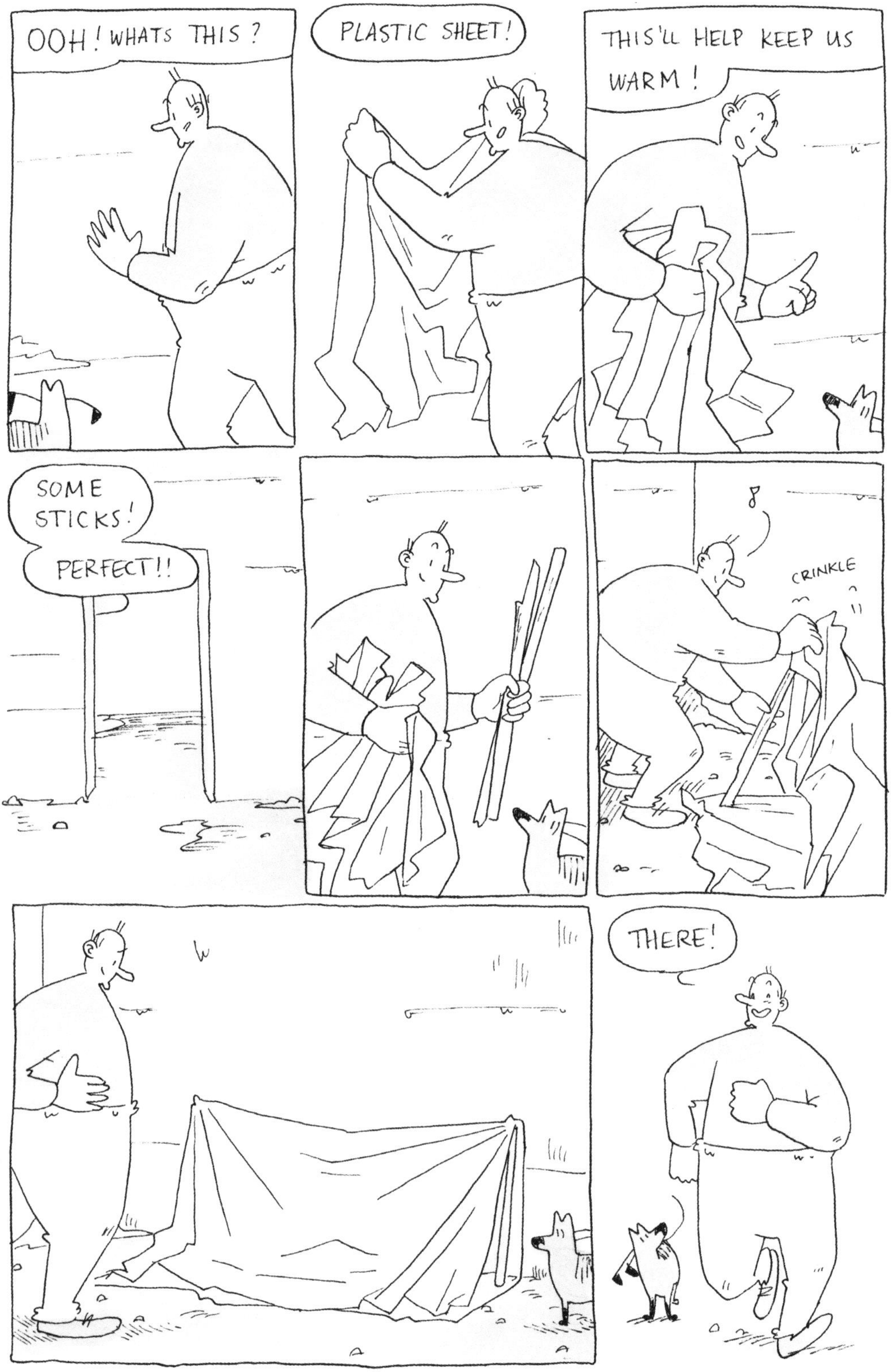
OOH! WHATS THIS?
PLASTIC SHEET!
THIS'LL HELP KEEP US WARM!
SOME STICKS!
PERFECT!!
CRINKLE
THERE!

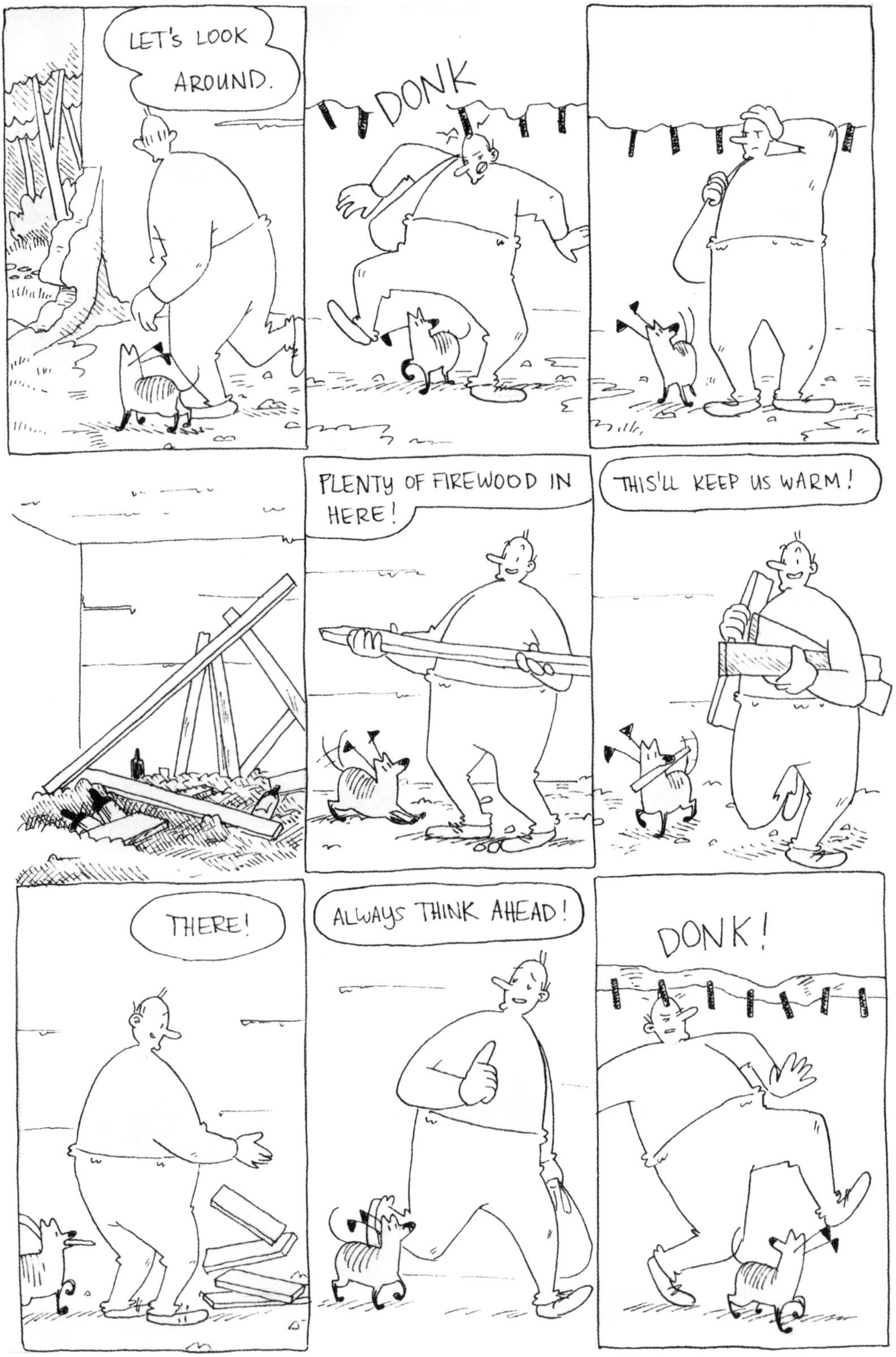
LET'S LOOK AROUND.
DONK
PLENTY OF FIREWOOD IN HERE!
THIS'LL KEEP US WARM!
THERE!
ALWAYS THINK AHEAD!
DONK!

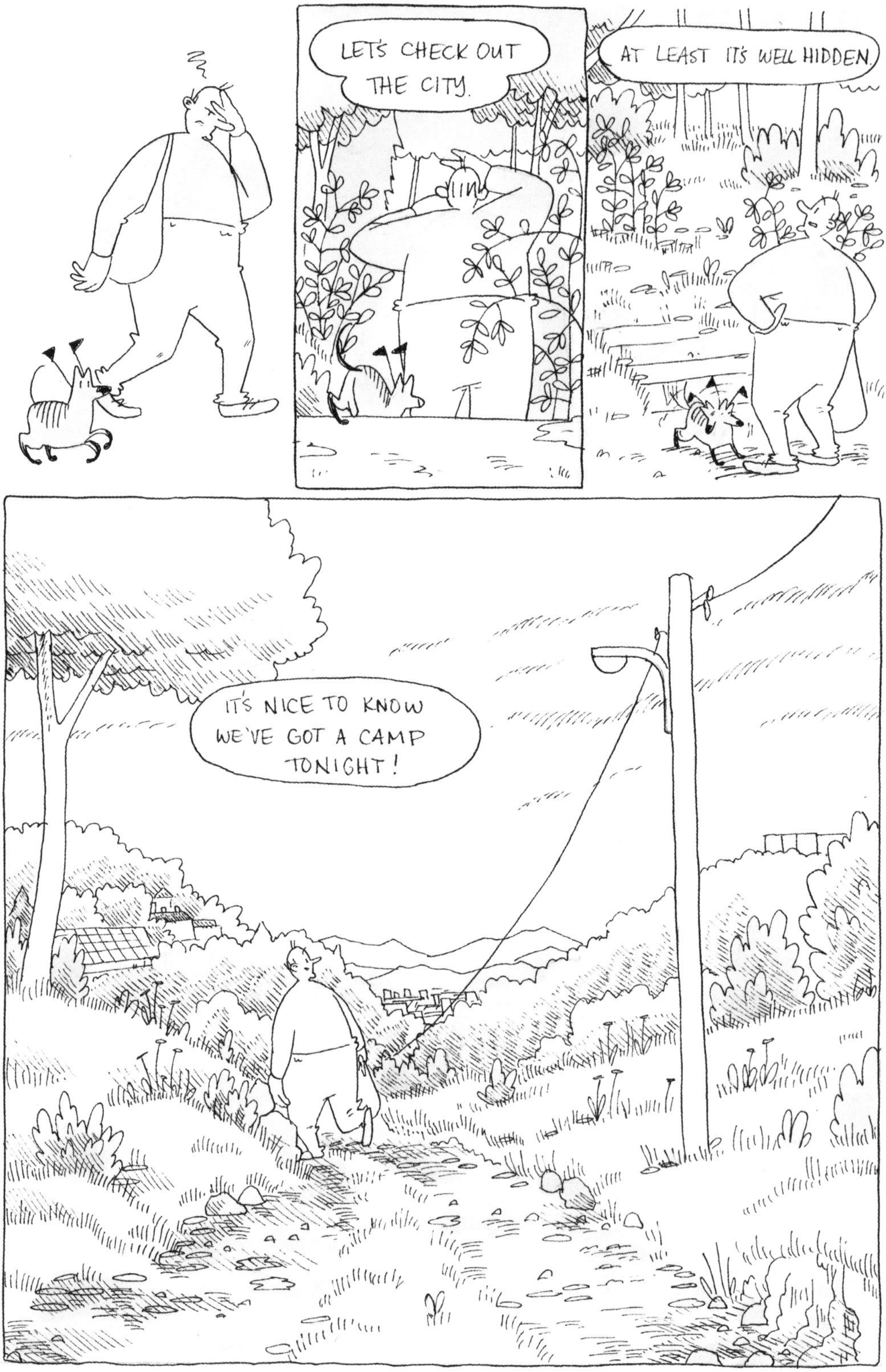
LET'S CHECK OUT THE CITY.
AT LEAST IT'S WELL HIDDEN.
IT'S NICE TO KNOW WE'VE GOT A CAMP TONIGHT!

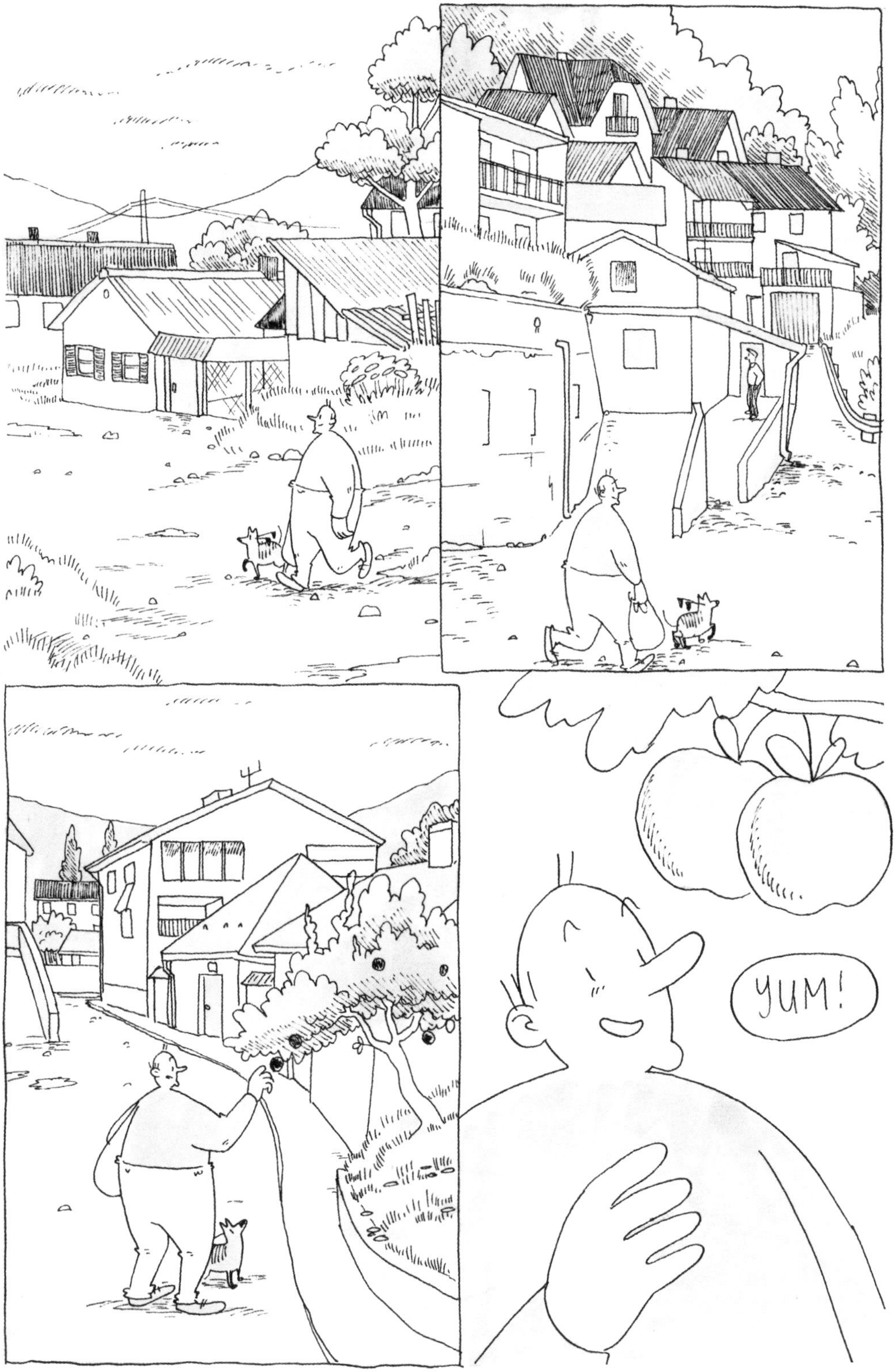
YUM!

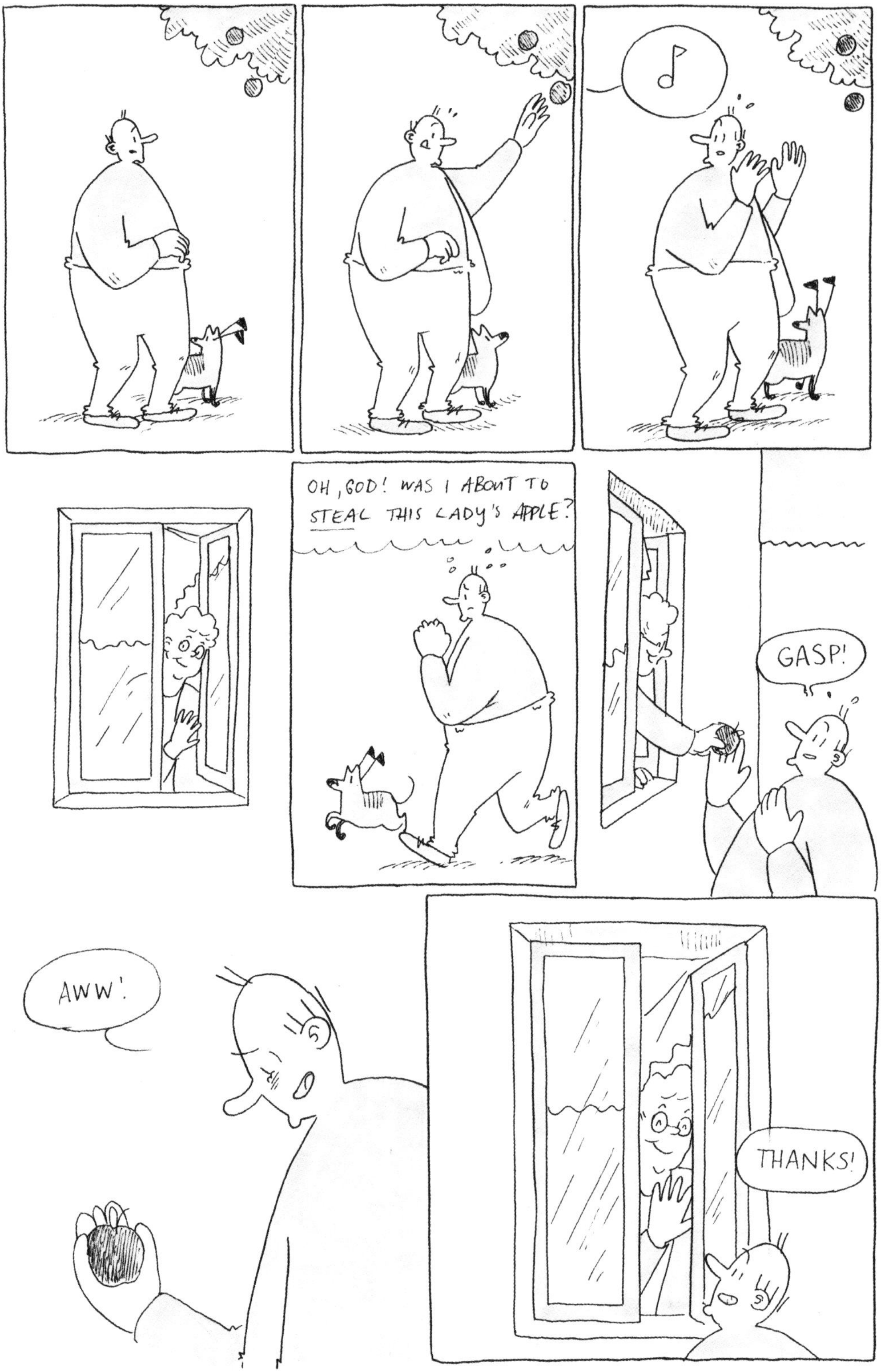
OH, GOD! WAS I ABOUT TO STEAL THIS LADY'S APPLE?
GASP!
AWW!
THANKS!

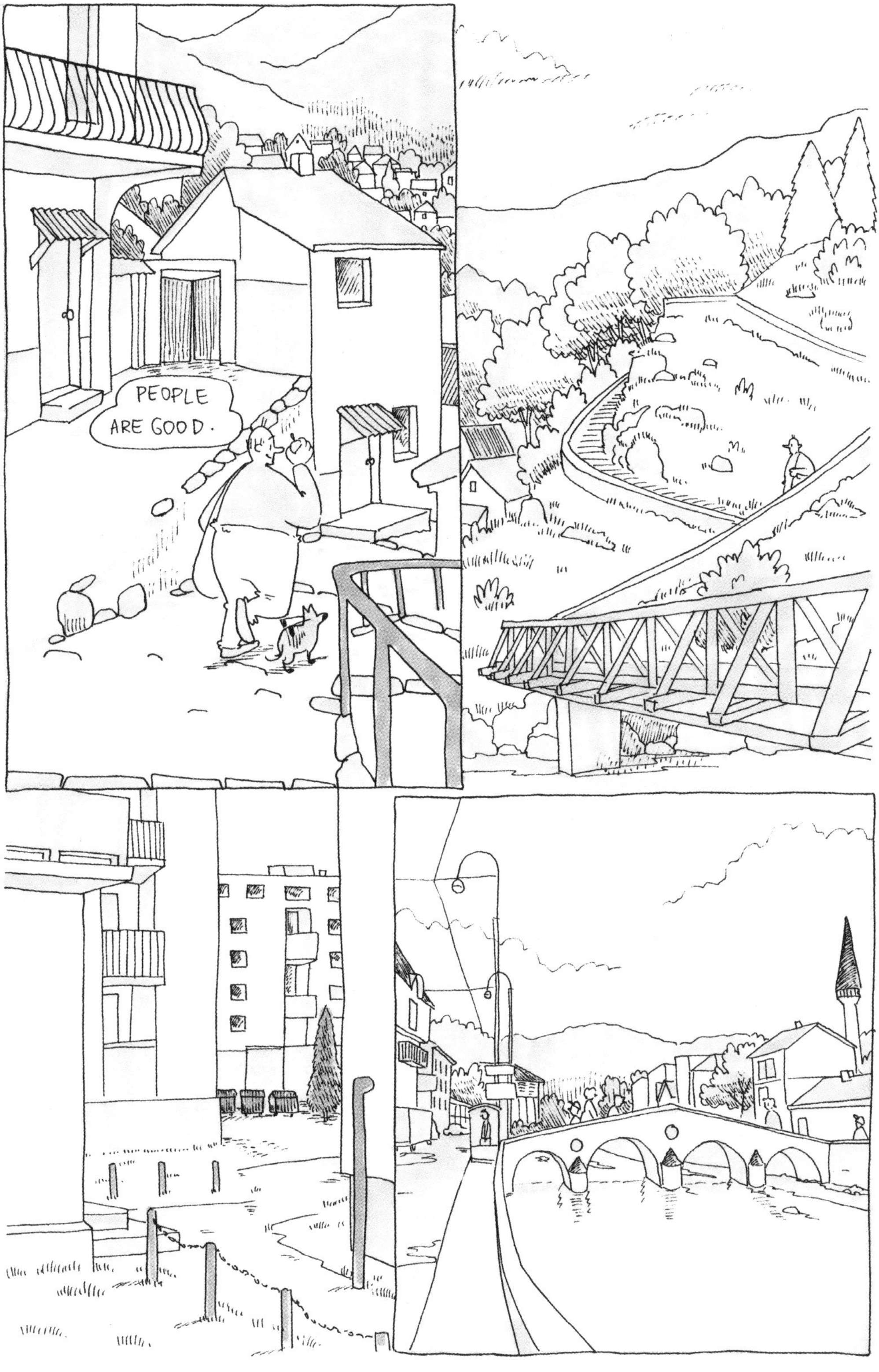
PEOPLE ARE GOOD.

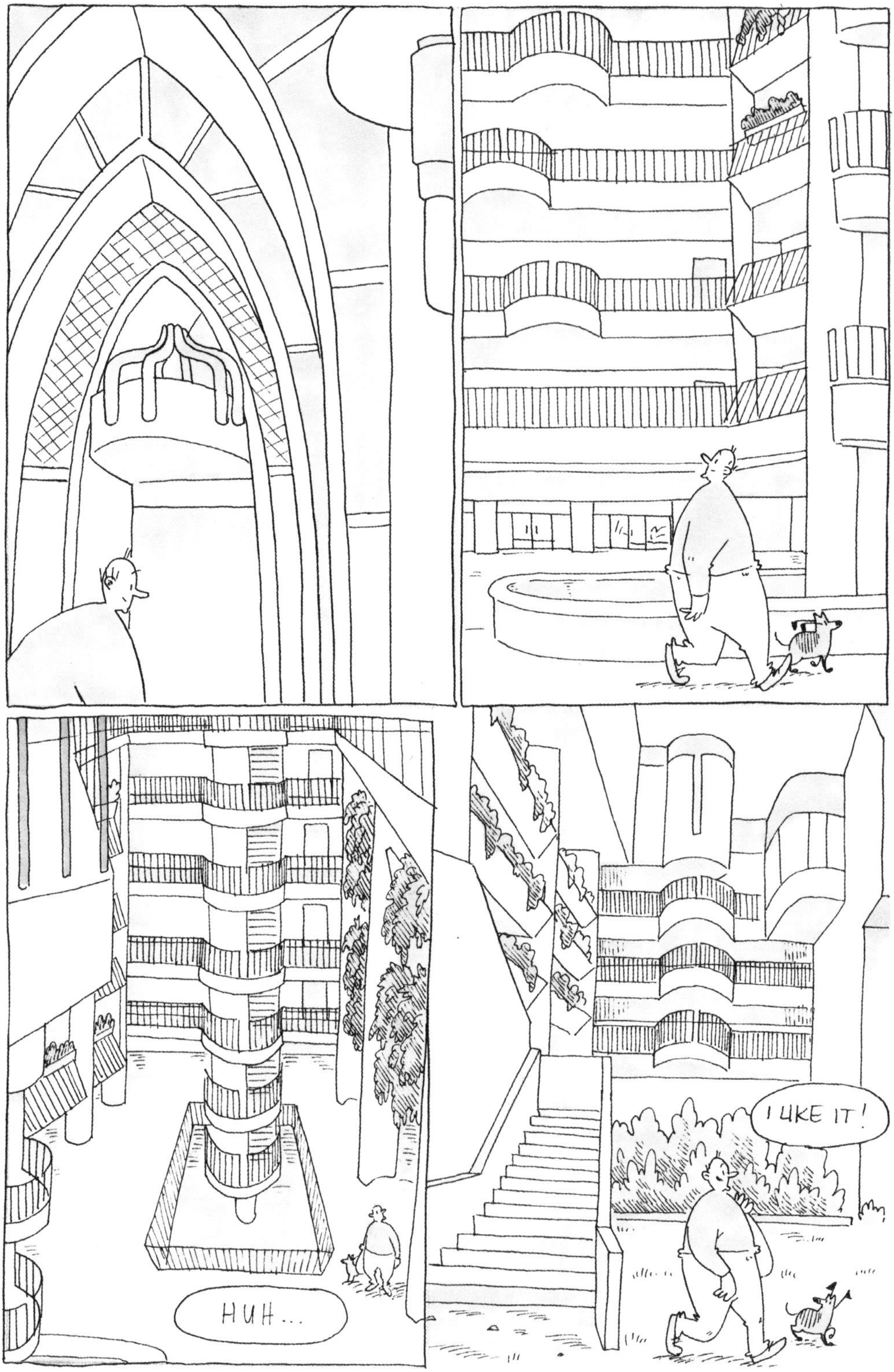
HUH...
I LIKE IT!

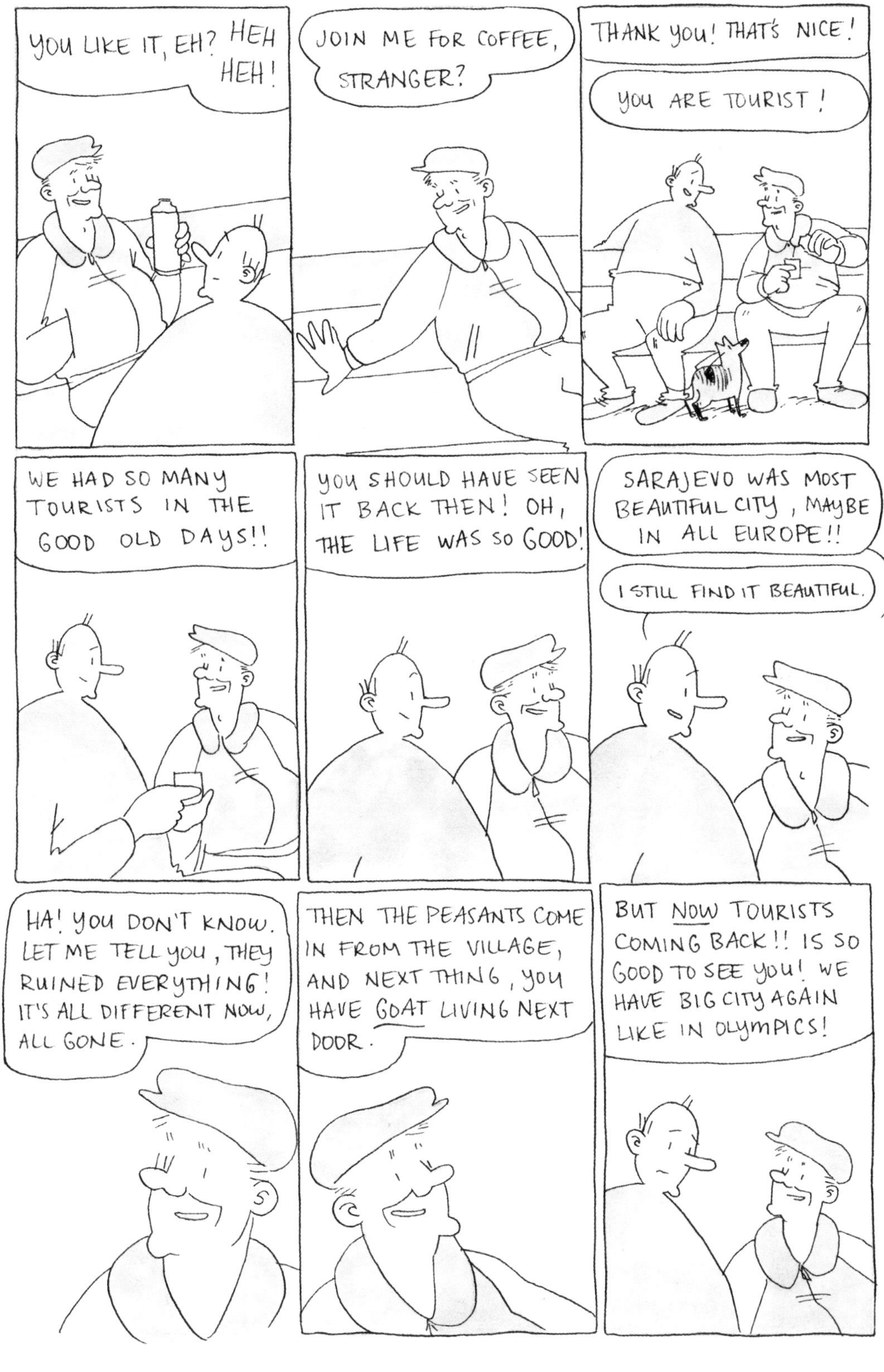
YOU LIKE IT, EH? HEH HEH!
JOIN ME FOR COFFEE, STRANGER?
THANK YOU! THAT'S NICE!
YOU ARE TOURIST!
WE HAD SO MANY TOURISTS IN THE GOOD OLD DAYS!!
YOU SHOULD HAVE SEEN IT BACK THEN! OH, THE LIFE WAS SO GOOD!
SARAJEVO WAS MOST BEAUTIFUL CITY, MAYBE IN ALL EUROPE!!
I STILL FIND IT BEAUTIFUL.
HA! YOU DON'T KNOW. LET ME TELL YOU, THEY RUINED EVERYTHING! IT'S ALL DIFFERENT NOW, ALL GONE.
THEN THE PEASANTS COME IN FROM THE VILLAGE, AND NEXT THING, YOU HAVE GOAT LIVING NEXT DOOR.
BUT NOW TOURISTS COMING BACK!! IS SO GOOD TO SEE YOU! WE HAVE BIG CITY AGAIN LIKE IN OLYMPICS!

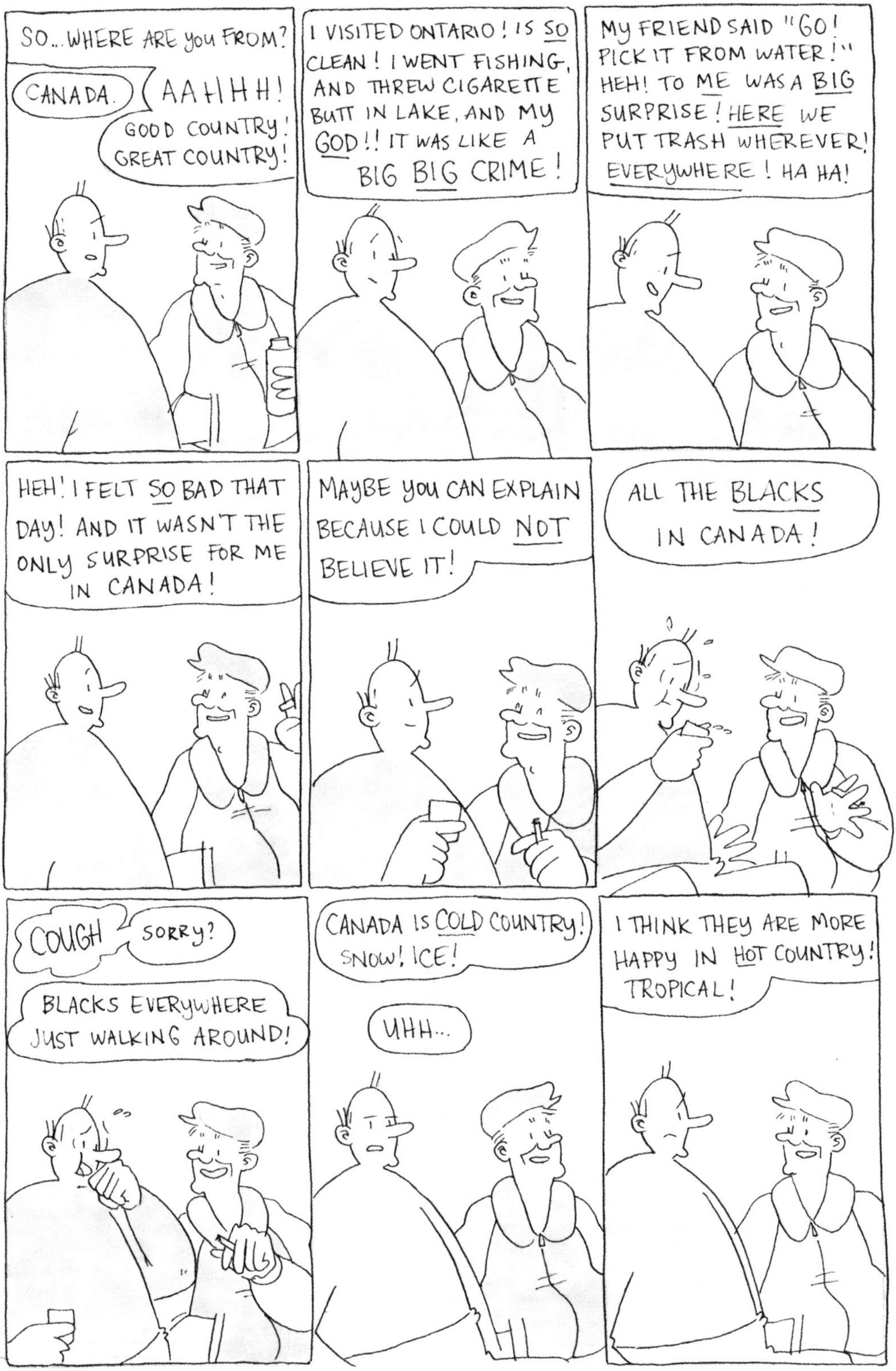
SO... WHERE ARE YOU FROM?
CANADA.
AAHHHH! GOOD COUNTRY! GREAT COUNTRY!
I VISITED ONTARIO! IS SO CLEAN! I WENT FISHING, AND THREW CIGARETTE BUTT IN LAKE, AND MY GOD!! IT WAS LIKE A BIG BIG CRIME!
MY FRIEND SAID "GO! PICK IT FROM WATER!" HEH! TO ME WAS A BIG SURPRISE! HERE WE PUT TRASH WHEREVER! EVERYWHERE! HA HA!
HEH! I FELT SO BAD THAT DAY! AND IT WASN'T THE ONLY SURPRISE FOR ME IN CANADA!
MAYBE YOU CAN EXPLAIN BECAUSE I COULD NOT BELIEVE IT!
ALL THE BLACKS IN CANADA!
COUGH
SORRY?
BLACKS EVERYWHERE JUST WALKING AROUND!
CANADA IS COLD COUNTRY! SNOW! ICE!
UHH...
I THINK THEY ARE MORE HAPPY IN HOT COUNTRY! TROPICAL!

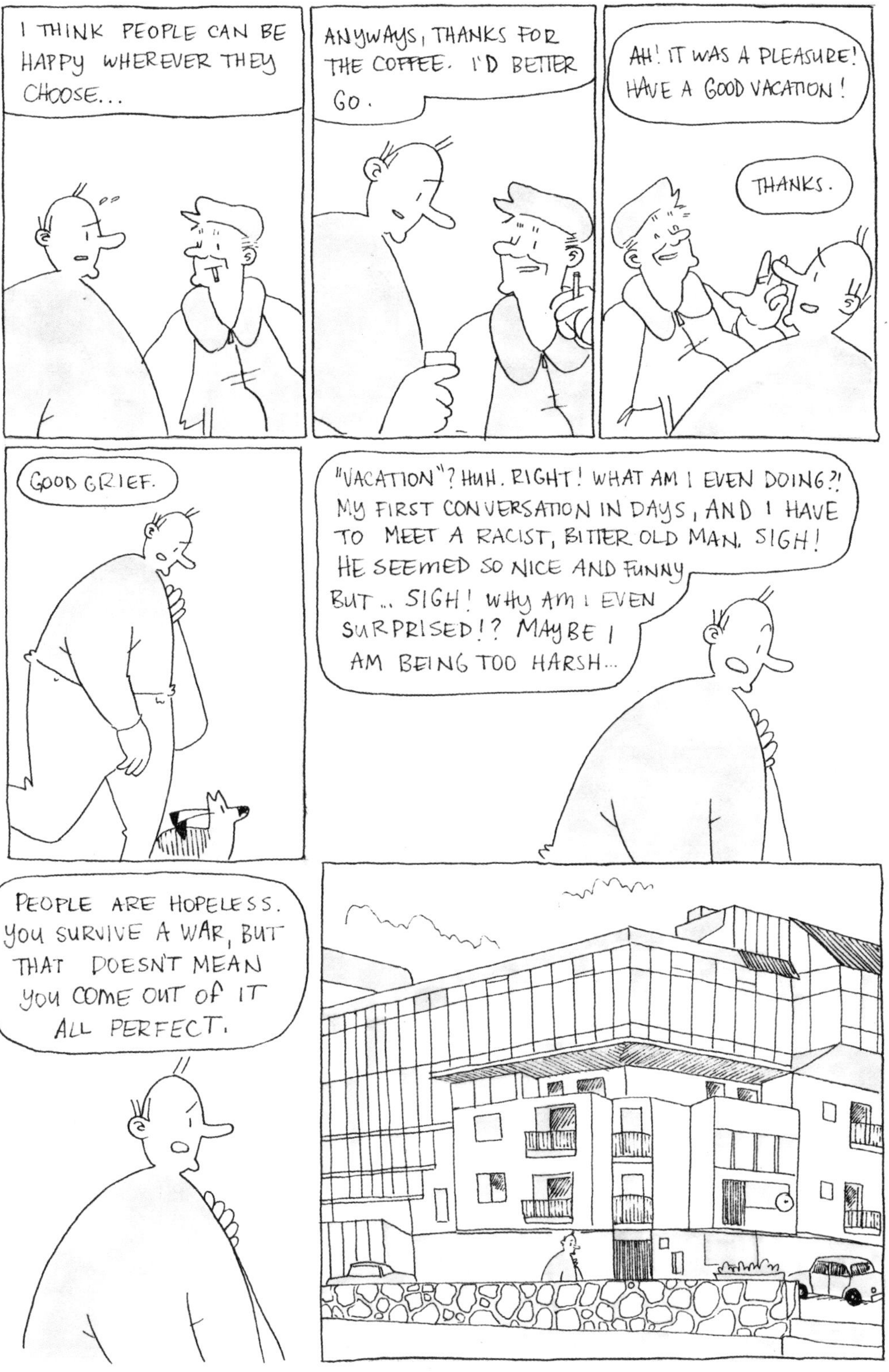
I THINK PEOPLE CAN BE HAPPY WHEREVER THEY CHOOSE...
ANYWAYS, THANKS FOR THE COFFEE. I'D BETTER GO.
AH! IT WAS A PLEASURE! HAVE A GOOD VACATION!
THANKS.
GOOD GRIEF.
"VACATION"? HUH. RIGHT! WHAT AM I EVEN DOING?! MY FIRST CONVERSATION IN DAYS, AND I HAVE TO MEET A RACIST, BITTER OLD MAN. SIGH! HE SEEMED SO NICE AND FUNNY BUT... SIGH! WHY AM I EVEN SURPRISED!? MAYBE I AM BEING TOO HARSH...
PEOPLE ARE HOPELESS. YOU SURVIVE A WAR, BUT THAT DOESN'T MEAN YOU COME OUT OF IT ALL PERFECT.

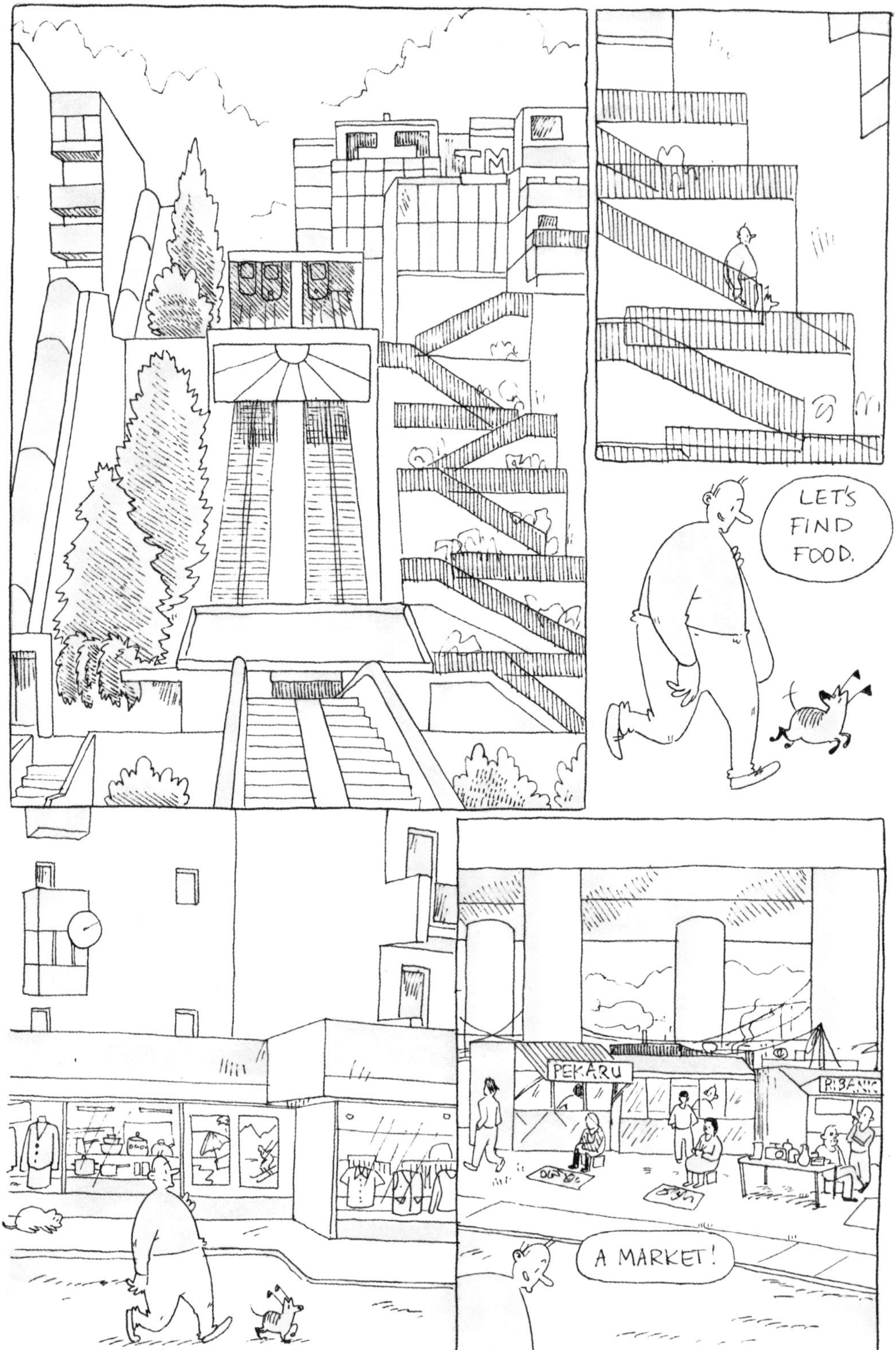
LET'S FIND FOOD.
PEKARU
A MARKET!

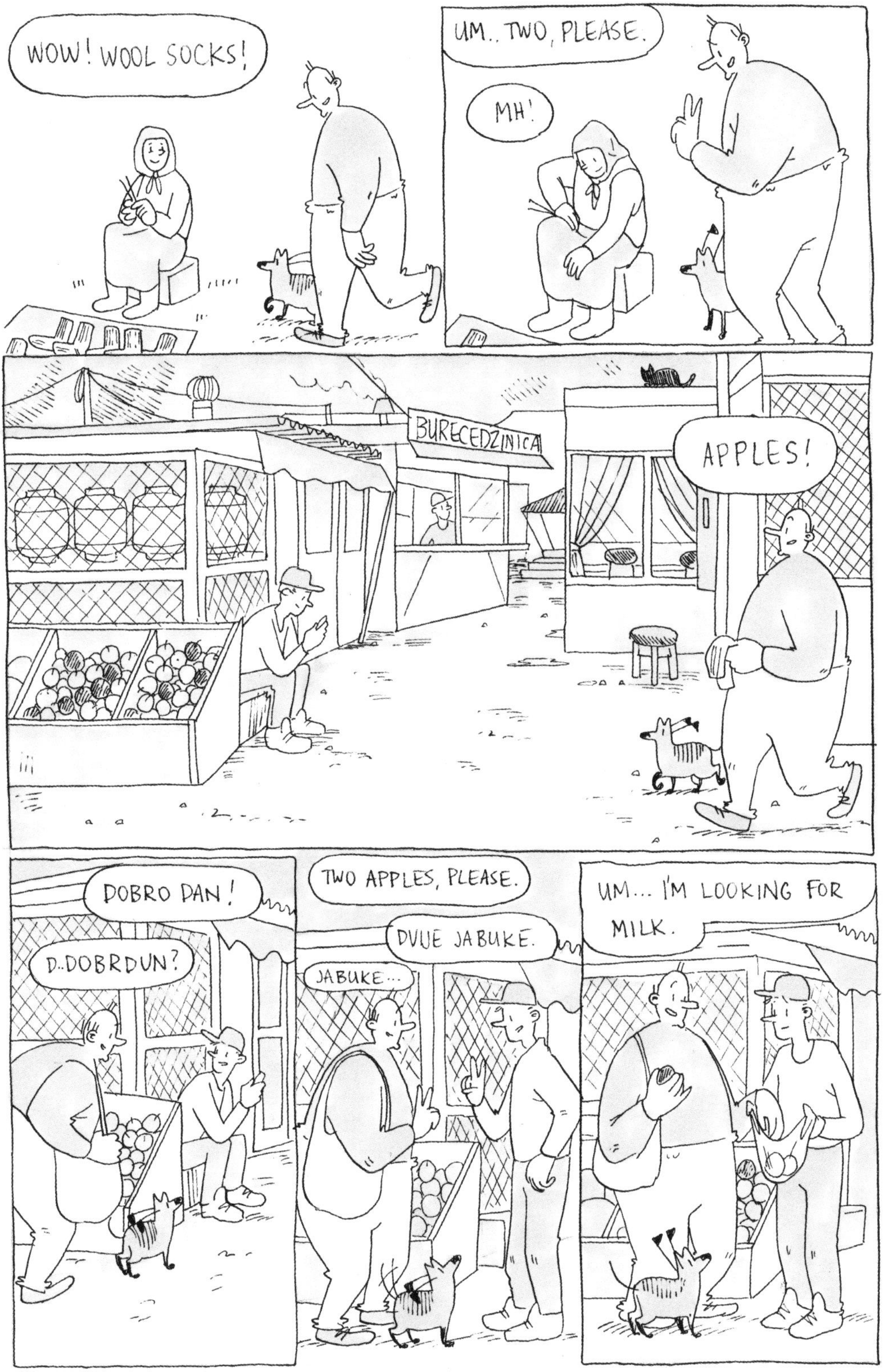
WOW! WOOL SOCKS!
UM.. TWO, PLEASE.
MH!
BURECEDZINICA
APPLES!
DOBRO DAN!
D..DOBRDUN?
TWO APPLES, PLEASE.
DVIJE JABUKE.
JABUKE...
UM... I'M LOOKING FOR MILK.

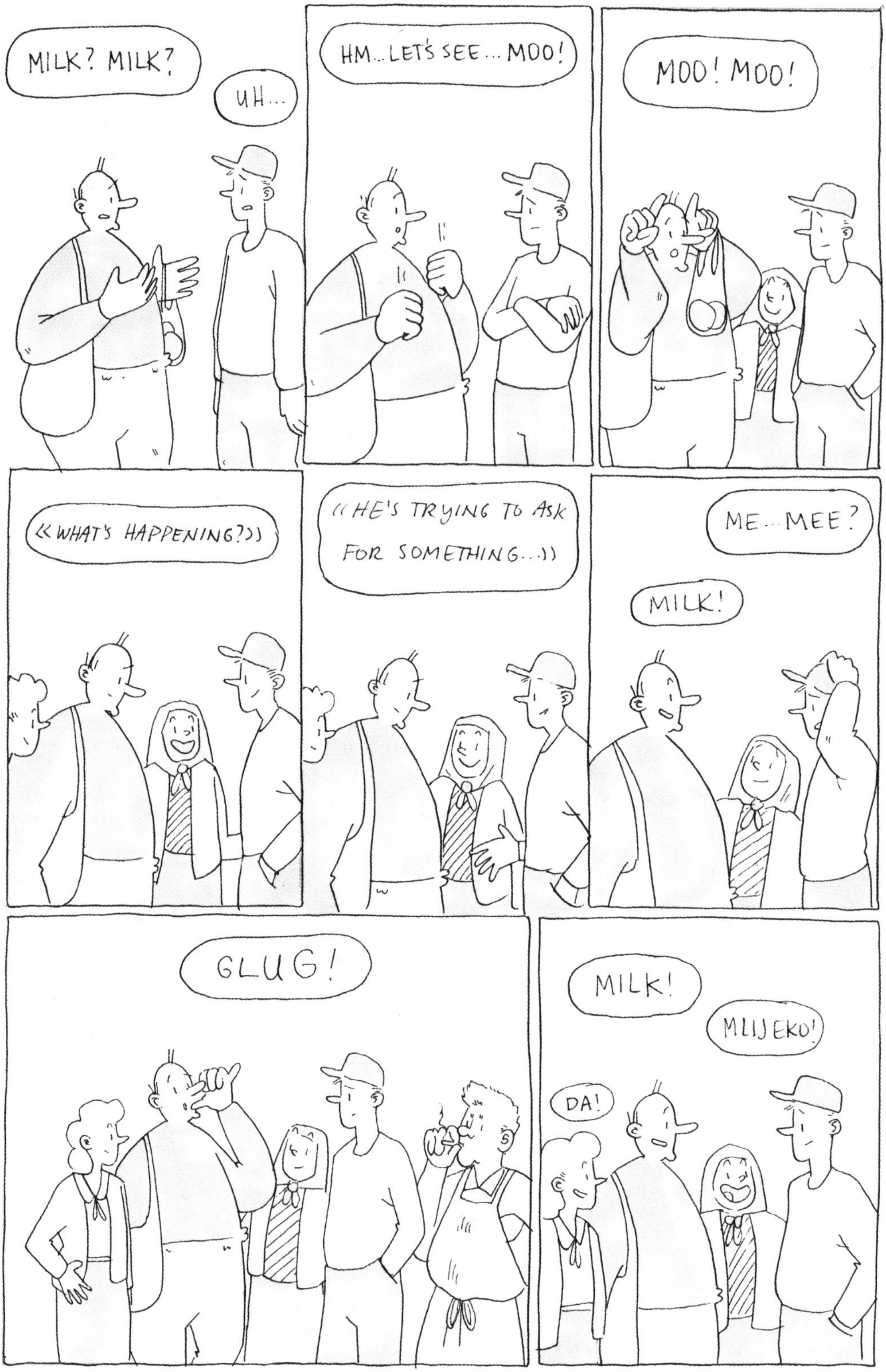
MILK? MILK?
UH...
HM... LET'S SEE... MOO!
MOO! MOO!
«WHAT'S HAPPENING?»
«HE'S TRYING TO ASK FOR SOMETHING...»
ME... MEE?
MILK!
GLUG!
MILK!
MLIJEKO!
DA!

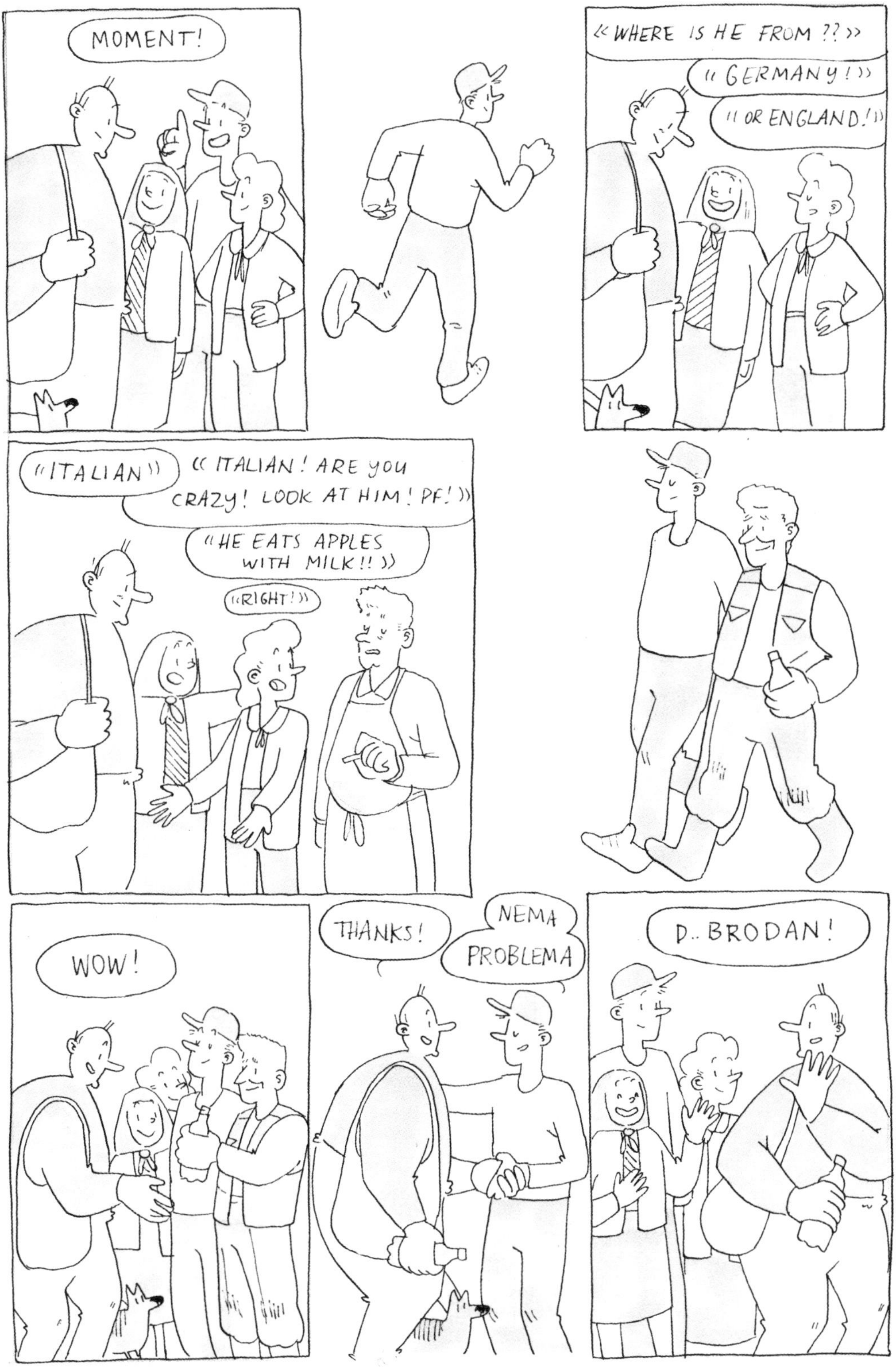
MOMENT!
« WHERE IS HE FROM ?? »
« GERMANY! »
« OR ENGLAND! »
« ITALIAN »
« ITALIAN! ARE YOU CRAZY! LOOK AT HIM! PF! »
« HE EATS APPLES WITH MILK!! »
« RIGHT! »
WOW!
THANKS!
NEMA PROBLEMA
D.. BRODAN!

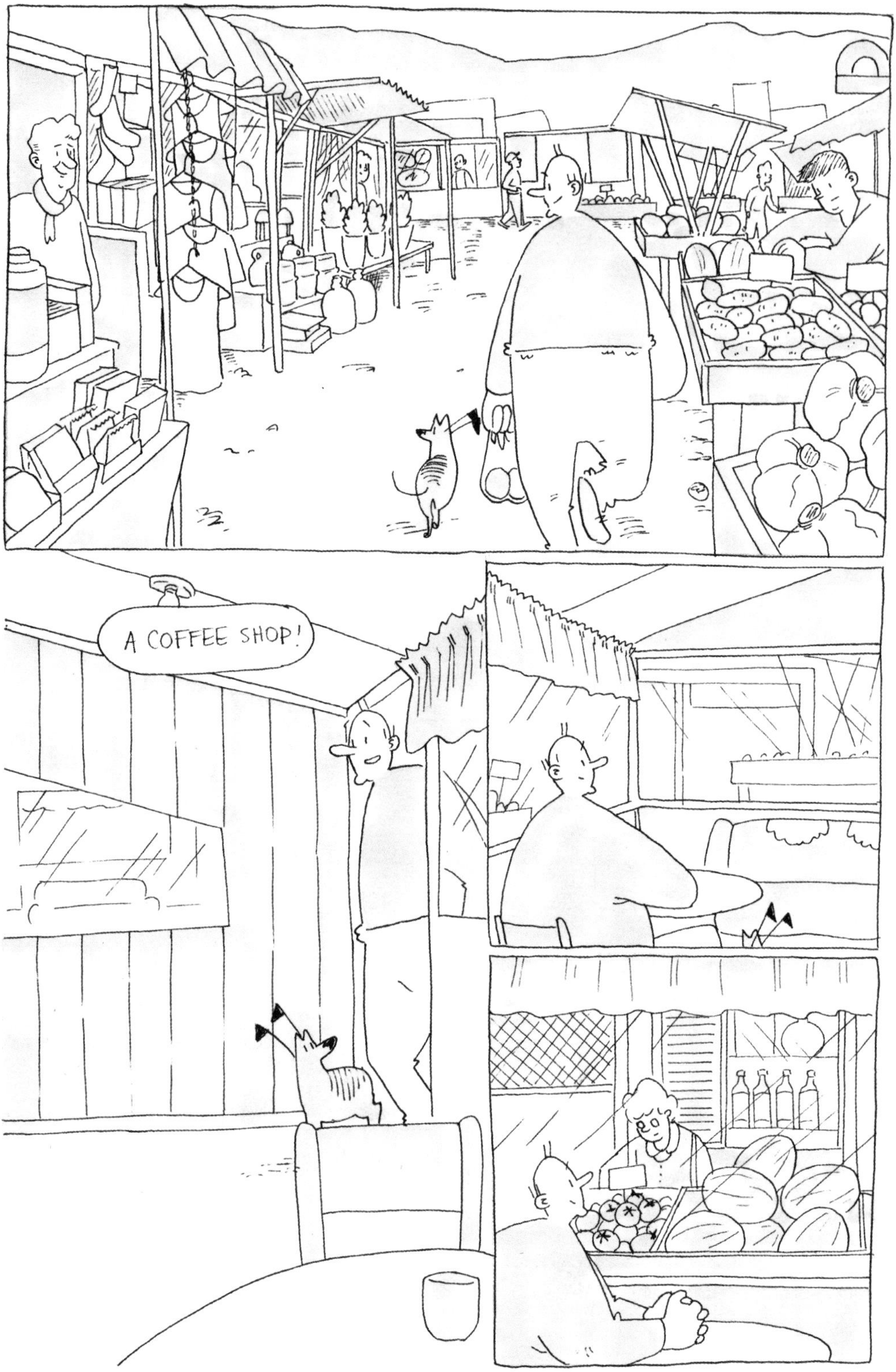
A COFFEE SHOP!

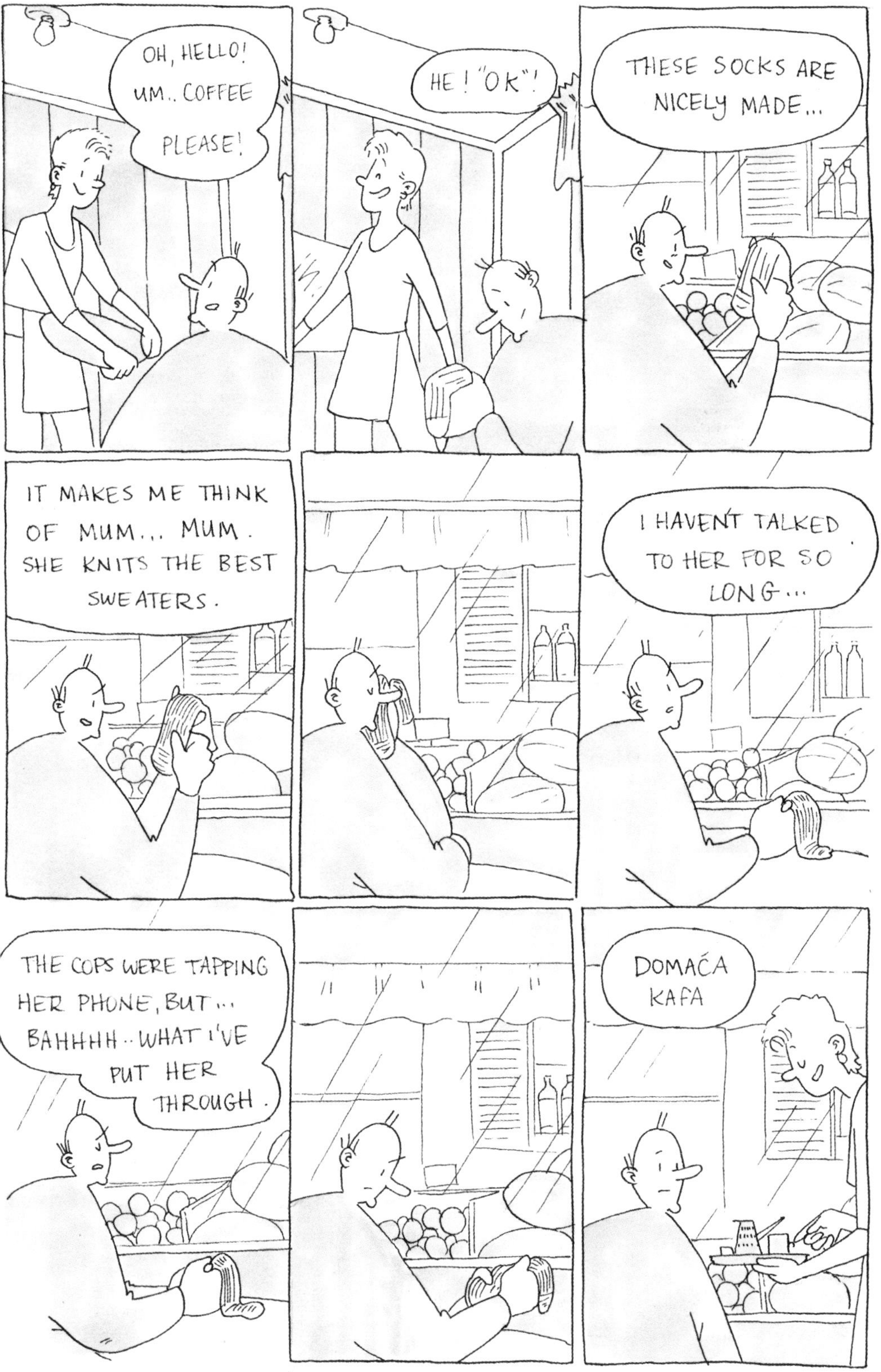
OH, HELLO! UM.. COFFEE PLEASE!
HE! "OK"!
THESE SOCKS ARE NICELY MADE...
IT MAKES ME THINK OF MUM... MUM. SHE KNITS THE BEST SWEATERS.
I HAVEN'T TALKED TO HER FOR SO LONG...
THE COPS WERE TAPPING HER PHONE, BUT... BAHHHH.. WHAT I'VE PUT HER THROUGH.
DOMAĆA KAFA

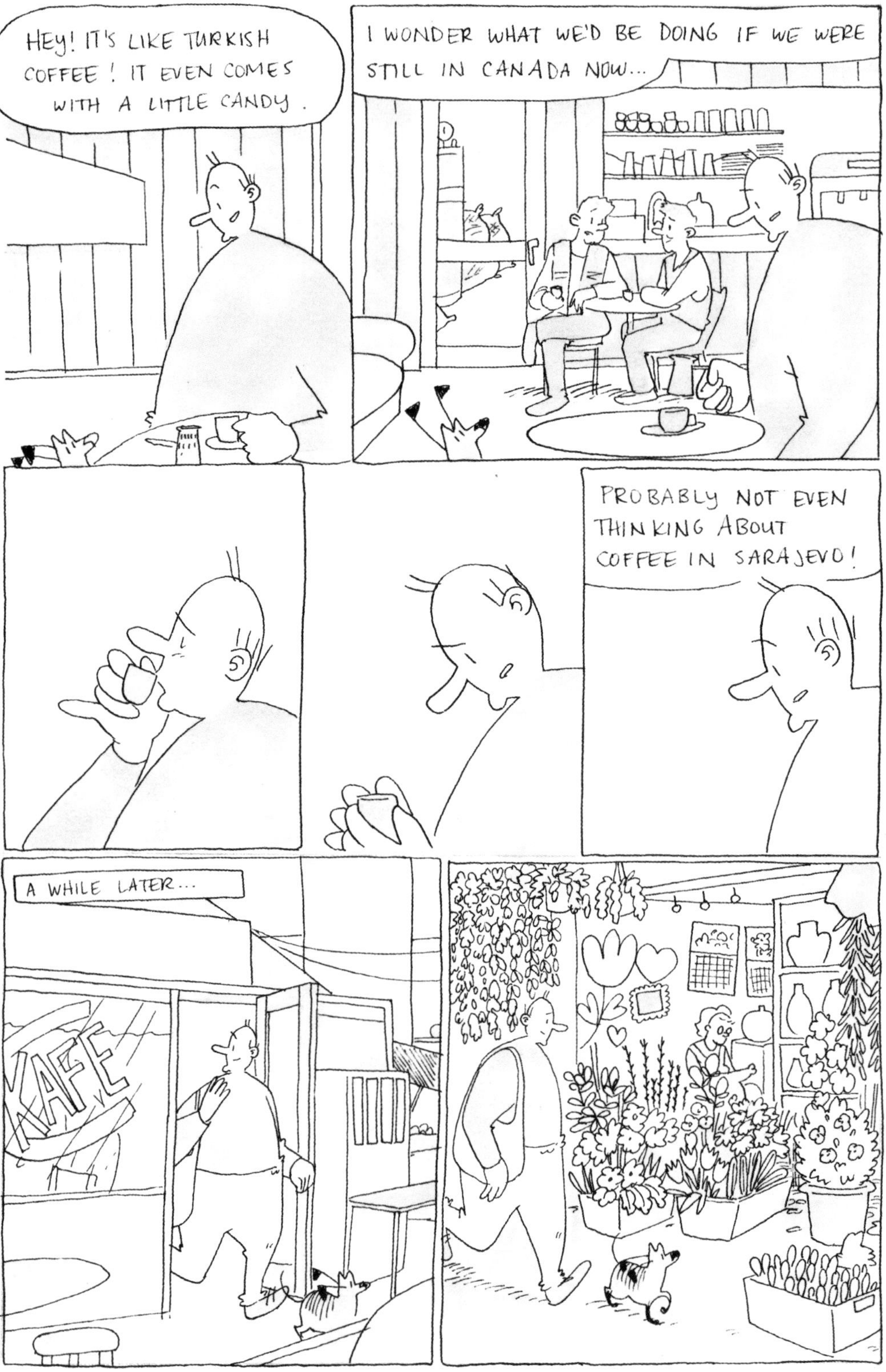
HEY! IT'S LIKE TURKISH COFFEE! IT EVEN COMES WITH A LITTLE CANDY.
I WONDER WHAT WE'D BE DOING IF WE WERE STILL IN CANADA NOW...
PROBABLY NOT EVEN THINKING ABOUT COFFEE IN SARAJEVO!
A WHILE LATER...
KAFE

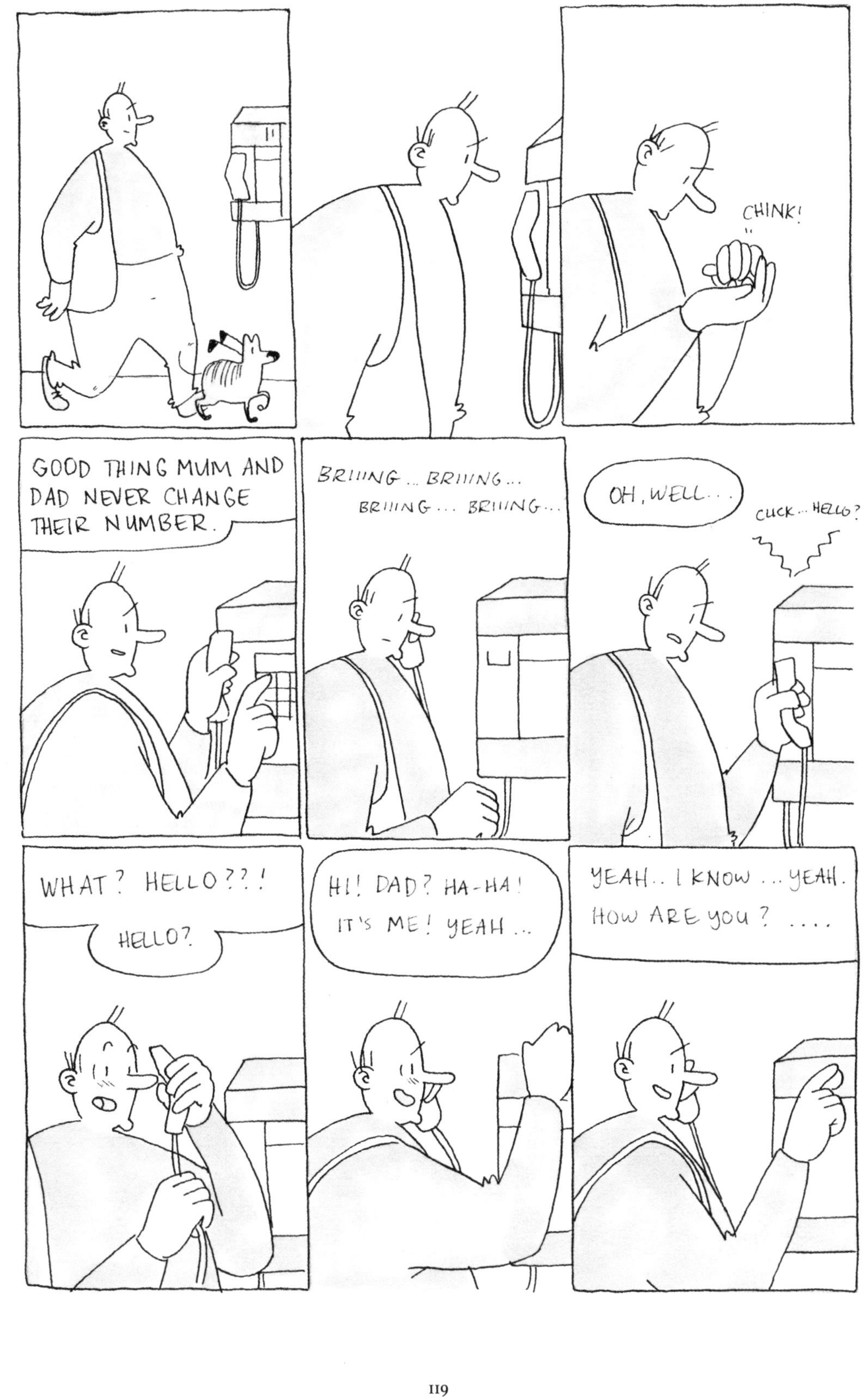
CHINK!
GOOD THING MUM AND DAD NEVER CHANGE THEIR NUMBER.
BRIIING... BRIIING...
BRIIING... BRIIING...
OH, WELL...
CLICK... HELLO?
WHAT? HELLO??!
HELLO?
HI! DAD? HA-HA! IT'S ME! YEAH...
YEAH.. I KNOW ... YEAH. HOW ARE YOU? ....

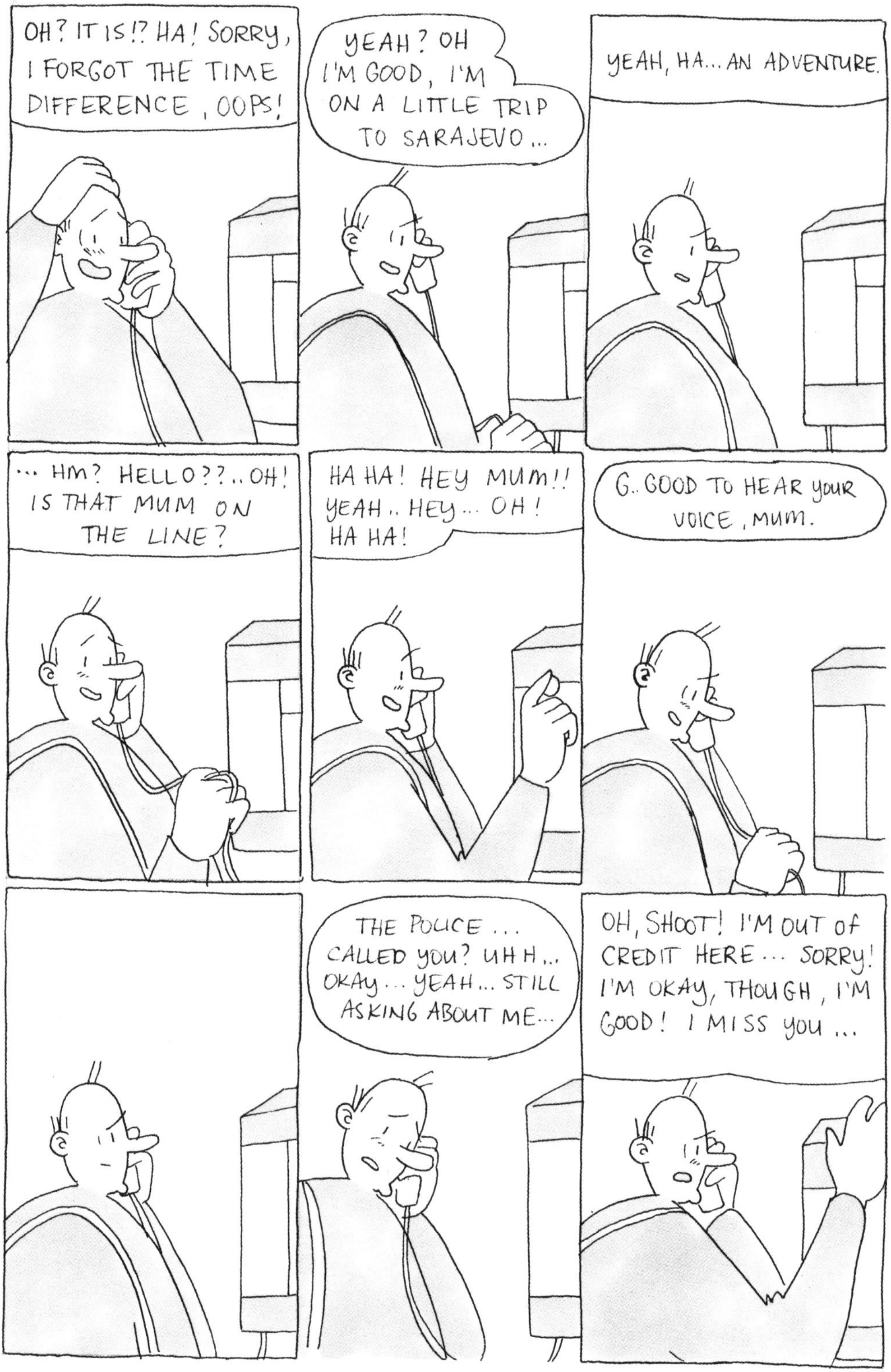
OH? IT IS!? HA! SORRY, I FORGOT THE TIME DIFFERENCE, OOPS!
YEAH? OH I'M GOOD, I'M ON A LITTLE TRIP TO SARAJEVO...
YEAH, HA... AN ADVENTURE.
... HM? HELLO??.. OH! IS THAT MUM ON THE LINE?
HA HA! HEY MUM!! YEAH.. HEY... OH! HA HA!
G.. GOOD TO HEAR YOUR VOICE, MUM.
THE POLICE... CALLED YOU? UHH... OKAY... YEAH... STILL ASKING ABOUT ME...
OH, SHOOT! I'M OUT OF CREDIT HERE... SORRY! I'M OKAY, THOUGH, I'M GOOD! I MISS YOU...

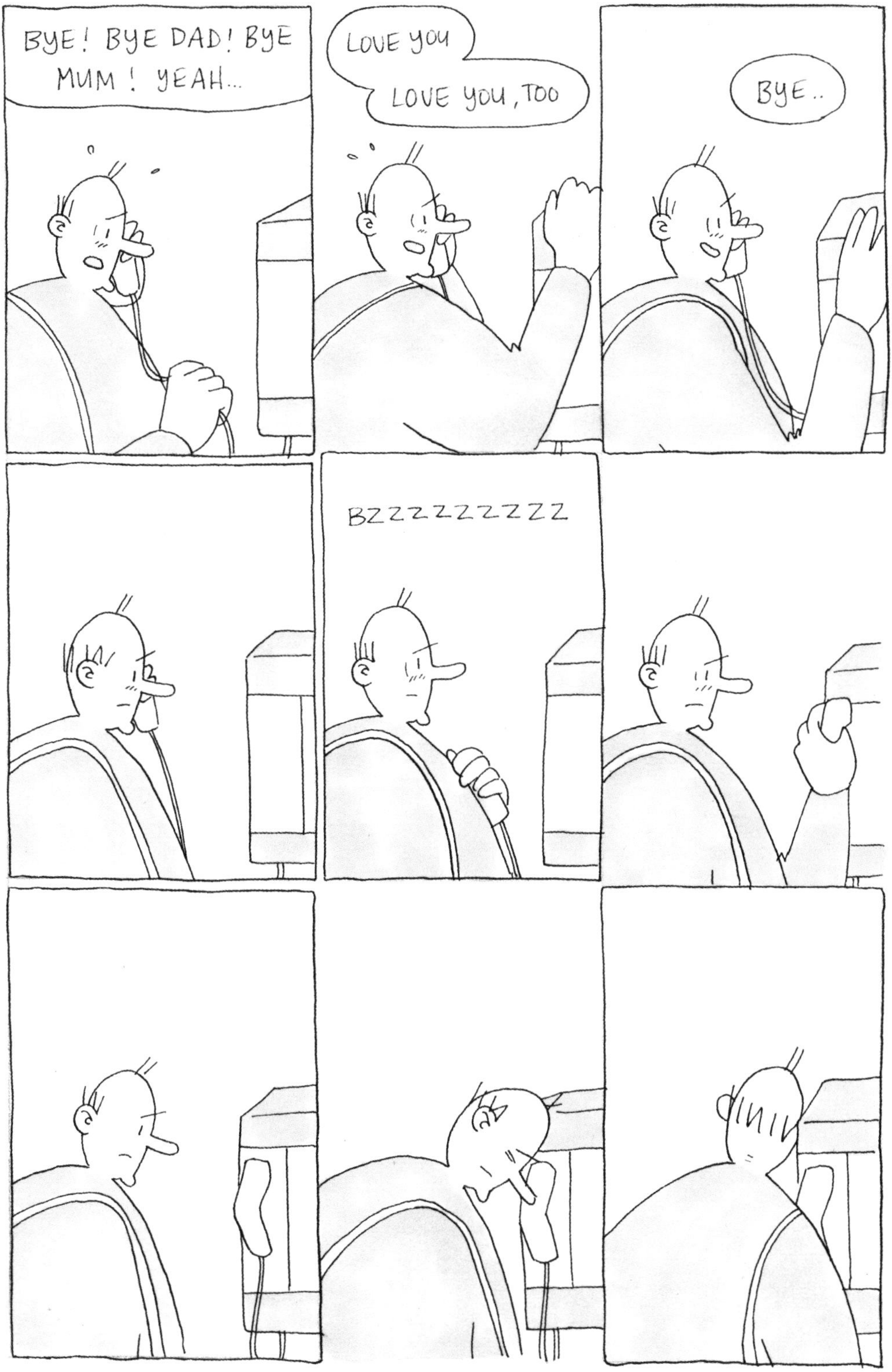
BYE! BYE DAD! BYE MUM! YEAH...
LOVE YOU
LOVE YOU, TOO
BYE..
BZZZZZZZZZ

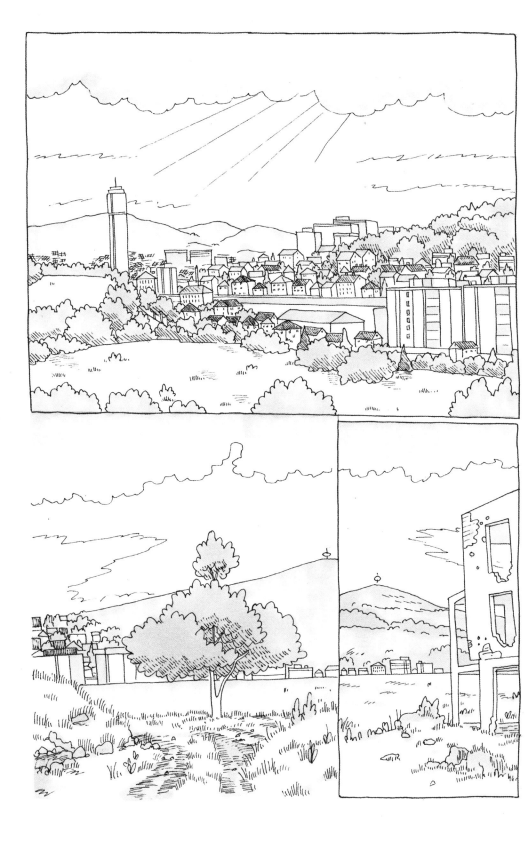

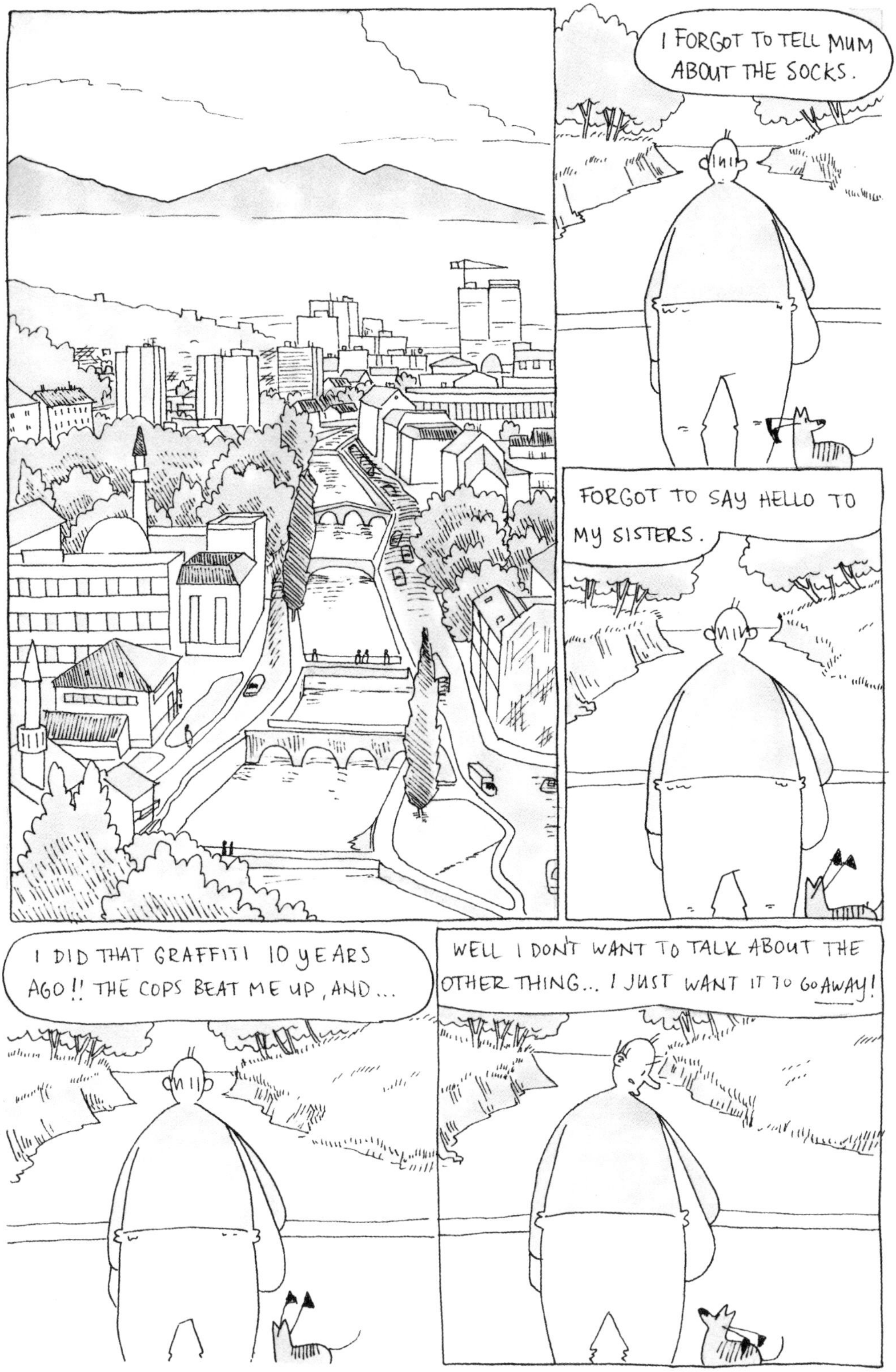
I FORGOT TO TELL MUM ABOUT THE SOCKS.
FORGOT TO SAY HELLO TO MY SISTERS.
I DID THAT GRAFFITI 10 YEARS AGO!! THE COPS BEAT ME UP, AND...
WELL I DON'T WANT TO TALK ABOUT THE OTHER THING... I JUST WANT IT TO GO AWAY!

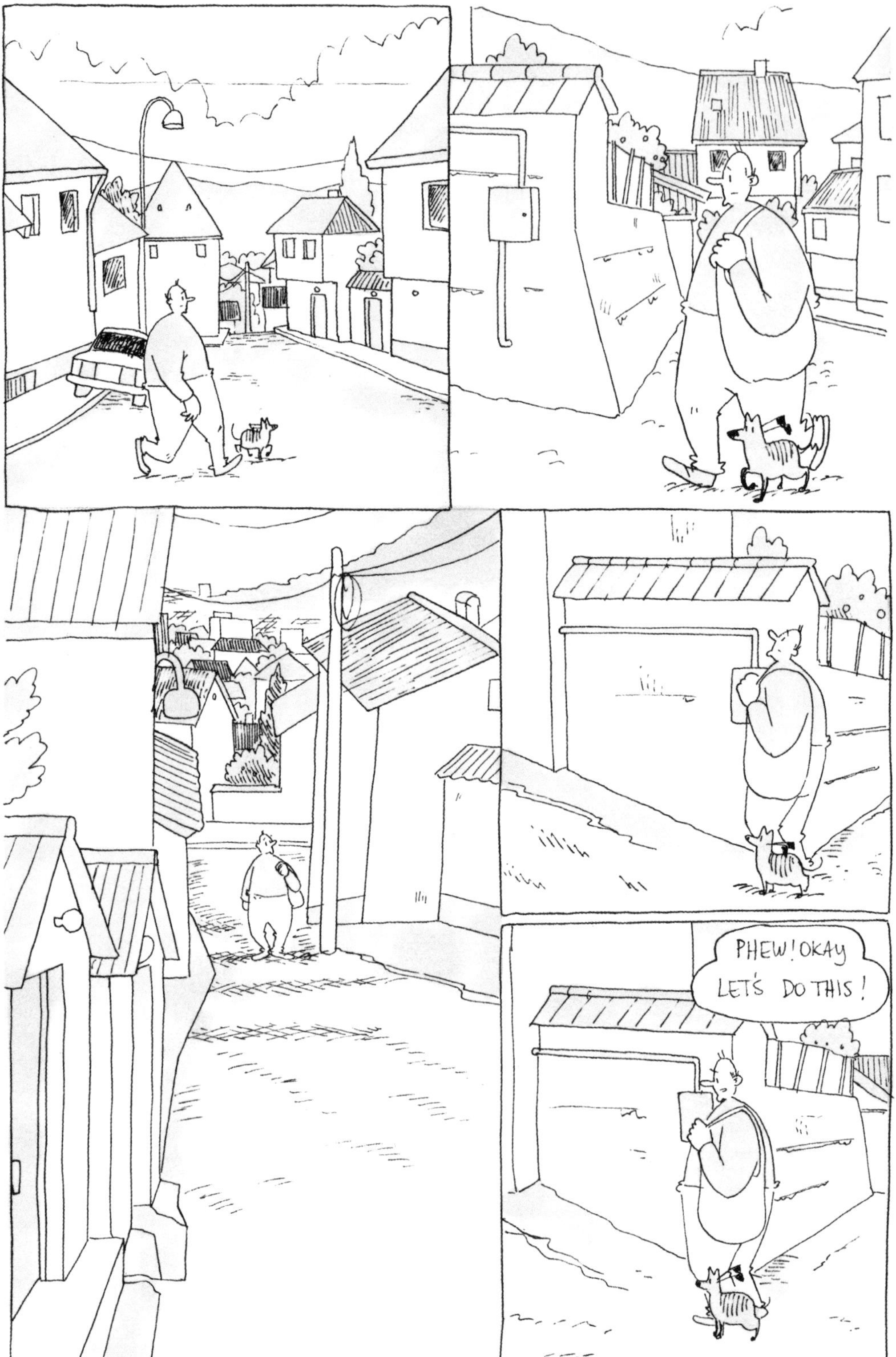
PHEW! OKAY
LET'S DO THIS!

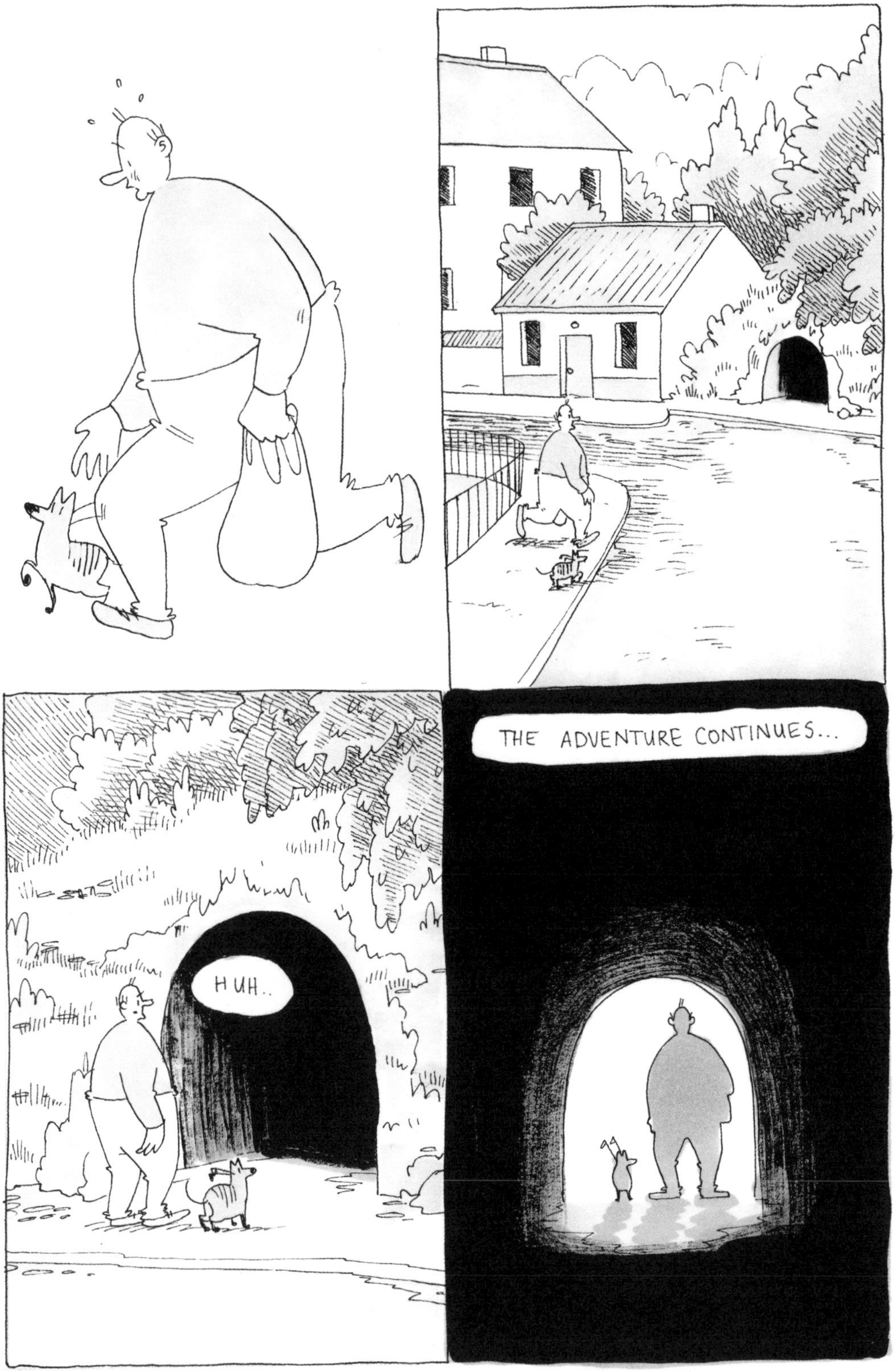
HUH..
THE ADVENTURE CONTINUES...

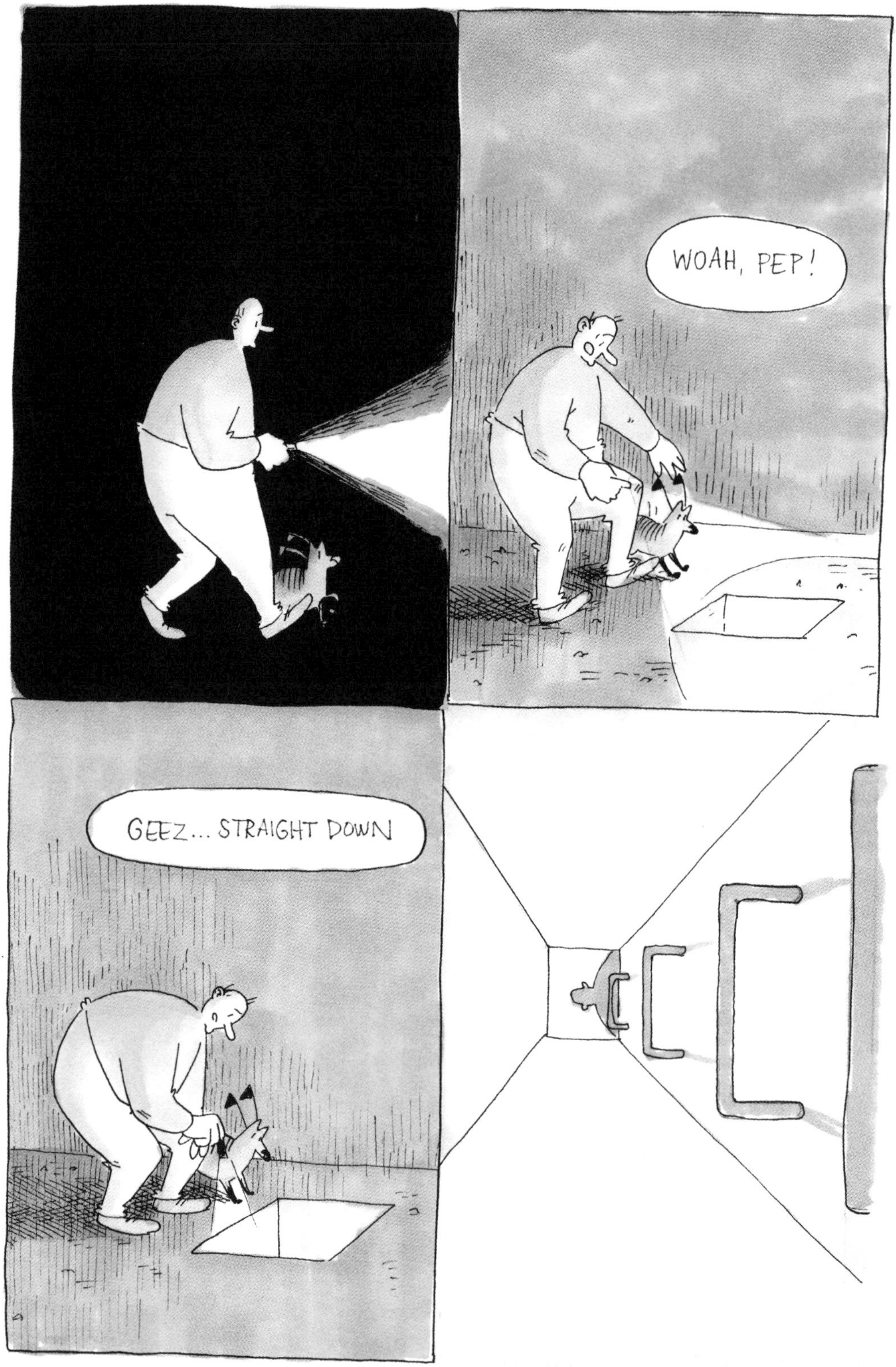
WOAH, PEP!
GEEZ... STRAIGHT DOWN

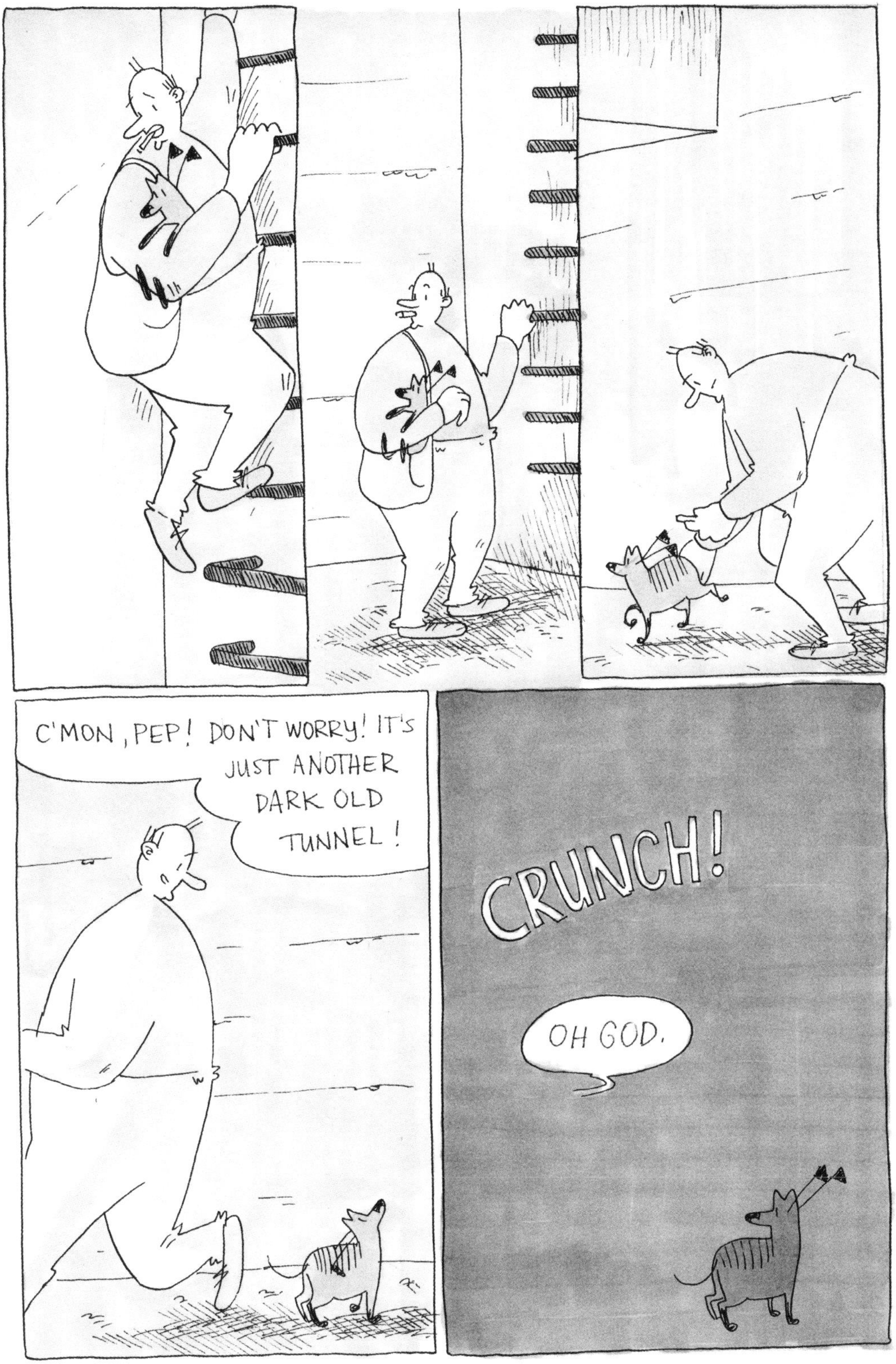
C'MON, PEP! DON'T WORRY! IT'S JUST ANOTHER DARK OLD TUNNEL!
CRUNCH!
OH GOD.

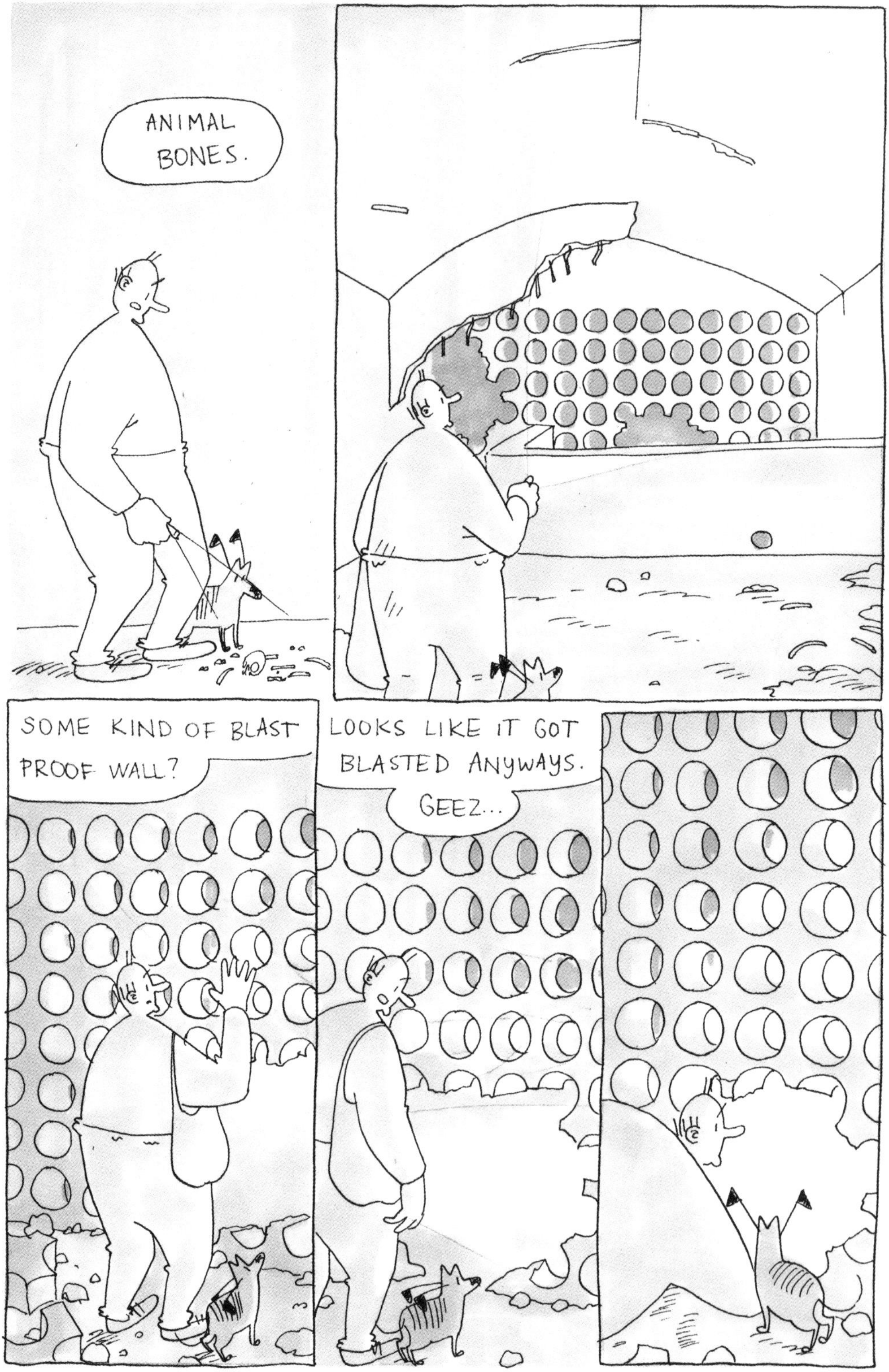
ANIMAL BONES.
SOME KIND OF BLAST PROOF WALL?
LOOKS LIKE IT GOT BLASTED ANYWAYS.
GEEZ...

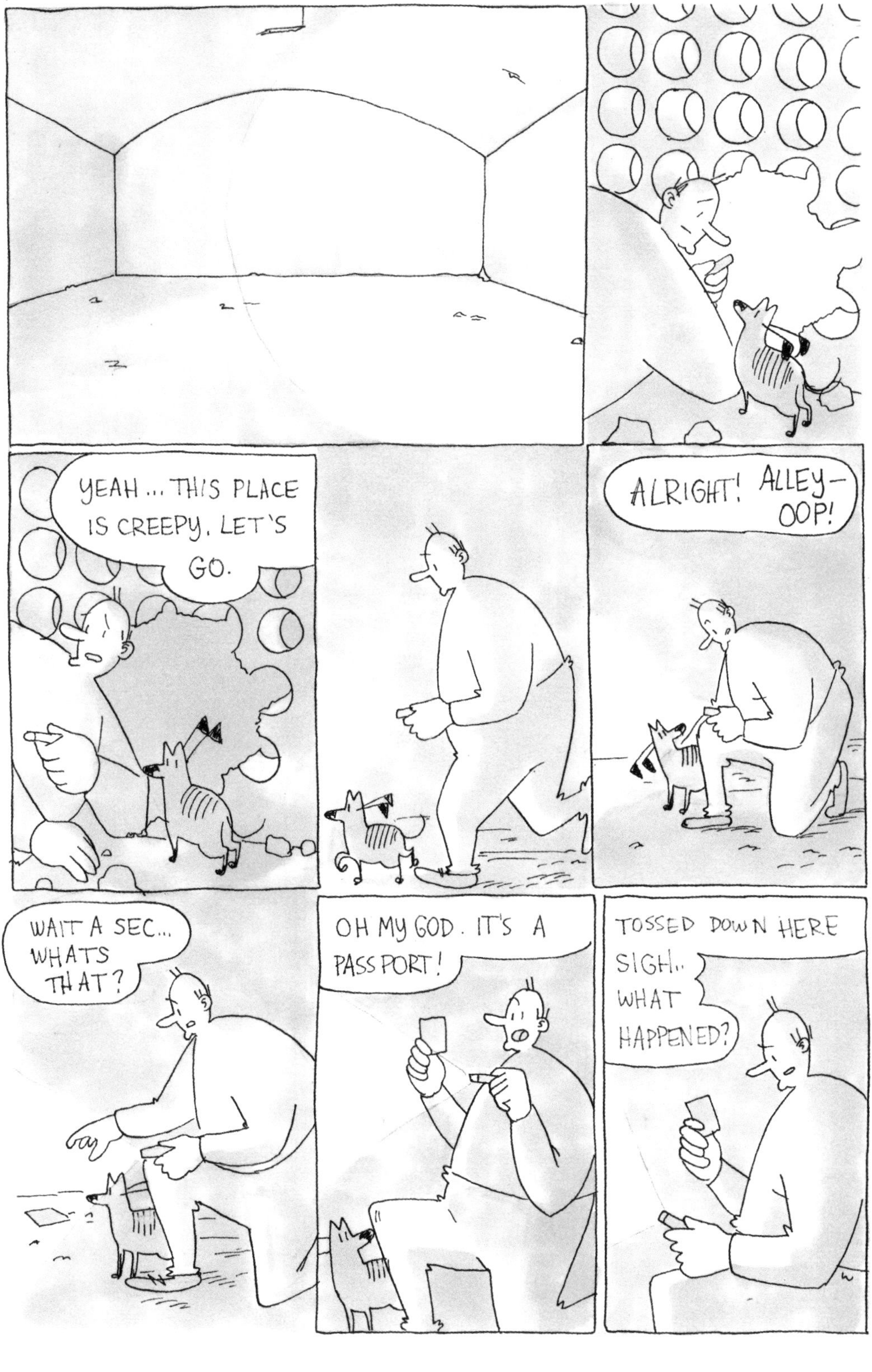
YEAH... THIS PLACE IS CREEPY. LET'S GO.
ALRIGHT! ALLEY-OOP!
WAIT A SEC... WHATS THAT?
OH MY GOD. IT'S A PASSPORT!
TOSSED DOWN HERE
SIGH.. WHAT HAPPENED?

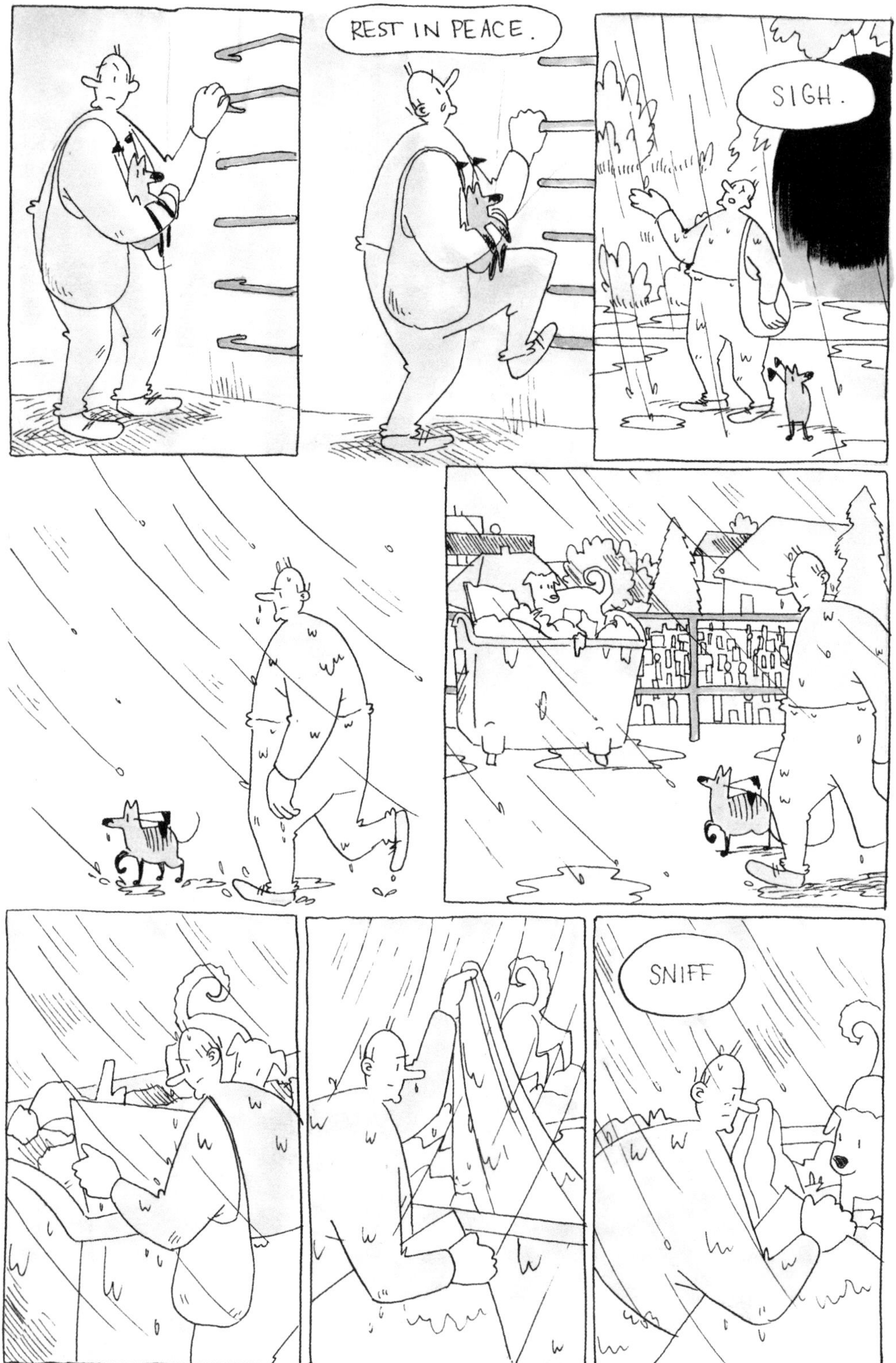
REST IN PEACE.
SIGH.
SNIFF

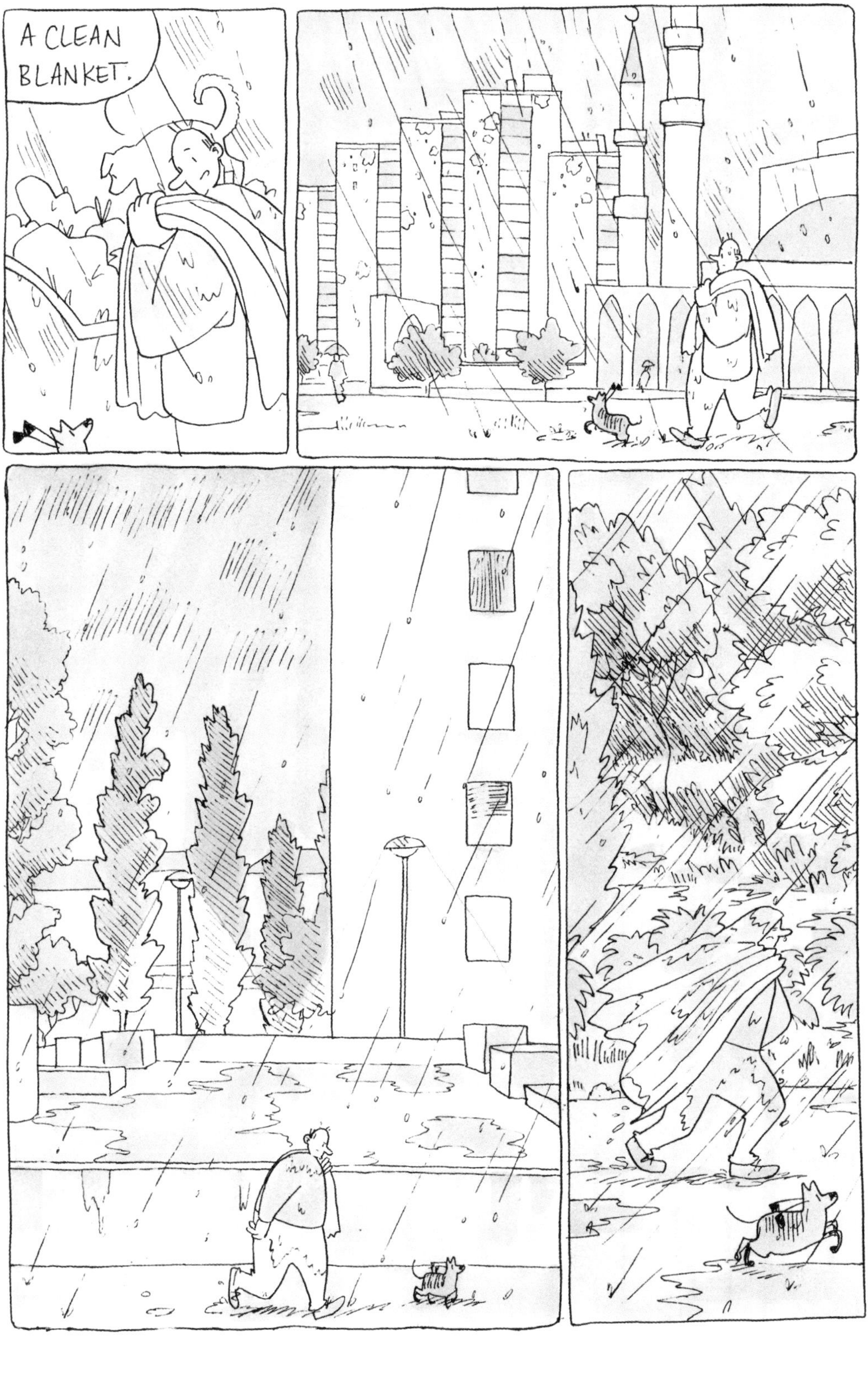
A CLEAN BLANKET.

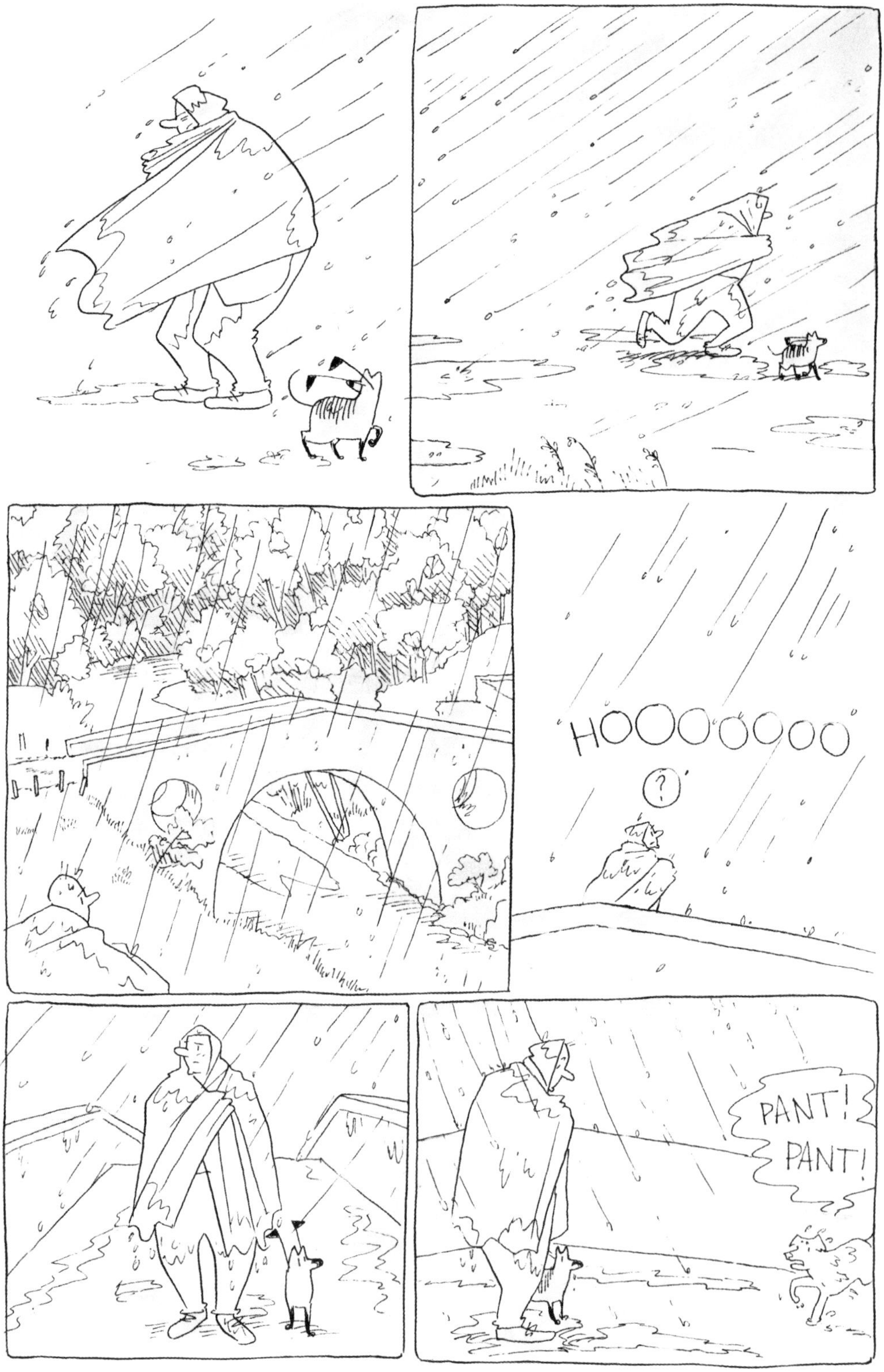
HOOOOOOOO
?
PANT!
PANT!

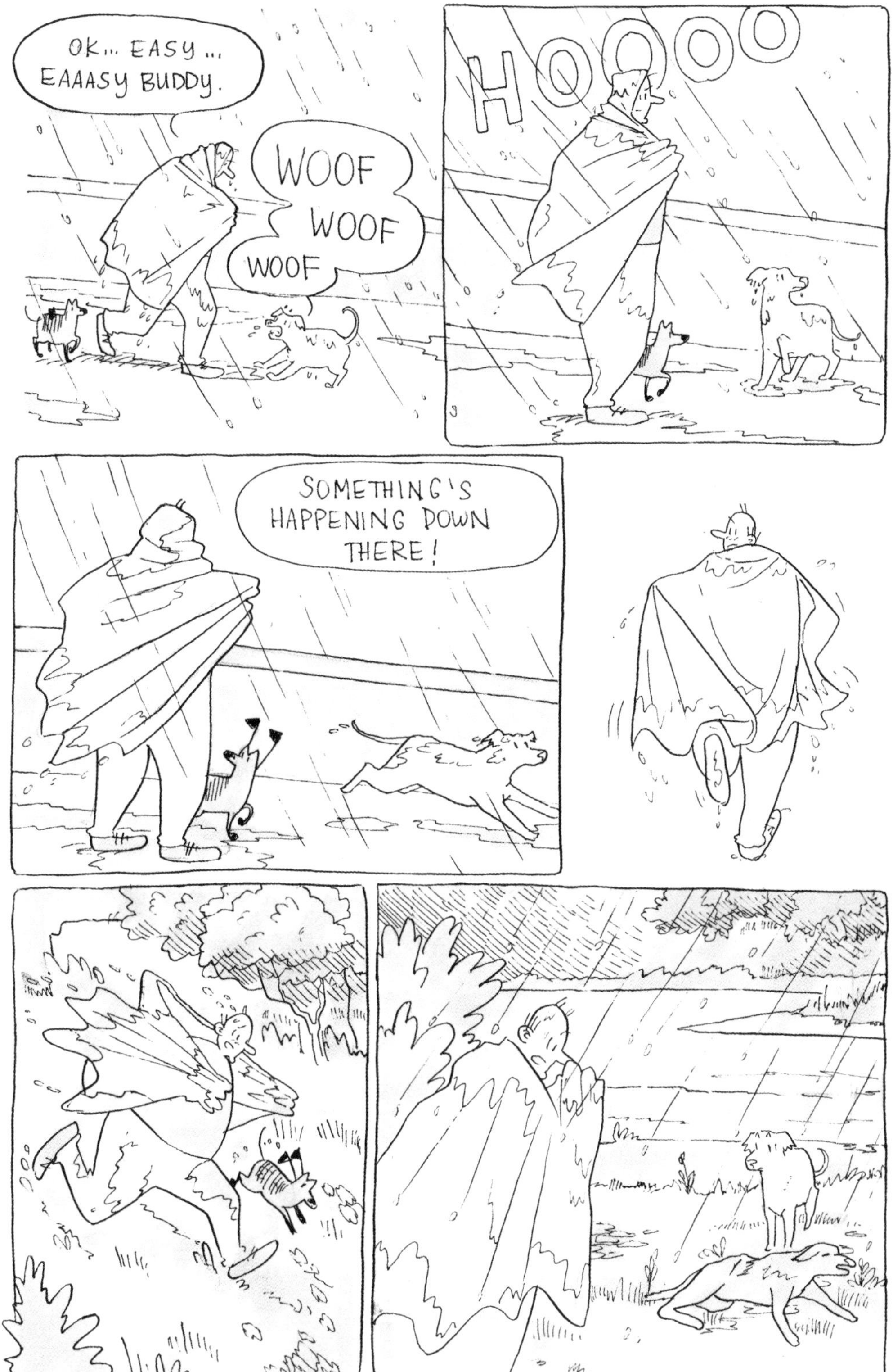
OK... EASY...
EAAASY BUDDY.
WOOF
WOOF
WOOF
HOOOOO
SOMETHING'S
HAPPENING DOWN
THERE!

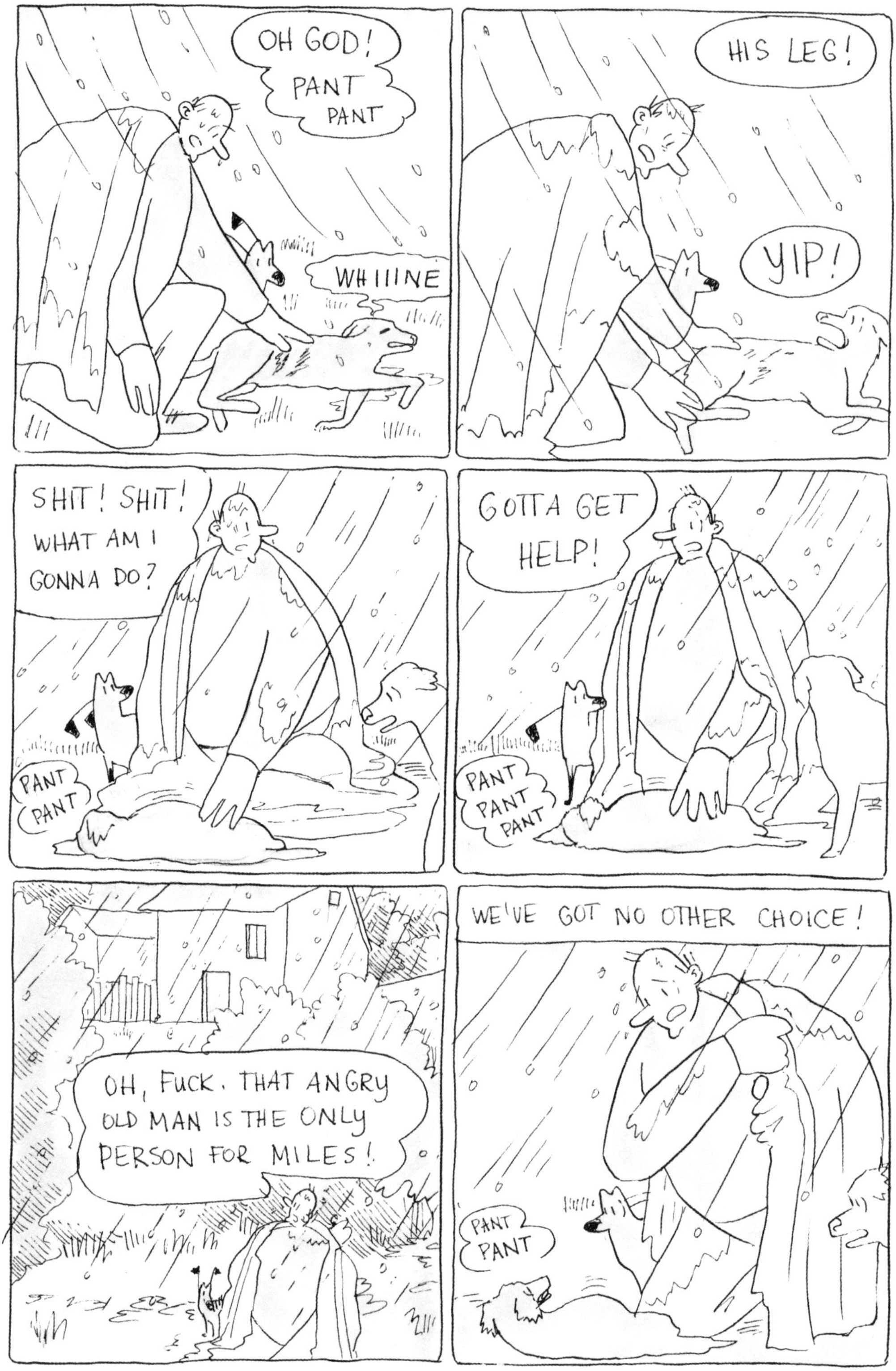

OH GOD! PANT PANT
WHIIINE
HIS LEG!
YIP!
SHIT! SHIT! WHAT AM I GONNA DO?
PANT PANT
GOTTA GET HELP!
PANT PANT PANT
OH, FUCK. THAT ANGRY OLD MAN IS THE ONLY PERSON FOR MILES!
WE'VE GOT NO OTHER CHOICE!
PANT PANT

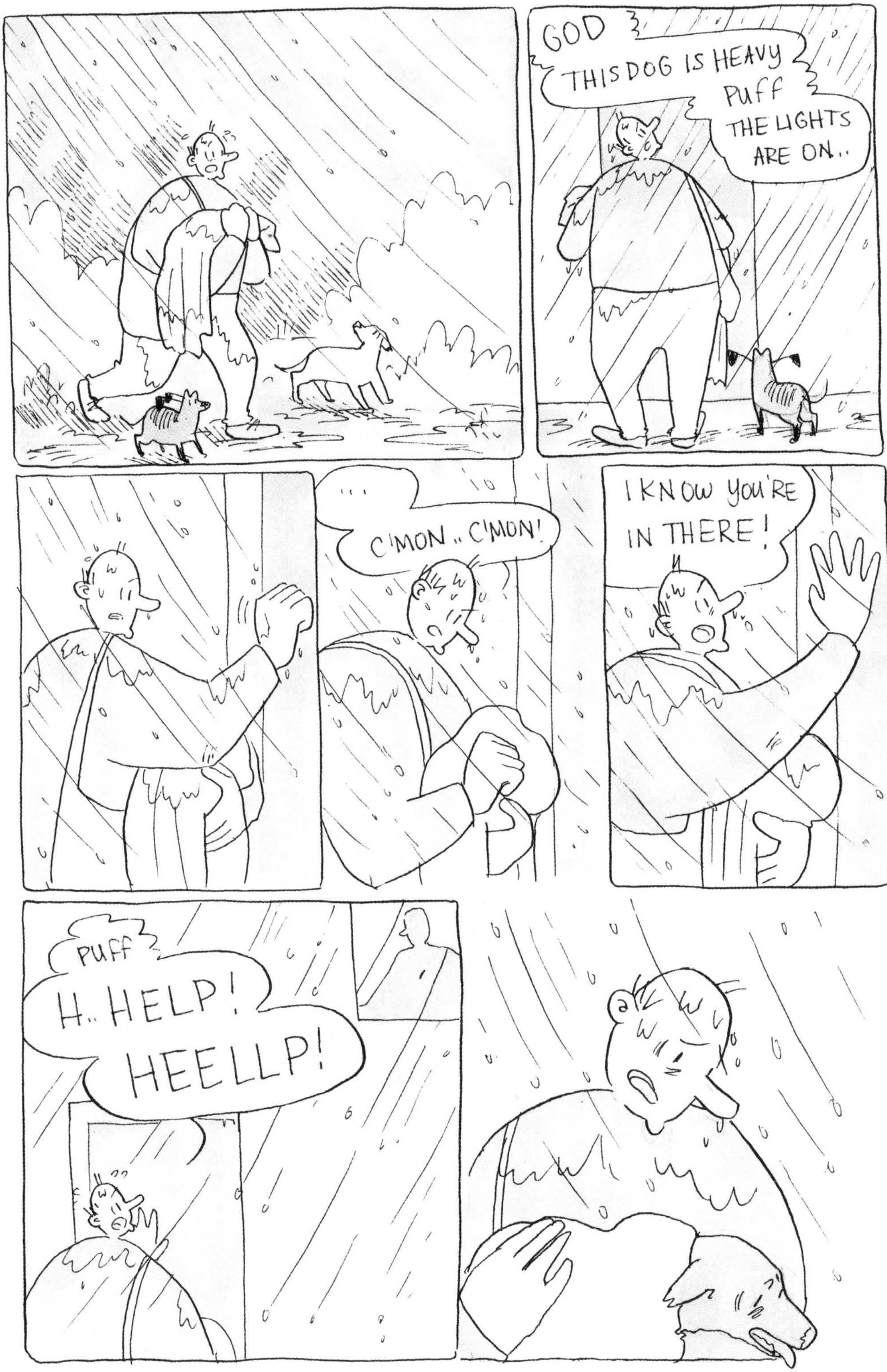
GOD
THIS DOG IS HEAVY
PUFF
THE LIGHTS ARE ON..
...
C'MON.. C'MON!
I KNOW YOU'RE IN THERE!
PUFF
H.. HELP!
HEELLP!

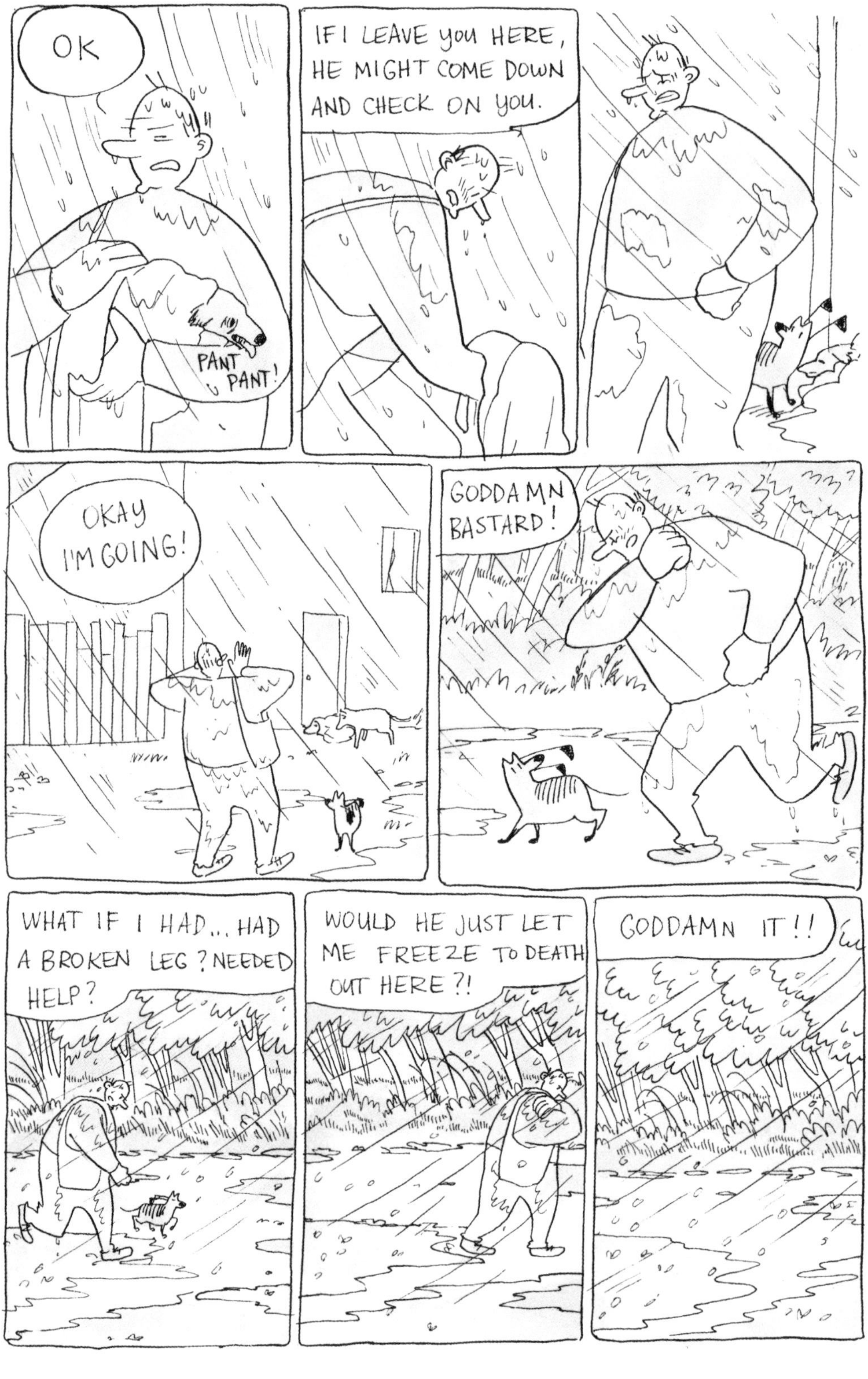
OK
PANT PANT!
IF I LEAVE YOU HERE, HE MIGHT COME DOWN AND CHECK ON YOU.
OKAY I'M GOING!
GODDAMN BASTARD!
WHAT IF I HAD... HAD A BROKEN LEG? NEEDED HELP?
WOULD HE JUST LET ME FREEZE TO DEATH OUT HERE?!
GODDAMN IT!!

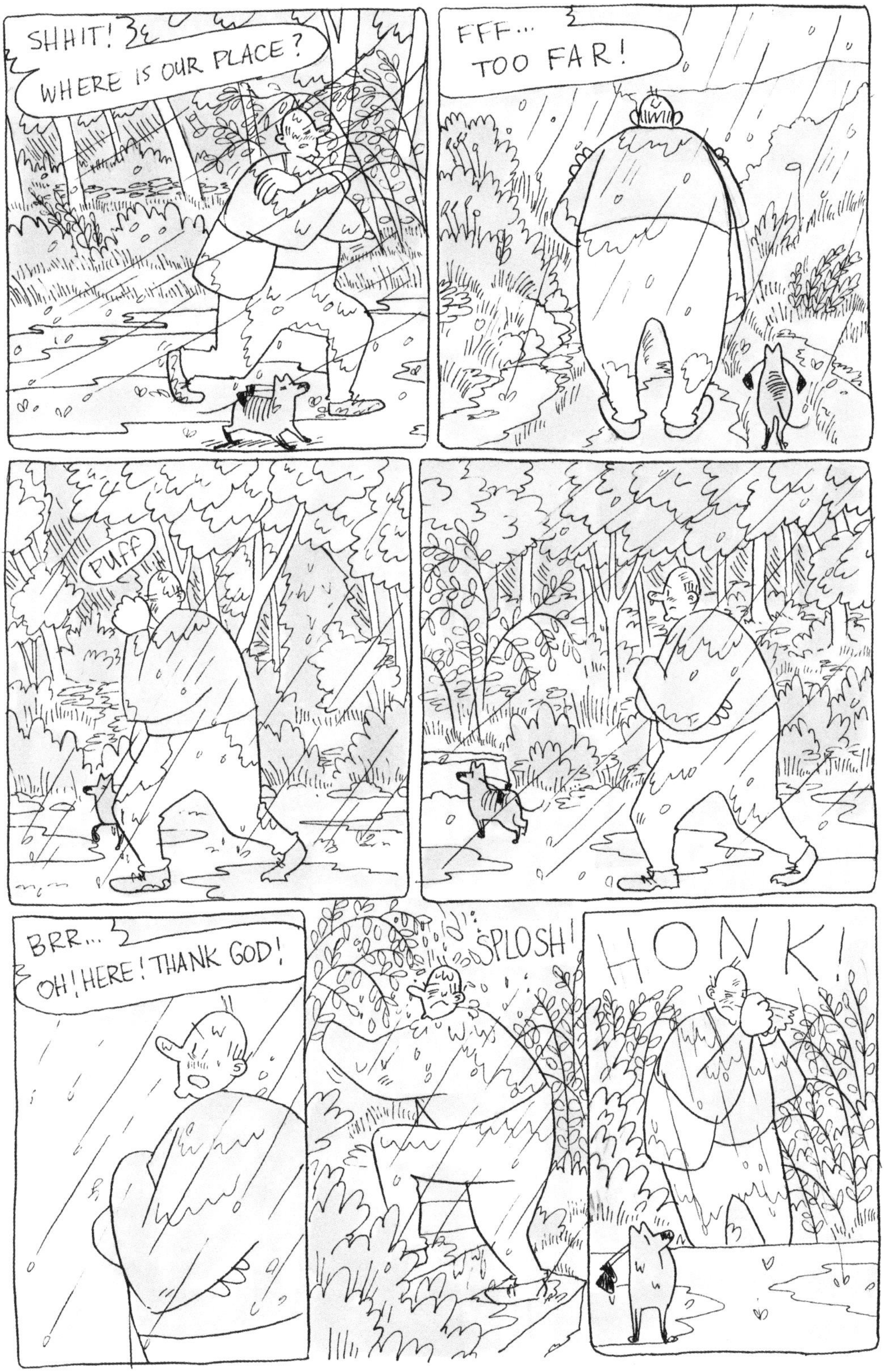
SHHIT!
WHERE IS OUR PLACE?
FFF... TOO FAR!
PUFF
BRR...
OH! HERE! THANK GOD!
SPLOSH!
HONK!

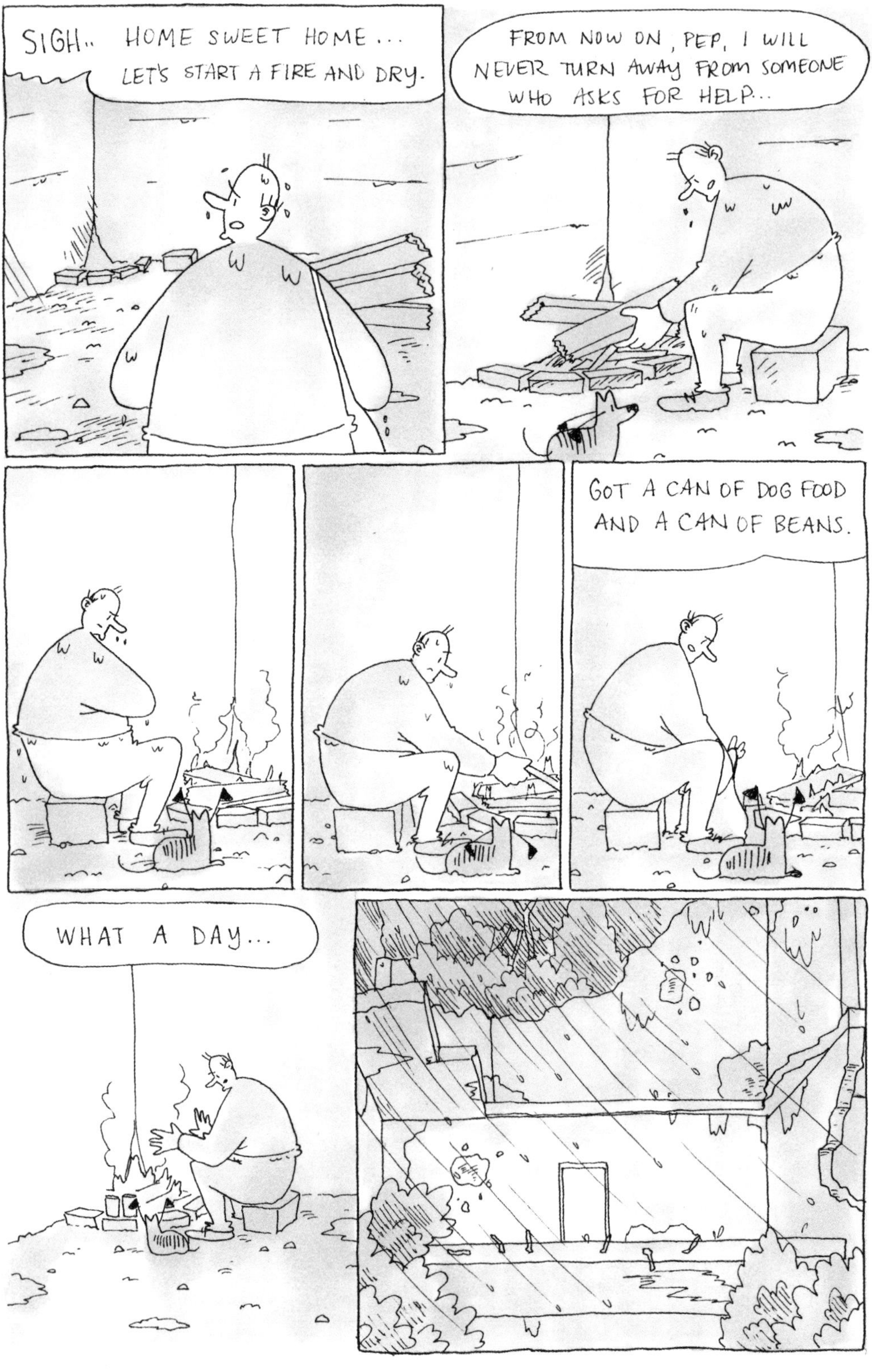
SIGH.. HOME SWEET HOME...
LET'S START A FIRE AND DRY.
FROM NOW ON, PEP, I WILL NEVER TURN AWAY FROM SOMEONE WHO ASKS FOR HELP...
GOT A CAN OF DOG FOOD AND A CAN OF BEANS.
WHAT A DAY...

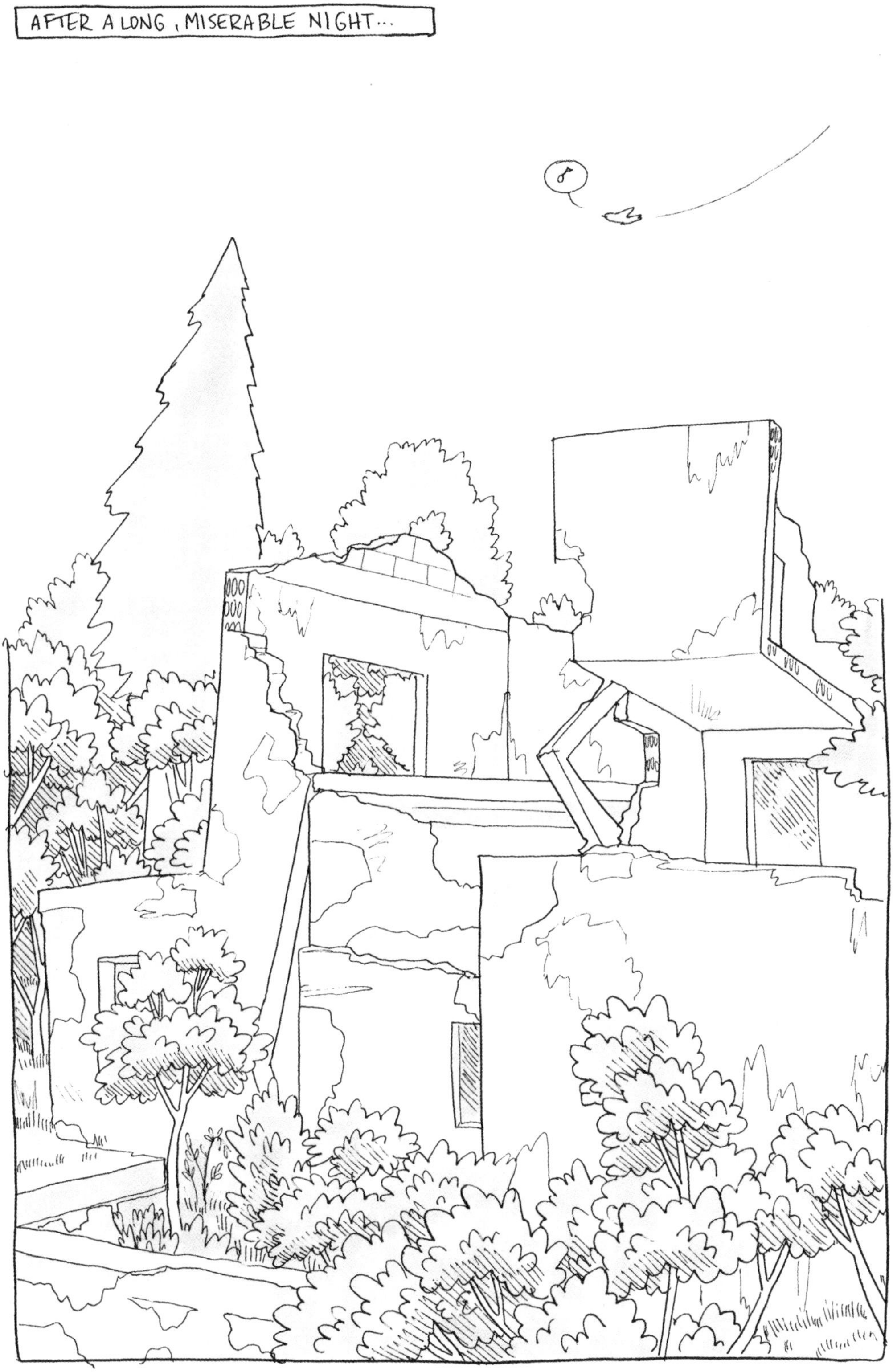
AFTER A LONG, MISERABLE NIGHT...

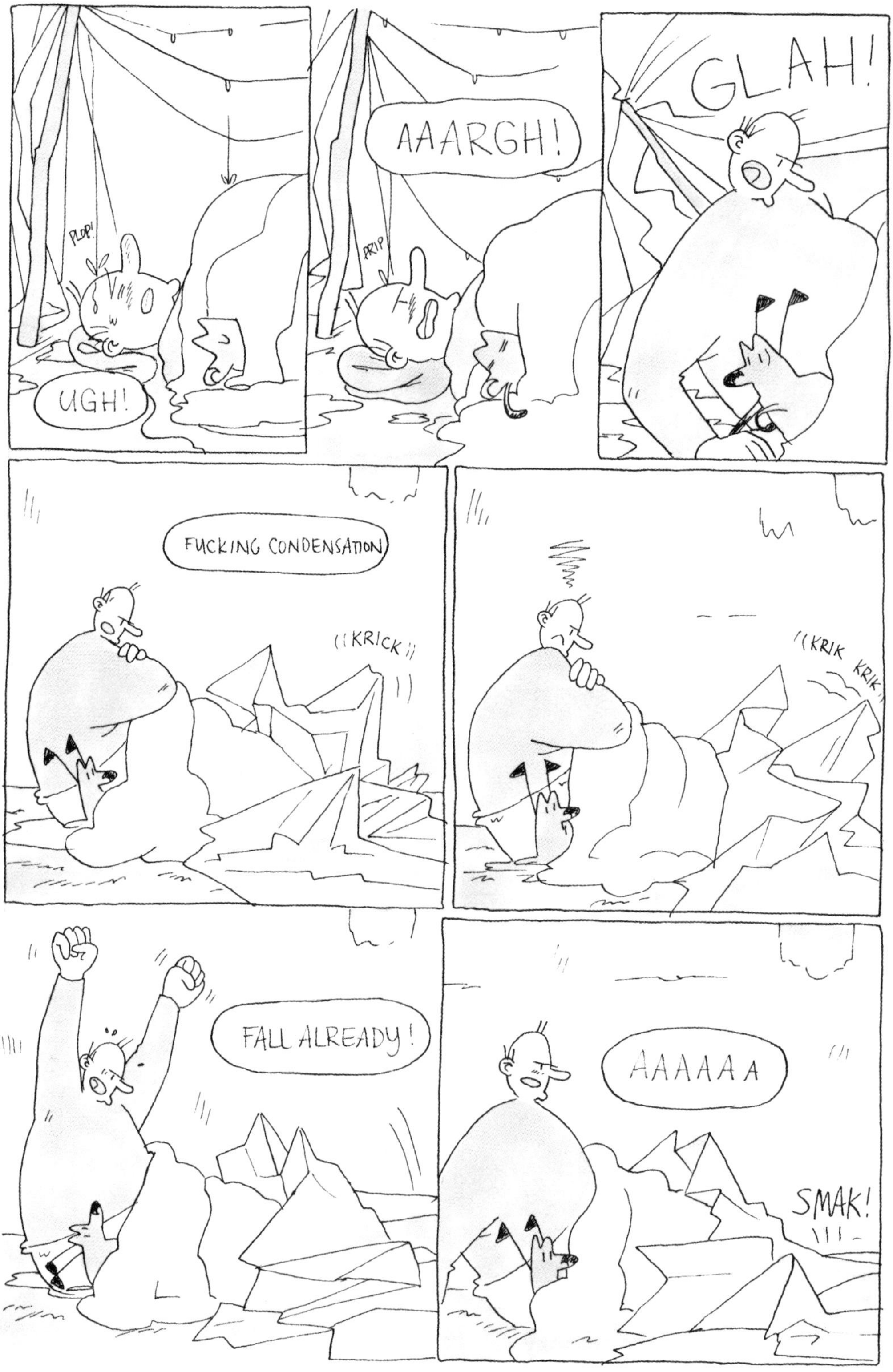
PLOP!
UGH!
DRIP
AAARGH!
GLAH!
FUCKING CONDENSATION
KRICK
KRIK KRIK
FALL ALREADY!
AAAAAA
SMAK!

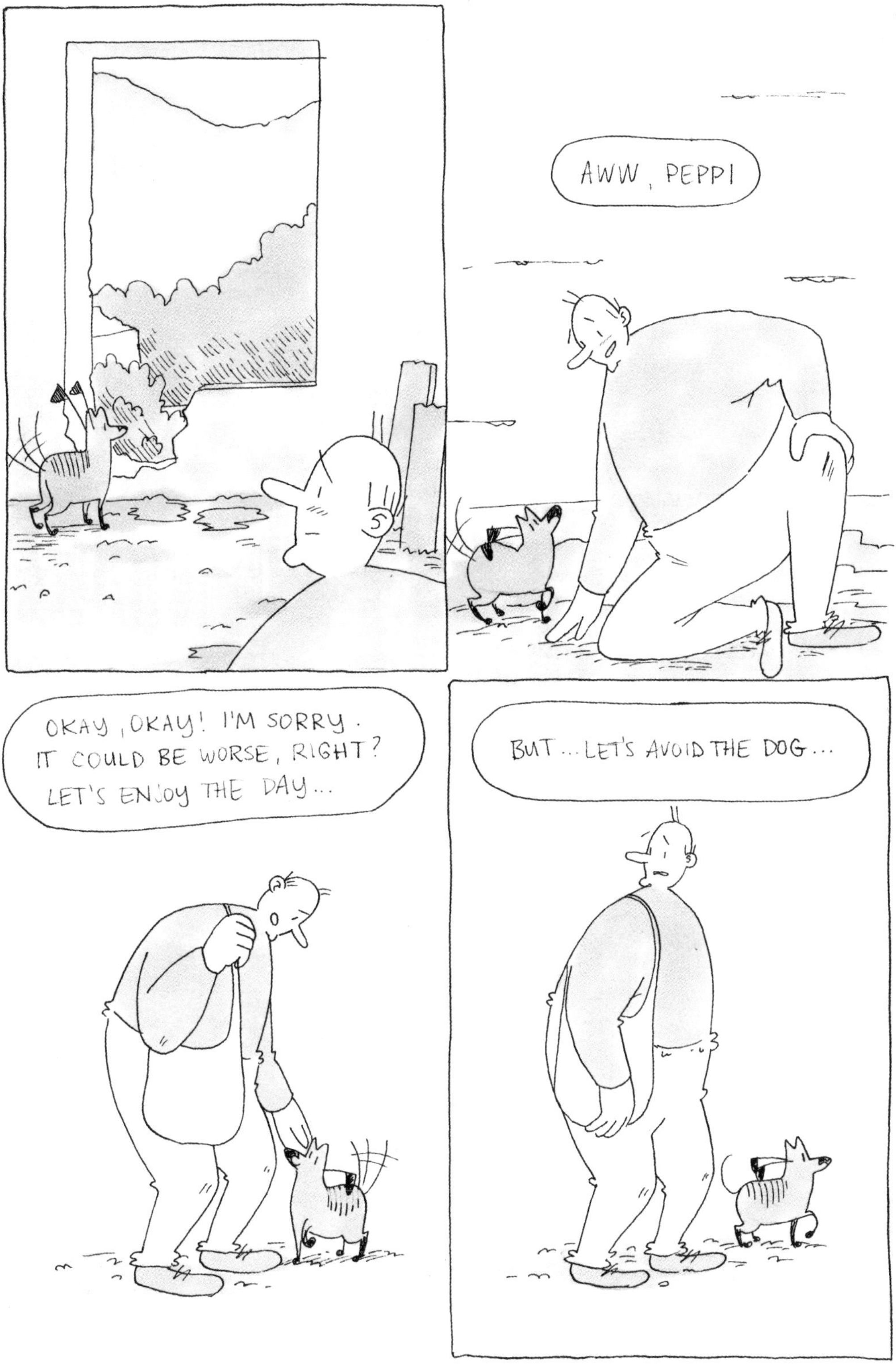
AWW, PEPPI
OKAY, OKAY! I'M SORRY. IT COULD BE WORSE, RIGHT? LET'S ENJOY THE DAY...
BUT... LET'S AVOID THE DOG...

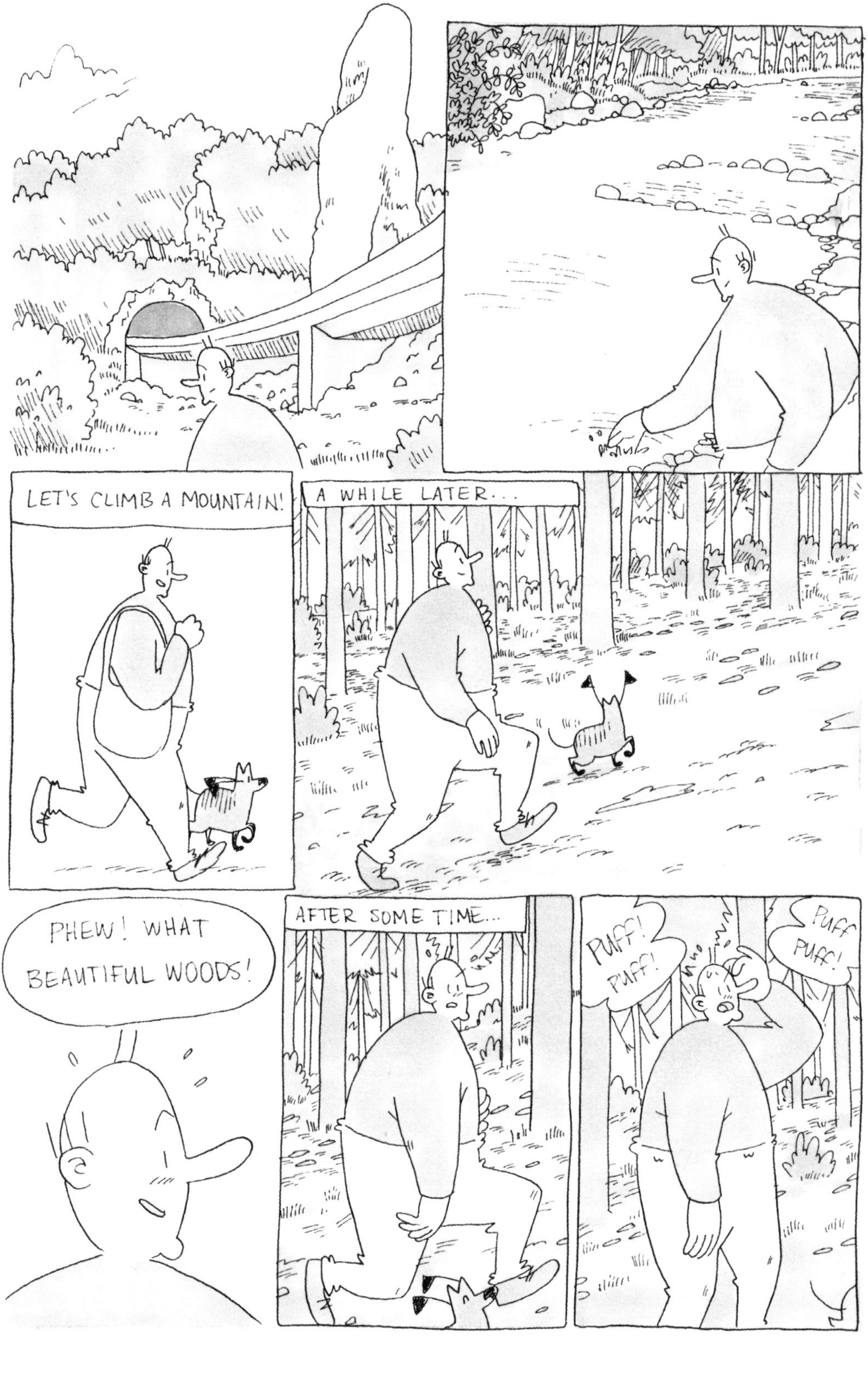
LET'S CLIMB A MOUNTAIN!
A WHILE LATER...
PHEW! WHAT BEAUTIFUL WOODS!
AFTER SOME TIME...
PUFF! PUFF!
PUFF PUFF!

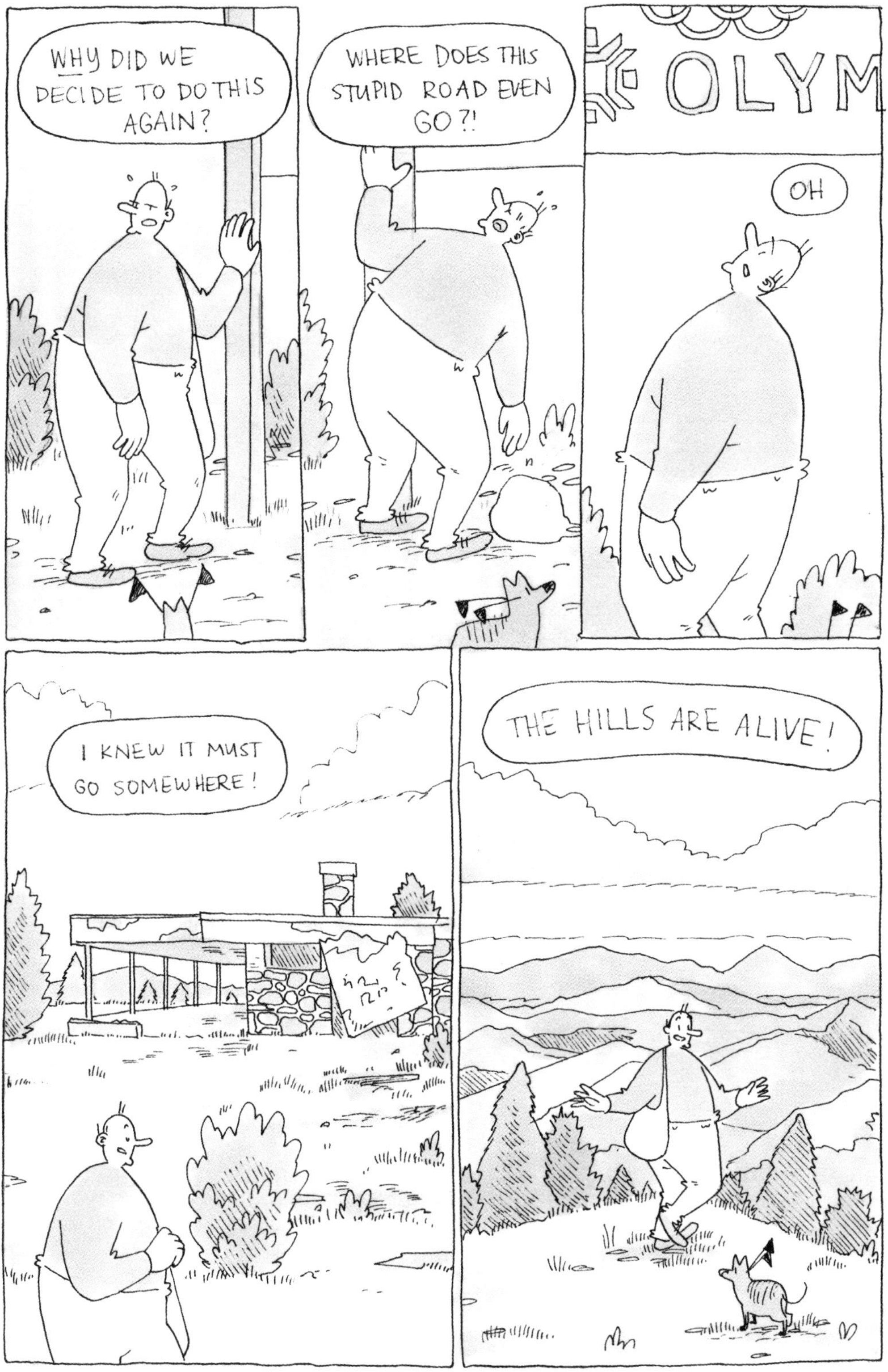
WHY DID WE DECIDE TO DO THIS AGAIN?
WHERE DOES THIS STUPID ROAD EVEN GO?!
OLYM
OH
I KNEW IT MUST GO SOMEWHERE!
THE HILLS ARE ALIVE!

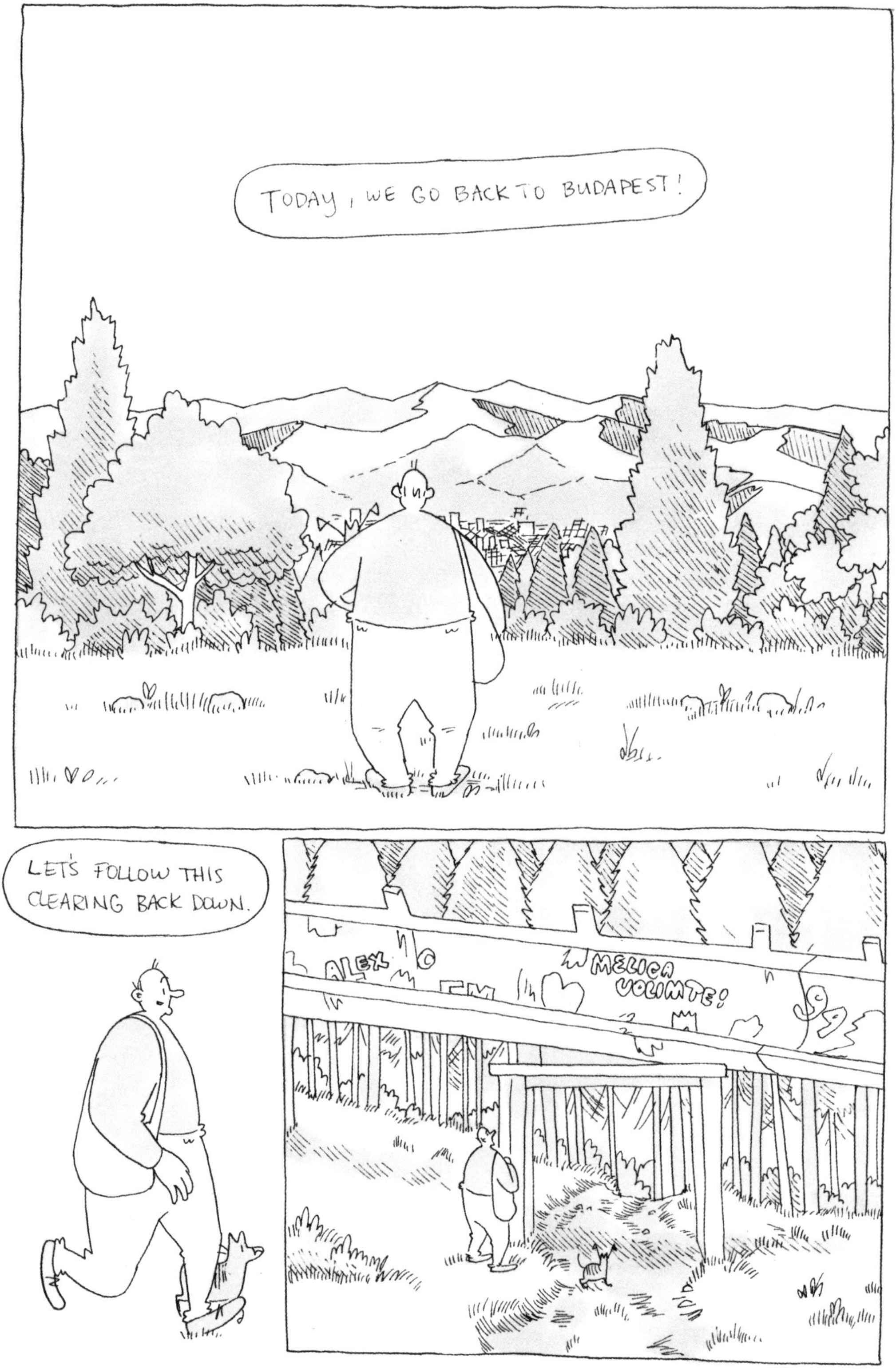
TODAY, WE GO BACK TO BUDAPEST!
LET'S FOLLOW THIS CLEARING BACK DOWN.
ALEX
MELICA VOLIMTE!

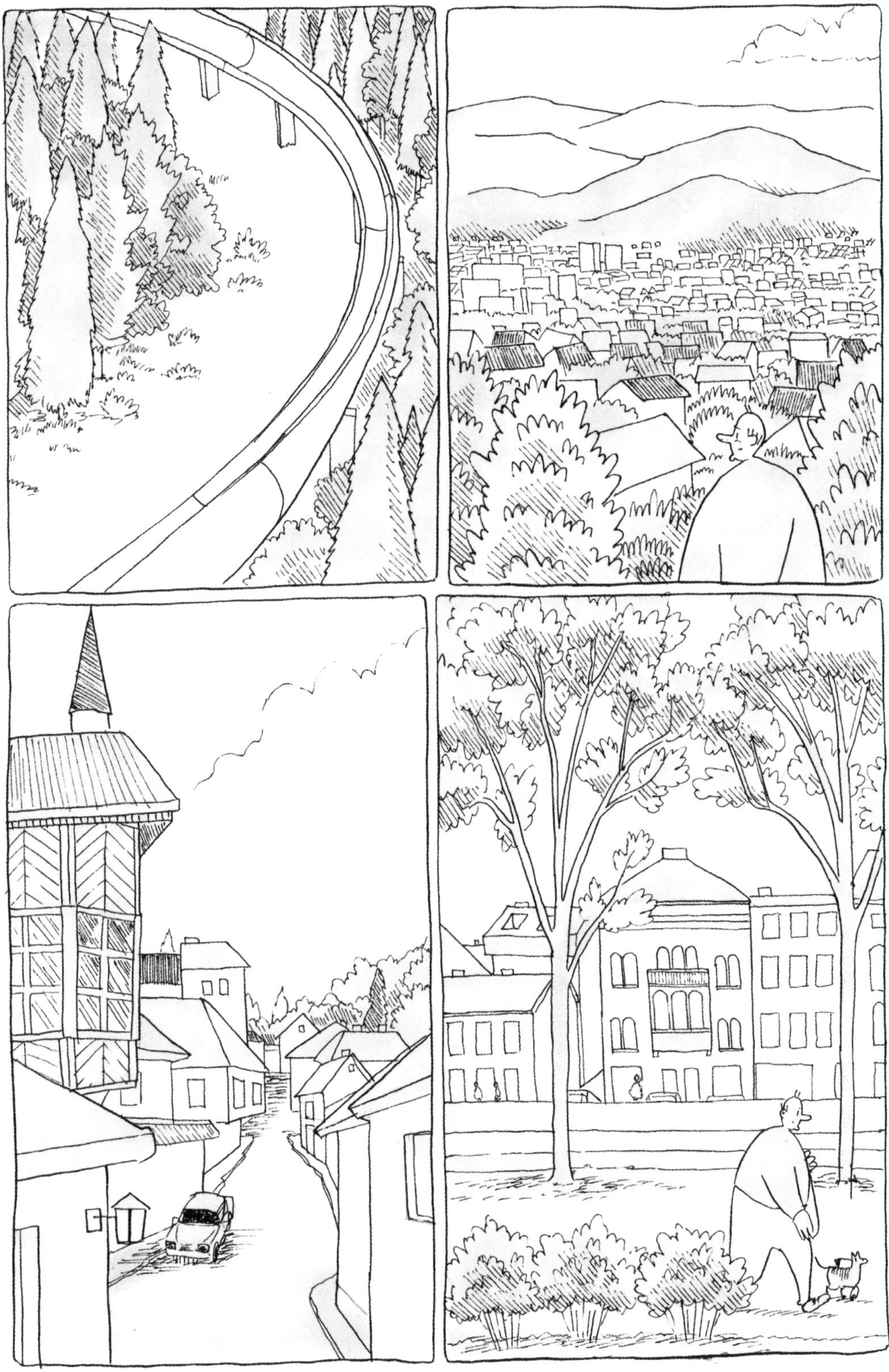

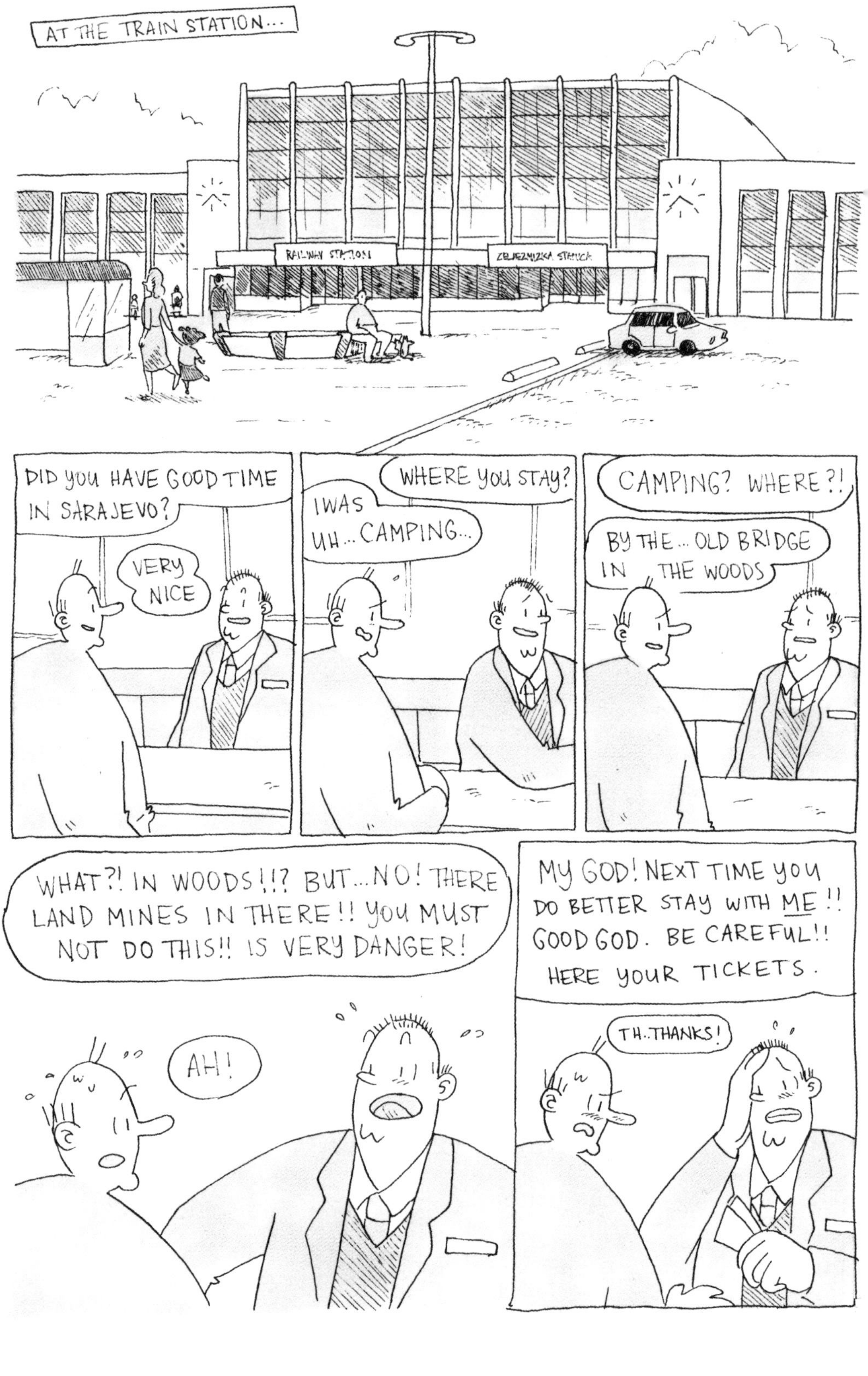
AT THE TRAIN STATION...
RAILWAY STATION
DID YOU HAVE GOOD TIME IN SARAJEVO?
VERY NICE
WHERE YOU STAY?
I WAS UH... CAMPING...
CAMPING? WHERE?!
BY THE... OLD BRIDGE IN THE WOODS
WHAT?! IN WOODS!!? BUT... NO! THERE LAND MINES IN THERE!! YOU MUST NOT DO THIS!! IS VERY DANGER!
AH!
MY GOD! NEXT TIME YOU DO BETTER STAY WITH ME!! GOOD GOD. BE CAREFUL!! HERE YOUR TICKETS.
TH..THANKS!

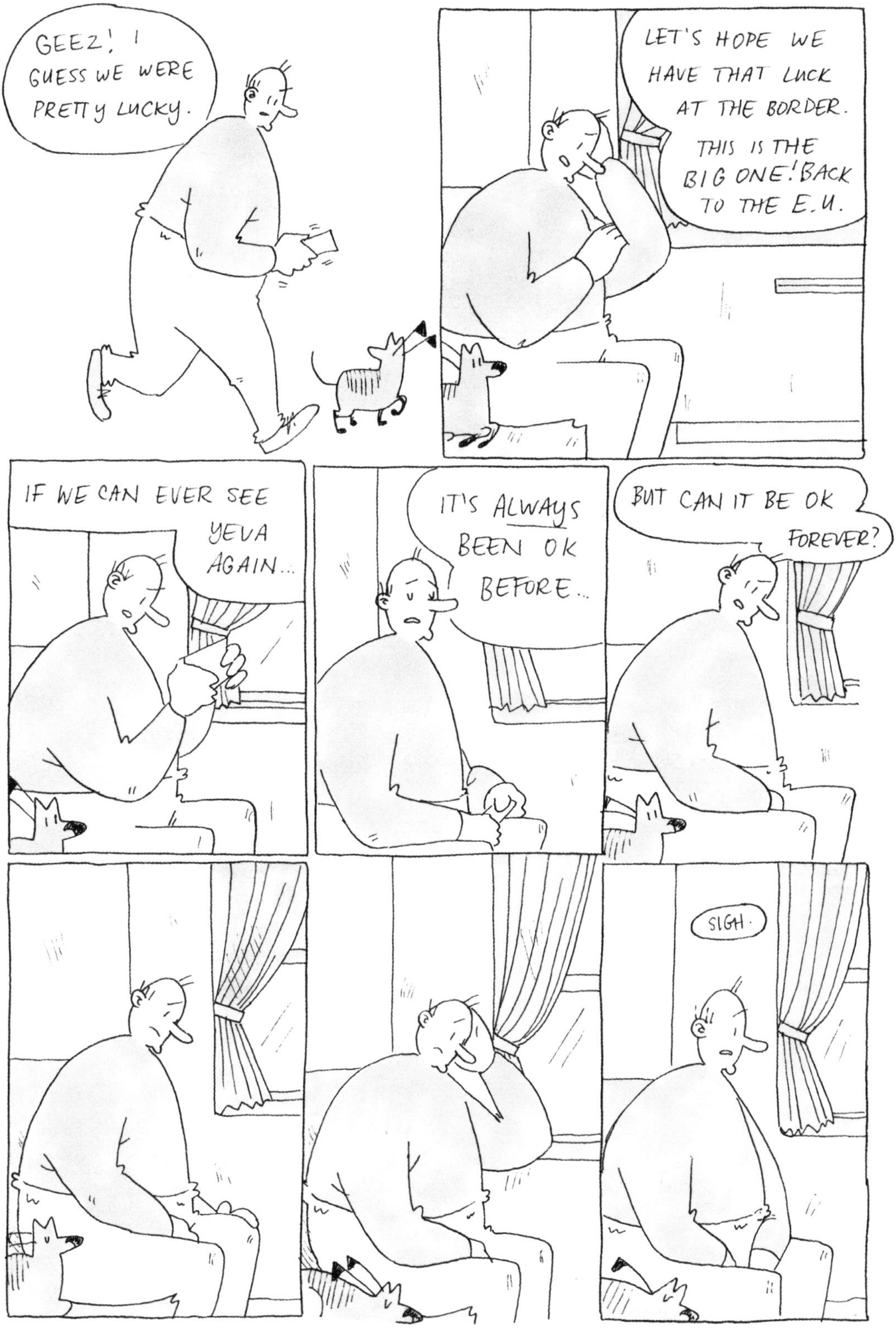
GEEZ! I GUESS WE WERE PRETTY LUCKY.
LET'S HOPE WE HAVE THAT LUCK AT THE BORDER.
THIS IS THE BIG ONE! BACK TO THE E.U.
IF WE CAN EVER SEE YEVA AGAIN...
IT'S ALWAYS BEEN OK BEFORE...
BUT CAN IT BE OK FOREVER?
SIGH.

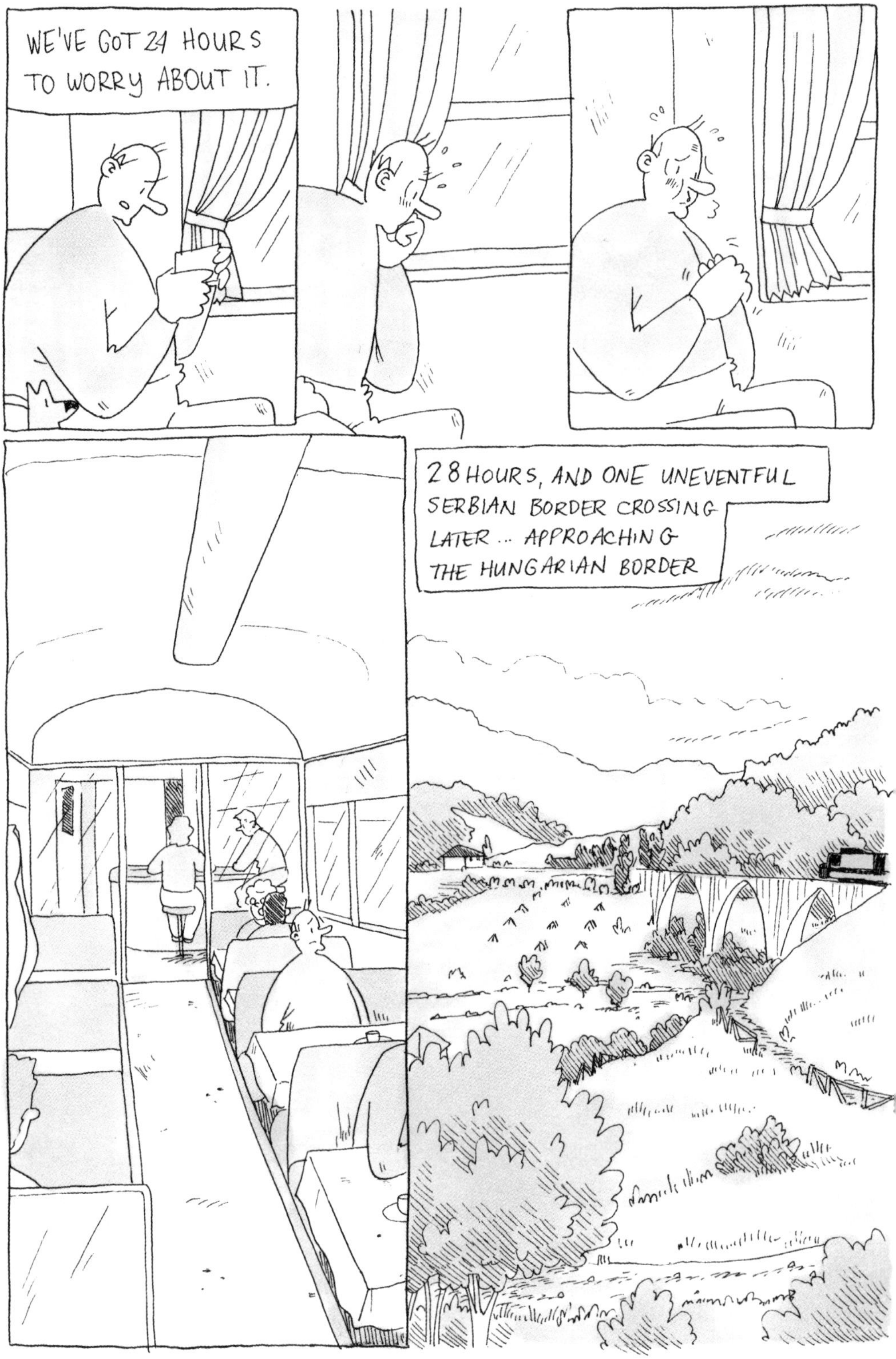
WE'VE GOT 24 HOURS TO WORRY ABOUT IT.
28 HOURS, AND ONE UNEVENTFUL SERBIAN BORDER CROSSING LATER... APPROACHING THE HUNGARIAN BORDER

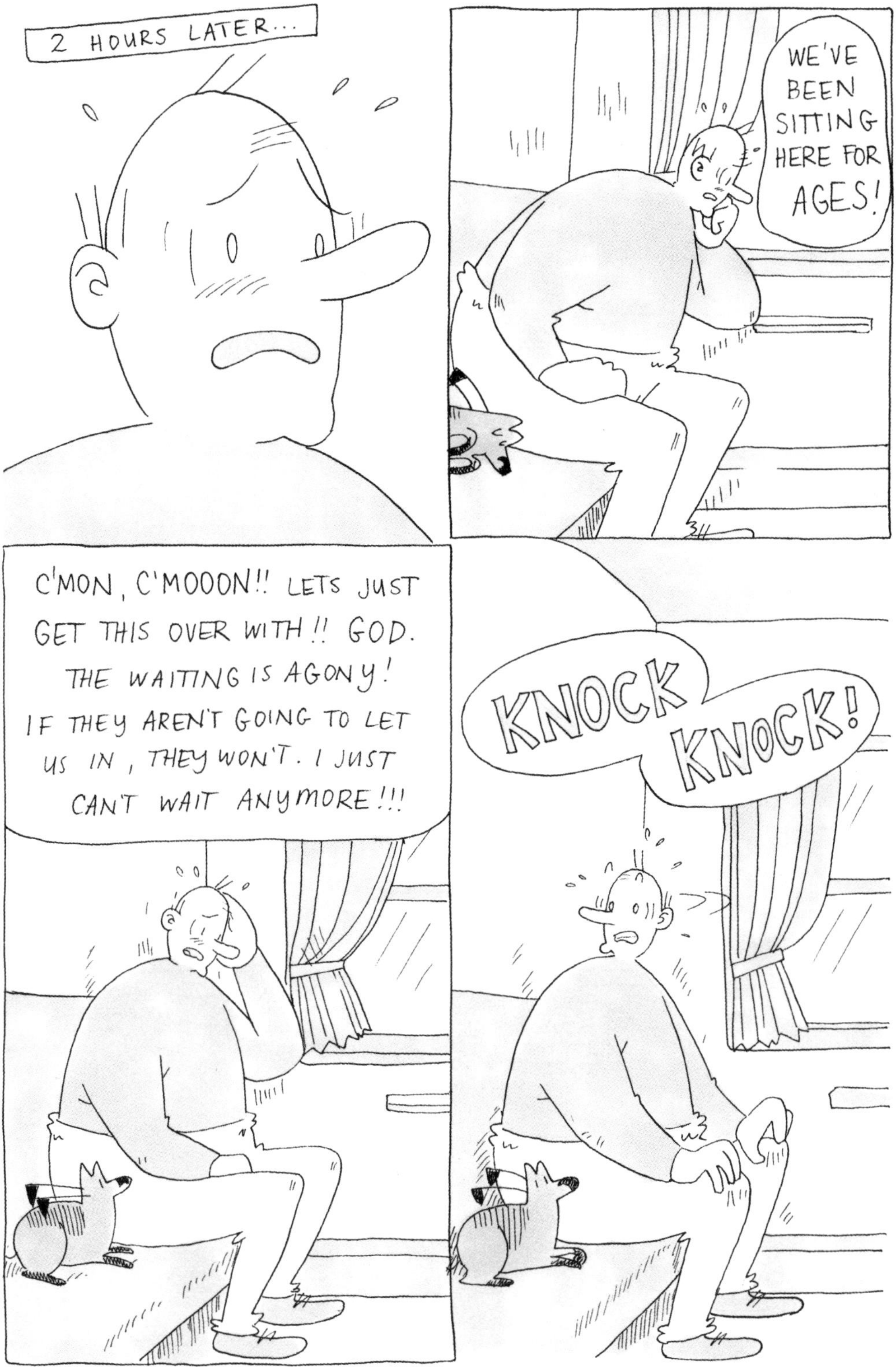
2 HOURS LATER...
WE'VE BEEN SITTING HERE FOR AGES!
C'MON, C'MOOON!! LETS JUST GET THIS OVER WITH!! GOD. THE WAITING IS AGONY! IF THEY AREN'T GOING TO LET US IN, THEY WON'T. I JUST CAN'T WAIT ANYMORE!!!
KNOCK KNOCK!

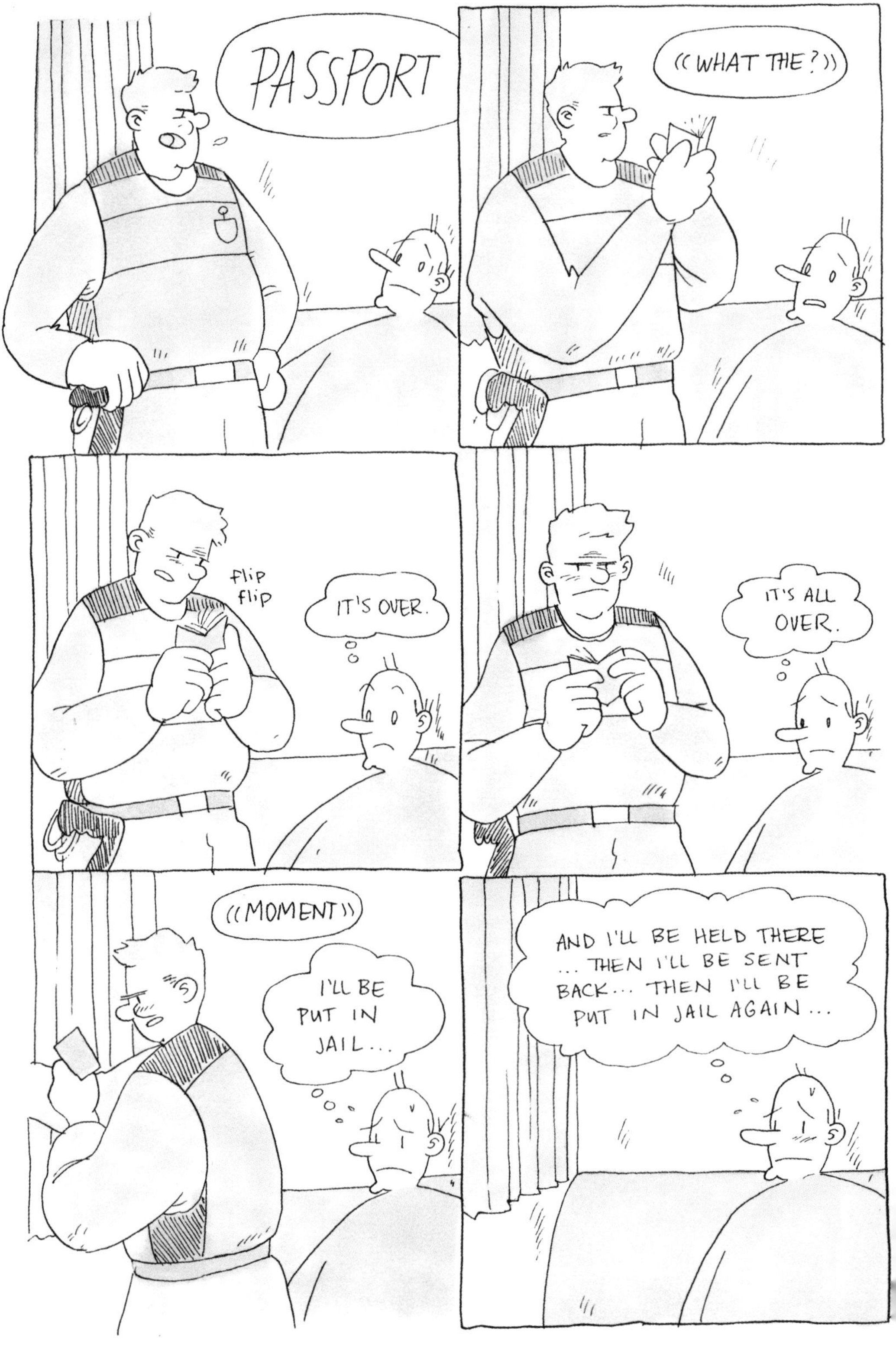
PASSPORT
((WHAT THE?))
flip flip
IT'S OVER.
IT'S ALL OVER.
((MOMENT))
I'LL BE PUT IN JAIL...
AND I'LL BE HELD THERE ... THEN I'LL BE SENT BACK... THEN I'LL BE PUT IN JAIL AGAIN...

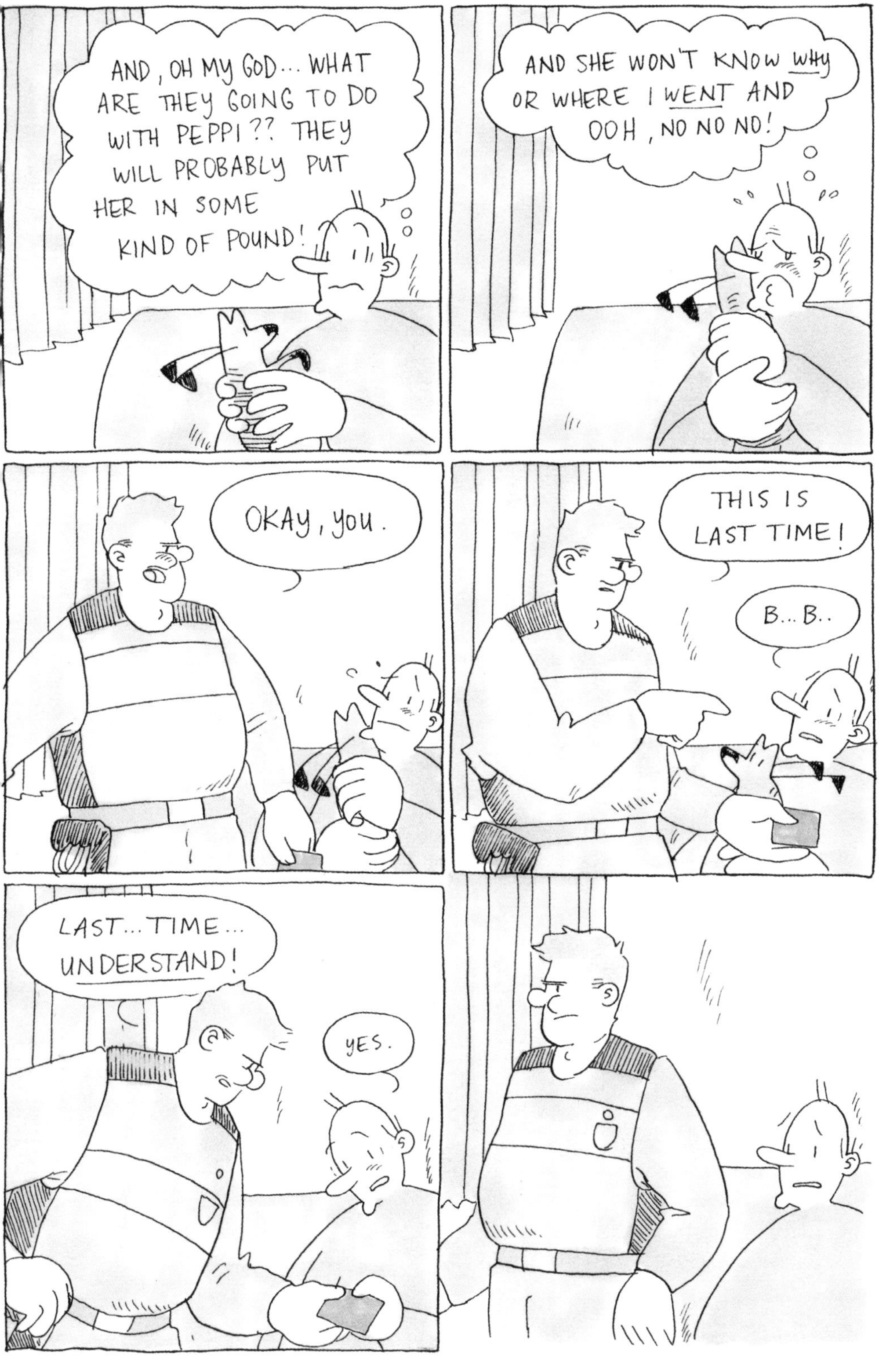
AND, OH MY GOD... WHAT ARE THEY GOING TO DO WITH PEPPI?? THEY WILL PROBABLY PUT HER IN SOME KIND OF POUND!
AND SHE WON'T KNOW WHY OR WHERE I WENT AND OOH, NO NO NO!
OKAY, YOU.
THIS IS LAST TIME!
B... B..
LAST... TIME... UNDERSTAND!
YES.

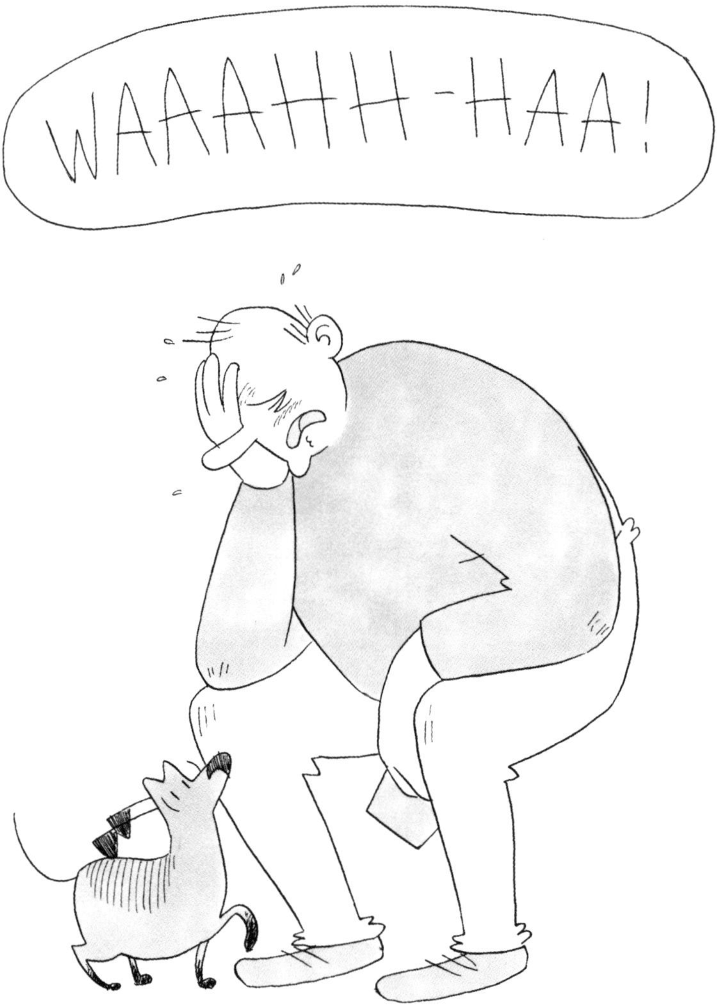
WAAAHH-HAA!

CHAPTER THREE

TIME TO THINK

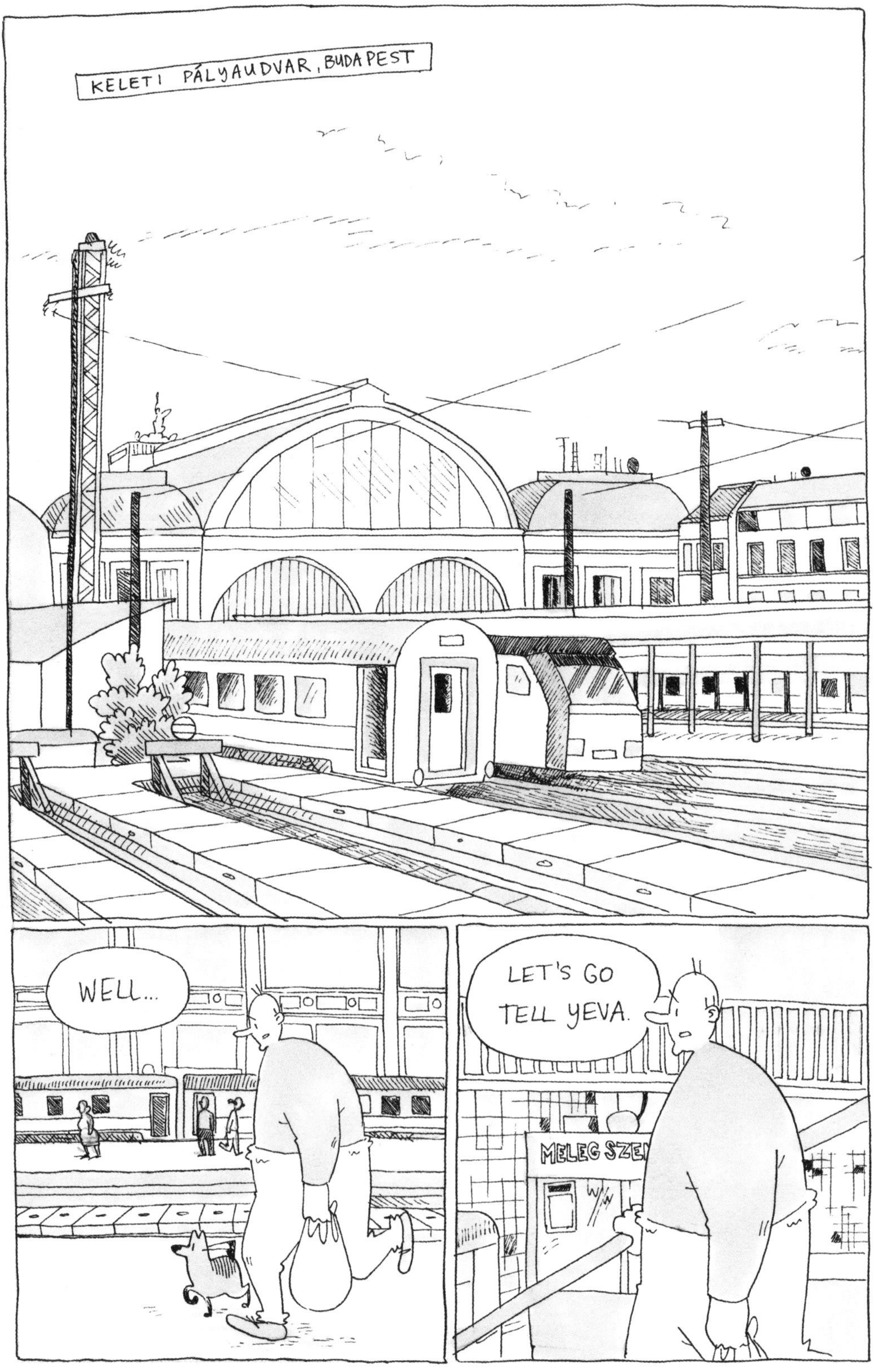
KELETI PÁLYAUDVAR, BUDAPEST
WELL...
LET'S GO TELL YEVA.

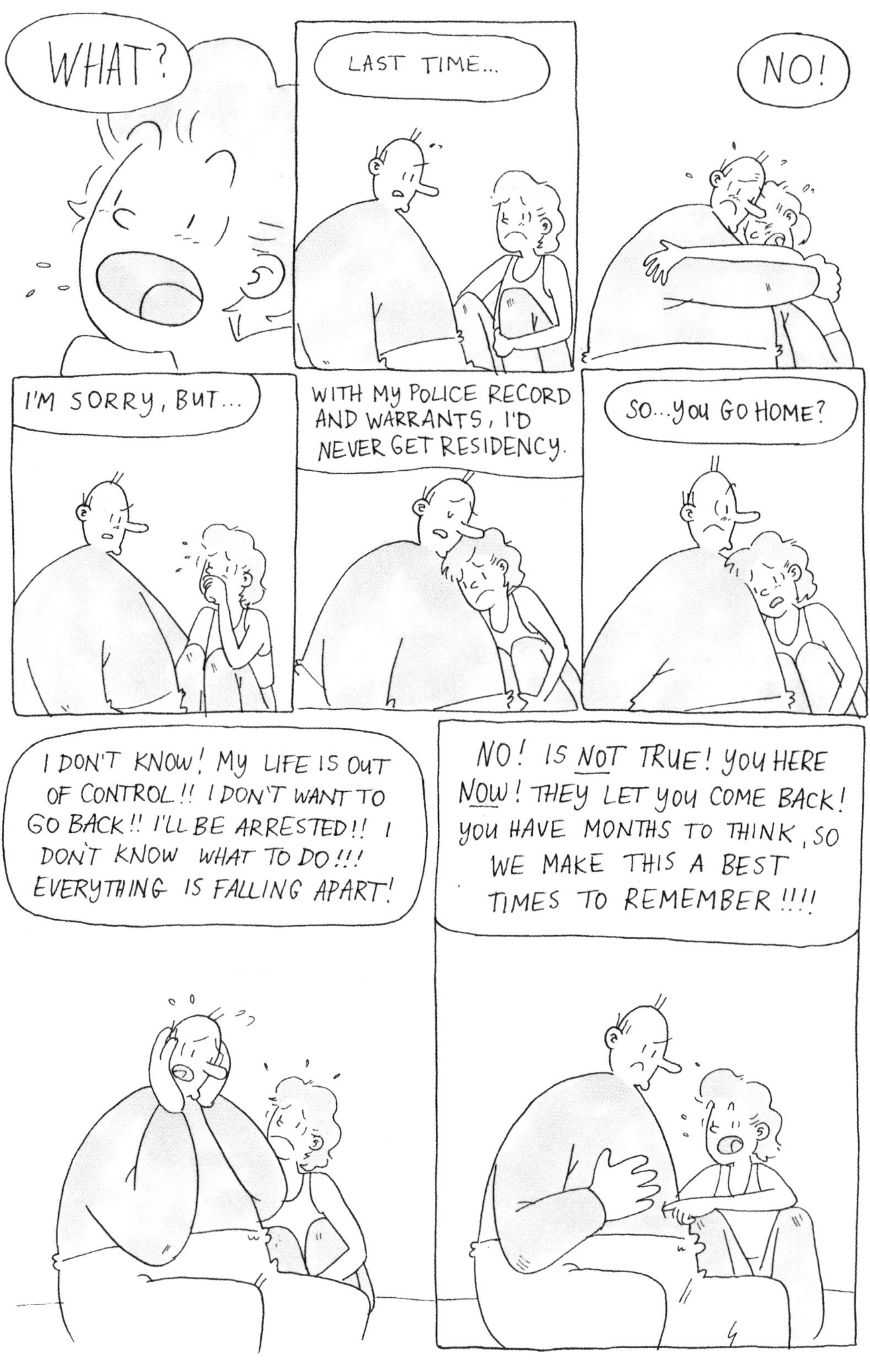
WHAT?
LAST TIME...
NO!
I'M SORRY, BUT...
WITH MY POLICE RECORD AND WARRANTS, I'D NEVER GET RESIDENCY.
SO...YOU GO HOME?
I DON'T KNOW! MY LIFE IS OUT OF CONTROL!! I DON'T WANT TO GO BACK!! I'LL BE ARRESTED!! I DON'T KNOW WHAT TO DO!!! EVERYTHING IS FALLING APART!
NO! IS NOT TRUE! YOU HERE NOW! THEY LET YOU COME BACK! YOU HAVE MONTHS TO THINK, SO WE MAKE THIS A BEST TIMES TO REMEMBER!!!!

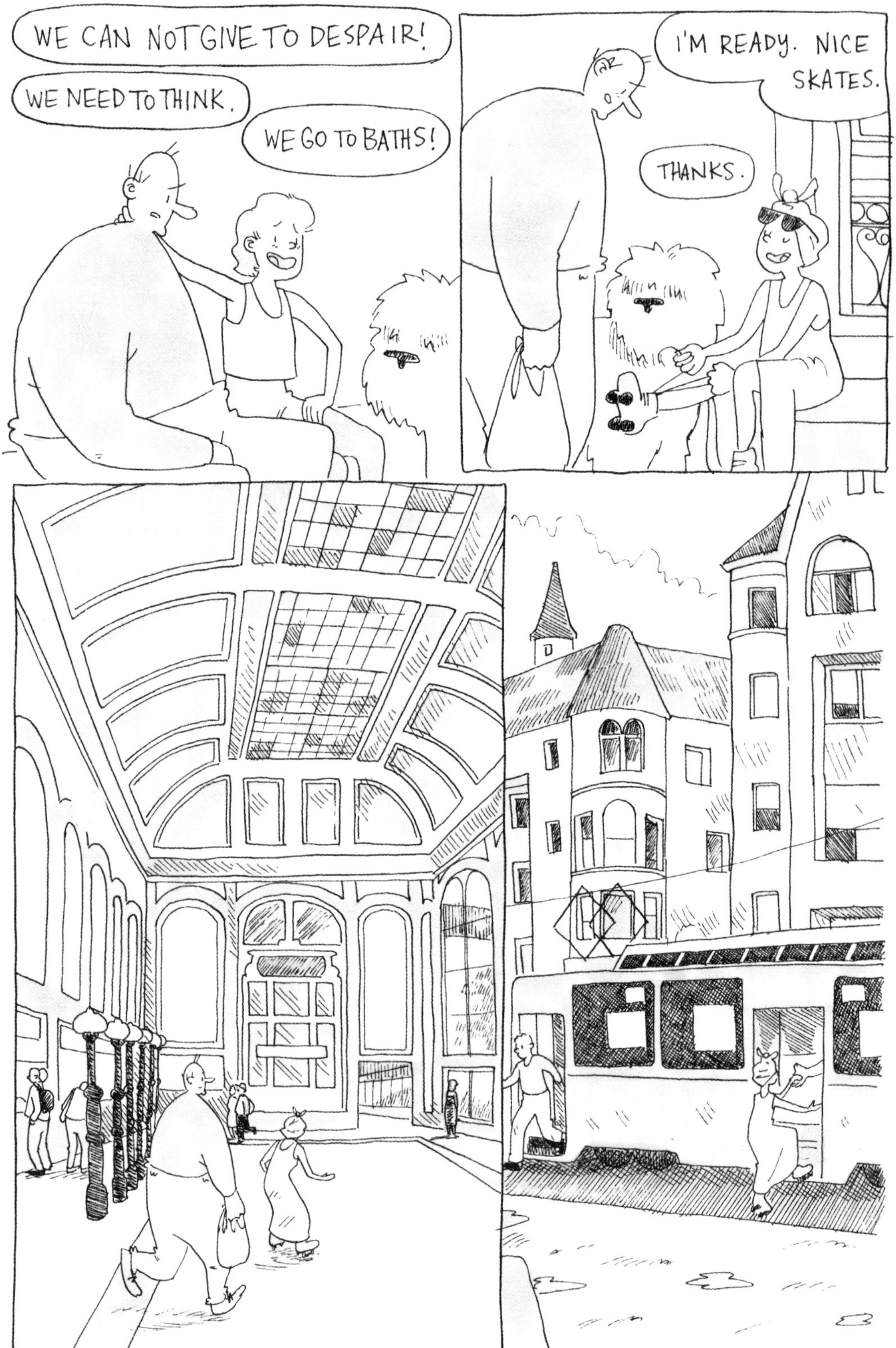
WE CAN NOT GIVE TO DESPAIR!
WE NEED TO THINK.
WE GO TO BATHS!
I'M READY. NICE SKATES.
THANKS.

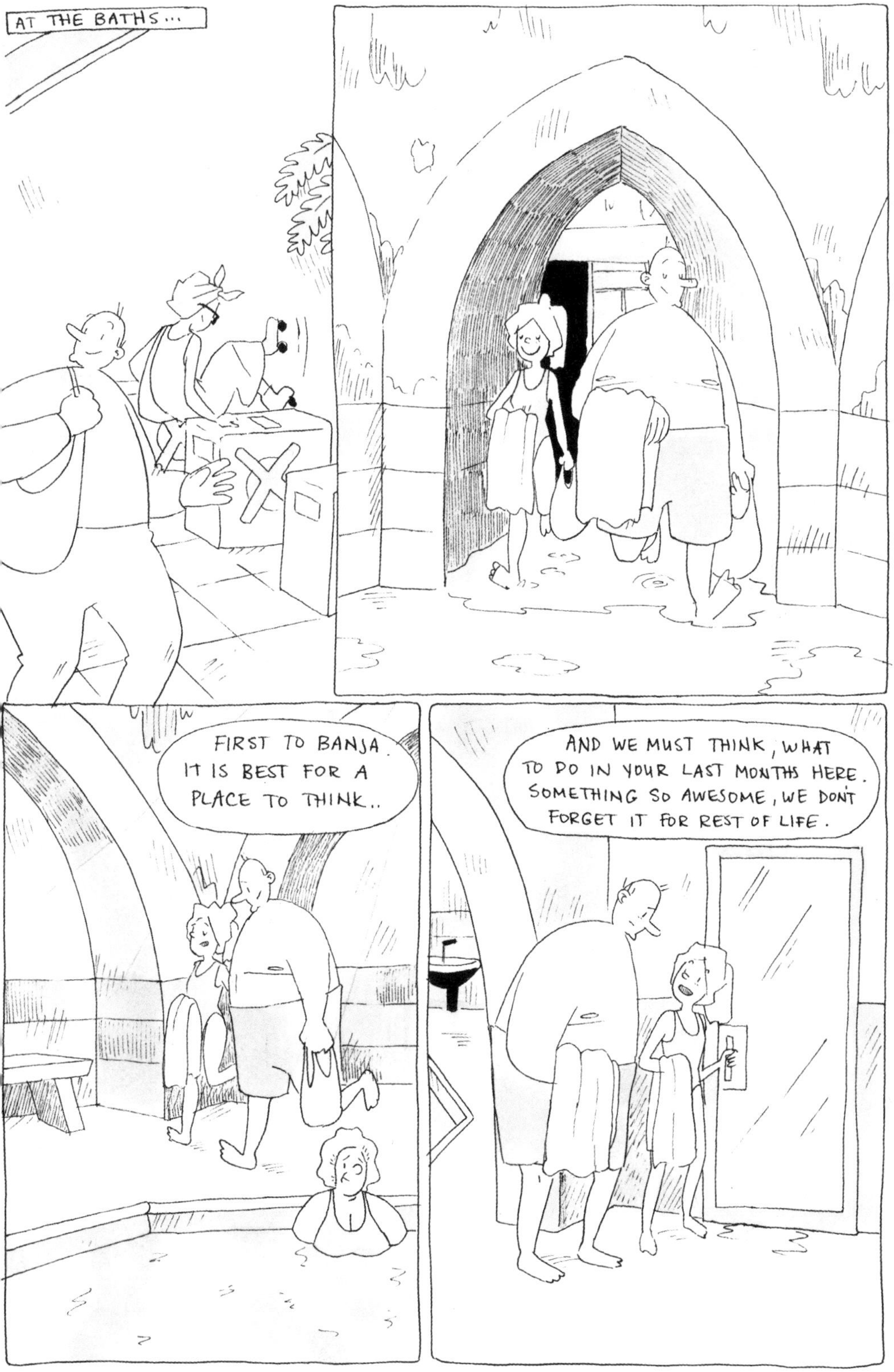
AT THE BATHS...
FIRST TO BANJA. IT IS BEST FOR A PLACE TO THINK..
AND WE MUST THINK, WHAT TO DO IN YOUR LAST MONTHS HERE. SOMETHING SO AWESOME, WE DON'T FORGET IT FOR REST OF LIFE.

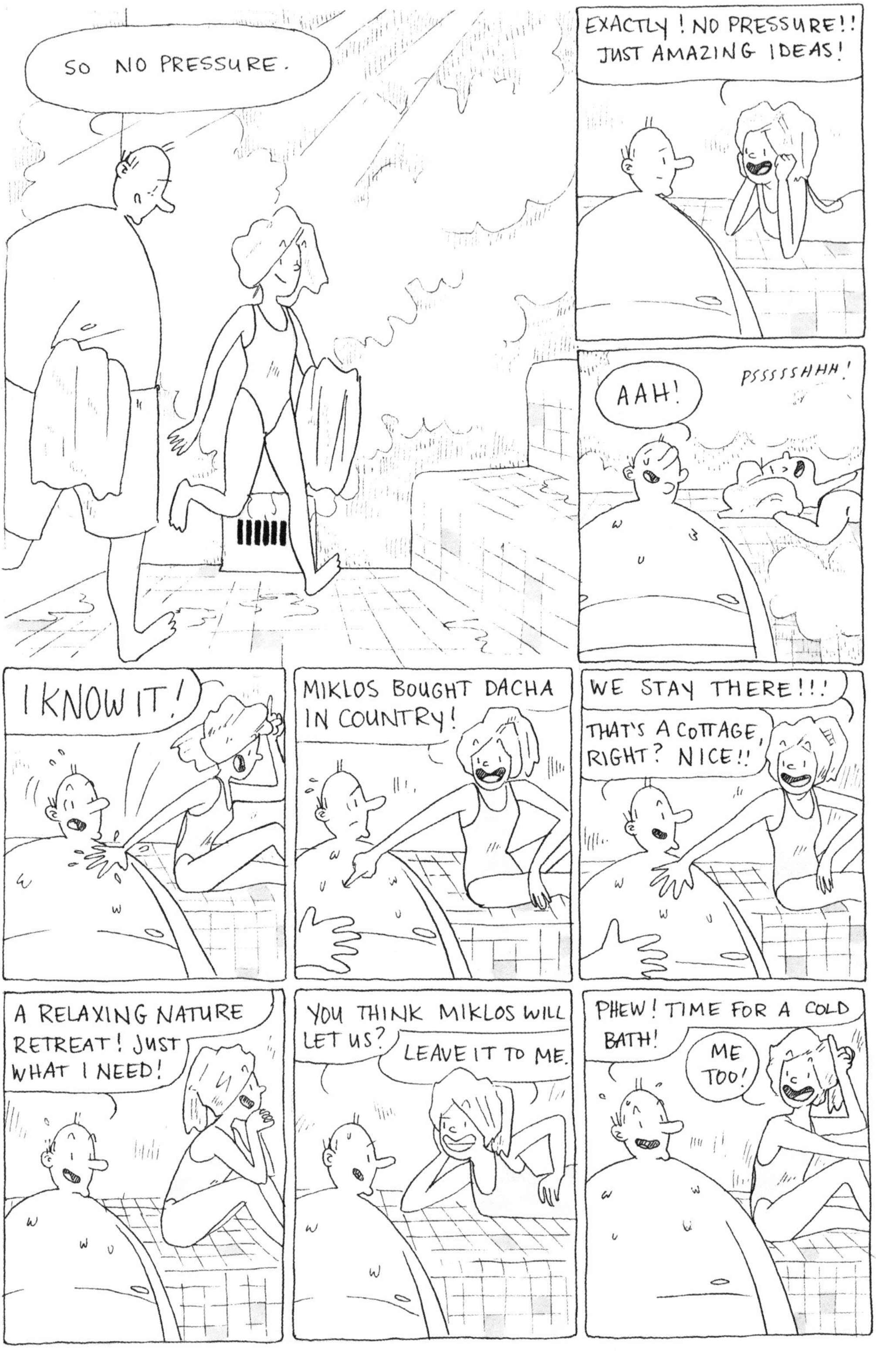
SO NO PRESSURE.
EXACTLY! NO PRESSURE!! JUST AMAZING IDEAS!
AAH!
PSSSSSHHH!
I KNOW IT!
MIKLOS BOUGHT DACHA IN COUNTRY!
WE STAY THERE!!!
THAT'S A COTTAGE, RIGHT? NICE!!
A RELAXING NATURE RETREAT! JUST WHAT I NEED!
YOU THINK MIKLOS WILL LET US?
LEAVE IT TO ME.
PHEW! TIME FOR A COLD BATH!
ME TOO!

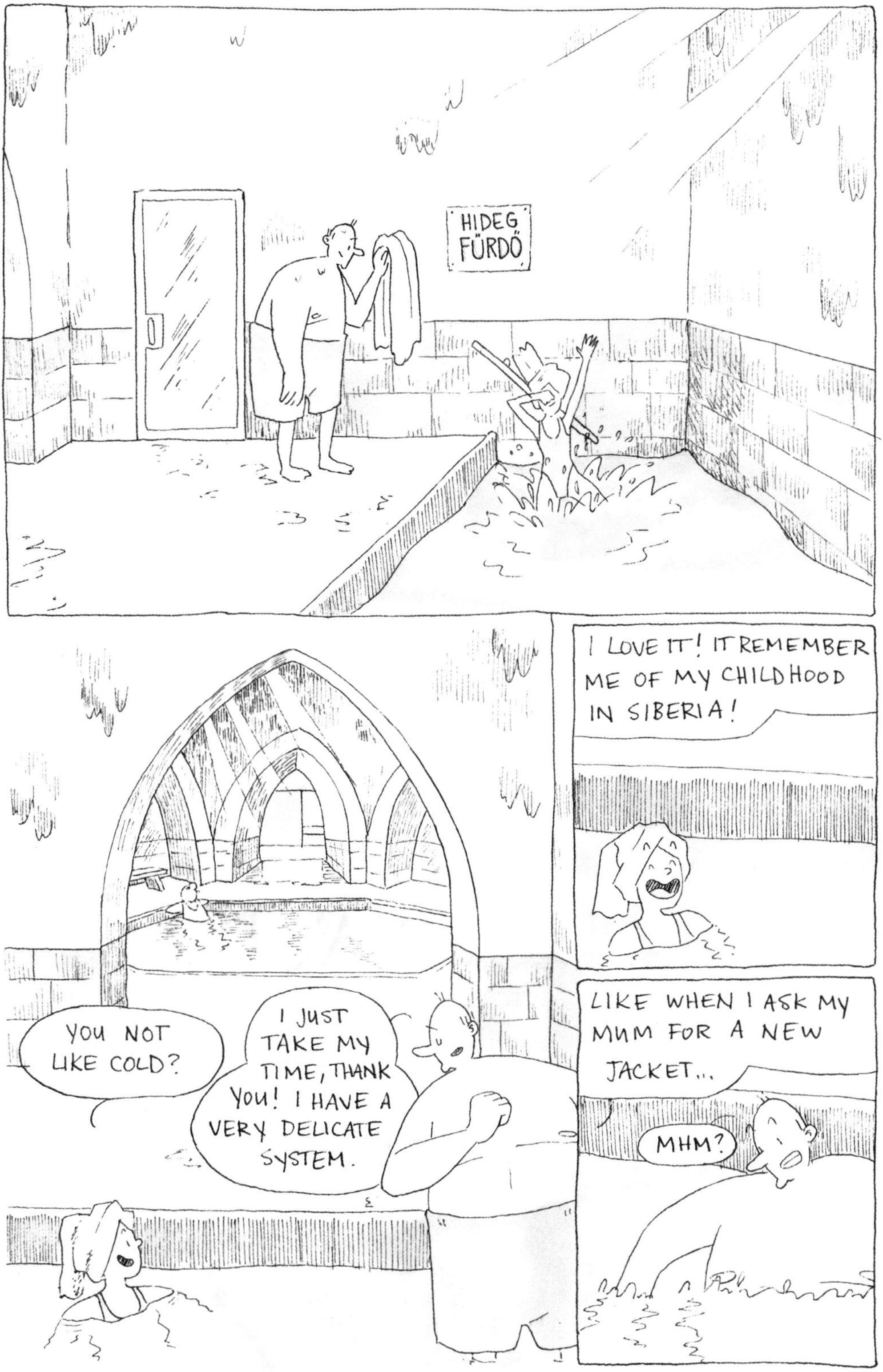
HIDEG FÜRDŐ
YOU NOT LIKE COLD?
I JUST TAKE MY TIME, THANK YOU! I HAVE A VERY DELICATE SYSTEM.
I LOVE IT! IT REMEMBER ME OF MY CHILDHOOD IN SIBERIA!
LIKE WHEN I ASK MY MUM FOR A NEW JACKET...
MHM?

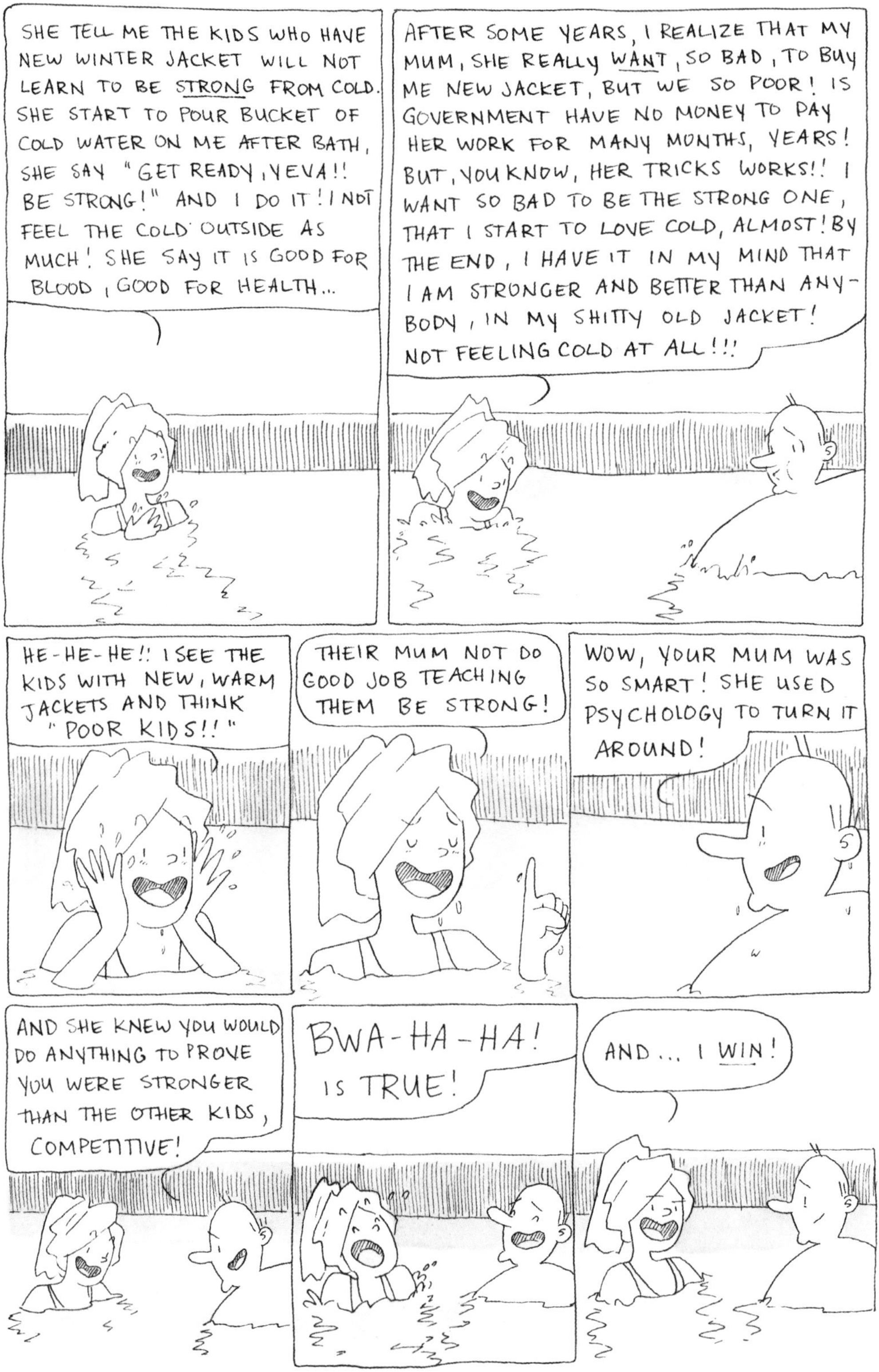
SHE TELL ME THE KIDS WHO HAVE NEW WINTER JACKET WILL NOT LEARN TO BE STRONG FROM COLD. SHE START TO POUR BUCKET OF COLD WATER ON ME AFTER BATH, SHE SAY "GET READY, YEVA!! BE STRONG!" AND I DO IT! I NOT FEEL THE COLD OUTSIDE AS MUCH! SHE SAY IT IS GOOD FOR BLOOD, GOOD FOR HEALTH...
AFTER SOME YEARS, I REALIZE THAT MY MUM, SHE REALLY WANT, SO BAD, TO BUY ME NEW JACKET, BUT WE SO POOR! IS GOVERNMENT HAVE NO MONEY TO PAY HER WORK FOR MANY MONTHS, YEARS! BUT, YOU KNOW, HER TRICKS WORKS!! I WANT SO BAD TO BE THE STRONG ONE, THAT I START TO LOVE COLD, ALMOST! BY THE END, I HAVE IT IN MY MIND THAT I AM STRONGER AND BETTER THAN ANYBODY, IN MY SHITTY OLD JACKET! NOT FEELING COLD AT ALL!!!
HE-HE-HE!! I SEE THE KIDS WITH NEW, WARM JACKETS AND THINK "POOR KIDS!!"
THEIR MUM NOT DO GOOD JOB TEACHING THEM BE STRONG!
WOW, YOUR MUM WAS SO SMART! SHE USED PSYCHOLOGY TO TURN IT AROUND!
AND SHE KNEW YOU WOULD DO ANYTHING TO PROVE YOU WERE STRONGER THAN THE OTHER KIDS, COMPETITIVE!
BWA-HA-HA! IS TRUE!
AND... I WIN!

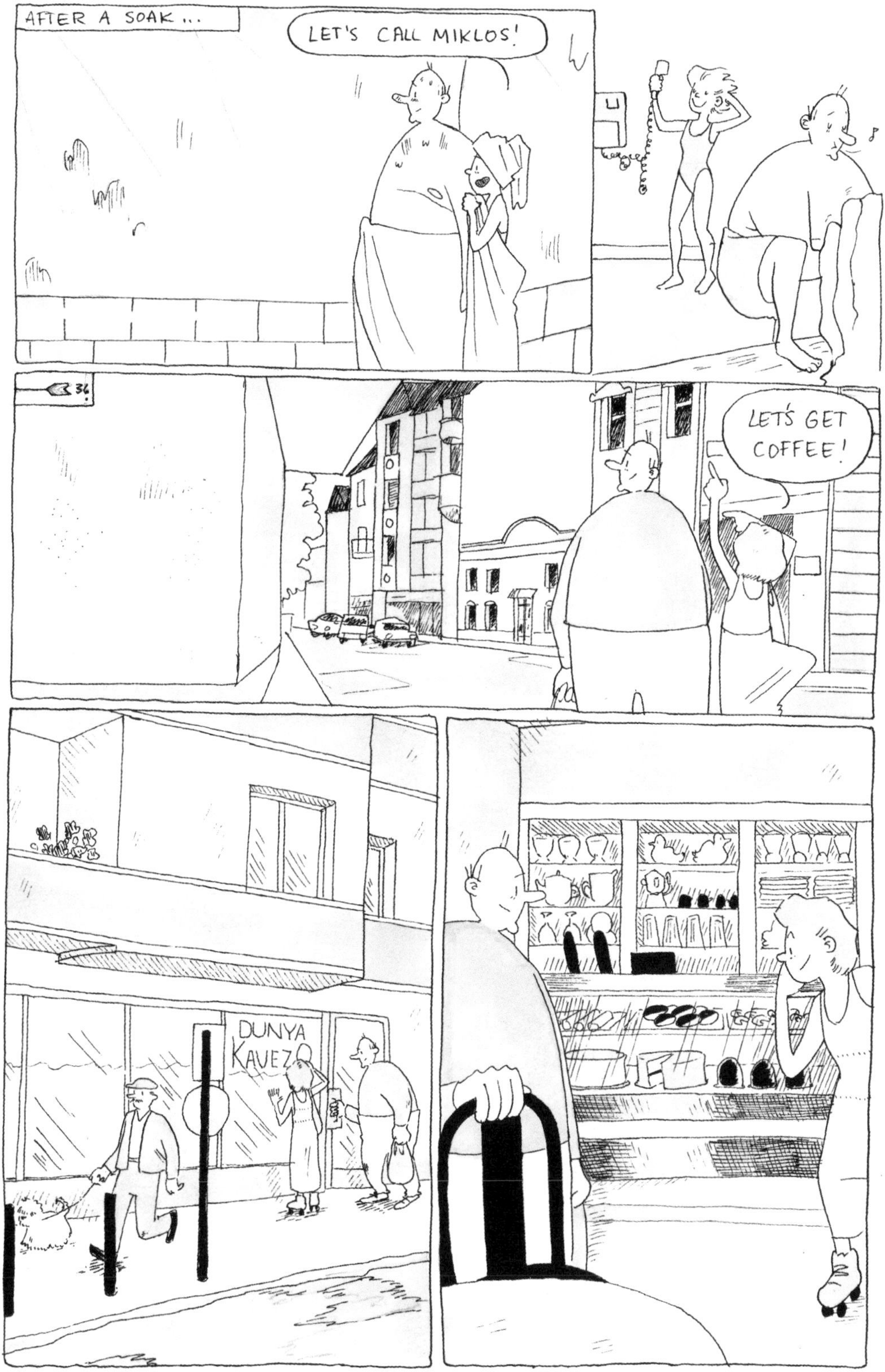
AFTER A SOAK...
LET'S CALL MIKLOS!
LET'S GET COFFEE!
DUNYA KAVEZ

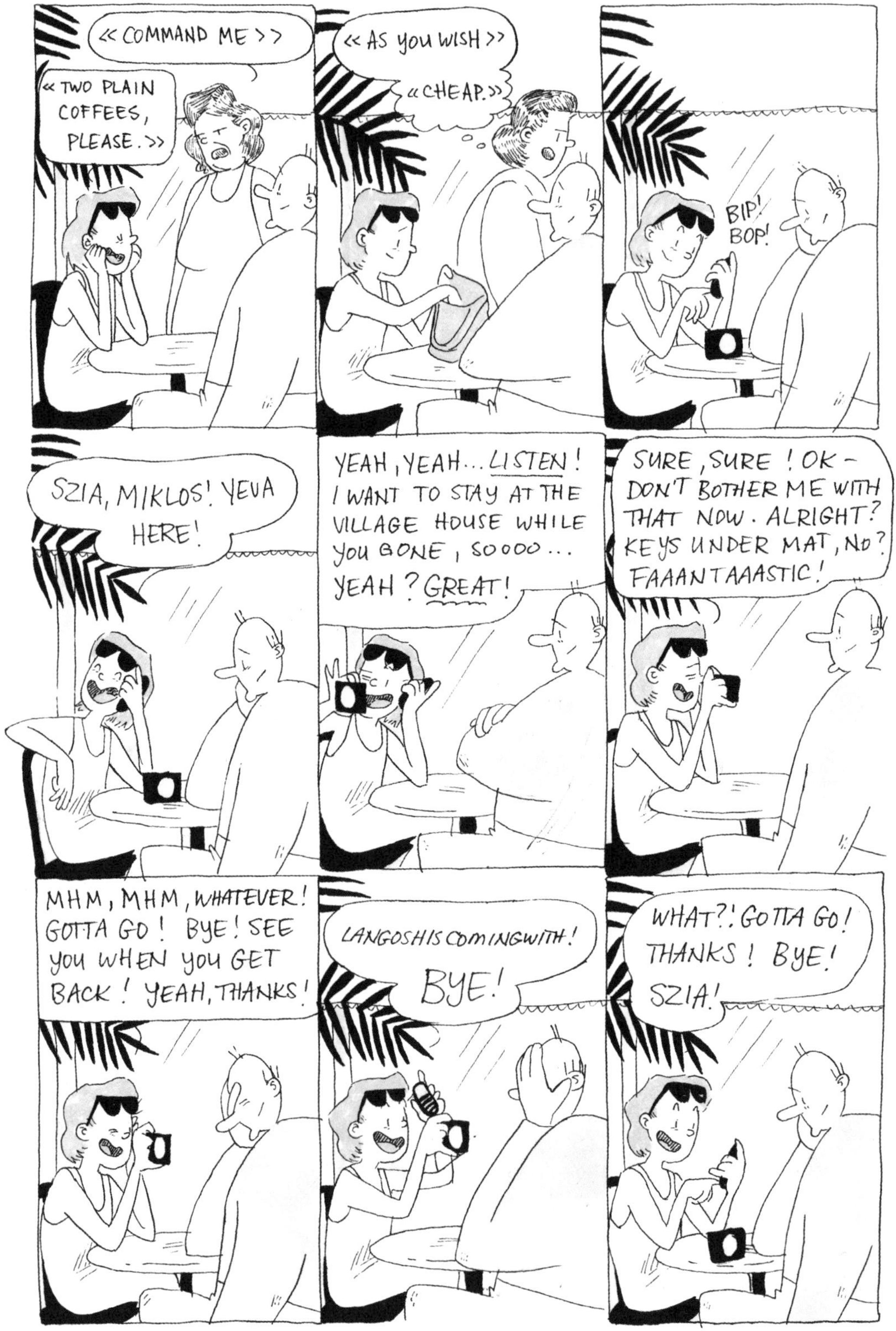
« COMMAND ME »
« TWO PLAIN COFFEES, PLEASE. »
« AS YOU WISH »
« CHEAP. »
BIP! BOP!
SZIA, MIKLOS! YEVA HERE!
YEAH, YEAH... LISTEN! I WANT TO STAY AT THE VILLAGE HOUSE WHILE YOU GONE, SOOOO... YEAH? GREAT!
SURE, SURE! OK - DON'T BOTHER ME WITH THAT NOW. ALRIGHT? KEYS UNDER MAT, NO? FAAANTAAASTIC!
MHM, MHM, WHATEVER! GOTTA GO! BYE! SEE YOU WHEN YOU GET BACK! YEAH, THANKS!
LANGOSHISCOMINGWITH!
BYE!
WHAT?! GOTTA GO! THANKS! BYE! SZIA!

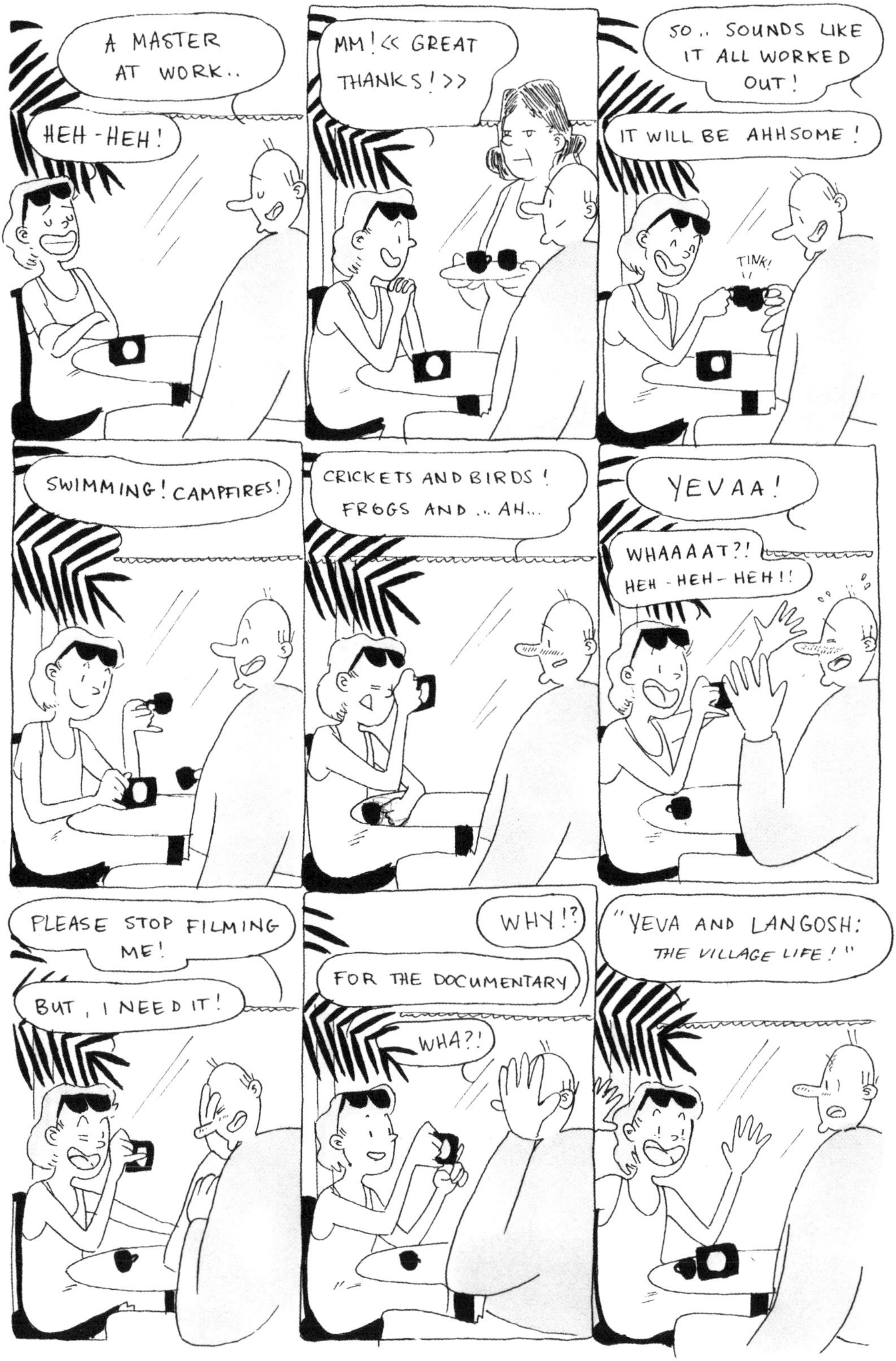
A MASTER AT WORK..
HEH-HEH!
MM! << GREAT THANKS! >>
SO.. SOUNDS LIKE IT ALL WORKED OUT!
IT WILL BE AHHSOME!
TINK!
SWIMMING! CAMPFIRES!
CRICKETS AND BIRDS! FROGS AND .. AH...
YEVAA!
WHAAAAT?! HEH-HEH-HEH!!
PLEASE STOP FILMING ME!
BUT, I NEED IT!
WHY!?
FOR THE DOCUMENTARY
WHA?!
"YEVA AND LANGOSH: THE VILLAGE LIFE!"

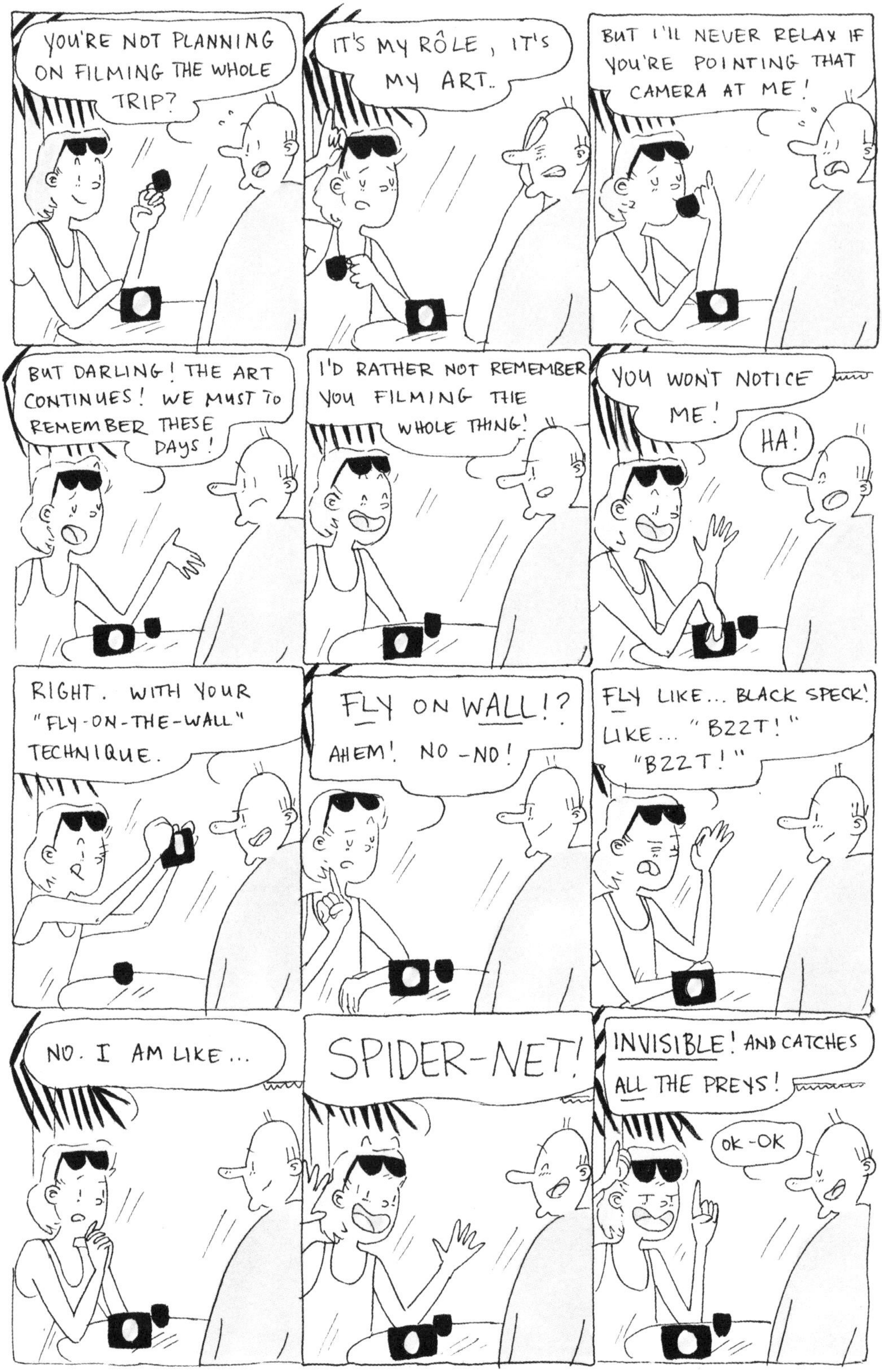
YOU'RE NOT PLANNING ON FILMING THE WHOLE TRIP?
IT'S MY RÔLE, IT'S MY ART..
BUT I'LL NEVER RELAX IF YOU'RE POINTING THAT CAMERA AT ME!
BUT DARLING! THE ART CONTINUES! WE MUST TO REMEMBER THESE DAYS!
I'D RATHER NOT REMEMBER YOU FILMING THE WHOLE THING!
YOU WON'T NOTICE ME!
HA!
RIGHT. WITH YOUR "FLY-ON-THE-WALL" TECHNIQUE.
FLY ON WALL!? AHEM! NO-NO!
FLY LIKE... BLACK SPECK! LIKE... "BZZT!" "BZZT!"
NO. I AM LIKE...
SPIDER-NET!
INVISIBLE! AND CATCHES ALL THE PREYS!
OK-OK

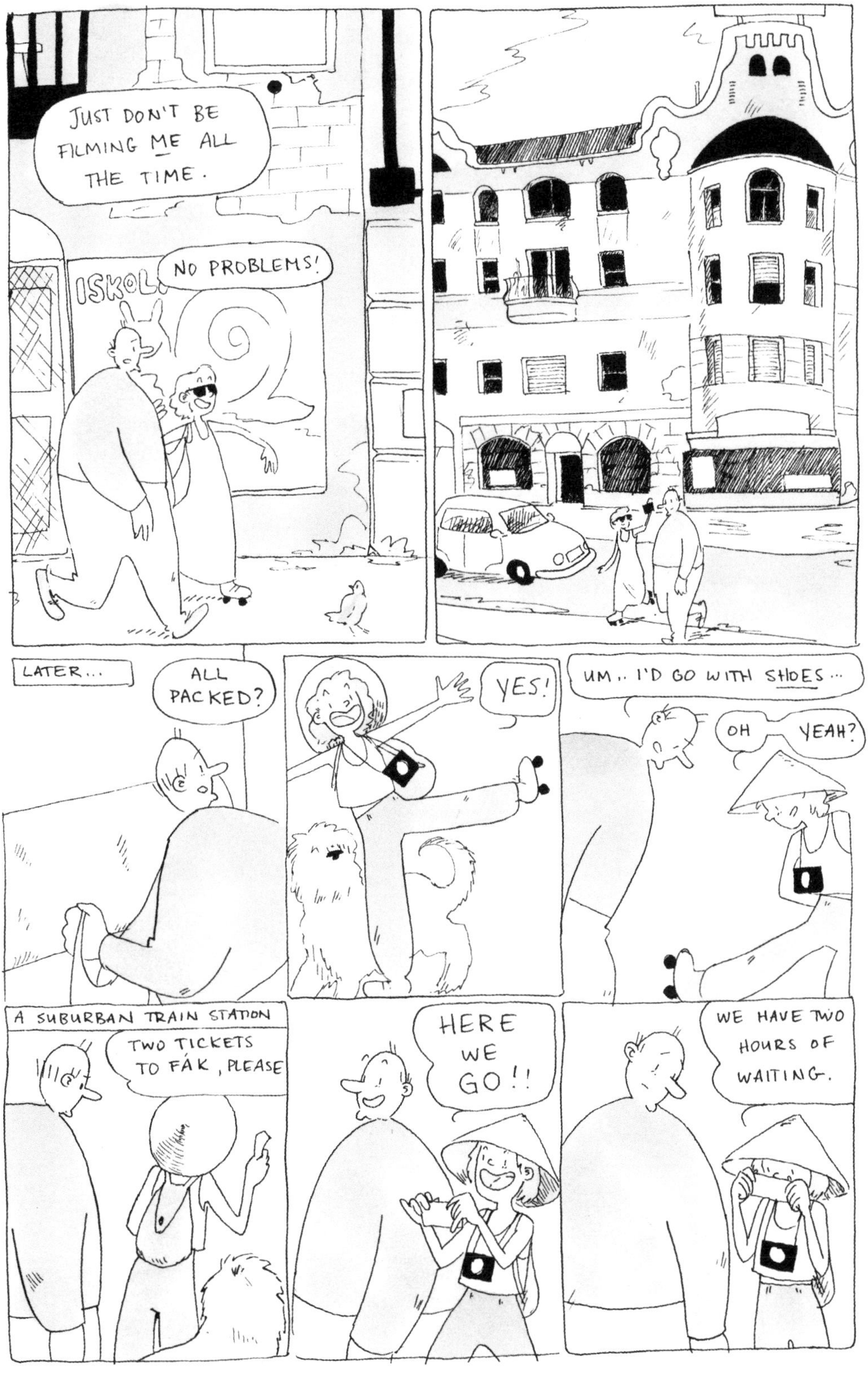
JUST DON'T BE FILMING ME ALL THE TIME.
NO PROBLEMS!
ISKOL
LATER...
ALL PACKED?
YES!
UM.. I'D GO WITH SHOES...
OH YEAH?
A SUBURBAN TRAIN STATION
TWO TICKETS TO FÁK, PLEASE
HERE WE GO!!
WE HAVE TWO HOURS OF WAITING.

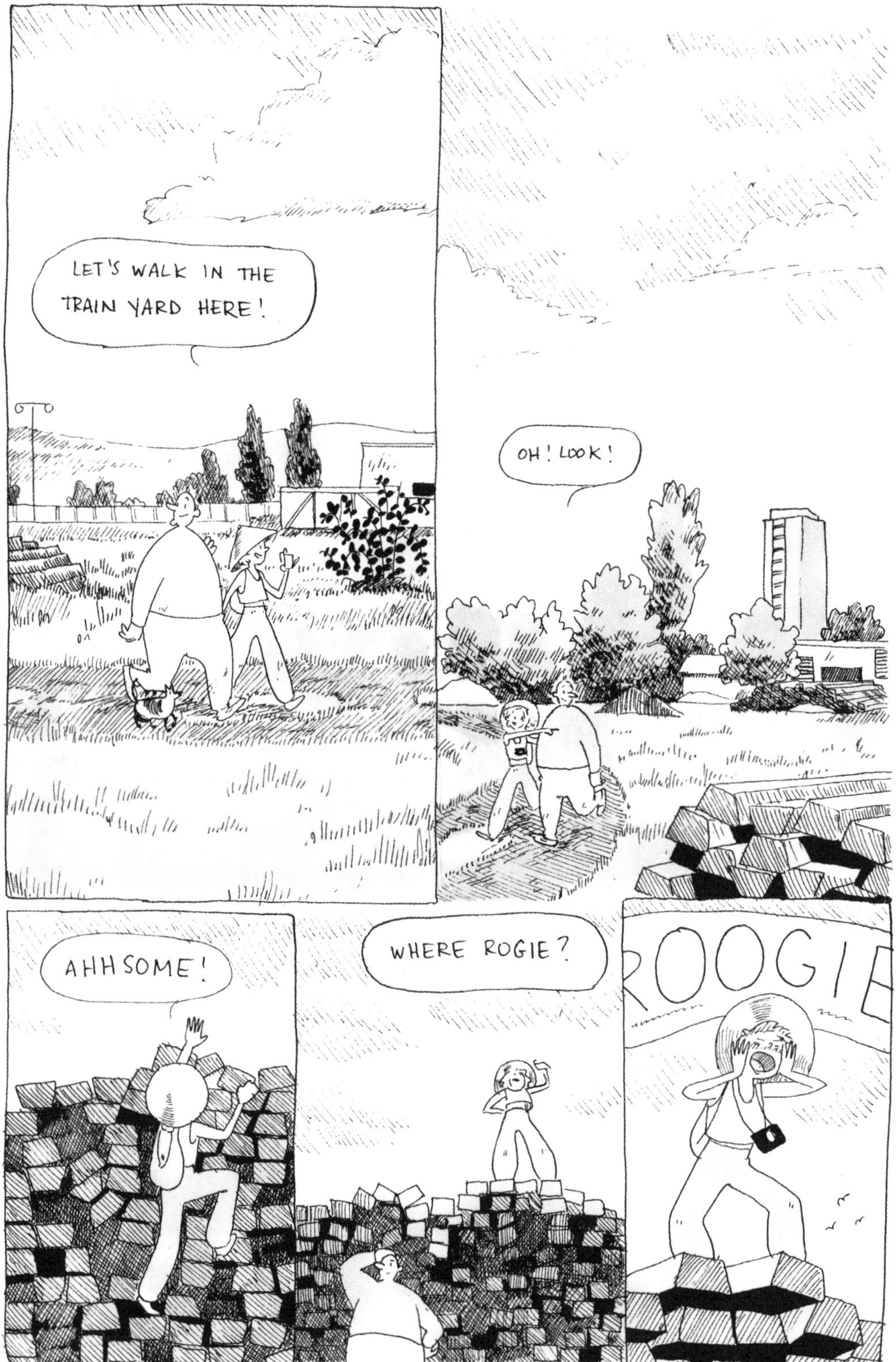
LET'S WALK IN THE TRAIN YARD HERE!
OH! LOOK!
AHHSOME!
WHERE ROGIE?
ROOGIE

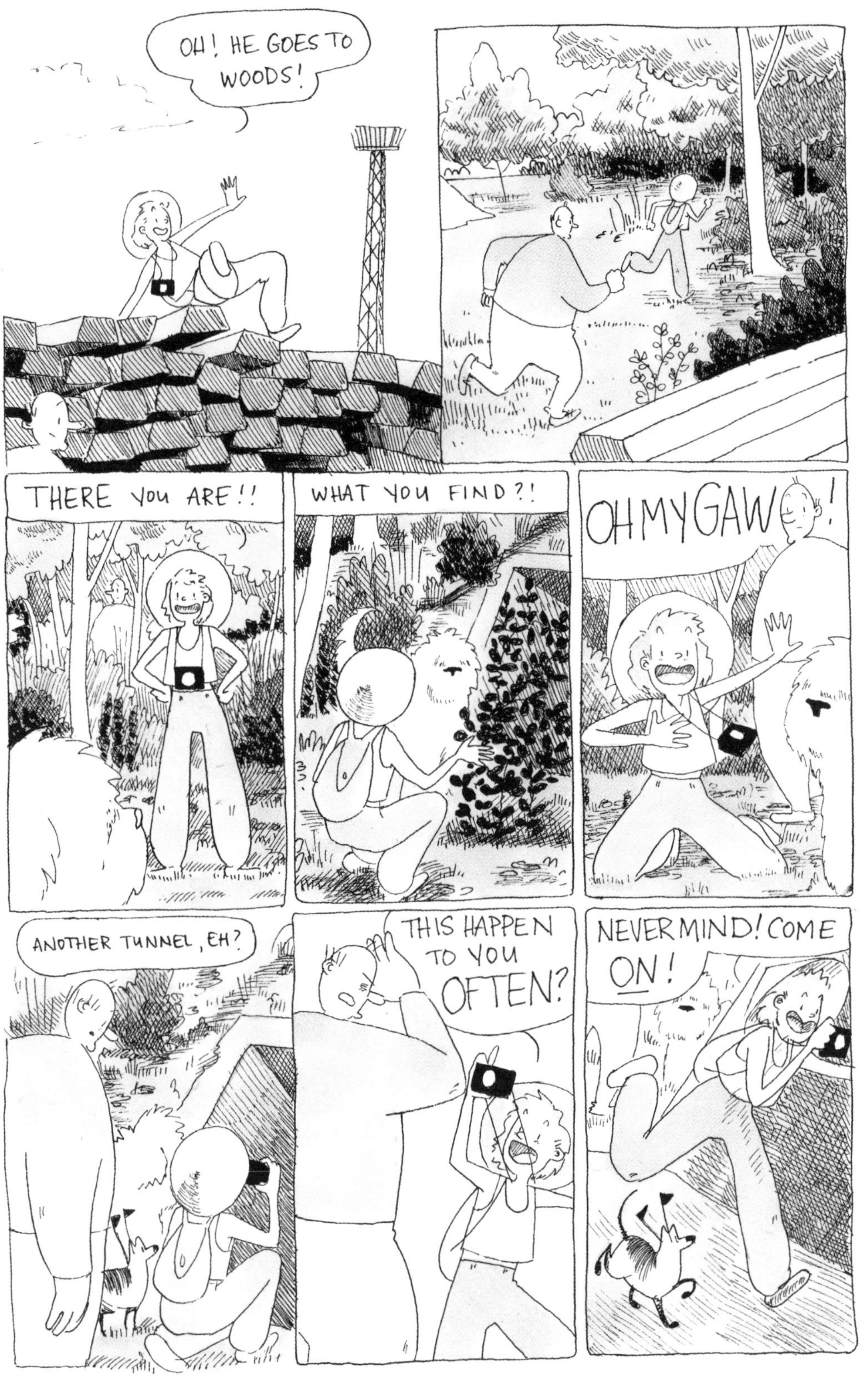
OH! HE GOES TO WOODS!
THERE YOU ARE!!
WHAT YOU FIND?!
OHMYGAWD!
ANOTHER TUNNEL, EH?
THIS HAPPEN TO YOU OFTEN?
NEVERMIND! COME ON!

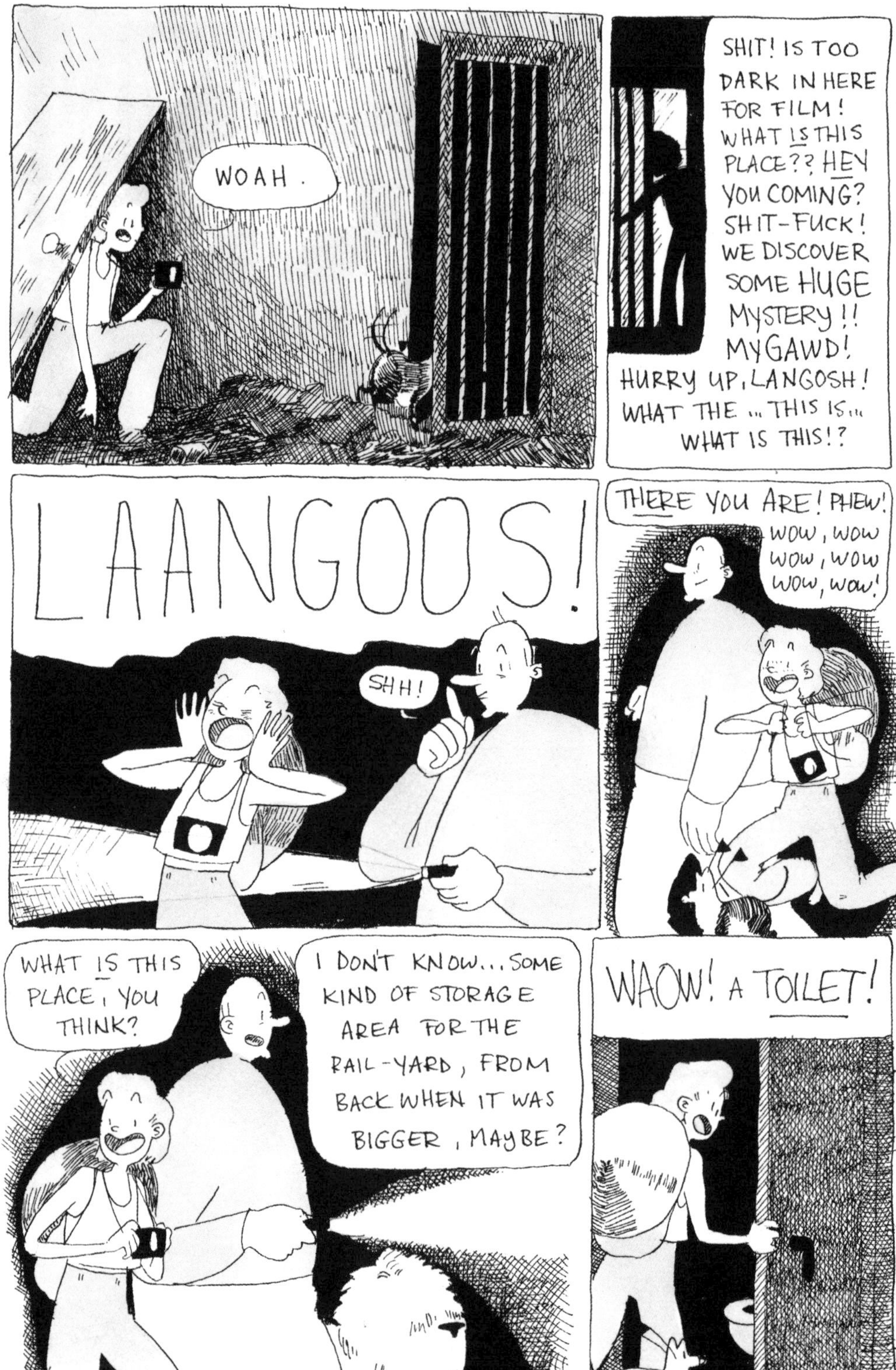
WOAH.
SHIT! IS TOO DARK IN HERE FOR FILM! WHAT IS THIS PLACE?? HEY YOU COMING? SHIT-FUCK! WE DISCOVER SOME HUGE MYSTERY!! MYGAWD! HURRY UP, LANGOSH! WHAT THE ... THIS IS... WHAT IS THIS!?
LAANGOOS!
SHH!
THERE YOU ARE! PHEW!
WOW, WOW WOW, WOW WOW, WOW!
WHAT IS THIS PLACE, YOU THINK?
I DON'T KNOW... SOME KIND OF STORAGE AREA FOR THE RAIL-YARD, FROM BACK WHEN IT WAS BIGGER, MAYBE?
WAOW! A TOILET!

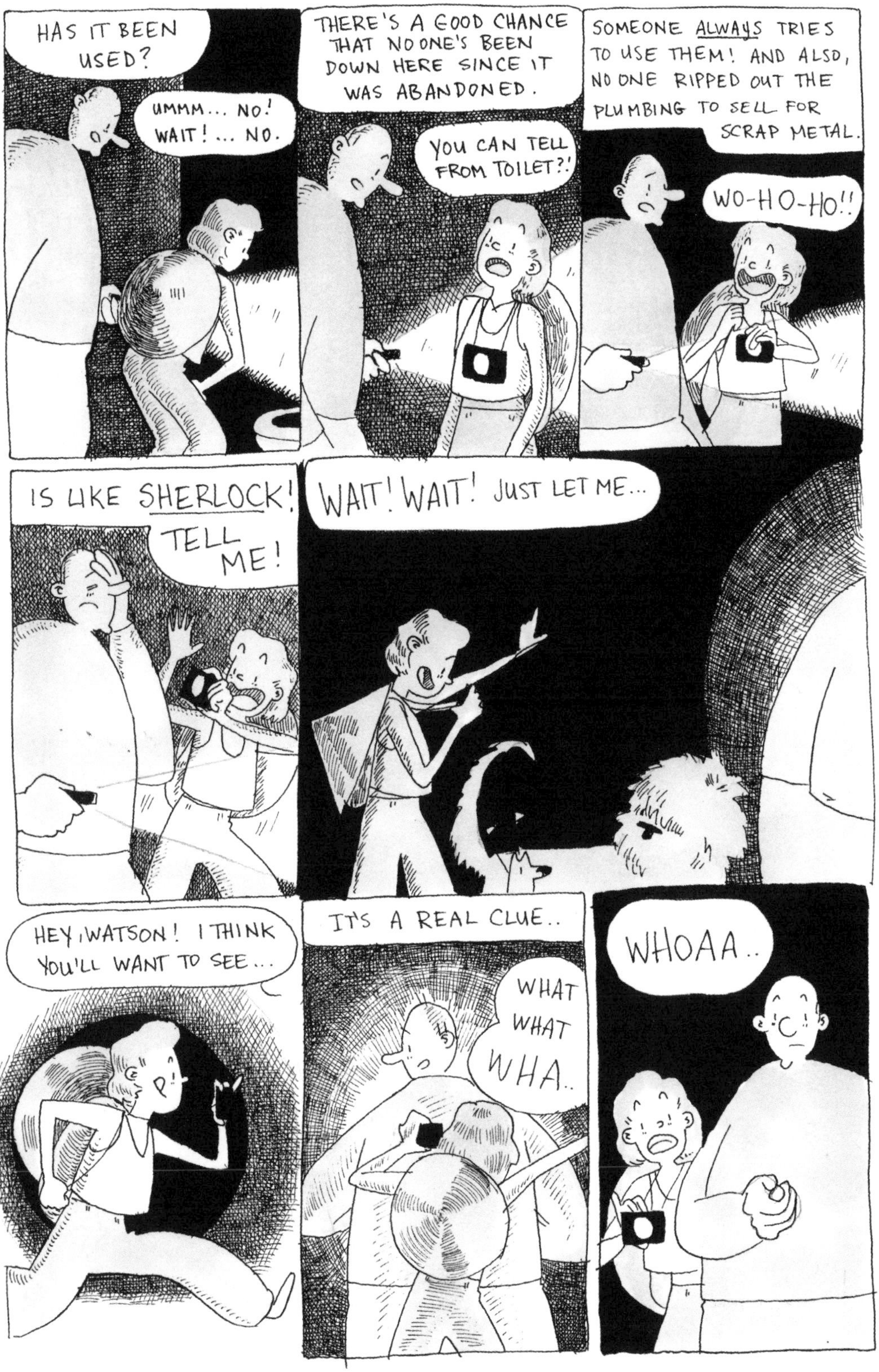
HAS IT BEEN USED?
UMMM... NO! WAIT! ... NO.
THERE'S A GOOD CHANCE THAT NO ONE'S BEEN DOWN HERE SINCE IT WAS ABANDONED.
YOU CAN TELL FROM TOILET?!
SOMEONE ALWAYS TRIES TO USE THEM! AND ALSO, NO ONE RIPPED OUT THE PLUMBING TO SELL FOR SCRAP METAL.
WO-HO-HO!!
IS LIKE SHERLOCK!
TELL ME!
WAIT! WAIT! JUST LET ME...
HEY, WATSON! I THINK YOU'LL WANT TO SEE...
IT'S A REAL CLUE..
WHAT WHAT WHA..
WHOAA..

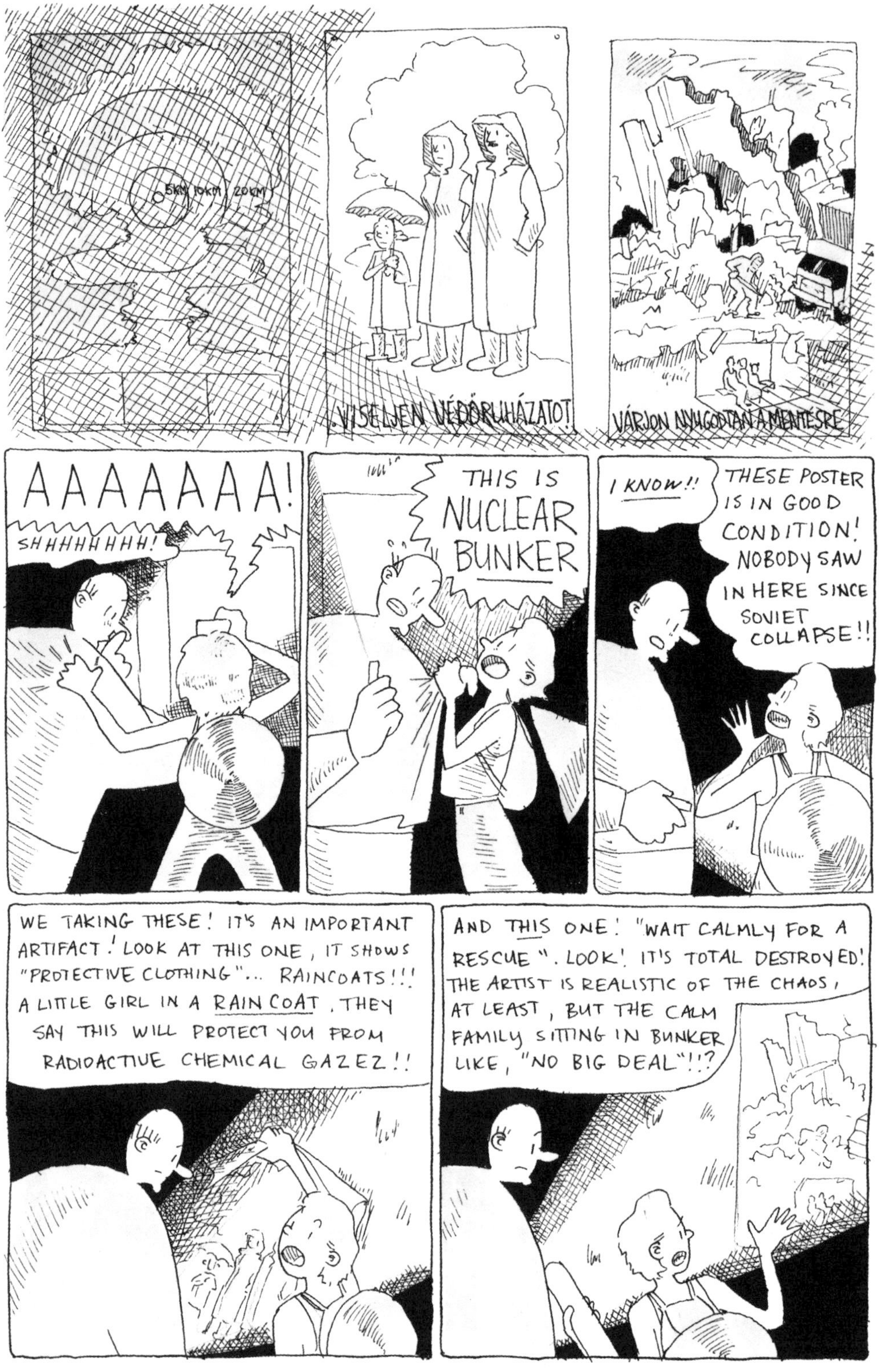

5KM 10KM 20KM
VISELJEN VÉDŐRUHÁZATOT!
VÁRJON NYUGODTAN A MENTÉSRE
AAAAAAA!
SHHHHHHHH!
THIS IS NUCLEAR BUNKER
I KNOW!!
THESE POSTER IS IN GOOD CONDITION! NOBODY SAW IN HERE SINCE SOVIET COLLAPSE!!
WE TAKING THESE! IT'S AN IMPORTANT ARTIFACT! LOOK AT THIS ONE, IT SHOWS "PROTECTIVE CLOTHING"... RAINCOATS!!! A LITTLE GIRL IN A RAIN COAT. THEY SAY THIS WILL PROTECT YOU FROM RADIOACTIVE CHEMICAL GAZEZ!!
AND THIS ONE! "WAIT CALMLY FOR A RESCUE". LOOK! IT'S TOTAL DESTROYED! THE ARTIST IS REALISTIC OF THE CHAOS, AT LEAST, BUT THE CALM FAMILY SITTING IN BUNKER LIKE, "NO BIG DEAL"!!?

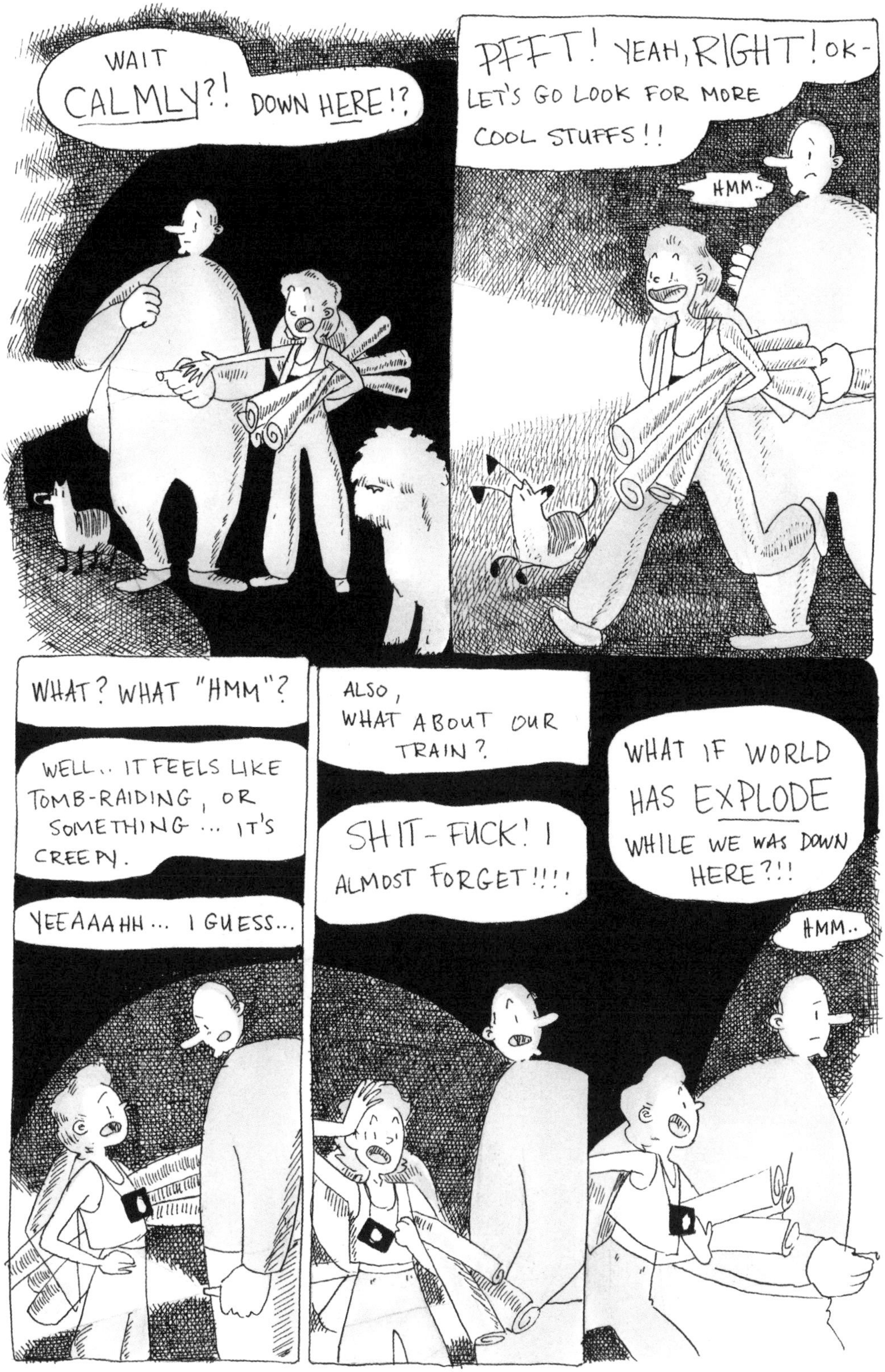
WAIT CALMLY?! DOWN HERE!?
PFFT! YEAH, RIGHT! OK-
LET'S GO LOOK FOR MORE COOL STUFFS!!
HMM..
WHAT? WHAT "HMM"?
WELL.. IT FEELS LIKE TOMB-RAIDING, OR SOMETHING... IT'S CREEPY.
YEEAAAHH... I GUESS...
ALSO, WHAT ABOUT OUR TRAIN?
SHIT-FUCK! I ALMOST FORGET!!!!
WHAT IF WORLD HAS EXPLODE WHILE WE WAS DOWN HERE?!!
HMM..

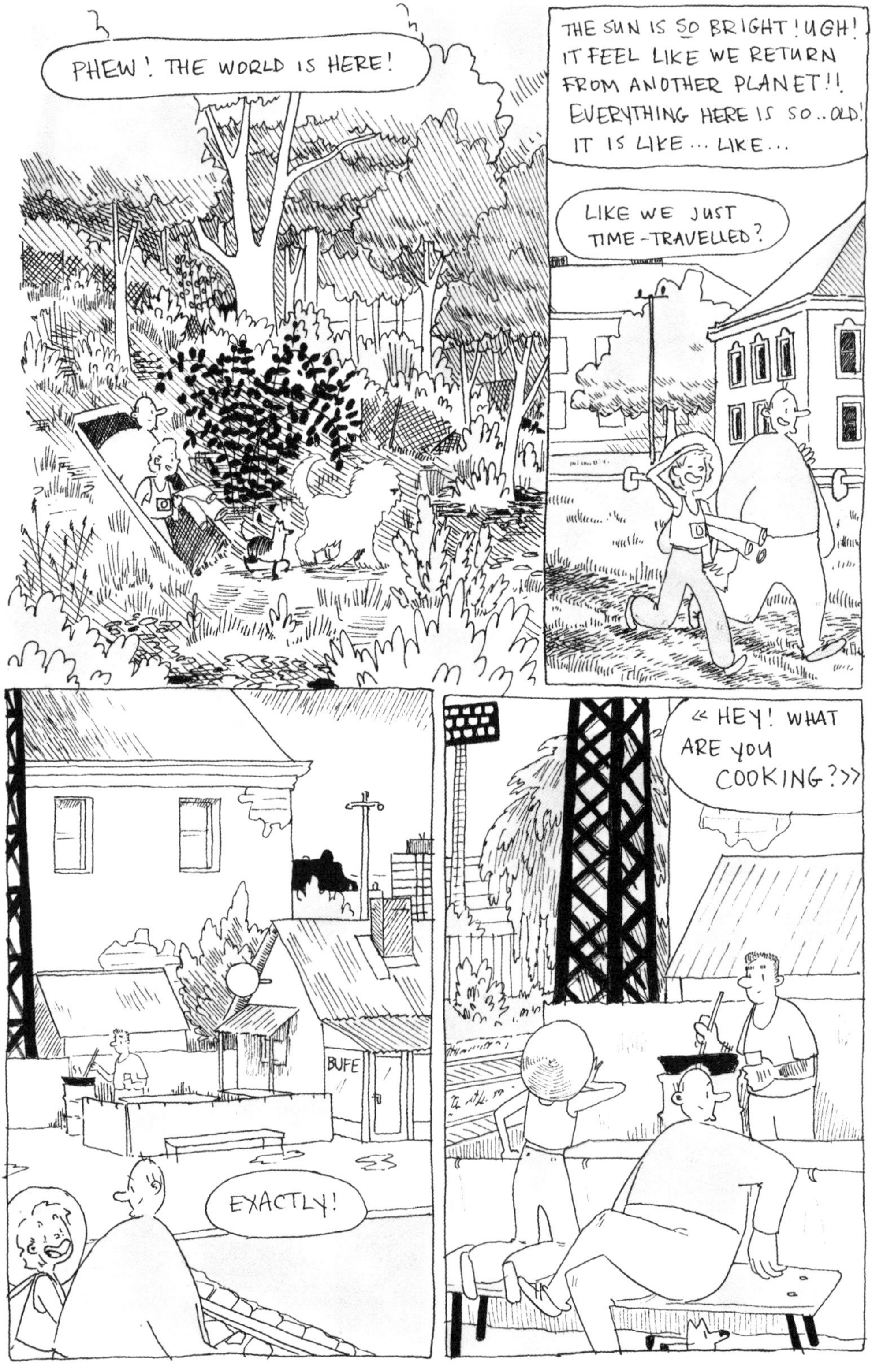
PHEW! THE WORLD IS HERE!
THE SUN IS SO BRIGHT! UGH! IT FEEL LIKE WE RETURN FROM ANOTHER PLANET!! EVERYTHING HERE IS SO..OLD! IT IS LIKE... LIKE...
LIKE WE JUST TIME-TRAVELLED?
BUFE
EXACTLY!
« HEY! WHAT ARE YOU COOKING? »

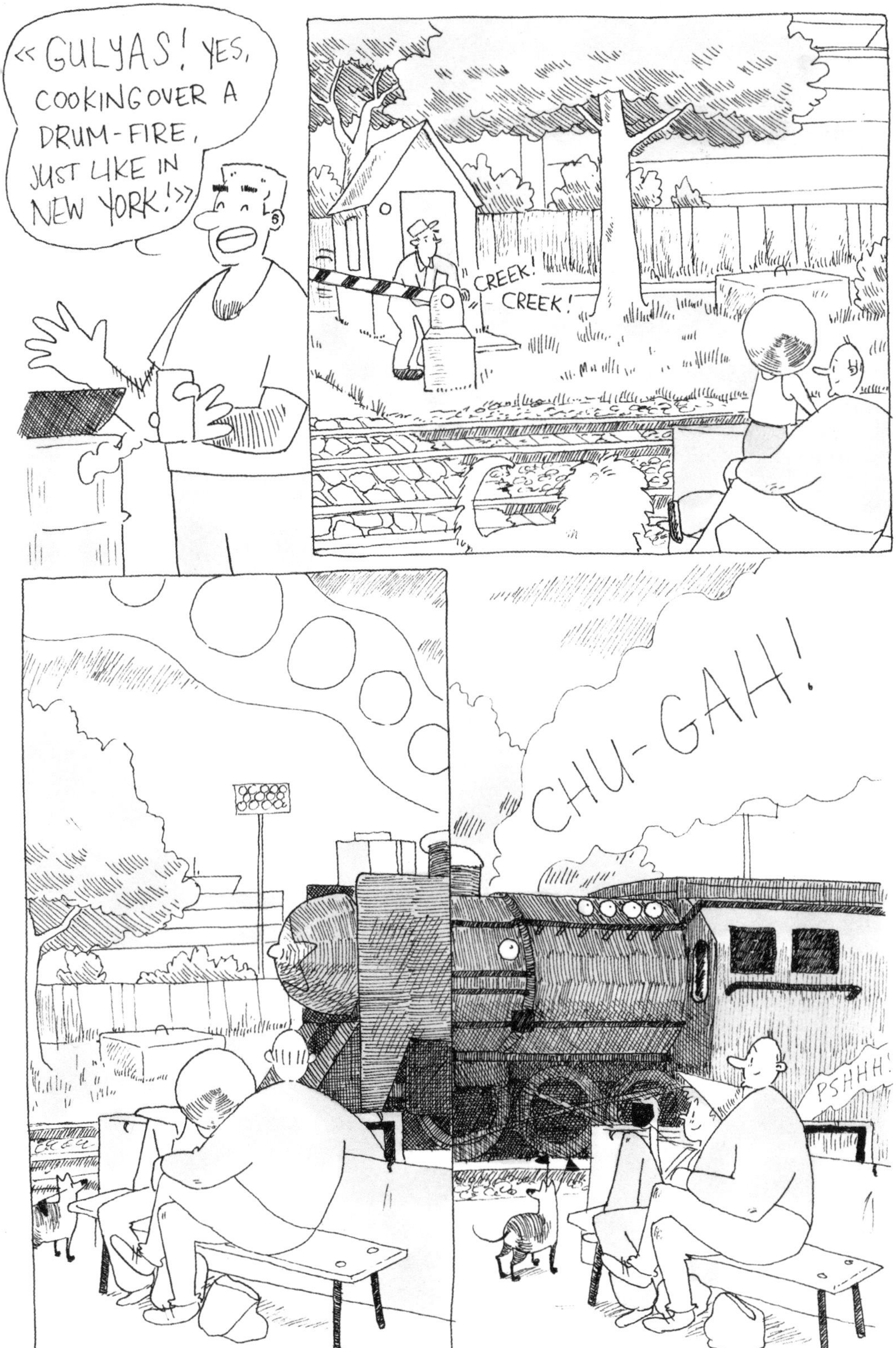
«GULYAS! YES, COOKING OVER A DRUM-FIRE, JUST LIKE IN NEW YORK!»
CREEK!
CREEK!
CHU-GAH!
PSHHH

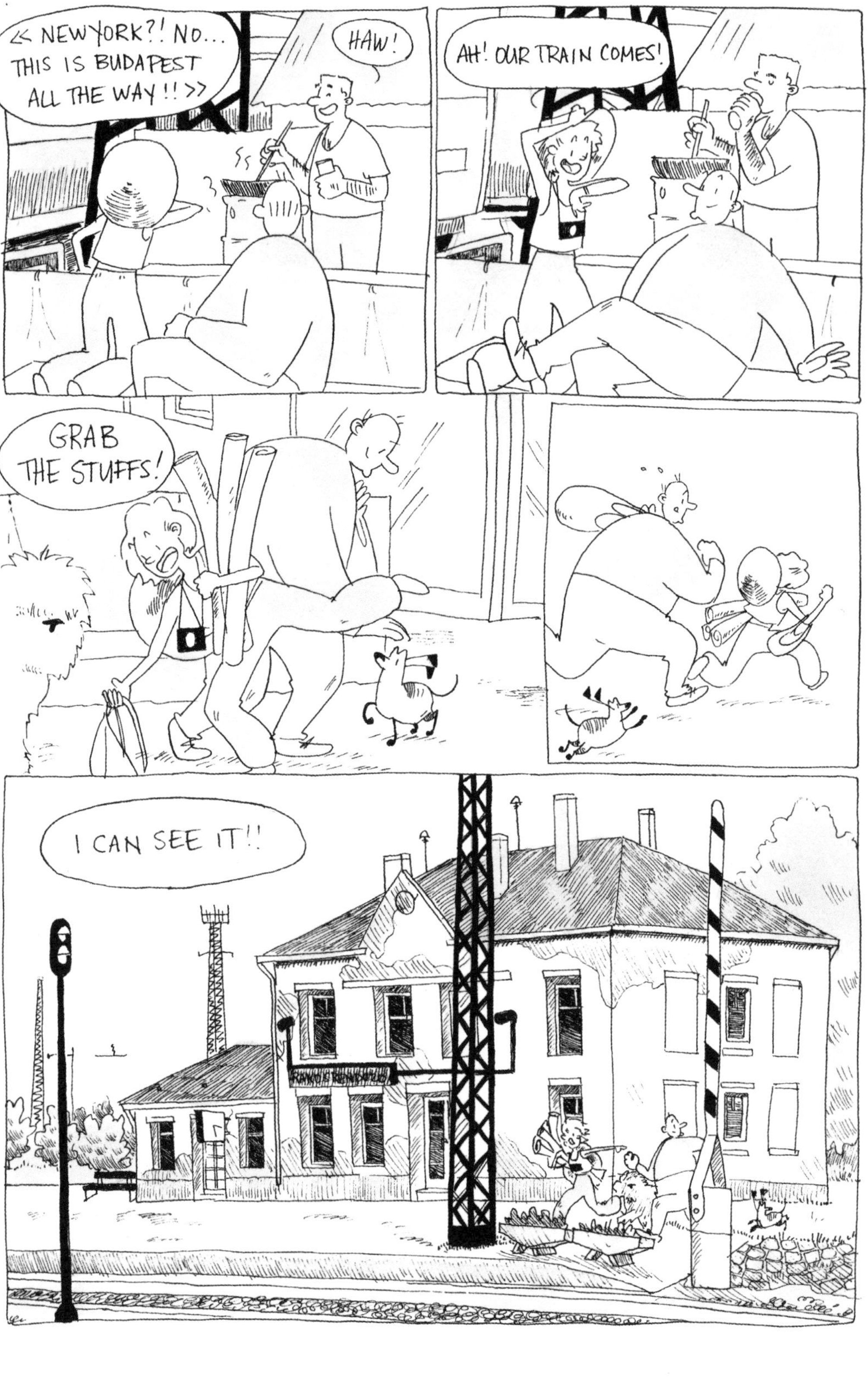
<< NEW YORK?! NO... THIS IS BUDAPEST ALL THE WAY!! >>
HAW!
AH! OUR TRAIN COMES!
GRAB THE STUFFS!
I CAN SEE IT!!

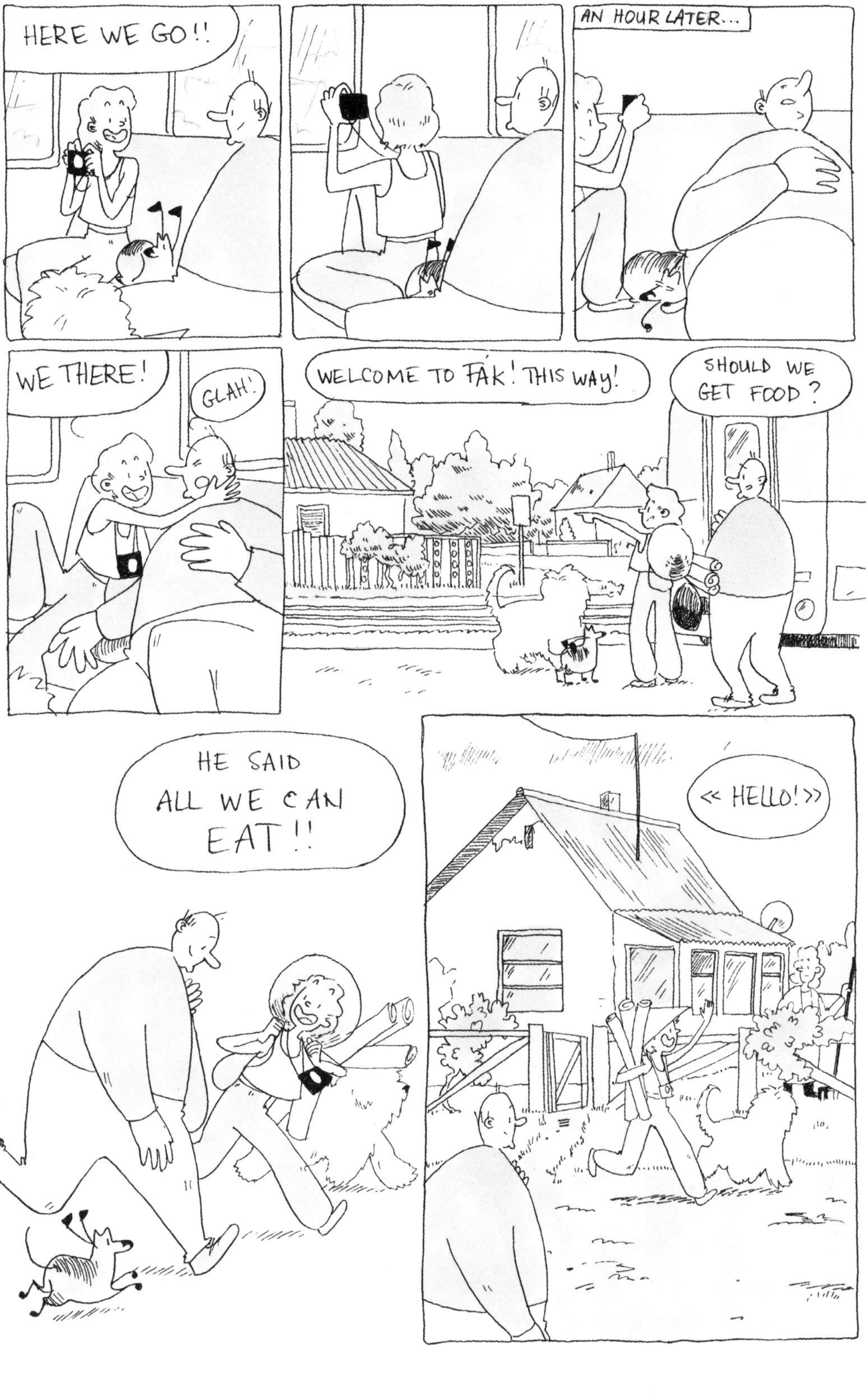
HERE WE GO!!
AN HOUR LATER...
WE THERE!
GLAH!
WELCOME TO FÁK! THIS WAY!
SHOULD WE GET FOOD?
HE SAID ALL WE CAN EAT!!
« HELLO! »

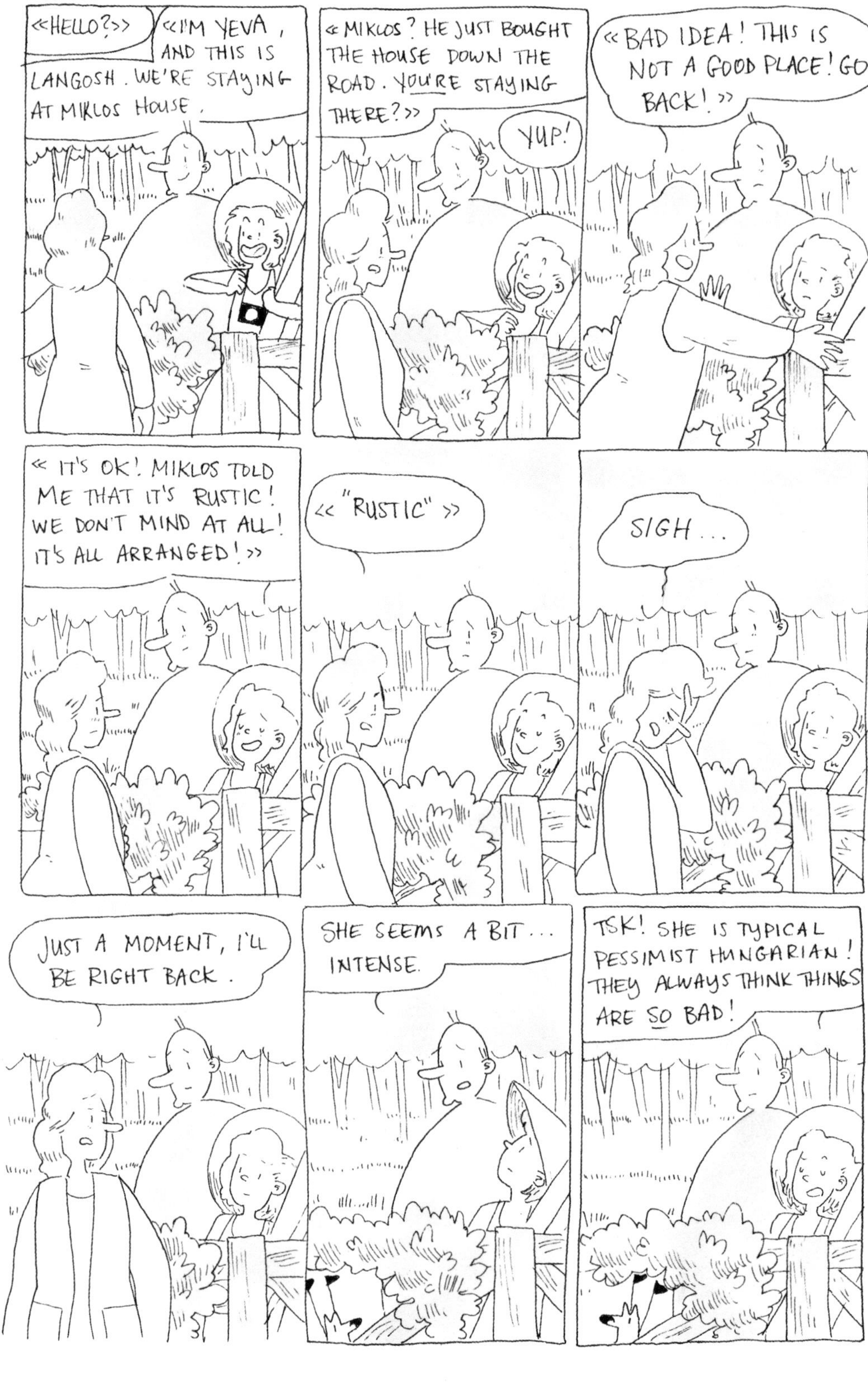
«HELLO?»
«I'M YEVA, AND THIS IS LANGOSH. WE'RE STAYING AT MIKLOS HOUSE.
«MIKLOS? HE JUST BOUGHT THE HOUSE DOWN THE ROAD. YOU'RE STAYING THERE?»
YUP!
«BAD IDEA! THIS IS NOT A GOOD PLACE! GO BACK!»
« IT'S OK! MIKLOS TOLD ME THAT IT'S RUSTIC! WE DON'T MIND AT ALL! IT'S ALL ARRANGED!»
« "RUSTIC" »
SIGH...
JUST A MOMENT, I'LL BE RIGHT BACK.
SHE SEEMS A BIT... INTENSE.
TSK! SHE IS TYPICAL PESSIMIST HUNGARIAN! THEY ALWAYS THINK THINGS ARE SO BAD!

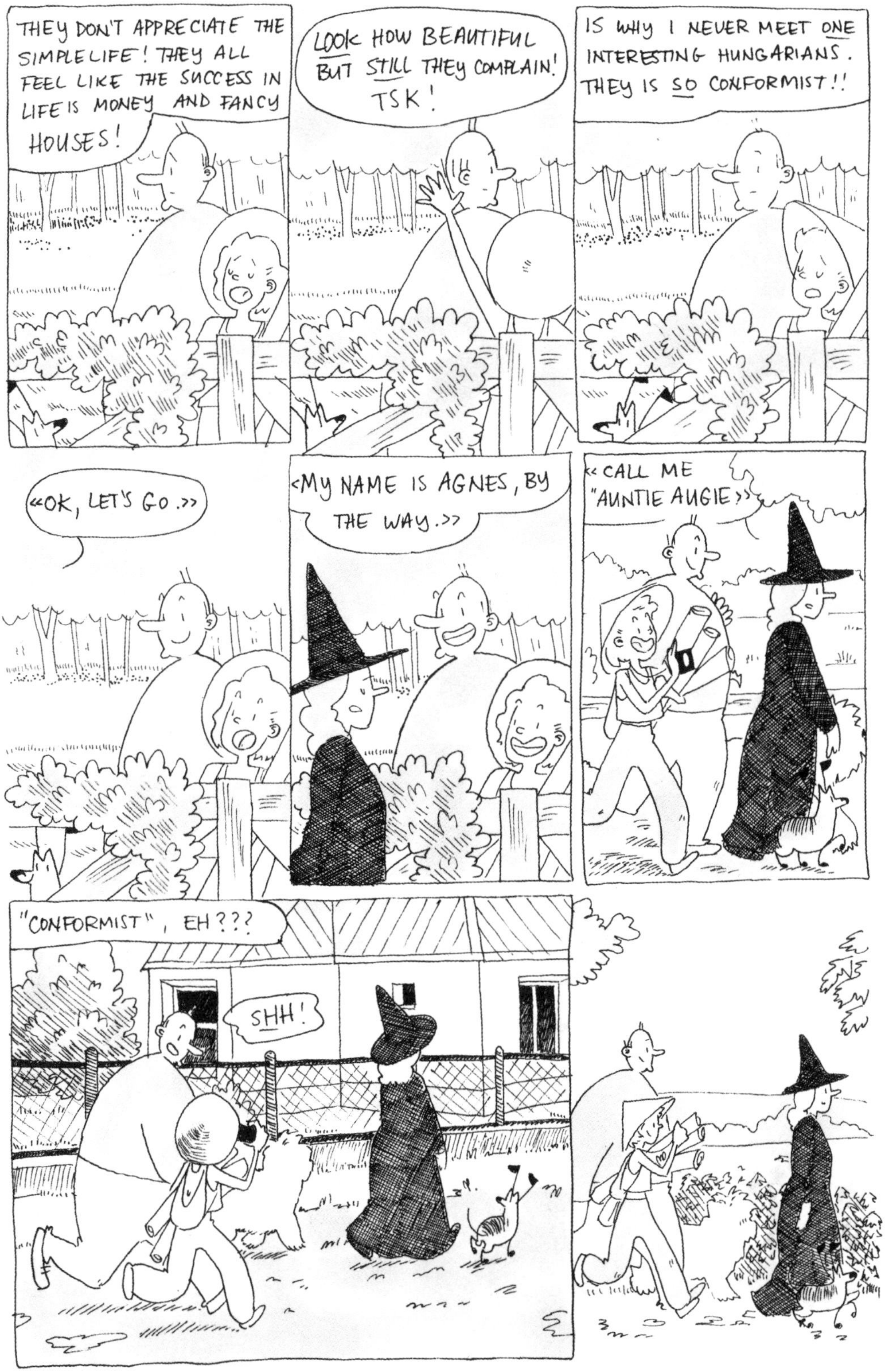
THEY DON'T APPRECIATE THE SIMPLE LIFE! THEY ALL FEEL LIKE THE SUCCESS IN LIFE IS MONEY AND FANCY HOUSES!
LOOK HOW BEAUTIFUL BUT STILL THEY COMPLAIN! TSK!
IS WHY I NEVER MEET ONE INTERESTING HUNGARIANS. THEY IS SO CONFORMIST!!
«OK, LET'S GO.»
«MY NAME IS AGNES, BY THE WAY.»
«CALL ME "AUNTIE AUGIE"»
"CONFORMIST", EH???
SHH!

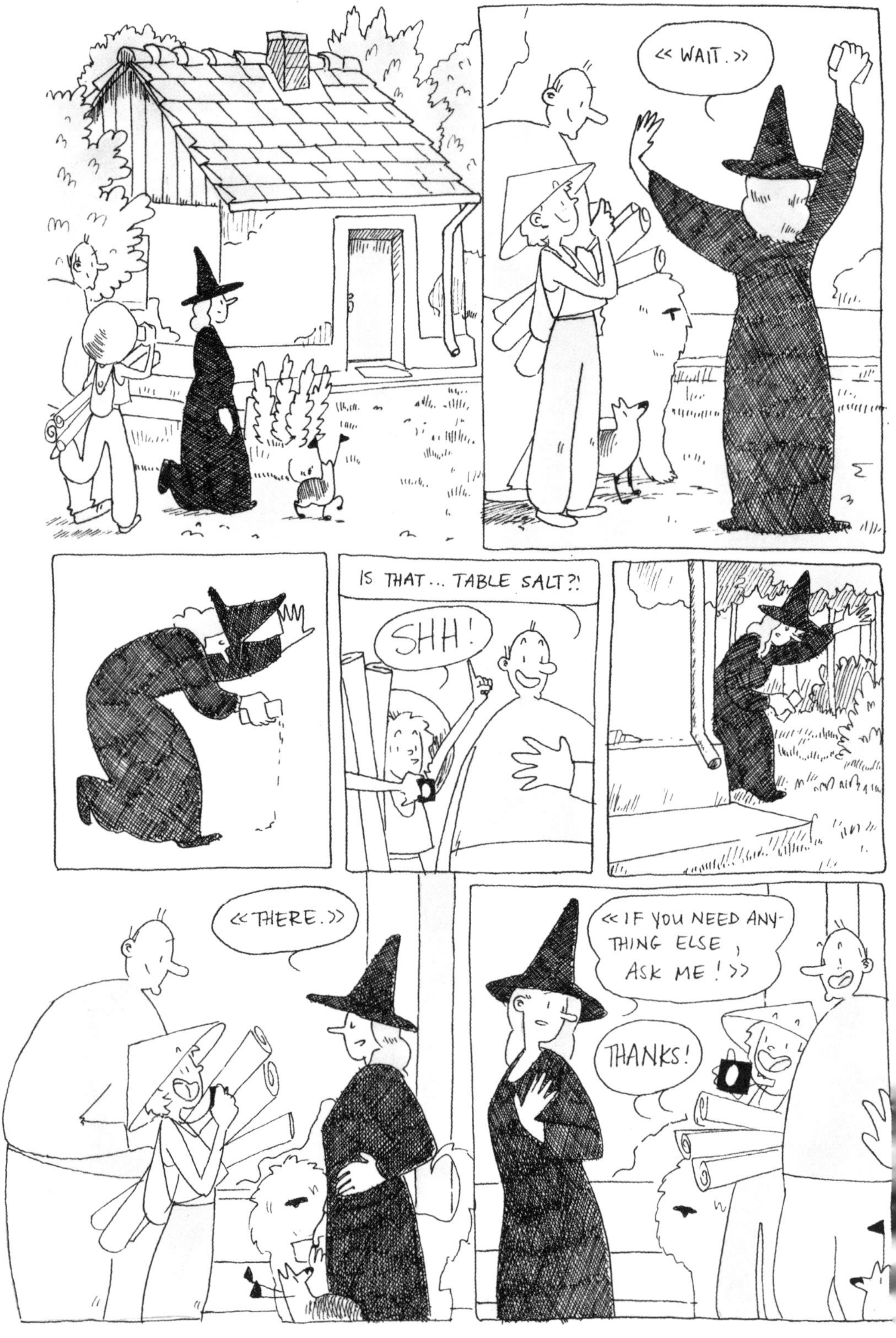

<< WAIT. >>
IS THAT... TABLE SALT?!
SHH!
<< THERE. >>
<< IF YOU NEED ANY-THING ELSE, ASK ME! >>
THANKS!

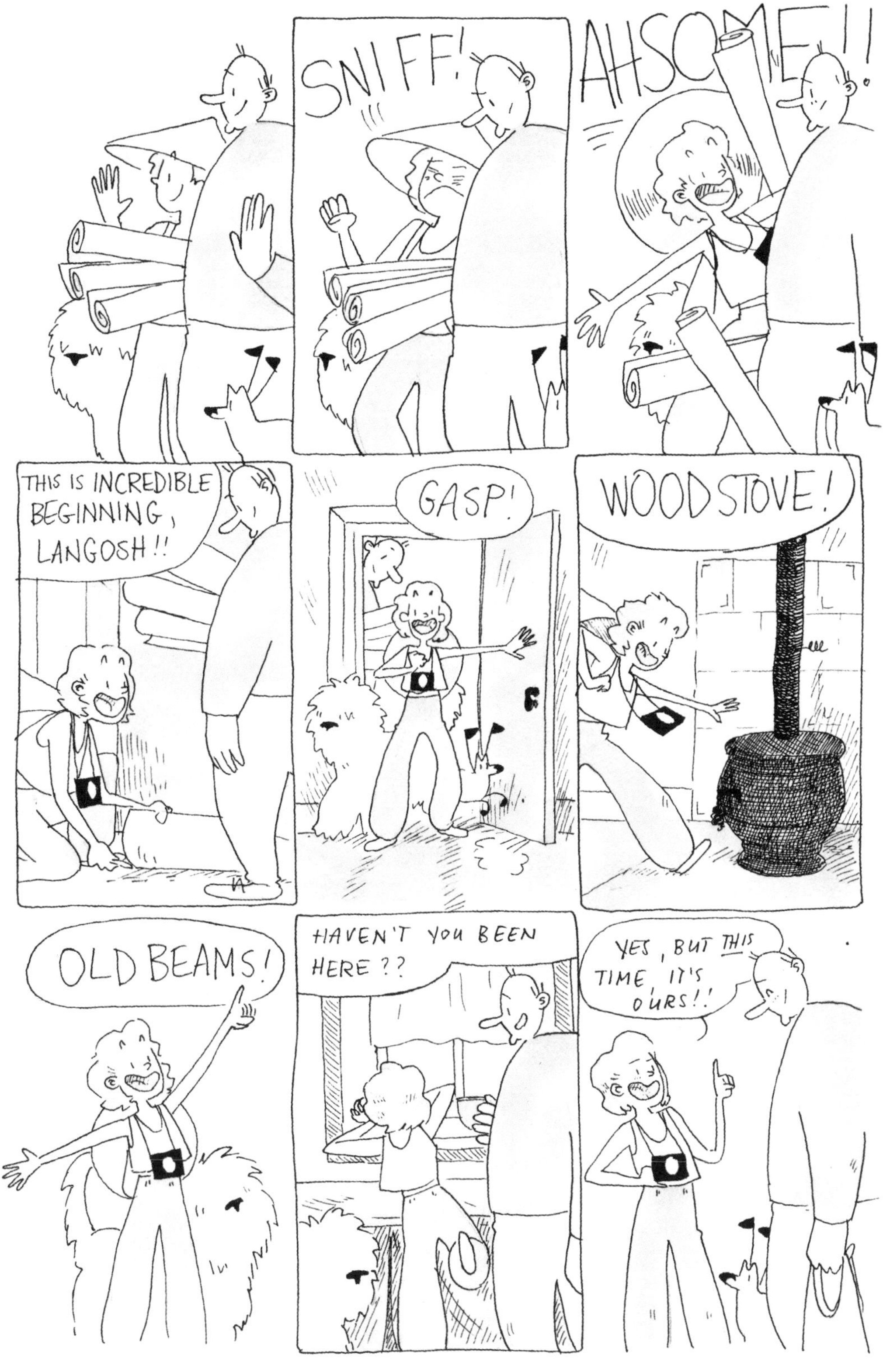
SNIFF!
AHSOME!!
THIS IS INCREDIBLE BEGINNING, LANGOSH!!
GASP!
WOODSTOVE!
OLD BEAMS!
HAVEN'T YOU BEEN HERE??
YES, BUT THIS TIME, IT'S OURS!!

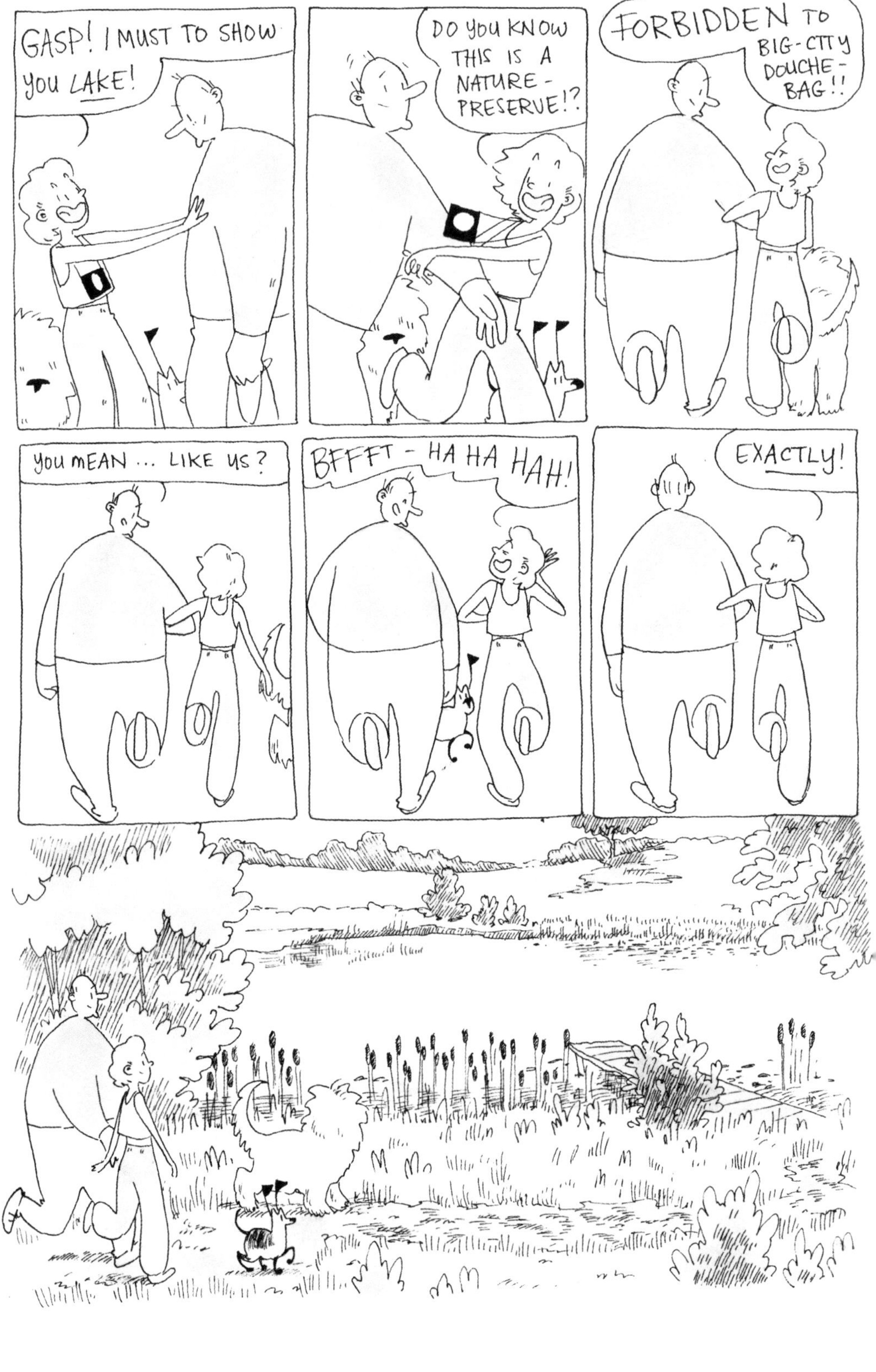
GASP! I MUST TO SHOW YOU LAKE!
DO YOU KNOW THIS IS A NATURE-PRESERVE!?
FORBIDDEN TO BIG-CITY DOUCHE-BAG!!
YOU MEAN ... LIKE US?
BFFFT-HA HA HAH!
EXACTLY!

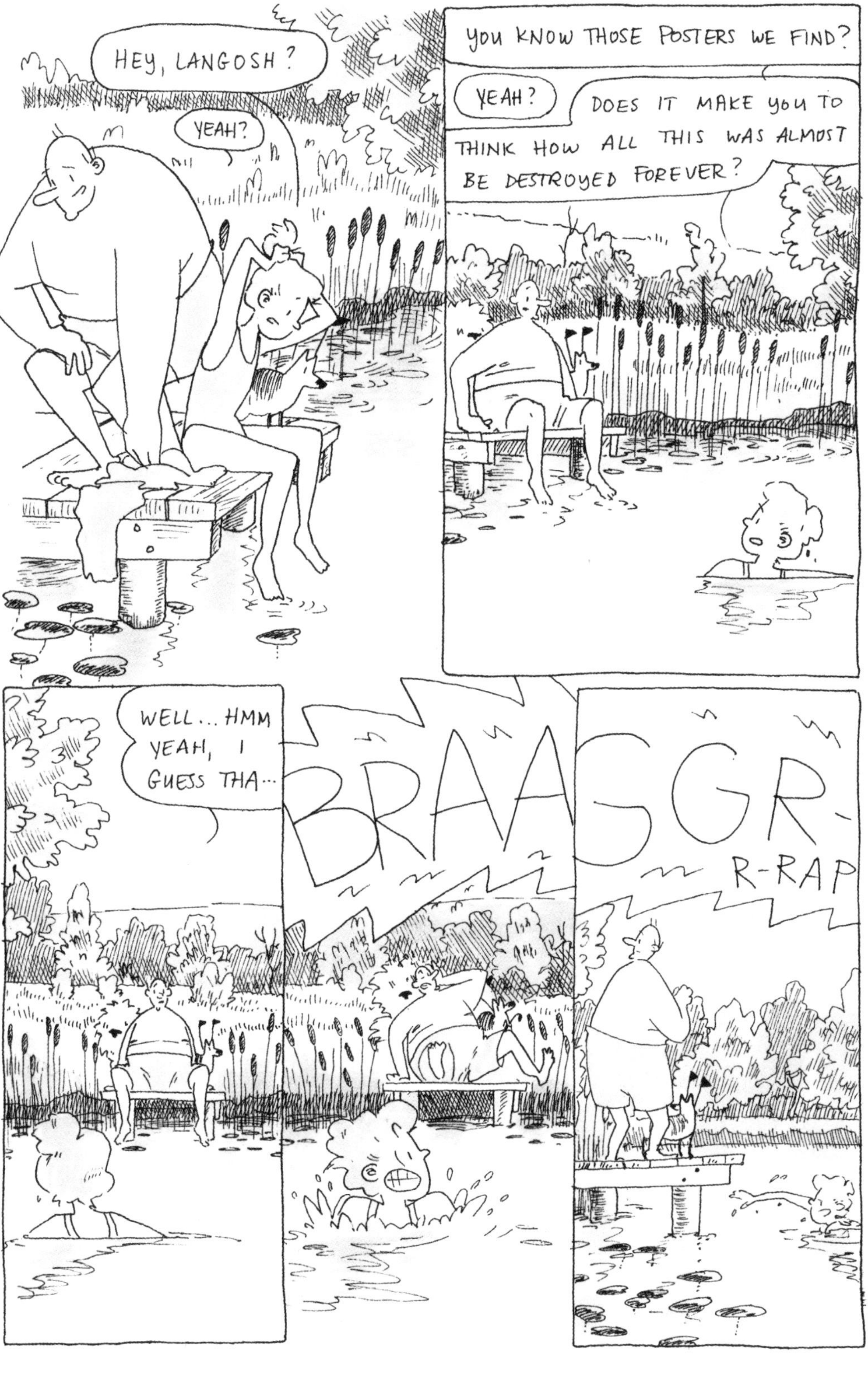
HEY, LANGOSH?
YEAH?
YOU KNOW THOSE POSTERS WE FIND?
YEAH?
DOES IT MAKE YOU TO THINK HOW ALL THIS WAS ALMOST BE DESTROYED FOREVER?
WELL... HMM YEAH, I GUESS THA...
BRAAAGGR-
R-RAP

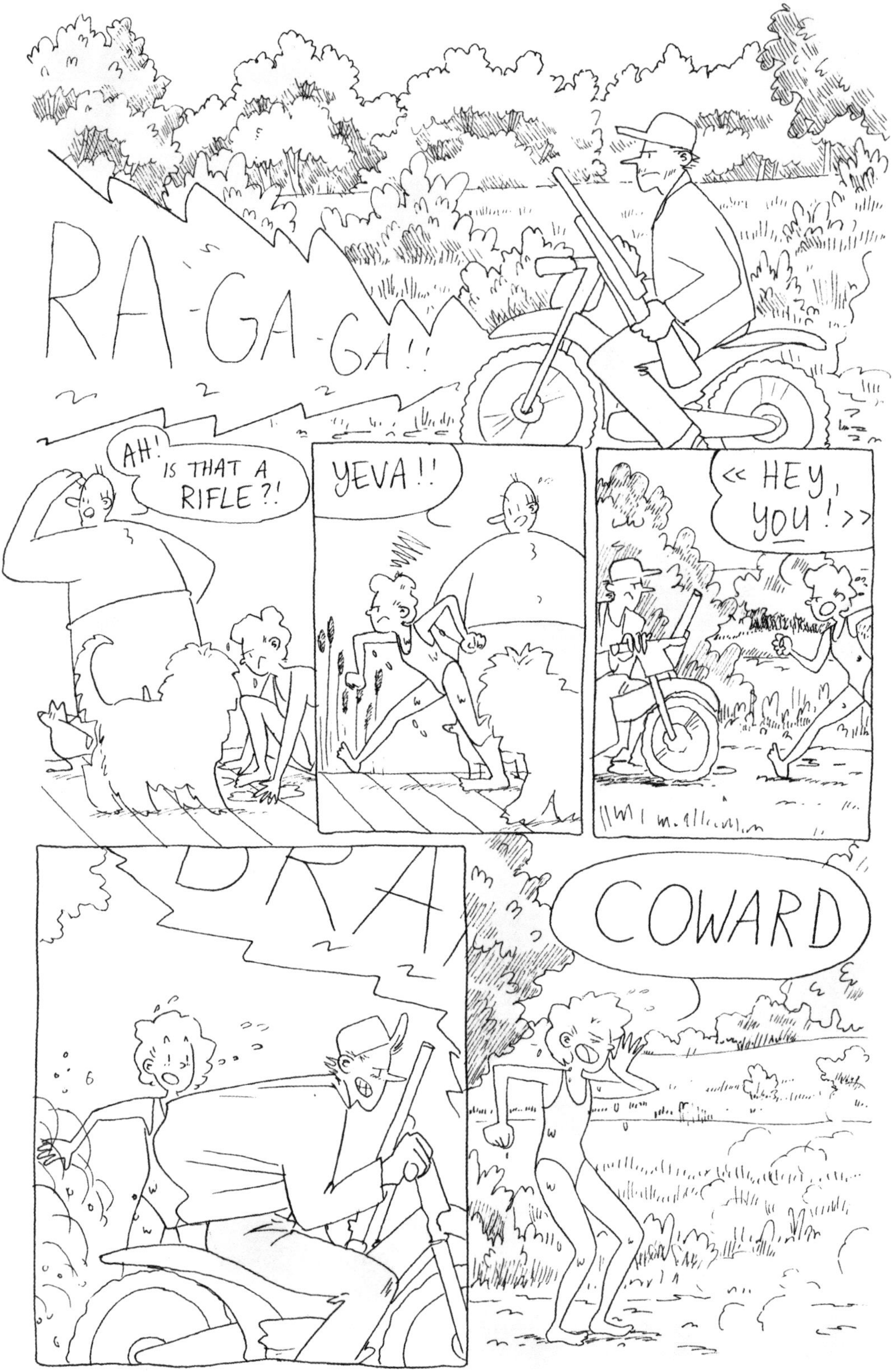
RA-GA-GA!!
AH! IS THAT A RIFLE?!
YEVA!!
« HEY, YOU! »
COWARD

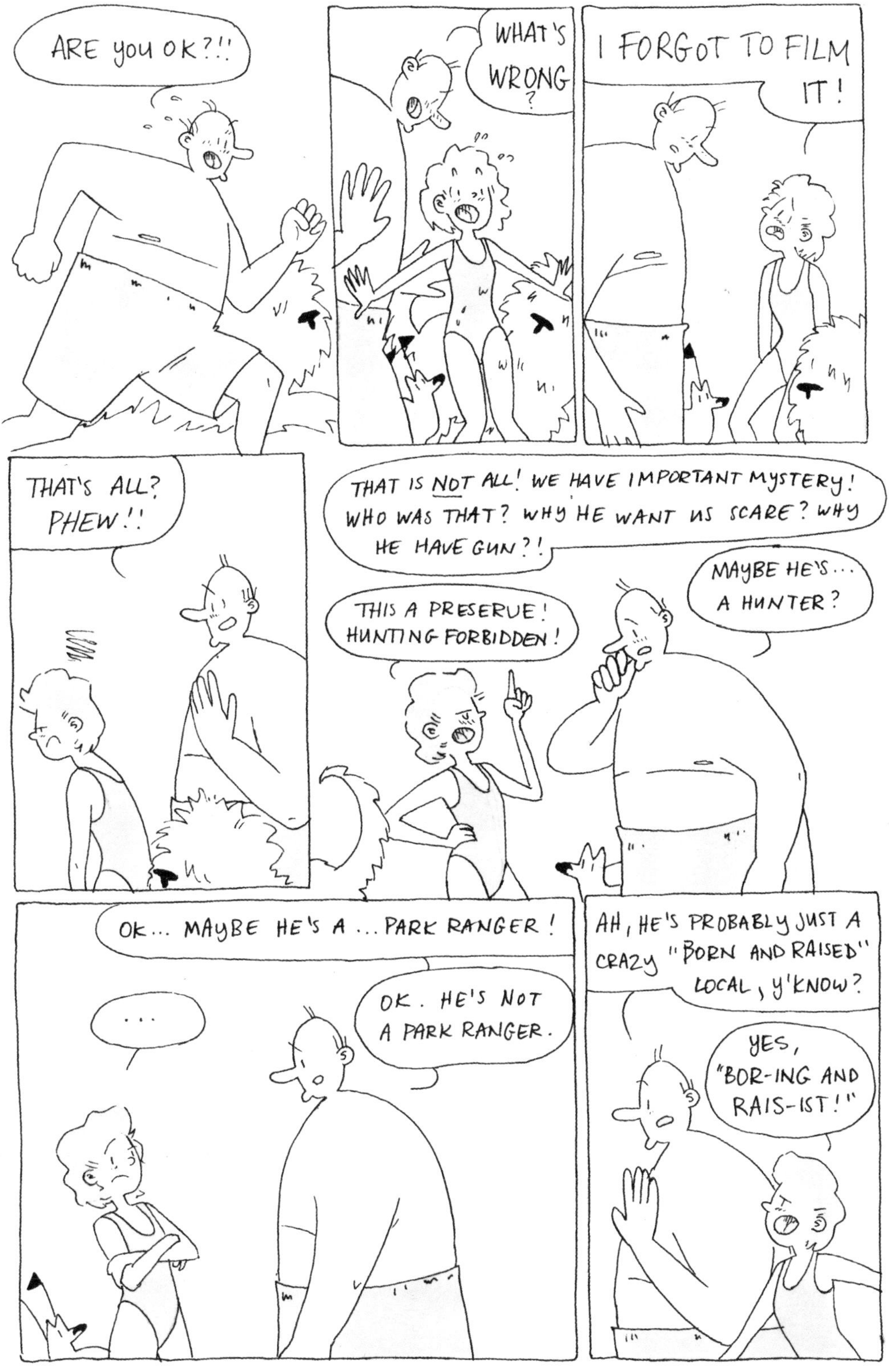
ARE YOU OK?!!
WHAT'S WRONG?
I FORGOT TO FILM IT!
THAT'S ALL? PHEW!!
THAT IS NOT ALL! WE HAVE IMPORTANT MYSTERY! WHO WAS THAT? WHY HE WANT US SCARE? WHY HE HAVE GUN?!
MAYBE HE'S... A HUNTER?
THIS A PRESERVE! HUNTING FORBIDDEN!
OK... MAYBE HE'S A ... PARK RANGER!
...
OK. HE'S NOT A PARK RANGER.
AH, HE'S PROBABLY JUST A CRAZY "BORN AND RAISED" LOCAL, Y'KNOW?
YES, "BOR-ING AND RAIS-IST!"

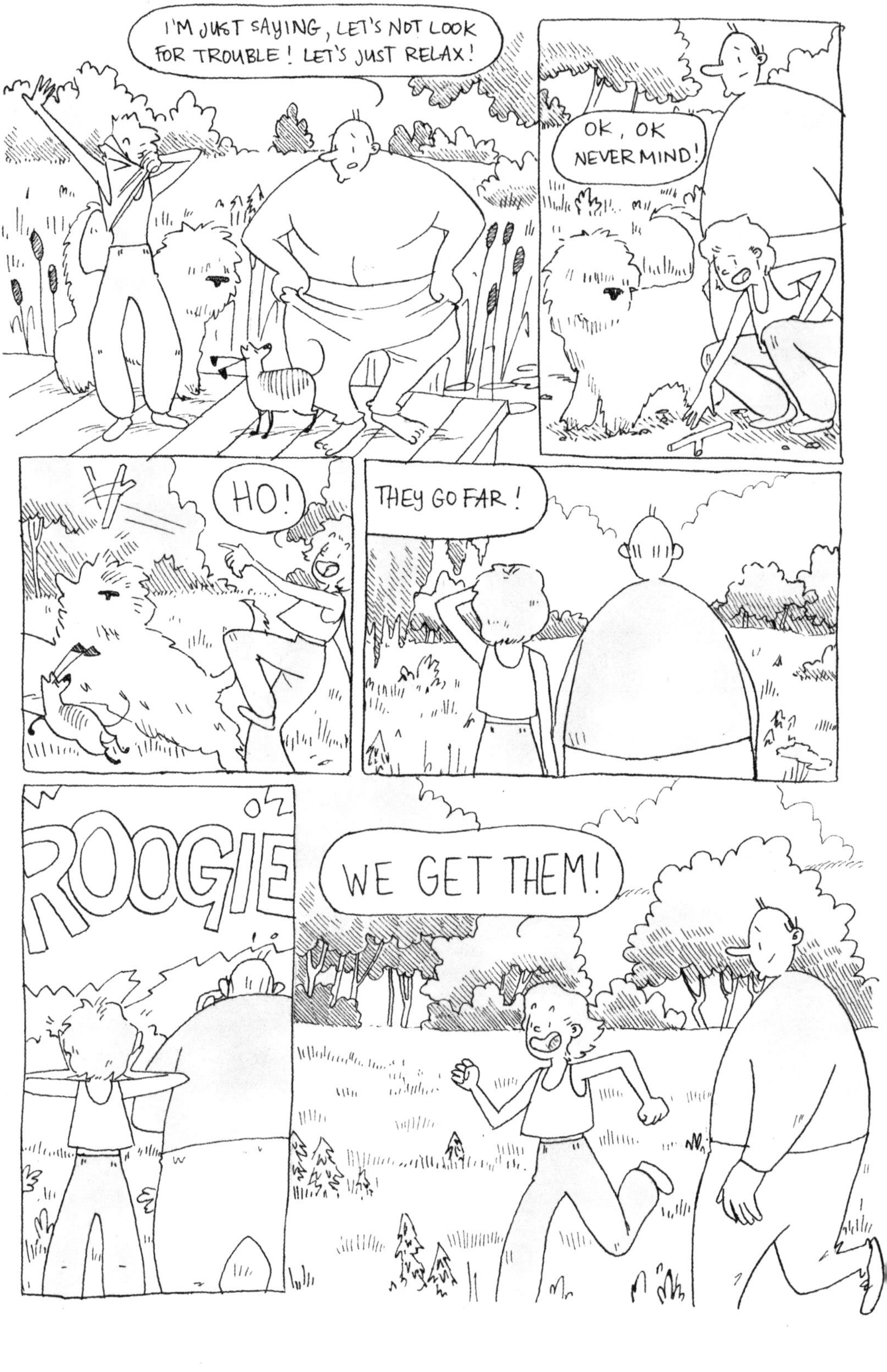
I'M JUST SAYING, LET'S NOT LOOK FOR TROUBLE! LET'S JUST RELAX!
OK, OK NEVERMIND!
HO!
THEY GO FAR!
ROOGIE
WE GET THEM!

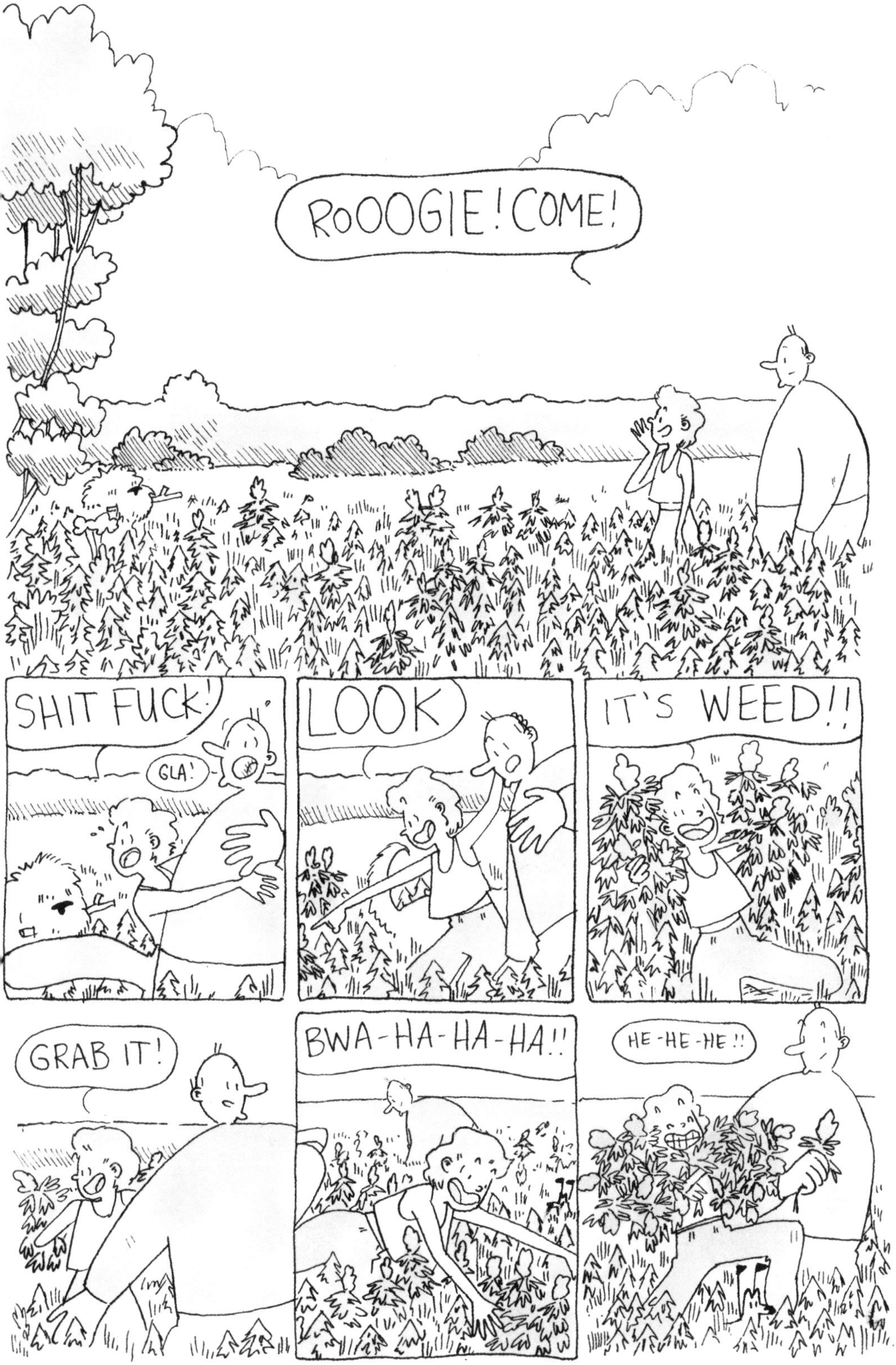
ROOOGIE! COME!
SHIT FUCK!
GLA!
LOOK
IT'S WEED!!
GRAB IT!
BWA-HA-HA-HA!!
HE-HE-HE!!

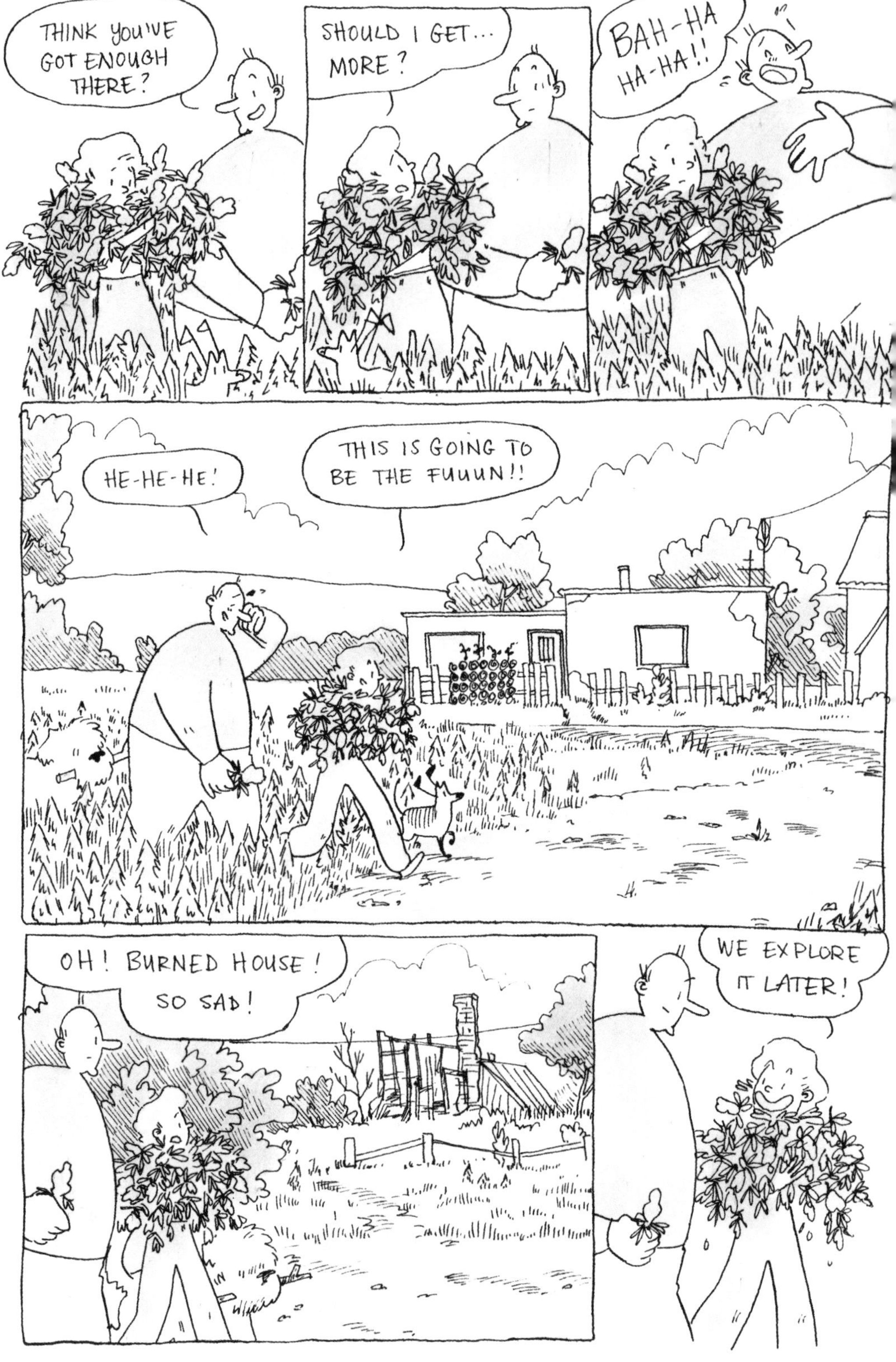
THINK YOU'VE GOT ENOUGH THERE?
SHOULD I GET... MORE?
BAH-HA HA-HA!!
HE-HE-HE!
THIS IS GOING TO BE THE FUUUN!!
OH! BURNED HOUSE! SO SAD!
WE EXPLORE IT LATER!

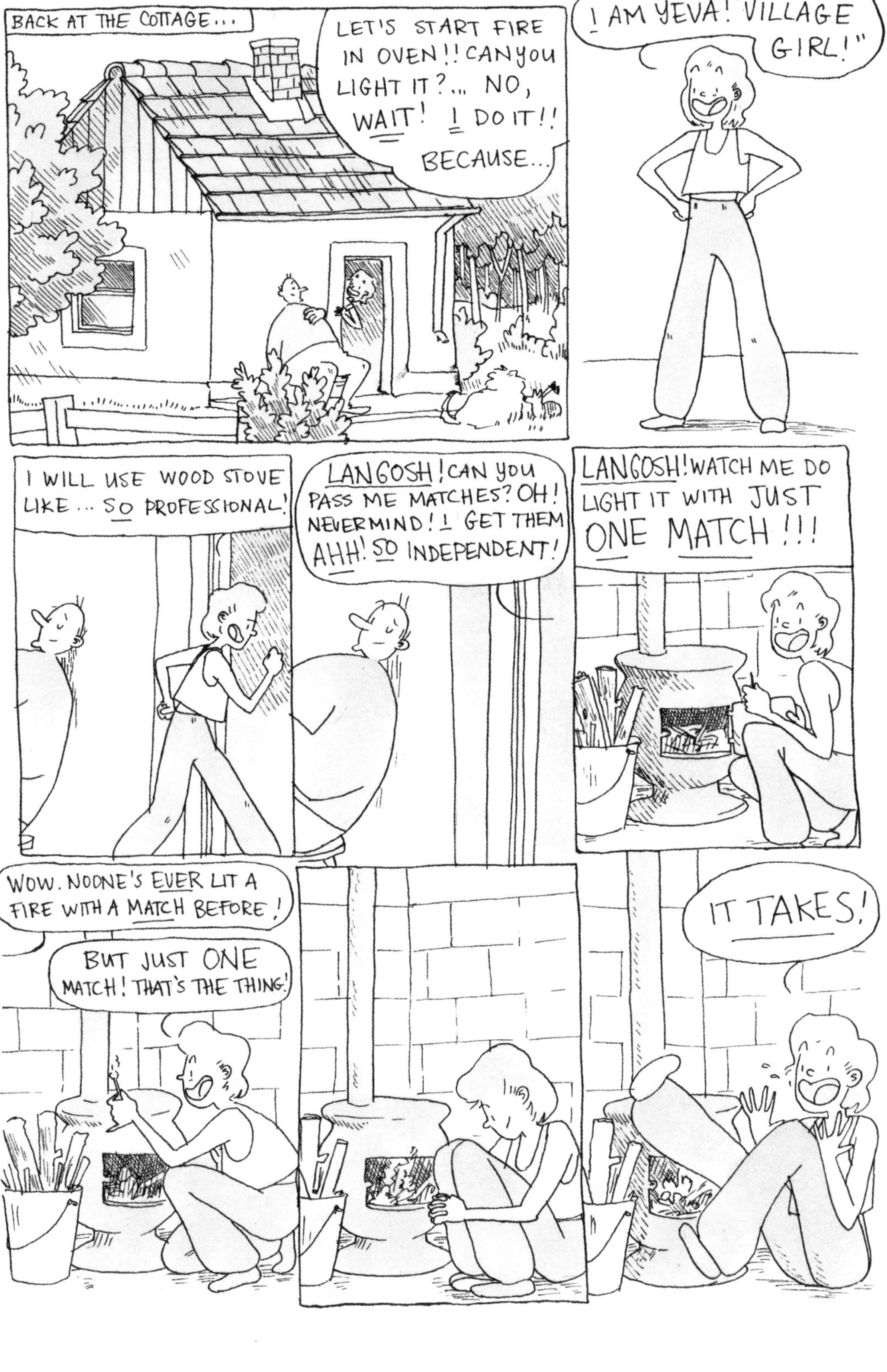
BACK AT THE COTTAGE...
LET'S START FIRE IN OVEN!! CAN YOU LIGHT IT?... NO, WAIT! I DO IT!! BECAUSE...
I AM YEVA! "VILLAGE GIRL!"
I WILL USE WOOD STOVE LIKE... SO PROFESSIONAL!
LANGOSH! CAN YOU PASS ME MATCHES? OH! NEVERMIND! I GET THEM AHH! SO INDEPENDENT!
LANGOSH! WATCH ME DO LIGHT IT WITH JUST ONE MATCH!!!
WOW. NOONE'S EVER LIT A FIRE WITH A MATCH BEFORE!
BUT JUST ONE MATCH! THAT'S THE THING!
IT TAKES!

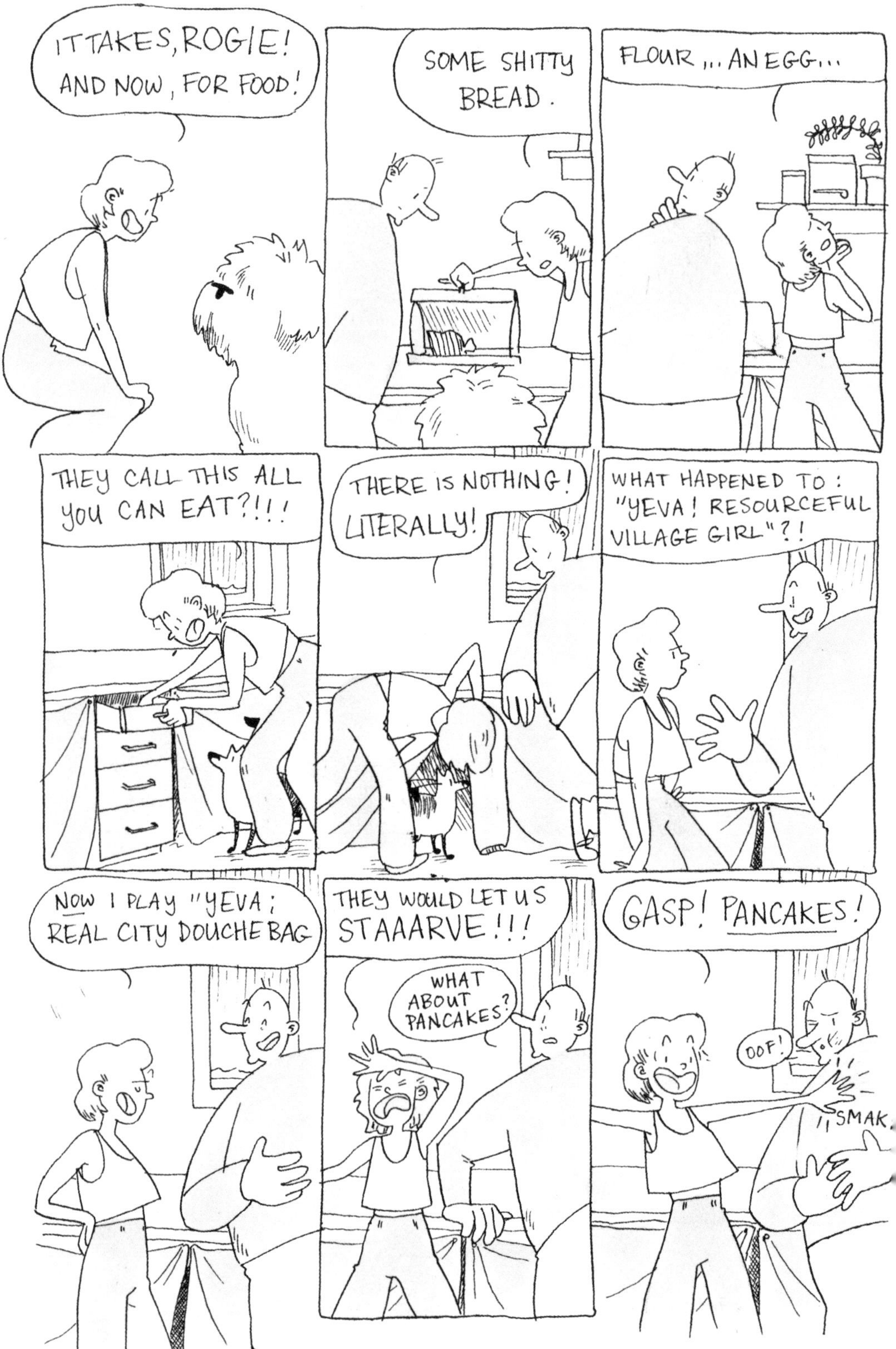

IT TAKES, ROGIE! AND NOW, FOR FOOD!
SOME SHITTY BREAD.
FLOUR ... AN EGG...
THEY CALL THIS ALL YOU CAN EAT?!!!
THERE IS NOTHING! LITERALLY!
WHAT HAPPENED TO: "YEVA! RESOURCEFUL VILLAGE GIRL"?!
NOW I PLAY "YEVA; REAL CITY DOUCHEBAG
THEY WOULD LET US STAAARVE!!!
WHAT ABOUT PANCAKES?
GASP! PANCAKES!
OOF!
SMAK

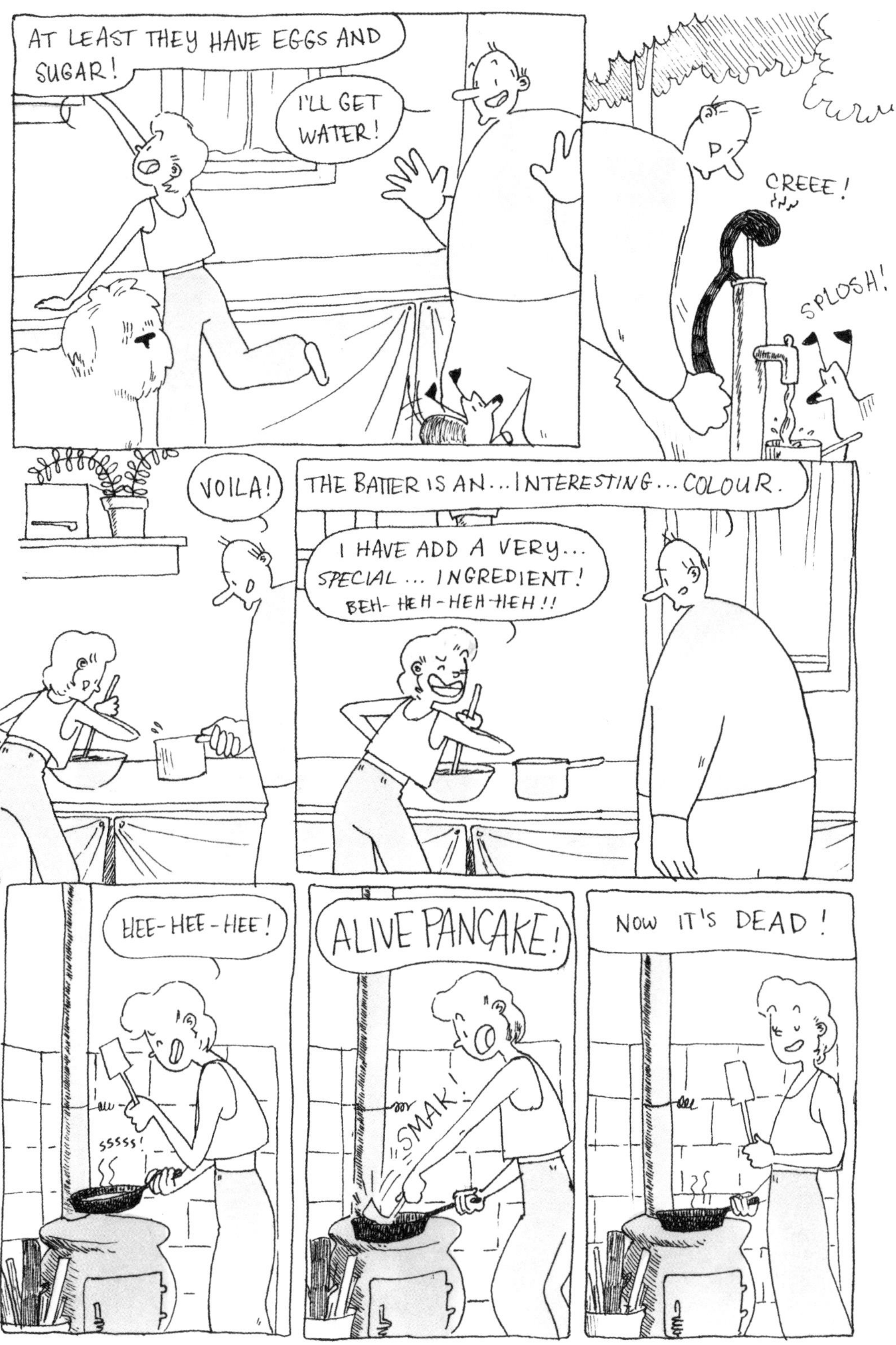
AT LEAST THEY HAVE EGGS AND SUGAR!
I'LL GET WATER!
CREEE!
SPLOSH!
VOILA!
THE BATTER IS AN... INTERESTING... COLOUR.
I HAVE ADD A VERY... SPECIAL... INGREDIENT! BEH-HEH-HEH-HEH!!
HEE-HEE-HEE!
sssss!
ALIVE PANCAKE!
SMAK!
NOW IT'S DEAD!

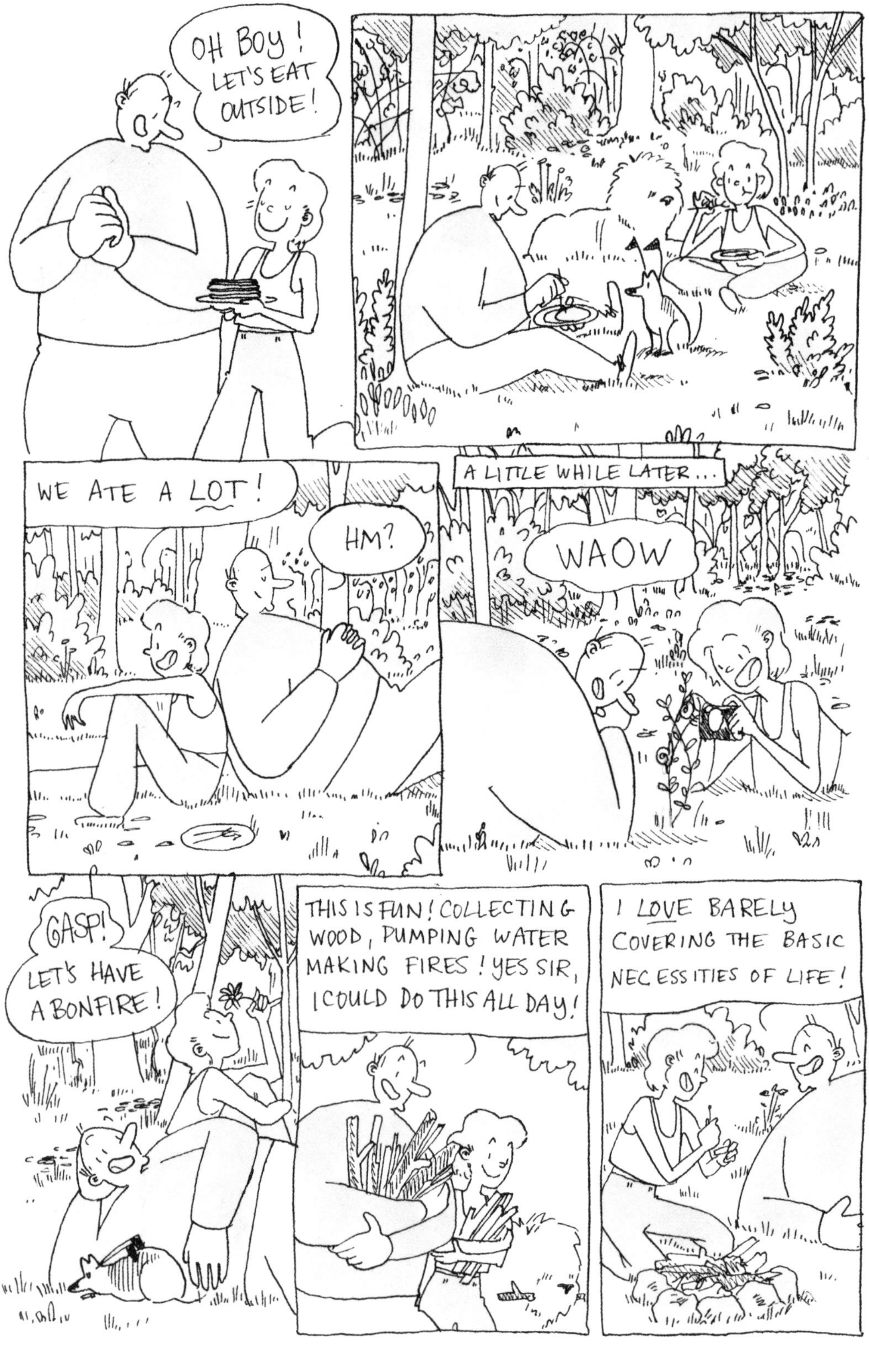
OH BOY! LET'S EAT OUTSIDE!
WE ATE A LOT!
HM?
A LITTLE WHILE LATER...
WAOW
GASP! LET'S HAVE A BONFIRE!
THIS IS FUN! COLLECTING WOOD, PUMPING WATER MAKING FIRES! YES SIR, I COULD DO THIS ALL DAY!
I LOVE BARELY COVERING THE BASIC NECESSITIES OF LIFE!

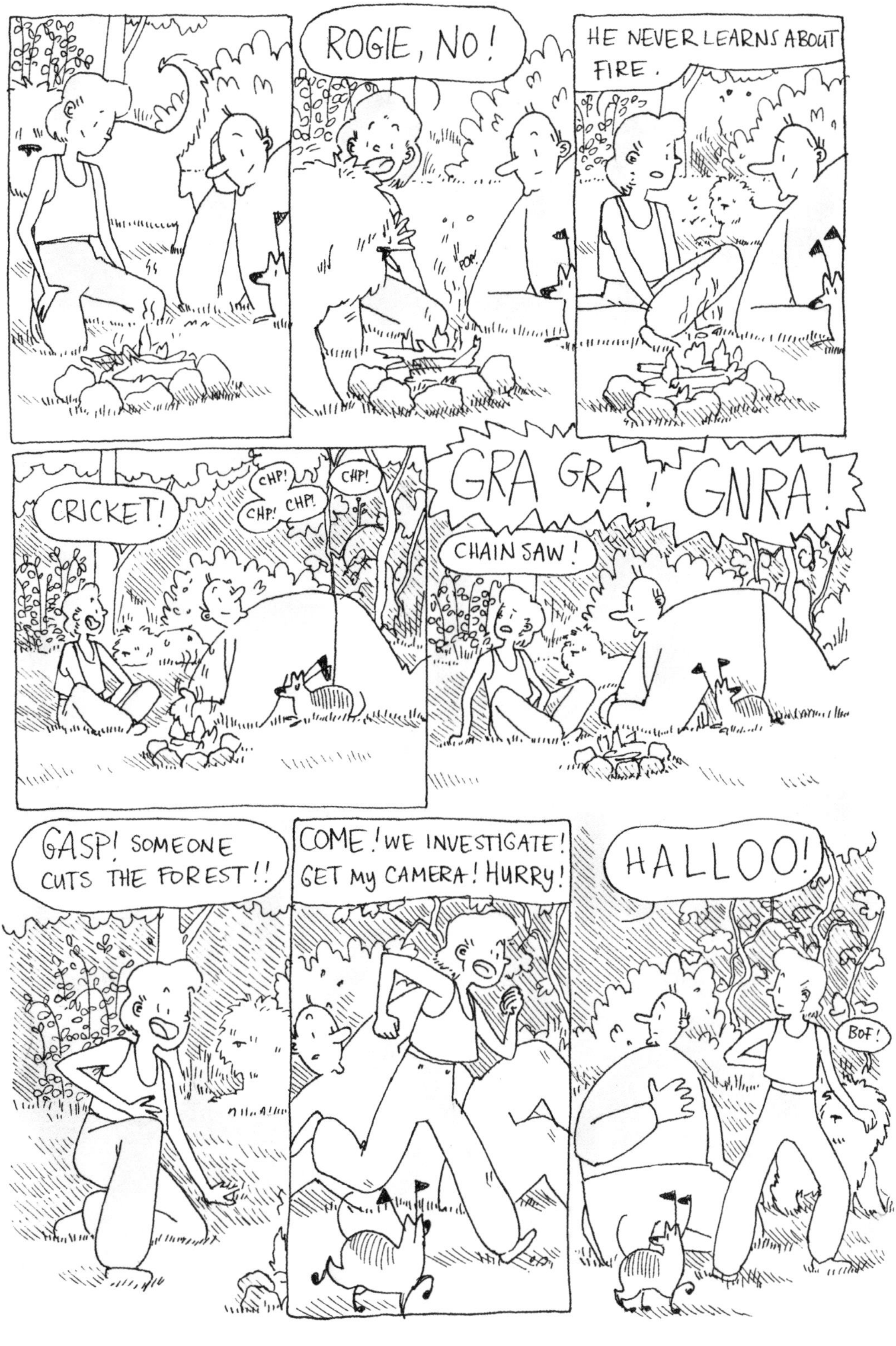
ROGIE, NO!
POP!
HE NEVER LEARNS ABOUT FIRE.
CRICKET!
CHP!
CHP!
CHP!
CHP!
GRA GRA! GNRA!
CHAINSAW!
GASP! SOMEONE CUTS THE FOREST!!
COME! WE INVESTIGATE! GET MY CAMERA! HURRY!
HALLOO!
BOF!

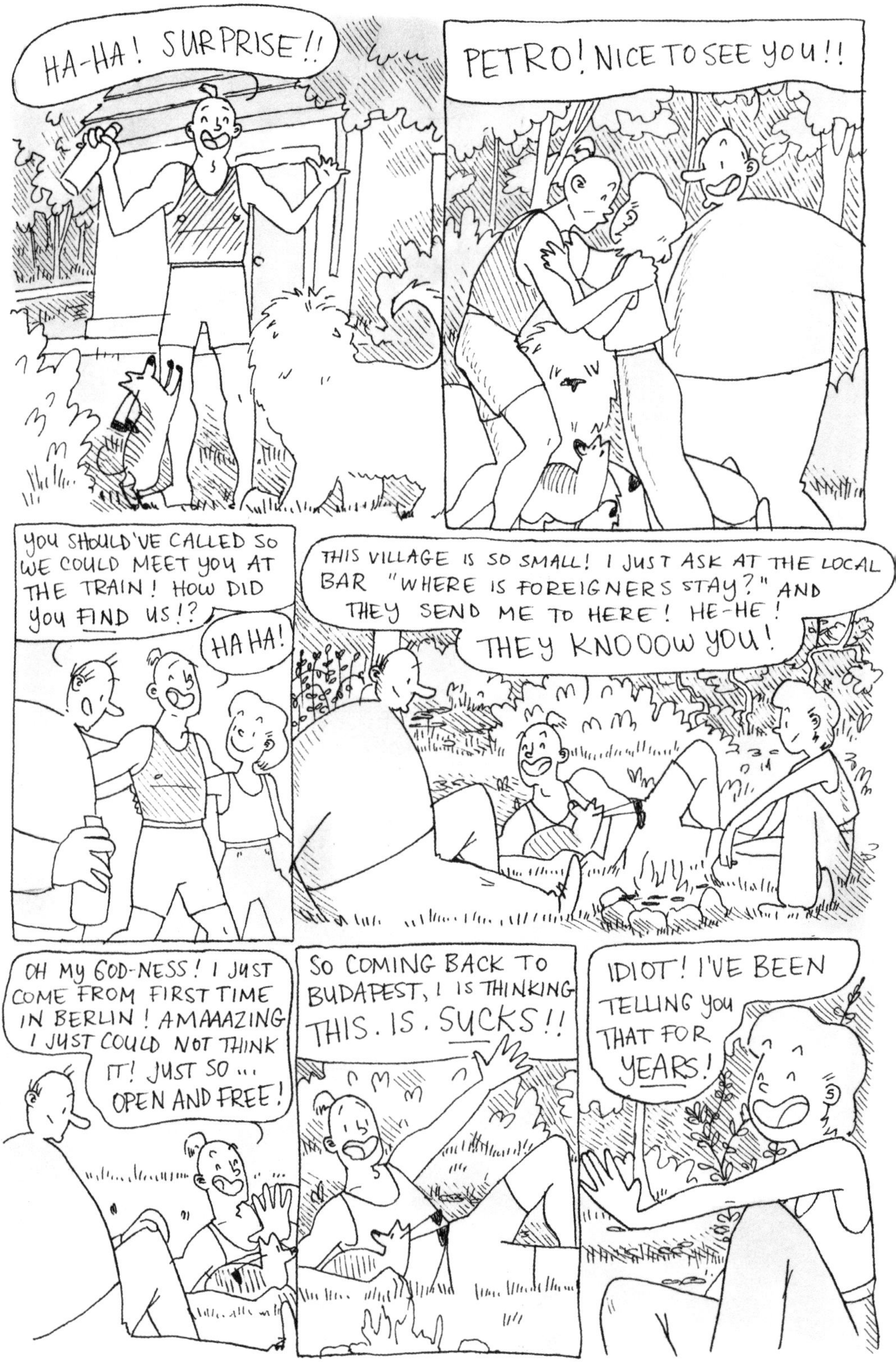

HA-HA! SURPRISE!!
PETRO! NICE TO SEE YOU!!
YOU SHOULD'VE CALLED SO WE COULD MEET YOU AT THE TRAIN! HOW DID YOU FIND US!?
HA HA!
THIS VILLAGE IS SO SMALL! I JUST ASK AT THE LOCAL BAR "WHERE IS FOREIGNERS STAY?" AND THEY SEND ME TO HERE! HE-HE! THEY KNOOOW YOU!
OH MY GOD-NESS! I JUST COME FROM FIRST TIME IN BERLIN! AMAAAZING I JUST COULD NOT THINK IT! JUST SO... OPEN AND FREE!
SO COMING BACK TO BUDAPEST, I IS THINKING THIS. IS. SUCKS!!
IDIOT! I'VE BEEN TELLING YOU THAT FOR YEARS!

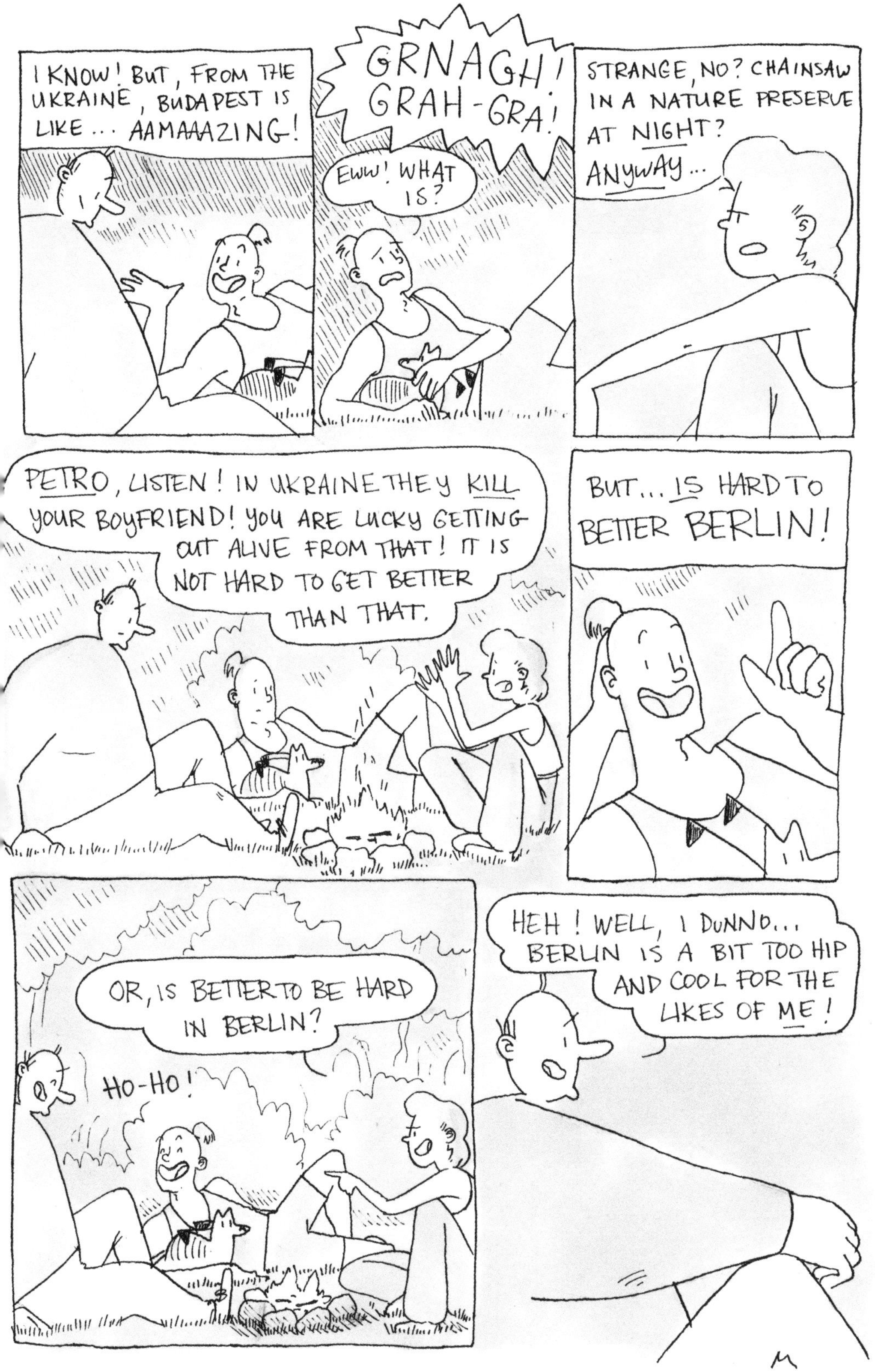

I KNOW! BUT, FROM THE UKRAINE, BUDAPEST IS LIKE... AAMAAAZING!
GRNAGH! GRAH-GRA!
EWW! WHAT IS?
STRANGE, NO? CHAINSAW IN A NATURE PRESERVE AT NIGHT? ANYWAY...
PETRO, LISTEN! IN UKRAINE THEY KILL YOUR BOYFRIEND! YOU ARE LUCKY GETTING OUT ALIVE FROM THAT! IT IS NOT HARD TO GET BETTER THAN THAT.
BUT... IS HARD TO BETTER BERLIN!
OR, IS BETTER TO BE HARD IN BERLIN?
HO-HO!
HEH! WELL, I DUNNO... BERLIN IS A BIT TOO HIP AND COOL FOR THE LIKES OF ME!

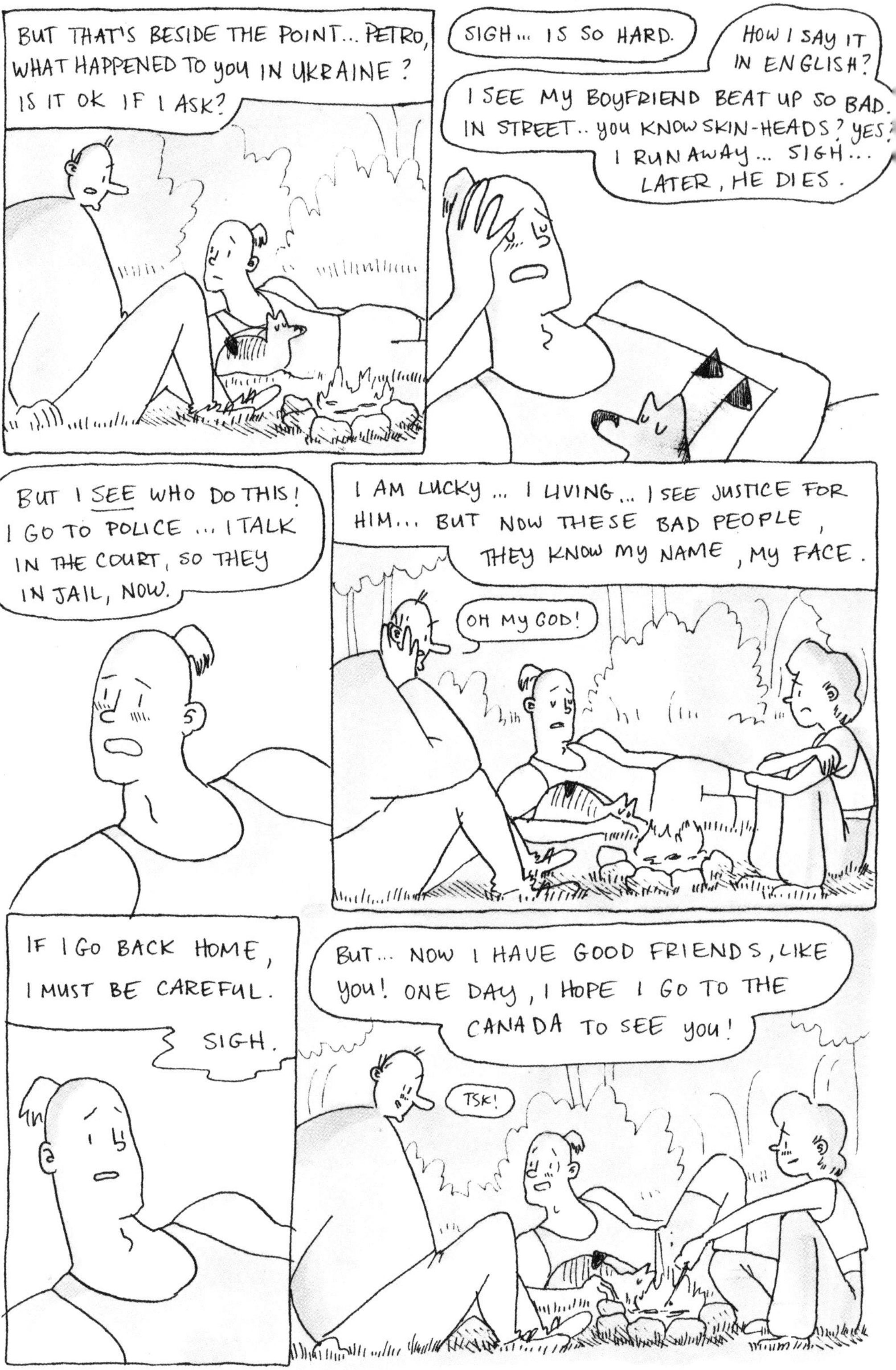

BUT THAT'S BESIDE THE POINT... PETRO, WHAT HAPPENED TO YOU IN UKRAINE? IS IT OK IF I ASK?
SIGH... IS SO HARD.
HOW I SAY IT IN ENGLISH?
I SEE MY BOYFRIEND BEAT UP SO BAD. IN STREET.. YOU KNOW SKIN-HEADS? YES? I RUN AWAY... SIGH... LATER, HE DIES.
BUT I SEE WHO DO THIS! I GO TO POLICE ... I TALK IN THE COURT, SO THEY IN JAIL, NOW.
I AM LUCKY ... I LIVING... I SEE JUSTICE FOR HIM... BUT NOW THESE BAD PEOPLE, THEY KNOW MY NAME, MY FACE.
OH MY GOD!
IF I GO BACK HOME, I MUST BE CAREFUL.
SIGH.
BUT... NOW I HAVE GOOD FRIENDS, LIKE YOU! ONE DAY, I HOPE I GO TO THE CANADA TO SEE YOU!
TSK!

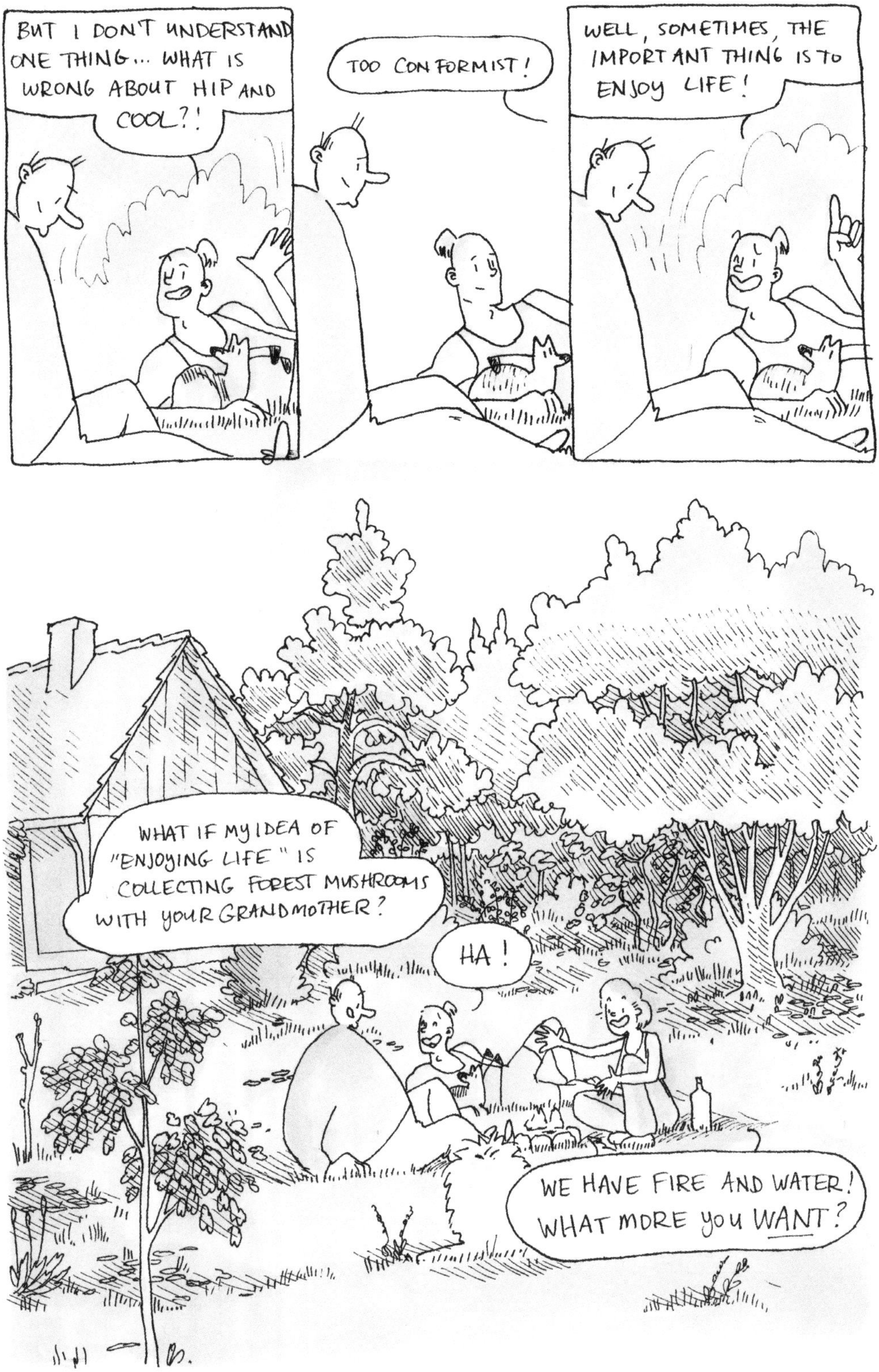
BUT I DON'T UNDERSTAND ONE THING... WHAT IS WRONG ABOUT HIP AND COOL?!
TOO CONFORMIST!
WELL, SOMETIMES, THE IMPORTANT THING IS TO ENJOY LIFE!
WHAT IF MY IDEA OF "ENJOYING LIFE" IS COLLECTING FOREST MUSHROOMS WITH YOUR GRANDMOTHER?
HA!
WE HAVE FIRE AND WATER! WHAT MORE YOU WANT?

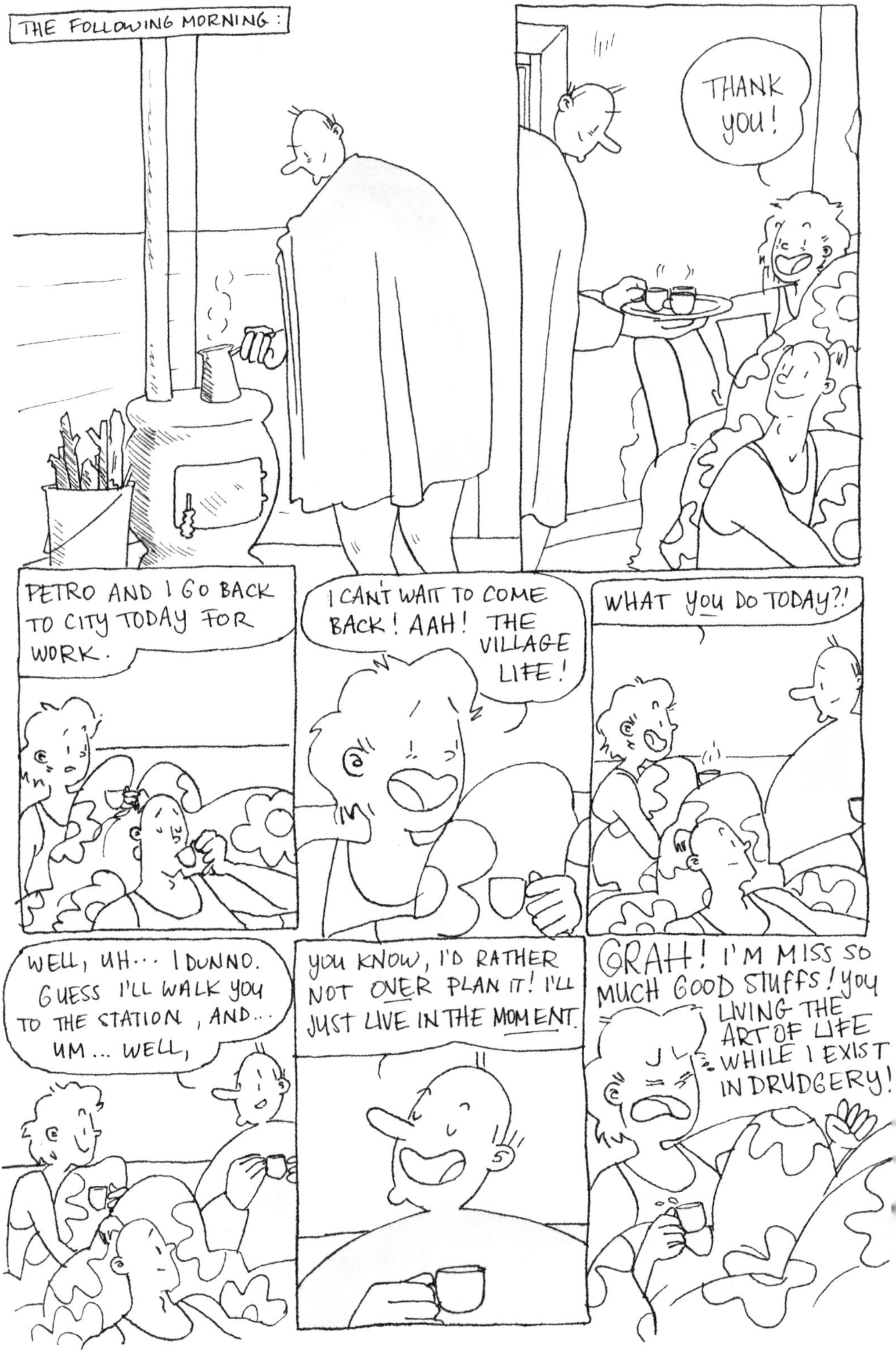
THE FOLLOWING MORNING:
THANK YOU!
PETRO AND I GO BACK TO CITY TODAY FOR WORK.
I CAN'T WAIT TO COME BACK! AAH! THE VILLAGE LIFE!
WHAT YOU DO TODAY?!
WELL, UH... I DUNNO. GUESS I'LL WALK YOU TO THE STATION, AND... UM... WELL,
YOU KNOW, I'D RATHER NOT OVER PLAN IT! I'LL JUST LIVE IN THE MOMENT.
GRAH! I'M MISS SO MUCH GOOD STUFFS! YOU LIVING THE ART OF LIFE WHILE I EXIST IN DRUDGERY!

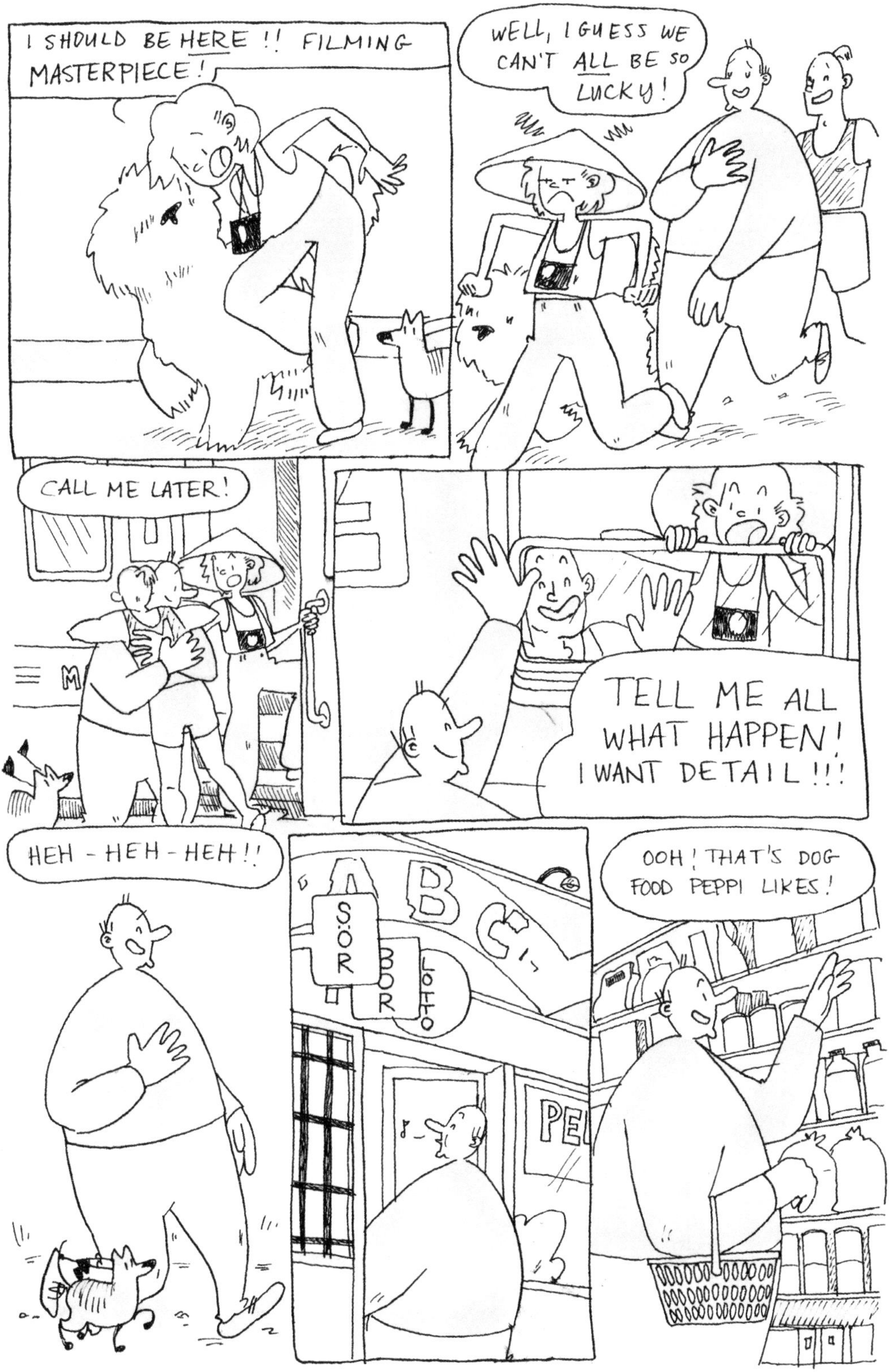
I SHOULD BE HERE !! FILMING MASTERPIECE !
WELL, I GUESS WE CAN'T ALL BE SO LUCKY !
CALL ME LATER !
TELL ME ALL WHAT HAPPEN ! I WANT DETAIL !!!
HEH - HEH - HEH !!
ABC
SÖR
BOR
LOTTO
PE
OOH ! THAT'S DOG FOOD PEPPI LIKES !

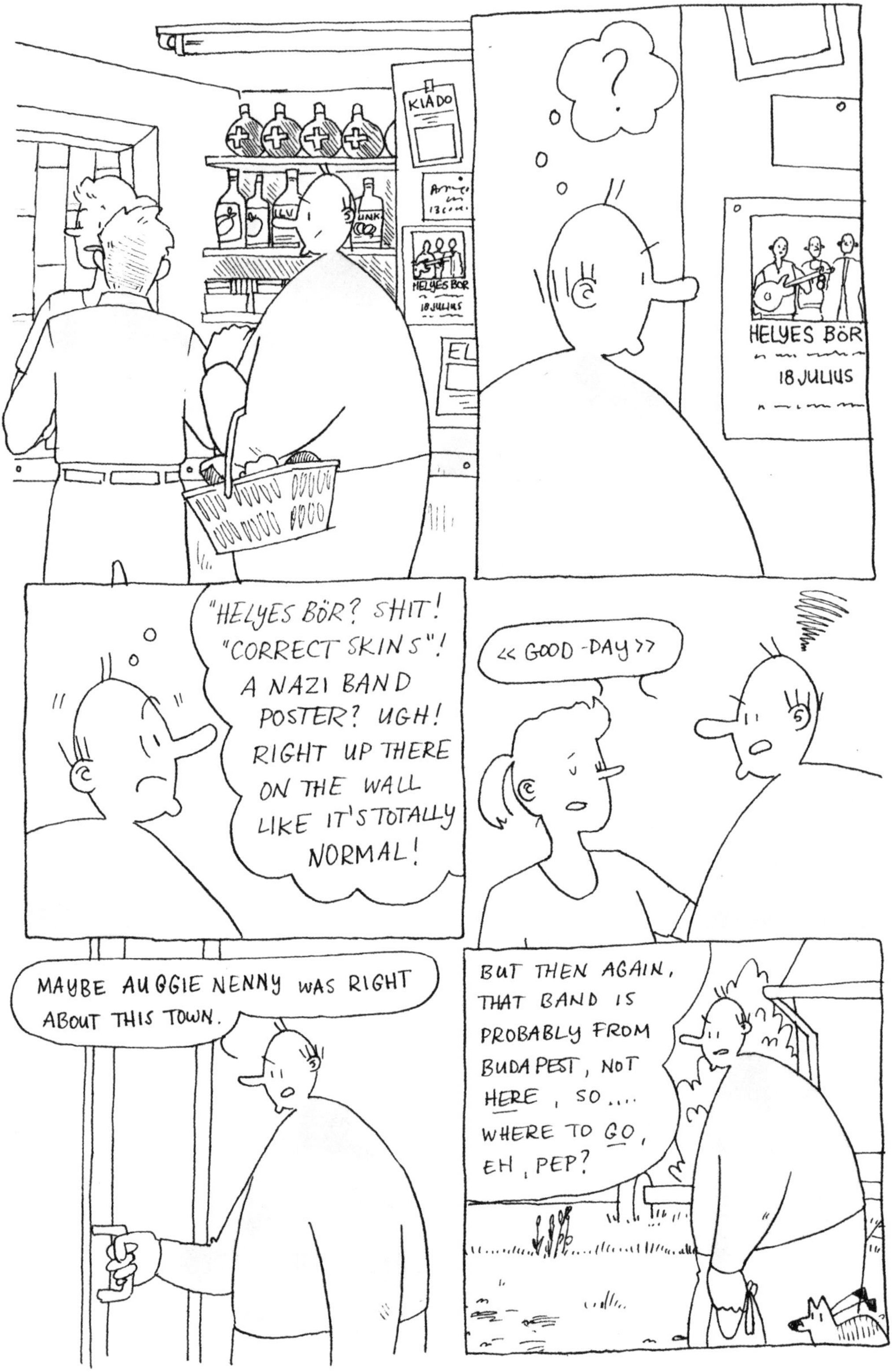
KIADO
HELYES BÖR
18 JULIUS
?
HELYES BÖR
18 JULIUS
"HELYES BÖR? SHIT! "CORRECT SKINS"! A NAZI BAND POSTER? UGH! RIGHT UP THERE ON THE WALL LIKE IT'S TOTALLY NORMAL!
<< GOOD-DAY >>
MAYBE AUGGIE NENNY WAS RIGHT ABOUT THIS TOWN.
BUT THEN AGAIN, THAT BAND IS PROBABLY FROM BUDAPEST, NOT HERE, SO.... WHERE TO GO, EH, PEP?

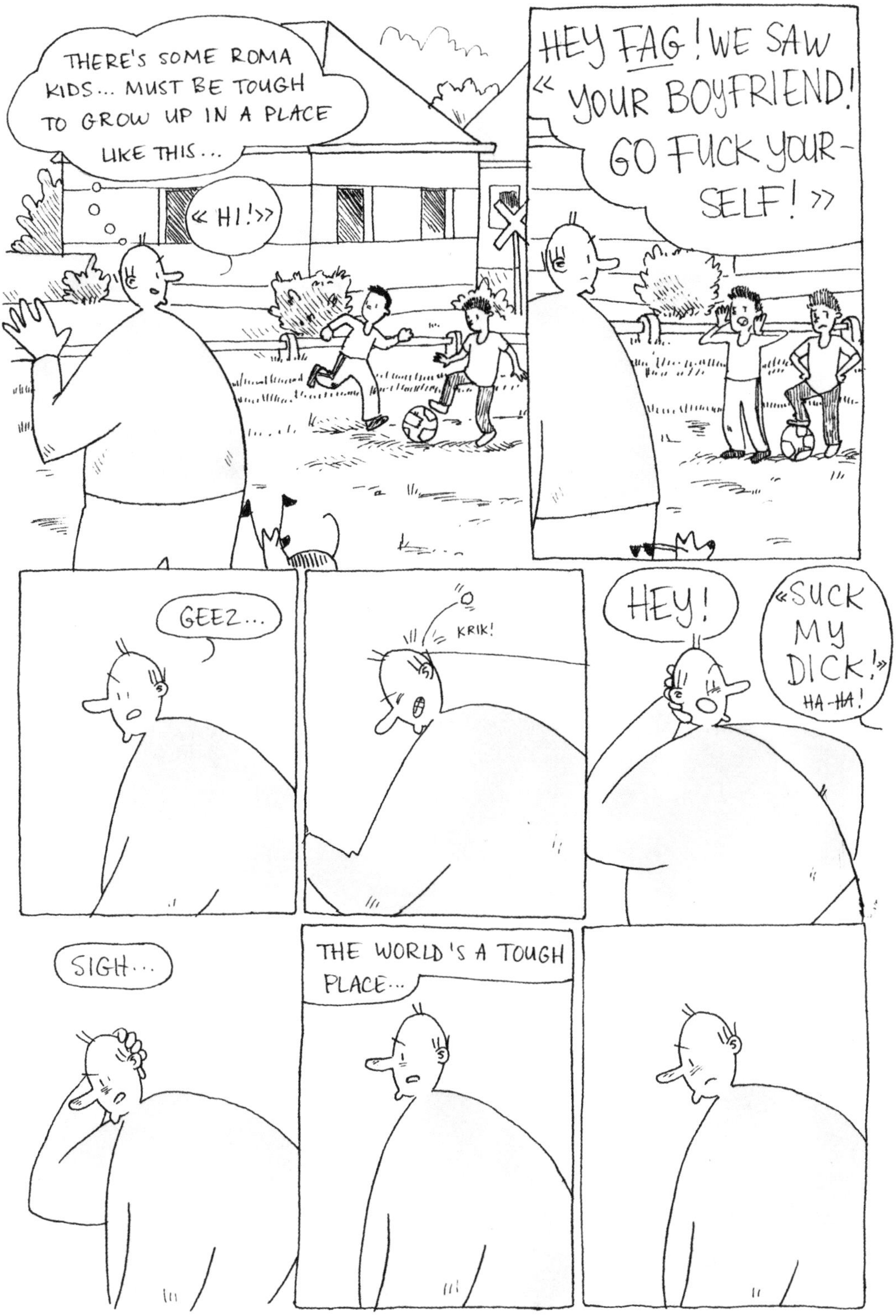
THERE'S SOME ROMA KIDS... MUST BE TOUGH TO GROW UP IN A PLACE LIKE THIS...
«HI!»
HEY FAG! WE SAW YOUR BOYFRIEND! GO FUCK YOURSELF!»
GEEZ...
KRIK!
HEY!
«SUCK MY DICK!» HA-HA!
SIGH...
THE WORLD'S A TOUGH PLACE...

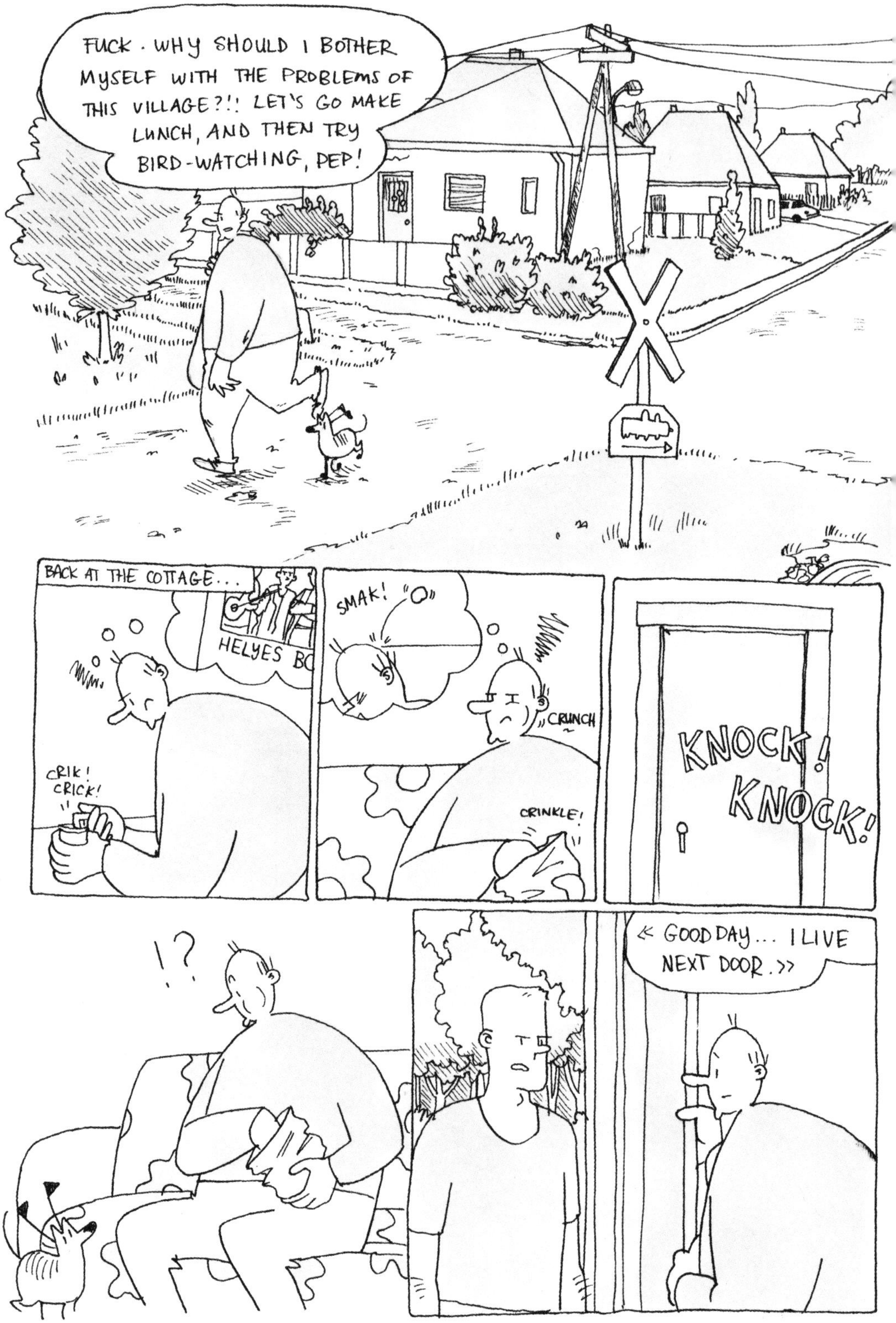
FUCK. WHY SHOULD I BOTHER MYSELF WITH THE PROBLEMS OF THIS VILLAGE?!! LET'S GO MAKE LUNCH, AND THEN TRY BIRD-WATCHING, PEP!
BACK AT THE COTTAGE...
HELYES BO
CRIK! CRICK!
SMAK!
CRUNCH
CRINKLE!
KNOCK! KNOCK!
!?
« GOOD DAY... I LIVE NEXT DOOR.»

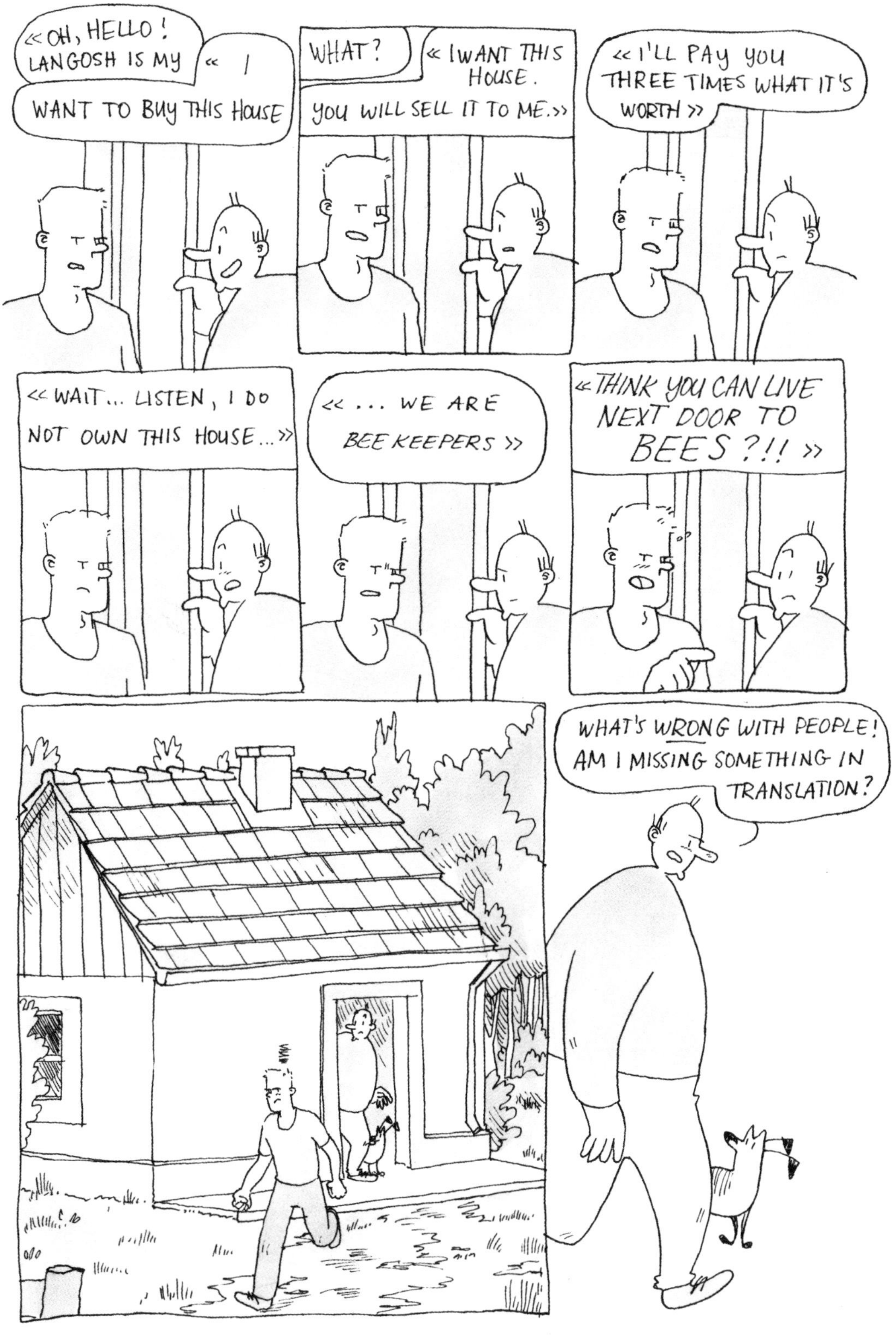
«OH, HELLO! LANGOSH IS MY
« I WANT TO BUY THIS HOUSE
WHAT?
«I WANT THIS HOUSE. YOU WILL SELL IT TO ME.»
«I'LL PAY YOU THREE TIMES WHAT IT'S WORTH»
«WAIT... LISTEN, I DO NOT OWN THIS HOUSE...»
«... WE ARE BEE KEEPERS»
«THINK YOU CAN LIVE NEXT DOOR TO BEES?!!»
WHAT'S WRONG WITH PEOPLE! AM I MISSING SOMETHING IN TRANSLATION?

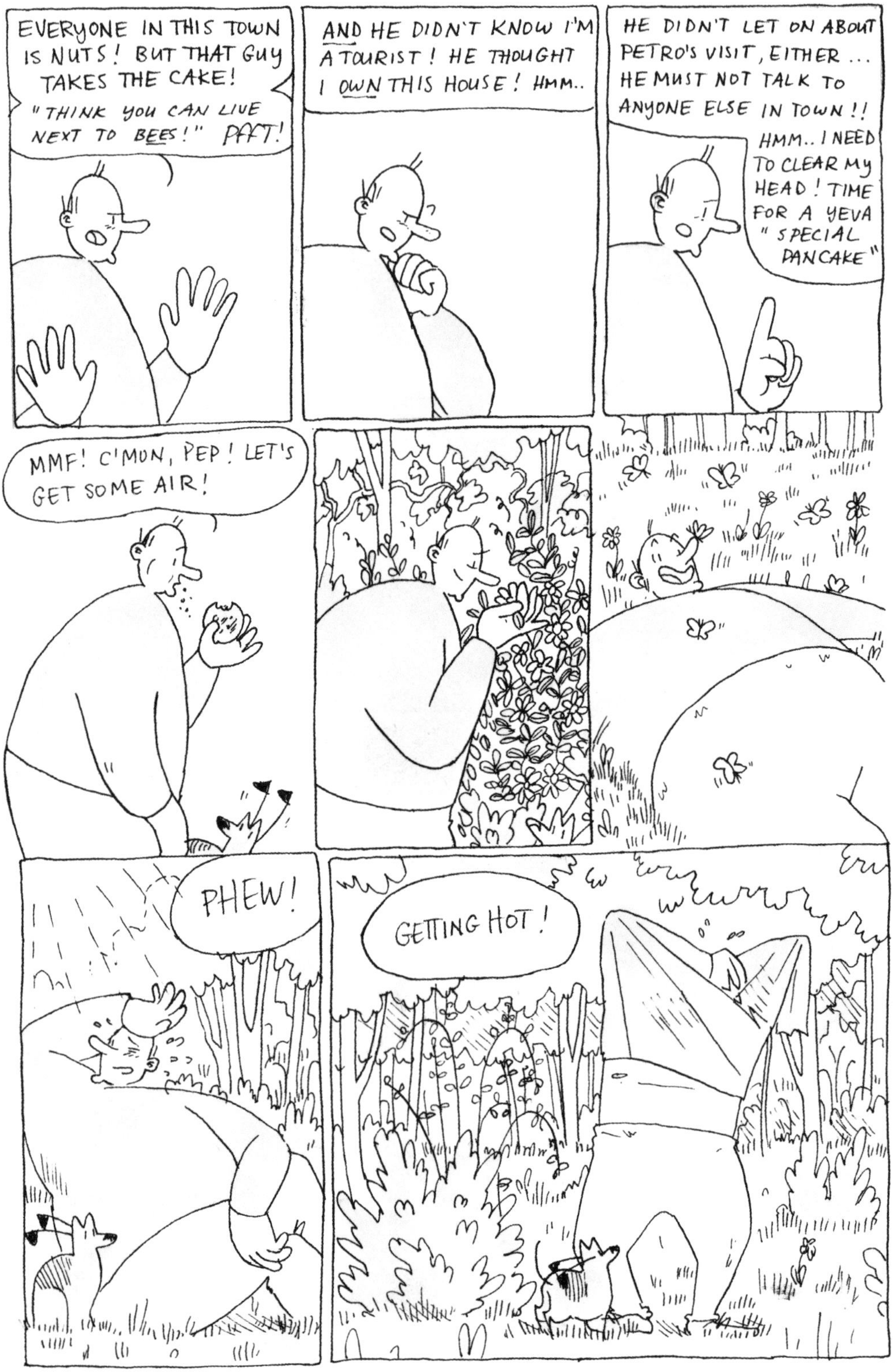

EVERYONE IN THIS TOWN IS NUTS! BUT THAT GUY TAKES THE CAKE! "THINK YOU CAN LIVE NEXT TO BEES!" PFFT!
AND HE DIDN'T KNOW I'M A TOURIST! HE THOUGHT I OWN THIS HOUSE! HMM..
HE DIDN'T LET ON ABOUT PETRO'S VISIT, EITHER... HE MUST NOT TALK TO ANYONE ELSE IN TOWN!!
HMM.. I NEED TO CLEAR MY HEAD! TIME FOR A YEVA "SPECIAL PANCAKE"
MMF! C'MON, PEP! LET'S GET SOME AIR!
PHEW!
GETTING HOT!

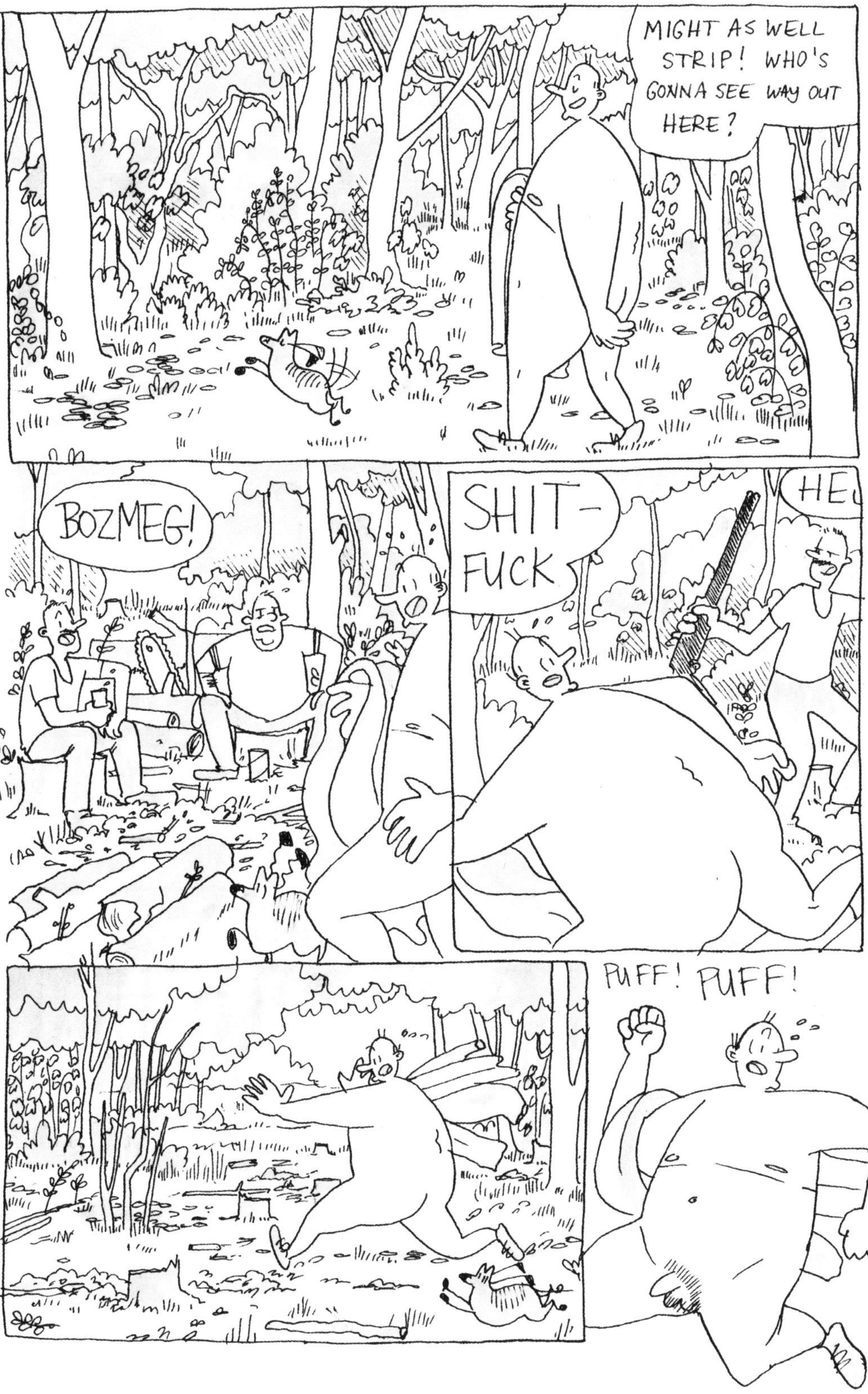
MIGHT AS WELL STRIP! WHO'S GONNA SEE WAY OUT HERE?
BOZMEG!
SHIT-FUCK
HE
PUFF! PUFF!

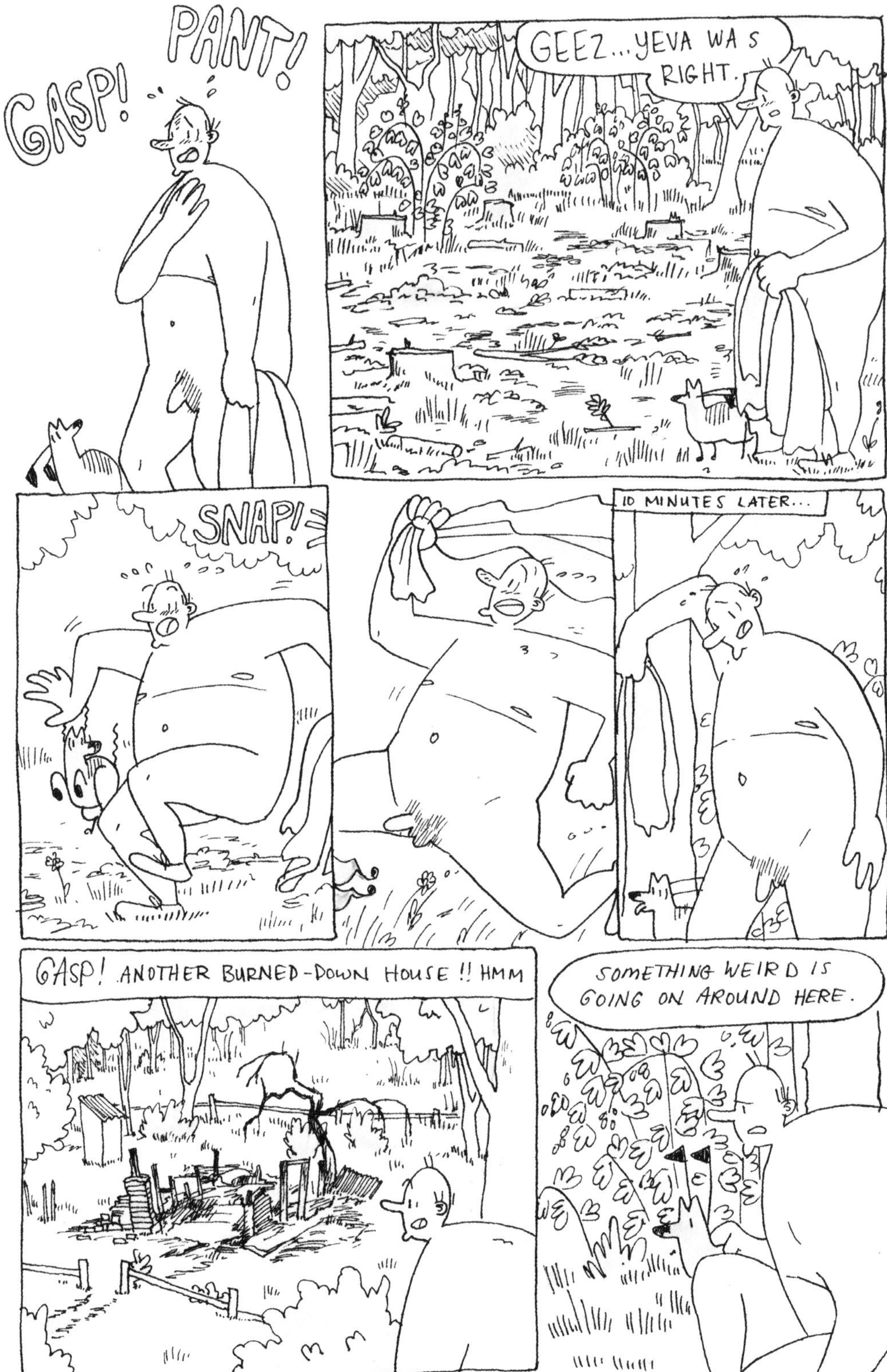
GASP!
PANT!
GEEZ... YEVA WAS RIGHT.
SNAP!
10 MINUTES LATER...
GASP! ANOTHER BURNED-DOWN HOUSE!! HMM
SOMETHING WEIRD IS GOING ON AROUND HERE.

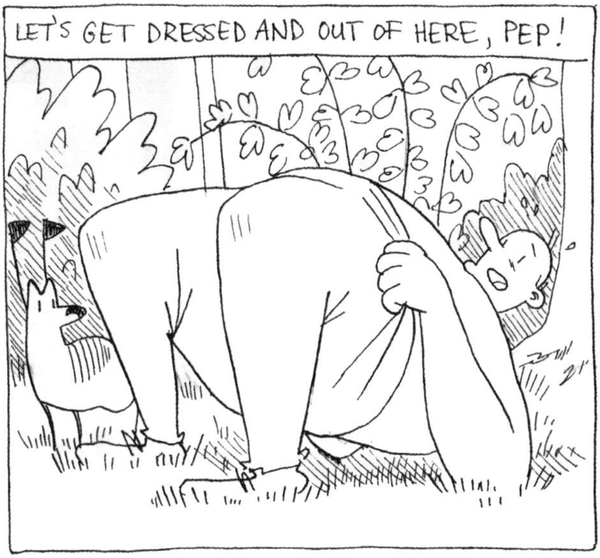
LET'S GET DRESSED AND OUT OF HERE, PEP!

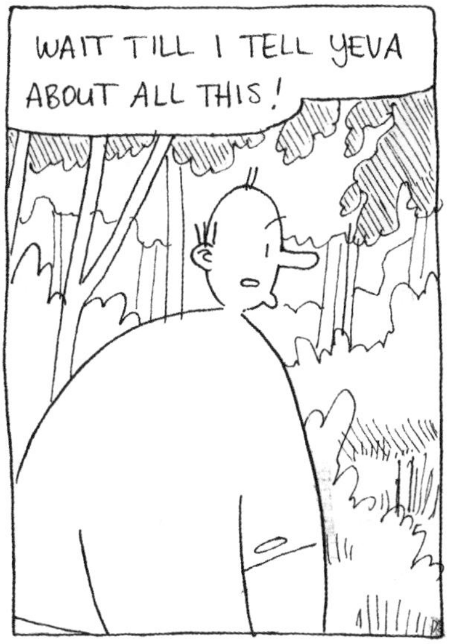
WAIT TILL I TELL YEVA ABOUT ALL THIS!

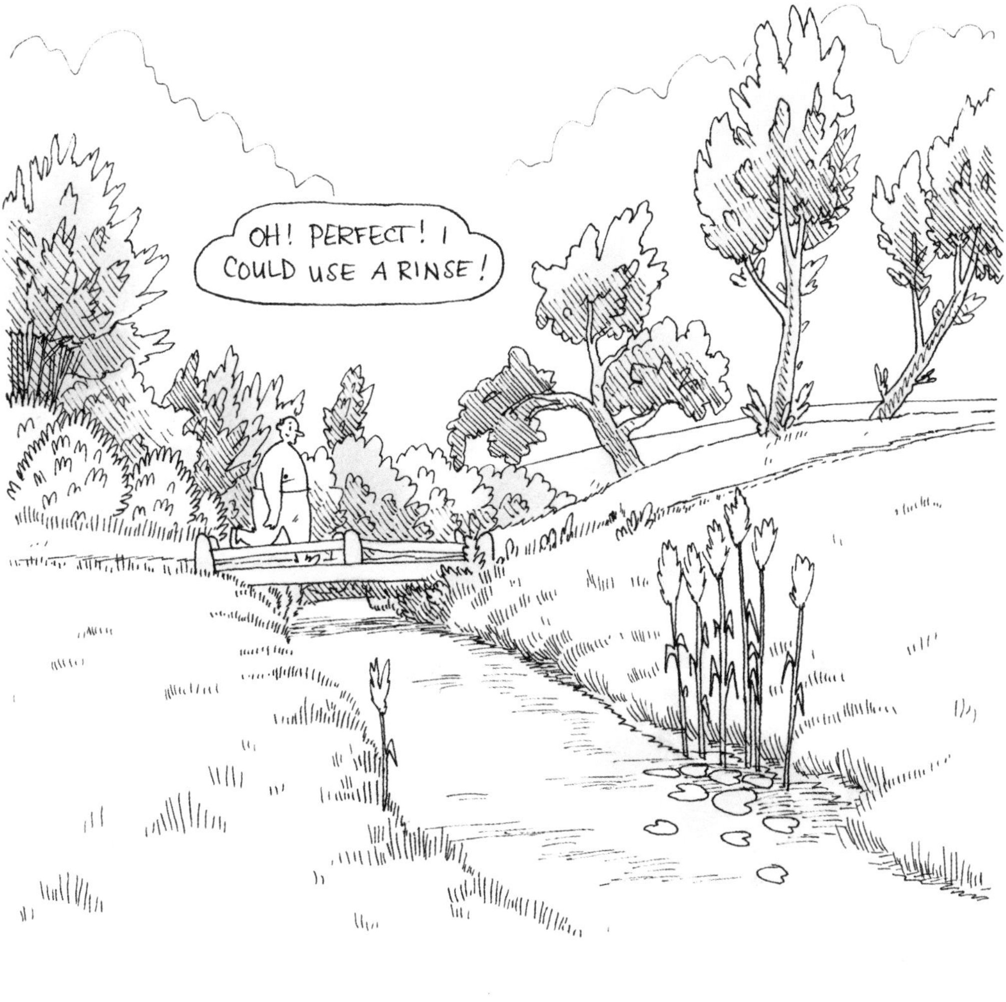
OH! PERFECT! I COULD USE A RINSE!

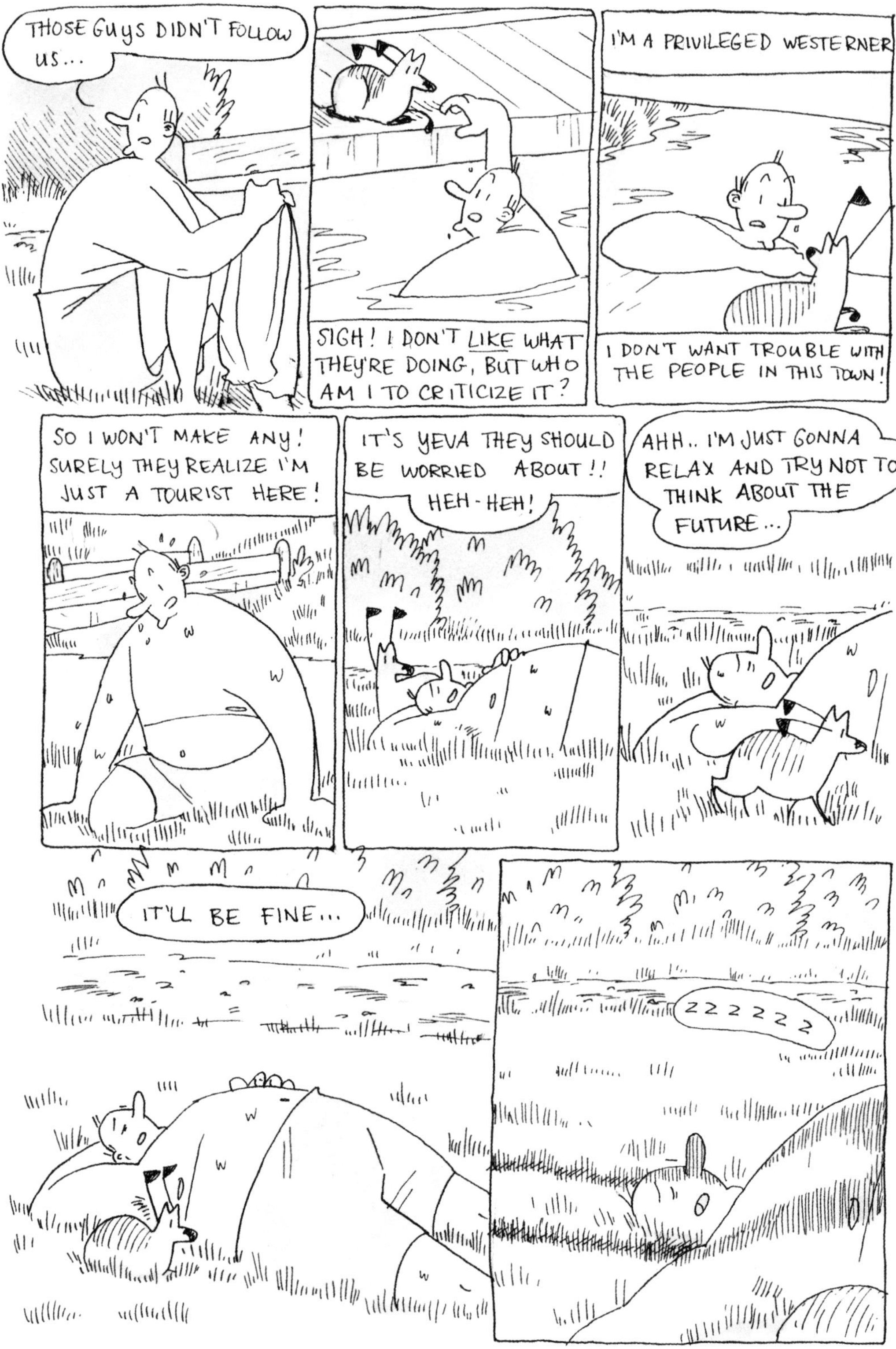
THOSE GUYS DIDN'T FOLLOW US...
SIGH! I DON'T LIKE WHAT THEY'RE DOING, BUT WHO AM I TO CRITICIZE IT?
I'M A PRIVILEGED WESTERNER
I DON'T WANT TROUBLE WITH THE PEOPLE IN THIS TOWN!
SO I WON'T MAKE ANY! SURELY THEY REALIZE I'M JUST A TOURIST HERE!
IT'S YEVA THEY SHOULD BE WORRIED ABOUT!!
HEH-HEH!
AHH.. I'M JUST GONNA RELAX AND TRY NOT TO THINK ABOUT THE FUTURE...
IT'LL BE FINE...
ZZZZZZ

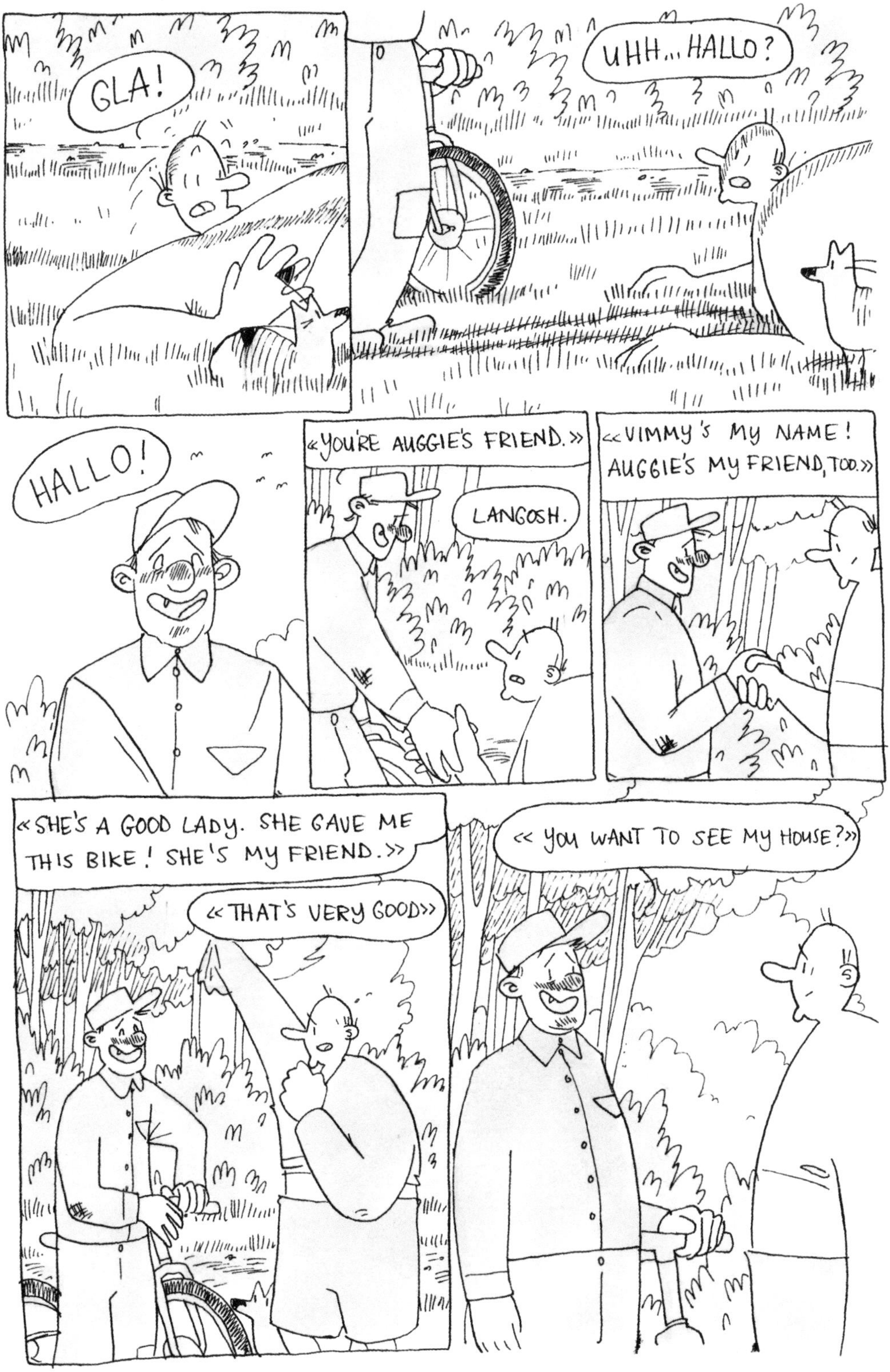
GLA!
UHH... HALLO?
HALLO!
«YOU'RE AUGGIE'S FRIEND.»
LANGOSH.
«VIMMY'S MY NAME! AUGGIE'S MY FRIEND, TOO.»
«SHE'S A GOOD LADY. SHE GAVE ME THIS BIKE! SHE'S MY FRIEND.»
«THAT'S VERY GOOD»
«YOU WANT TO SEE MY HOUSE?»

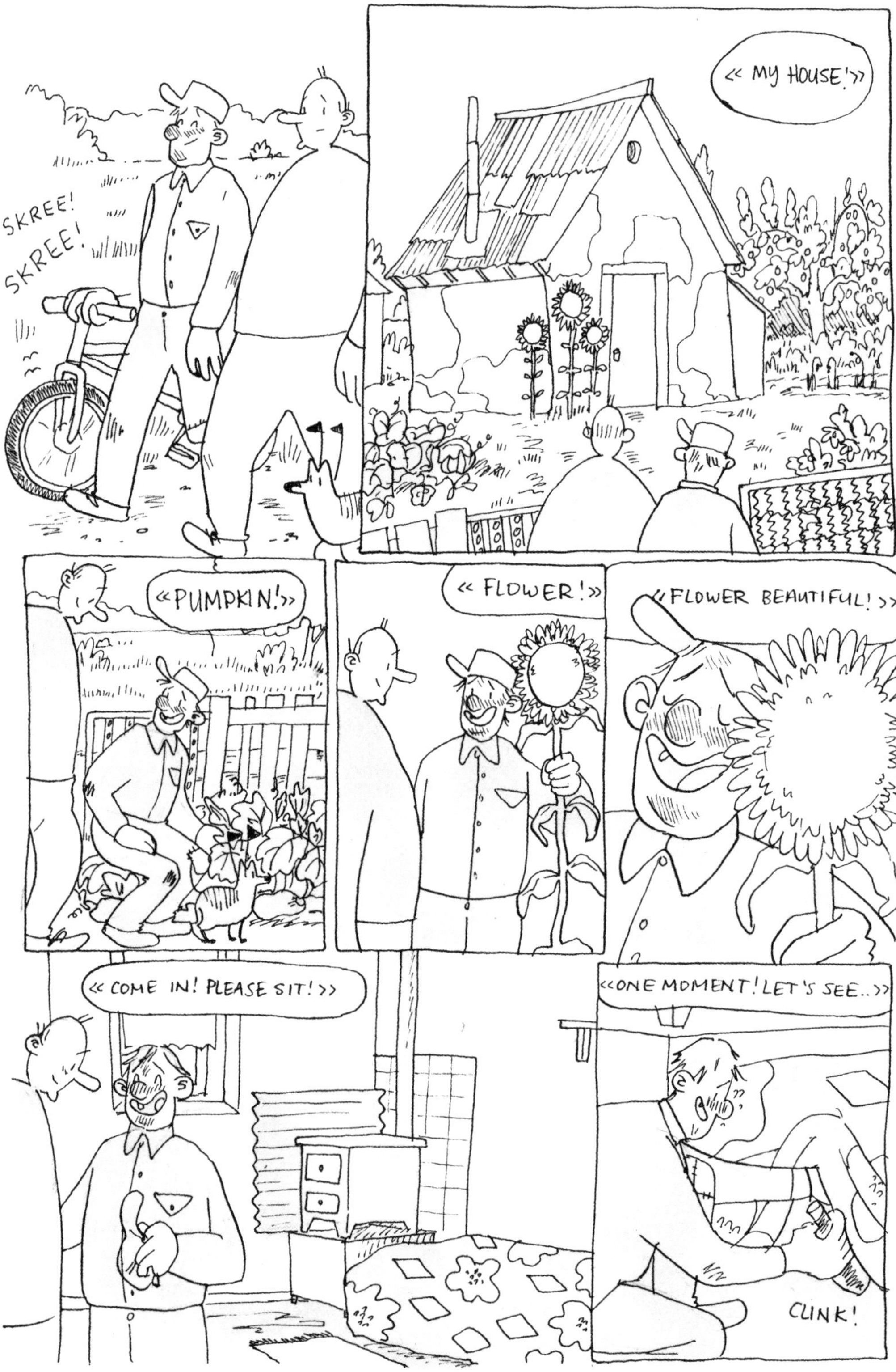
SKREE!
SKREE!
« MY HOUSE! »
« PUMPKIN! »
« FLOWER! »
« FLOWER BEAUTIFUL! »
« COME IN! PLEASE SIT! »
« ONE MOMENT! LET'S SEE.. »
CLINK!

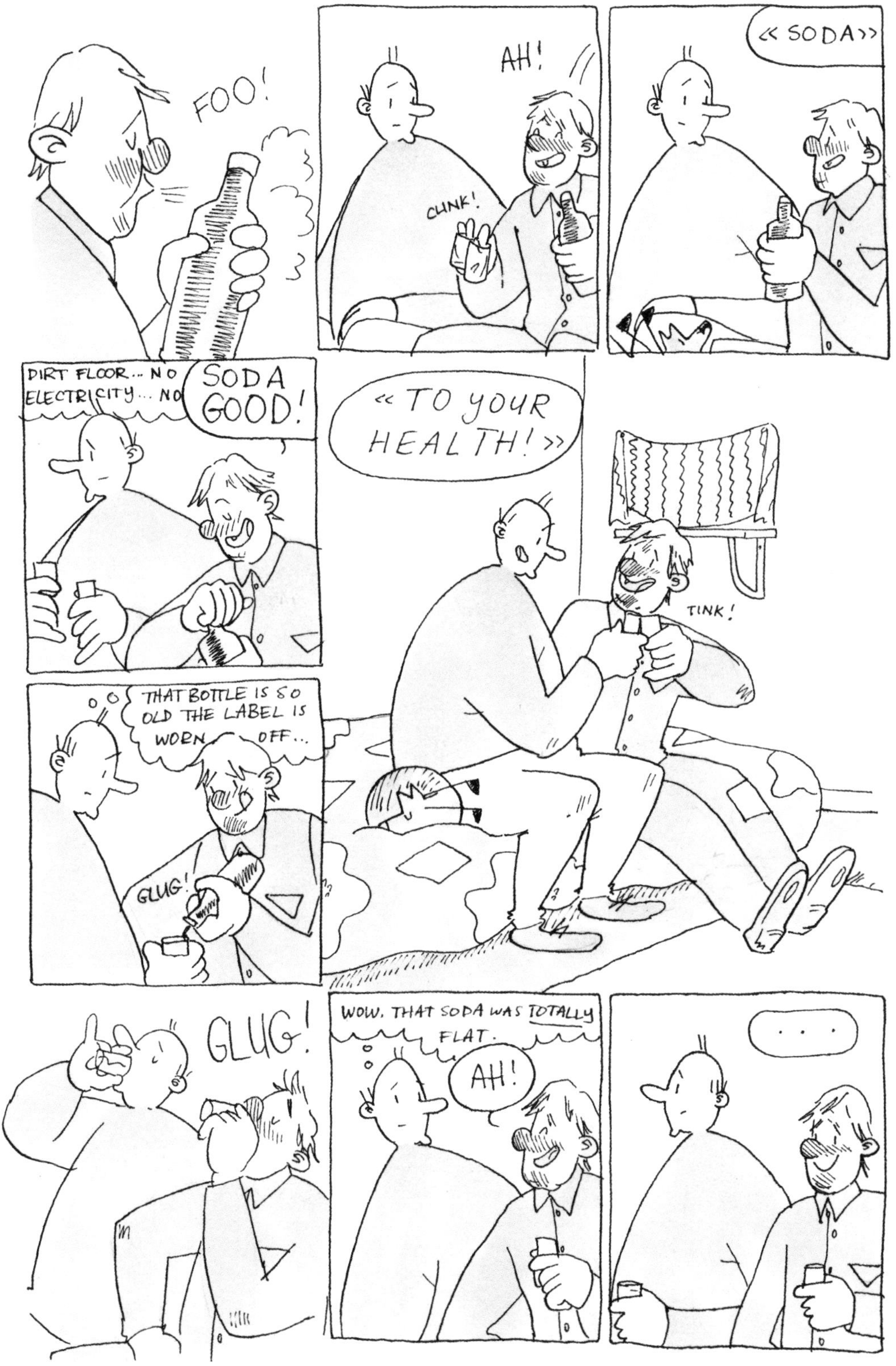
FOO!
AH!
CLINK!
« SODA »
DIRT FLOOR... NO ELECTRICITY... NO
SODA GOOD!
« TO YOUR HEALTH! »
TINK!
THAT BOTTLE IS SO OLD THE LABEL IS WORN OFF...
GLUG!
GLUG!
WOW. THAT SODA WAS TOTALLY FLAT.
AH!
. . .

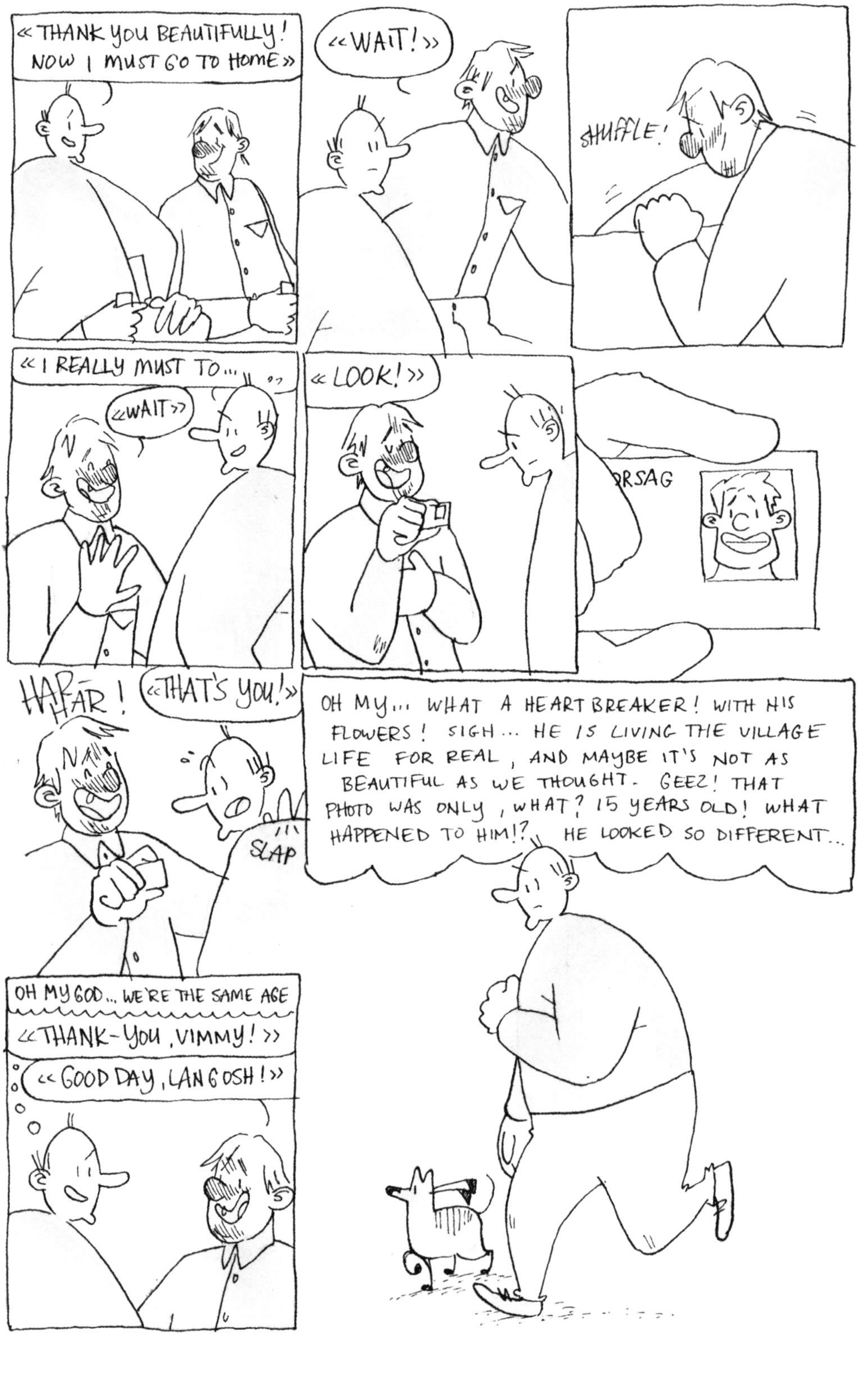

«THANK YOU BEAUTIFULLY! NOW I MUST GO TO HOME»
«WAIT!»
SHUFFLE!
«I REALLY MUST TO...
«WAIT»
«LOOK!»
RSAG
HAR HAR!
«THAT'S YOU!»
SLAP
OH MY... WHAT A HEARTBREAKER! WITH HIS FLOWERS! SIGH... HE IS LIVING THE VILLAGE LIFE FOR REAL, AND MAYBE IT'S NOT AS BEAUTIFUL AS WE THOUGHT. GEEZ! THAT PHOTO WAS ONLY, WHAT? 15 YEARS OLD! WHAT HAPPENED TO HIM!? HE LOOKED SO DIFFERENT...
OH MY GOD... WE'RE THE SAME AGE
«THANK-YOU, VIMMY!»
«GOOD DAY, LANGOSH!»

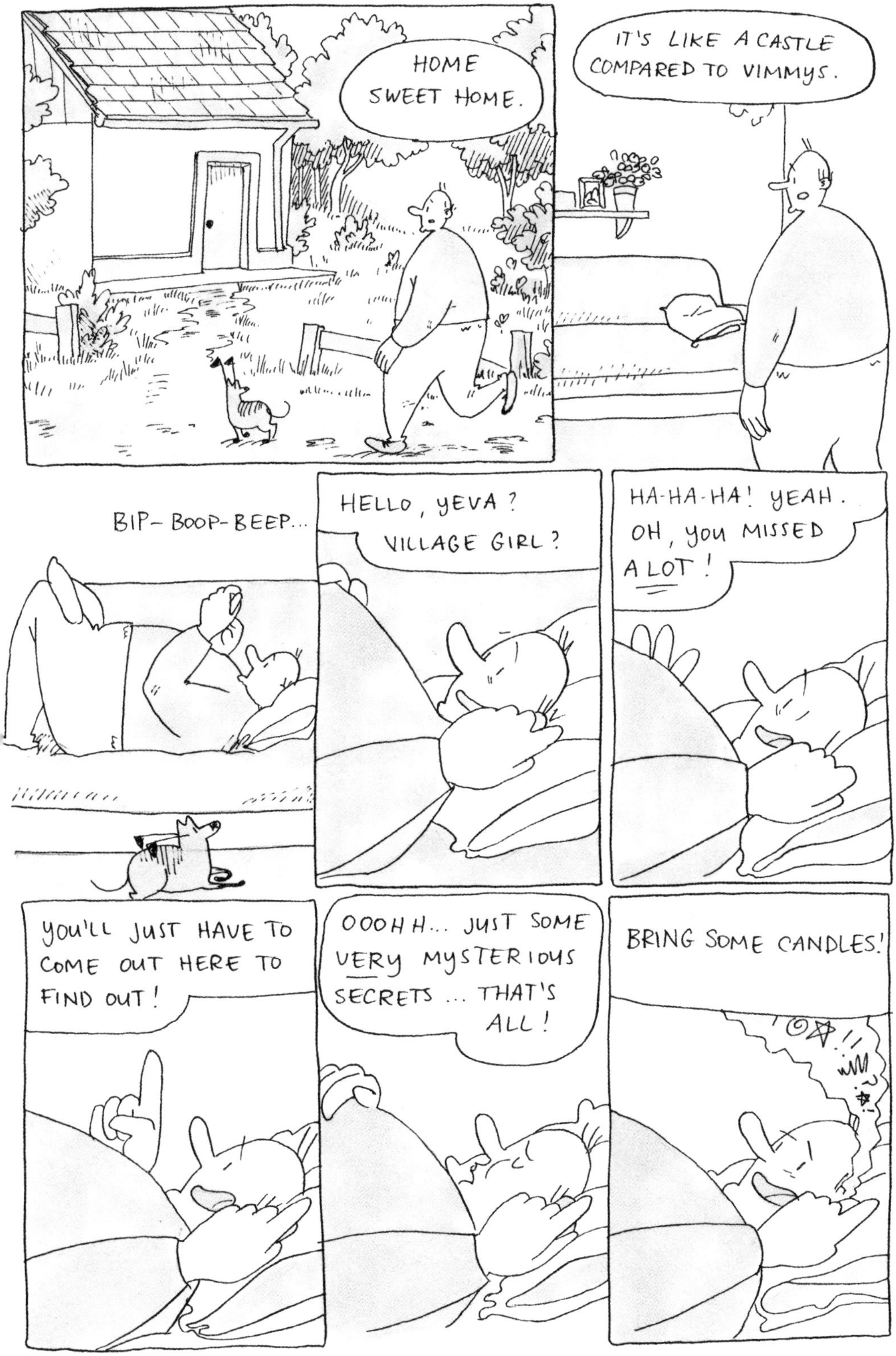
HOME SWEET HOME.
IT'S LIKE A CASTLE COMPARED TO VIMMYS.
BIP-BOOP-BEEP...
HELLO, YEVA? VILLAGE GIRL?
HA-HA-HA! YEAH. OH, YOU MISSED A LOT!
YOU'LL JUST HAVE TO COME OUT HERE TO FIND OUT!
OOOHH... JUST SOME VERY MYSTERIOUS SECRETS... THAT'S ALL!
BRING SOME CANDLES!

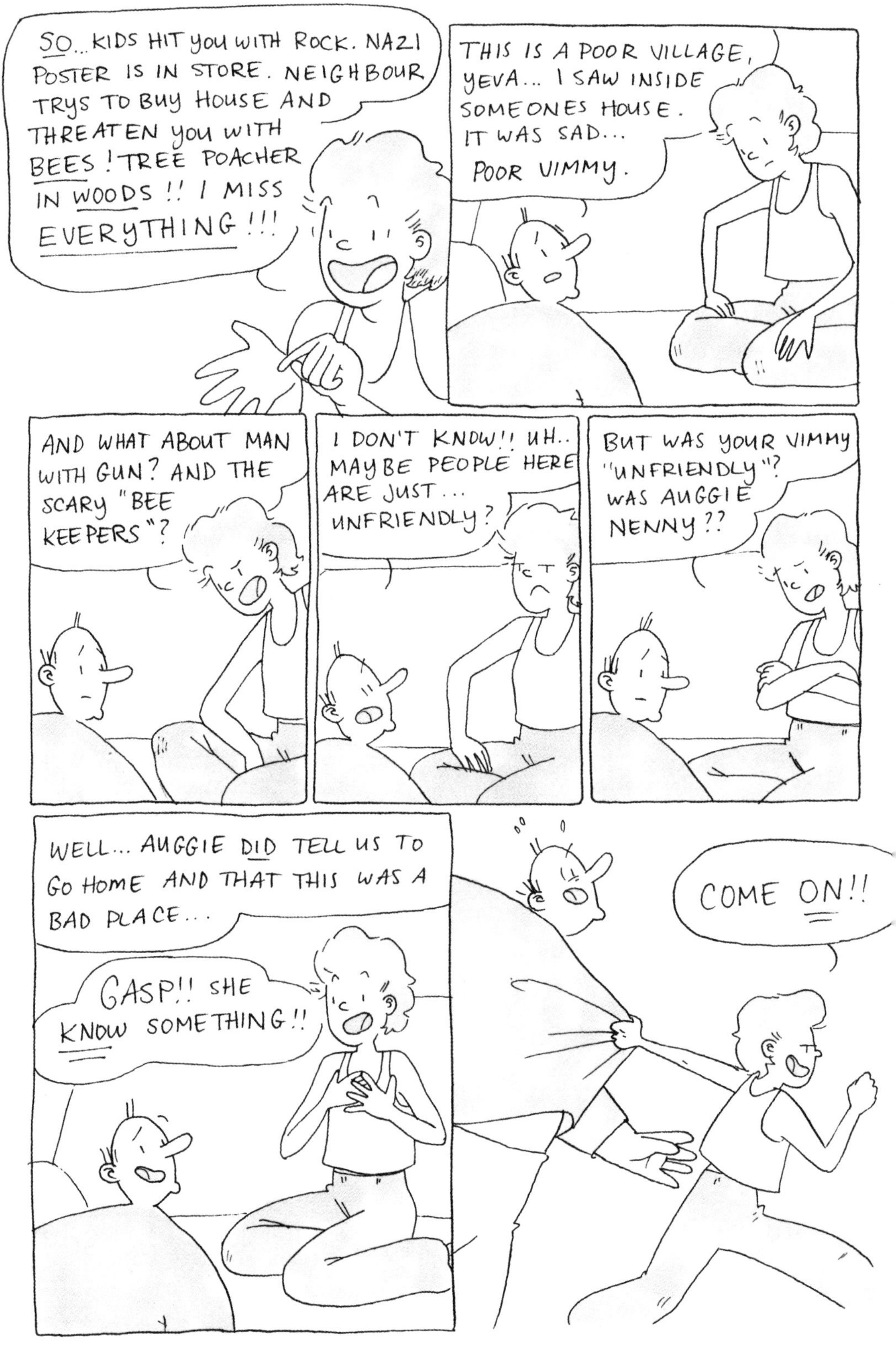
SO... KIDS HIT YOU WITH ROCK. NAZI POSTER IS IN STORE. NEIGHBOUR TRYS TO BUY HOUSE AND THREATEN YOU WITH BEES! TREE POACHER IN WOODS!! I MISS EVERYTHING!!!
THIS IS A POOR VILLAGE, YEVA... I SAW INSIDE SOMEONES HOUSE. IT WAS SAD... POOR VIMMY.
AND WHAT ABOUT MAN WITH GUN? AND THE SCARY "BEE KEEPERS"?
I DON'T KNOW!! UH.. MAYBE PEOPLE HERE ARE JUST... UNFRIENDLY?
BUT WAS YOUR VIMMY "UNFRIENDLY"? WAS AUGGIE NENNY??
WELL... AUGGIE DID TELL US TO GO HOME AND THAT THIS WAS A BAD PLACE...
GASP!! SHE KNOW SOMETHING!!
COME ON!!

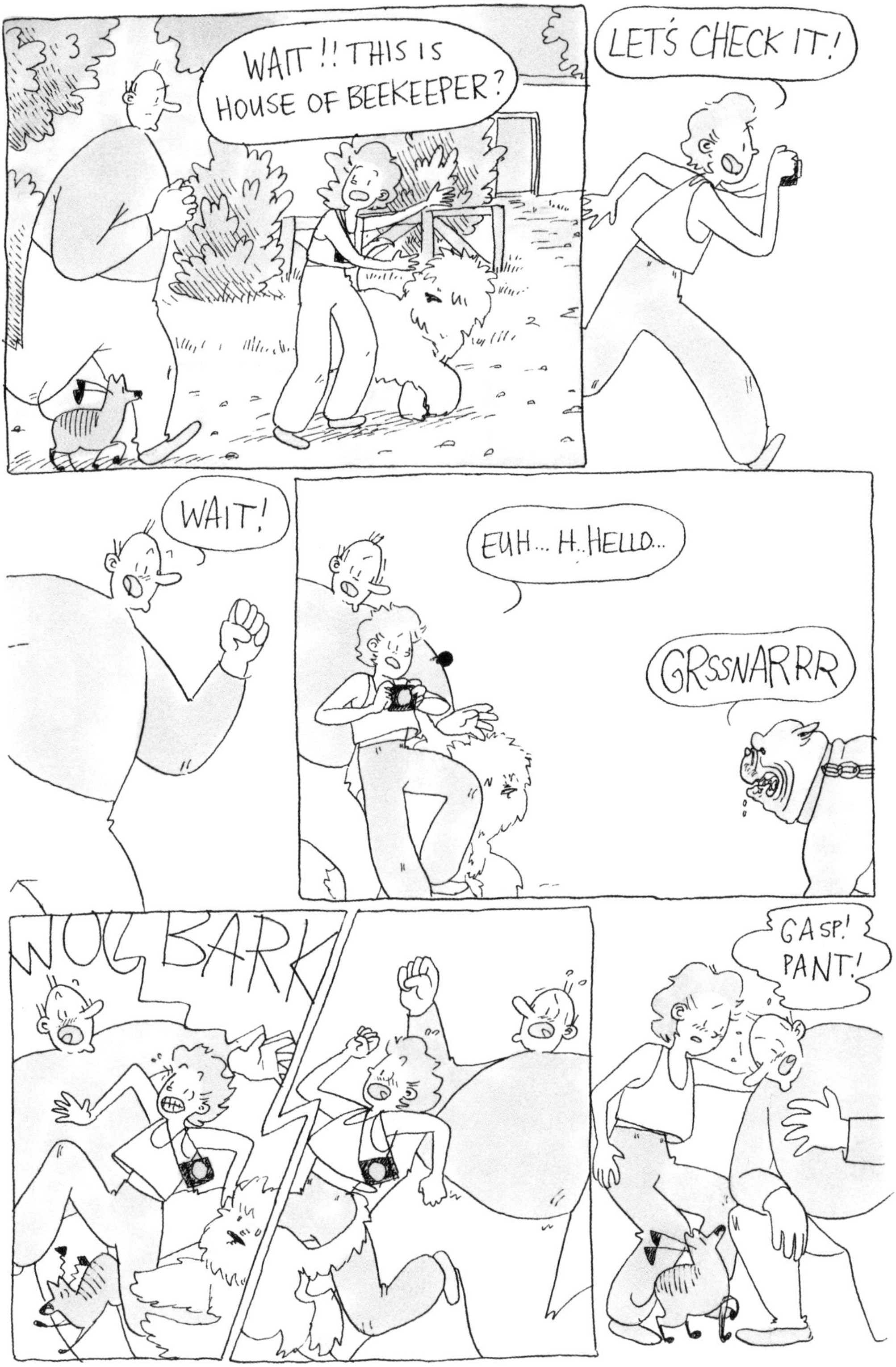
WAIT!! THIS IS HOUSE OF BEEKEEPER?
LET'S CHECK IT!
WAIT!
EUH... H..HELLO...
GRSSNARRR
WOG BARK
GASP! PANT!

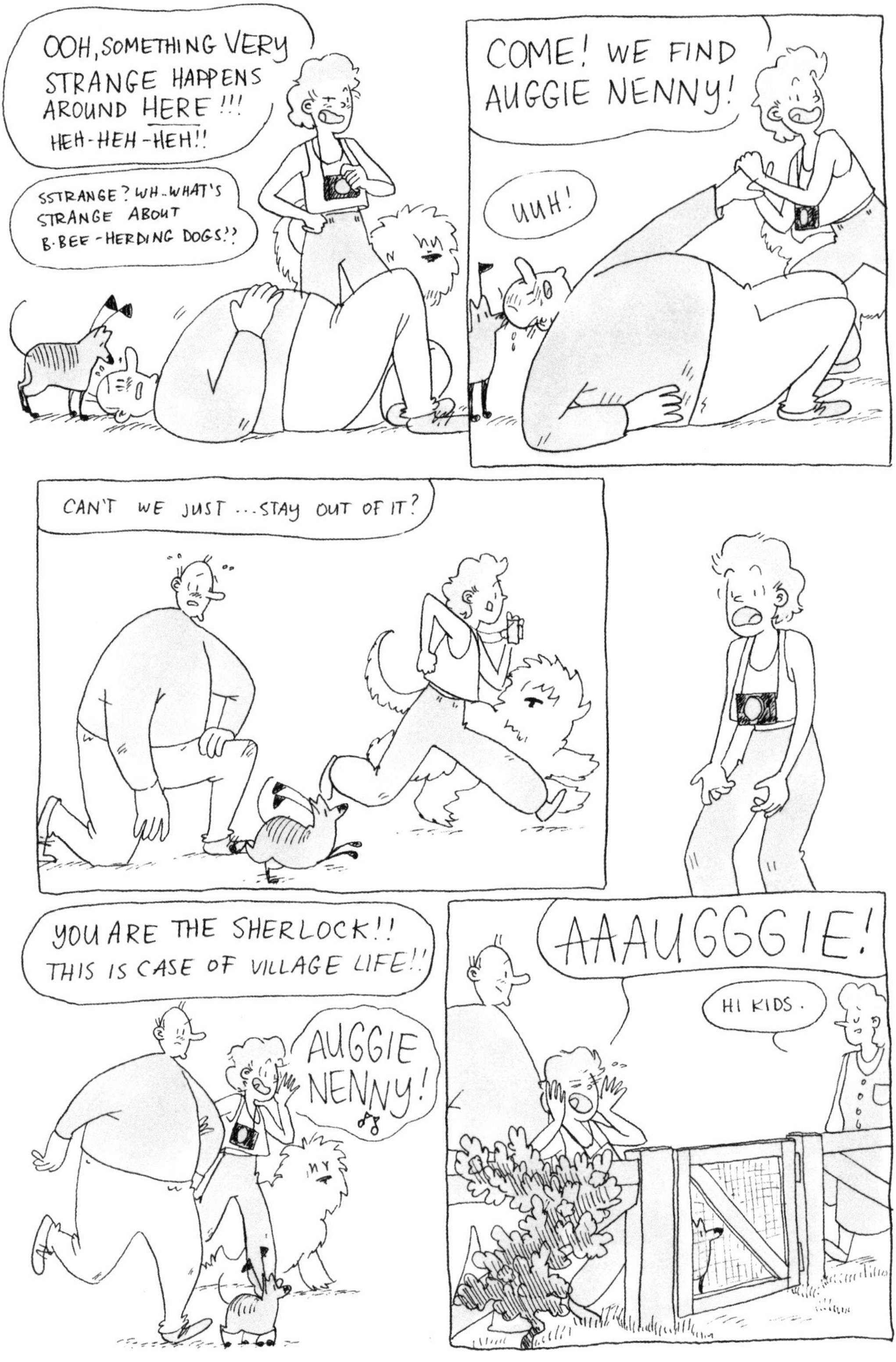
OOH, SOMETHING VERY STRANGE HAPPENS AROUND HERE!!! HEH-HEH-HEH!!
SSTRANGE? WH..WHAT'S STRANGE ABOUT B-BEE-HERDING DOGS!?
COME! WE FIND AUGGIE NENNY!
UUH!
CAN'T WE JUST ...STAY OUT OF IT?
YOU ARE THE SHERLOCK!! THIS IS CASE OF VILLAGE LIFE!!
AUGGIE NENNY!
AAAUGGGIE!
HI KIDS.

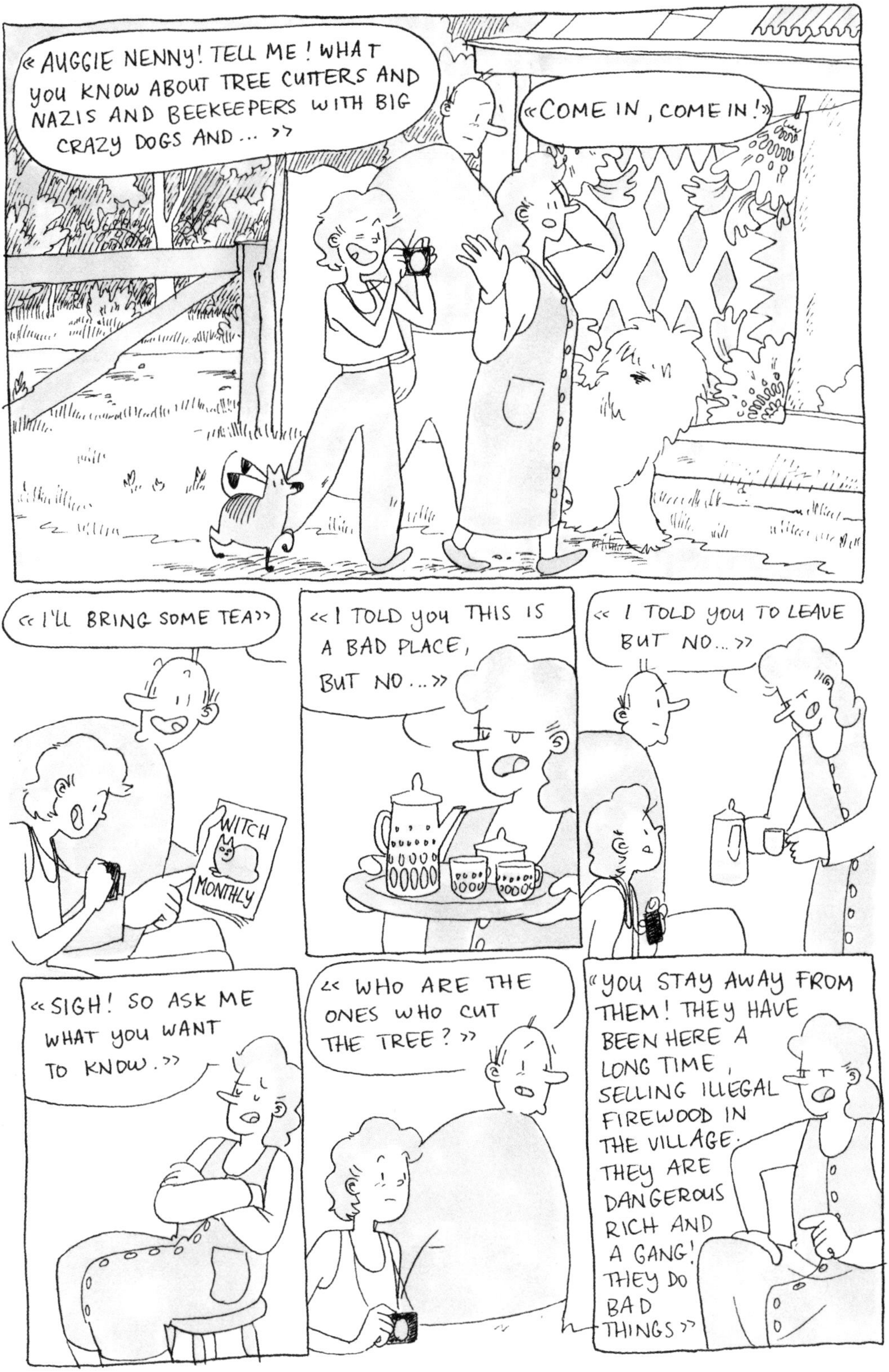
«AUGGIE NENNY! TELL ME! WHAT YOU KNOW ABOUT TREE CUTTERS AND NAZIS AND BEEKEEPERS WITH BIG CRAZY DOGS AND... »
«COME IN, COME IN!»
«I'LL BRING SOME TEA»
WITCH MONTHLY
«I TOLD YOU THIS IS A BAD PLACE, BUT NO...»
«I TOLD YOU TO LEAVE BUT NO...»
«SIGH! SO ASK ME WHAT YOU WANT TO KNOW.»
«WHO ARE THE ONES WHO CUT THE TREE?»
«YOU STAY AWAY FROM THEM! THEY HAVE BEEN HERE A LONG TIME, SELLING ILLEGAL FIREWOOD IN THE VILLAGE. THEY ARE DANGEROUS RICH AND A GANG! THEY DO BAD THINGS»

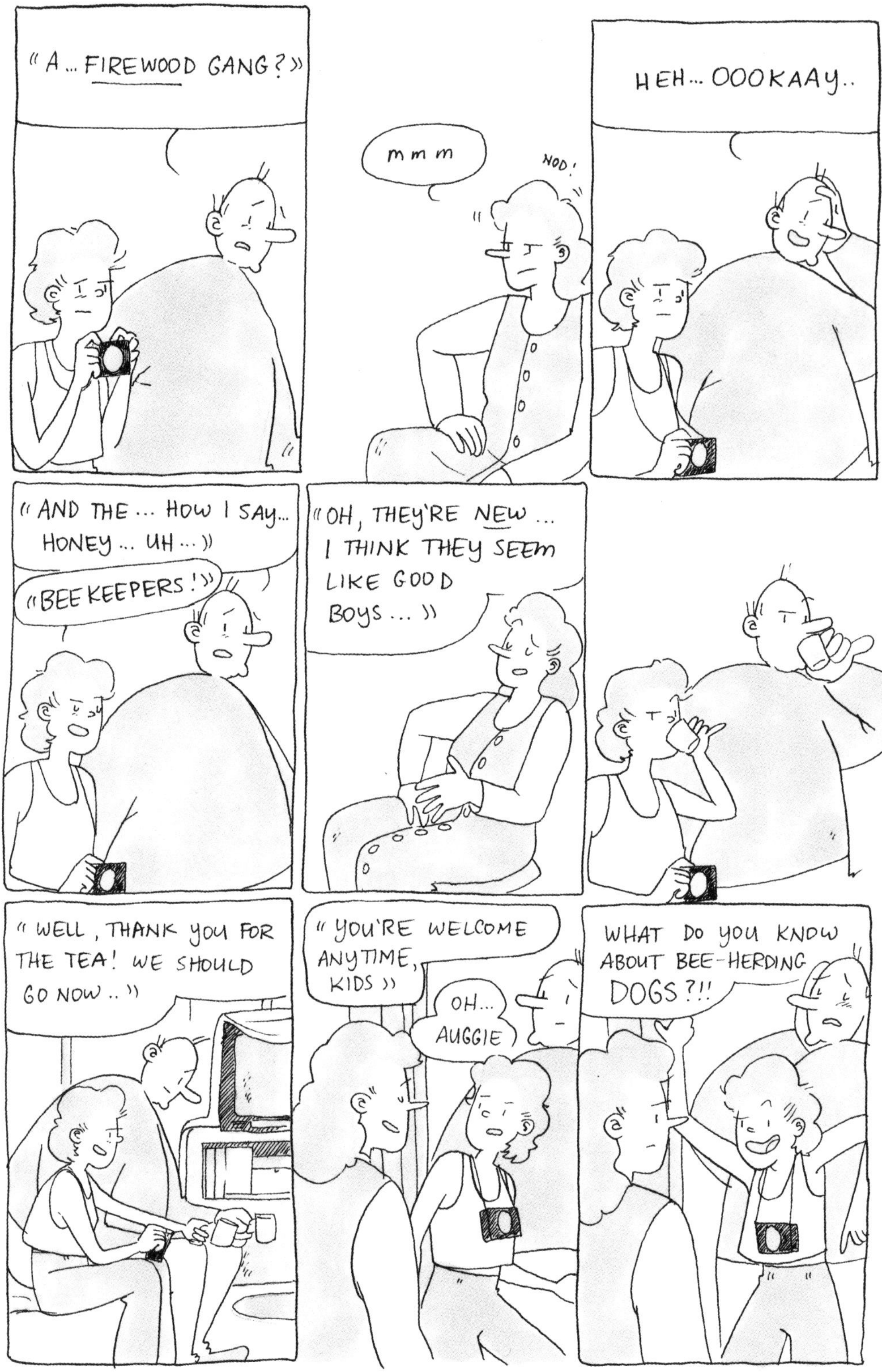
« A ... FIREWOOD GANG? »
mmm
NOD!
HEH... OOOKAAY..
« AND THE ... HOW I SAY... HONEY ... UH ... »
« BEEKEEPERS! »
« OH, THEY'RE NEW ... I THINK THEY SEEM LIKE GOOD BOYS ... »
« WELL, THANK YOU FOR THE TEA! WE SHOULD GO NOW .. »
« YOU'RE WELCOME ANYTIME, KIDS »
OH... AUGGIE
WHAT DO YOU KNOW ABOUT BEE-HERDING DOGS?!!

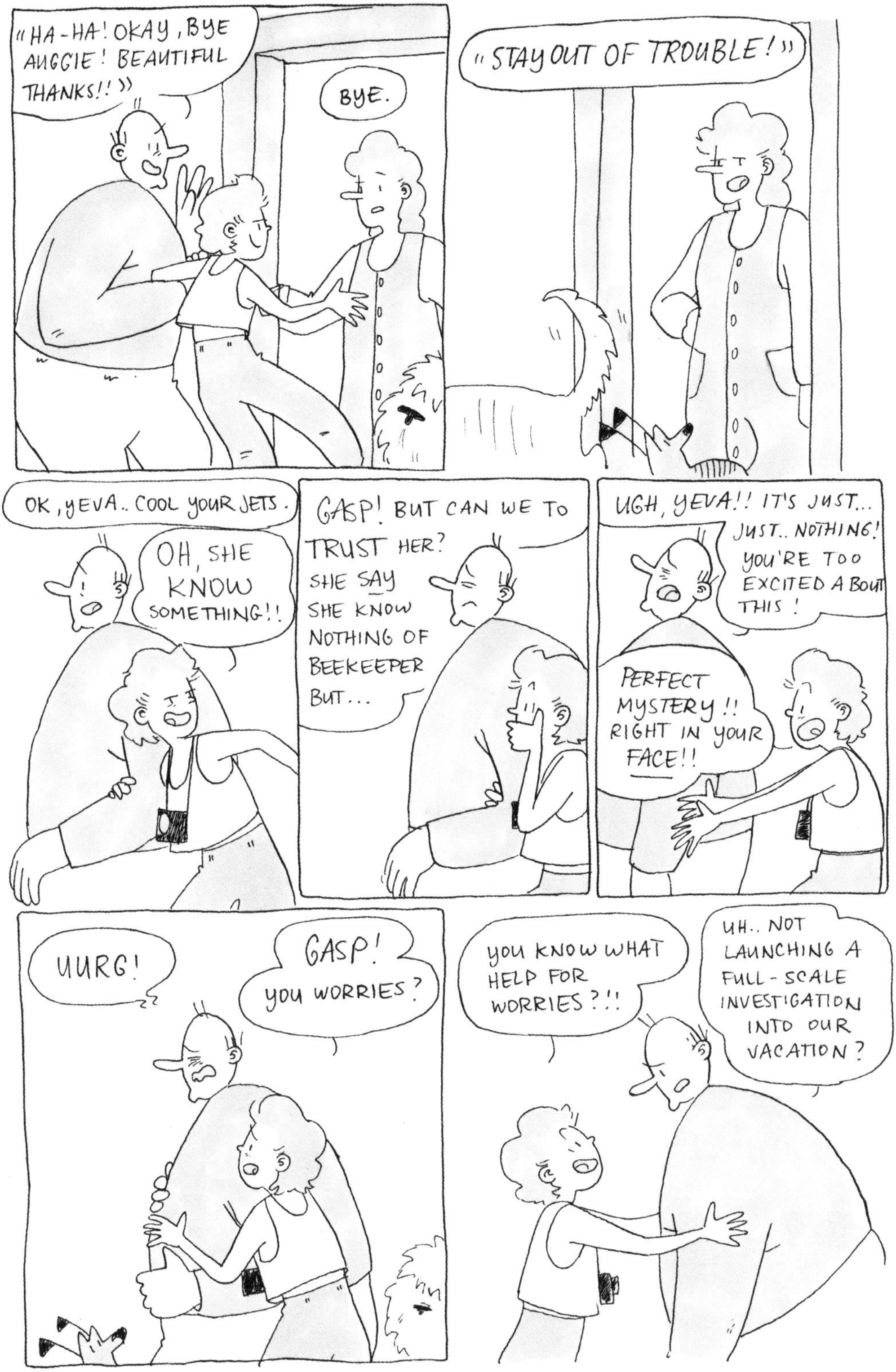
« HA-HA! OKAY, BYE AUGGIE! BEAUTIFUL THANKS!! »
BYE.
« STAY OUT OF TROUBLE! »
OK, YEVA.. COOL YOUR JETS.
OH, SHE KNOW SOMETHING!!
GASP! BUT CAN WE TO TRUST HER? SHE SAY SHE KNOW NOTHING OF BEEKEEPER BUT...
UGH, YEVA!! IT'S JUST... JUST.. NOTHING! YOU'RE TOO EXCITED ABOUT THIS!
PERFECT MYSTERY!! RIGHT IN YOUR FACE!!
UURG!
GASP! YOU WORRIES?
YOU KNOW WHAT HELP FOR WORRIES?!!
UH.. NOT LAUNCHING A FULL-SCALE INVESTIGATION INTO OUR VACATION?

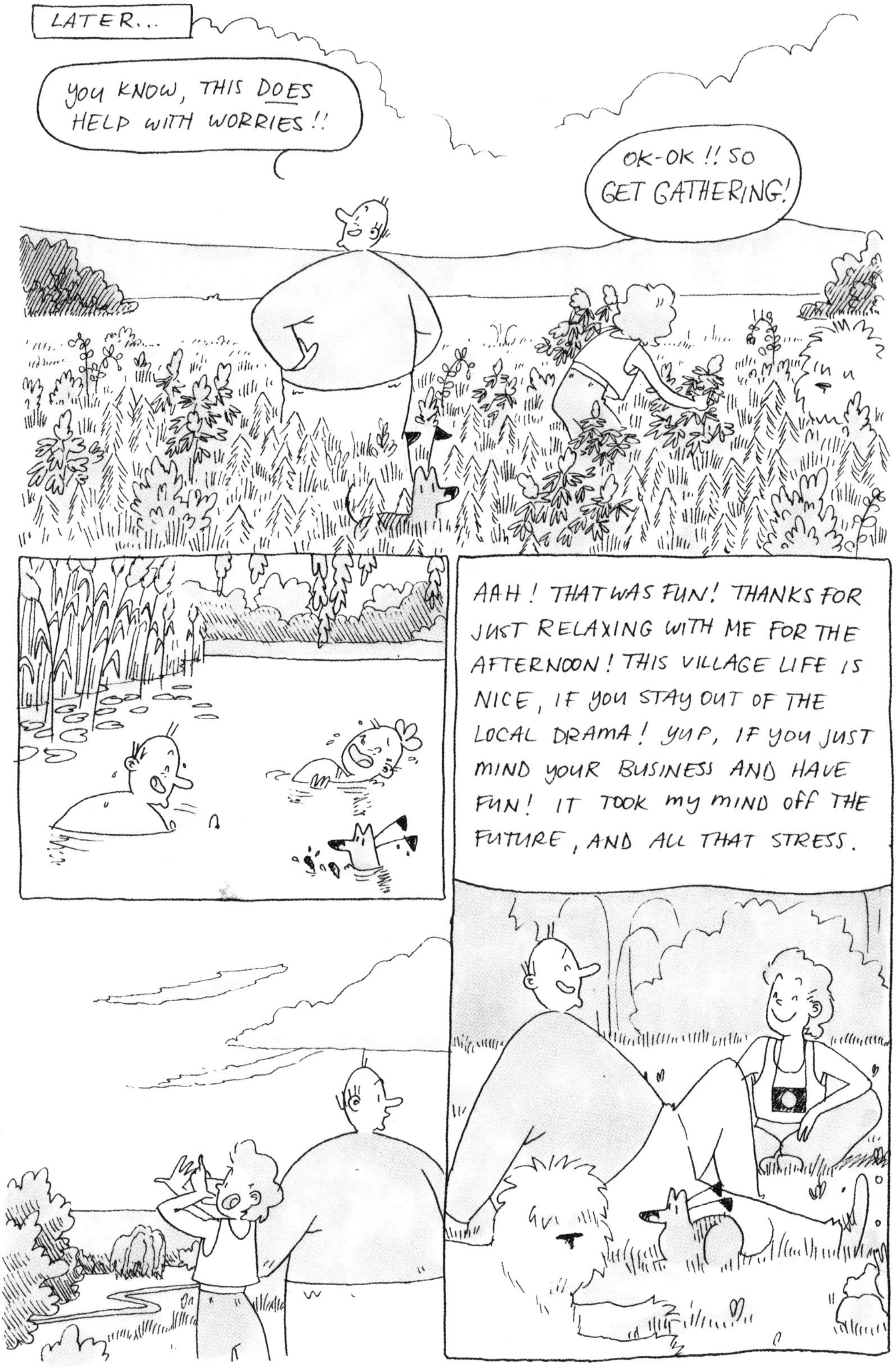
LATER...
YOU KNOW, THIS DOES HELP WITH WORRIES!!
OK-OK!! SO GET GATHERING!
AAH! THAT WAS FUN! THANKS FOR JUST RELAXING WITH ME FOR THE AFTERNOON! THIS VILLAGE LIFE IS NICE, IF YOU STAY OUT OF THE LOCAL DRAMA! YUP, IF YOU JUST MIND YOUR BUSINESS AND HAVE FUN! IT TOOK MY MIND OFF THE FUTURE, AND ALL THAT STRESS.

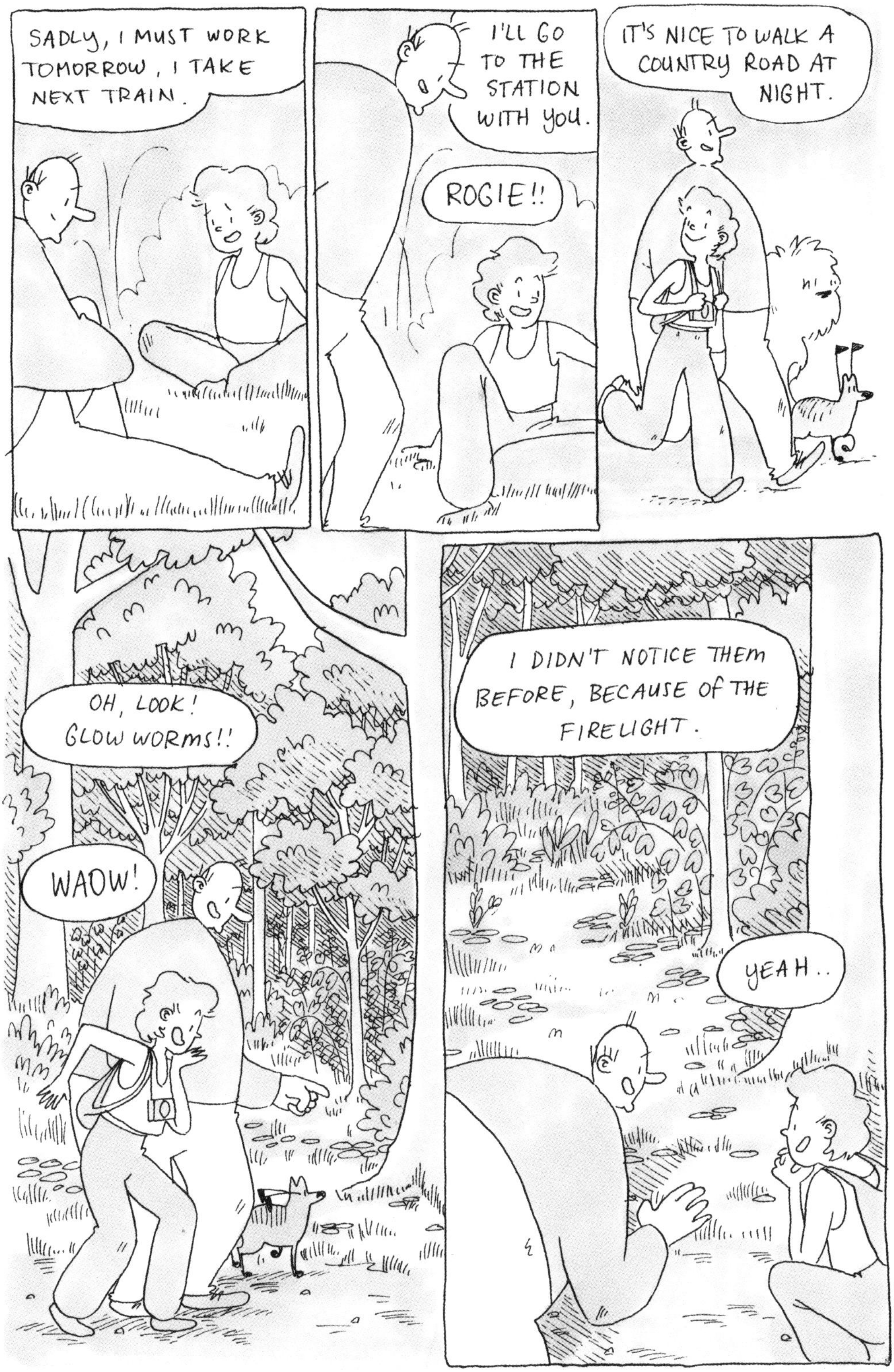
SADLY, I MUST WORK TOMORROW, I TAKE NEXT TRAIN.
I'LL GO TO THE STATION WITH YOU.
ROGIE!!
IT'S NICE TO WALK A COUNTRY ROAD AT NIGHT.
OH, LOOK! GLOW WORMS!!
WAOW!
I DIDN'T NOTICE THEM BEFORE, BECAUSE OF THE FIRELIGHT.
YEAH..

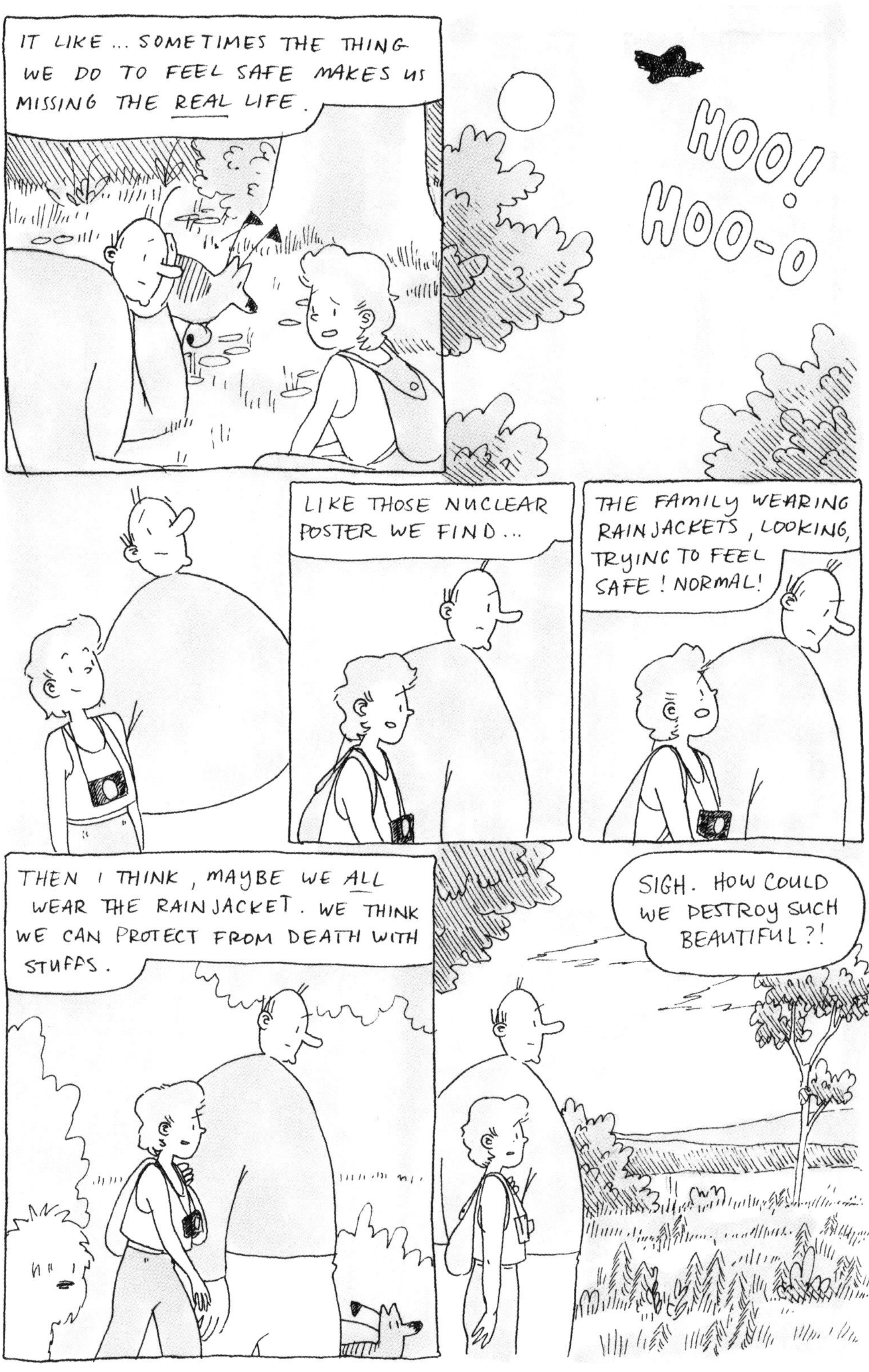
IT LIKE ... SOMETIMES THE THING WE DO TO FEEL SAFE MAKES US MISSING THE REAL LIFE.
HOO! HOO-O
LIKE THOSE NUCLEAR POSTER WE FIND...
THE FAMILY WEARING RAINJACKETS, LOOKING, TRYING TO FEEL SAFE! NORMAL!
THEN I THINK, MAYBE WE ALL WEAR THE RAINJACKET. WE THINK WE CAN PROTECT FROM DEATH WITH STUFFS.
SIGH. HOW COULD WE DESTROY SUCH BEAUTIFUL?!

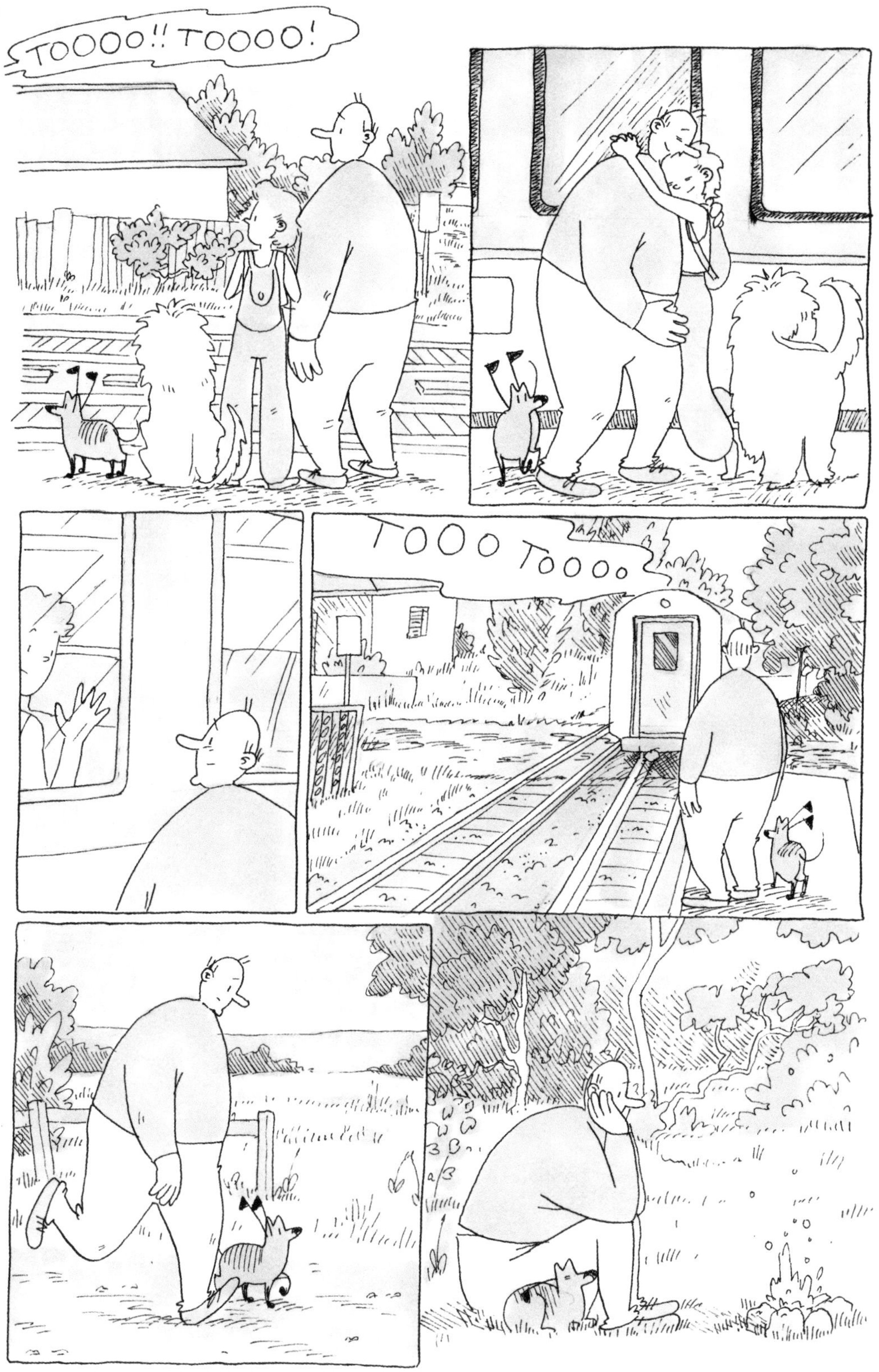
TOOOO!! TOOOO!
TOOO TOOOo

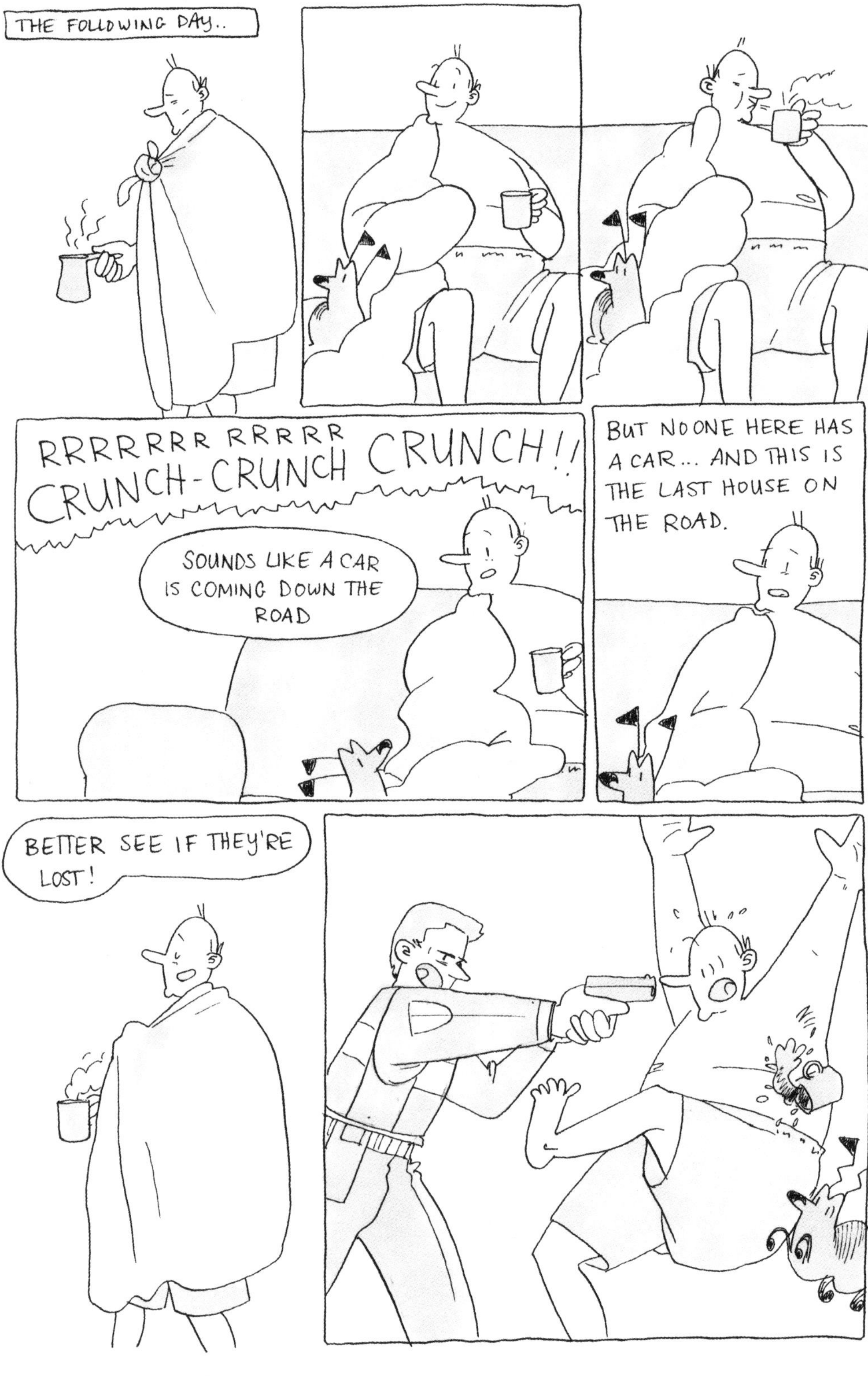
THE FOLLOWING DAY..
RRRRRRR RRRRR
CRUNCH-CRUNCH CRUNCH!!
SOUNDS LIKE A CAR IS COMING DOWN THE ROAD
BUT NO ONE HERE HAS A CAR... AND THIS IS THE LAST HOUSE ON THE ROAD.
BETTER SEE IF THEY'RE LOST!

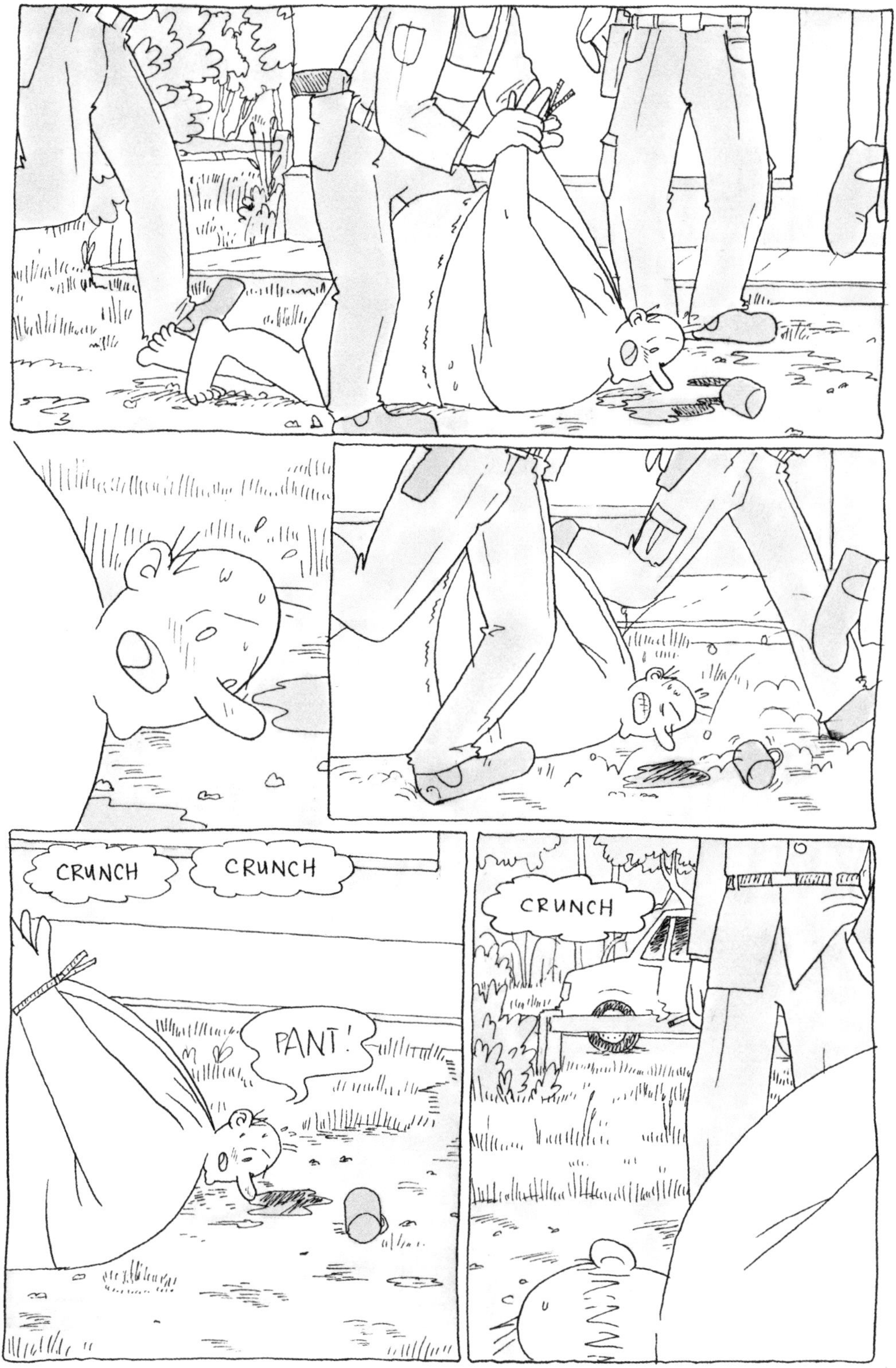
CRUNCH
CRUNCH
PANT!
CRUNCH

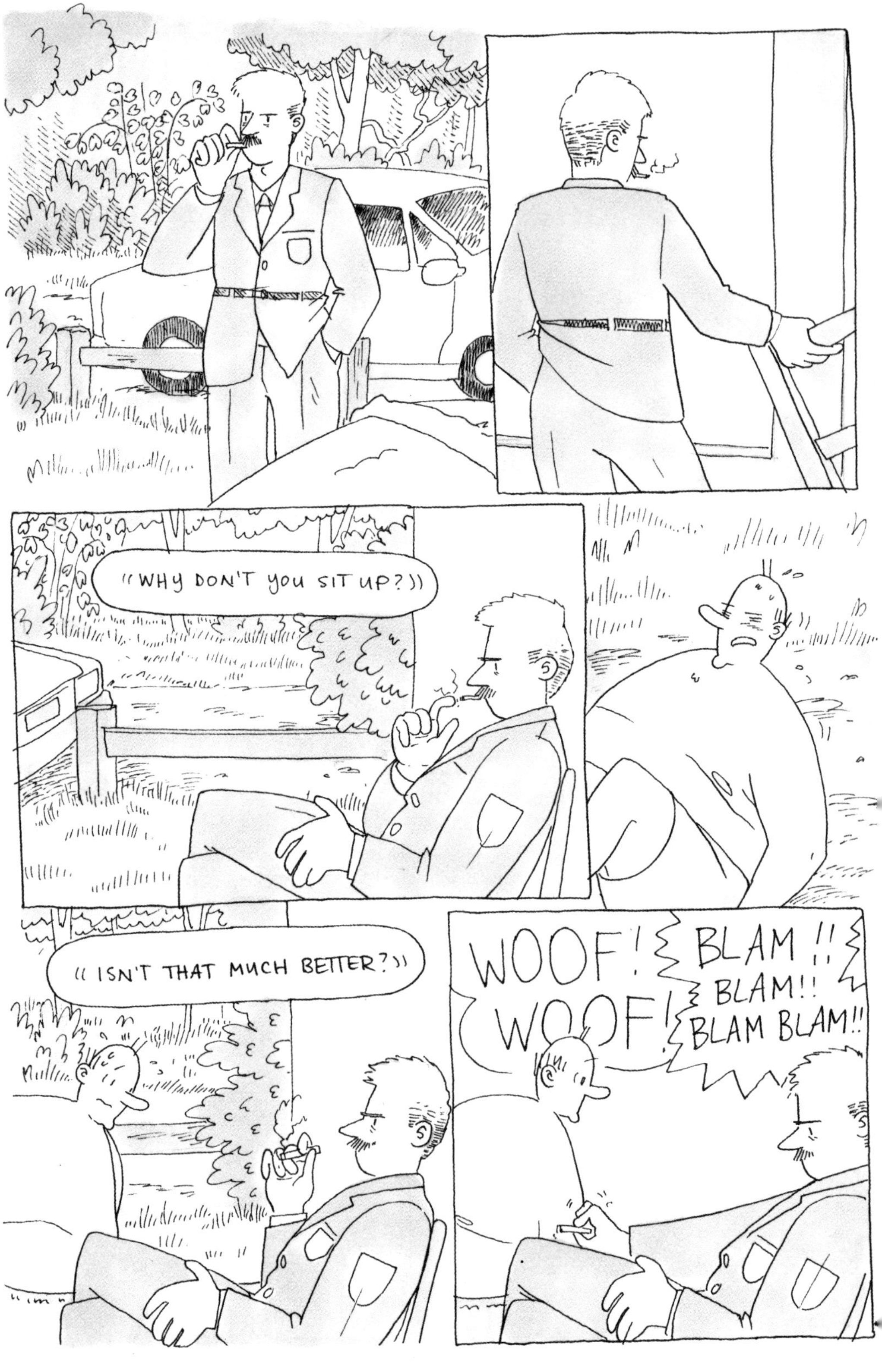
((WHY DON'T YOU SIT UP?))
((ISN'T THAT MUCH BETTER?))
WOOF! WOOF!
BLAM!! BLAM!! BLAM BLAM!!

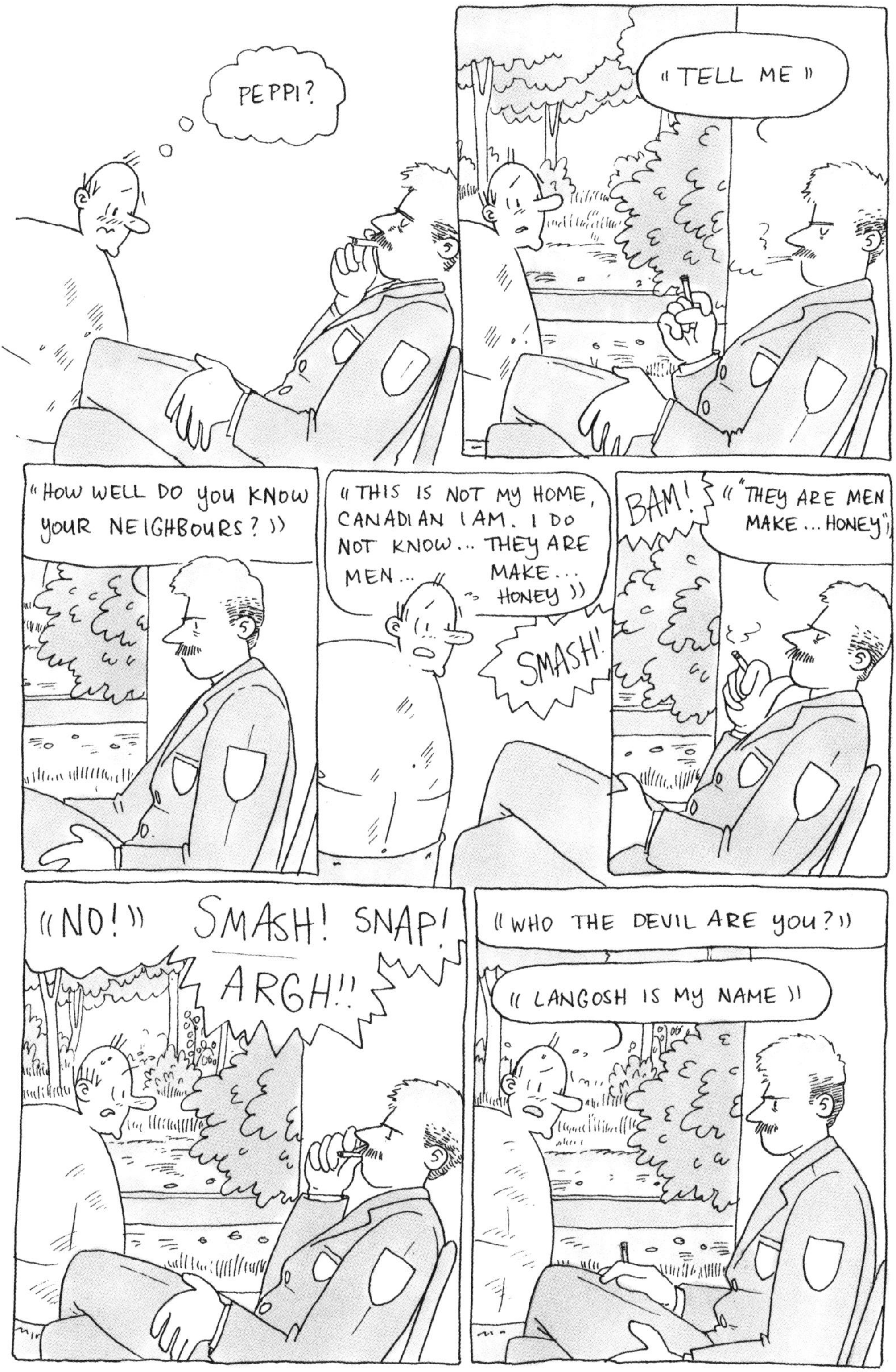
PEPPI?
« TELL ME »
« HOW WELL DO YOU KNOW YOUR NEIGHBOURS? »
« THIS IS NOT MY HOME, CANADIAN I AM. I DO NOT KNOW... THEY ARE MEN... MAKE... HONEY »
SMASH!
BAM!
« "THEY ARE MEN MAKE... HONEY"
« NO! »
SMASH! SNAP!
ARGH!!
« WHO THE DEVIL ARE YOU? »
« LANGOSH IS MY NAME »

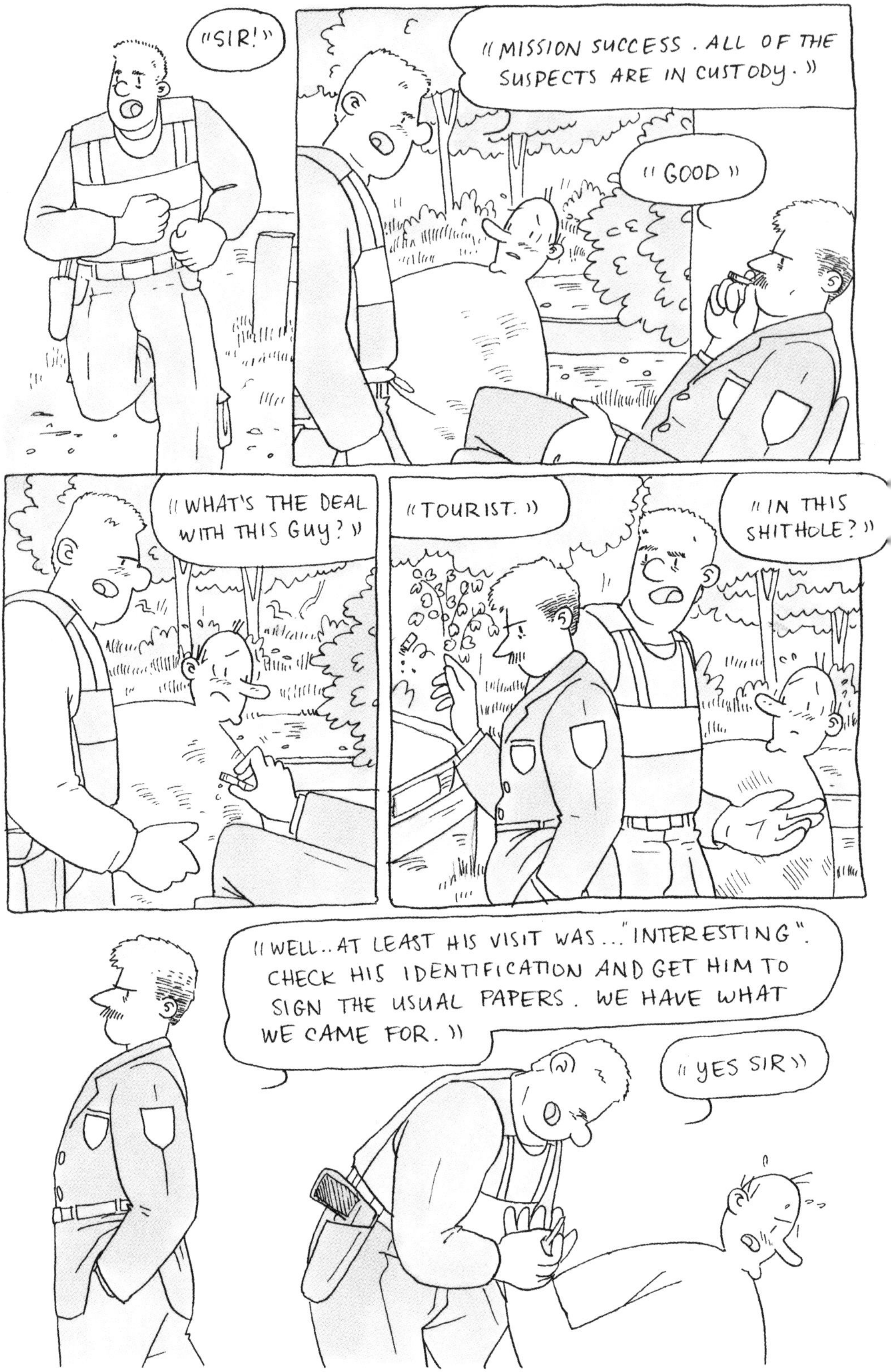
"SIR!"
« MISSION SUCCESS. ALL OF THE SUSPECTS ARE IN CUSTODY. »
« GOOD »
« WHAT'S THE DEAL WITH THIS GUY? »
« TOURIST. »
« IN THIS SHITHOLE? »
« WELL.. AT LEAST HIS VISIT WAS... "INTERESTING". CHECK HIS IDENTIFICATION AND GET HIM TO SIGN THE USUAL PAPERS. WE HAVE WHAT WE CAME FOR. »
« YES SIR »

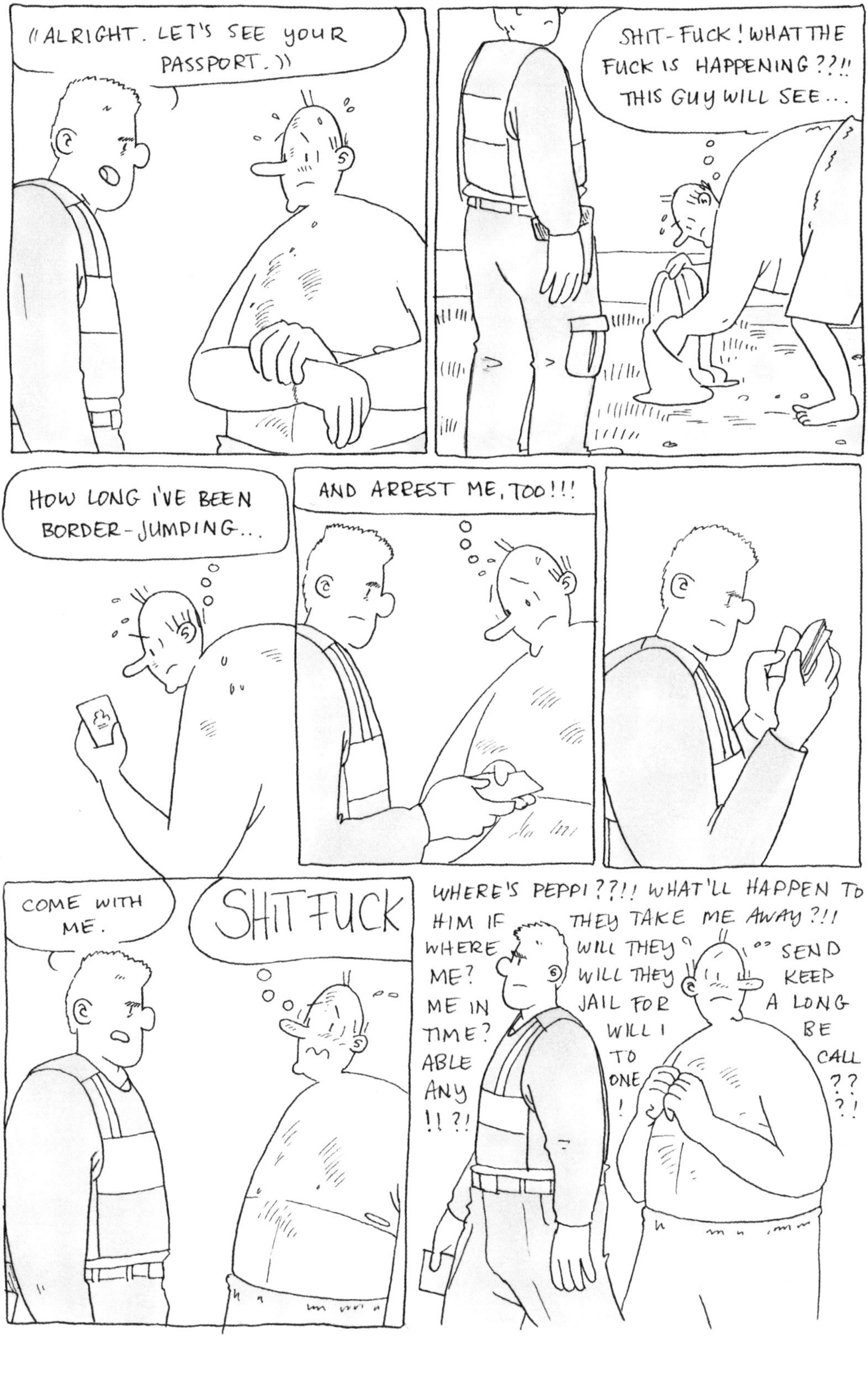

((ALRIGHT. LET'S SEE YOUR PASSPORT.))
SHIT-FUCK! WHAT THE FUCK IS HAPPENING??!! THIS GUY WILL SEE...
HOW LONG I'VE BEEN BORDER-JUMPING...
AND ARREST ME, TOO!!!
COME WITH ME.
SHIT FUCK
WHERE'S PEPPI??!! WHAT'LL HAPPEN TO HIM IF THEY TAKE ME AWAY?!!
WHERE WILL THEY SEND ME? WILL THEY KEEP ME IN JAIL FOR A LONG TIME? WILL I BE ABLE TO CALL ANY ONE
!!?! ! ??
?!

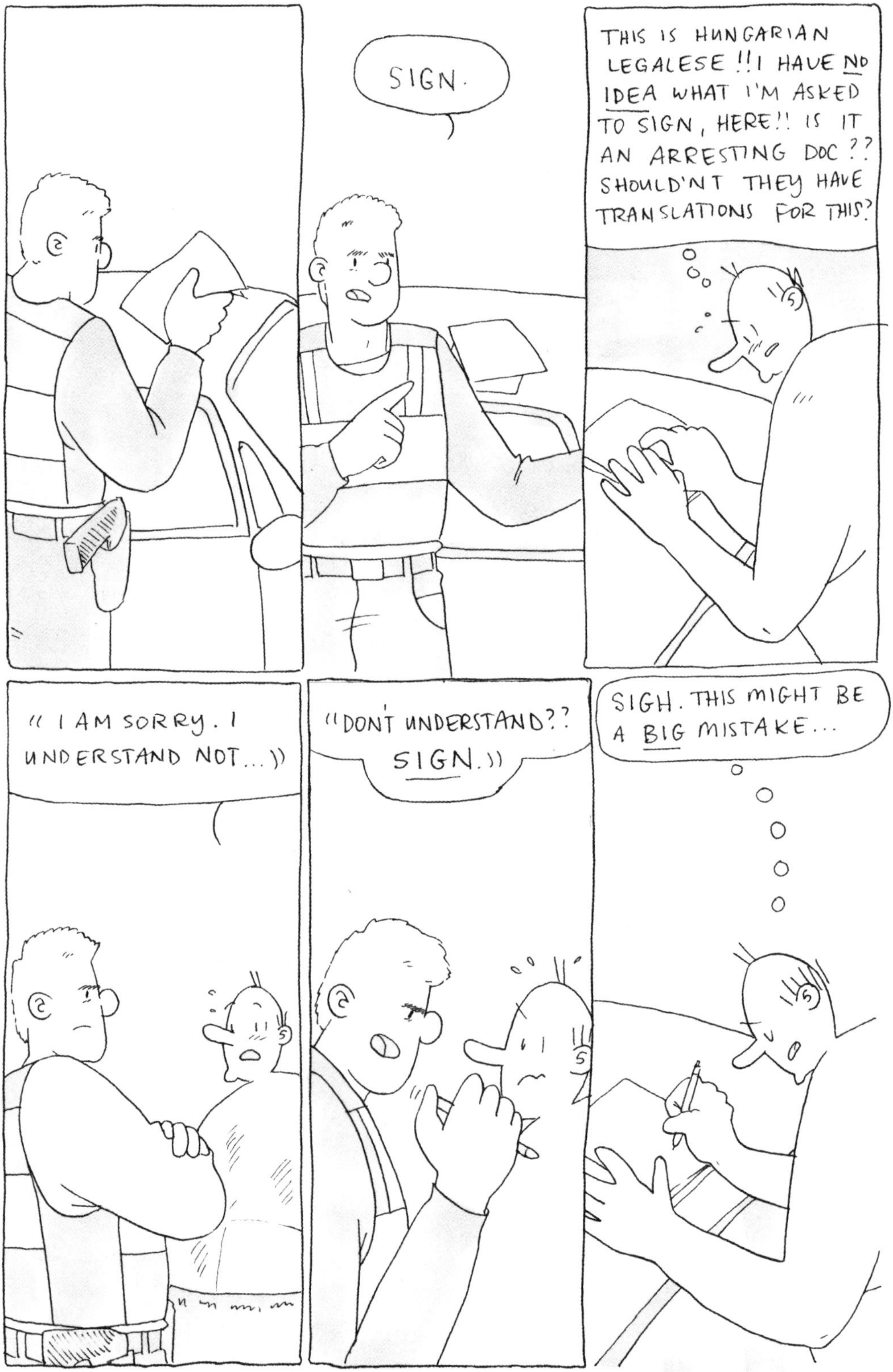
SIGN.
THIS IS HUNGARIAN LEGALESE !!! I HAVE NO IDEA WHAT I'M ASKED TO SIGN, HERE!! IS IT AN ARRESTING DOC?? SHOULD'NT THEY HAVE TRANSLATIONS FOR THIS?
« I AM SORRY. I UNDERSTAND NOT... »
« DON'T UNDERSTAND?? SIGN. »
SIGH. THIS MIGHT BE A BIG MISTAKE...

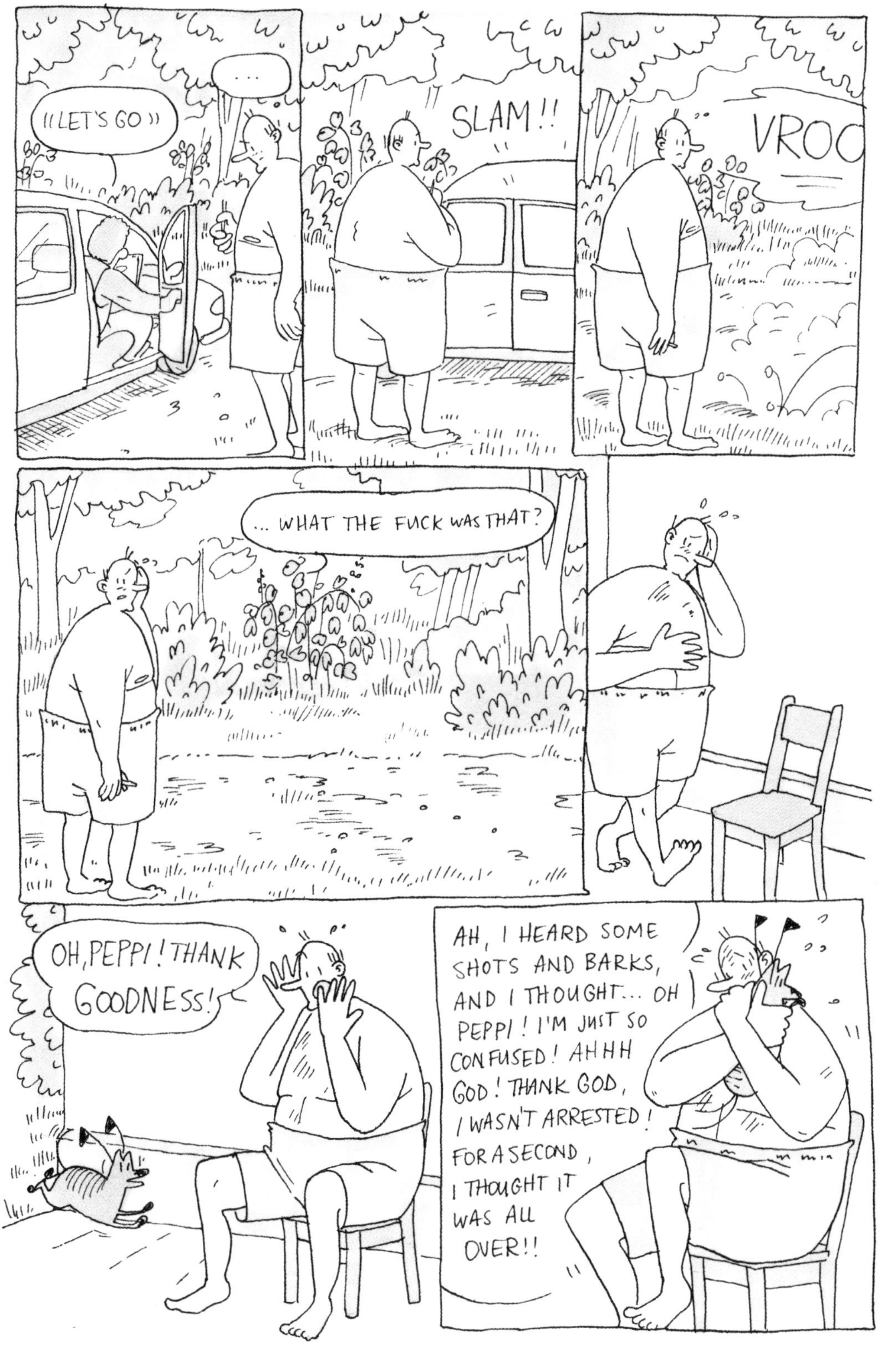

((LET'S GO))
...
SLAM!!
VROO
... WHAT THE FUCK WAS THAT?
OH, PEPPI! THANK GOODNESS!
AH, I HEARD SOME SHOTS AND BARKS, AND I THOUGHT... OH PEPPI! I'M JUST SO CONFUSED! AHHH GOD! THANK GOD, I WASN'T ARRESTED! FOR A SECOND, I THOUGHT IT WAS ALL OVER!!

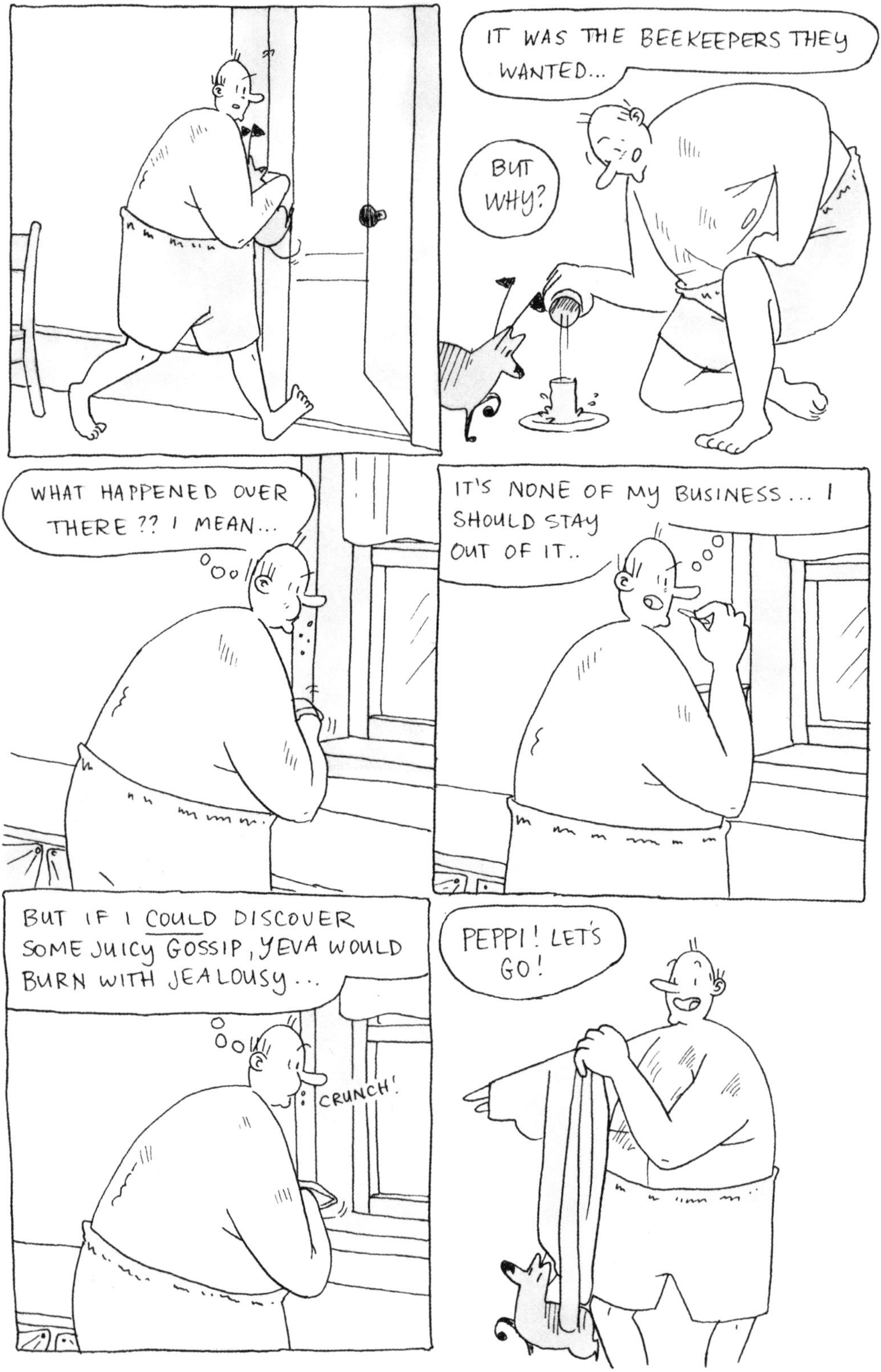
IT WAS THE BEEKEEPERS THEY WANTED...
BUT WHY?
WHAT HAPPENED OVER THERE?? I MEAN...
IT'S NONE OF MY BUSINESS... I SHOULD STAY OUT OF IT..
BUT IF I COULD DISCOVER SOME JUICY GOSSIP, YEVA WOULD BURN WITH JEALOUSY...
CRUNCH!
PEPPI! LET'S GO!

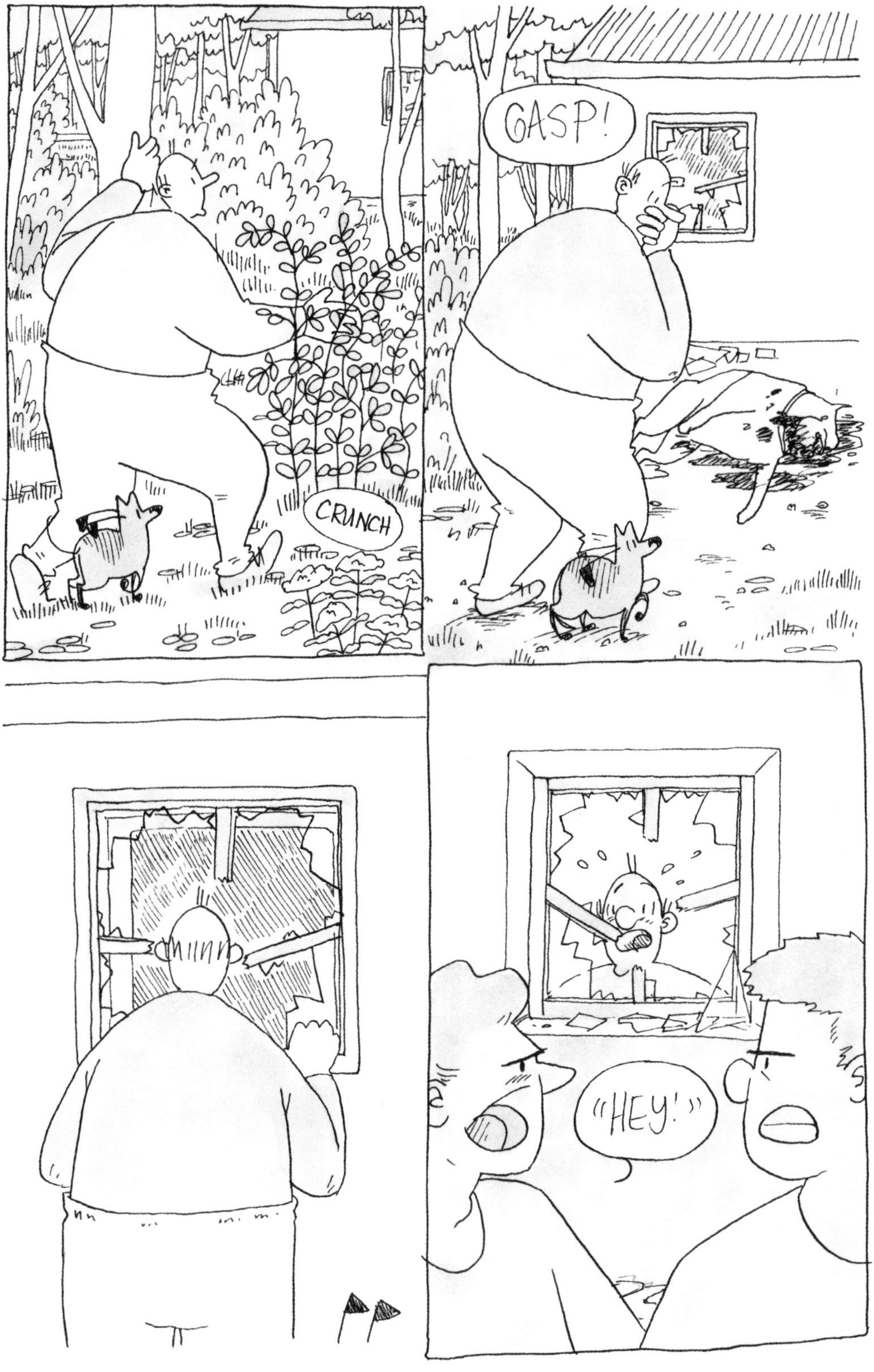
CRUNCH
GASP!
"HEY!"

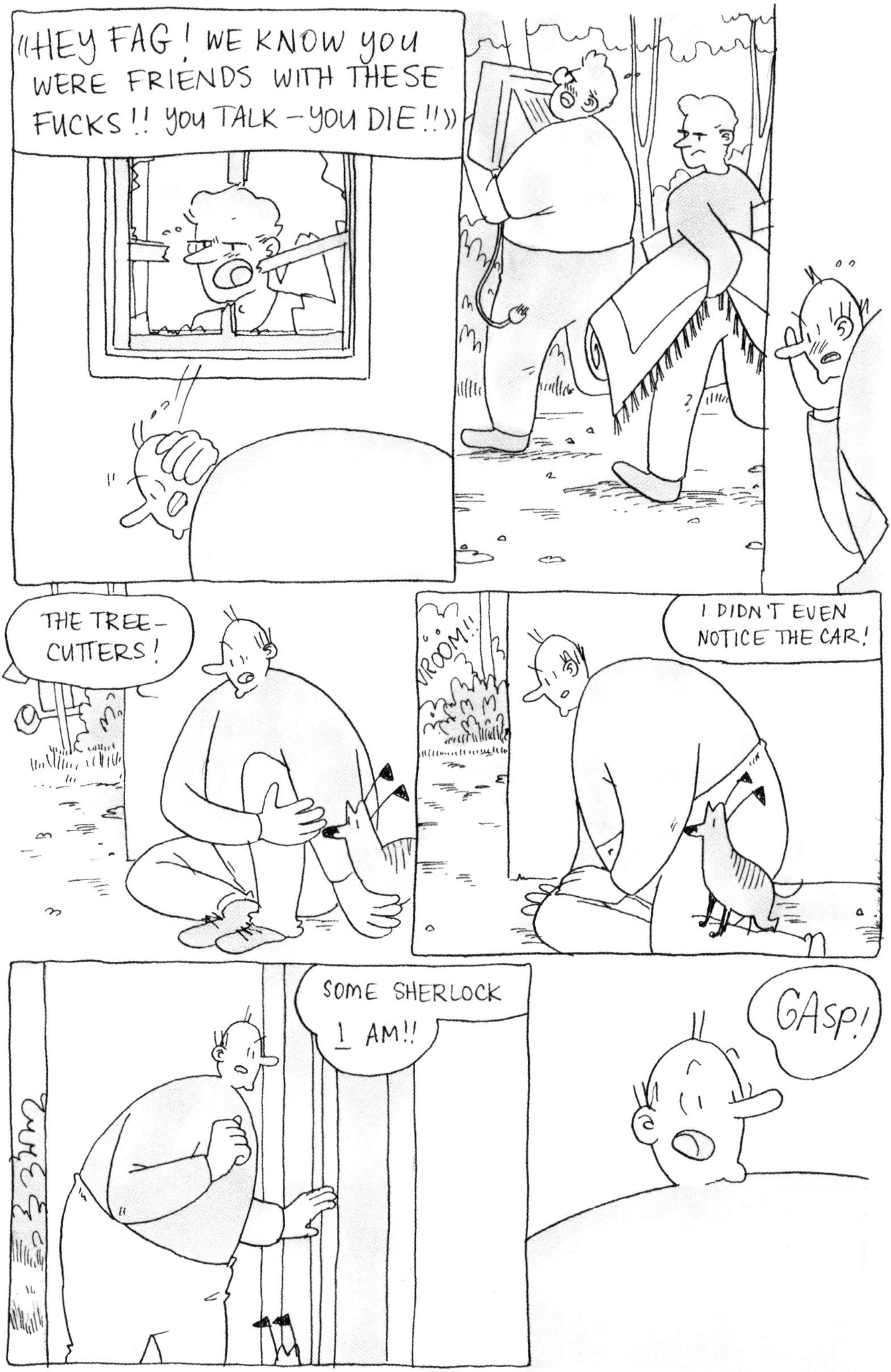

«HEY FAG! WE KNOW YOU WERE FRIENDS WITH THESE FUCKS!! YOU TALK—YOU DIE!!»
THE TREE-CUTTERS!
VROOM!!
I DIDN'T EVEN NOTICE THE CAR!
SOME SHERLOCK I AM!!
GASP!

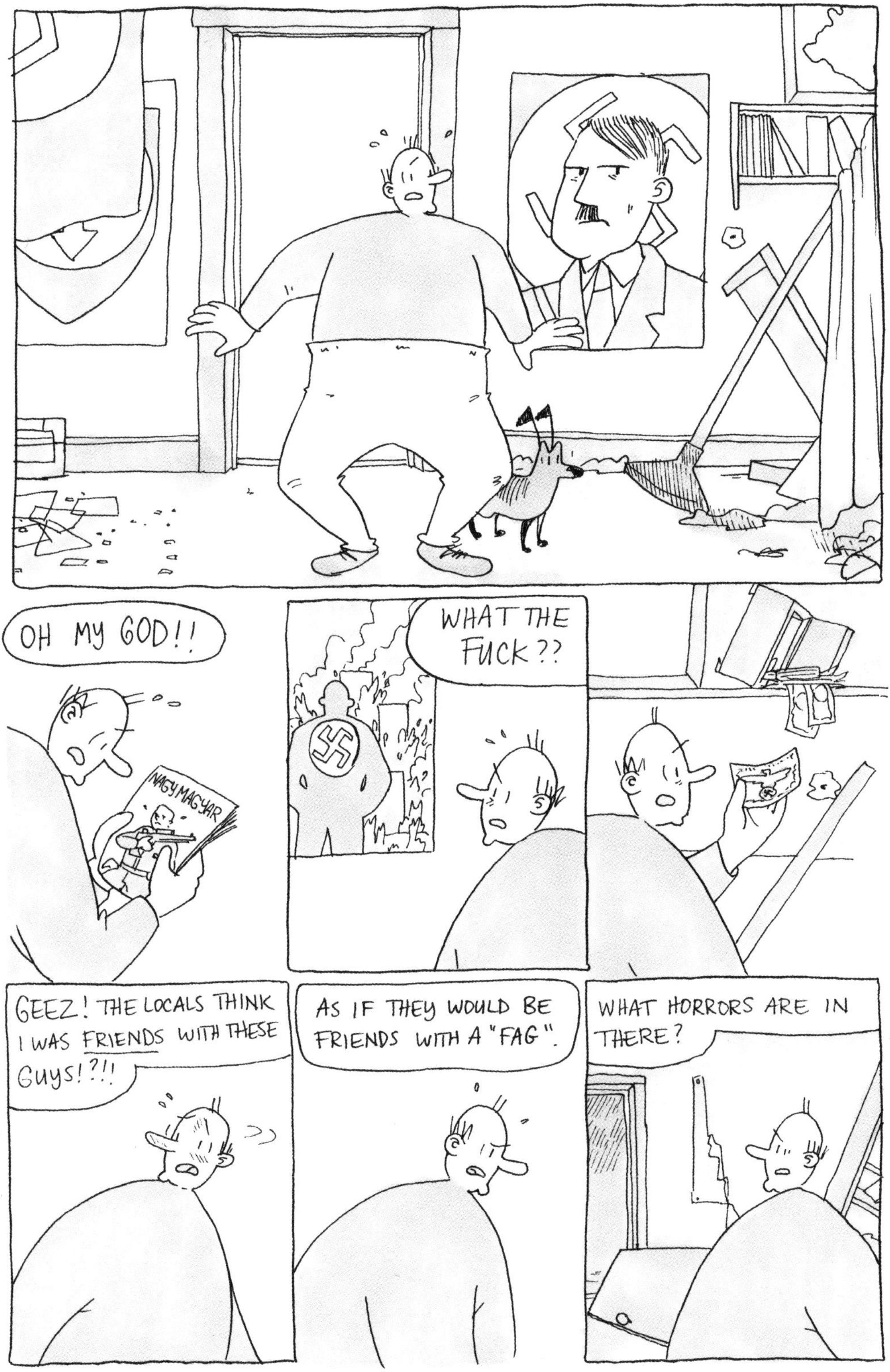
OH MY GOD!!
WHAT THE FUCK??
NAGY MAGYAR
GEEZ! THE LOCALS THINK I WAS FRIENDS WITH THESE GUYS!?!!
AS IF THEY WOULD BE FRIENDS WITH A "FAG".
WHAT HORRORS ARE IN THERE?

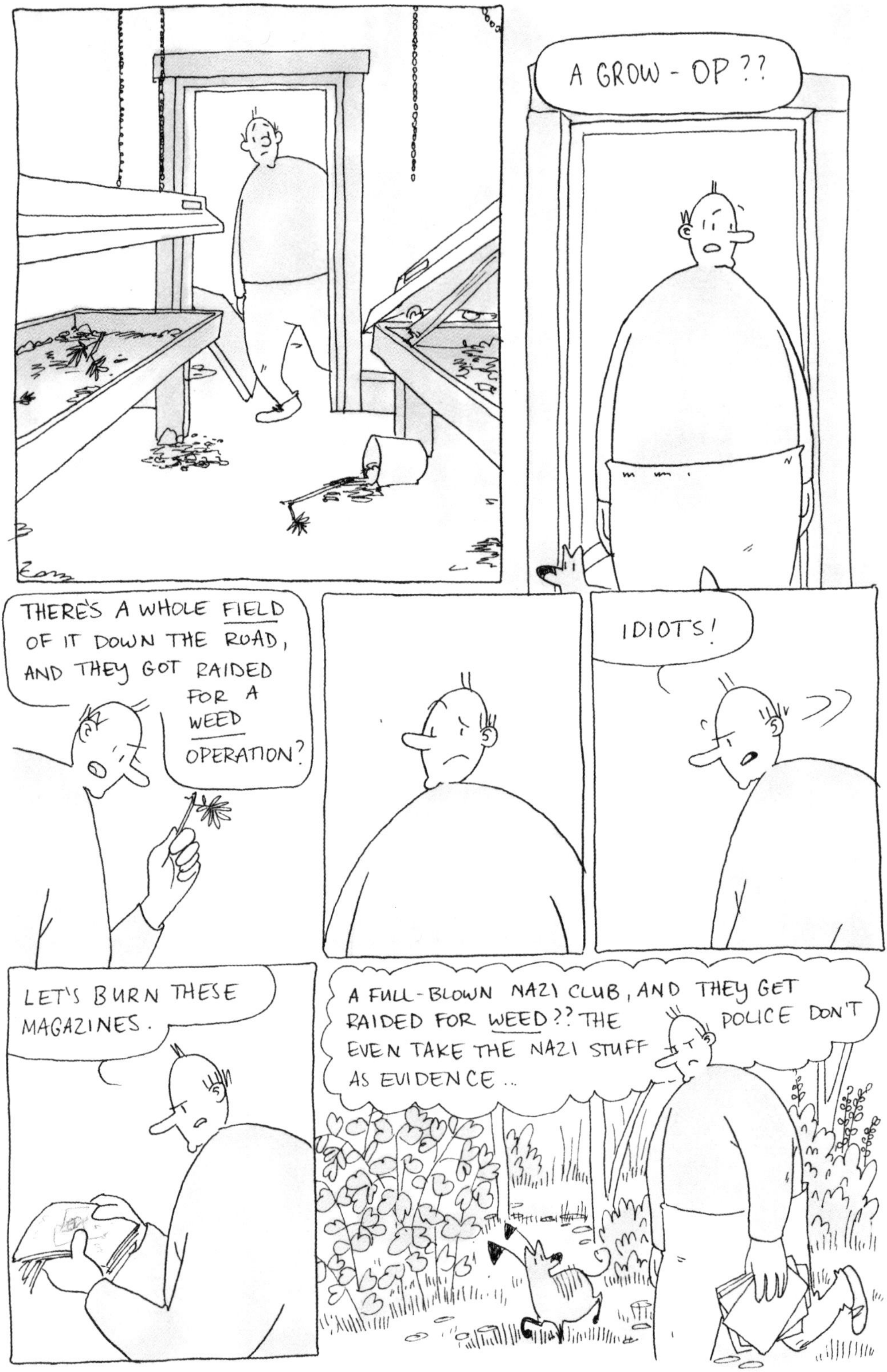
A GROW - OP ??
THERE'S A WHOLE FIELD OF IT DOWN THE ROAD, AND THEY GOT RAIDED FOR A WEED OPERATION?
IDIOTS!
LET'S BURN THESE MAGAZINES.
A FULL-BLOWN NAZI CLUB, AND THEY GET RAIDED FOR WEED?? THE POLICE DON'T EVEN TAKE THE NAZI STUFF AS EVIDENCE ...

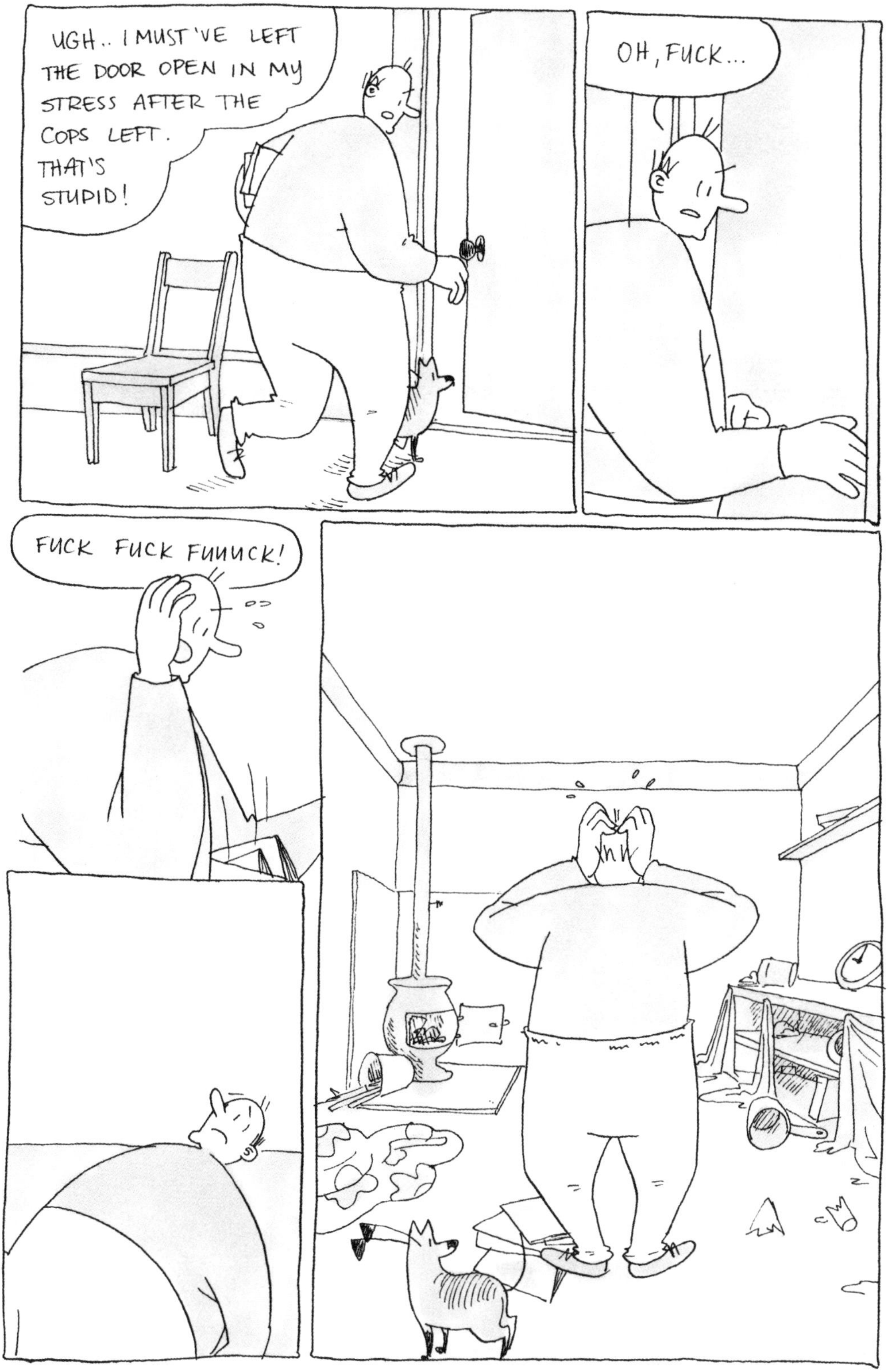
UGH.. I MUST'VE LEFT THE DOOR OPEN IN MY STRESS AFTER THE COPS LEFT. THAT'S STUPID!
OH, FUCK...
FUCK FUCK FUUUCK!

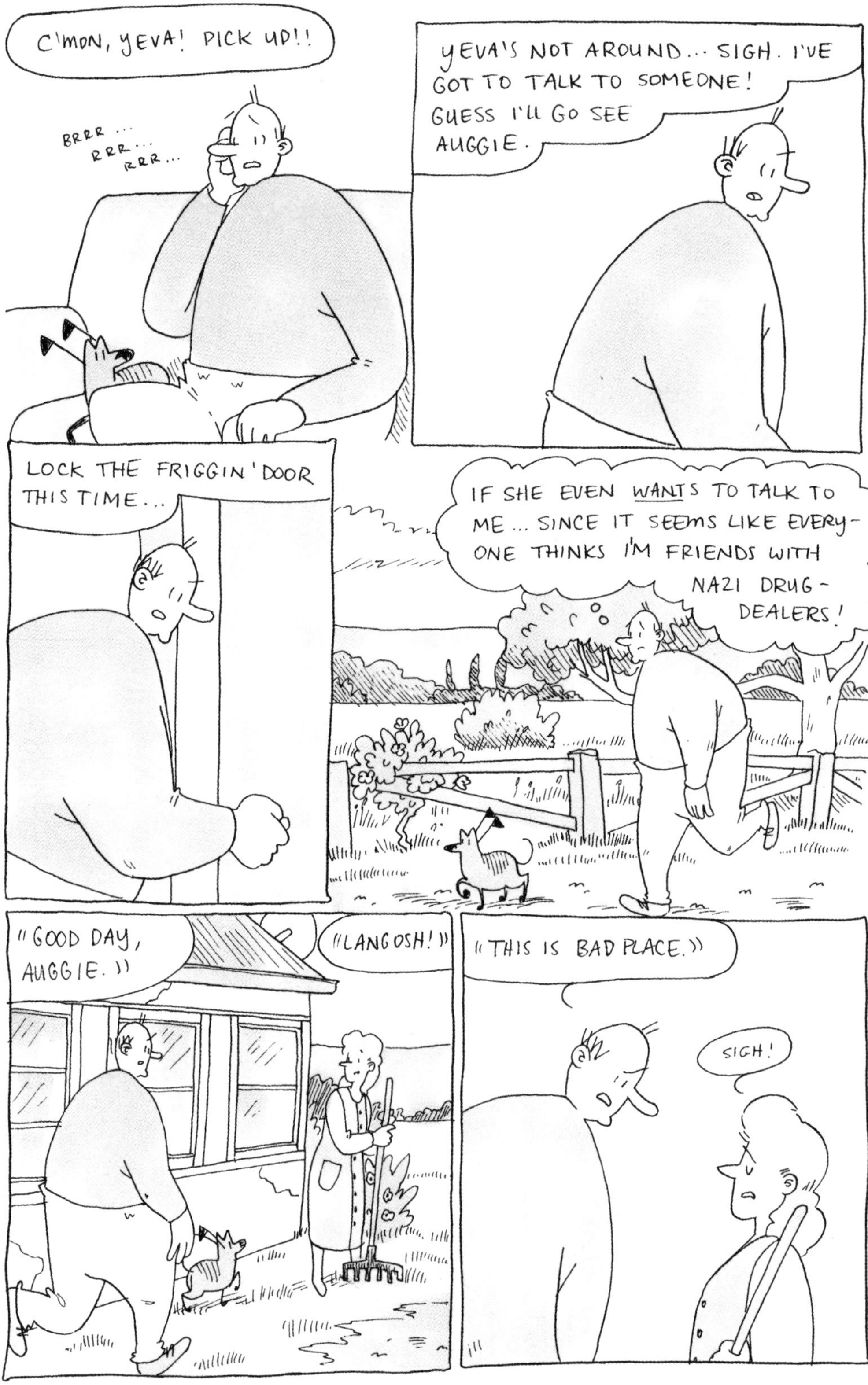
C'MON, YEVA! PICK UP!!
BRRR... RRR... RRR...
YEVA'S NOT AROUND... SIGH. I'VE GOT TO TALK TO SOMEONE! GUESS I'LL GO SEE AUGGIE.
LOCK THE FRIGGIN' DOOR THIS TIME...
IF SHE EVEN WANTS TO TALK TO ME... SINCE IT SEEMS LIKE EVERY-ONE THINKS I'M FRIENDS WITH NAZI DRUG-DEALERS!
«GOOD DAY, AUGGIE.»
«LANGOSH!»
«THIS IS BAD PLACE.»
SIGH!

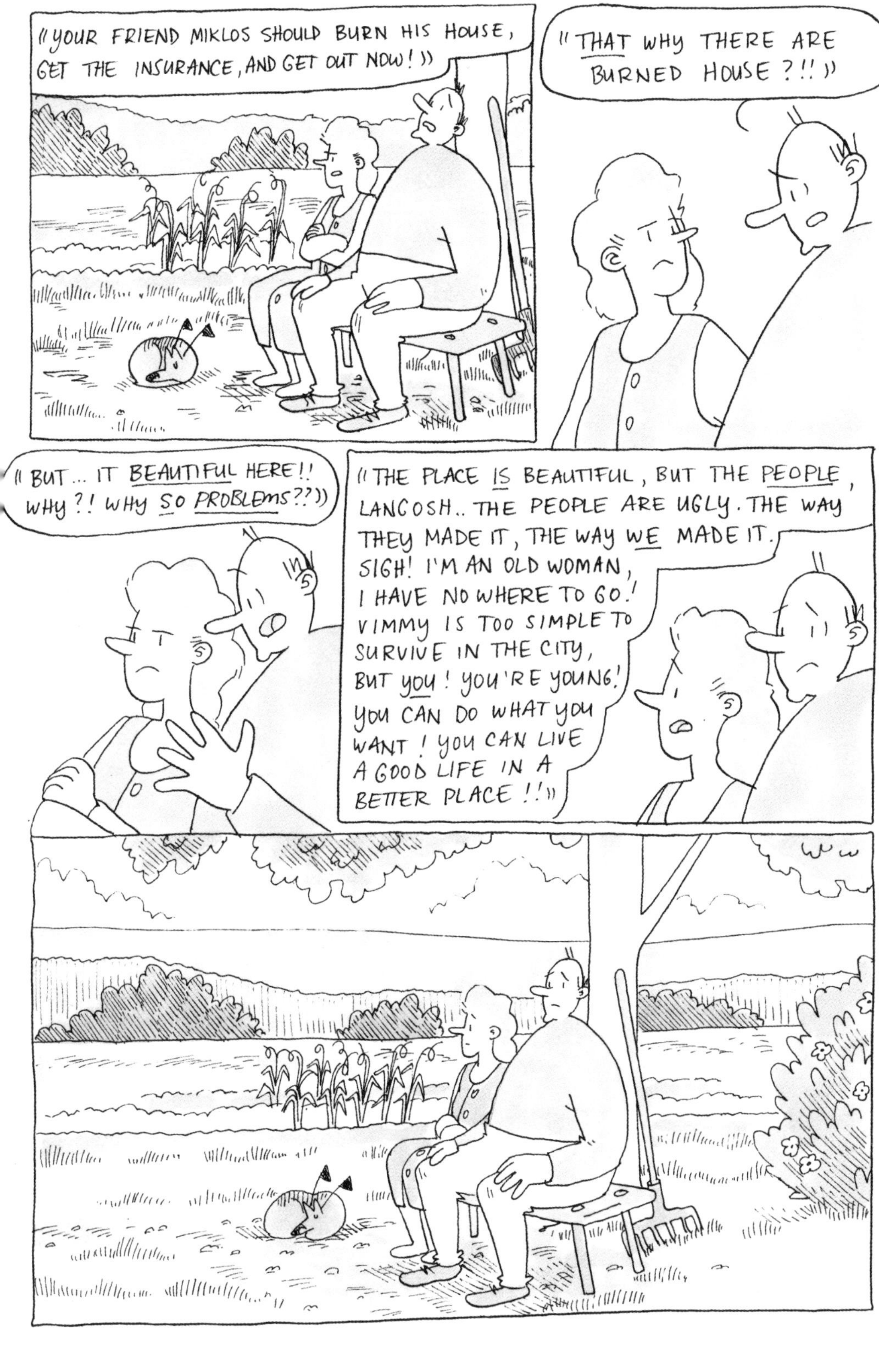

« YOUR FRIEND MIKLOS SHOULD BURN HIS HOUSE, GET THE INSURANCE, AND GET OUT NOW! »
« THAT WHY THERE ARE BURNED HOUSE ?!! »
« BUT... IT BEAUTIFUL HERE!! WHY ?! WHY SO PROBLEMS?? »
« THE PLACE IS BEAUTIFUL, BUT THE PEOPLE, LANCOSH.. THE PEOPLE ARE UGLY. THE WAY THEY MADE IT, THE WAY WE MADE IT. SIGH! I'M AN OLD WOMAN, I HAVE NO WHERE TO GO! VIMMY IS TOO SIMPLE TO SURVIVE IN THE CITY, BUT YOU! YOU'RE YOUNG! YOU CAN DO WHAT YOU WANT! YOU CAN LIVE A GOOD LIFE IN A BETTER PLACE!! »

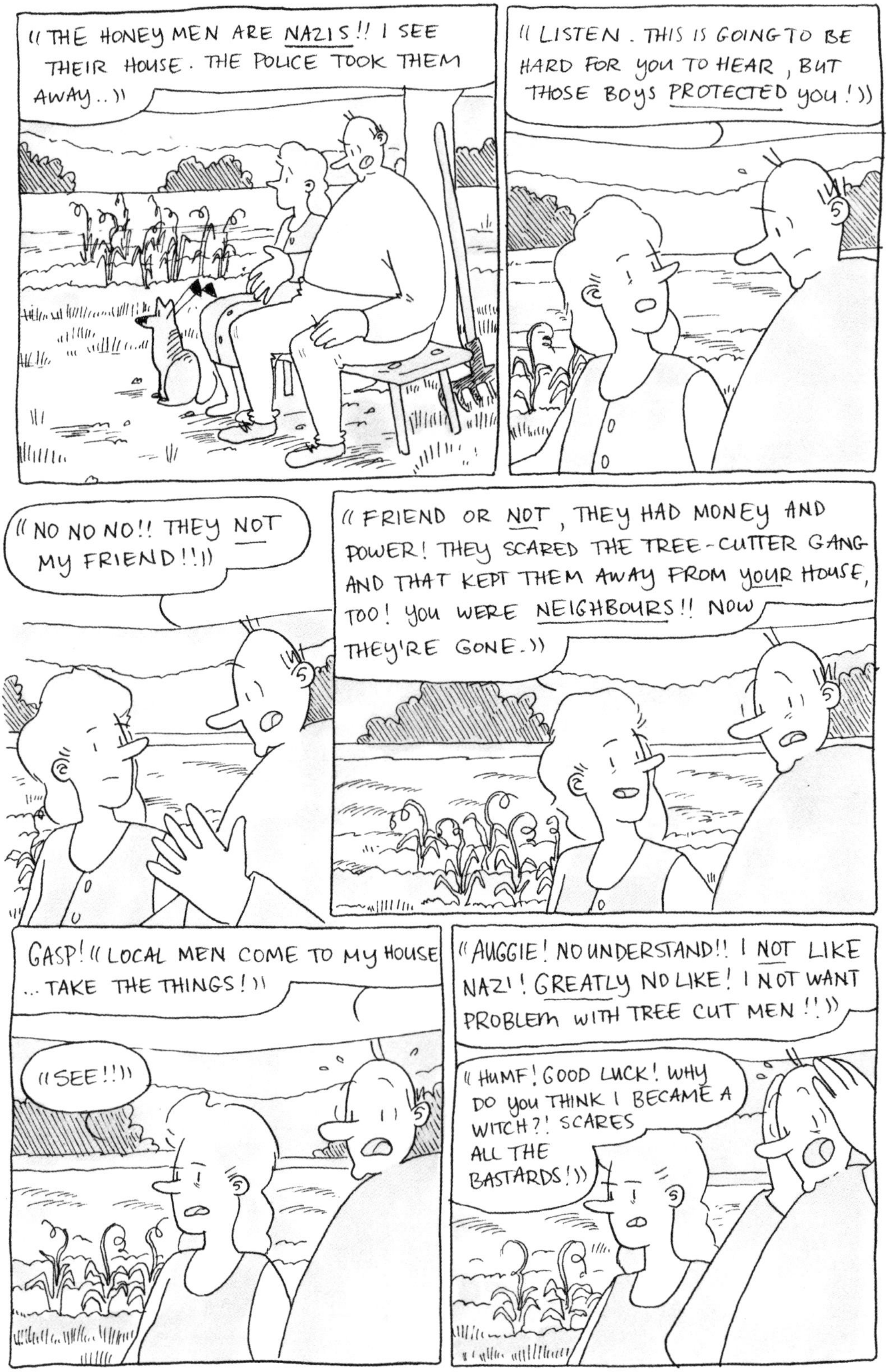

((THE HONEY MEN ARE NAZIS!! I SEE THEIR HOUSE. THE POLICE TOOK THEM AWAY..))
((LISTEN. THIS IS GOING TO BE HARD FOR YOU TO HEAR, BUT THOSE BOYS PROTECTED YOU!))
((NO NO NO!! THEY NOT MY FRIEND!!))
((FRIEND OR NOT, THEY HAD MONEY AND POWER! THEY SCARED THE TREE-CUTTER GANG AND THAT KEPT THEM AWAY FROM YOUR HOUSE, TOO! YOU WERE NEIGHBOURS!! NOW THEY'RE GONE.))
GASP! ((LOCAL MEN COME TO MY HOUSE ...TAKE THE THINGS!))
((SEE!!))
((AUGGIE! NO UNDERSTAND!! I NOT LIKE NAZI! GREATLY NO LIKE! I NOT WANT PROBLEM WITH TREE CUT MEN!!))
((HUMF! GOOD LUCK! WHY DO YOU THINK I BECAME A WITCH?! SCARES ALL THE BASTARDS!))

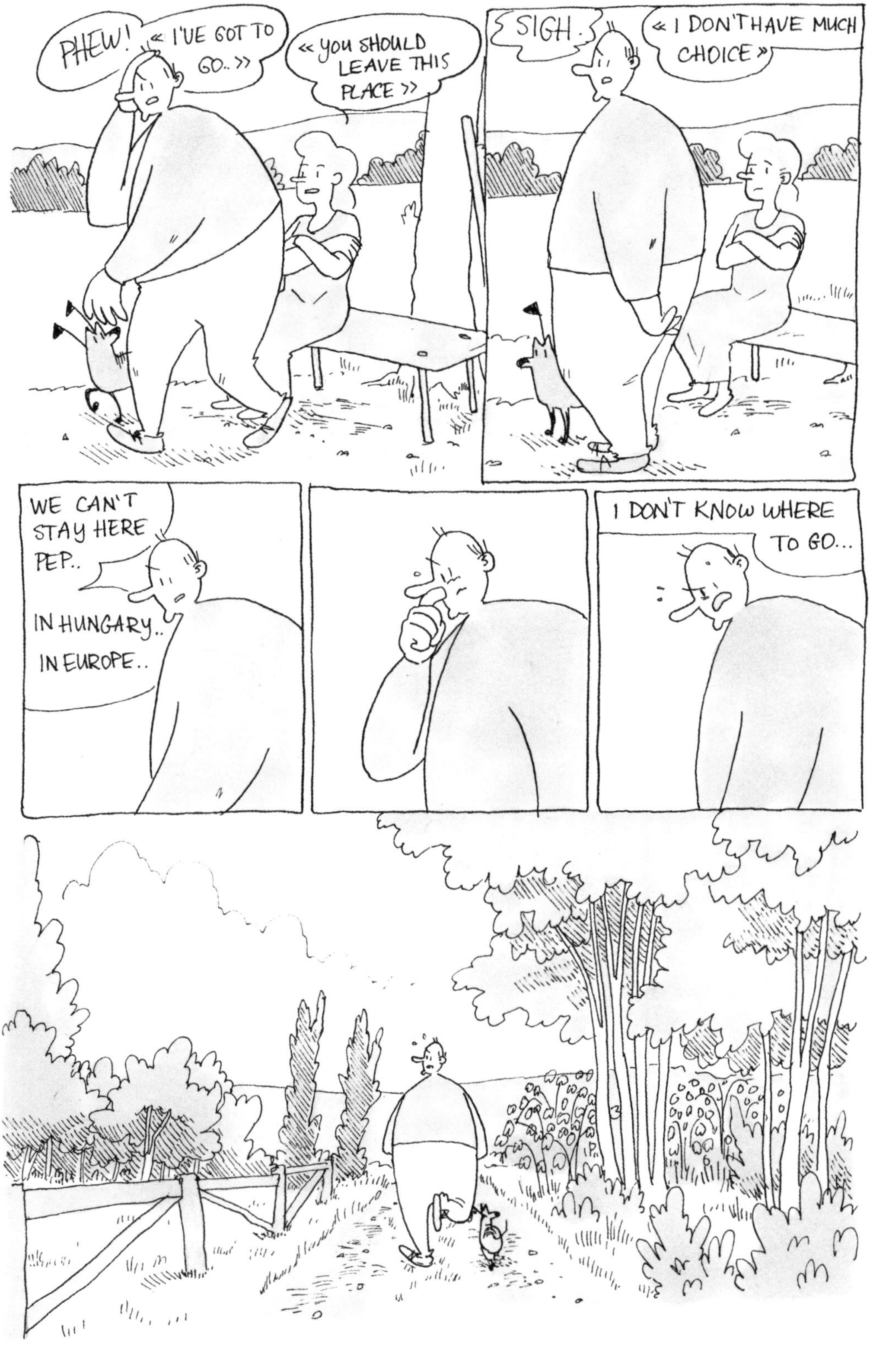
PHEW!
« I'VE GOT TO GO.. »
« YOU SHOULD LEAVE THIS PLACE »
SIGH.
« I DON'T HAVE MUCH CHOICE »
WE CAN'T STAY HERE PEP..
IN HUNGARY..
IN EUROPE..
I DON'T KNOW WHERE TO GO...

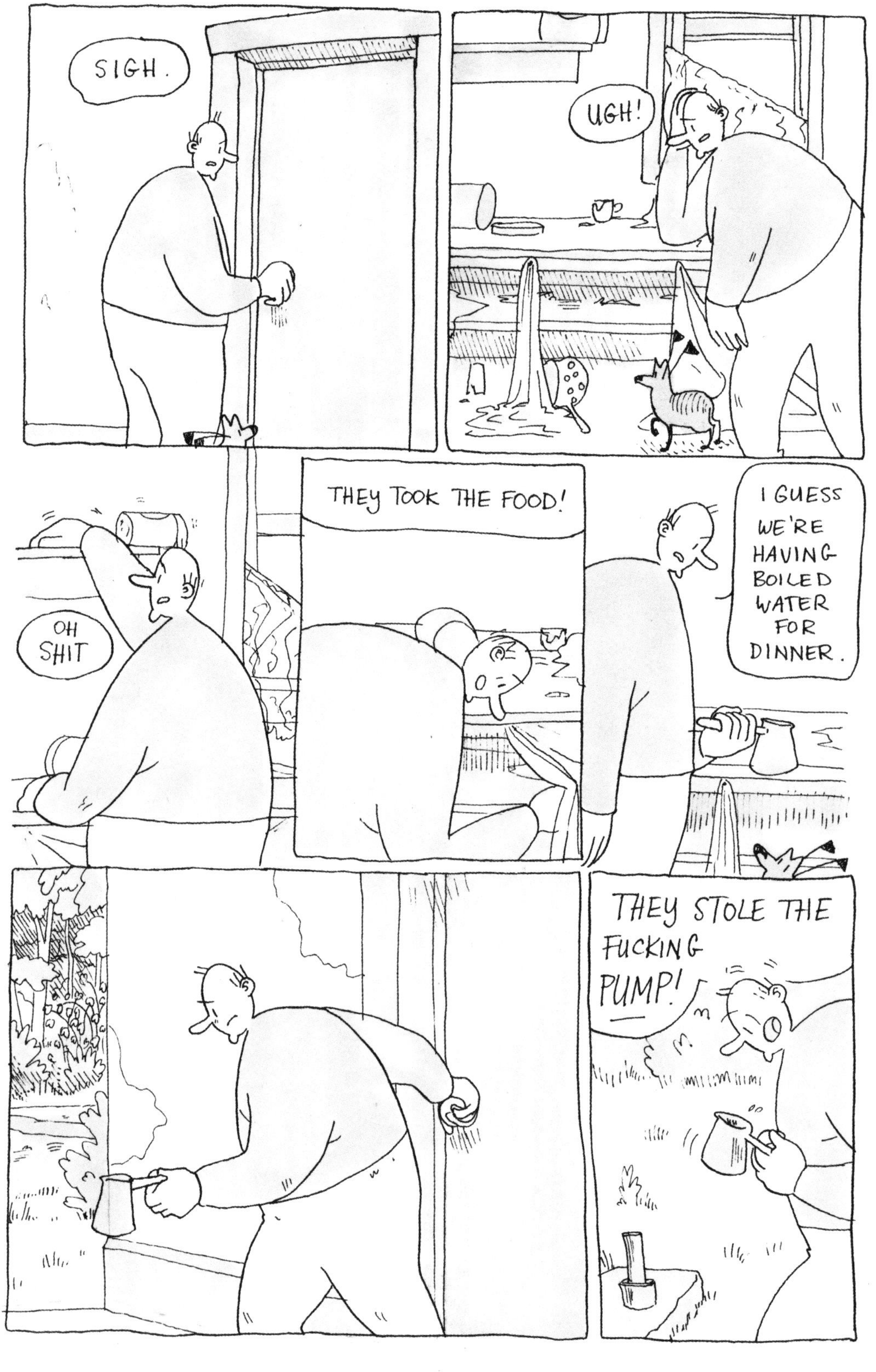
SIGH.
UGH!
OH SHIT
THEY TOOK THE FOOD!
I GUESS WE'RE HAVING BOILED WATER FOR DINNER.
THEY STOLE THE FUCKING PUMP!

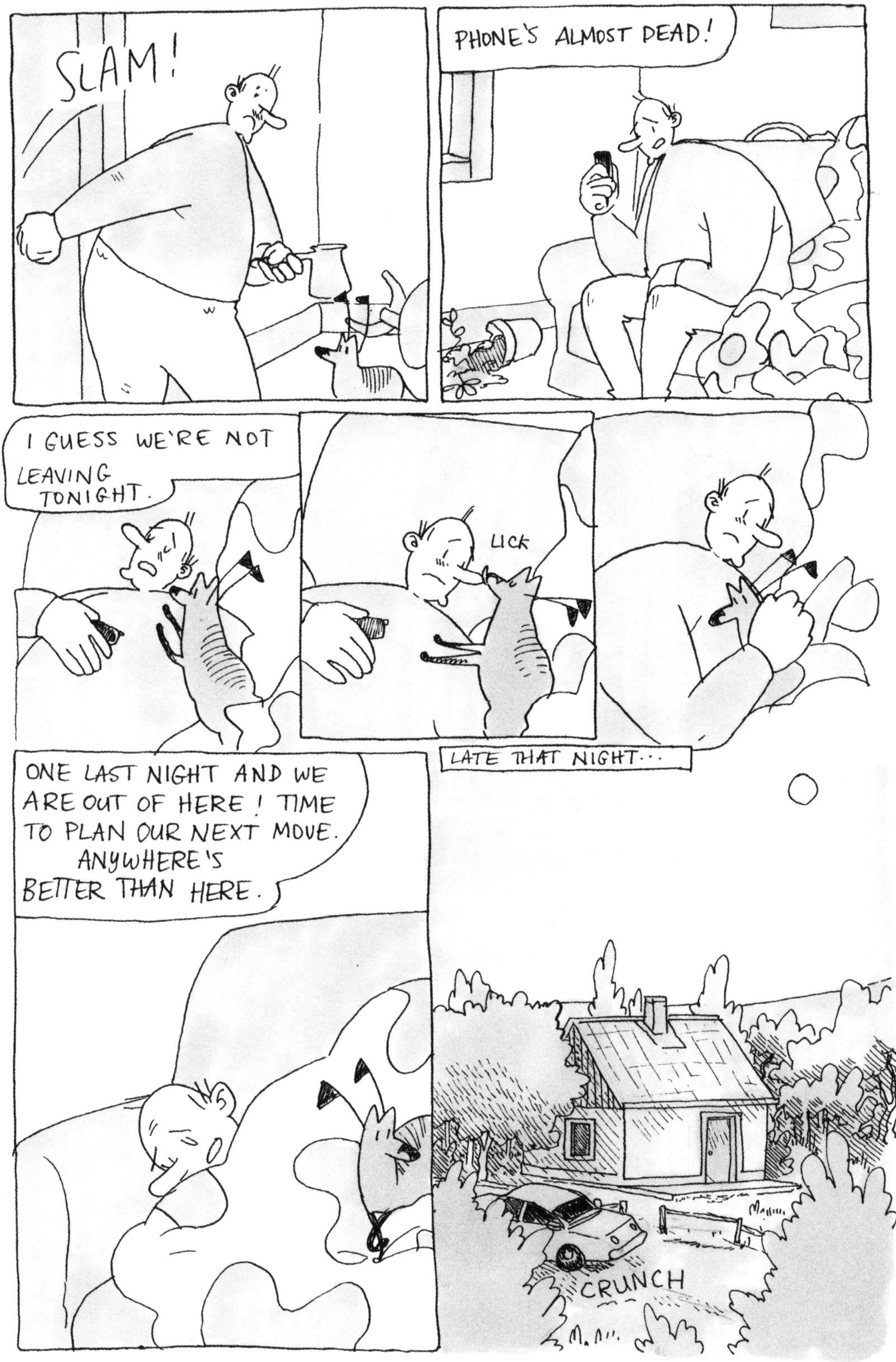
SLAM!
PHONE'S ALMOST DEAD!
I GUESS WE'RE NOT LEAVING TONIGHT.
LICK
ONE LAST NIGHT AND WE ARE OUT OF HERE! TIME TO PLAN OUR NEXT MOVE. ANYWHERE'S BETTER THAN HERE.
LATE THAT NIGHT...
CRUNCH

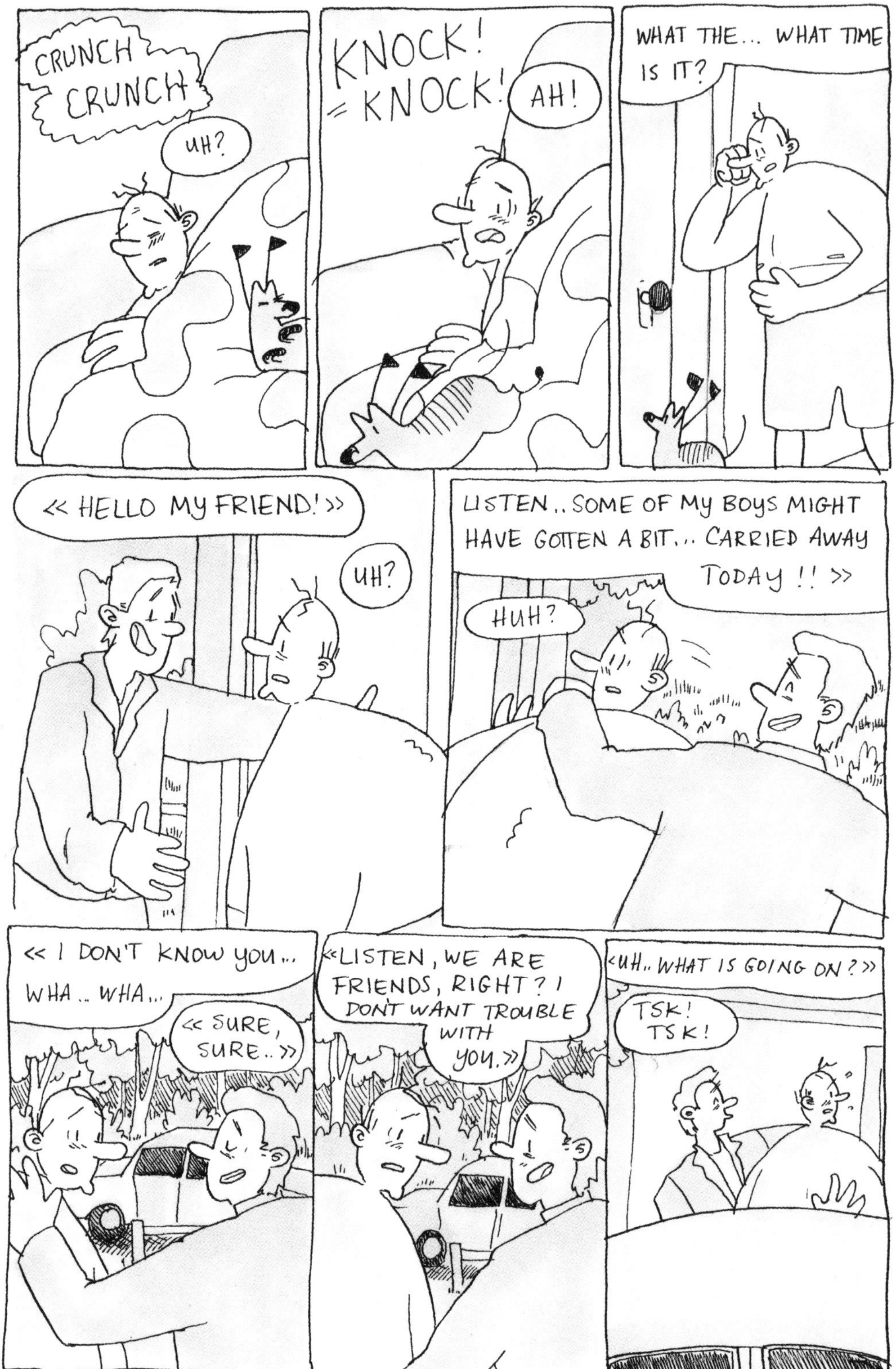
CRUNCH CRUNCH
UH?
KNOCK! KNOCK!
AH!
WHAT THE... WHAT TIME IS IT?
<< HELLO MY FRIEND! >>
UH?
LISTEN.. SOME OF MY BOYS MIGHT HAVE GOTTEN A BIT... CARRIED AWAY TODAY !! >>
HUH?
<< I DON'T KNOW YOU... WHA... WHA...
<< SURE, SURE.. >>
<<LISTEN, WE ARE FRIENDS, RIGHT? I DON'T WANT TROUBLE WITH YOU. >>
<UH.. WHAT IS GOING ON? >>
TSK! TSK!

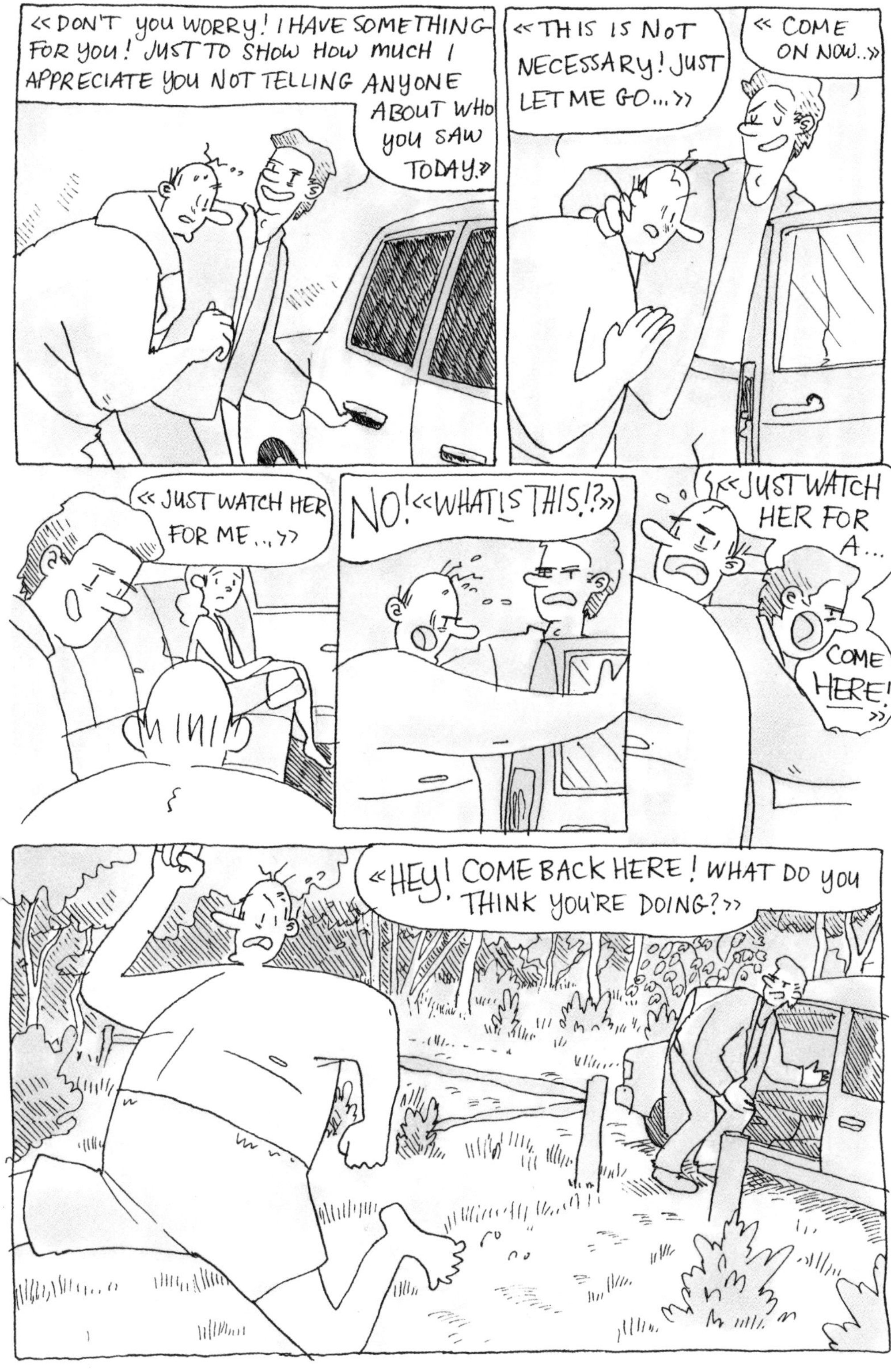
«DON'T YOU WORRY! I HAVE SOMETHING FOR YOU! JUST TO SHOW HOW MUCH I APPRECIATE YOU NOT TELLING ANYONE ABOUT WHO YOU SAW TODAY.»
«THIS IS NOT NECESSARY! JUST LET ME GO...»
«COME ON NOW...»
«JUST WATCH HER FOR ME...»
NO! «WHAT IS THIS!?»
«JUST WATCH HER FOR A...
COME HERE!»
«HEY! COME BACK HERE! WHAT DO YOU THINK YOU'RE DOING?»

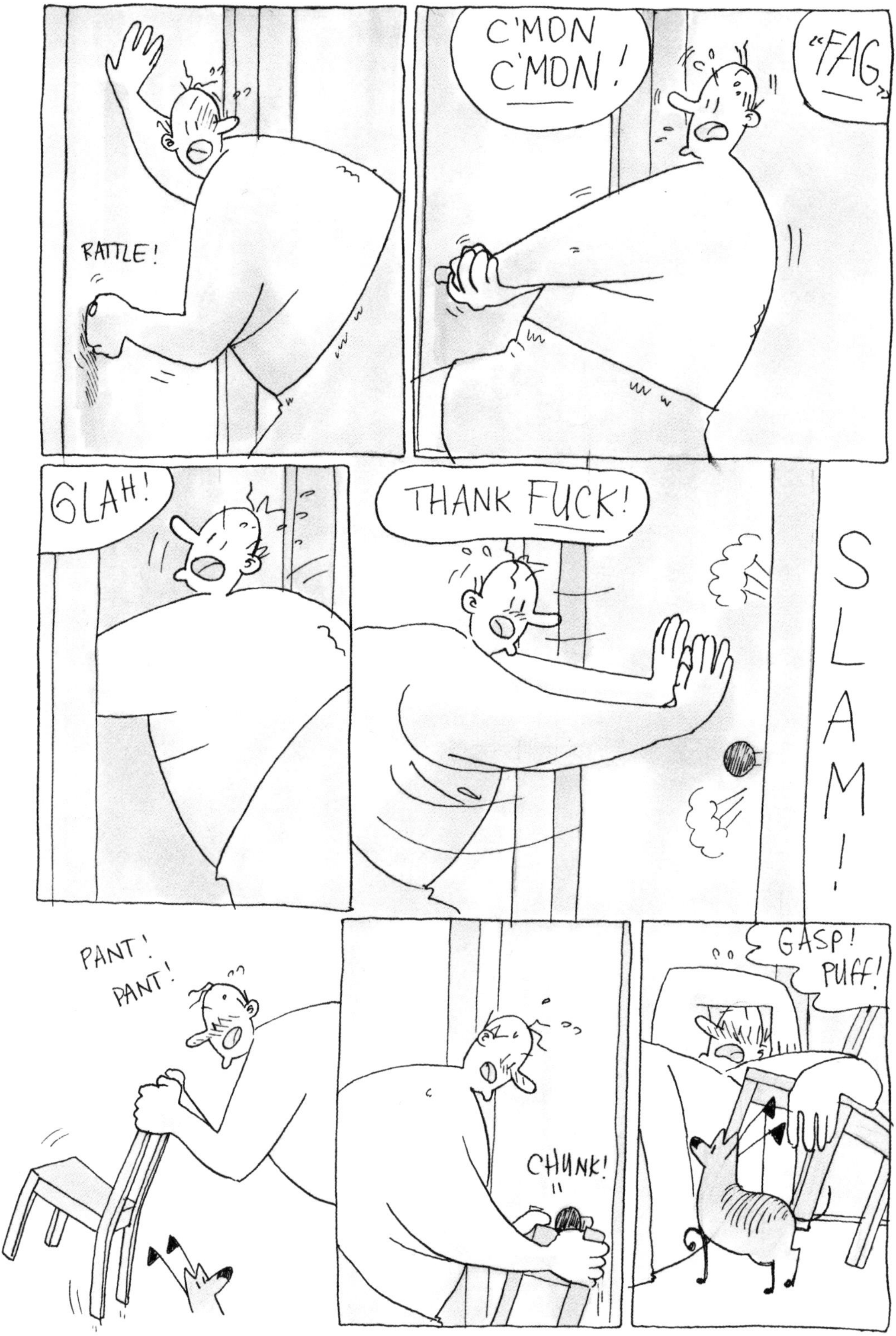
RATTLE!
C'MON C'MON!
"FAG"
GLAH!
THANK FUCK!
SLAM!
PANT! PANT!
CHUNK!
GASP! PUFF!

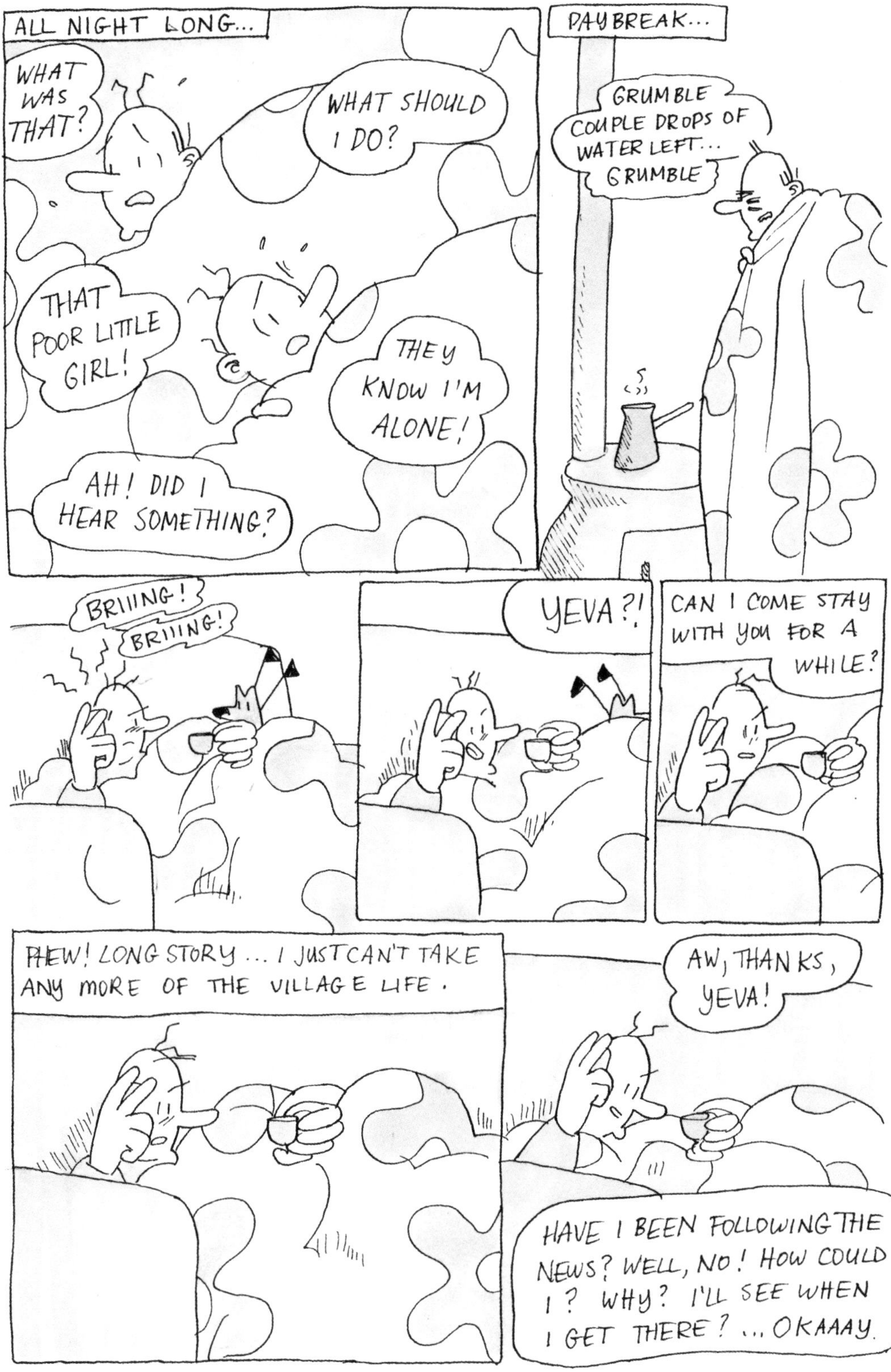
ALL NIGHT LONG...
WHAT WAS THAT?
WHAT SHOULD I DO?
THAT POOR LITTLE GIRL!
THEY KNOW I'M ALONE!
AH! DID I HEAR SOMETHING?
DAYBREAK...
GRUMBLE COUPLE DROPS OF WATER LEFT... GRUMBLE
BRIIING! BRIIING!
YEVA?!
CAN I COME STAY WITH YOU FOR A WHILE?
PHEW! LONG STORY ... I JUST CAN'T TAKE ANY MORE OF THE VILLAGE LIFE.
AW, THANKS, YEVA!
HAVE I BEEN FOLLOWING THE NEWS? WELL, NO! HOW COULD I? WHY? I'LL SEE WHEN I GET THERE? ... OKAAAY.

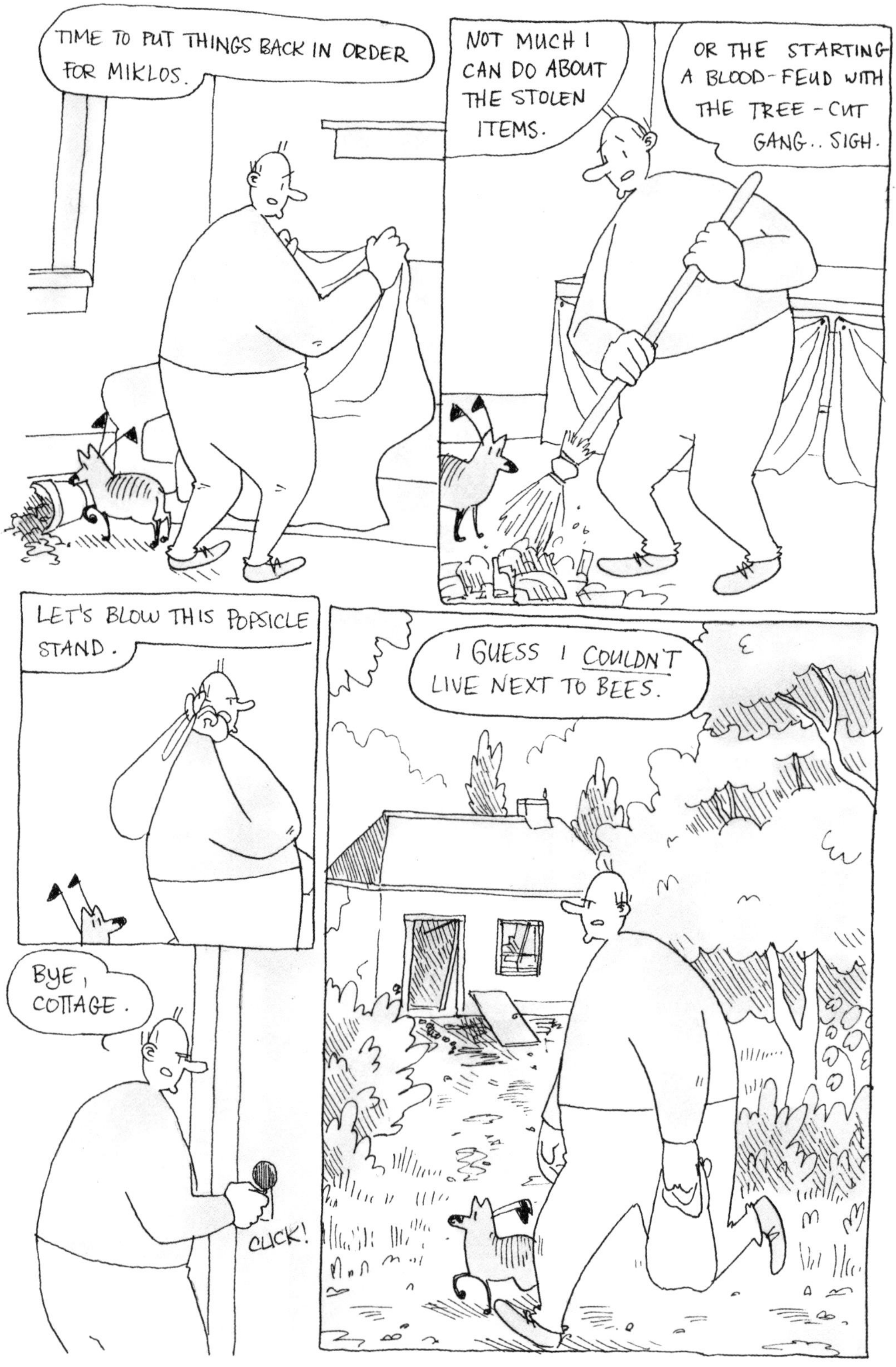
TIME TO PUT THINGS BACK IN ORDER FOR MIKLOS.
NOT MUCH I CAN DO ABOUT THE STOLEN ITEMS.
OR THE STARTING A BLOOD-FEUD WITH THE TREE-CUT GANG.. SIGH.
LET'S BLOW THIS POPSICLE STAND.
BYE, COTTAGE.
CLICK!
I GUESS I COULDN'T LIVE NEXT TO BEES.

CHAPTER FOUR

CHOICE

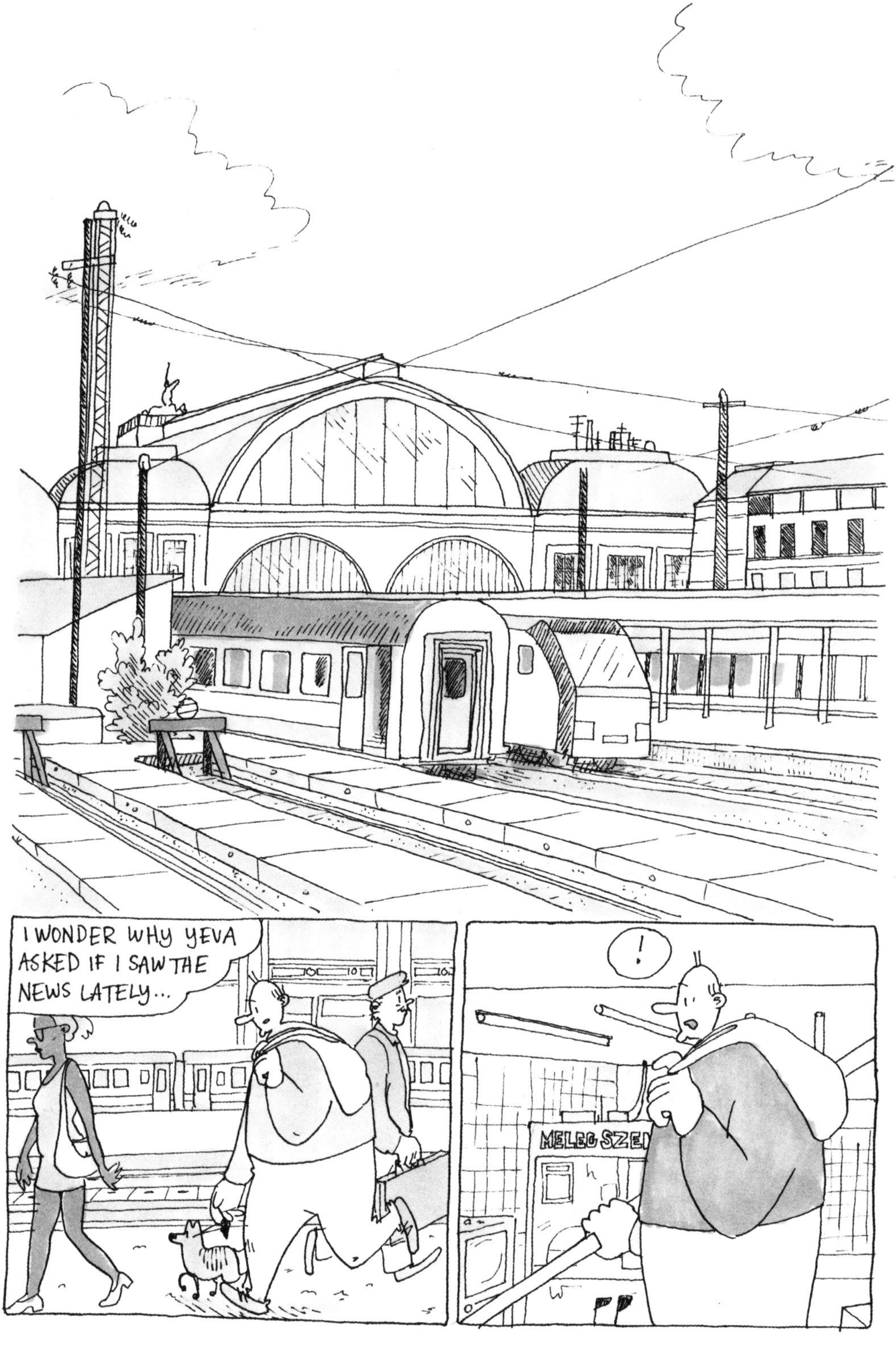
I WONDER WHY YEVA ASKED IF I SAW THE NEWS LATELY...
!
MELEG SZE

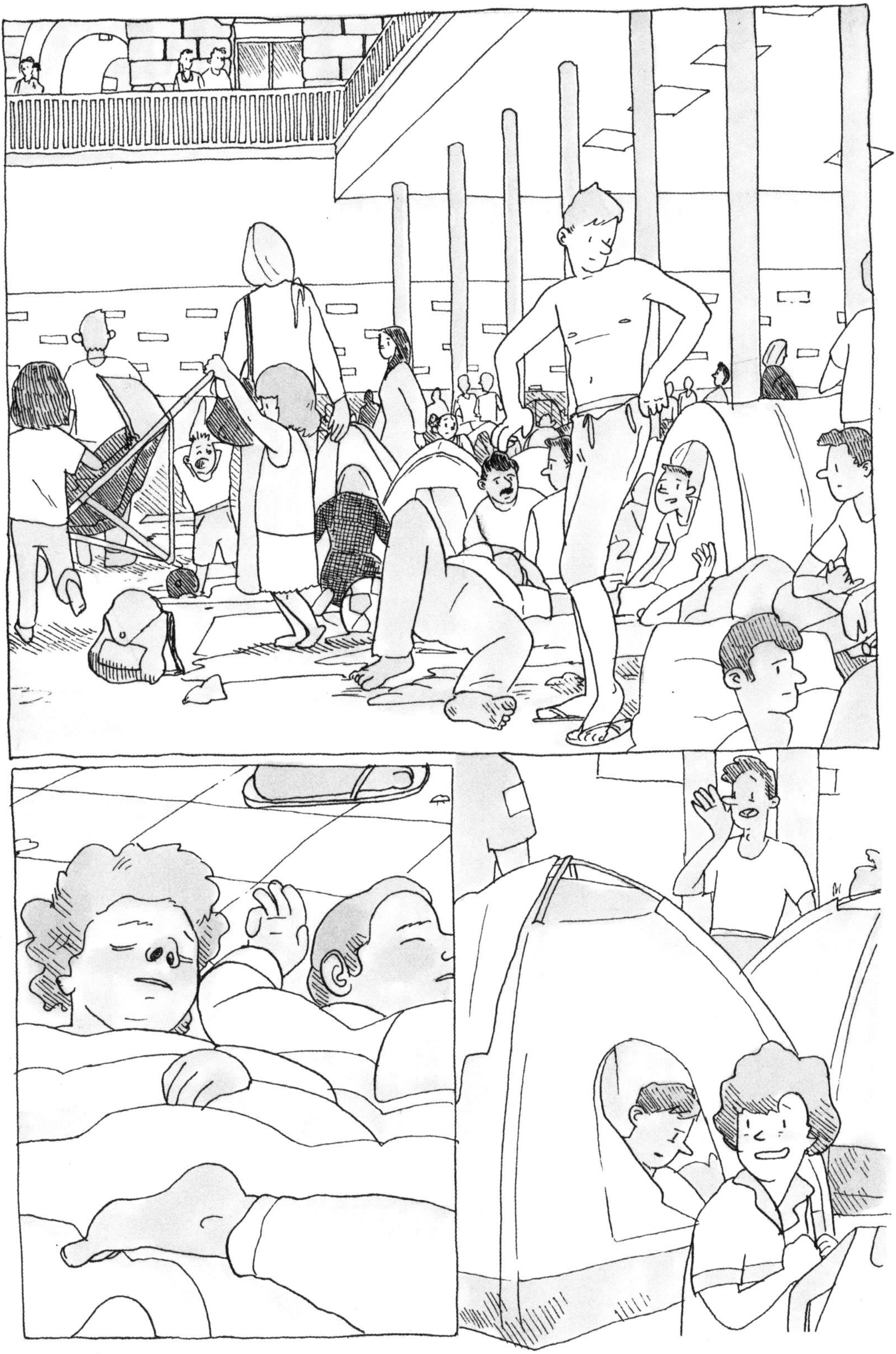

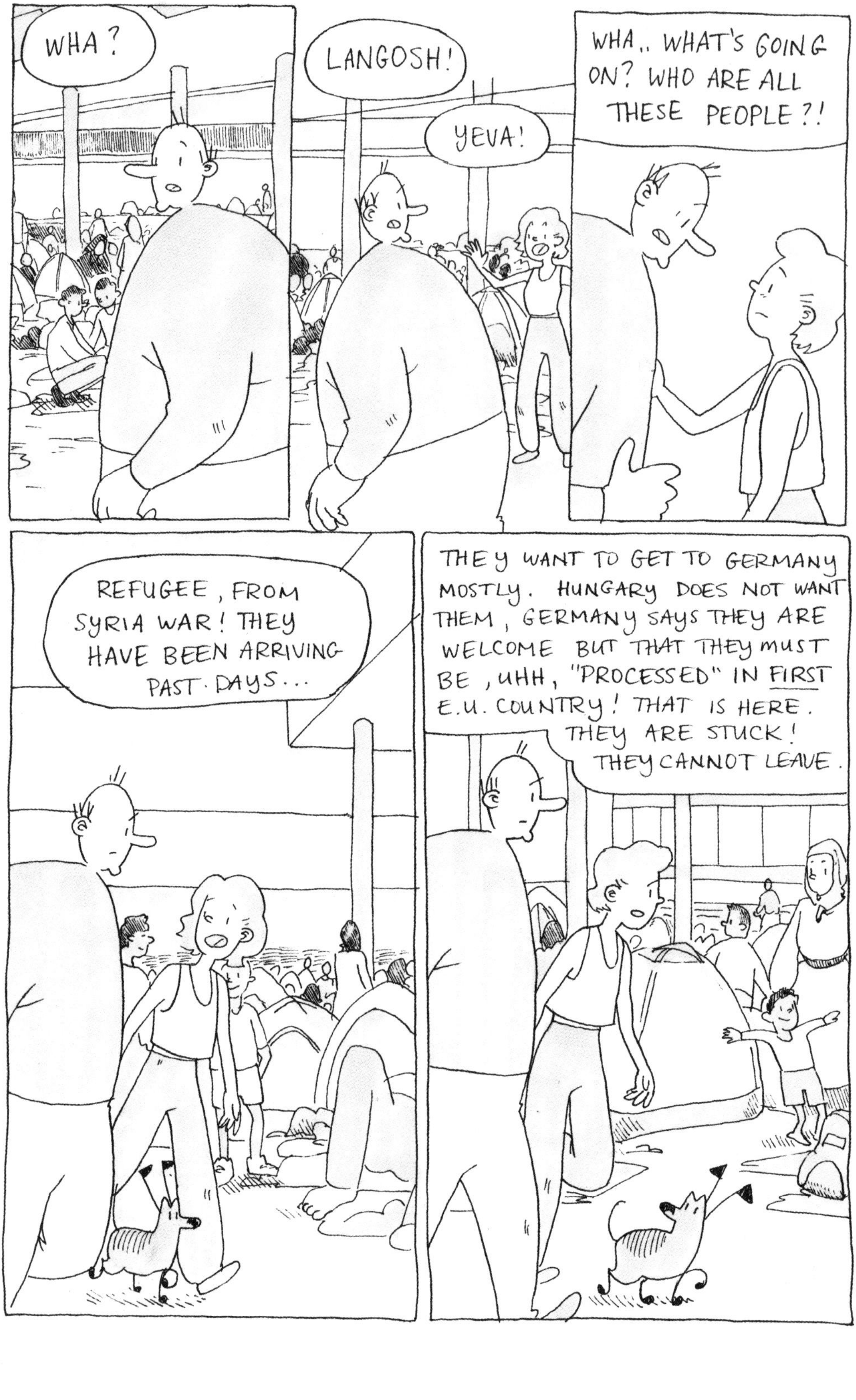
WHA?
LANGOSH!
YEVA!
WHA.. WHAT'S GOING ON? WHO ARE ALL THESE PEOPLE?!
REFUGEE, FROM SYRIA WAR! THEY HAVE BEEN ARRIVING PAST DAYS...
THEY WANT TO GET TO GERMANY MOSTLY. HUNGARY DOES NOT WANT THEM, GERMANY SAYS THEY ARE WELCOME BUT THAT THEY MUST BE, UHH, "PROCESSED" IN FIRST E.U. COUNTRY! THAT IS HERE.
THEY ARE STUCK! THEY CANNOT LEAVE.

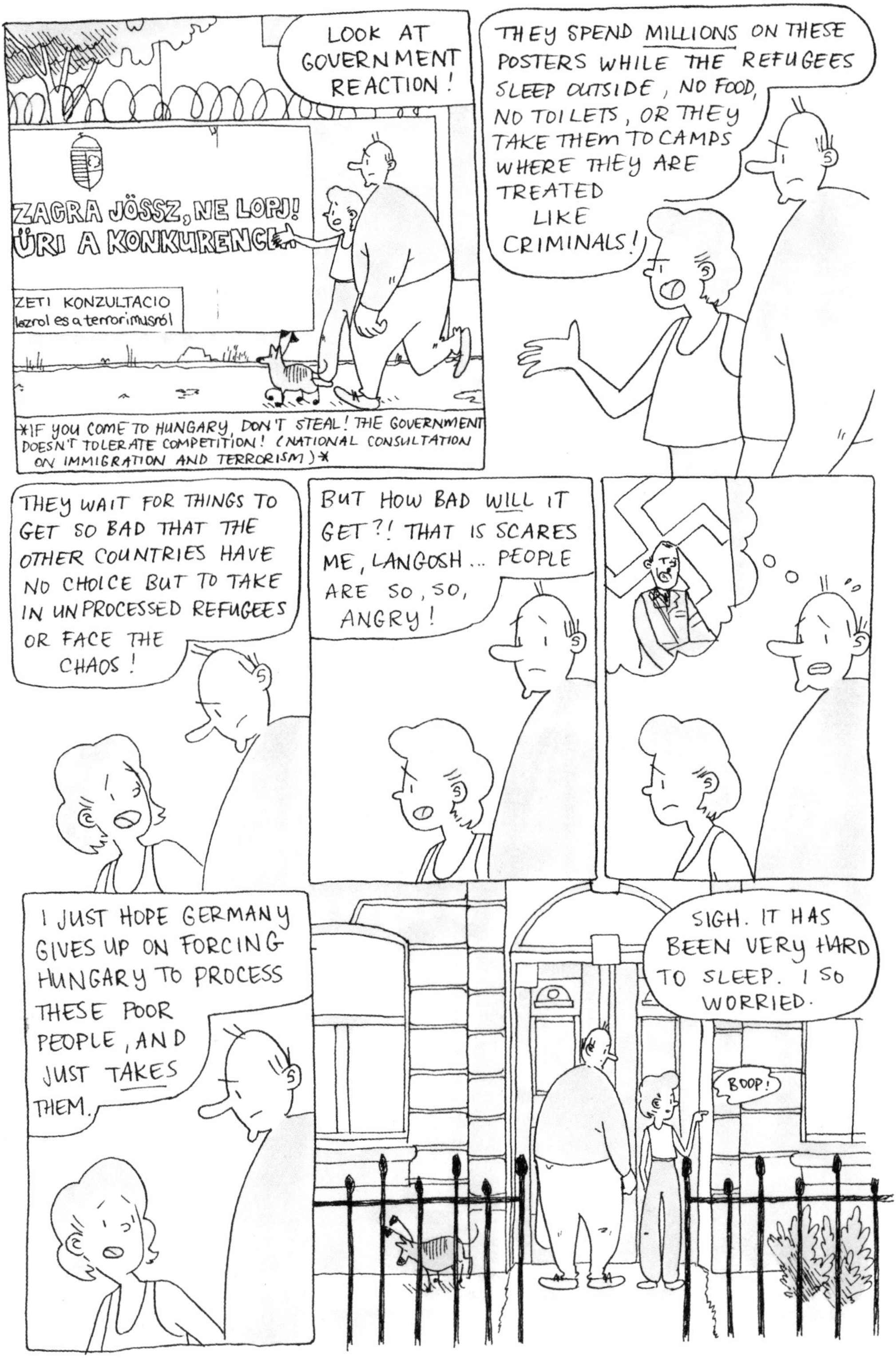
LOOK AT GOVERNMENT REACTION!
ZAGRA JÖSSZ, NE LOPJ! ÜRI A KONKURENCI
ZETI KONZULTACIO lazrol es a terrorimusról
IF YOU COME TO HUNGARY, DON'T STEAL! THE GOVERNMENT DOESN'T TOLERATE COMPETITION! (NATIONAL CONSULTATION ON IMMIGRATION AND TERRORISM)
THEY SPEND MILLIONS ON THESE POSTERS WHILE THE REFUGEES SLEEP OUTSIDE, NO FOOD, NO TOILETS, OR THEY TAKE THEM TO CAMPS WHERE THEY ARE TREATED LIKE CRIMINALS!
THEY WAIT FOR THINGS TO GET SO BAD THAT THE OTHER COUNTRIES HAVE NO CHOICE BUT TO TAKE IN UNPROCESSED REFUGEES OR FACE THE CHAOS!
BUT HOW BAD WILL IT GET?! THAT IS SCARES ME, LANGOSH... PEOPLE ARE SO, SO, ANGRY!
I JUST HOPE GERMANY GIVES UP ON FORCING HUNGARY TO PROCESS THESE POOR PEOPLE, AND JUST TAKES THEM.
SIGH. IT HAS BEEN VERY HARD TO SLEEP. I SO WORRIED.
BOOP!

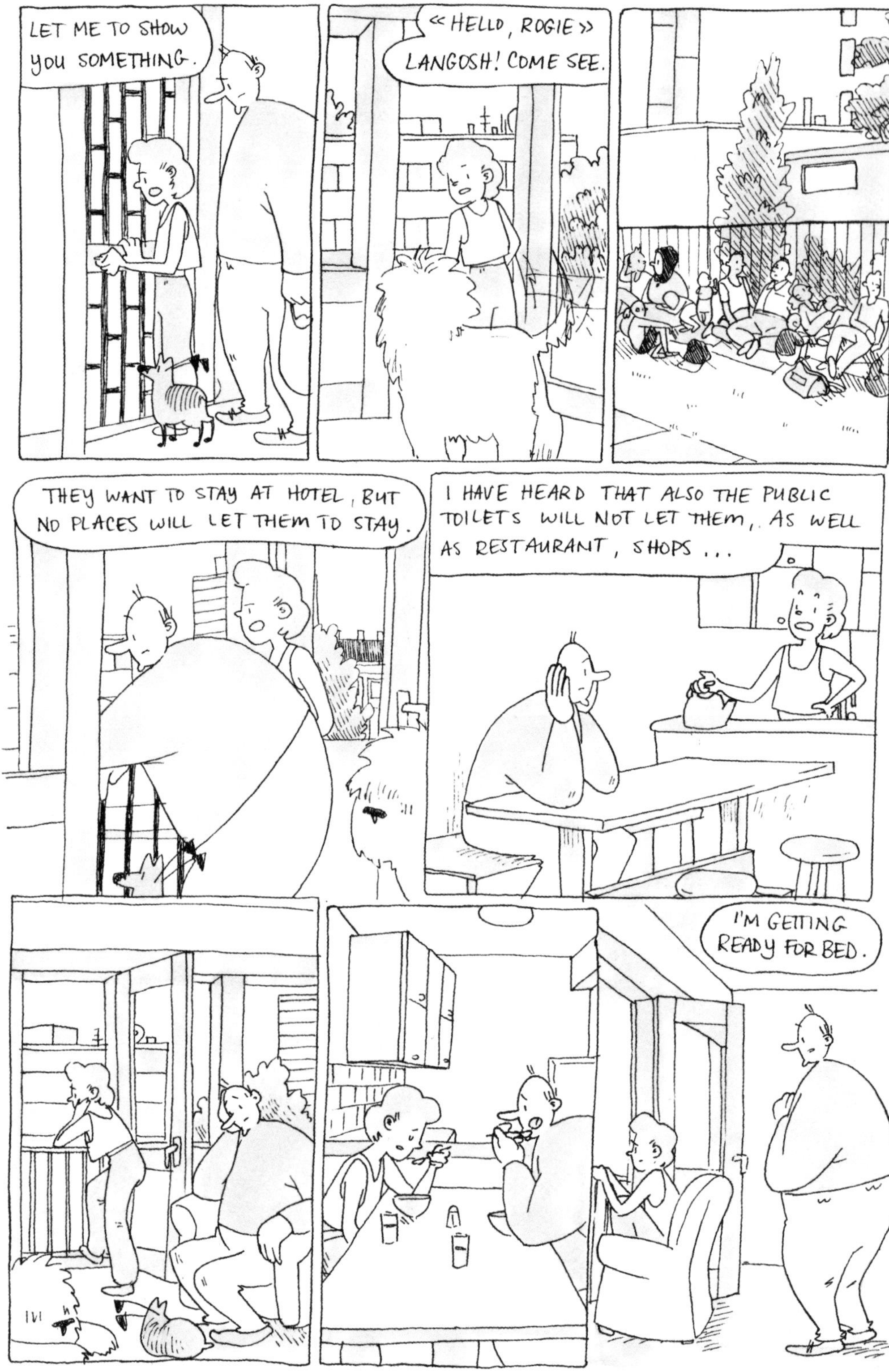
LET ME TO SHOW YOU SOMETHING.
«HELLO, ROGIE» LANGOSH! COME SEE.
THEY WANT TO STAY AT HOTEL, BUT NO PLACES WILL LET THEM TO STAY.
I HAVE HEARD THAT ALSO THE PUBLIC TOILETS WILL NOT LET THEM, AS WELL AS RESTAURANT, SHOPS...
I'M GETTING READY FOR BED.

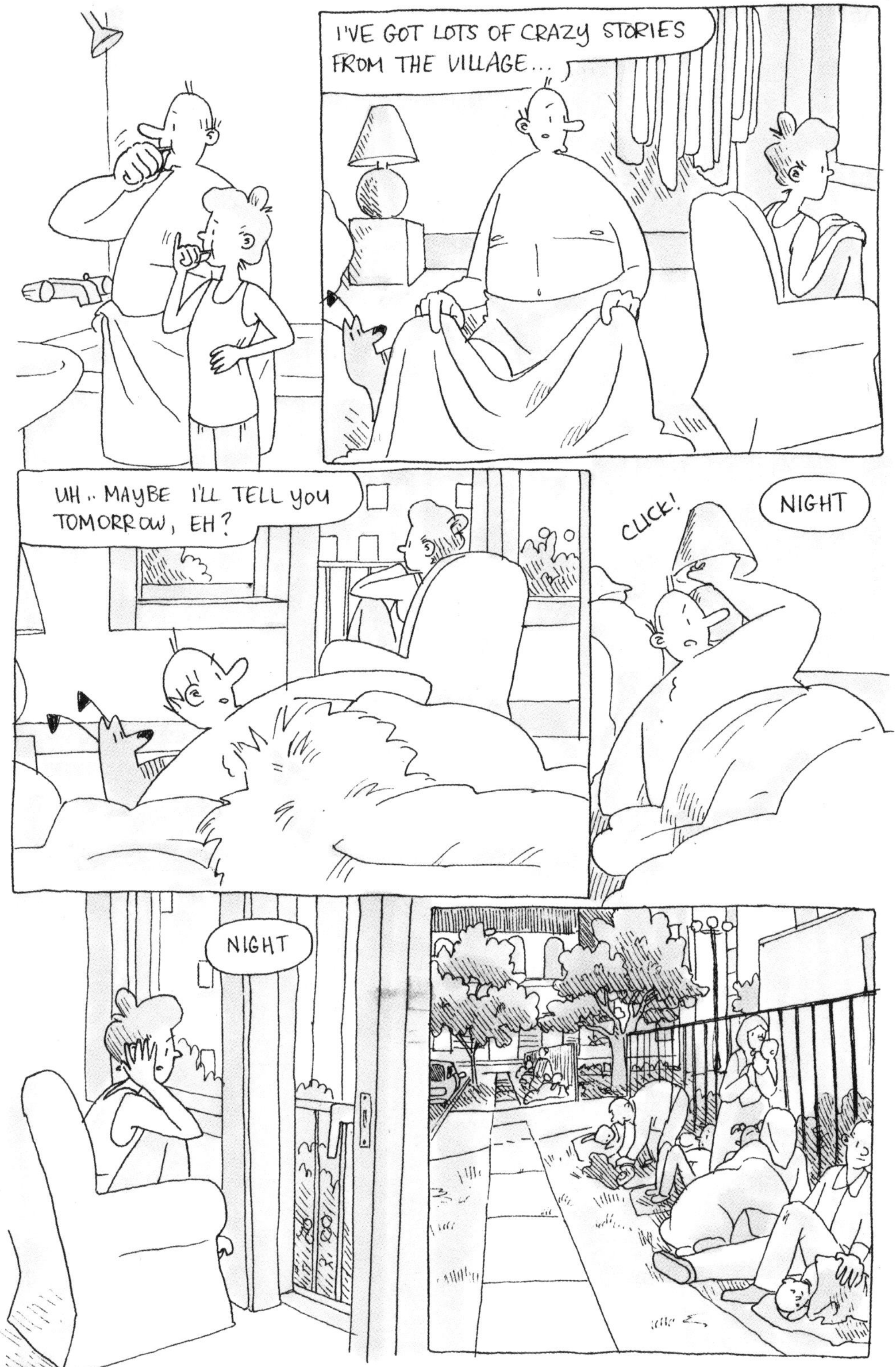
I'VE GOT LOTS OF CRAZY STORIES FROM THE VILLAGE...
UH.. MAYBE I'LL TELL YOU TOMORROW, EH?
CLICK!
NIGHT
NIGHT

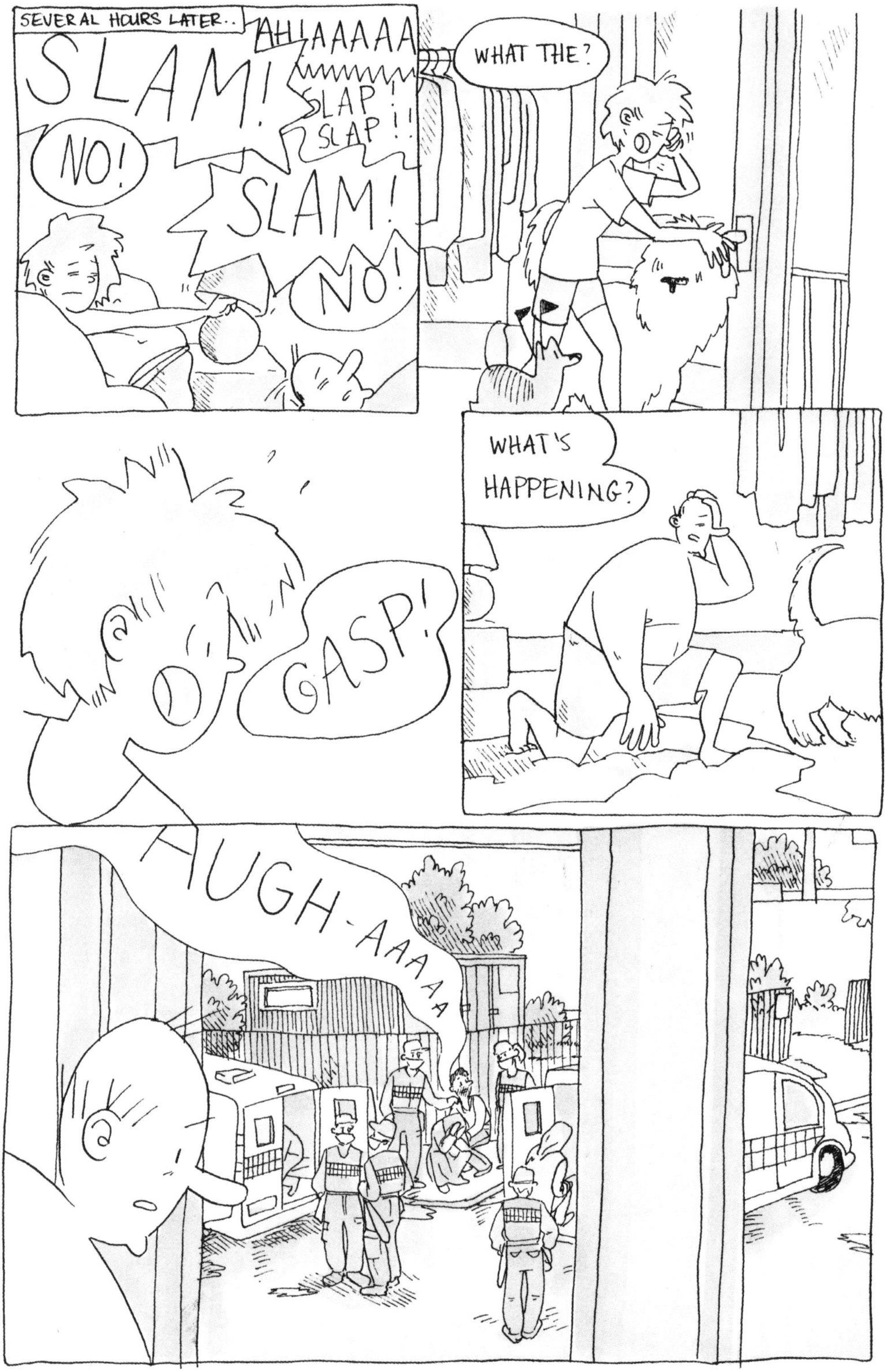
SEVERAL HOURS LATER..
SLAM!
AHHAAAAAA
SLAP! SLAP!!
NO!
SLAM!
NO!
WHAT THE?
WHAT'S HAPPENING?
GASP!
HUGH-AAAAAA

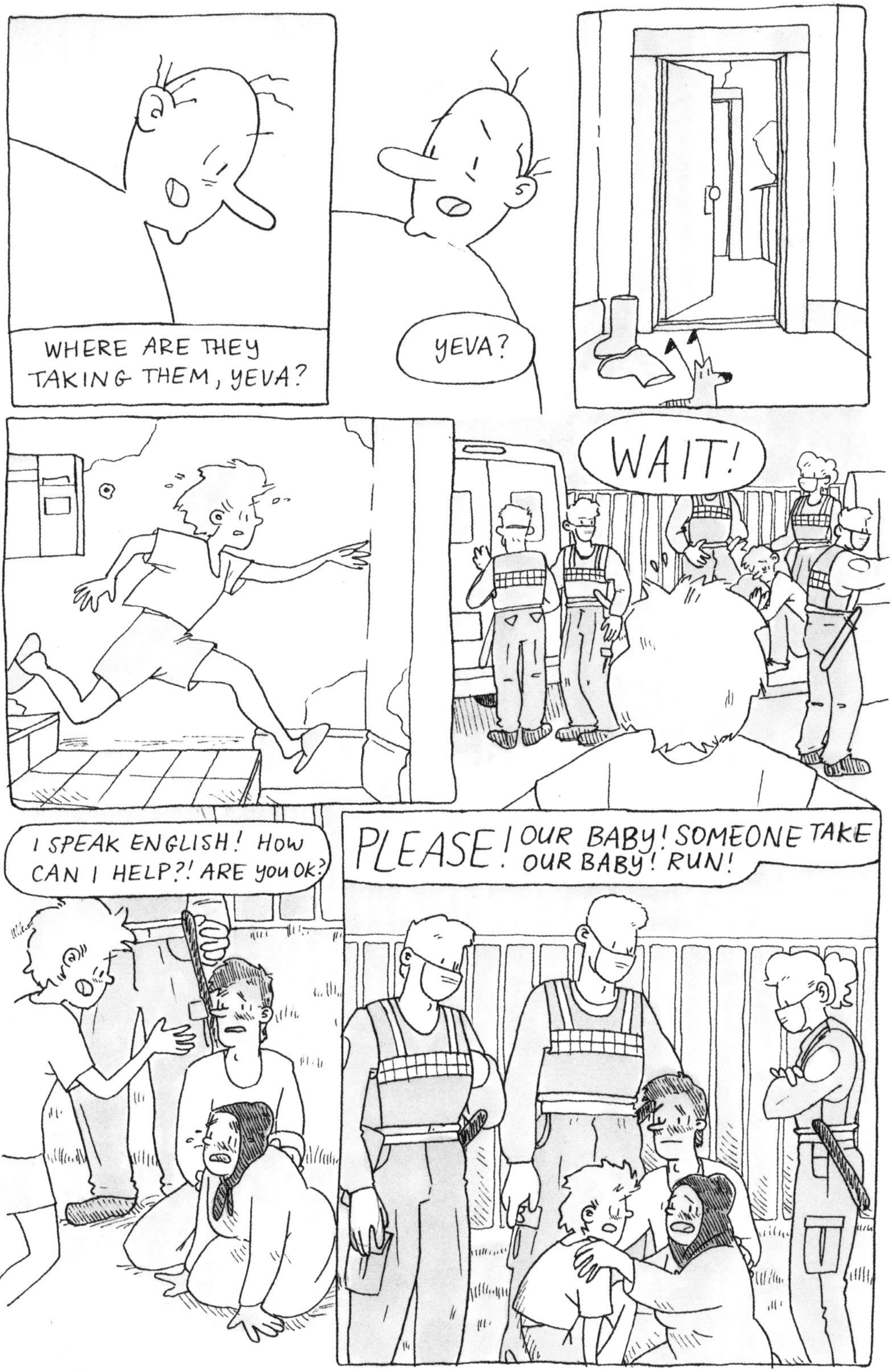
WHERE ARE THEY TAKING THEM, YEVA?
YEVA?
WAIT!
I SPEAK ENGLISH! HOW CAN I HELP?! ARE YOU OK?
PLEASE! OUR BABY! SOMEONE TAKE OUR BABY! RUN!

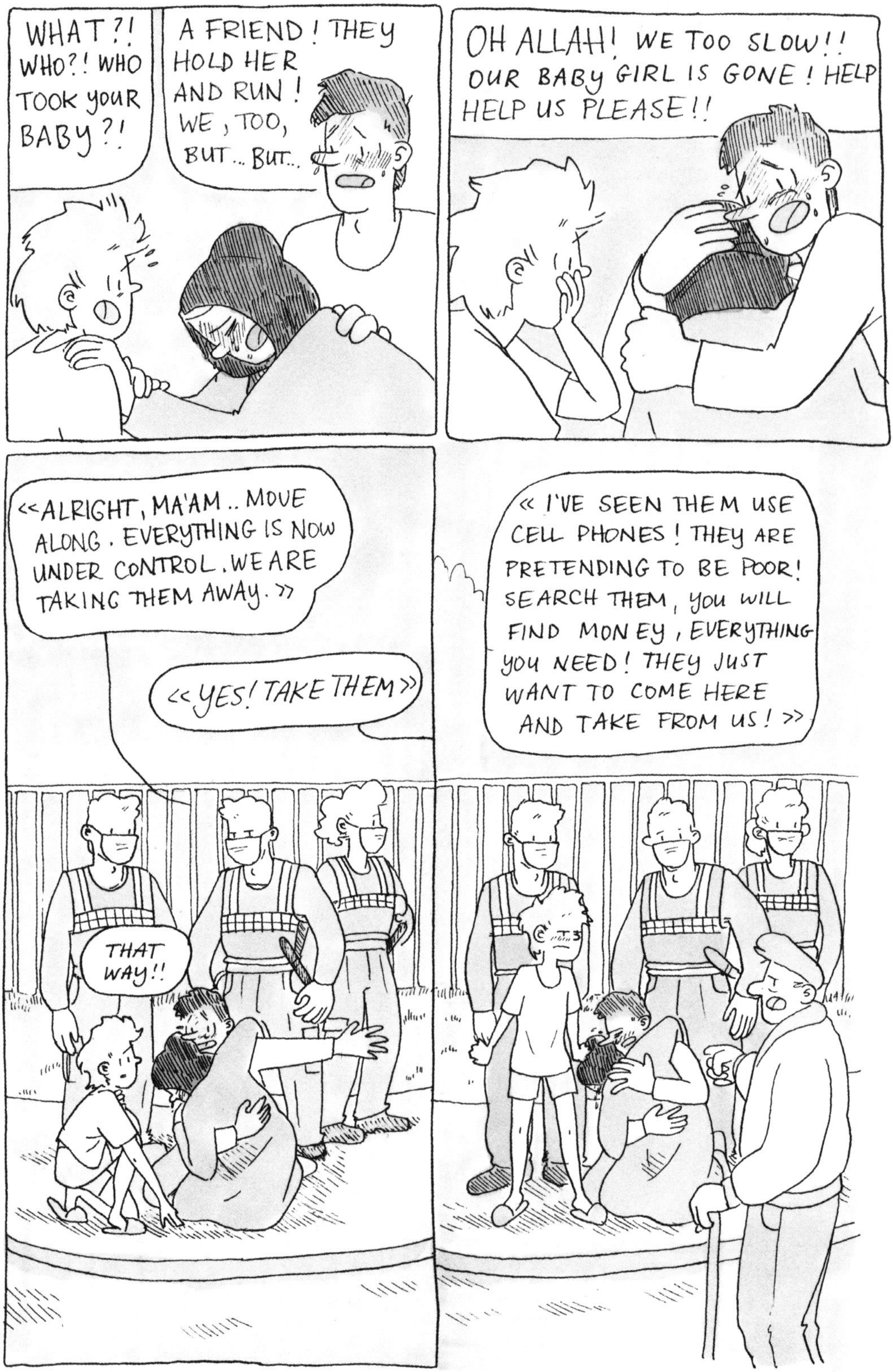
WHAT?! WHO?! WHO TOOK YOUR BABY?!
A FRIEND! THEY HOLD HER AND RUN! WE, TOO, BUT... BUT...
OH ALLAH! WE TOO SLOW!! OUR BABY GIRL IS GONE! HELP HELP US PLEASE!!
<<ALRIGHT, MA'AM .. MOVE ALONG. EVERYTHING IS NOW UNDER CONTROL. WE ARE TAKING THEM AWAY.>>
<<YES! TAKE THEM>>
THAT WAY!!
<<I'VE SEEN THEM USE CELL PHONES! THEY ARE PRETENDING TO BE POOR! SEARCH THEM, YOU WILL FIND MONEY, EVERYTHING YOU NEED! THEY JUST WANT TO COME HERE AND TAKE FROM US!>>

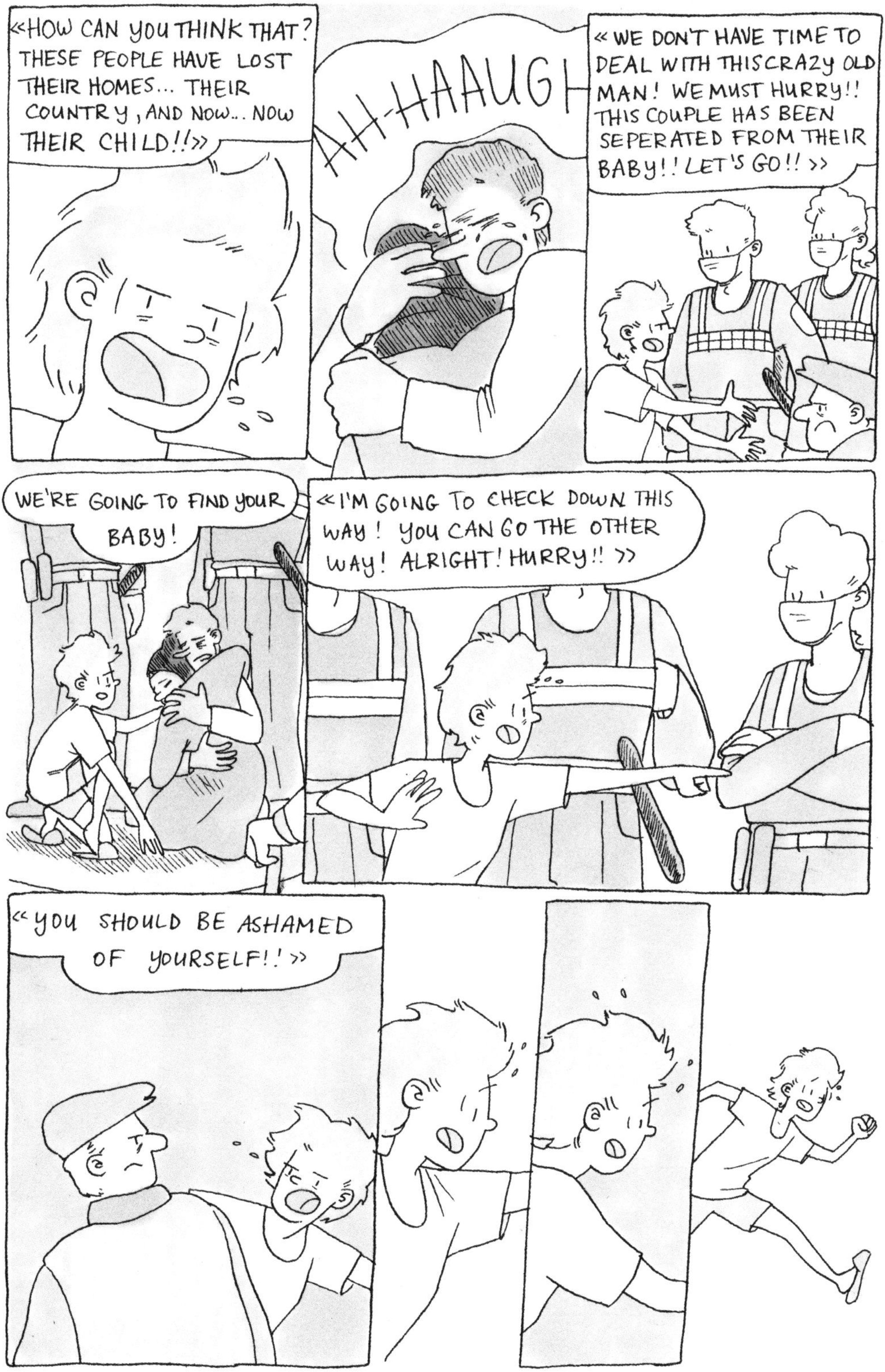
«HOW CAN YOU THINK THAT? THESE PEOPLE HAVE LOST THEIR HOMES... THEIR COUNTRY, AND NOW... NOW THEIR CHILD!!»
AH-HAAUGH
« WE DON'T HAVE TIME TO DEAL WITH THIS CRAZY OLD MAN! WE MUST HURRY!! THIS COUPLE HAS BEEN SEPERATED FROM THEIR BABY!! LET'S GO!! »
WE'RE GOING TO FIND YOUR BABY!
«I'M GOING TO CHECK DOWN THIS WAY! YOU CAN GO THE OTHER WAY! ALRIGHT! HURRY!! »
« YOU SHOULD BE ASHAMED OF YOURSELF!! »

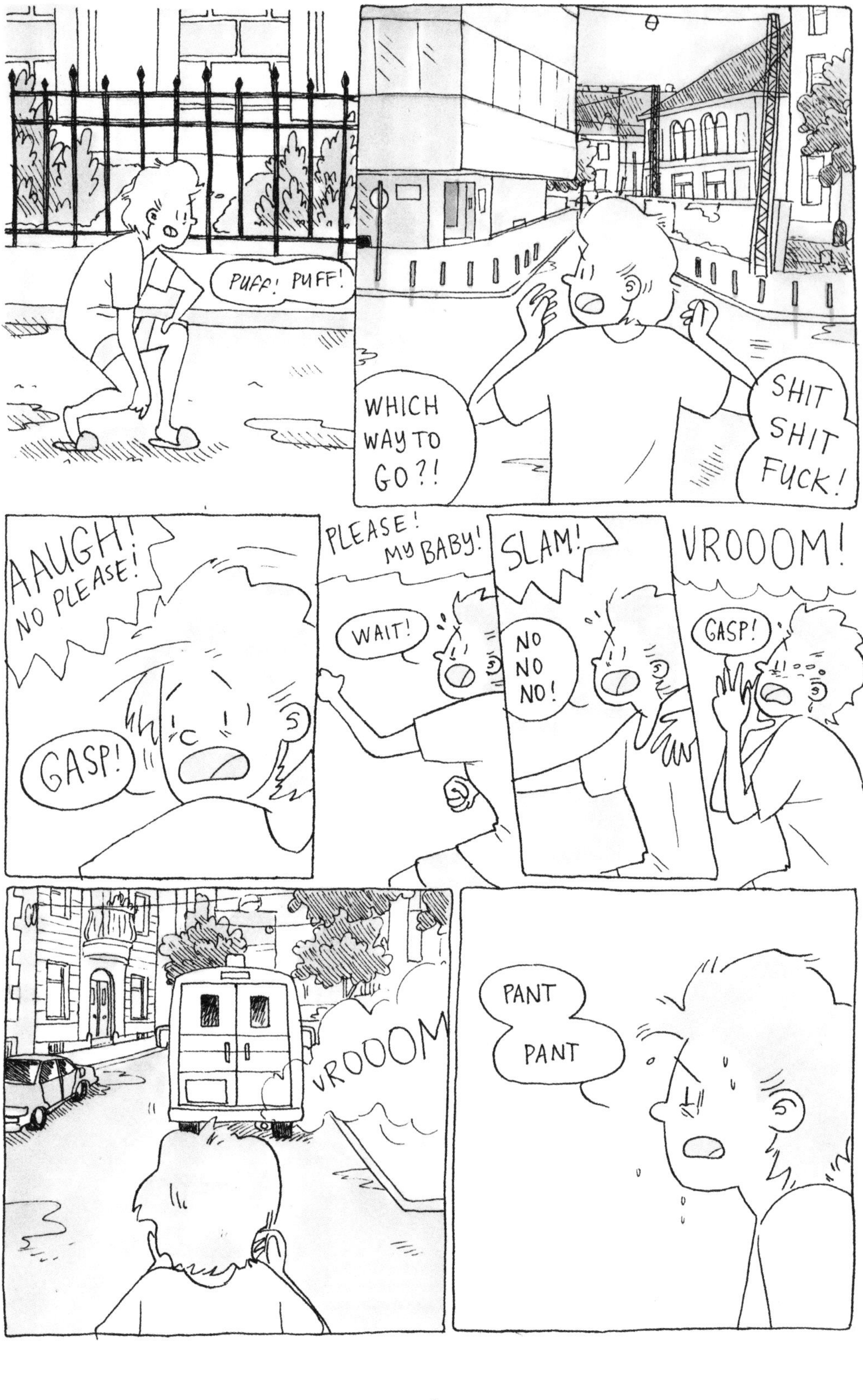
PUFF! PUFF!
WHICH WAY TO GO?!
SHIT SHIT FUCK!
AAUGH! NO PLEASE!
GASP!
PLEASE! MY BABY!
WAIT!
SLAM!
NO NO NO!
VROOOM!
GASP!
VROOOM
PANT
PANT

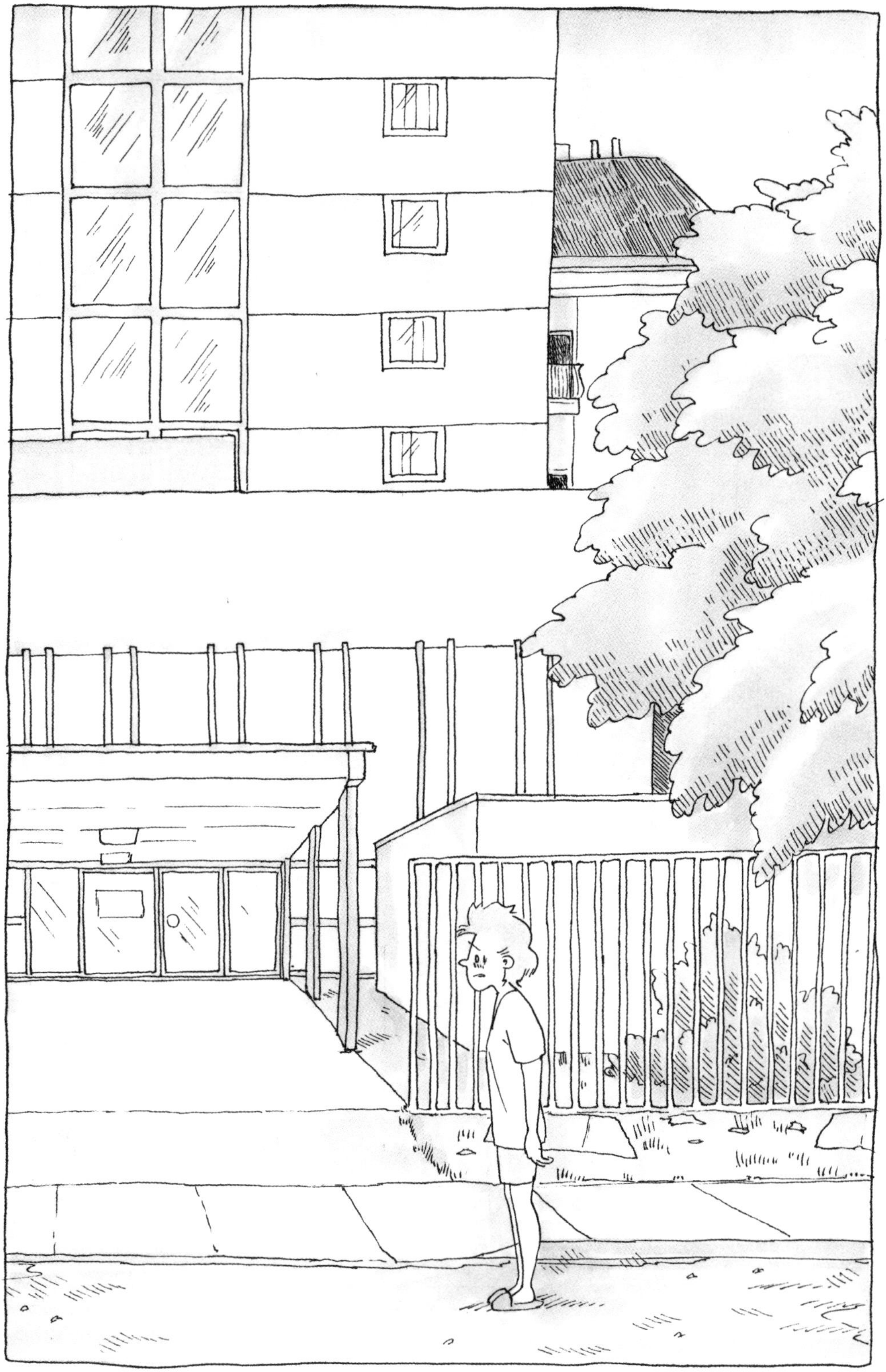

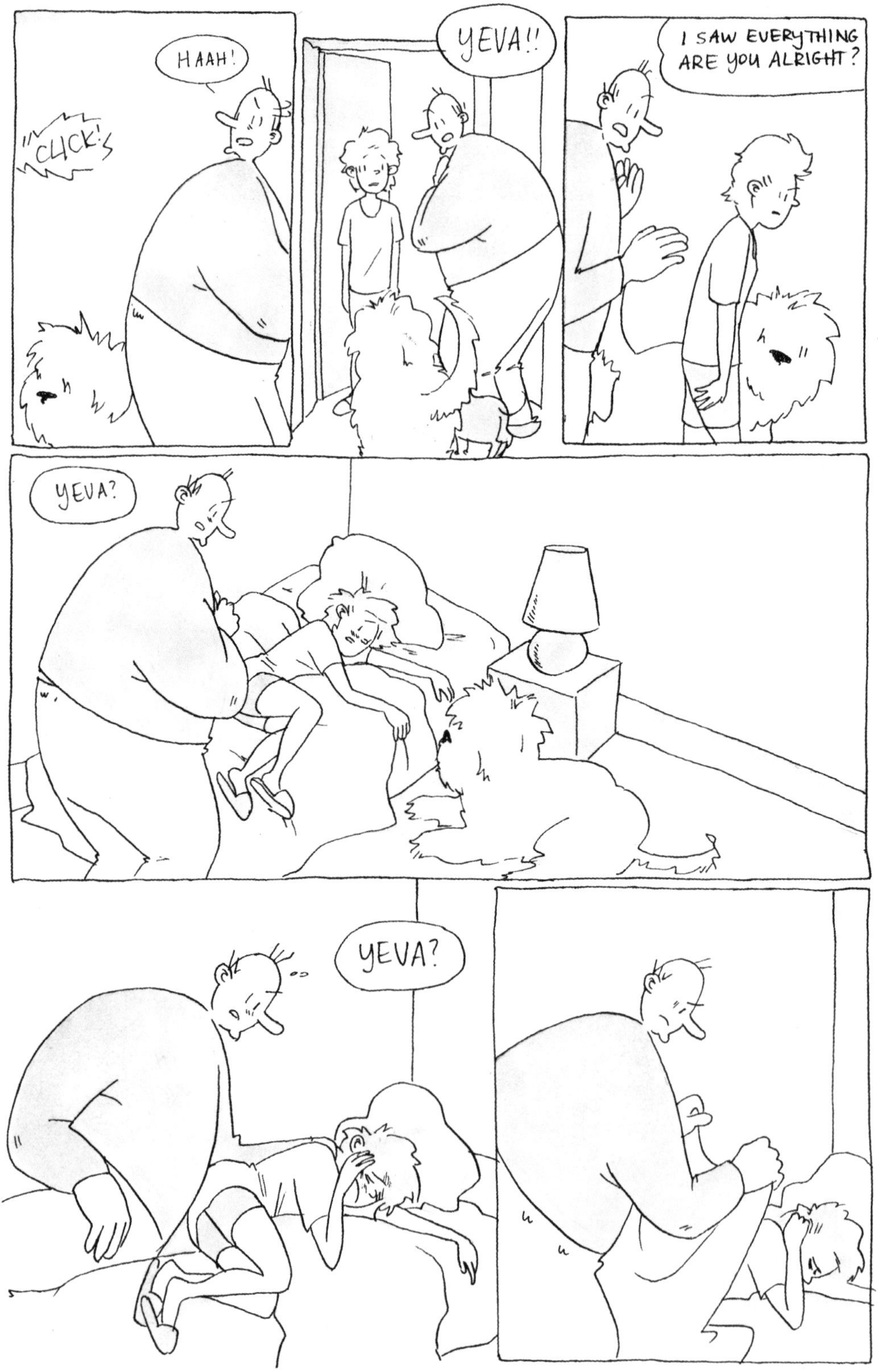
CLICK!
HAAH!
YEVA!!
I SAW EVERYTHING
ARE YOU ALRIGHT?
YEVA?
YEVA?

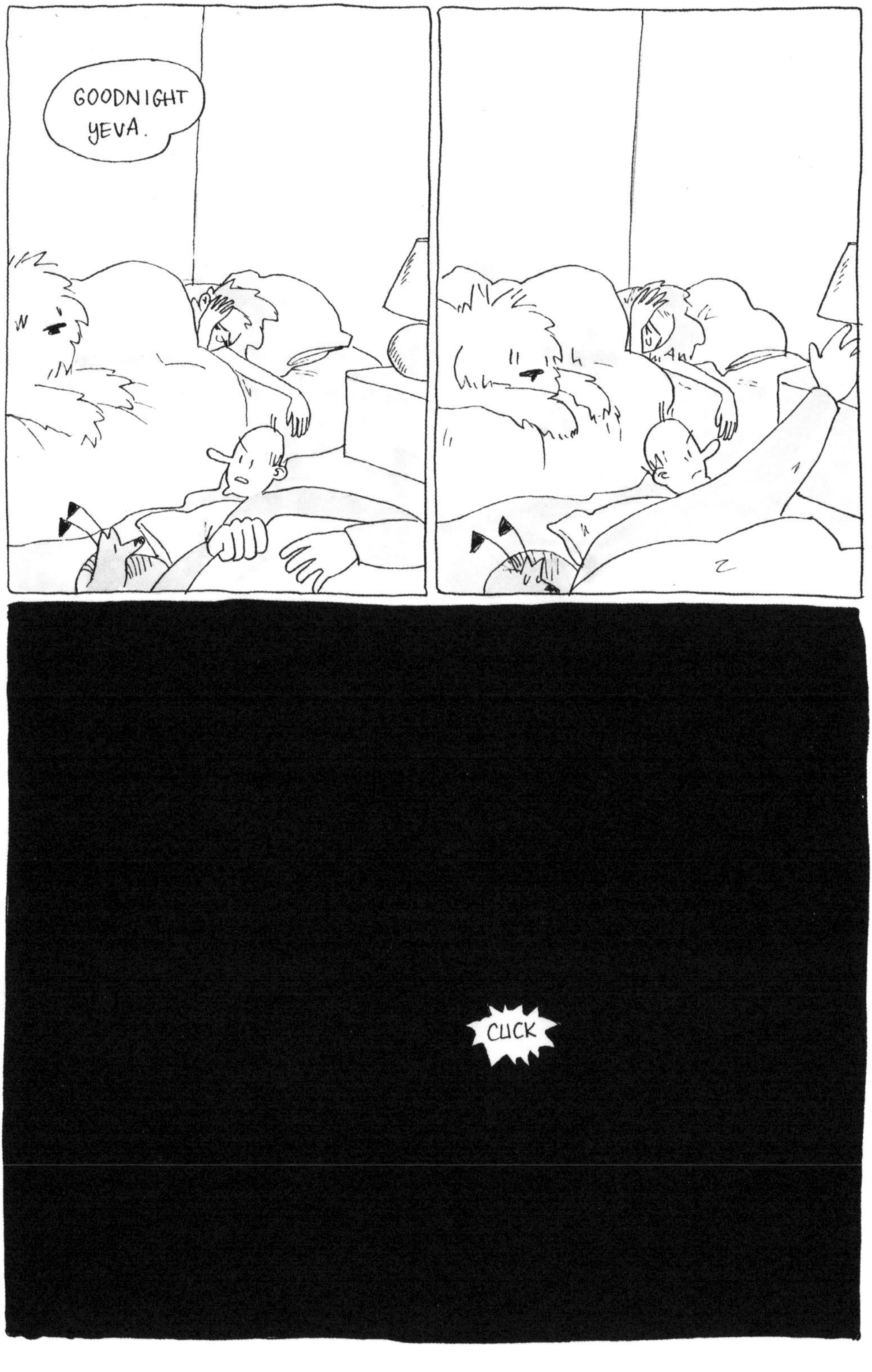
GOODNIGHT YEVA.
CLICK

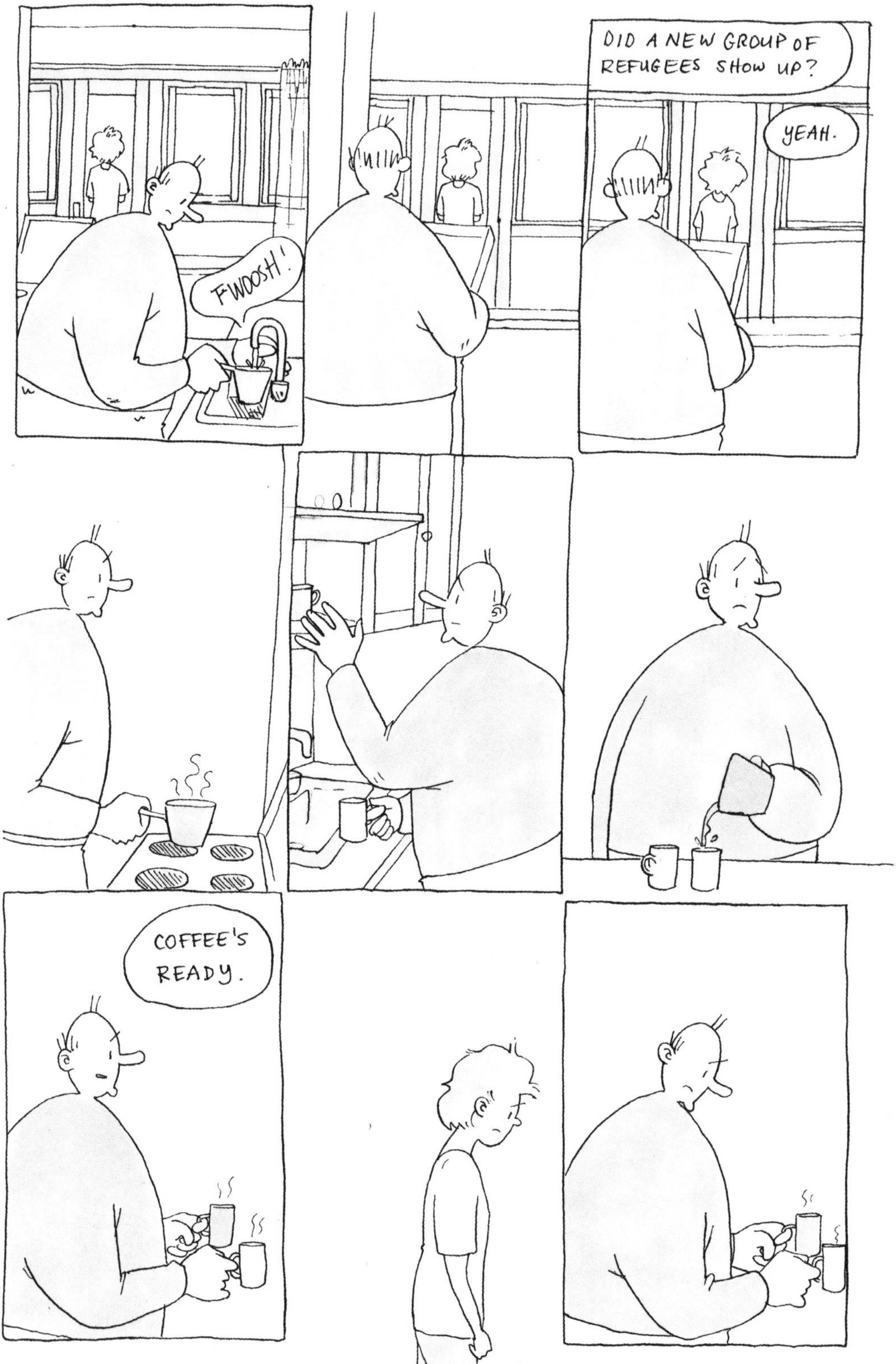
FWOOSH!
DID A NEW GROUP OF REFUGEES SHOW UP?
YEAH.
COFFEE'S READY.

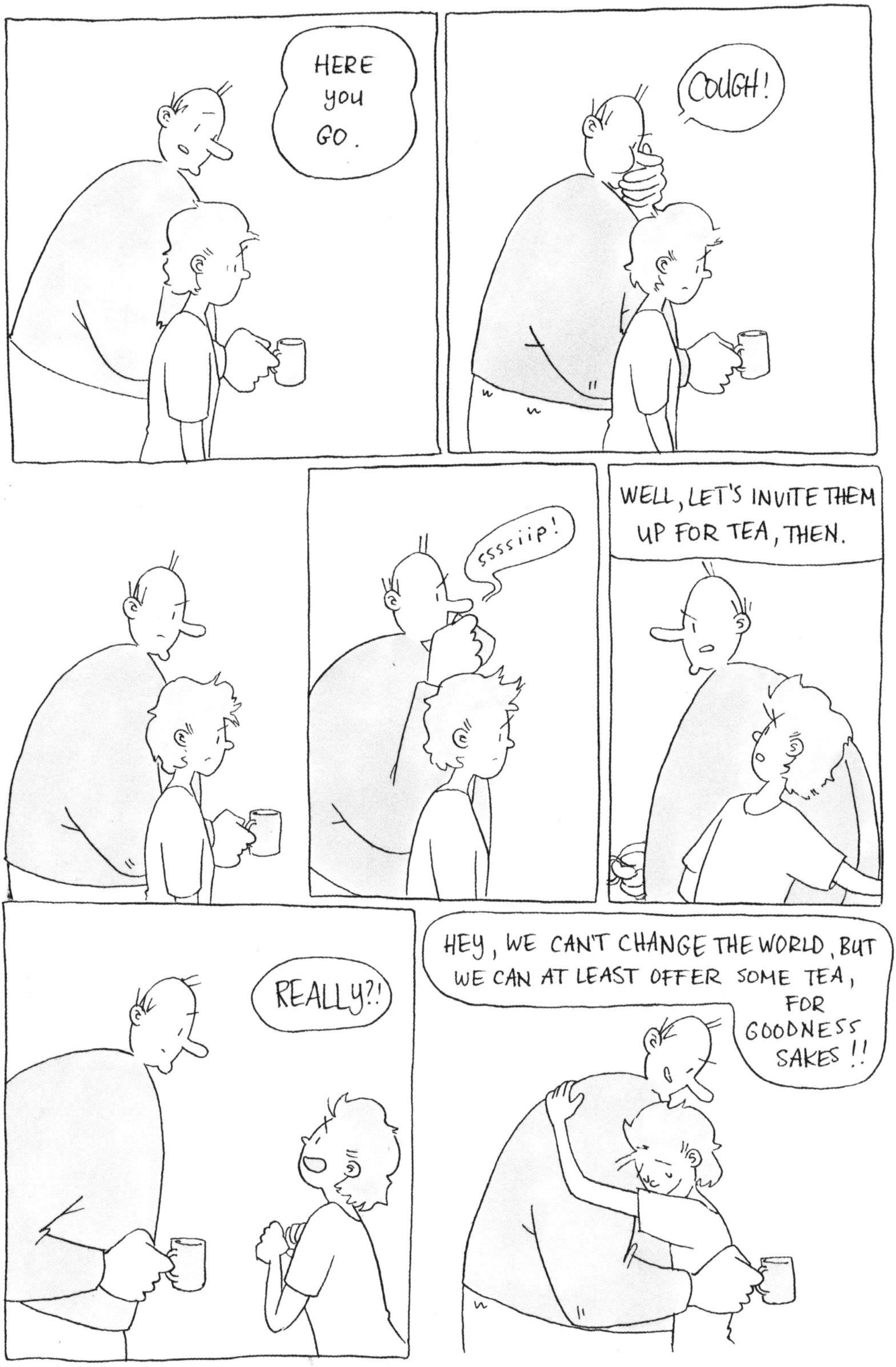
HERE you GO.
COUGH!
sssssiip!
WELL, LET'S INVITE THEM UP FOR TEA, THEN.
REALLY?!
HEY, WE CAN'T CHANGE THE WORLD, BUT WE CAN AT LEAST OFFER SOME TEA, FOR GOODNESS SAKES!!

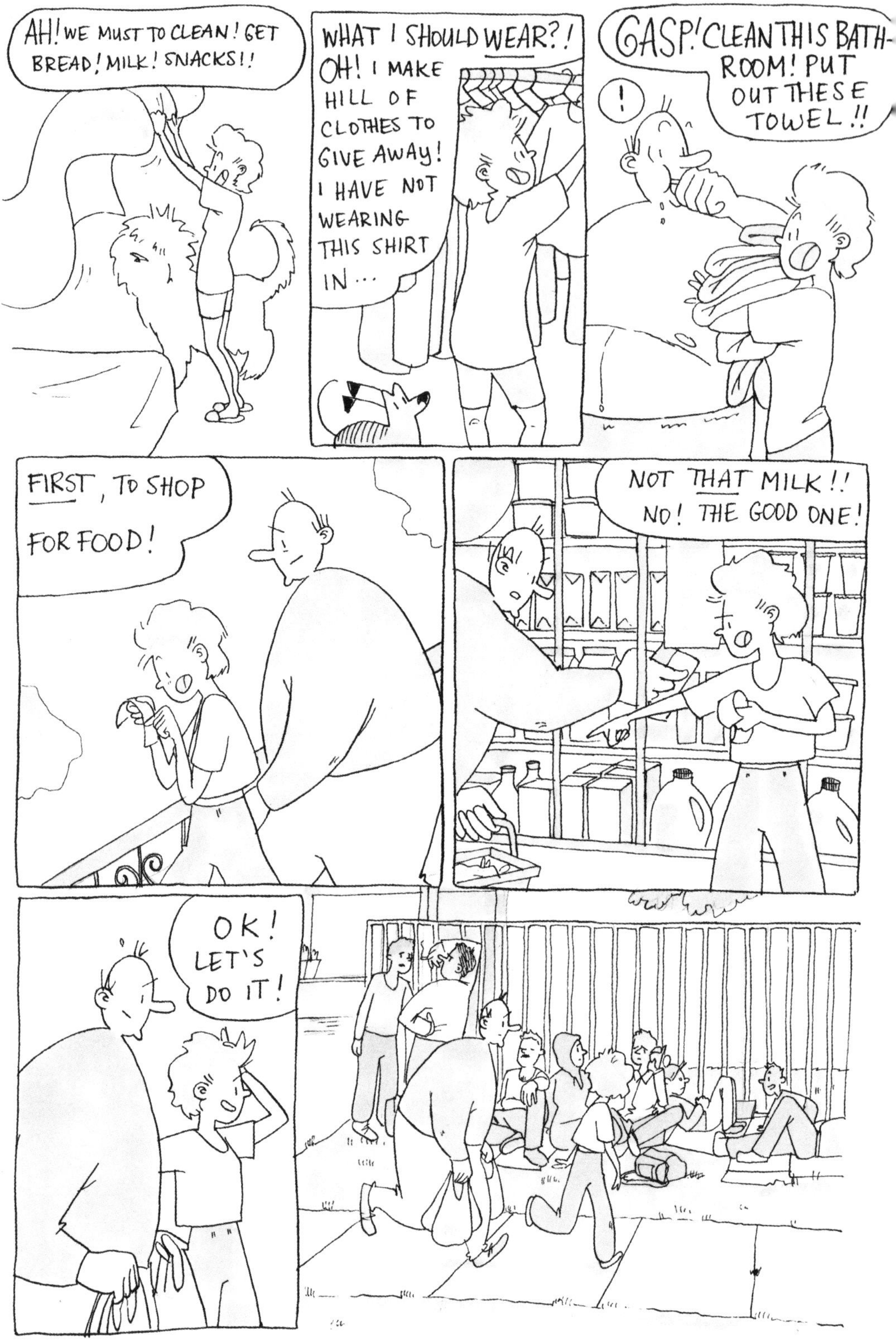
AH! WE MUST TO CLEAN! GET BREAD! MILK! SNACKS!!
WHAT I SHOULD WEAR?! OH! I MAKE HILL OF CLOTHES TO GIVE AWAY! I HAVE NOT WEARING THIS SHIRT IN...
GASP! CLEAN THIS BATHROOM! PUT OUT THESE TOWEL!!
!
FIRST, TO SHOP FOR FOOD!
NOT THAT MILK!! NO! THE GOOD ONE!
OK! LET'S DO IT!

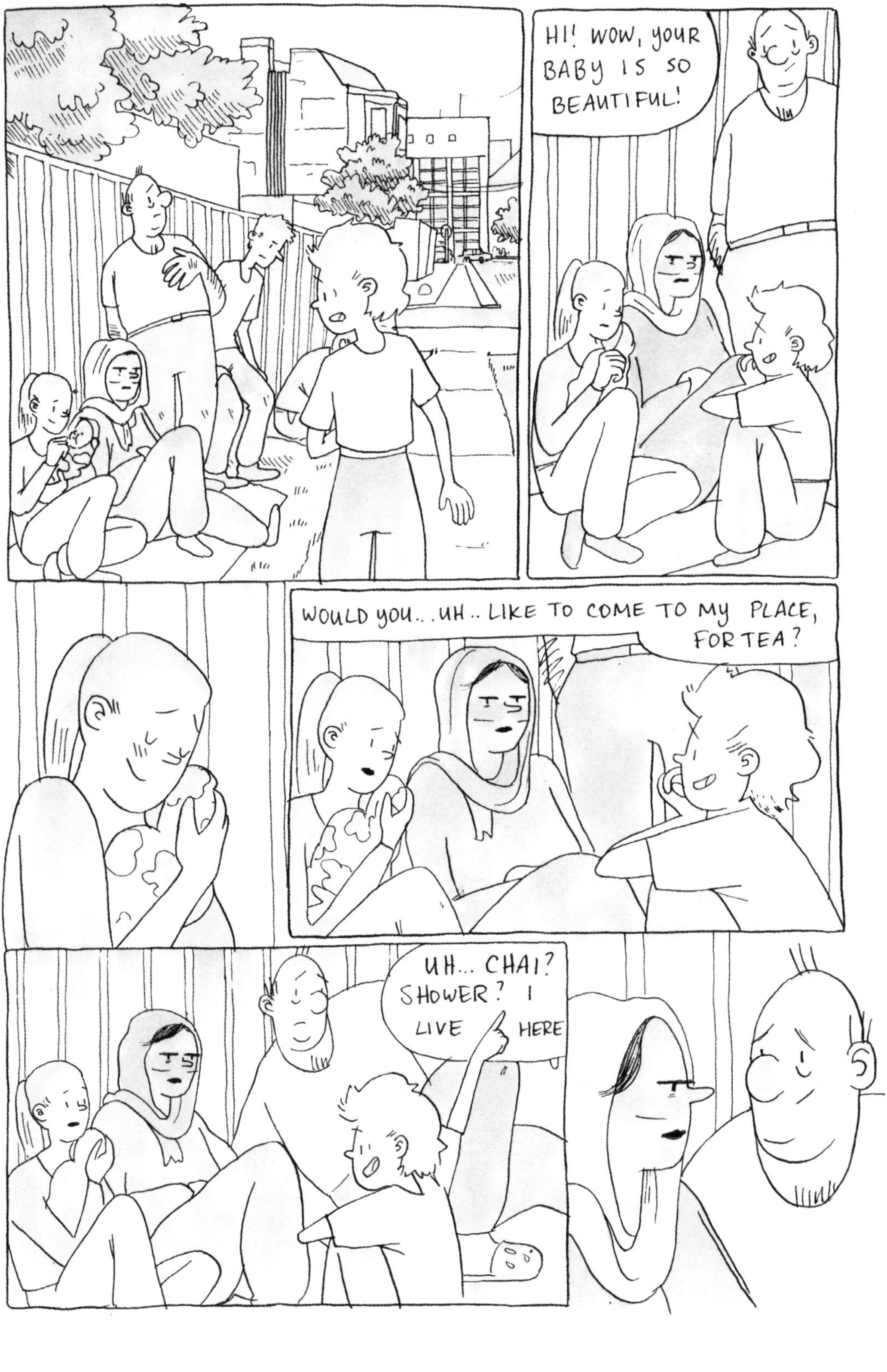
HI! WOW, YOUR BABY IS SO BEAUTIFUL!
WOULD YOU... UH.. LIKE TO COME TO MY PLACE, FOR TEA?
UH... CHAI? SHOWER? I LIVE HERE

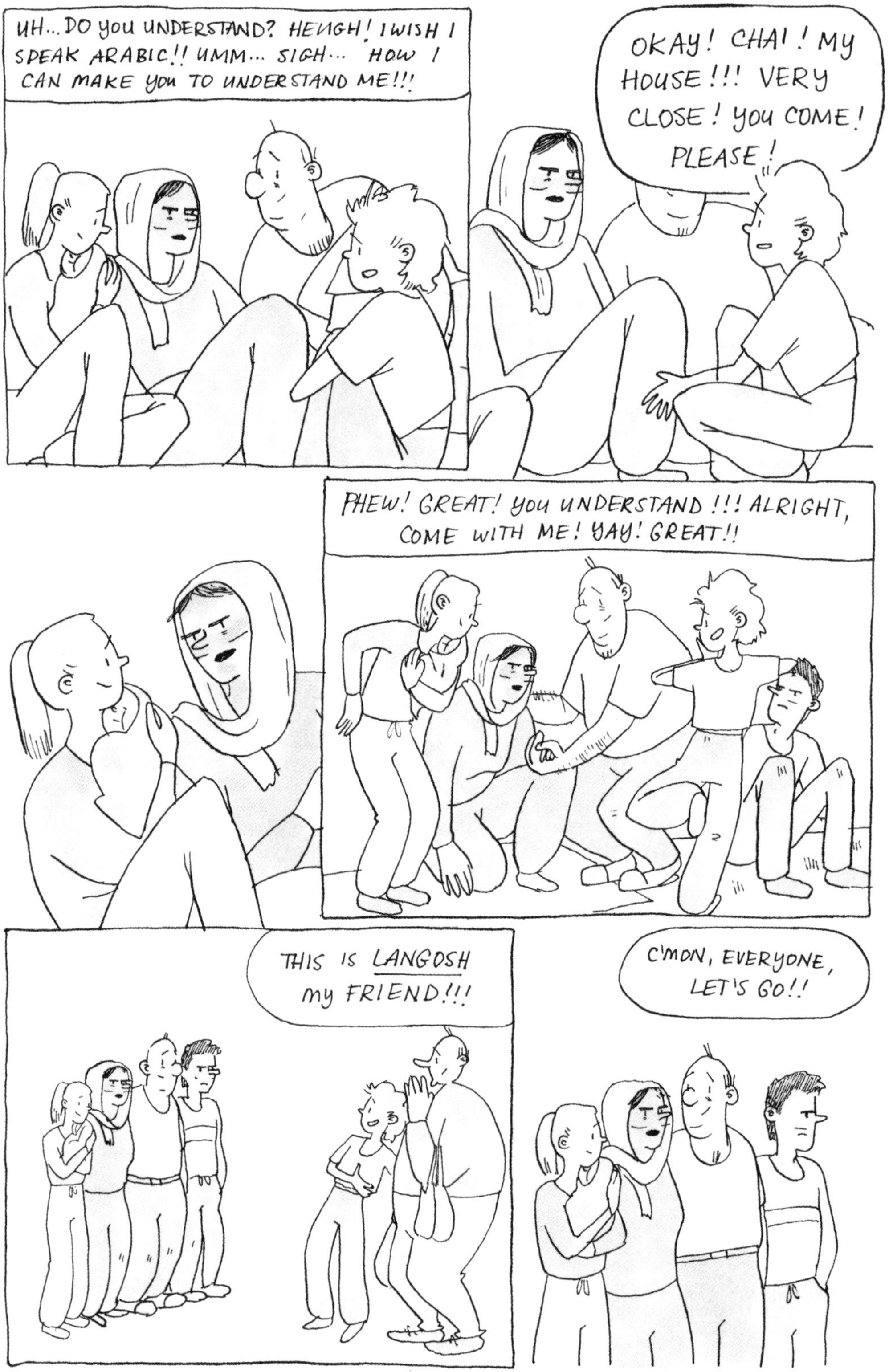
UH... DO YOU UNDERSTAND? HEUGH! I WISH I SPEAK ARABIC!! UMM... SIGH... HOW I CAN MAKE YOU TO UNDERSTAND ME!!!
OKAY! CHAI! MY HOUSE!!! VERY CLOSE! YOU COME! PLEASE!
PHEW! GREAT! YOU UNDERSTAND!!! ALRIGHT, COME WITH ME! YAY! GREAT!!
THIS IS LANGOSH MY FRIEND!!!
C'MON, EVERYONE, LET'S GO!!

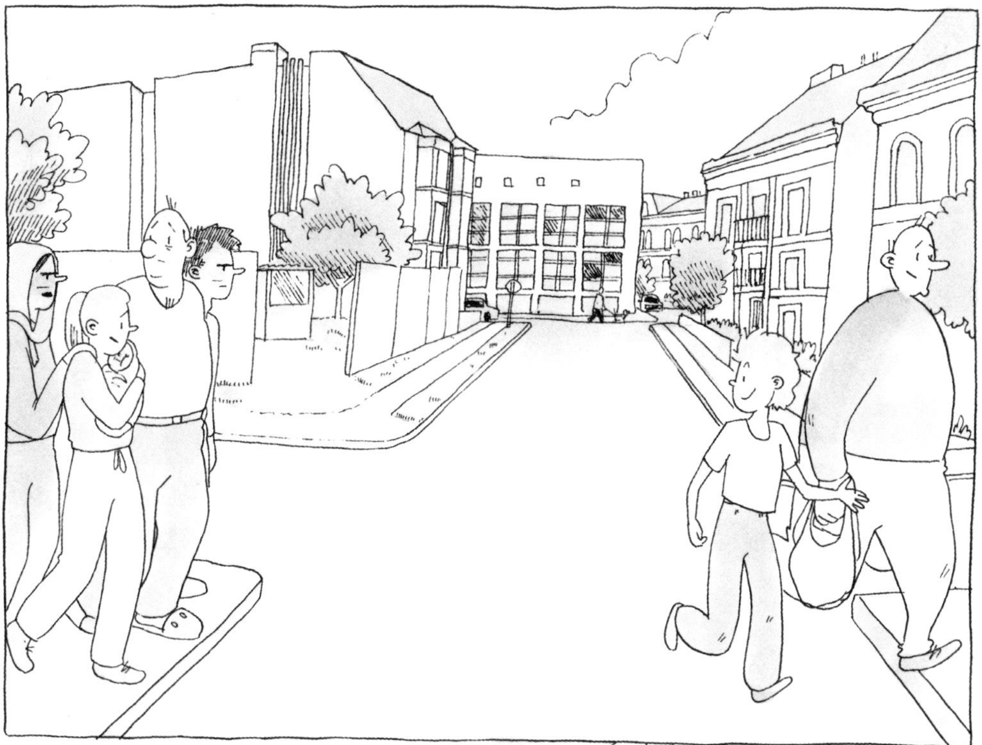

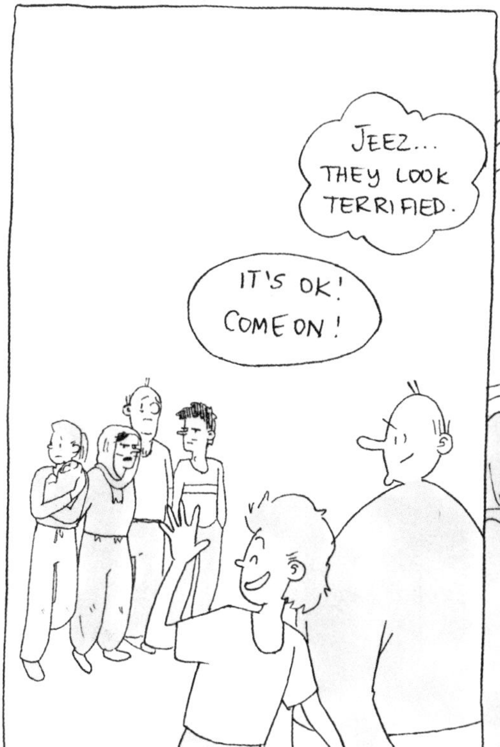
JEEZ...
THEY LOOK
TERRIFIED.
IT'S OK!
COME ON!

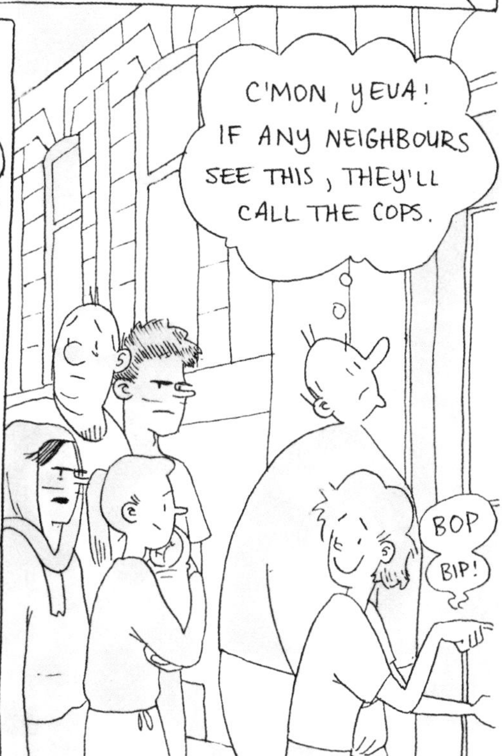
C'MON, YEVA!
IF ANY NEIGHBOURS
SEE THIS, THEY'LL
CALL THE COPS.
BOP
BIP!

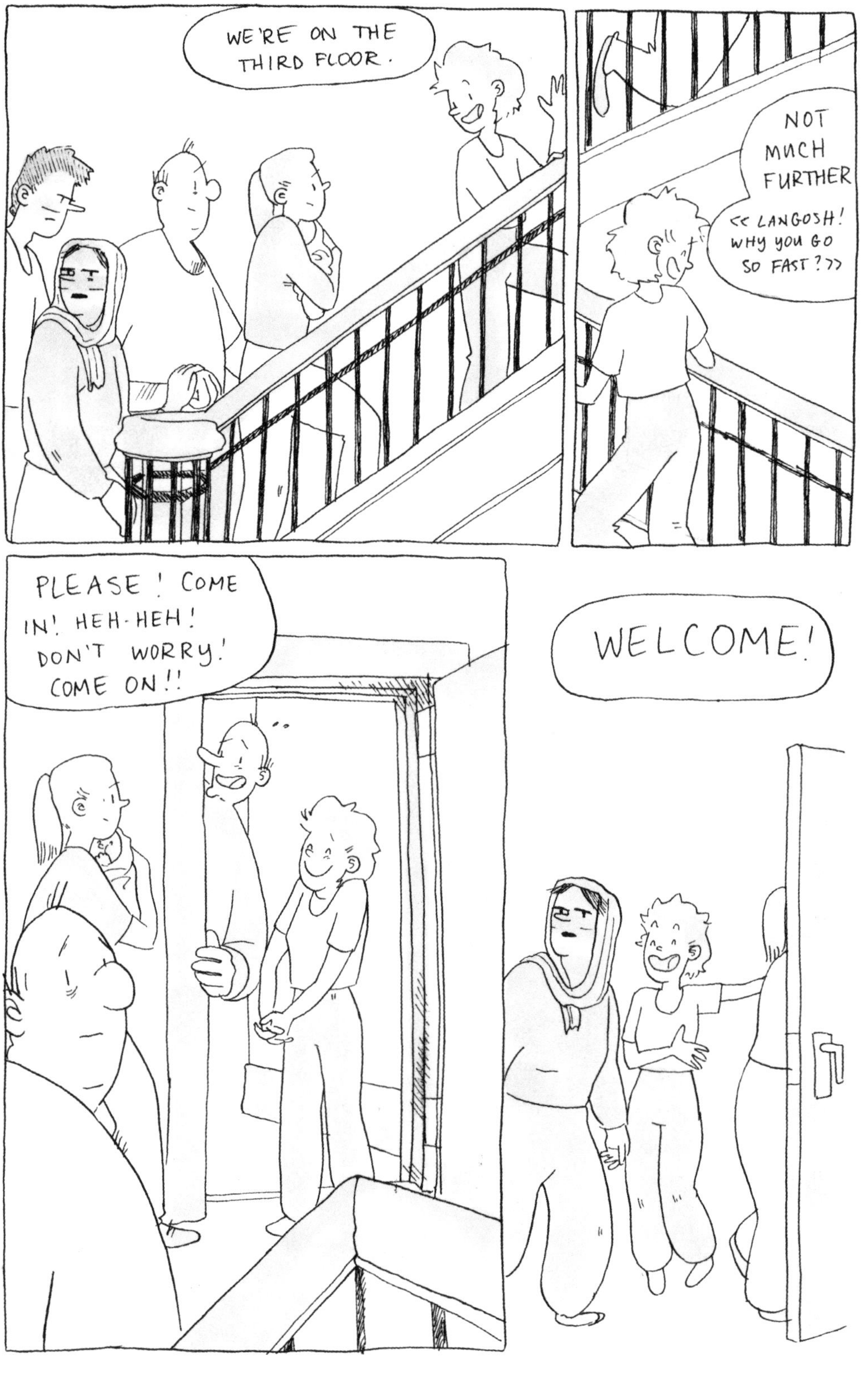
WE'RE ON THE THIRD FLOOR.
NOT MUCH FURTHER
<< LANGOSH! WHY YOU GO SO FAST? >>
PLEASE! COME IN! HEH-HEH! DON'T WORRY! COME ON!!
WELCOME!

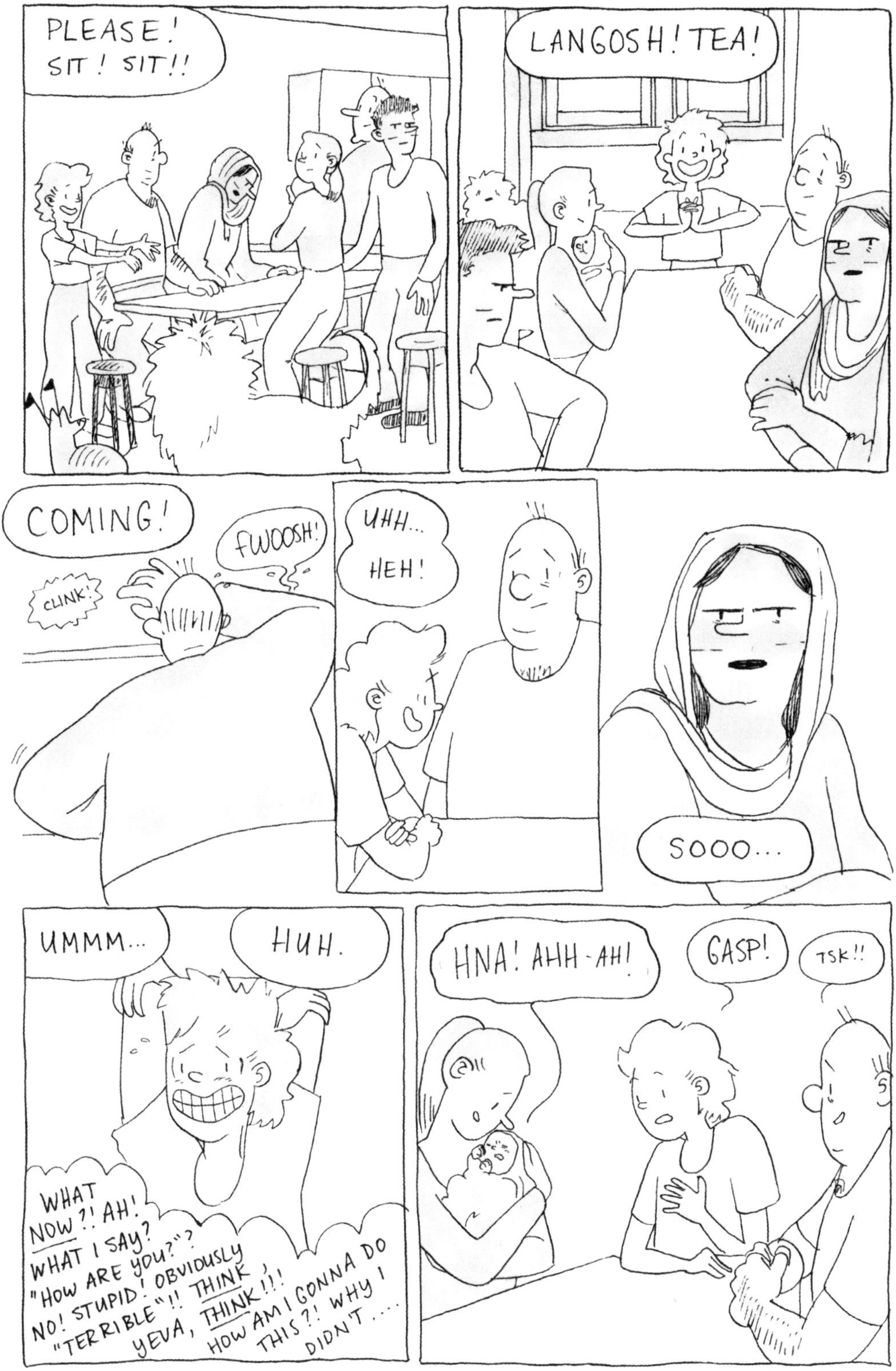
PLEASE! SIT! SIT!!
LANGOSH! TEA!
COMING!
CLINK!
FWOOSH!
UHH... HEH!
SOOO...
UMMM...
HUH.
WHAT NOW?! AH! WHAT I SAY? "HOW ARE YOU?"? NO! STUPID! OBVIOUSLY "TERRIBLE"!! THINK, YEVA, THINK!!! HOW AM I GONNA DO THIS?! WHY I DIDN'T....
HNA! AHH-AH!
GASP!
TSK!!

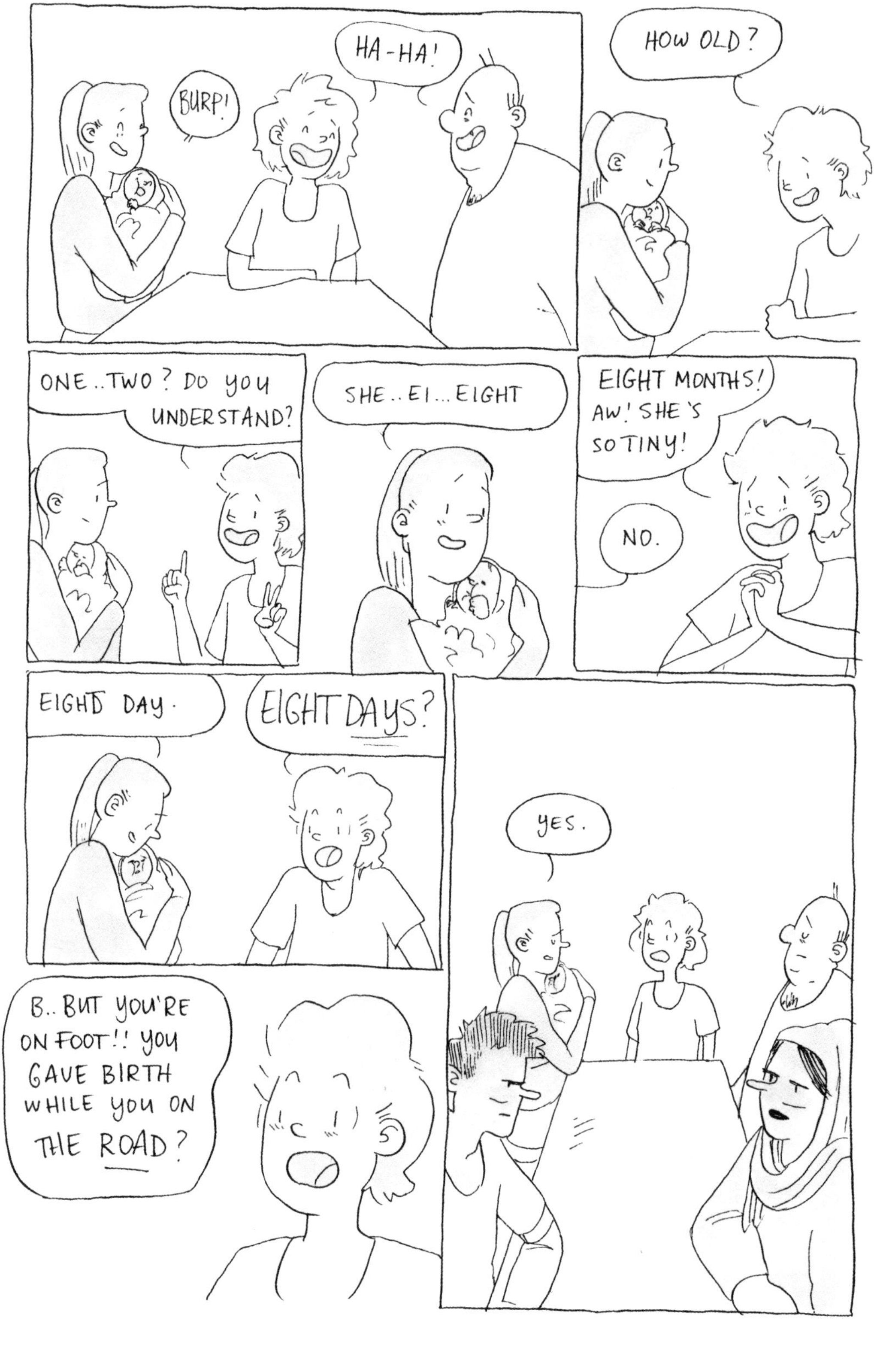
BURP!
HA-HA!
HOW OLD?
ONE..TWO? DO YOU UNDERSTAND?
SHE..EI...EIGHT
EIGHT MONTHS! AW! SHE'S SO TINY!
NO.
EIGHT DAY.
EIGHT DAYS?
B..BUT YOU'RE ON FOOT!! YOU GAVE BIRTH WHILE YOU ON THE ROAD?
YES.

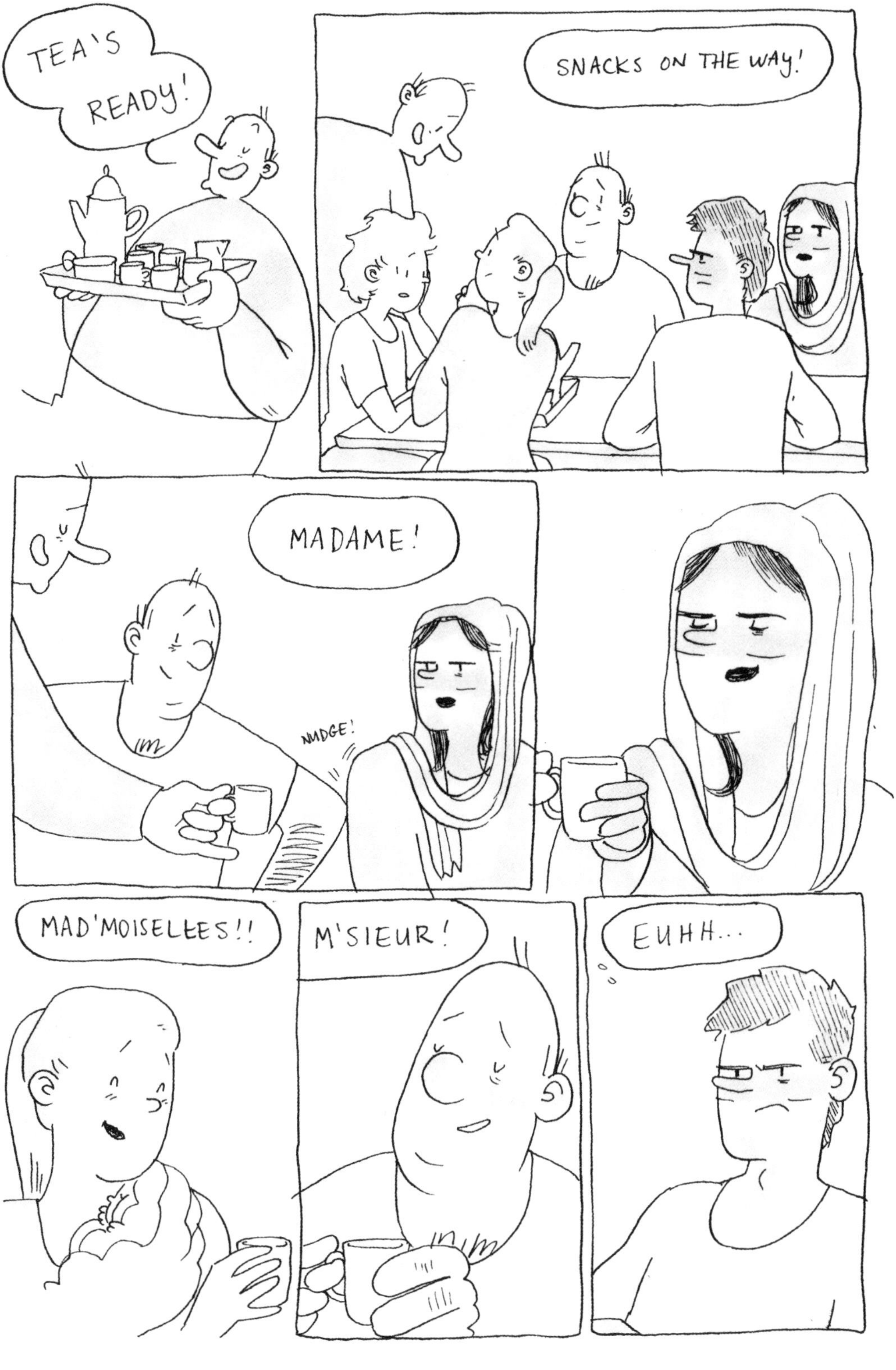
TEA'S READY!
SNACKS ON THE WAY!
MADAME!
NUDGE!
MAD'MOISELLES!!
M'SIEUR!
EUHH...

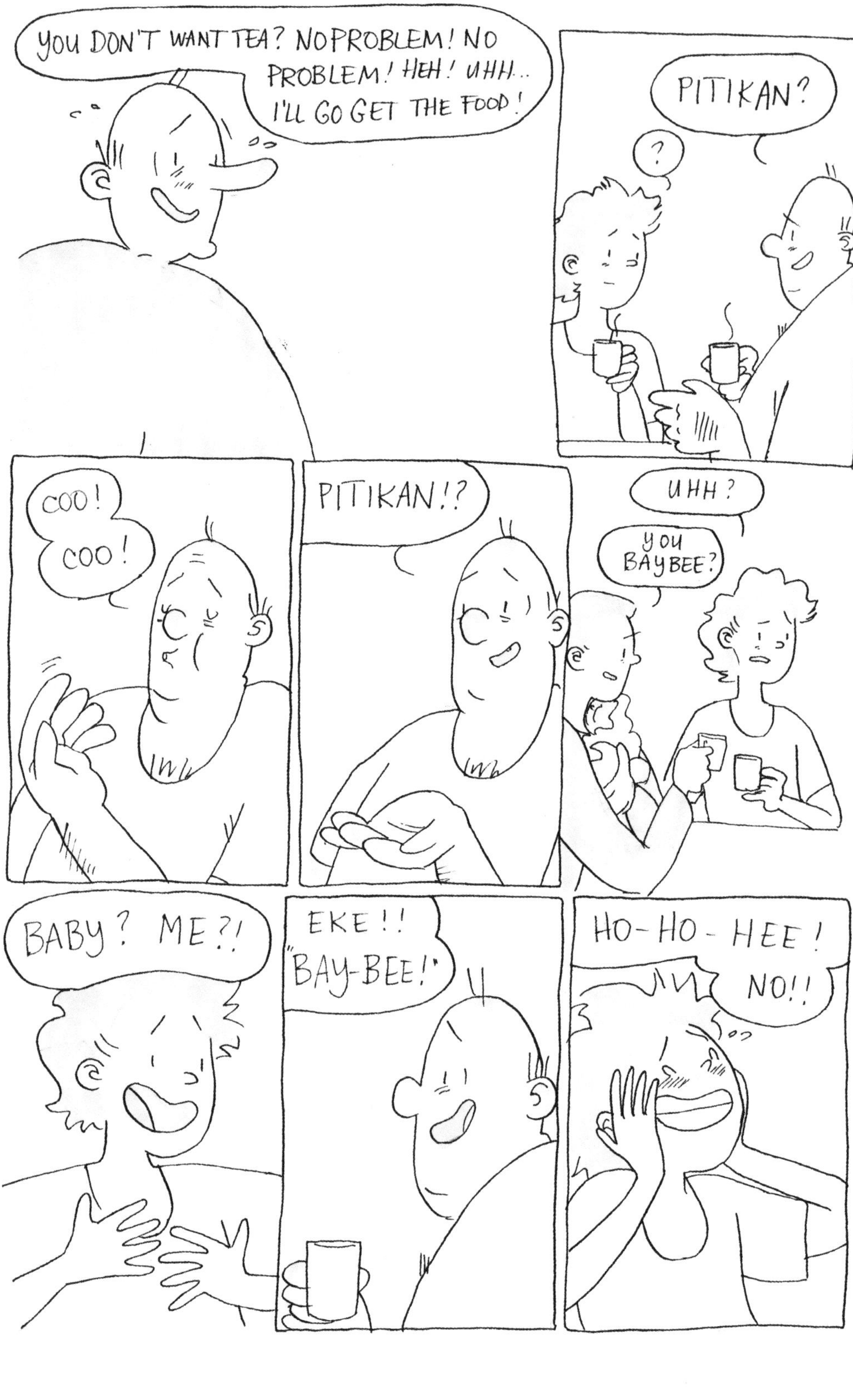
YOU DON'T WANT TEA? NO PROBLEM! NO PROBLEM! HEH! UHH... I'LL GO GET THE FOOD!
?
PITIKAN?
COO!
COO!
PITIKAN!?
UHH?
YOU BAYBEE?
BABY? ME?!
EKE!! "BAY-BEE!"
HO-HO-HEE!
NO!!

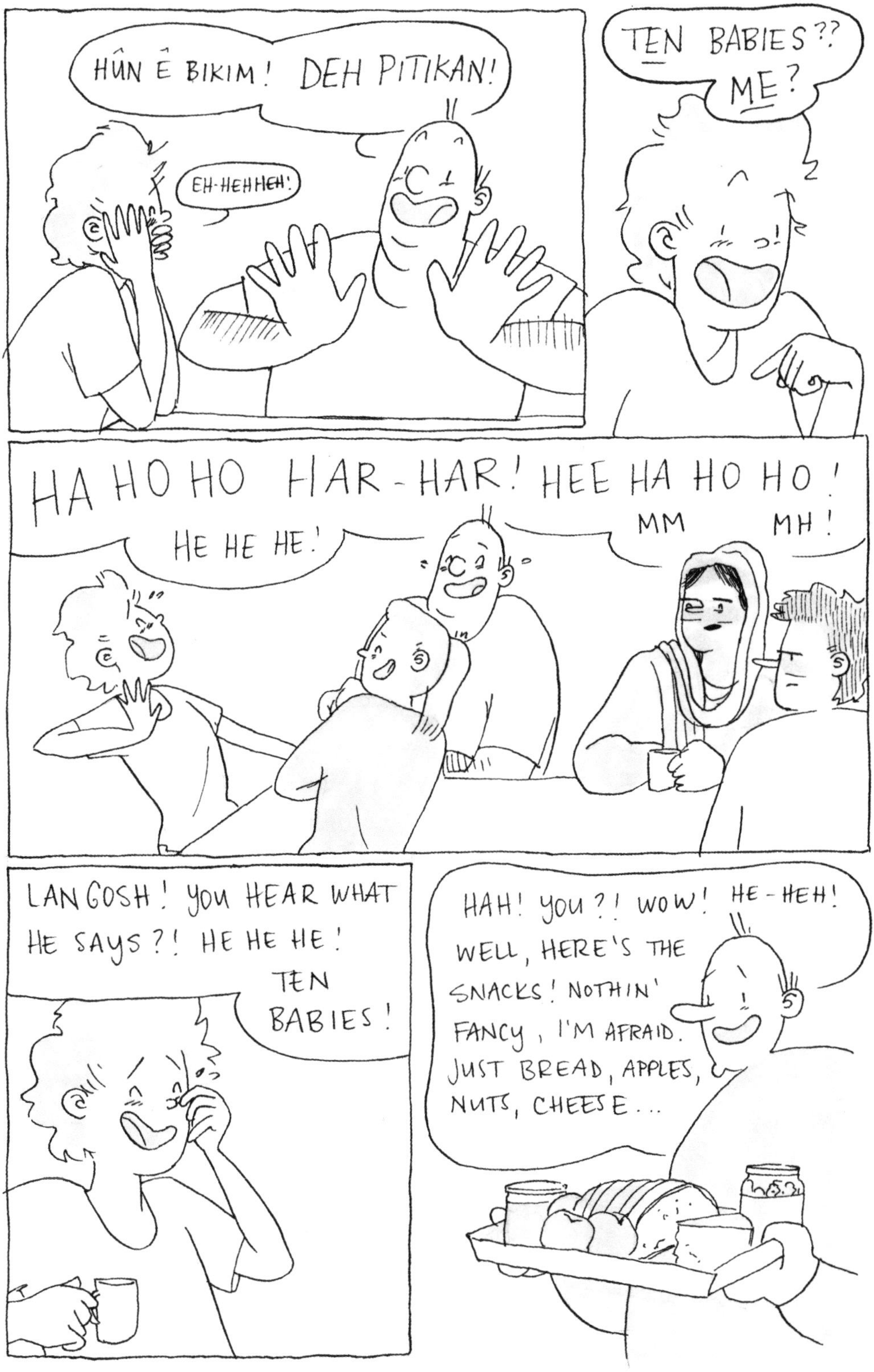
HÛN Ê BIKIM! DEH PITIKAN!
EH-HEHHEH!
TEN BABIES?? ME?
HA HO HO HAR-HAR! HEE HA HO HO!
HE HE HE!
MM MH!
LANGOSH! YOU HEAR WHAT HE SAYS?! HE HE HE!
TEN BABIES!
HAH! YOU?! WOW! HE-HEH!
WELL, HERE'S THE SNACKS! NOTHIN' FANCY, I'M AFRAID. JUST BREAD, APPLES, NUTS, CHEESE...

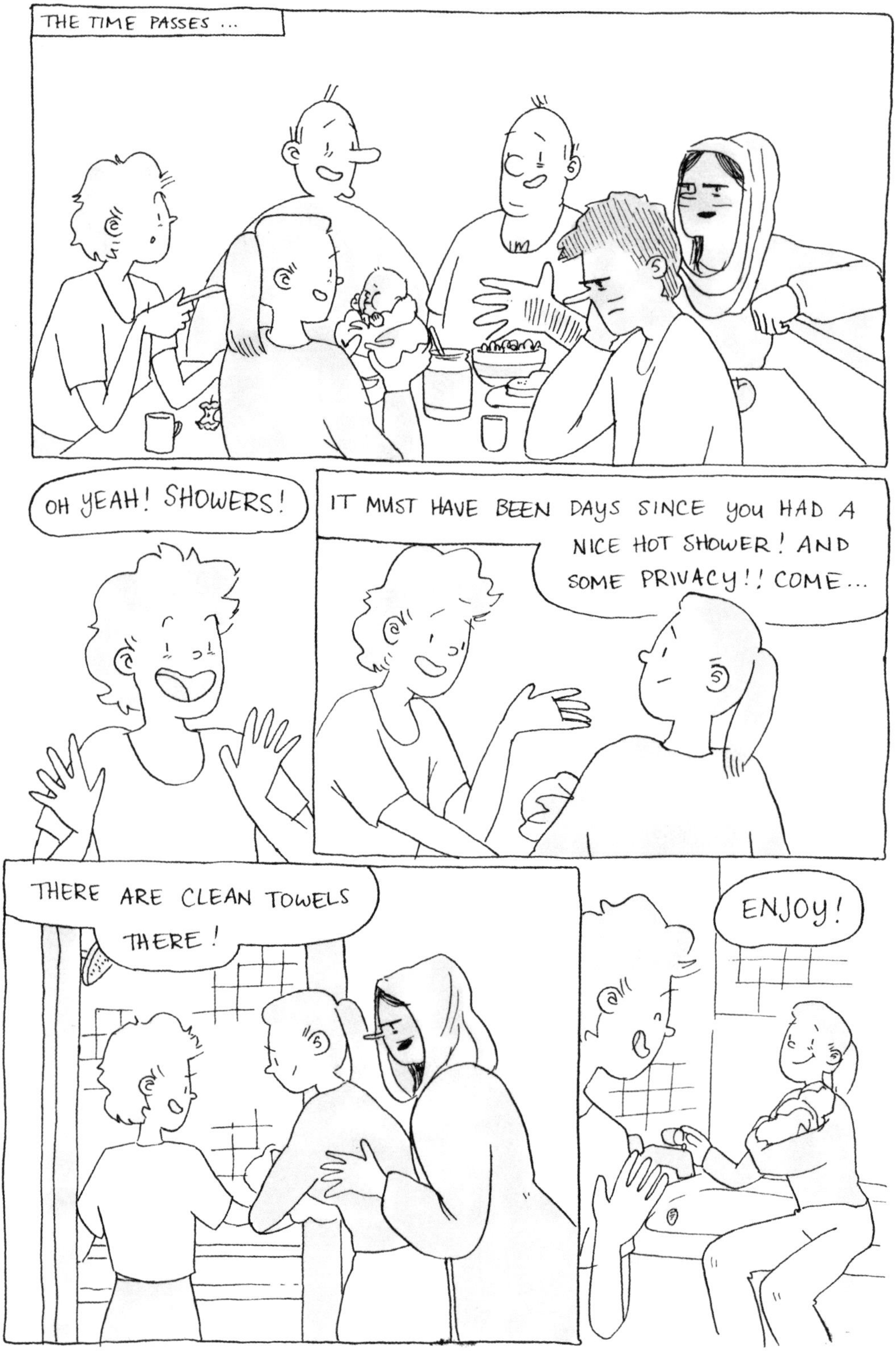
THE TIME PASSES ...
OH YEAH! SHOWERS!
IT MUST HAVE BEEN DAYS SINCE YOU HAD A NICE HOT SHOWER! AND SOME PRIVACY!! COME...
THERE ARE CLEAN TOWELS THERE!
ENJOY!

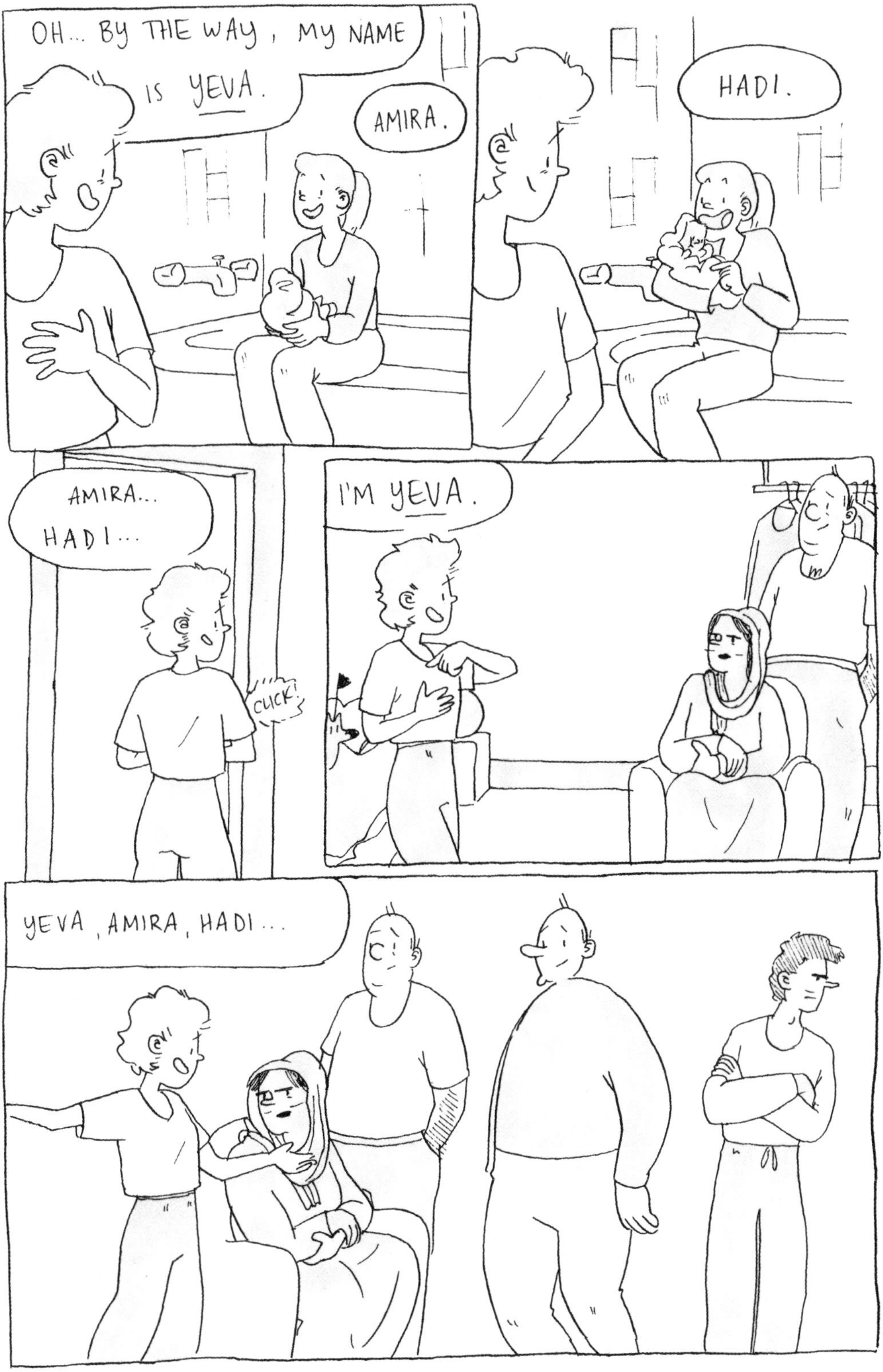
OH... BY THE WAY, MY NAME IS YEVA.
AMIRA.
HADI.
AMIRA... HADI...
CLICK!
I'M YEVA.
YEVA, AMIRA, HADI...

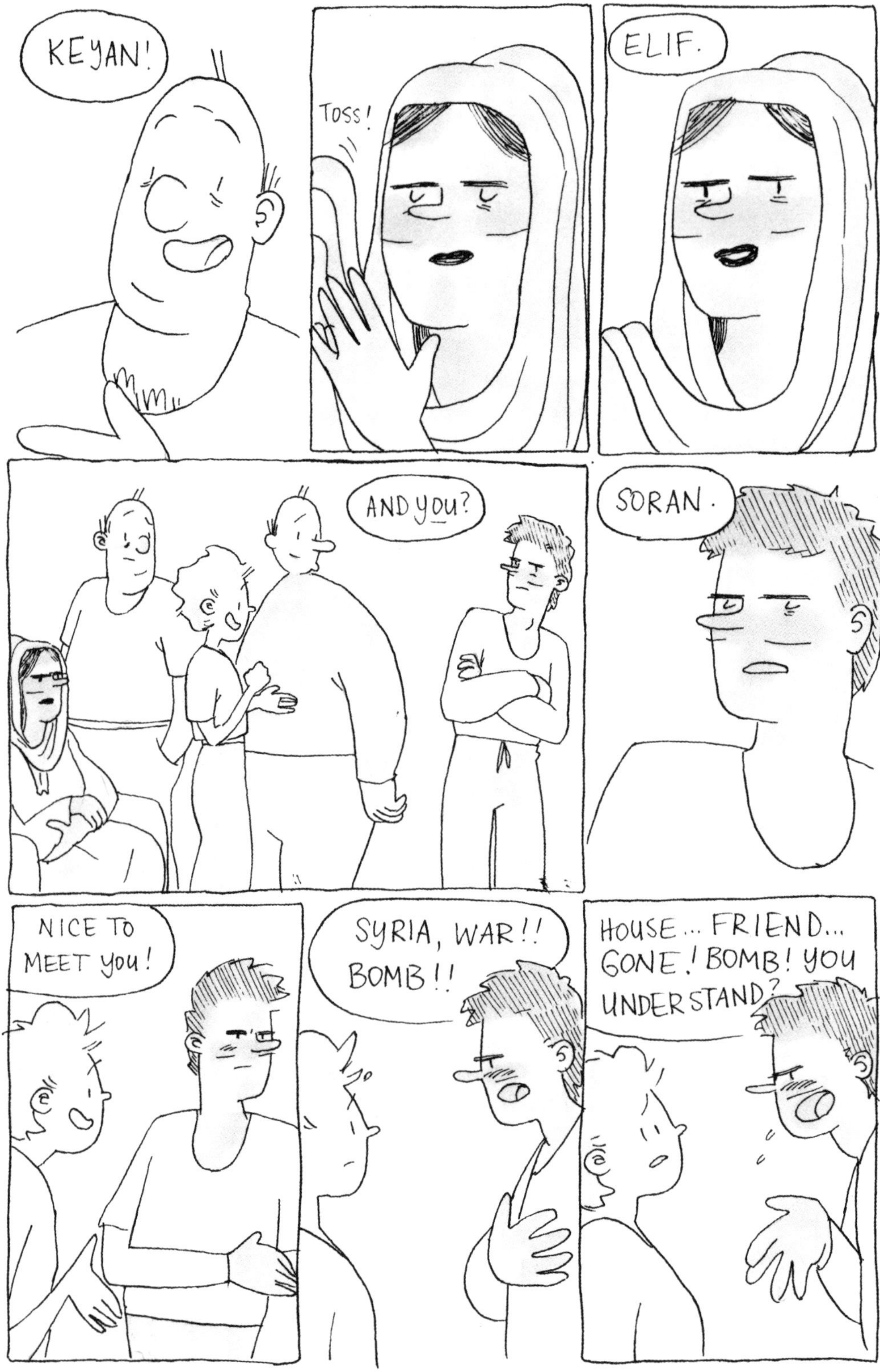
KEYAN!
TOSS!
ELIF.
AND YOU?
SORAN.
NICE TO MEET YOU!
SYRIA, WAR!! BOMB!!
HOUSE... FRIEND... GONE! BOMB! YOU UNDERSTAND?

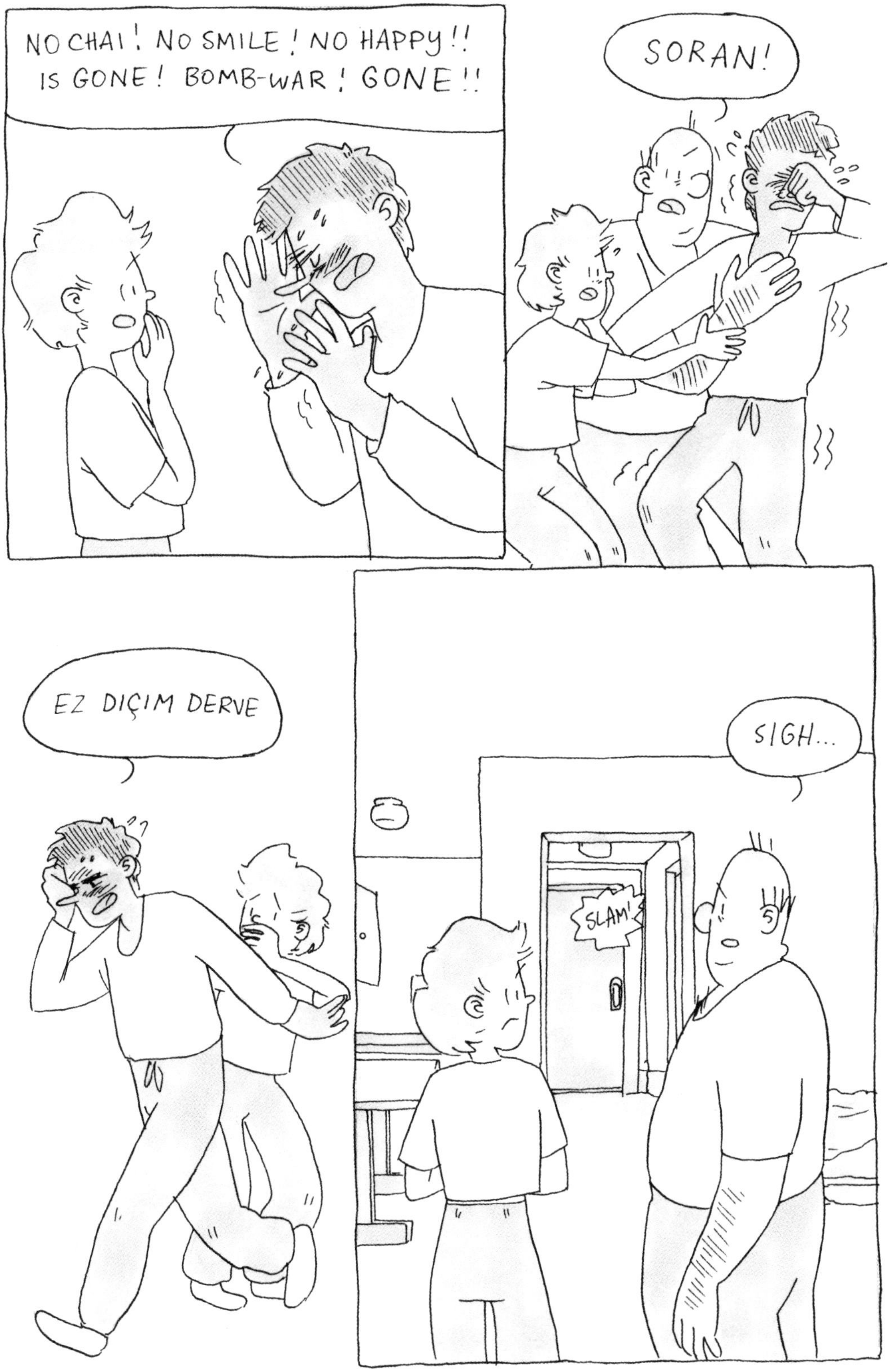
NO CHAI! NO SMILE! NO HAPPY!! IS GONE! BOMB-WAR! GONE!!
SORAN!
EZ DIÇIM DERVE
SLAM!
SIGH...

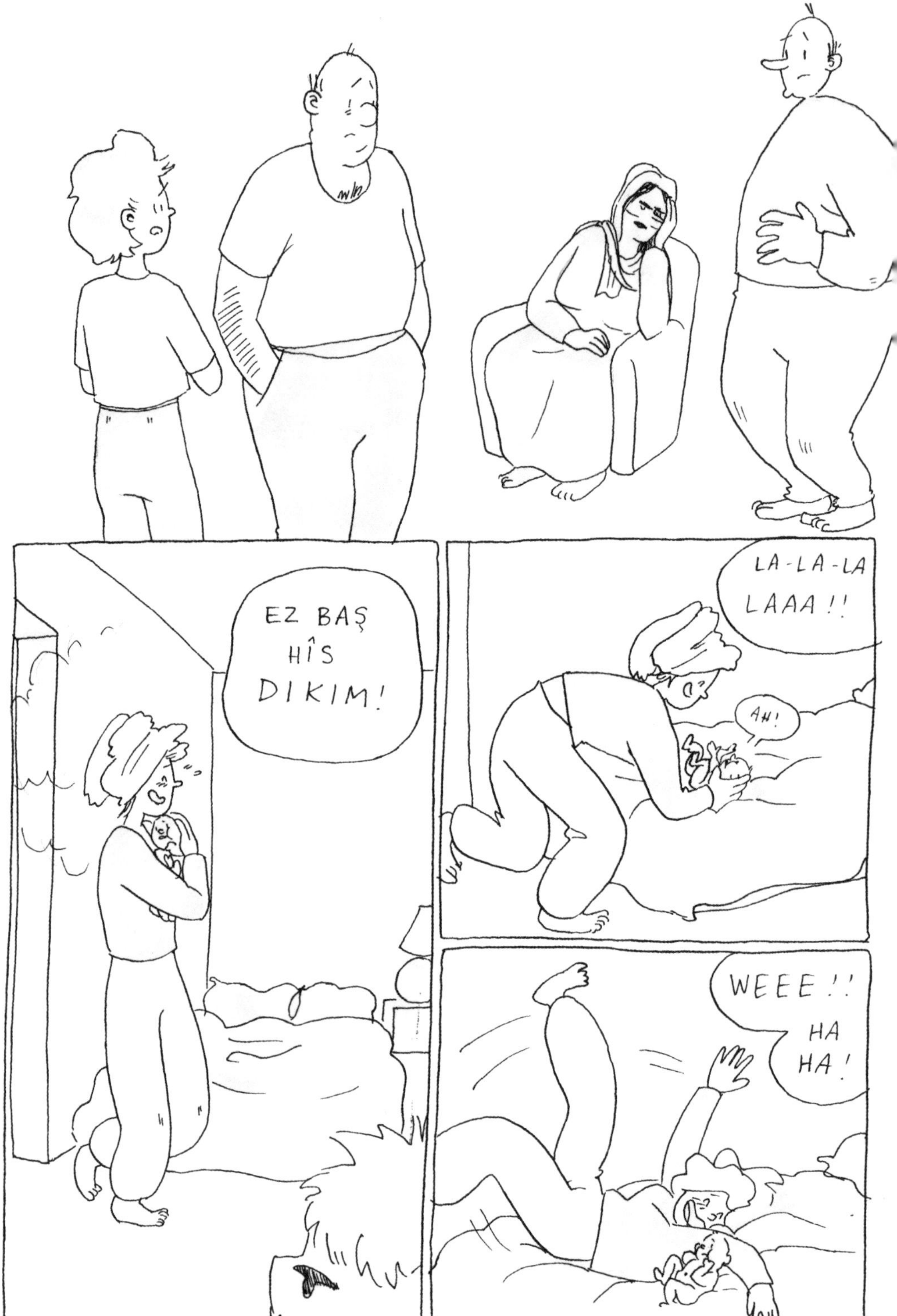
EZ BAŞ
HÎS
DIKIM!
LA-LA-LA
LAAA!!
AH!
WEEE!!
HA
HA!

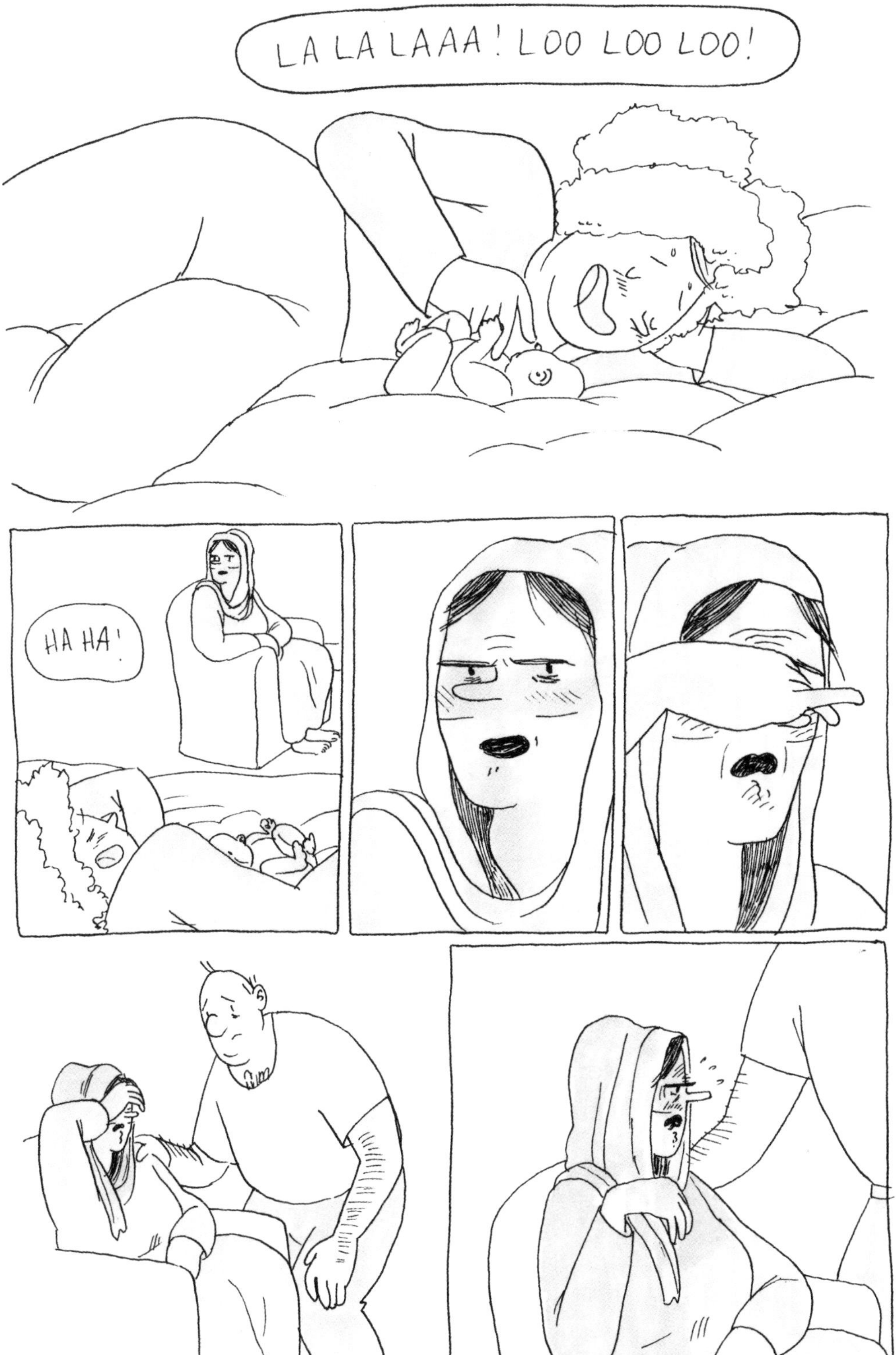
LA LA LAAA! LOO LOO LOO!
HA HA!

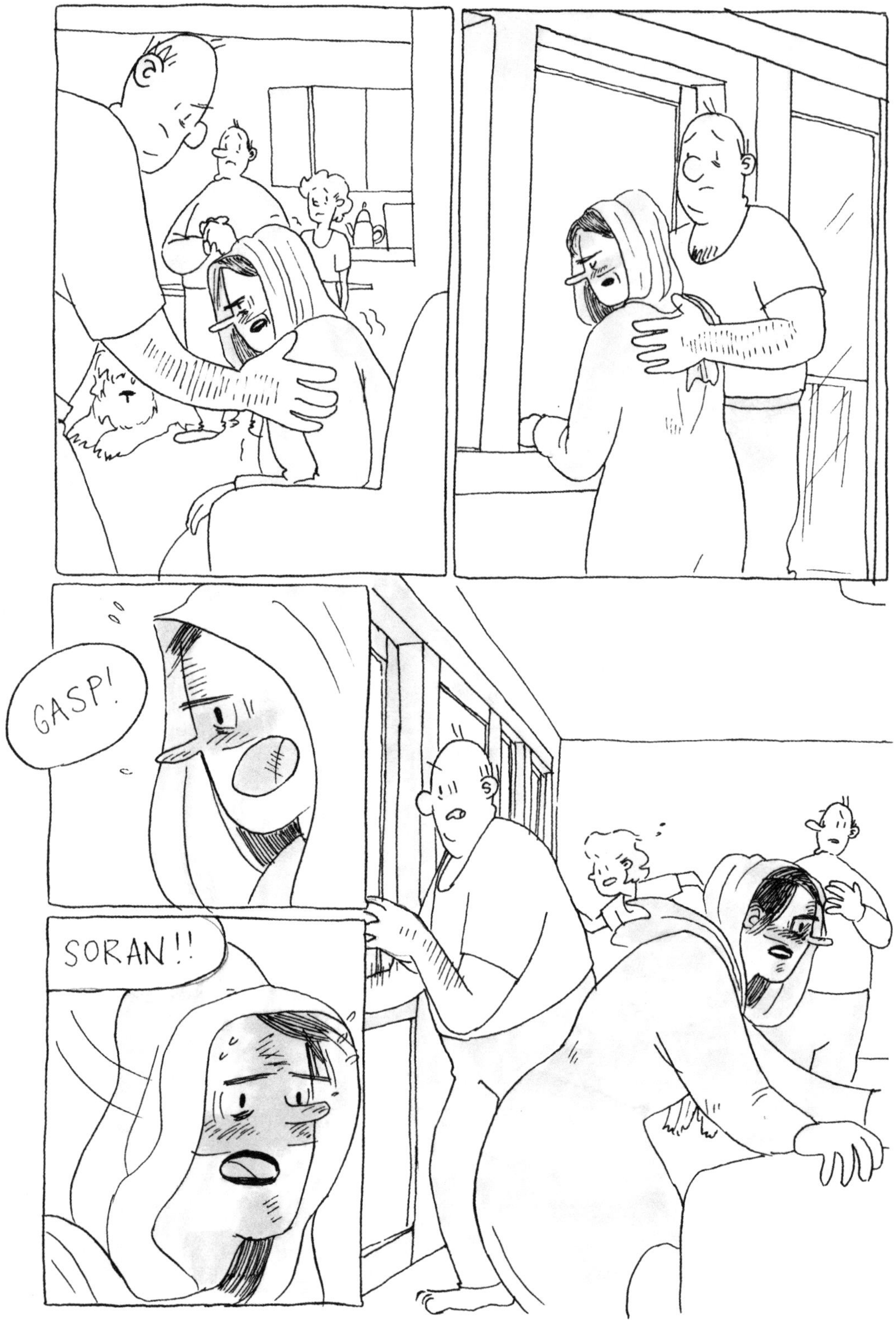
GASP!
SORAN!!

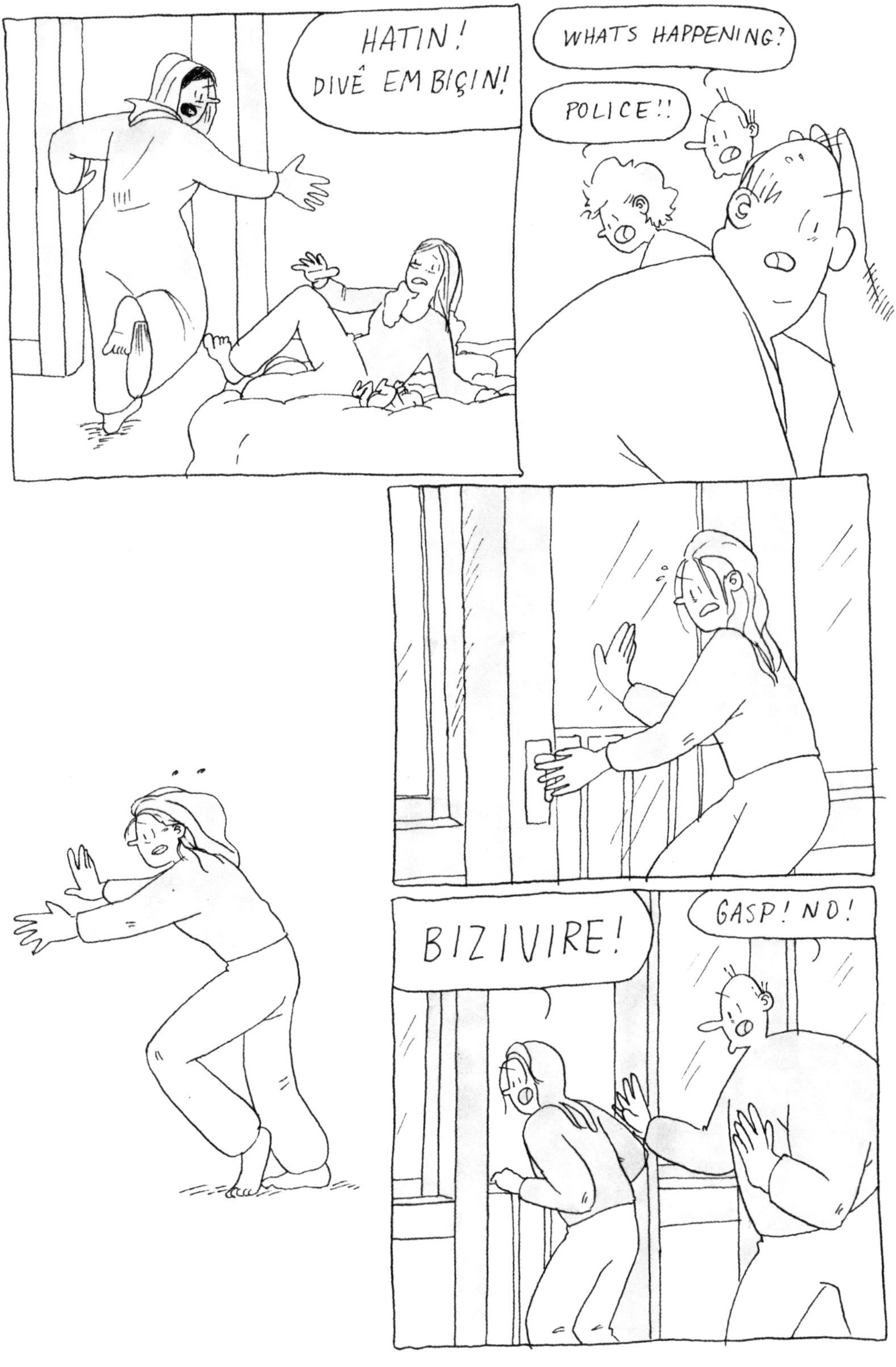
HATIN!
DIVÊ EM BIÇIN!
WHATS HAPPENING?
POLICE!!
BIZIVIRE!
GASP! NO!

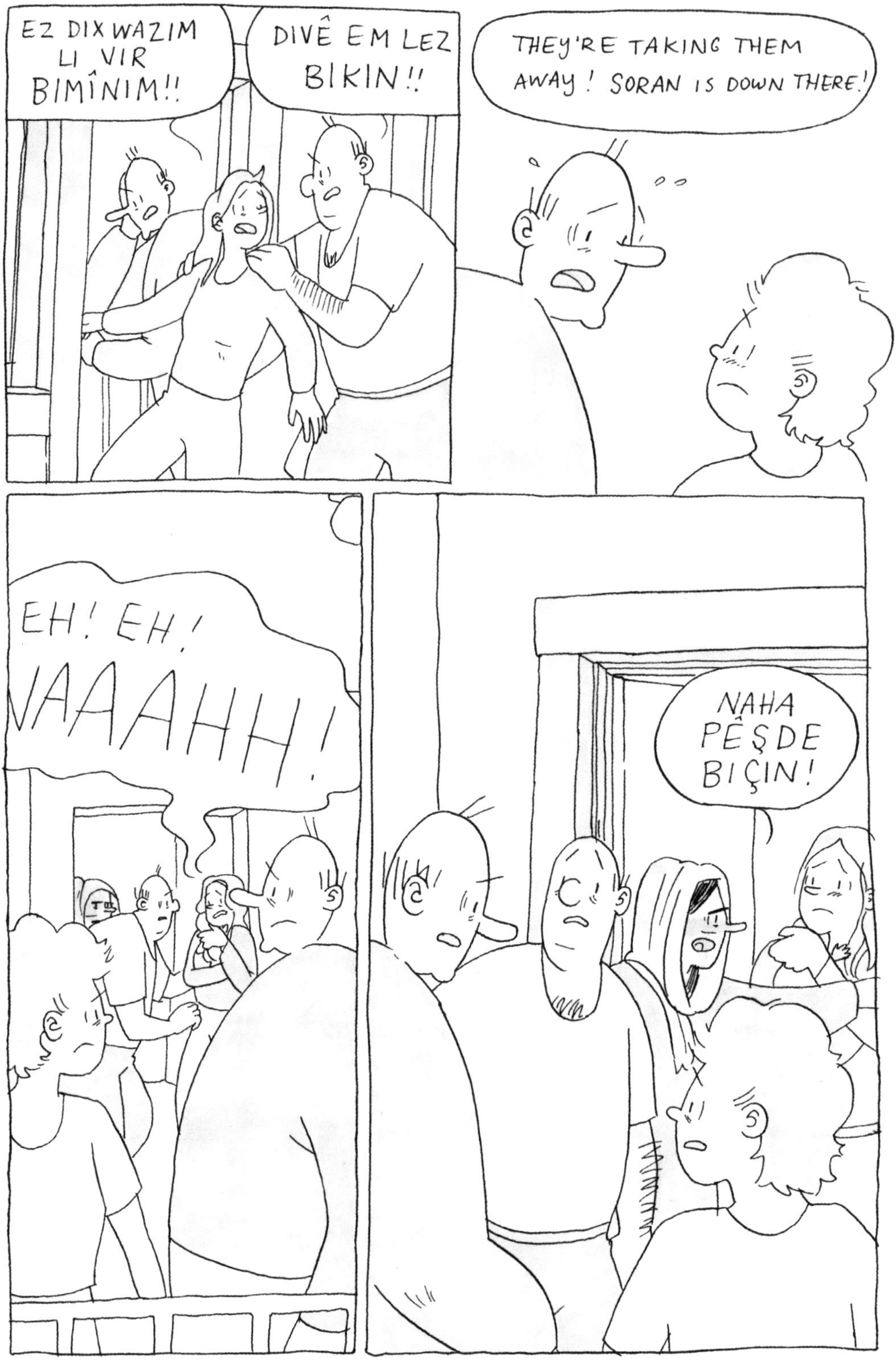
EZ DIXWAZIM LI VIR BIMÎNIM!!
DIVÊ EM LEZ BIKIN!!
THEY'RE TAKING THEM AWAY! SORAN IS DOWN THERE!
EH! EH! NAAAHH!
NAHA PÊŞDE BIÇIN!

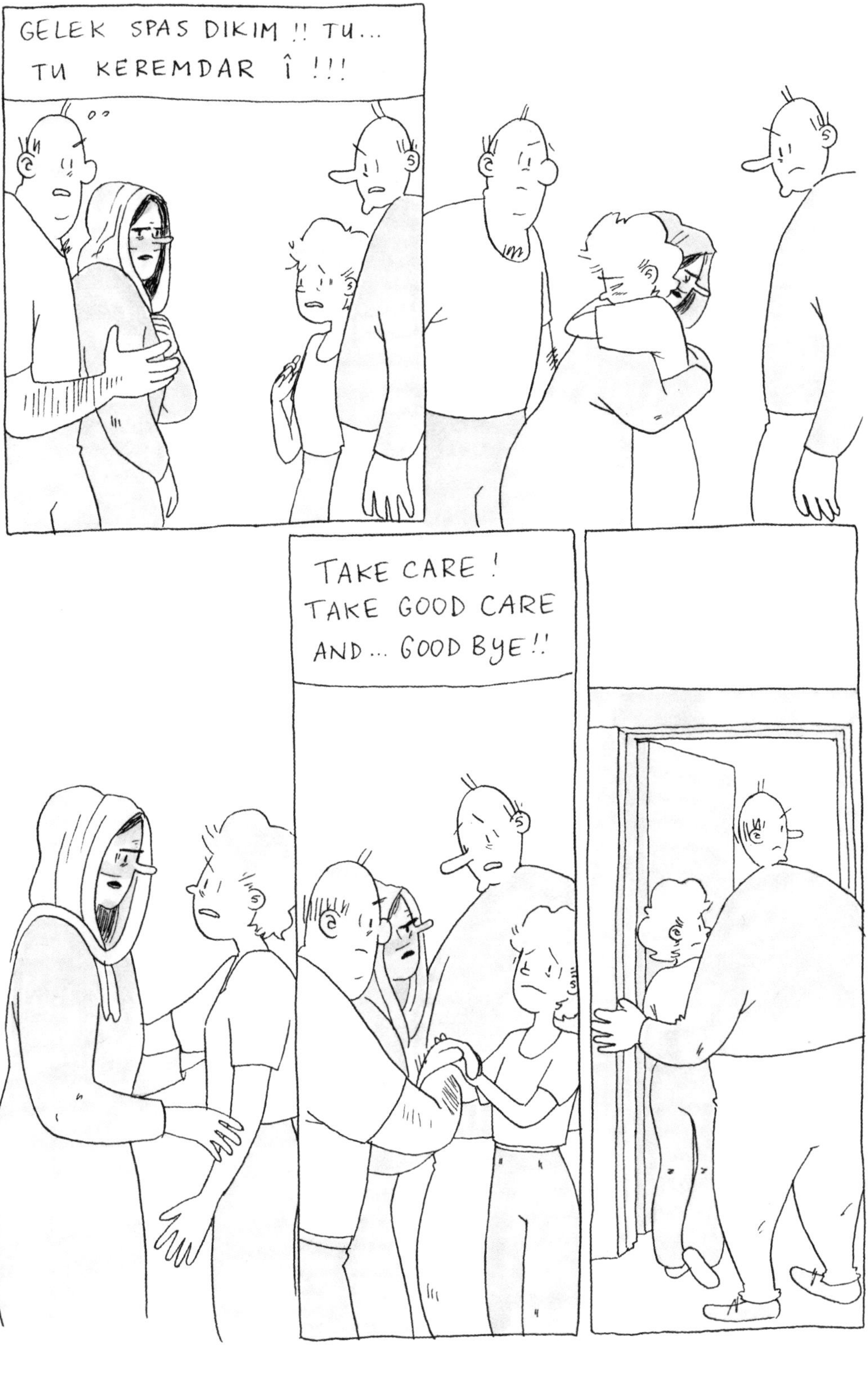
GELEK SPAS DIKIM !! TU...
TU KEREMDAR Î !!!
TAKE CARE !
TAKE GOOD CARE
AND... GOOD BYE !!

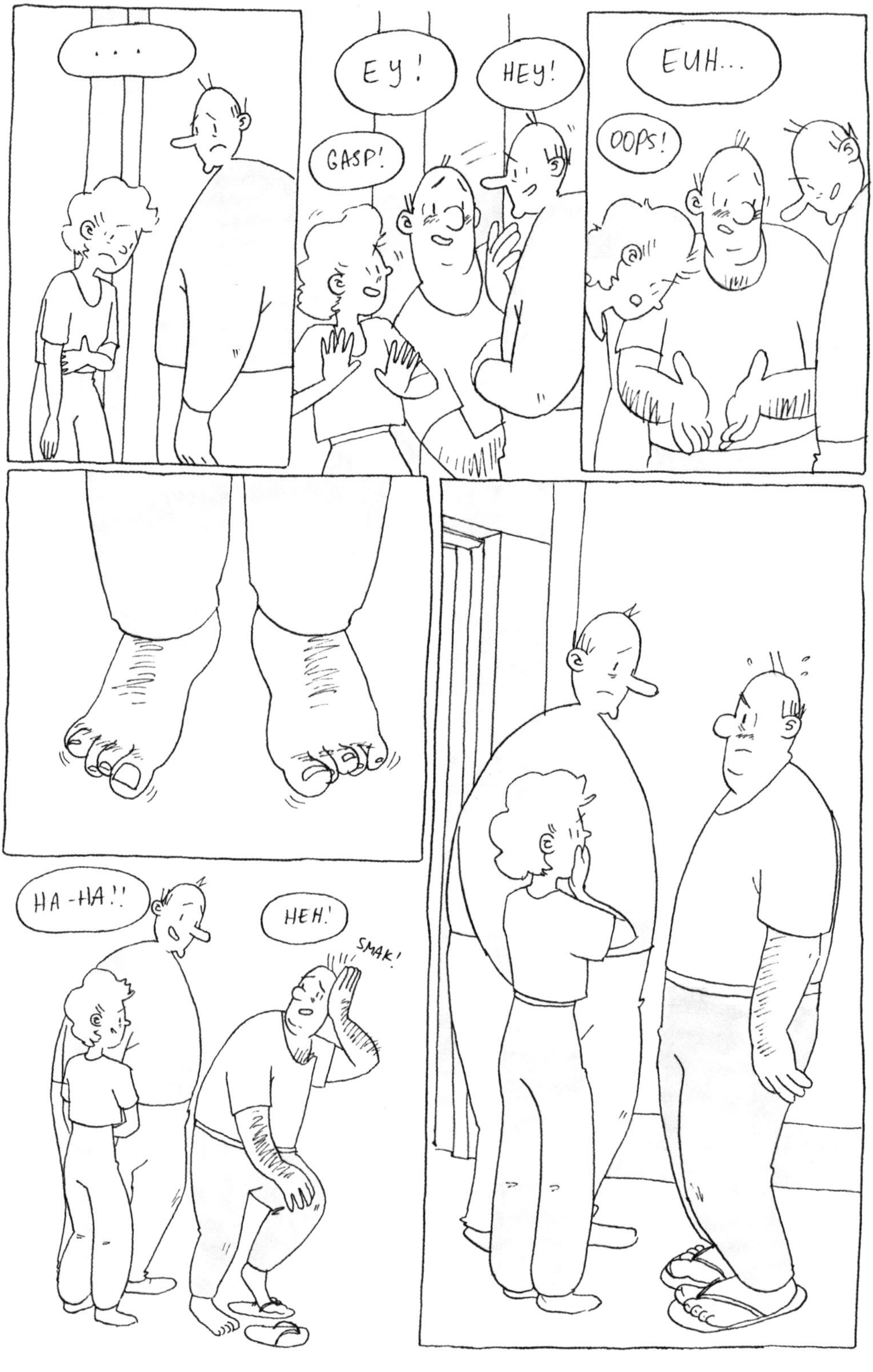
. . .
EY!
HEY!
GASP!
EUH...
OOPS!
HA-HA!!
HEH!
SMAK!

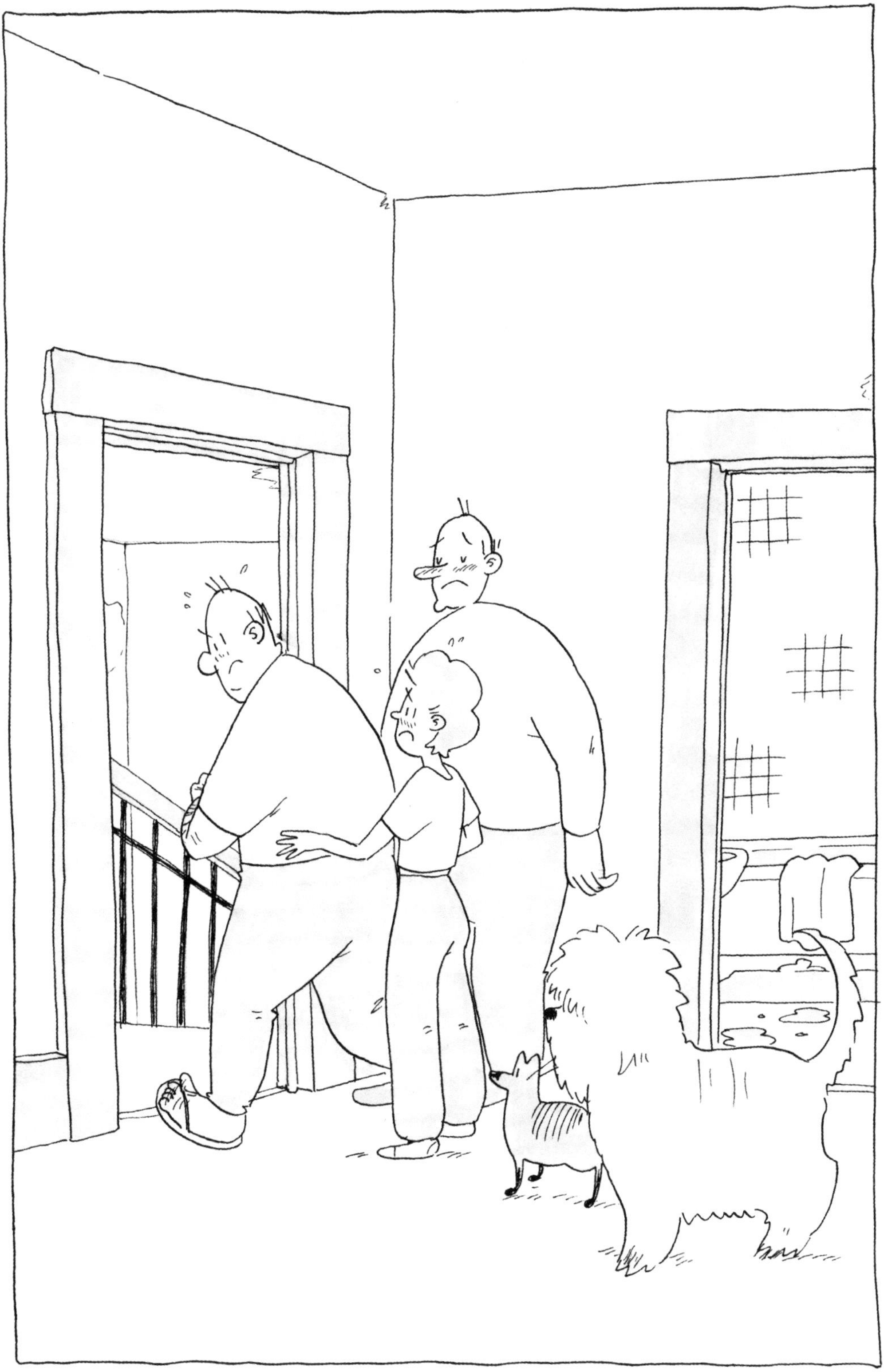

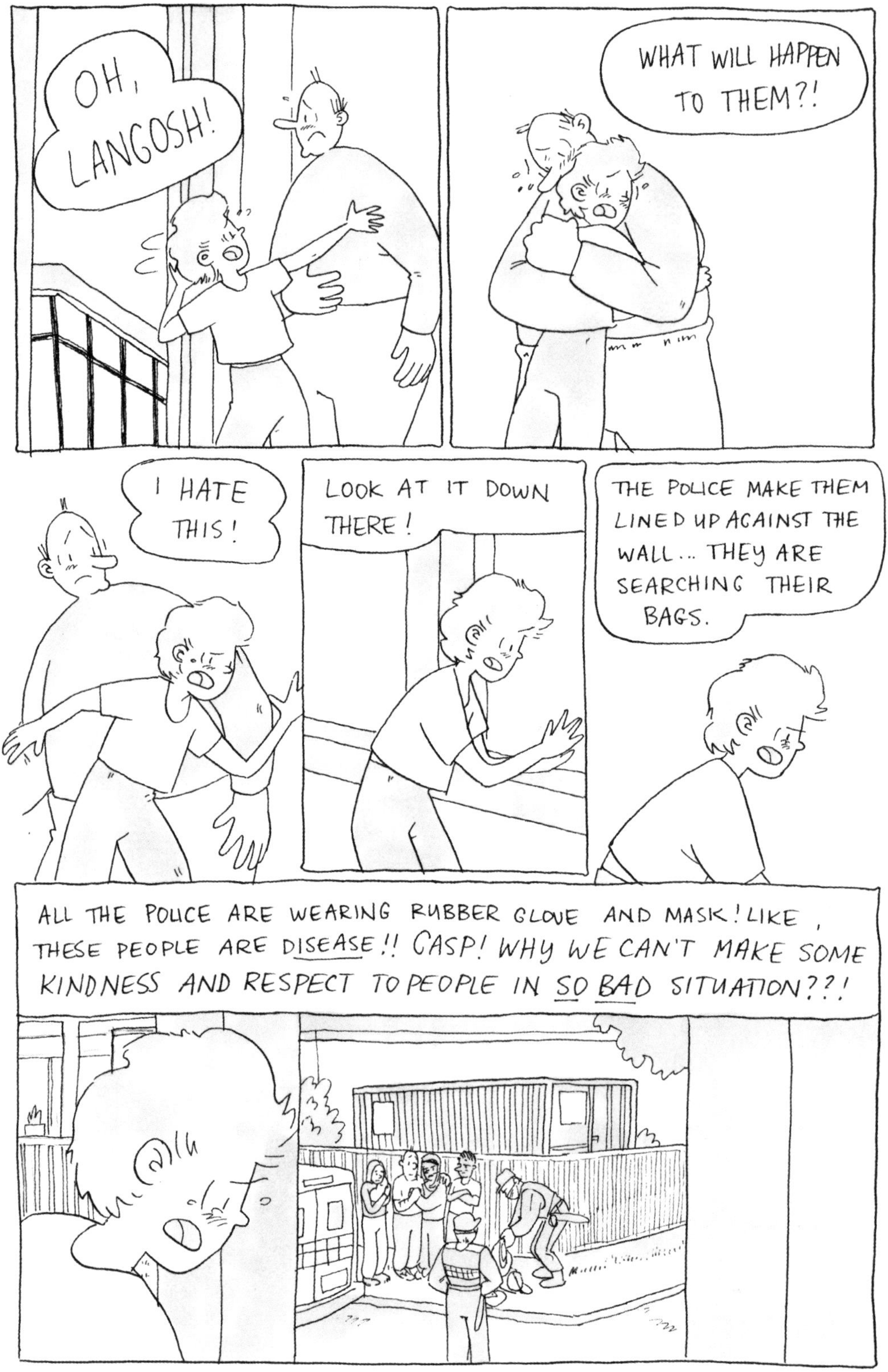
OH, LANGOSH!
WHAT WILL HAPPEN TO THEM?!
I HATE THIS!
LOOK AT IT DOWN THERE!
THE POLICE MAKE THEM LINED UP AGAINST THE WALL... THEY ARE SEARCHING THEIR BAGS.
ALL THE POLICE ARE WEARING RUBBER GLOVE AND MASK! LIKE, THESE PEOPLE ARE DISEASE!! GASP! WHY WE CAN'T MAKE SOME KINDNESS AND RESPECT TO PEOPLE IN SO BAD SITUATION??!

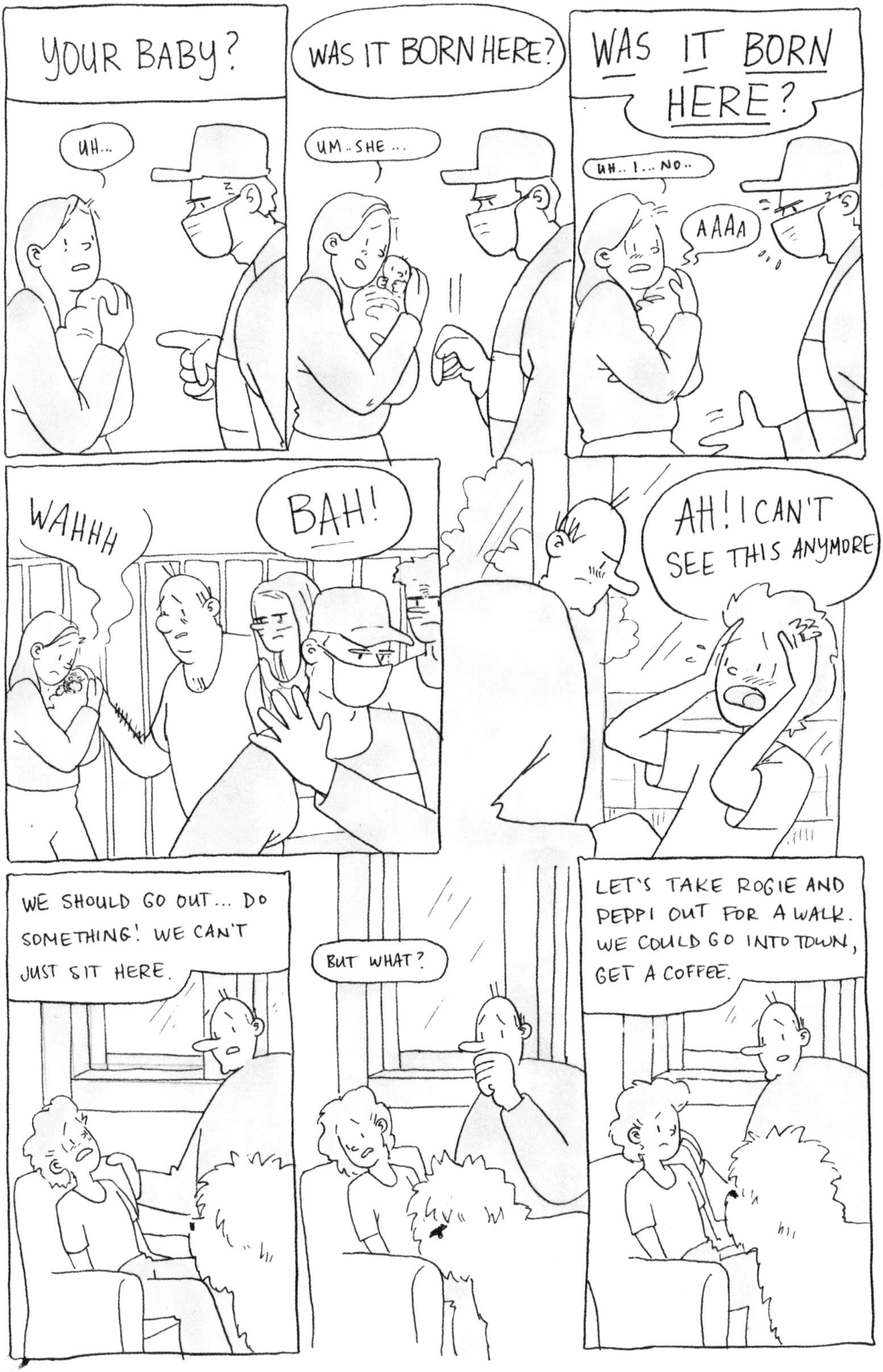
YOUR BABY?
UH...
WAS IT BORN HERE?
UM.. SHE ...
WAS IT BORN HERE?
UH.. I... NO..
AAAA
WAHHH
BAH!
AH! I CAN'T SEE THIS ANYMORE
WE SHOULD GO OUT... DO SOMETHING! WE CAN'T JUST SIT HERE.
BUT WHAT?
LET'S TAKE ROGIE AND PEPPI OUT FOR A WALK. WE COULD GO INTO TOWN, GET A COFFEE.

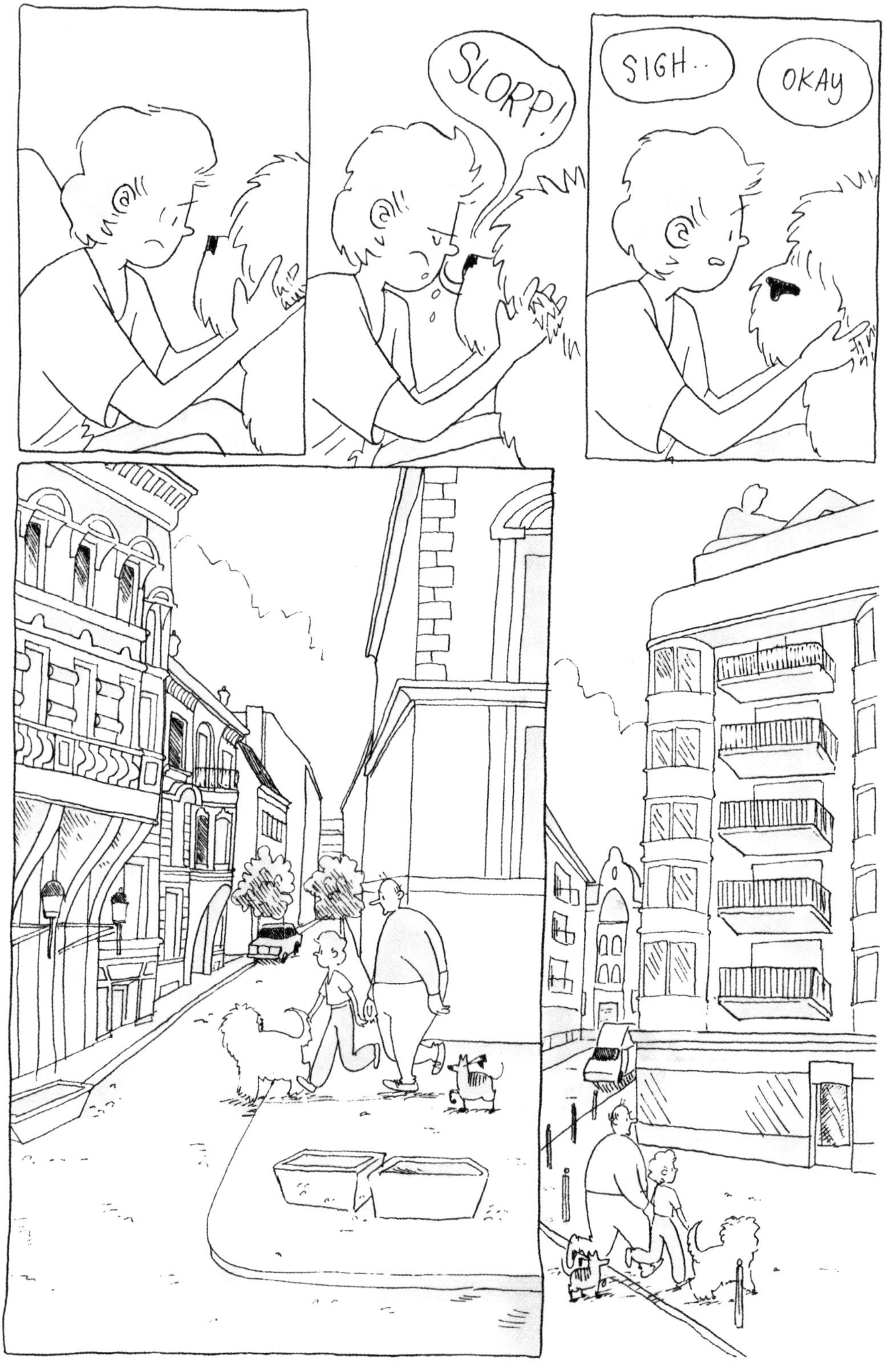
SLORP!
SIGH..
OKAY

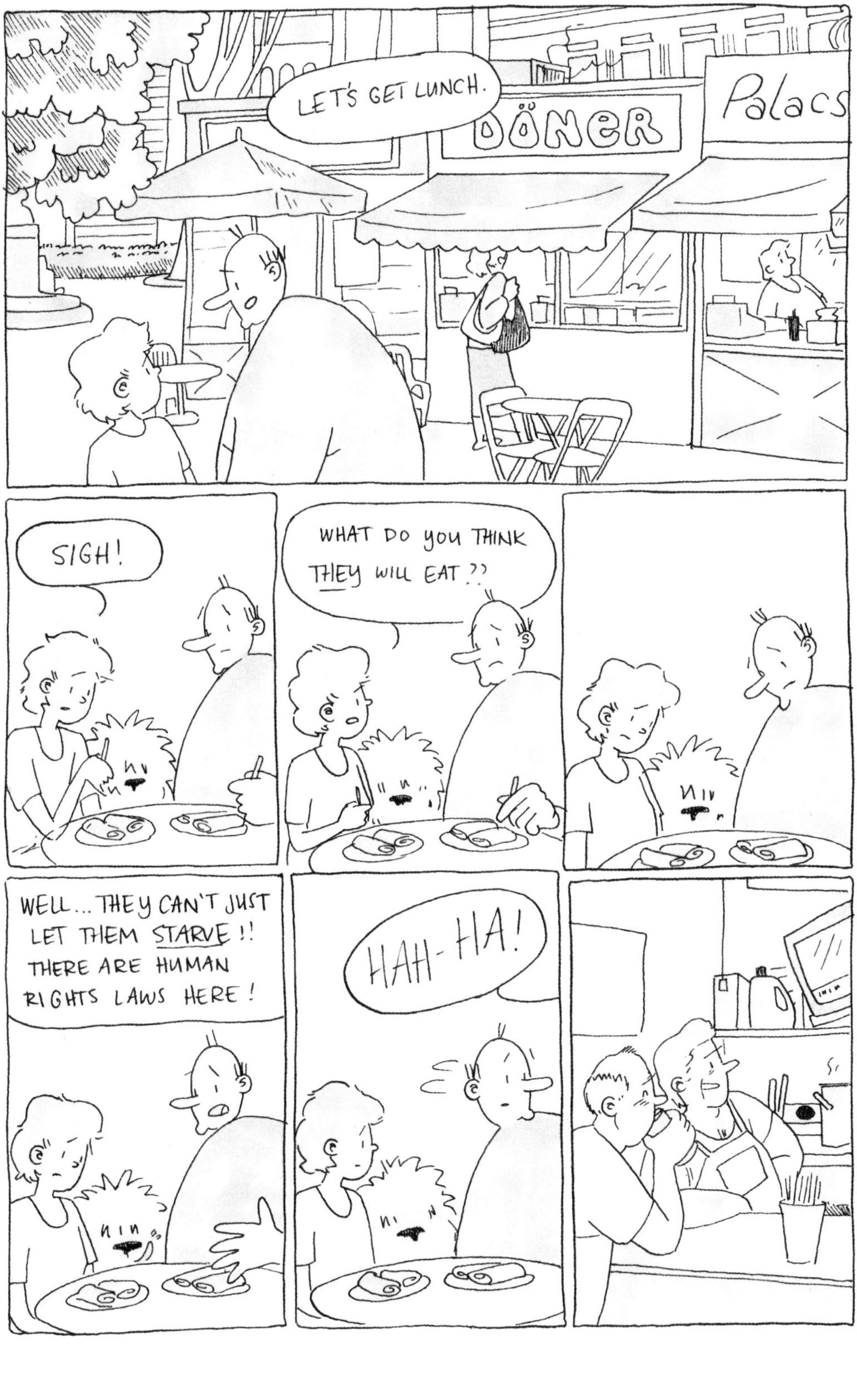
LET'S GET LUNCH.
DÖNER
Palacs
SIGH!
WHAT DO YOU THINK THEY WILL EAT ??
WELL... THEY CAN'T JUST LET THEM STARVE !! THERE ARE HUMAN RIGHTS LAWS HERE!
HAH-HA!

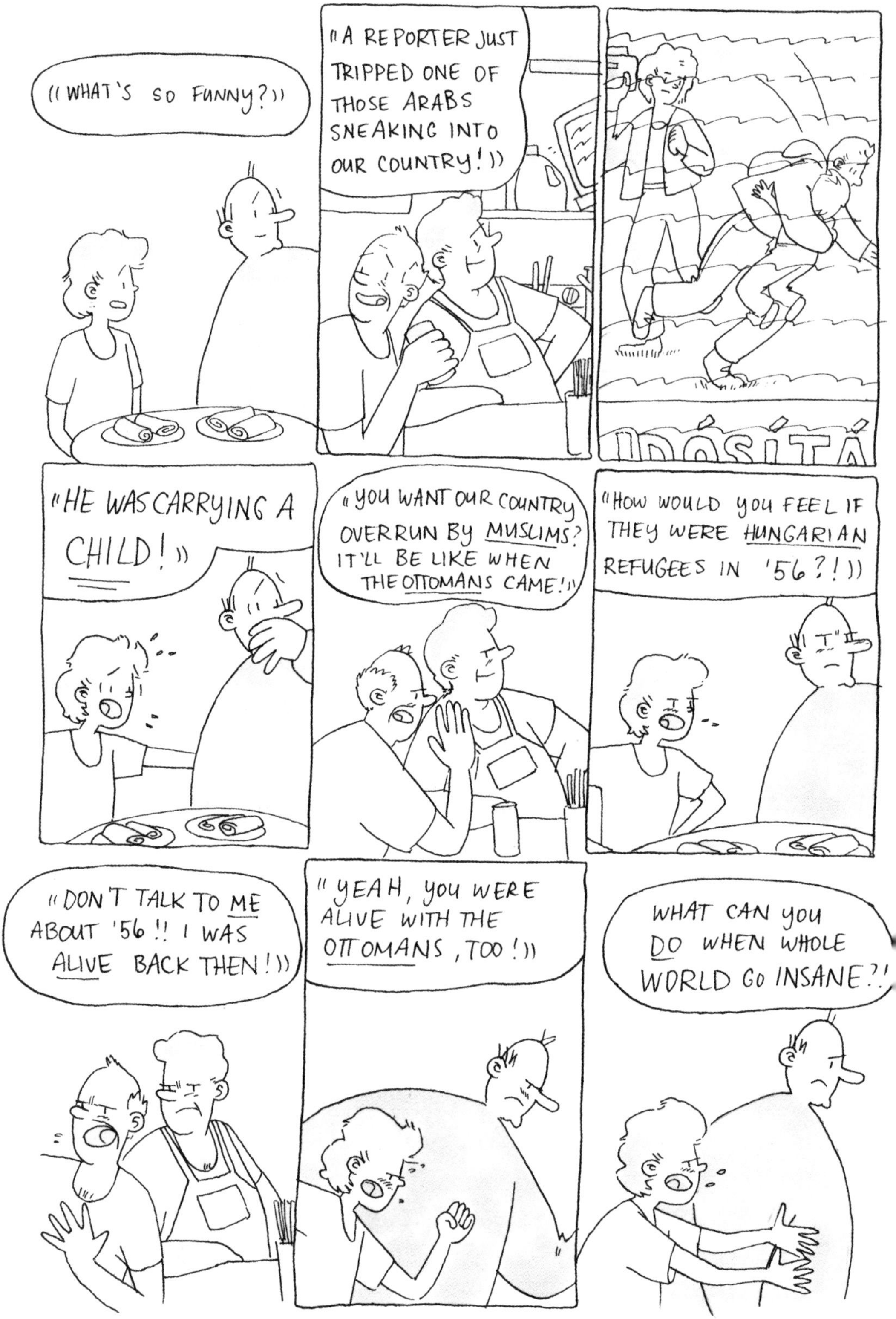
((WHAT'S SO FUNNY?))
((A REPORTER JUST TRIPPED ONE OF THOSE ARABS SNEAKING INTO OUR COUNTRY!))
((HE WAS CARRYING A CHILD!))
((YOU WANT OUR COUNTRY OVERRUN BY MUSLIMS? IT'LL BE LIKE WHEN THE OTTOMANS CAME!))
((HOW WOULD YOU FEEL IF THEY WERE HUNGARIAN REFUGEES IN '56?!))
((DON'T TALK TO ME ABOUT '56!! I WAS ALIVE BACK THEN!))
((YEAH, YOU WERE ALIVE WITH THE OTTOMANS, TOO!))
WHAT CAN YOU DO WHEN WHOLE WORLD GO INSANE?!

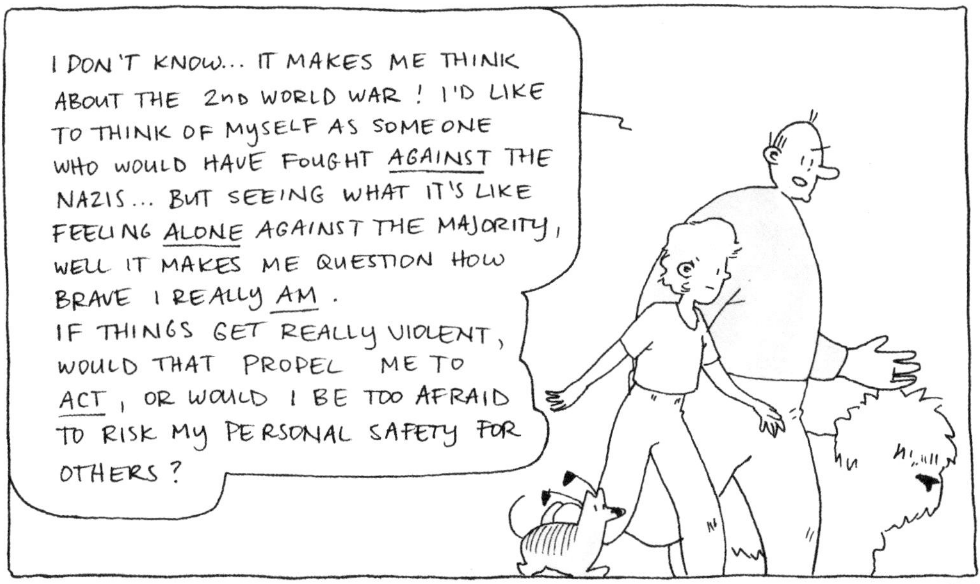
I DON'T KNOW... IT MAKES ME THINK ABOUT THE 2nd WORLD WAR! I'D LIKE TO THINK OF MYSELF AS SOMEONE WHO WOULD HAVE FOUGHT AGAINST THE NAZIS... BUT SEEING WHAT IT'S LIKE FEELING ALONE AGAINST THE MAJORITY, WELL IT MAKES ME QUESTION HOW BRAVE I REALLY AM.
IF THINGS GET REALLY VIOLENT, WOULD THAT PROPEL ME TO ACT, OR WOULD I BE TOO AFRAID TO RISK MY PERSONAL SAFETY FOR OTHERS?

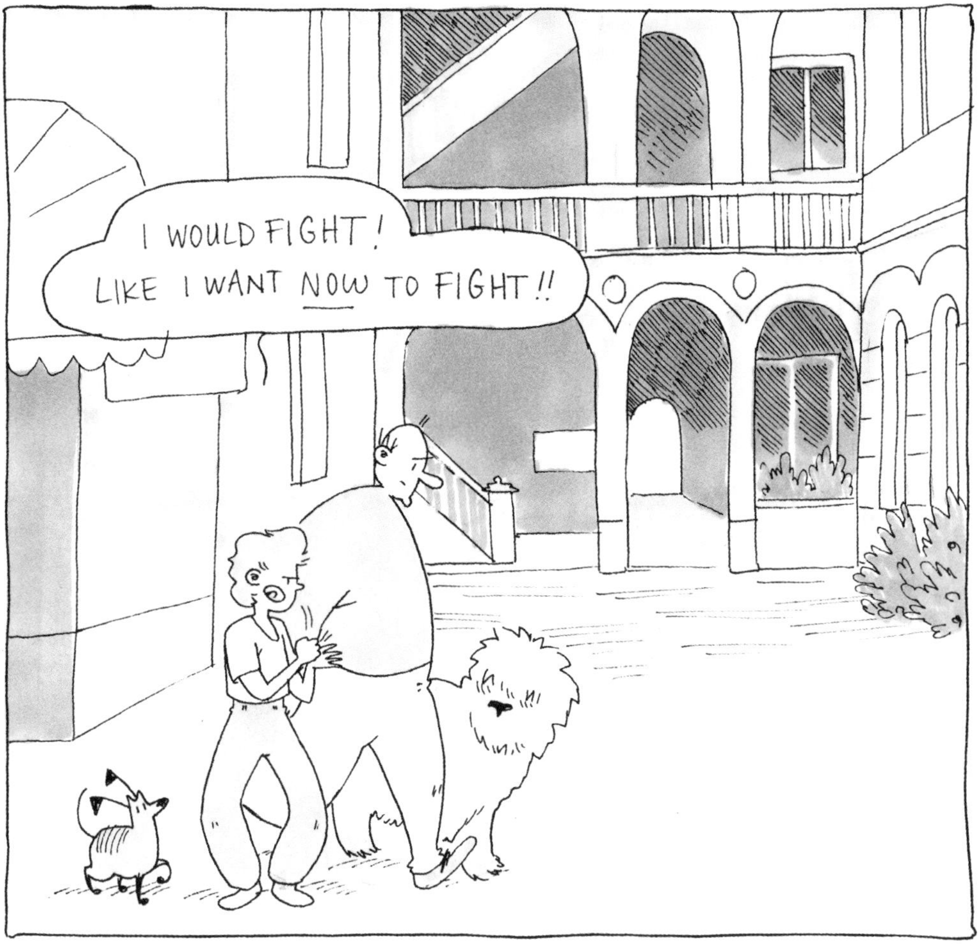
I WOULD FIGHT! LIKE I WANT NOW TO FIGHT!!

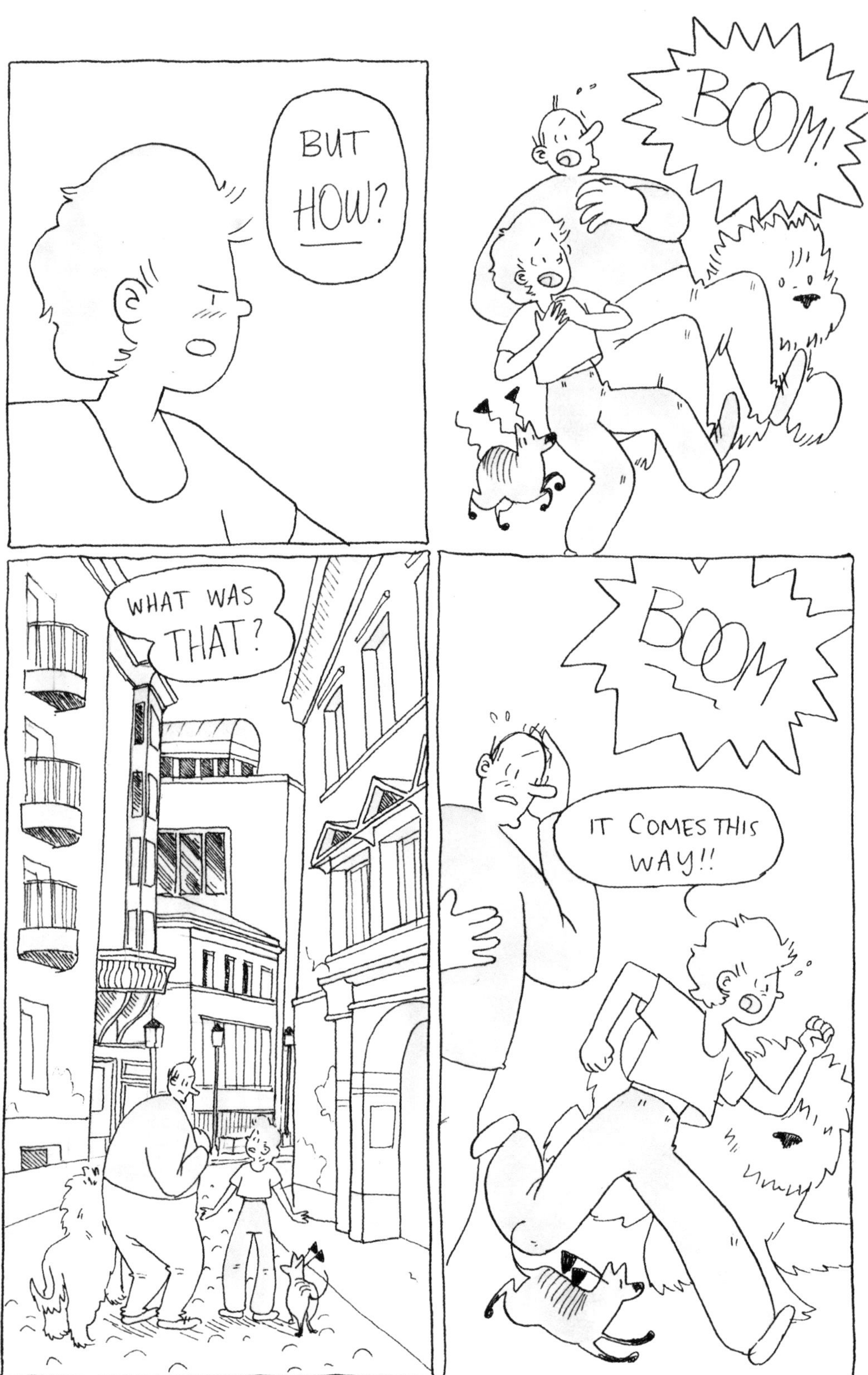
BUT HOW?
BOOM!
WHAT WAS THAT?
BOOM
IT COMES THIS WAY!!

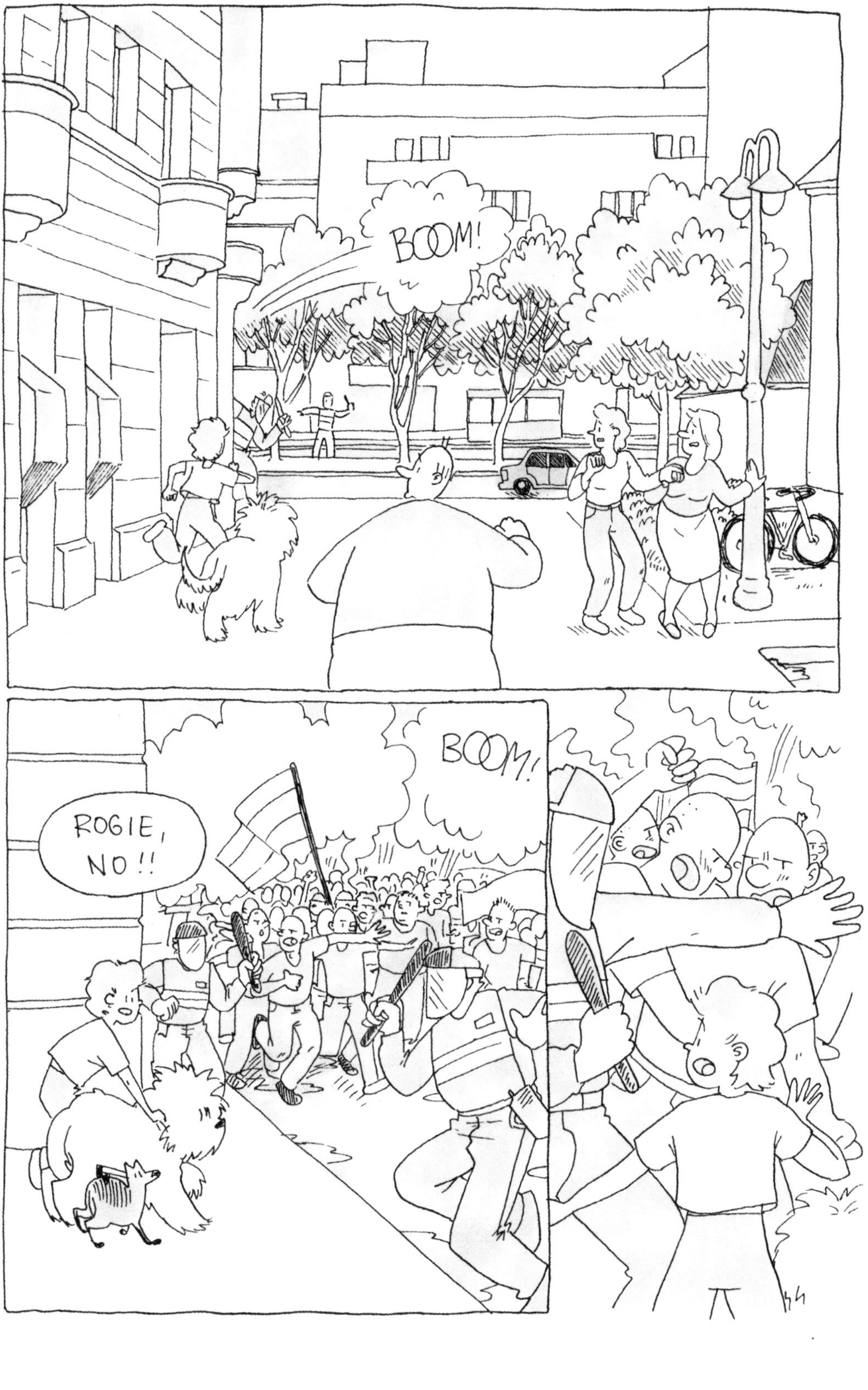
BOOM!
ROGIE, NO!!
BOOM!

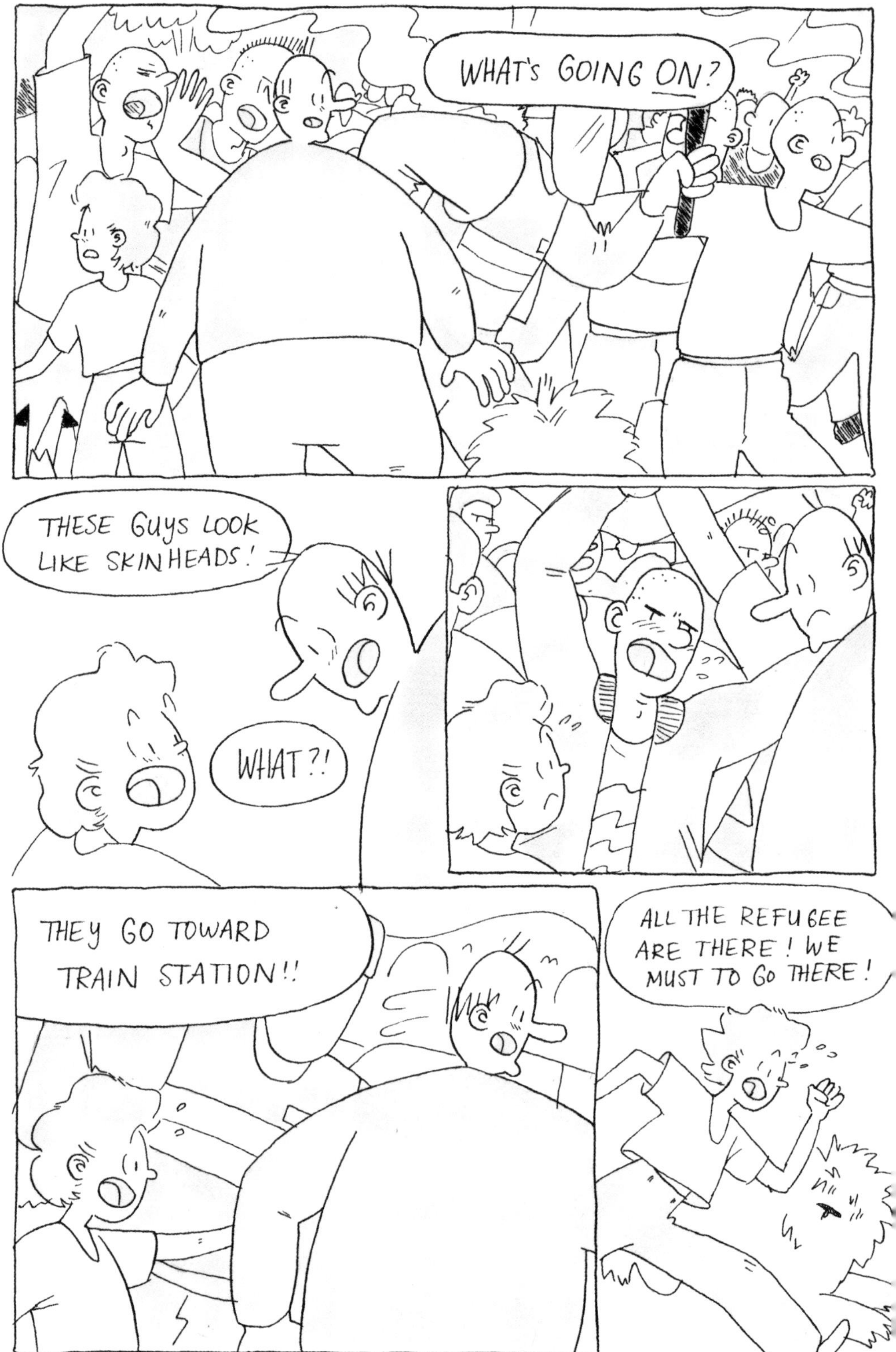
WHAT'S GOING ON?
THESE GUYS LOOK LIKE SKINHEADS!
WHAT?!
THEY GO TOWARD TRAIN STATION!!
ALL THE REFUGEE ARE THERE! WE MUST TO GO THERE!

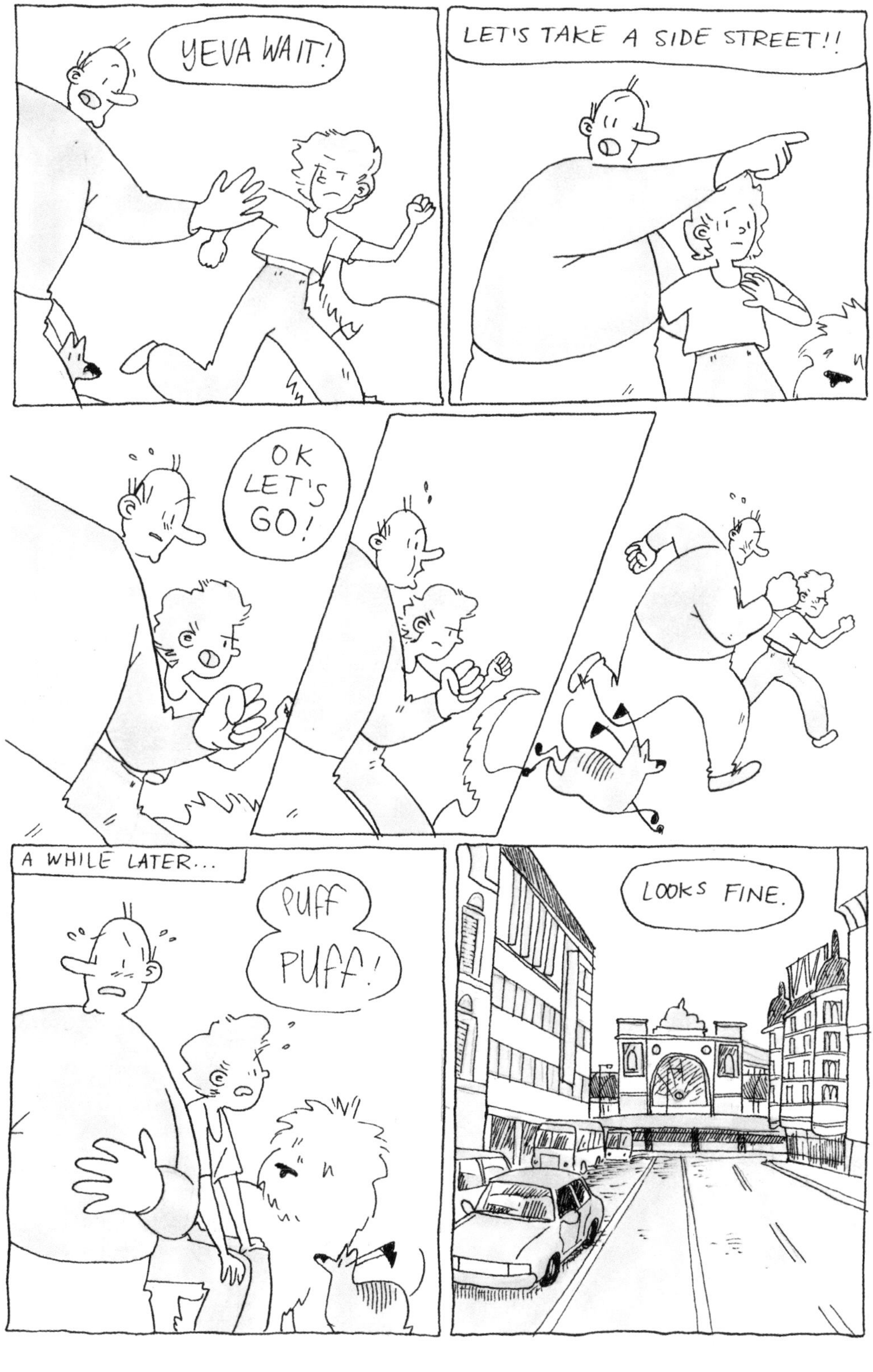
YEVA WAIT!
LET'S TAKE A SIDE STREET!!
OK LET'S GO!
A WHILE LATER...
PUFF
PUFF!
LOOKS FINE.

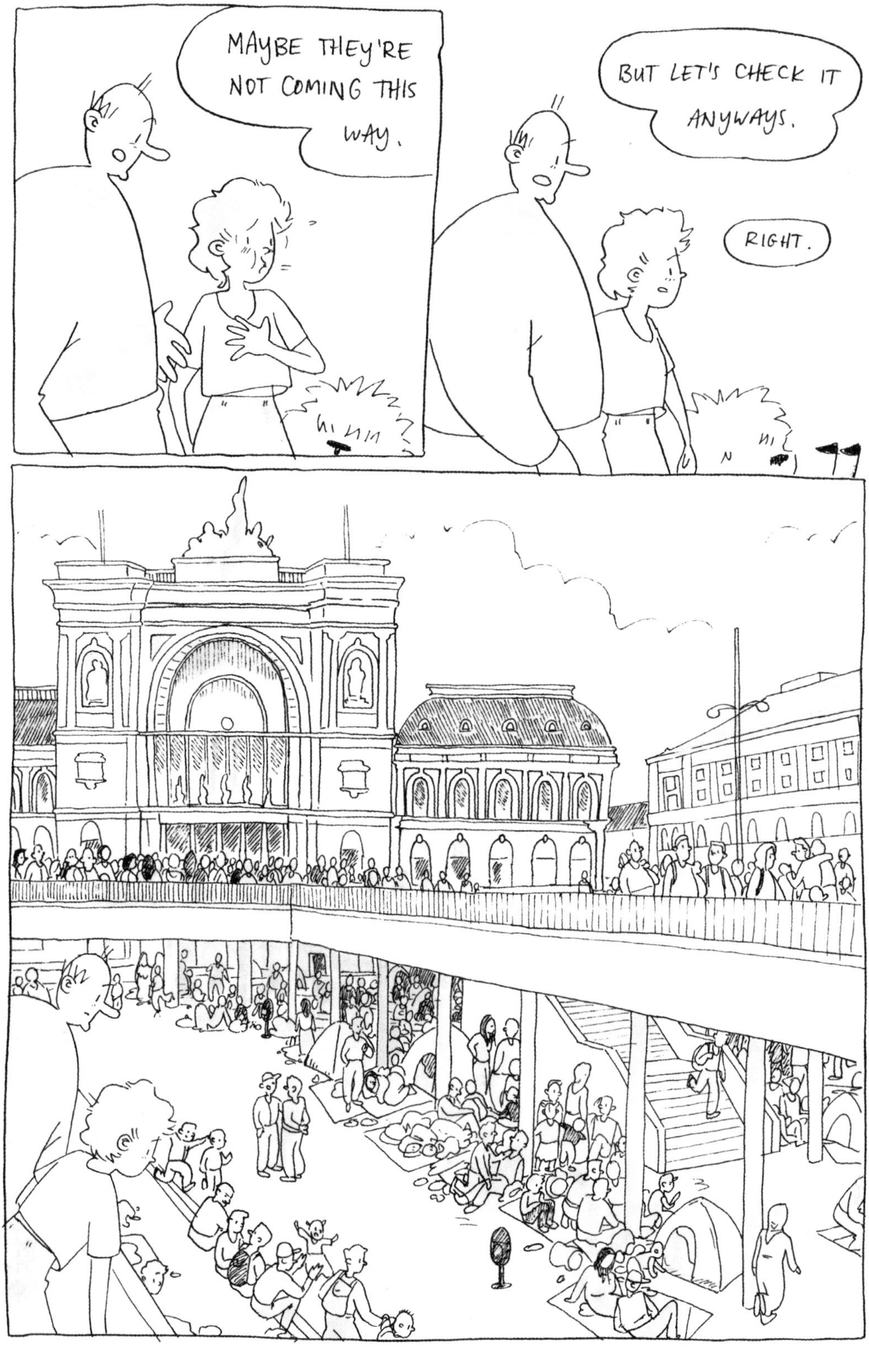
MAYBE THEY'RE NOT COMING THIS WAY.
BUT LET'S CHECK IT ANYWAYS.
RIGHT.

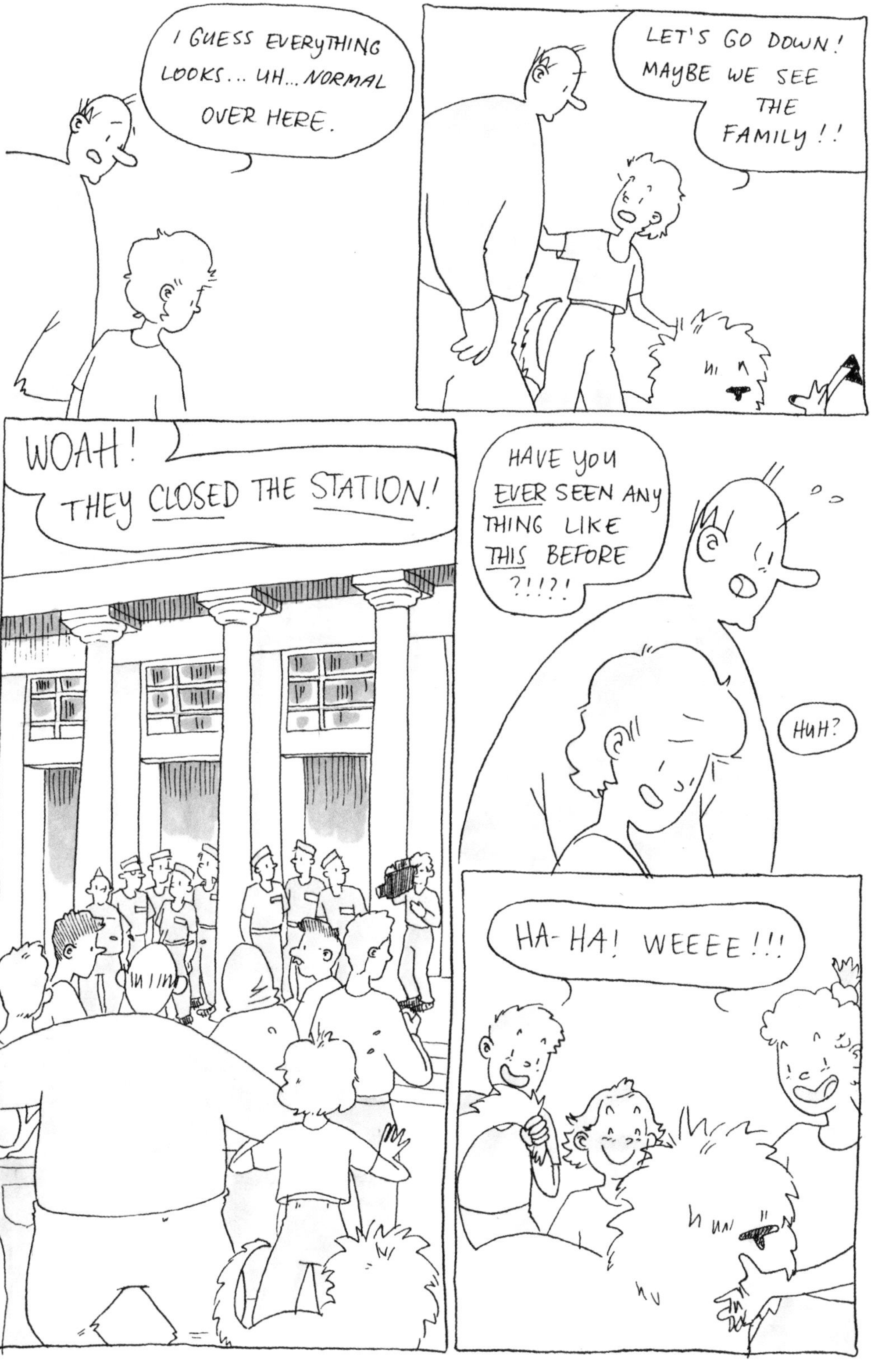
I GUESS EVERYTHING LOOKS... UH... NORMAL OVER HERE.
LET'S GO DOWN! MAYBE WE SEE THE FAMILY!!
WOAH! THEY CLOSED THE STATION!
HAVE YOU EVER SEEN ANYTHING LIKE THIS BEFORE ?!!?!
HUH?
HA-HA! WEEEE!!!

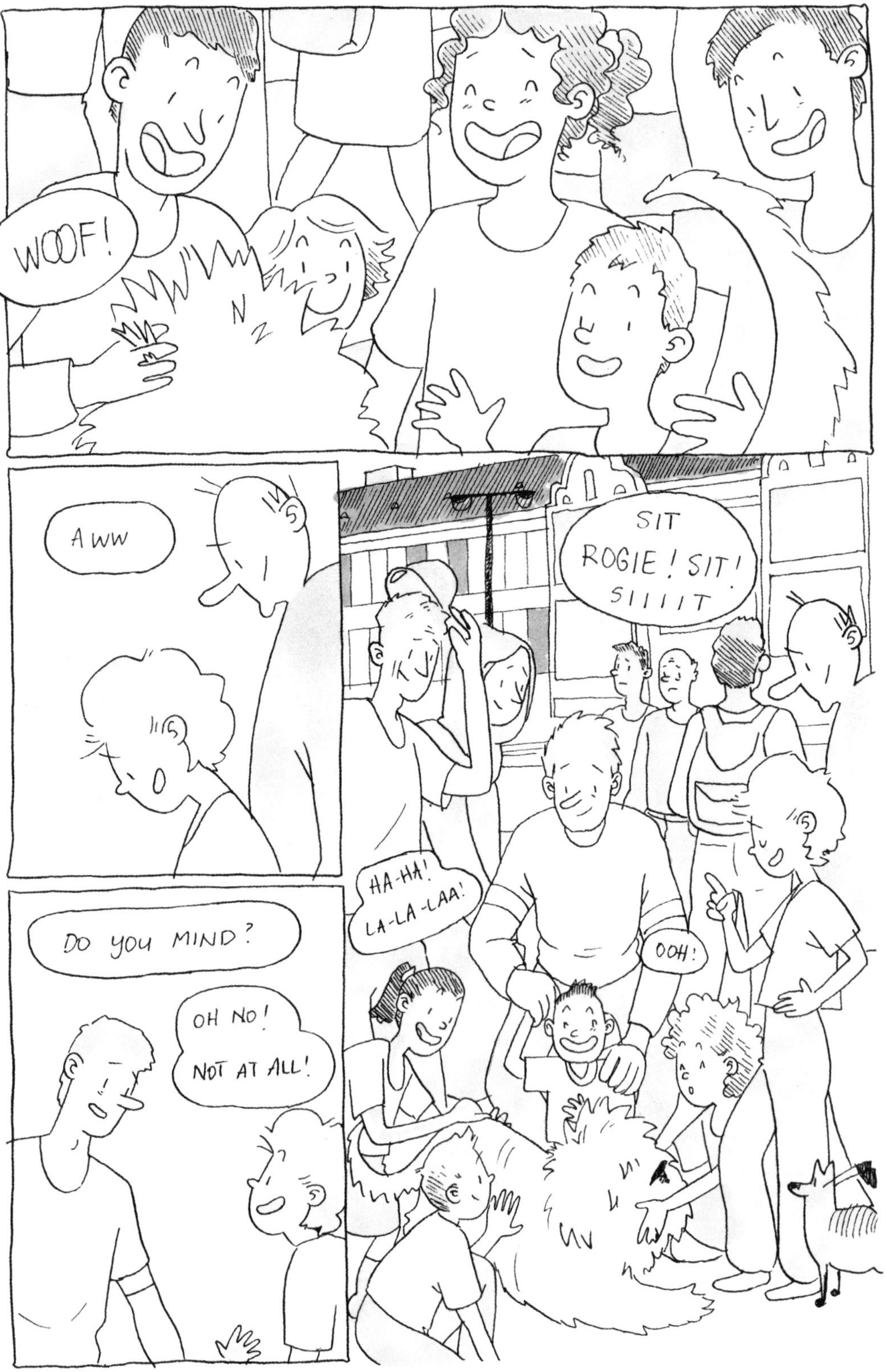
WOOF!
AWW
SIT ROGIE! SIT! SIIIIT
DO YOU MIND?
OH NO! NOT AT ALL!
HA-HA! LA-LA-LAA!
OOH!

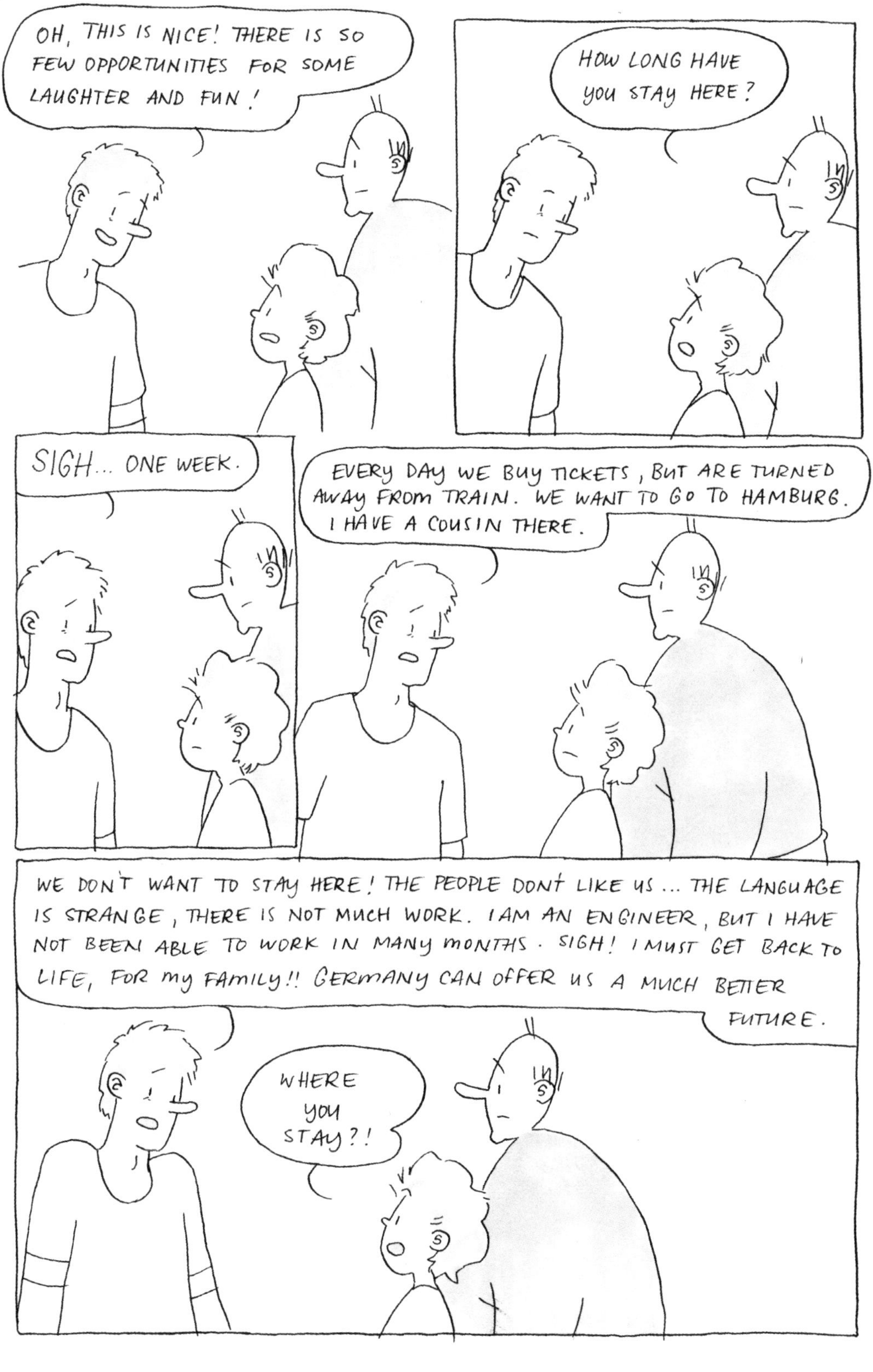
OH, THIS IS NICE! THERE IS SO FEW OPPORTUNITIES FOR SOME LAUGHTER AND FUN!
HOW LONG HAVE YOU STAY HERE?
SIGH... ONE WEEK.
EVERY DAY WE BUY TICKETS, BUT ARE TURNED AWAY FROM TRAIN. WE WANT TO GO TO HAMBURG. I HAVE A COUSIN THERE.
WE DON'T WANT TO STAY HERE! THE PEOPLE DON'T LIKE US ... THE LANGUAGE IS STRANGE, THERE IS NOT MUCH WORK. I AM AN ENGINEER, BUT I HAVE NOT BEEN ABLE TO WORK IN MANY MONTHS. SIGH! I MUST GET BACK TO LIFE, FOR MY FAMILY!! GERMANY CAN OFFER US A MUCH BETTER FUTURE.
WHERE YOU STAY?!

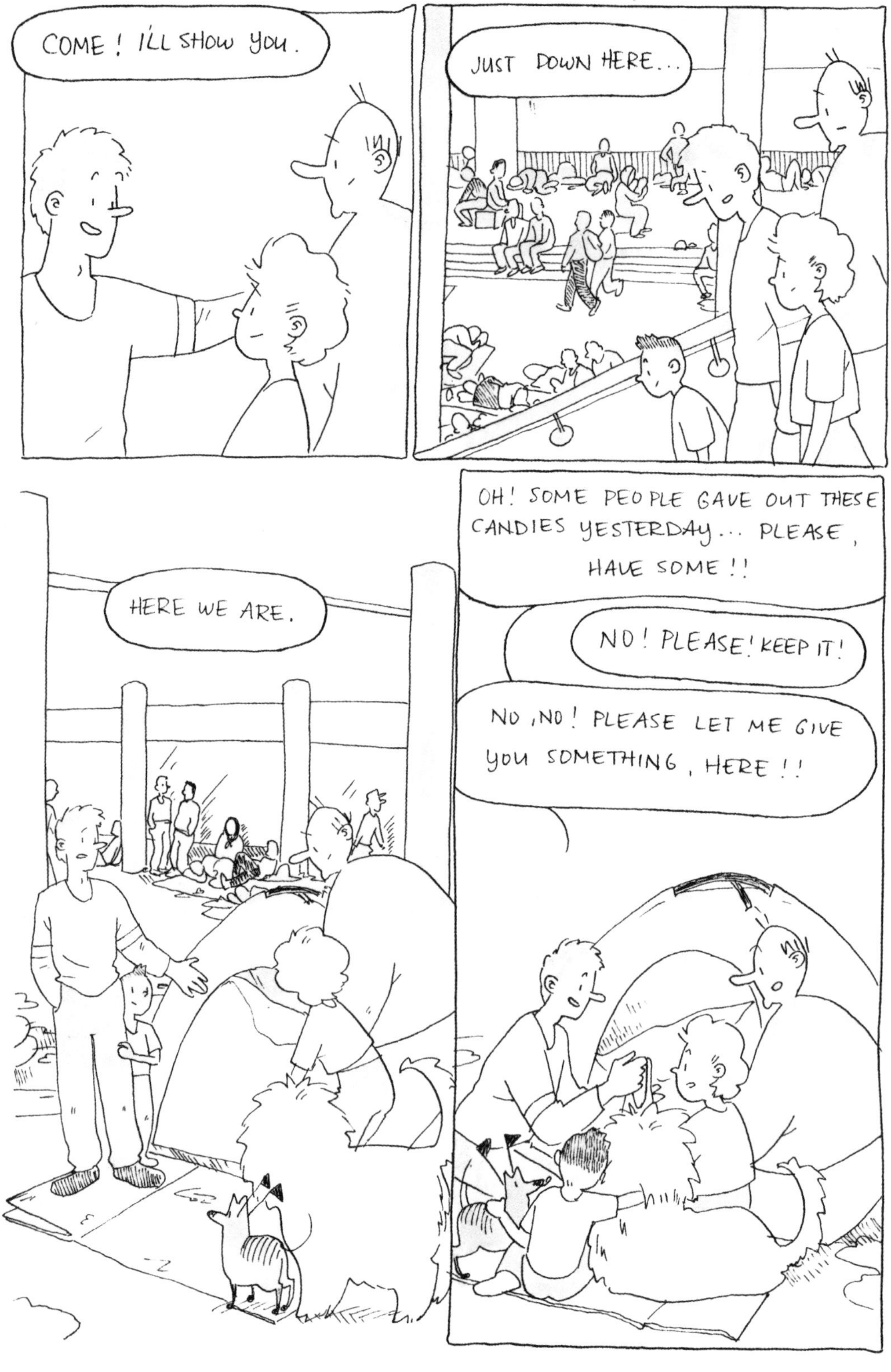
COME! I'LL SHOW YOU.
JUST DOWN HERE...
HERE WE ARE.
OH! SOME PEOPLE GAVE OUT THESE CANDIES YESTERDAY... PLEASE, HAVE SOME!!
NO! PLEASE! KEEP IT!
NO, NO! PLEASE LET ME GIVE YOU SOMETHING, HERE!!

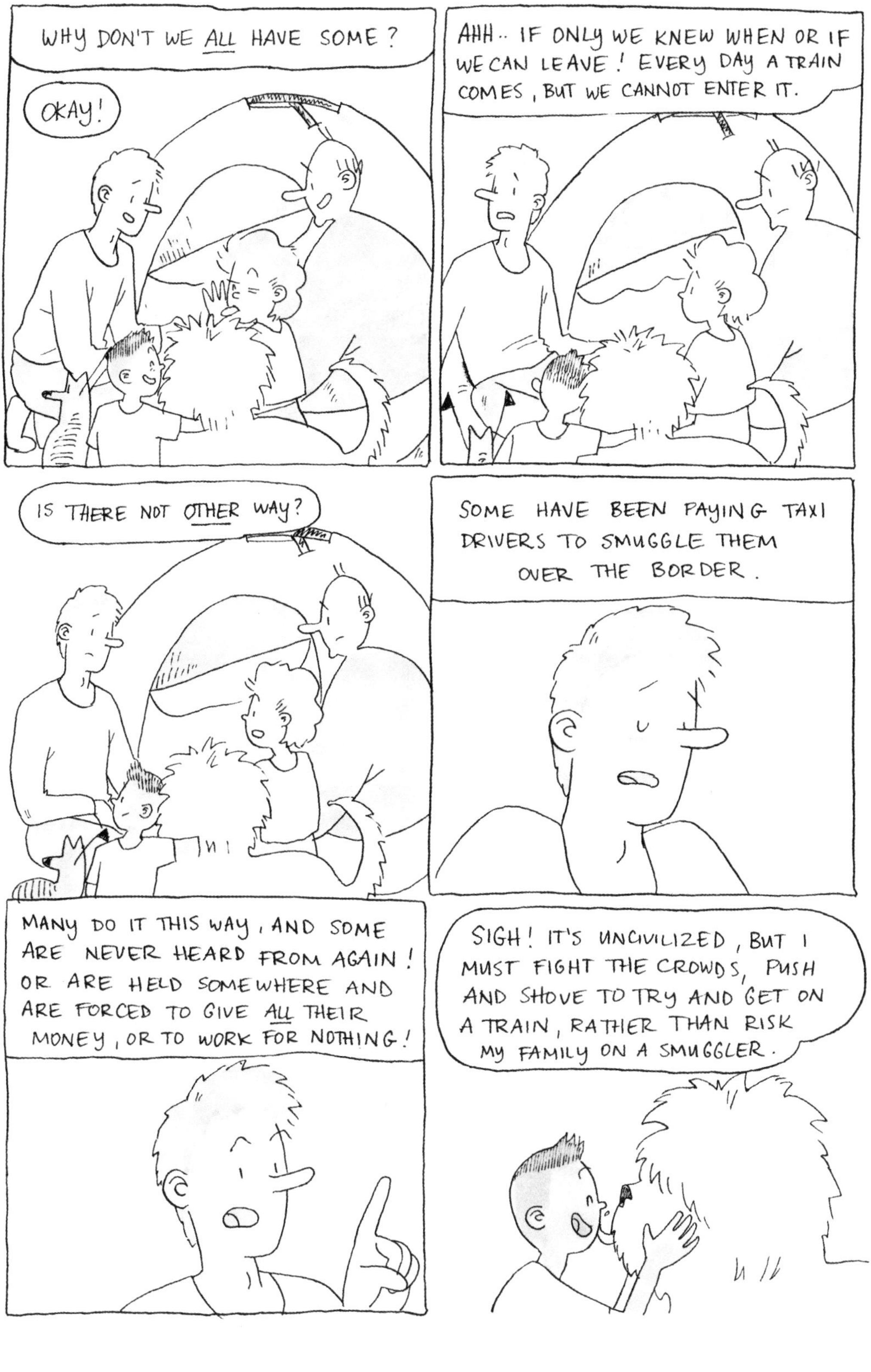
WHY DON'T WE ALL HAVE SOME?
OKAY!
AHH.. IF ONLY WE KNEW WHEN OR IF WE CAN LEAVE! EVERY DAY A TRAIN COMES, BUT WE CANNOT ENTER IT.
IS THERE NOT OTHER WAY?
SOME HAVE BEEN PAYING TAXI DRIVERS TO SMUGGLE THEM OVER THE BORDER.
MANY DO IT THIS WAY, AND SOME ARE NEVER HEARD FROM AGAIN! OR ARE HELD SOMEWHERE AND ARE FORCED TO GIVE ALL THEIR MONEY, OR TO WORK FOR NOTHING!
SIGH! IT'S UNCIVILIZED, BUT I MUST FIGHT THE CROWDS, PUSH AND SHOVE TO TRY AND GET ON A TRAIN, RATHER THAN RISK MY FAMILY ON A SMUGGLER.

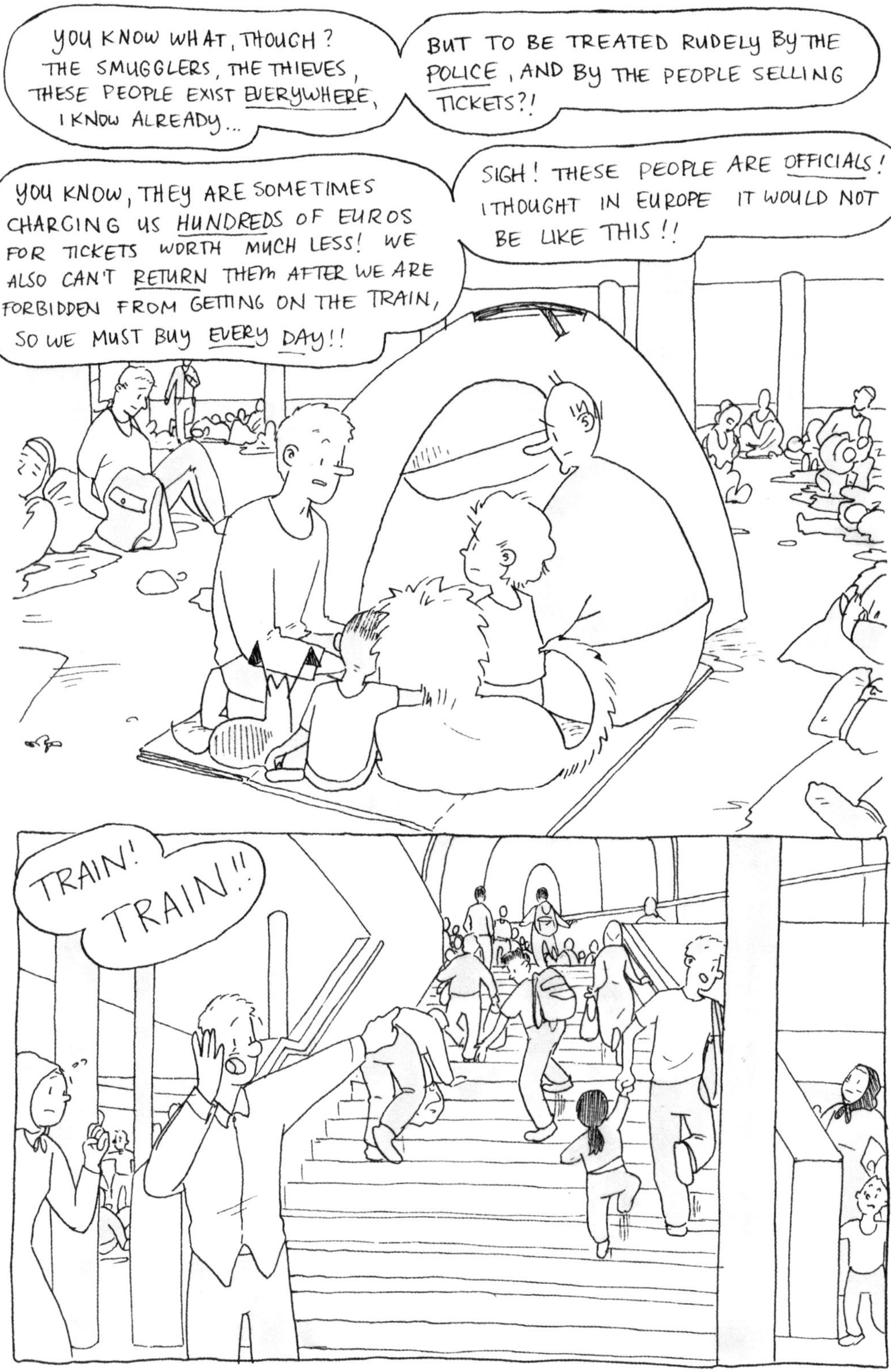
YOU KNOW WHAT, THOUGH? THE SMUGGLERS, THE THIEVES, THESE PEOPLE EXIST EVERYWHERE, I KNOW ALREADY...
BUT TO BE TREATED RUDELY BY THE POLICE, AND BY THE PEOPLE SELLING TICKETS?!
YOU KNOW, THEY ARE SOMETIMES CHARGING US HUNDREDS OF EUROS FOR TICKETS WORTH MUCH LESS! WE ALSO CAN'T RETURN THEM AFTER WE ARE FORBIDDEN FROM GETTING ON THE TRAIN, SO WE MUST BUY EVERY DAY!!
SIGH! THESE PEOPLE ARE OFFICIALS! I THOUGHT IN EUROPE IT WOULD NOT BE LIKE THIS!!
TRAIN! TRAIN!!

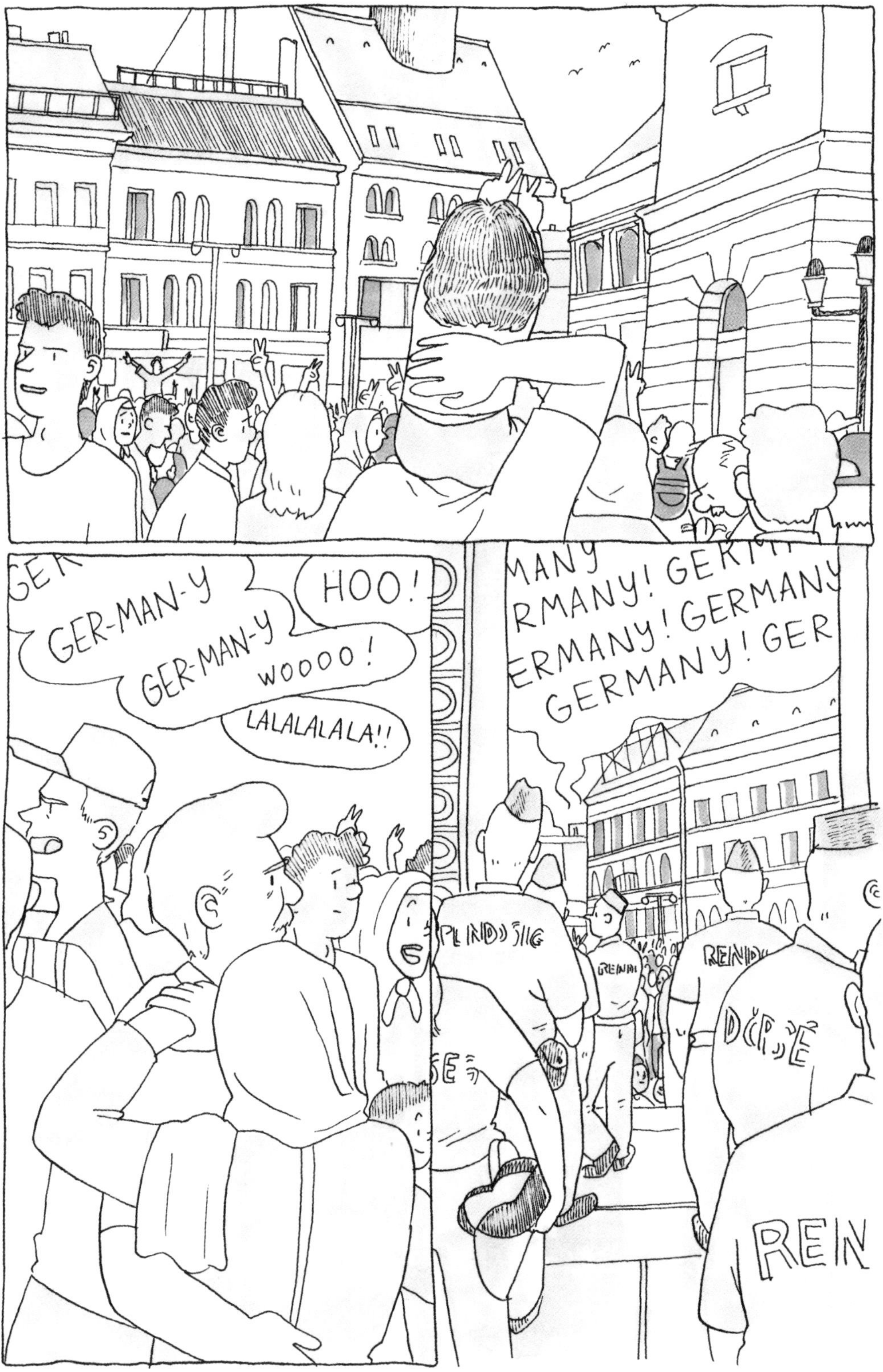

GER
GER-MAN-Y
GER-MAN-Y
HOO!
WOOOO!
LALALALALA!!
MANY
RMANY! GERM
ERMANY! GERMANY
GERMANY! GER
REN

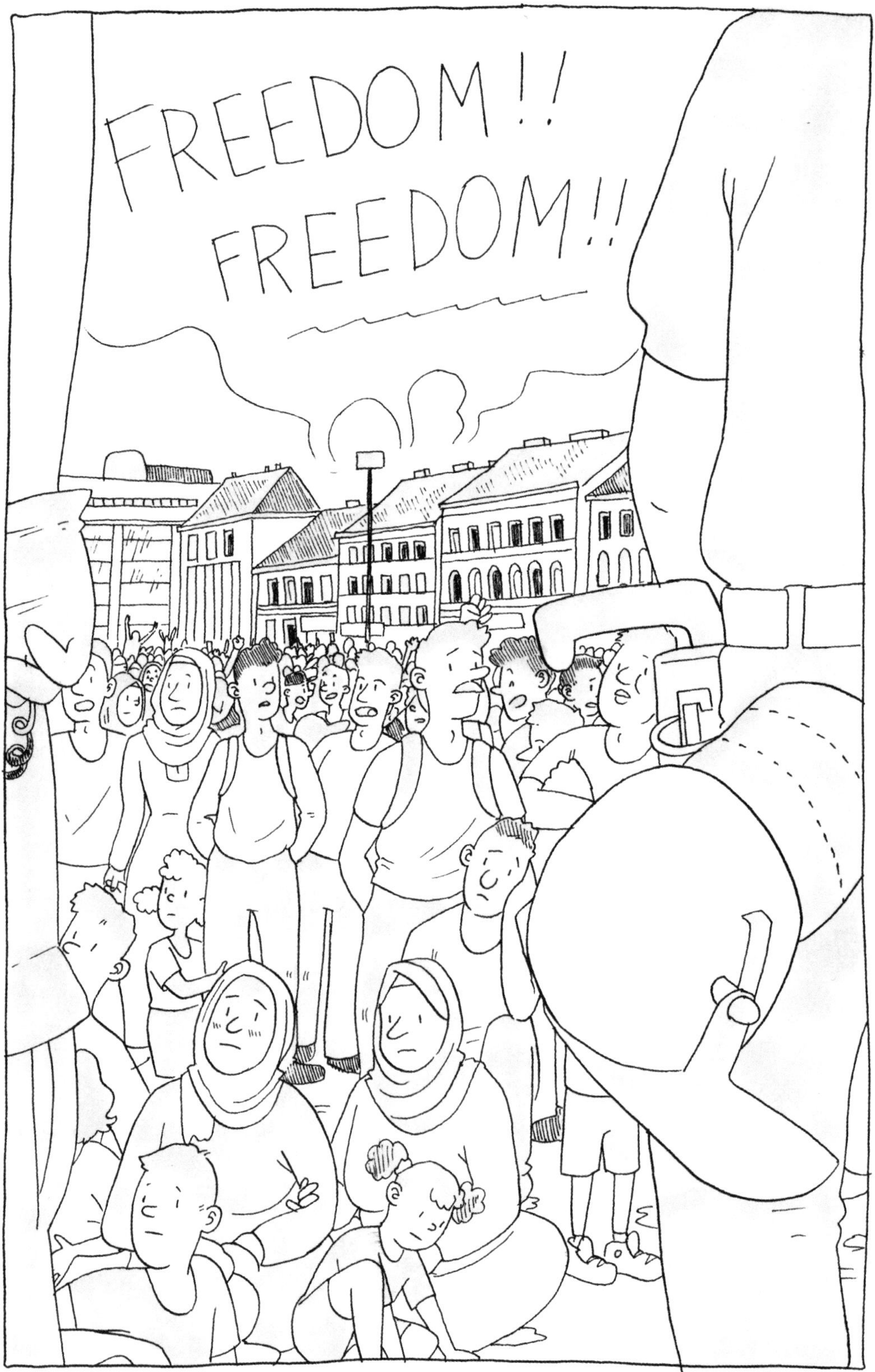
FREEDOM!!
FREEDOM!!

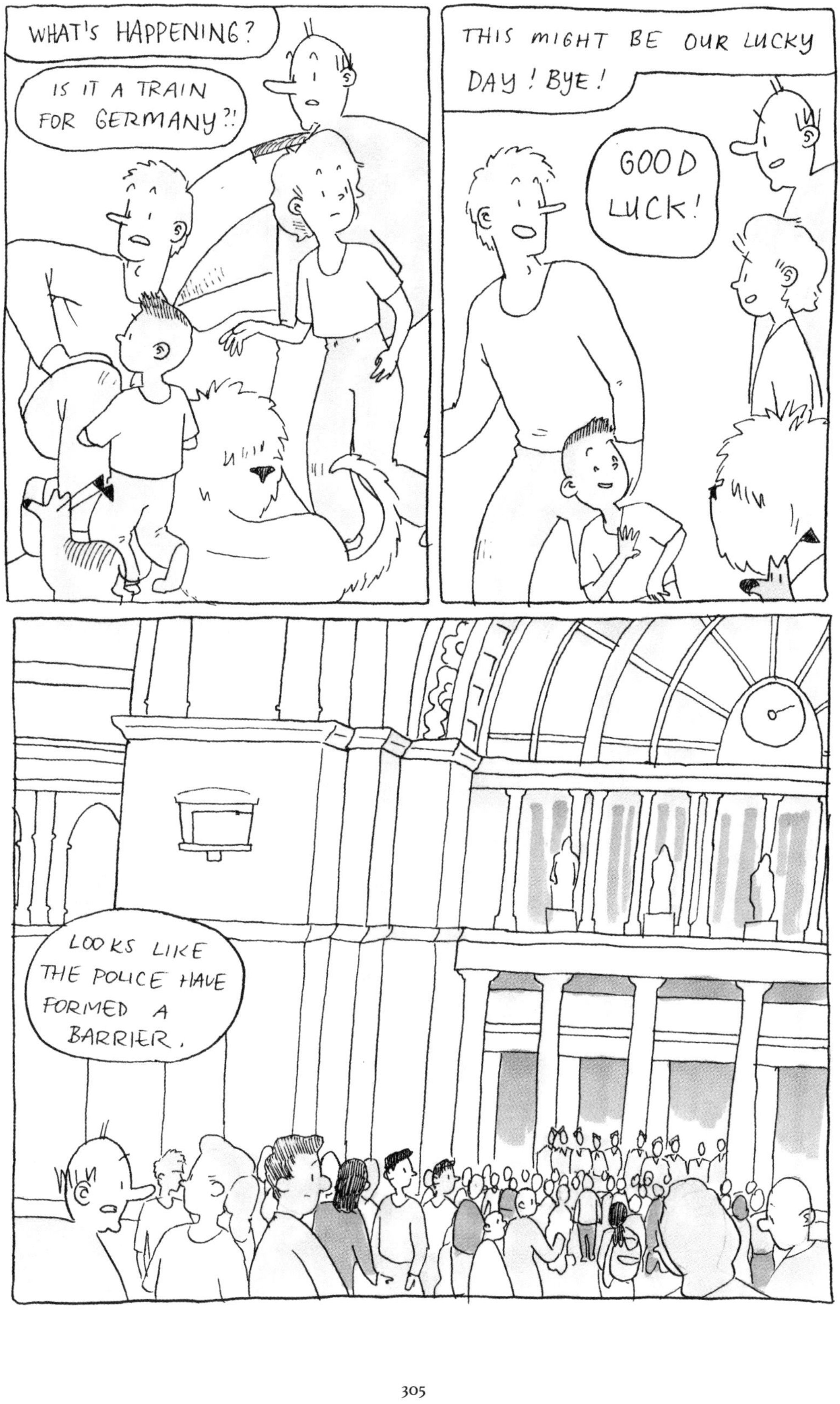
WHAT'S HAPPENING?
IS IT A TRAIN FOR GERMANY?!
THIS MIGHT BE OUR LUCKY DAY! BYE!
GOOD LUCK!
LOOKS LIKE THE POLICE HAVE FORMED A BARRIER.

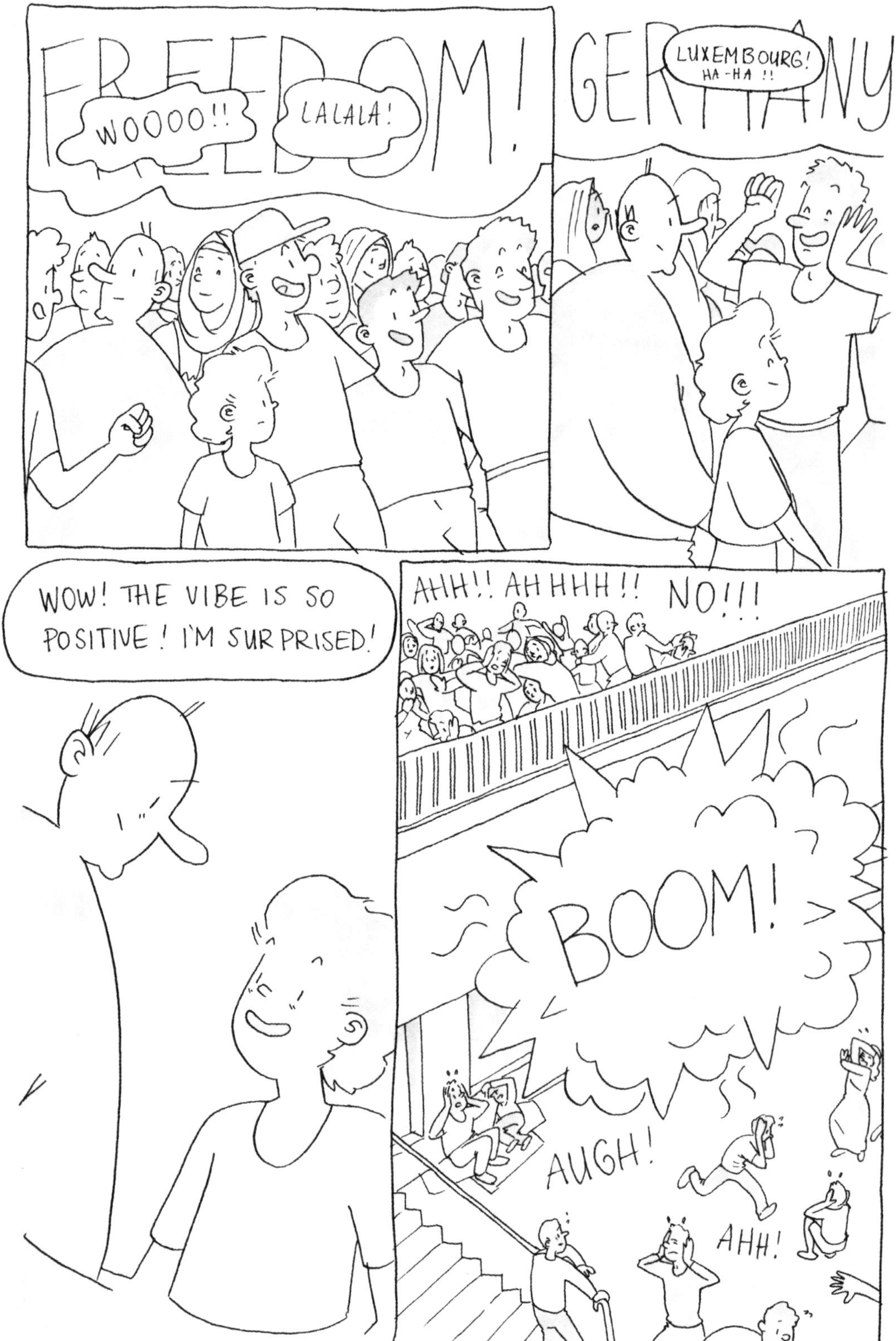
FREEDOM!
WOOOO!!
LALALA!
GERMANY
LUXEMBOURG! HA-HA!!
WOW! THE VIBE IS SO POSITIVE! I'M SURPRISED!
AHH!! AHHHH!! NO!!!
BOOM!
AUGH!
AHH!

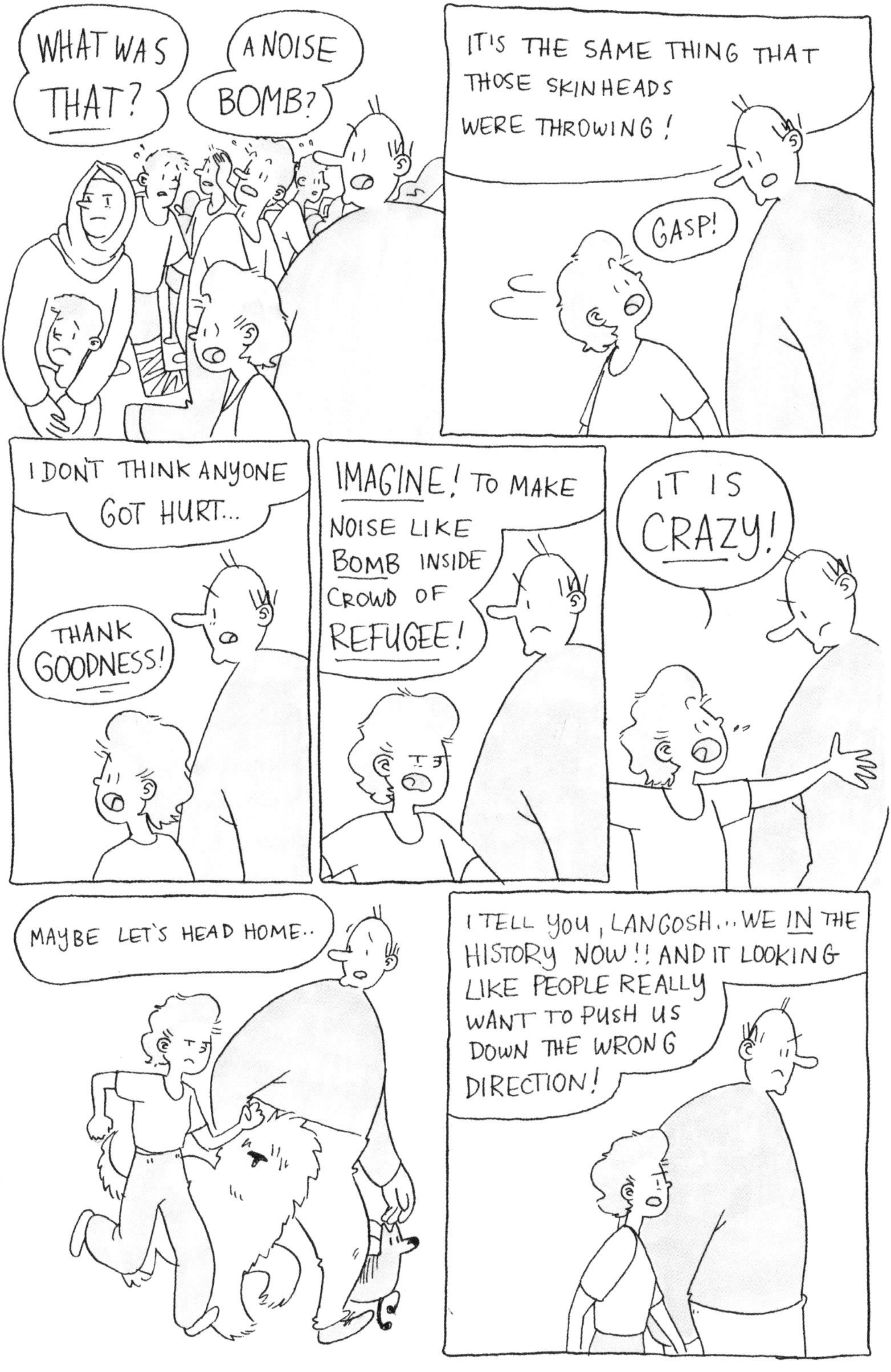
WHAT WAS THAT?
A NOISE BOMB?
IT'S THE SAME THING THAT THOSE SKINHEADS WERE THROWING!
GASP!
I DON'T THINK ANYONE GOT HURT...
THANK GOODNESS!
IMAGINE! TO MAKE NOISE LIKE BOMB INSIDE CROWD OF REFUGEE!
IT IS CRAZY!
MAYBE LET'S HEAD HOME..
I TELL YOU, LANGOSH...WE IN THE HISTORY NOW!! AND IT LOOKING LIKE PEOPLE REALLY WANT TO PUSH US DOWN THE WRONG DIRECTION!

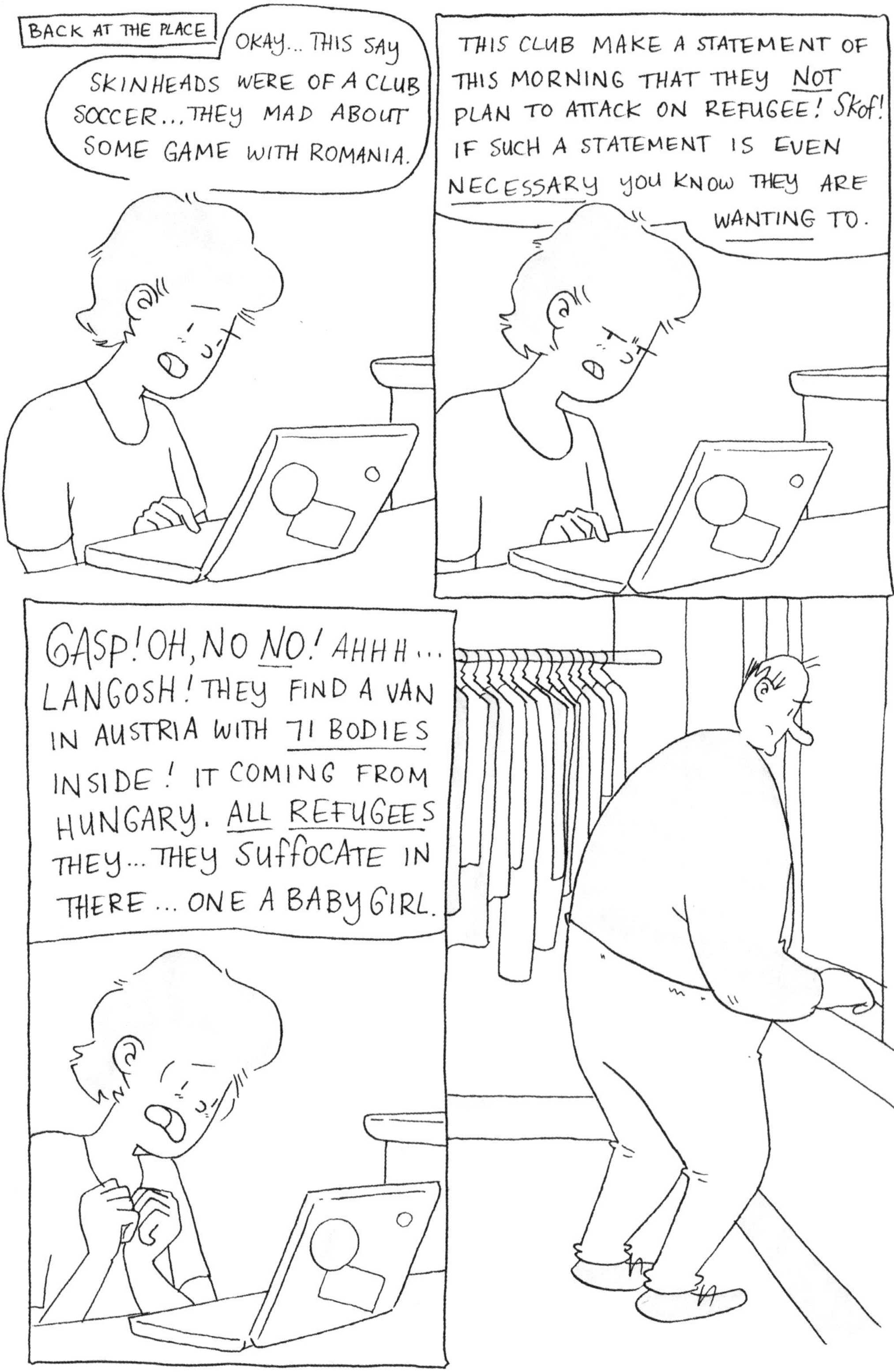
BACK AT THE PLACE
OKAY... THIS SAY SKINHEADS WERE OF A CLUB SOCCER... THEY MAD ABOUT SOME GAME WITH ROMANIA.
THIS CLUB MAKE A STATEMENT OF THIS MORNING THAT THEY NOT PLAN TO ATTACK ON REFUGEE! Skof! IF SUCH A STATEMENT IS EVEN NECESSARY YOU KNOW THEY ARE WANTING TO.
GASP! OH, NO NO! AHHH... LANGOSH! THEY FIND A VAN IN AUSTRIA WITH 71 BODIES INSIDE! IT COMING FROM HUNGARY. ALL REFUGEES THEY... THEY SUFFOCATE IN THERE... ONE A BABY GIRL.

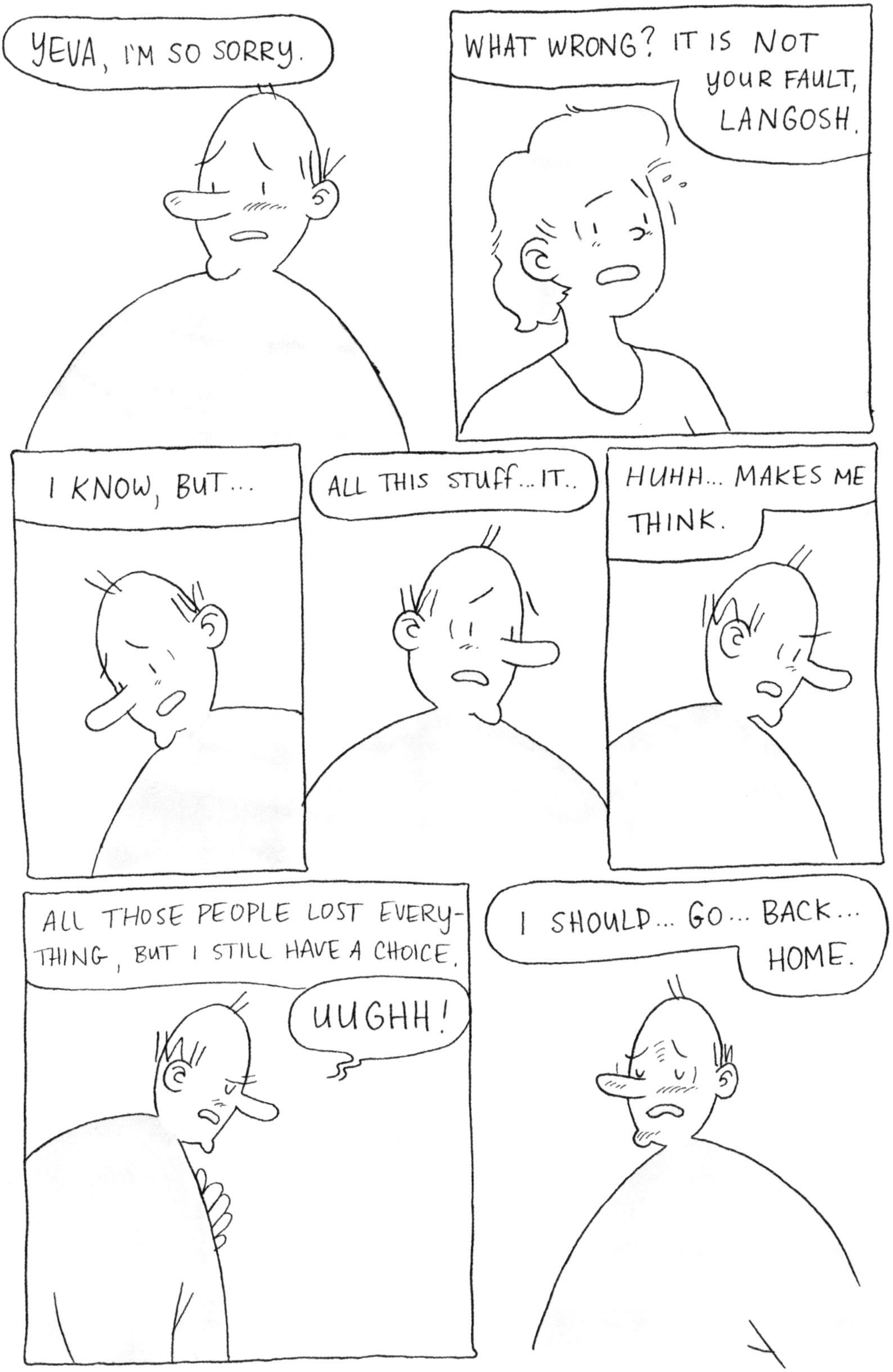
YEVA, I'M SO SORRY.
WHAT WRONG? IT IS NOT YOUR FAULT, LANGOSH.
I KNOW, BUT...
ALL THIS STUFF... IT..
HUHH... MAKES ME THINK.
ALL THOSE PEOPLE LOST EVERY-THING, BUT I STILL HAVE A CHOICE.
UUGHH!
I SHOULD... GO... BACK... HOME.

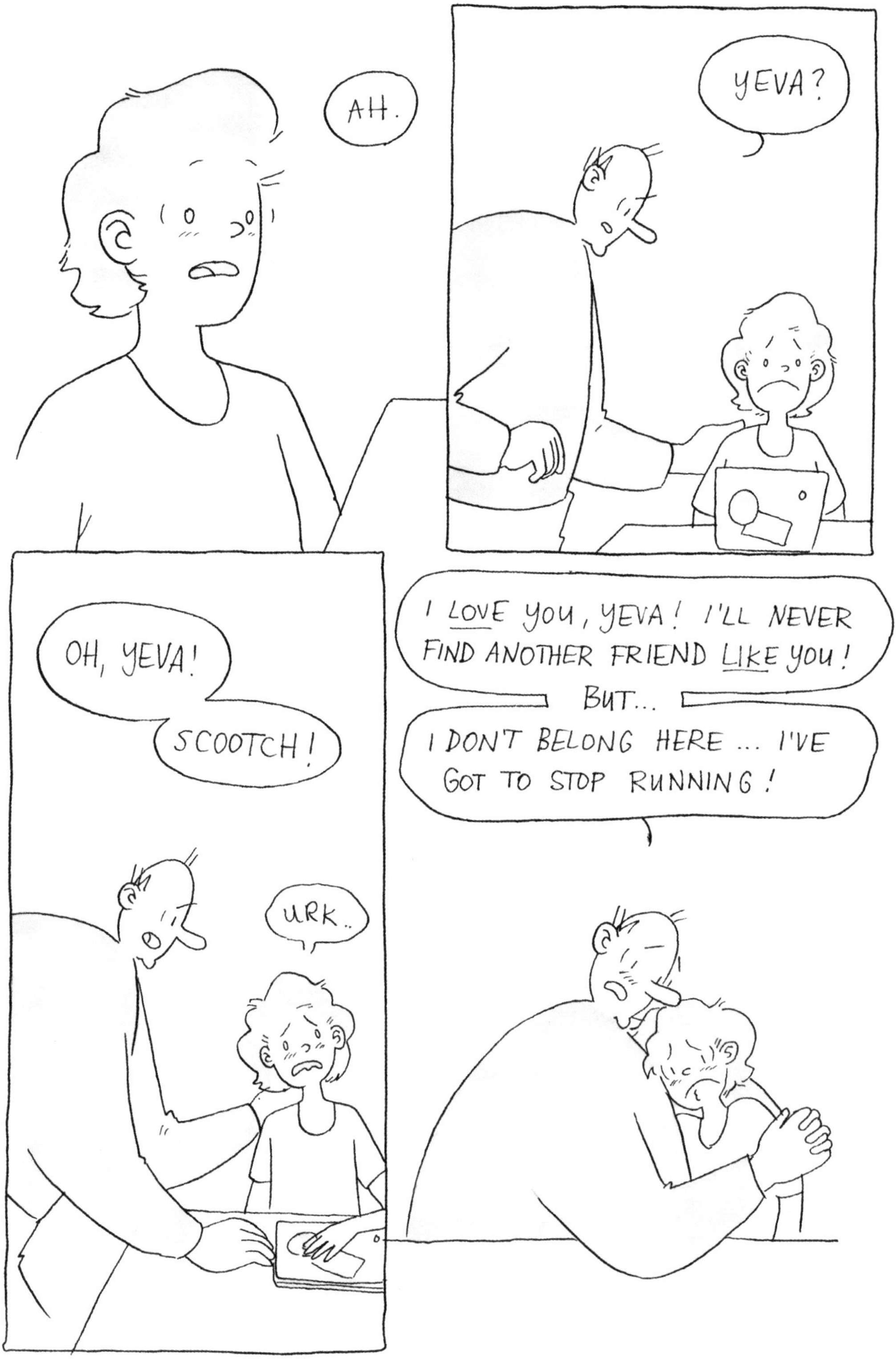
AH.
YEVA?
OH, YEVA!
SCOOTCH!
URK..
I LOVE YOU, YEVA! I'LL NEVER FIND ANOTHER FRIEND LIKE YOU!
BUT...
I DON'T BELONG HERE ... I'VE GOT TO STOP RUNNING!

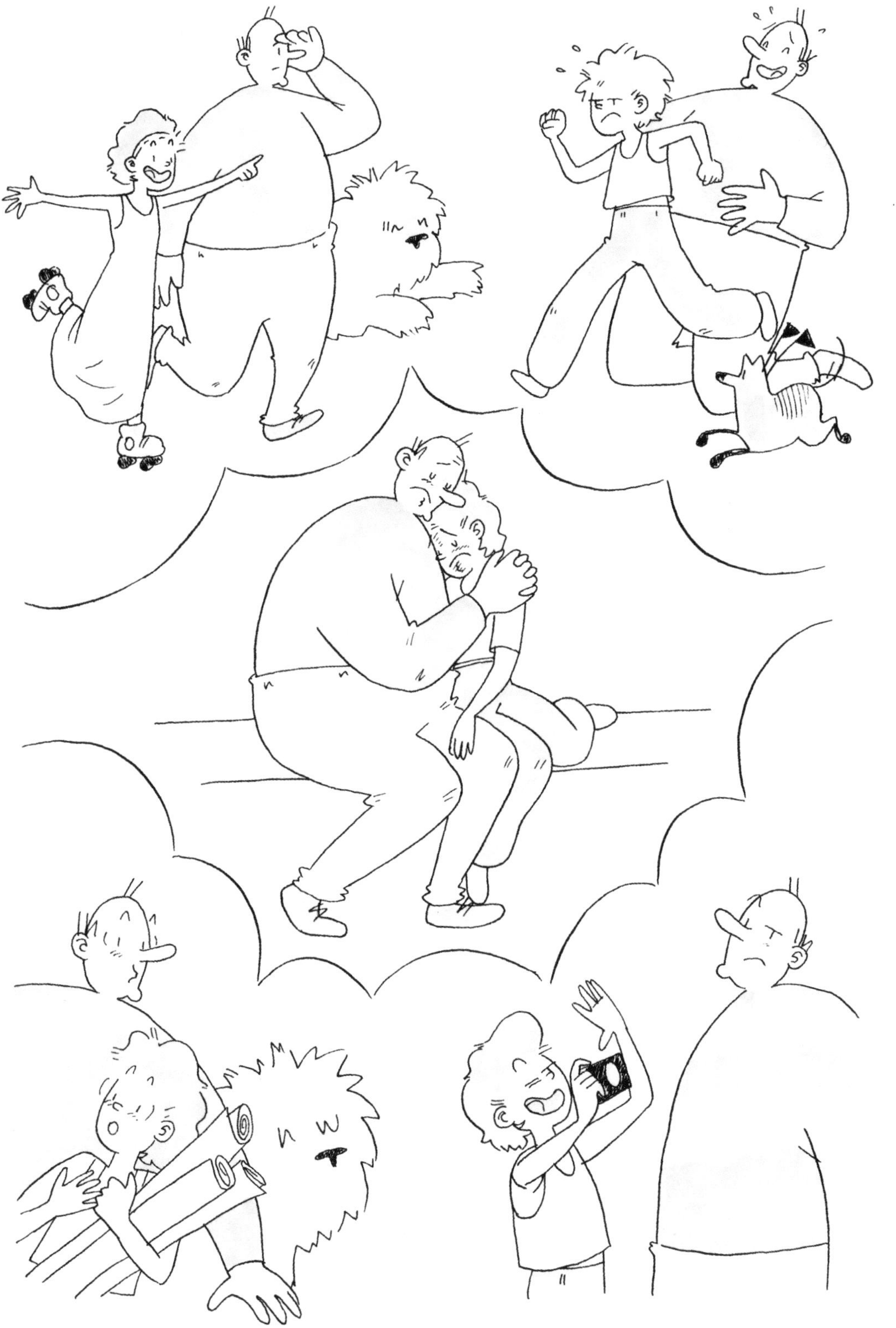

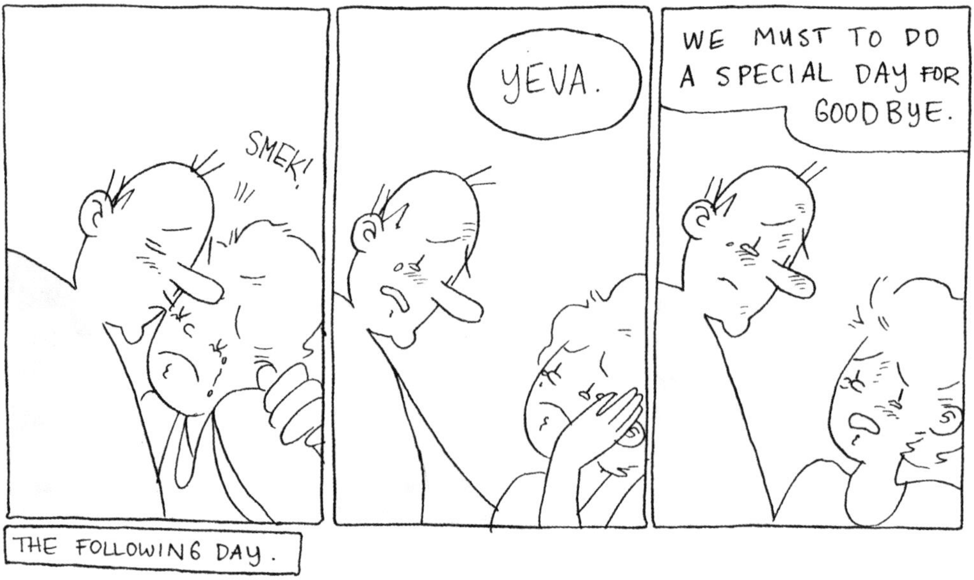
SMEK!
YEVA.
WE MUST TO DO A SPECIAL DAY FOR GOODBYE.
THE FOLLOWING DAY.

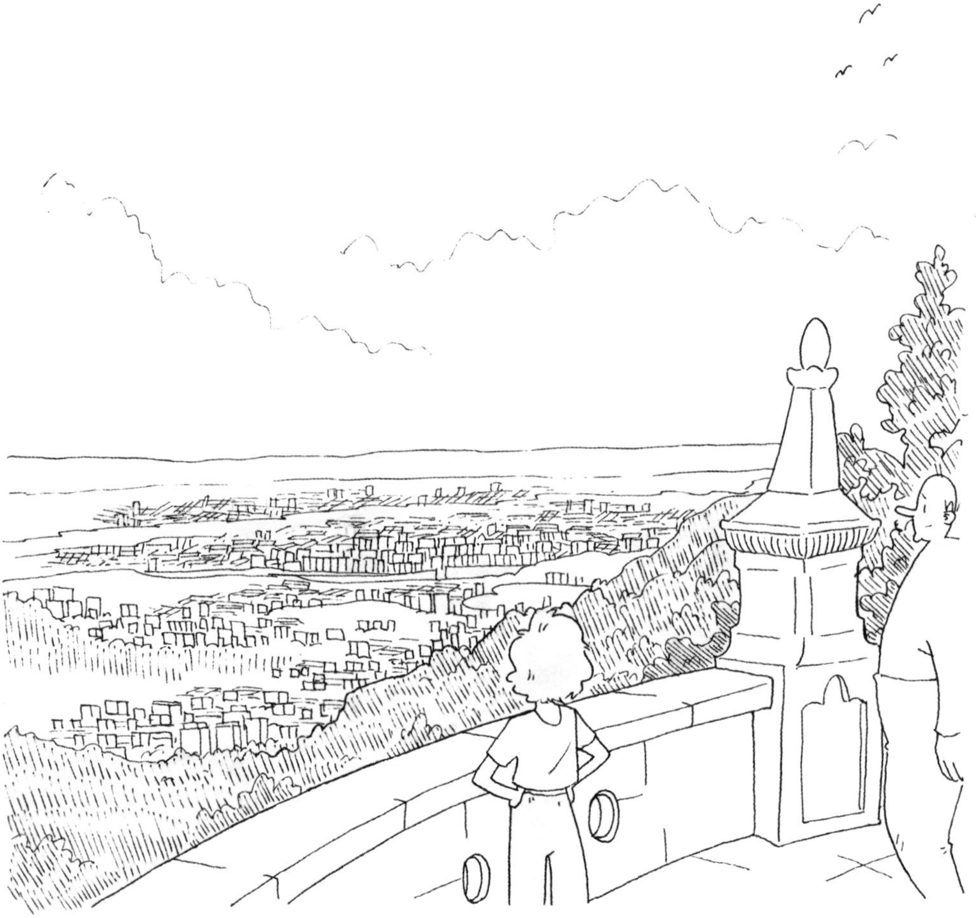

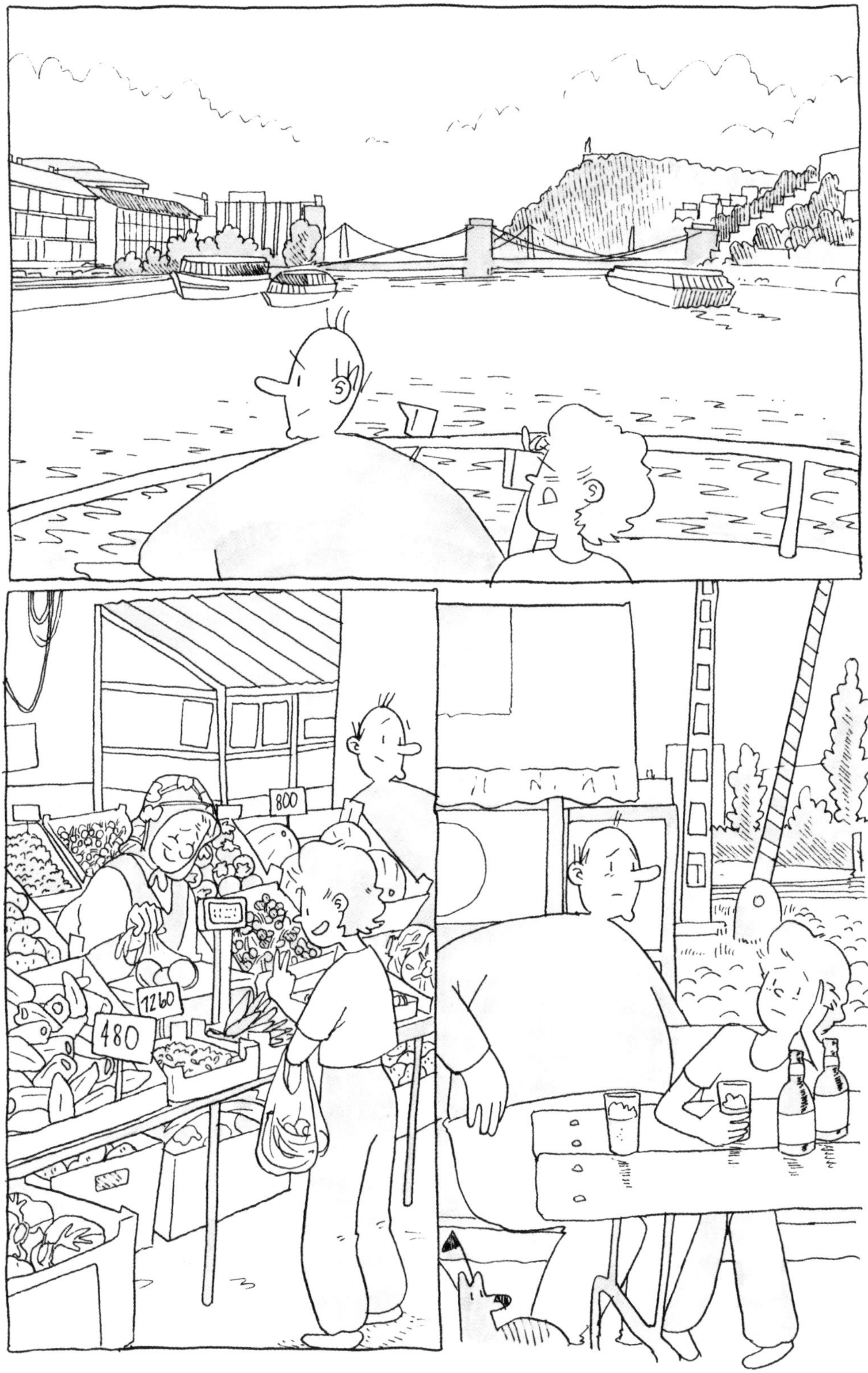
800
1260
480

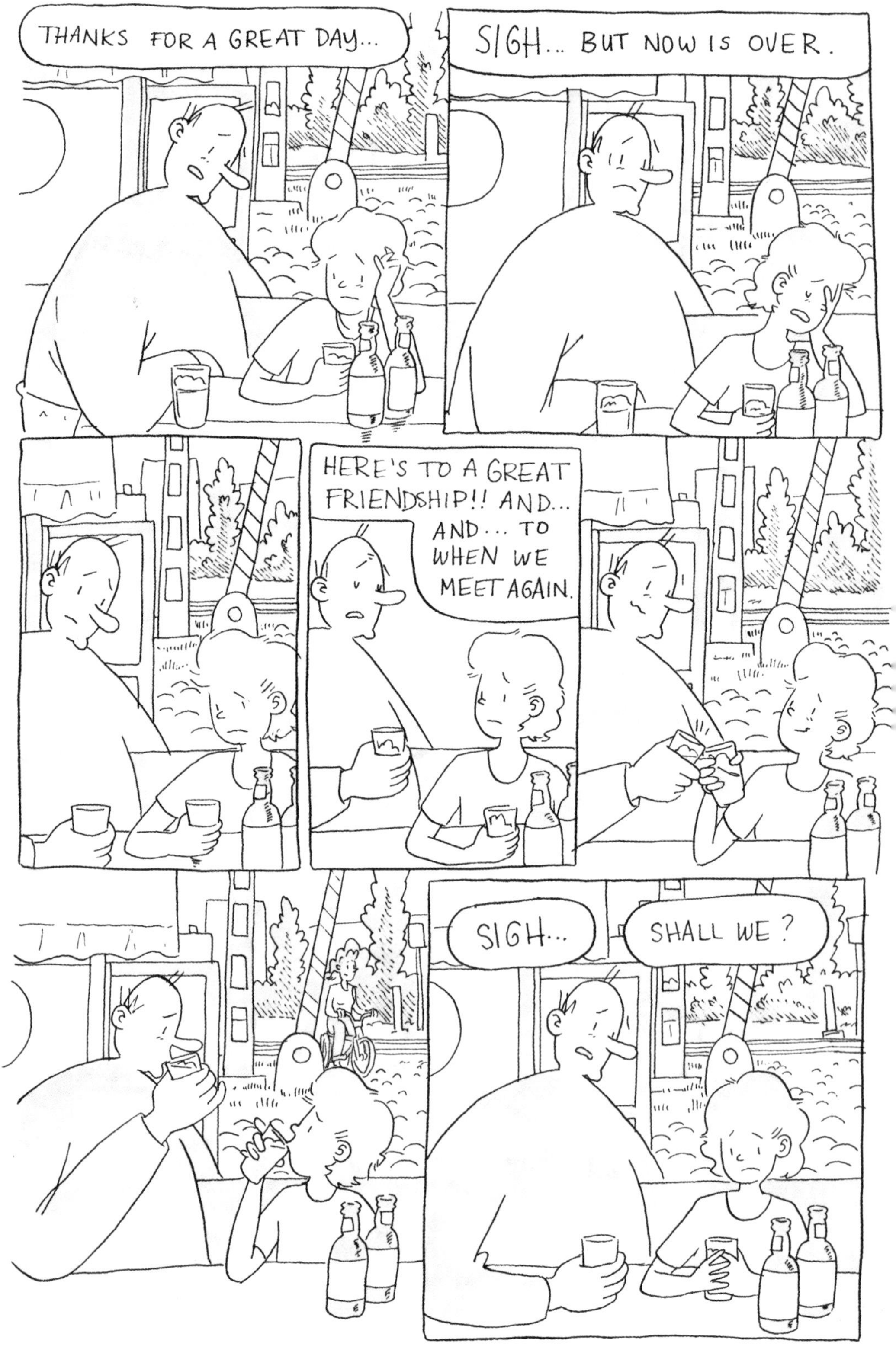
THANKS FOR A GREAT DAY...
SIGH... BUT NOW IS OVER.
HERE'S TO A GREAT FRIENDSHIP!! AND...
AND... TO WHEN WE MEET AGAIN.
SIGH...
SHALL WE?

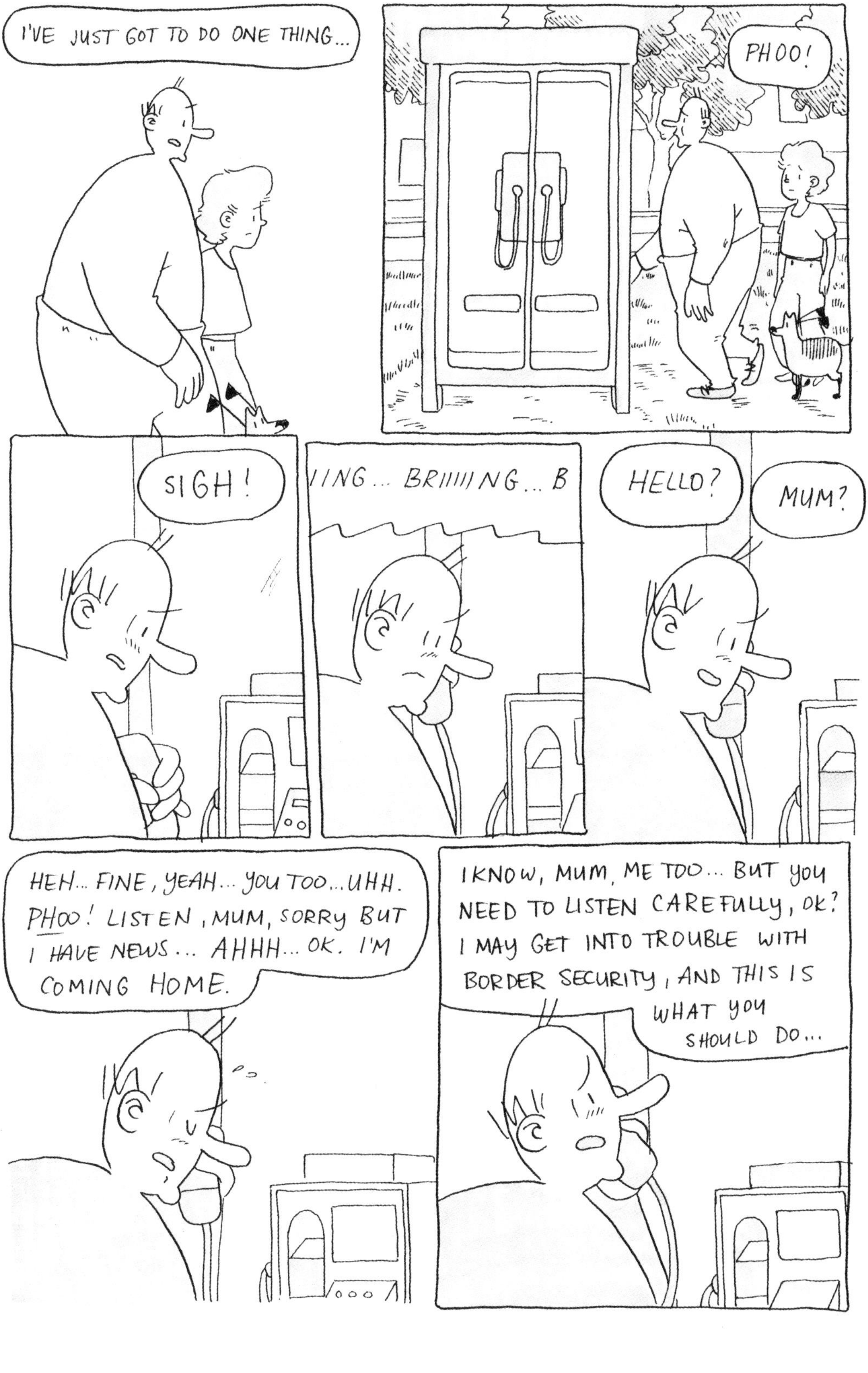
I'VE JUST GOT TO DO ONE THING...
PHOO!
SIGH!
IING... BRIIIIING... B
HELLO?
MUM?
HEH... FINE, YEAH... YOU TOO... UHH. PHOO! LISTEN, MUM, SORRY BUT I HAVE NEWS... AHHH... OK. I'M COMING HOME.
I KNOW, MUM, ME TOO... BUT YOU NEED TO LISTEN CAREFULLY, OK? I MAY GET INTO TROUBLE WITH BORDER SECURITY, AND THIS IS WHAT YOU SHOULD DO...

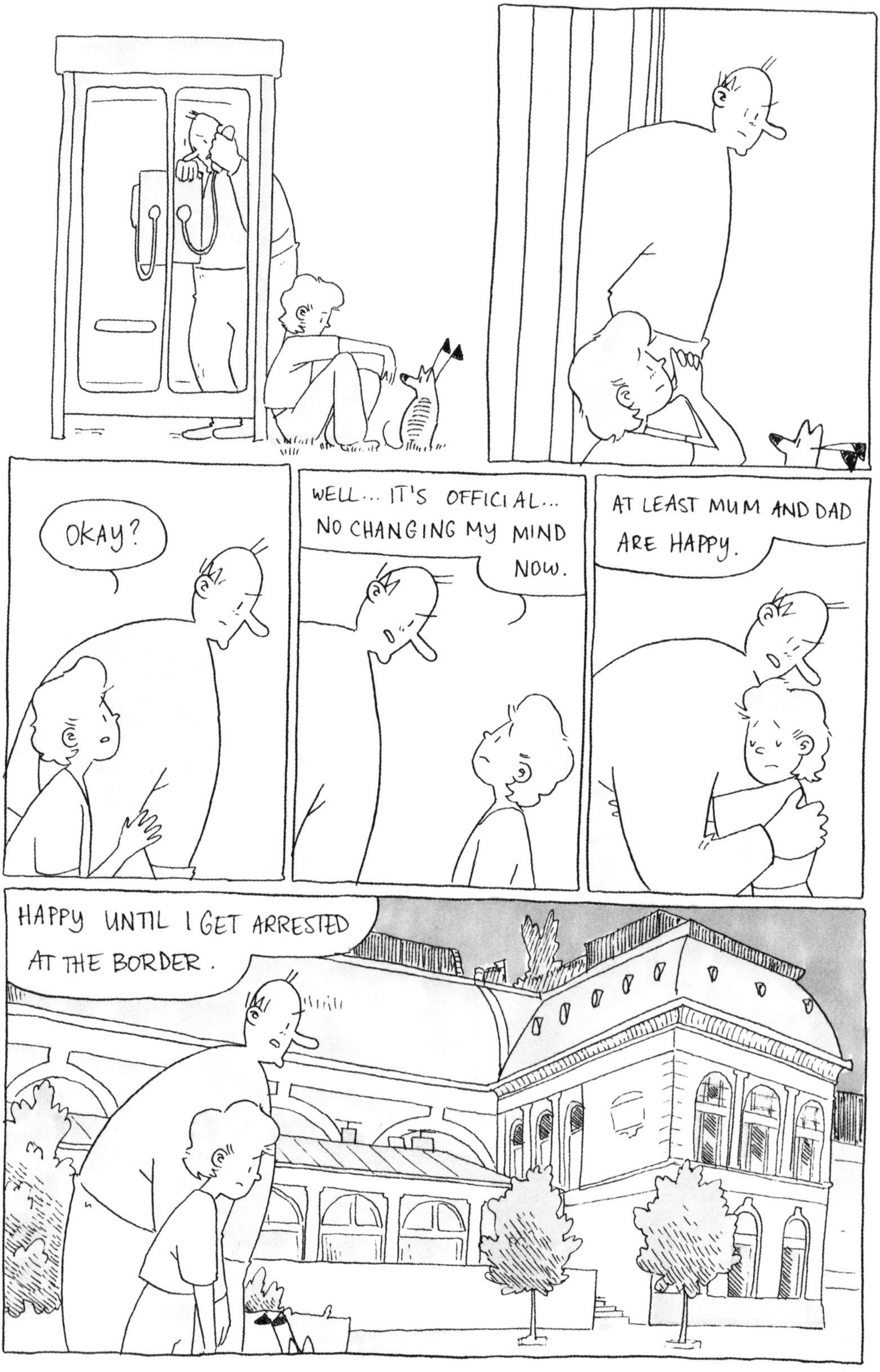
OKAY?
WELL... IT'S OFFICIAL... NO CHANGING MY MIND NOW.
AT LEAST MUM AND DAD ARE HAPPY.
HAPPY UNTIL I GET ARRESTED AT THE BORDER.

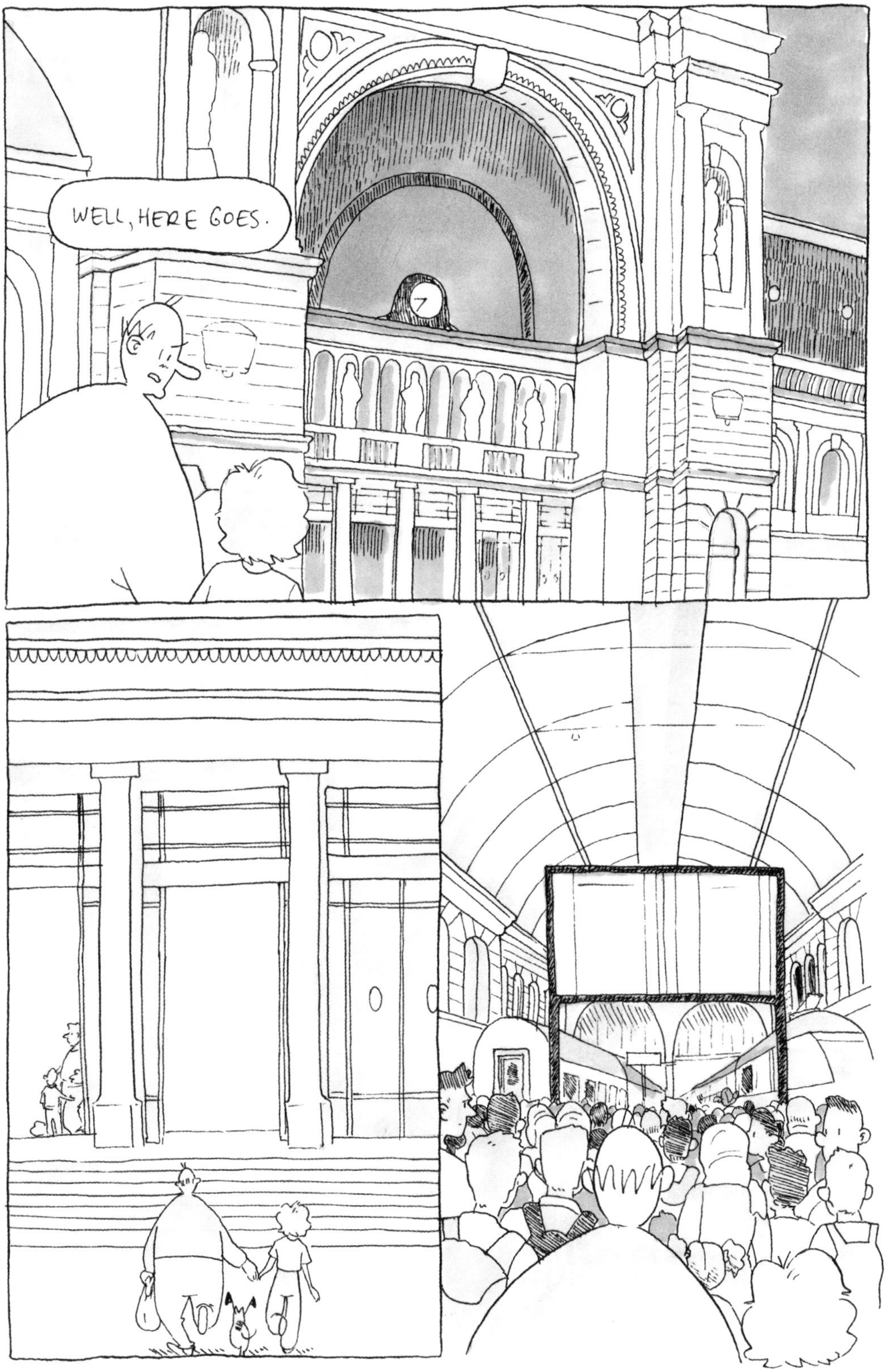
WELL, HERE GOES.

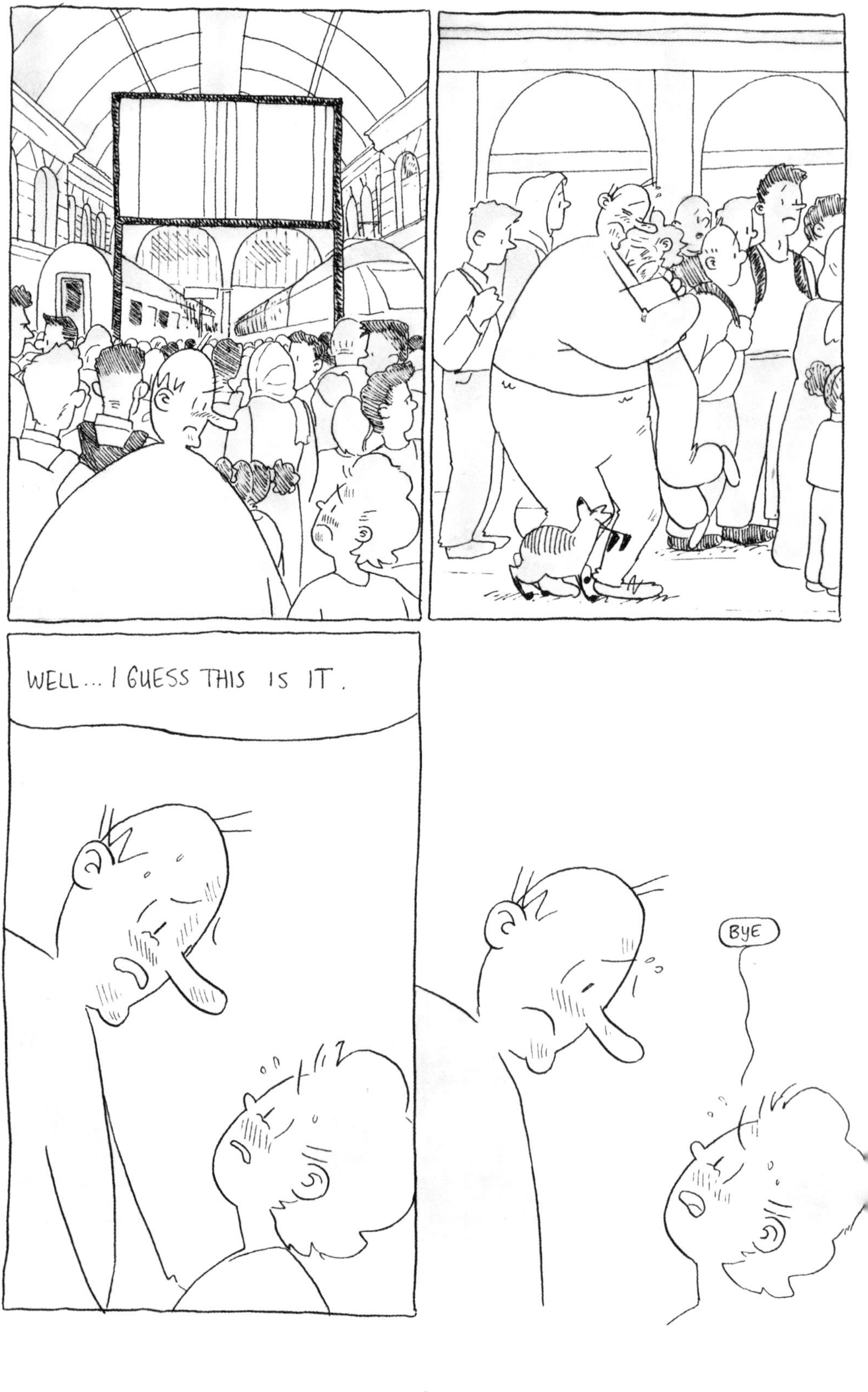
WELL... I GUESS THIS IS IT.
BYE

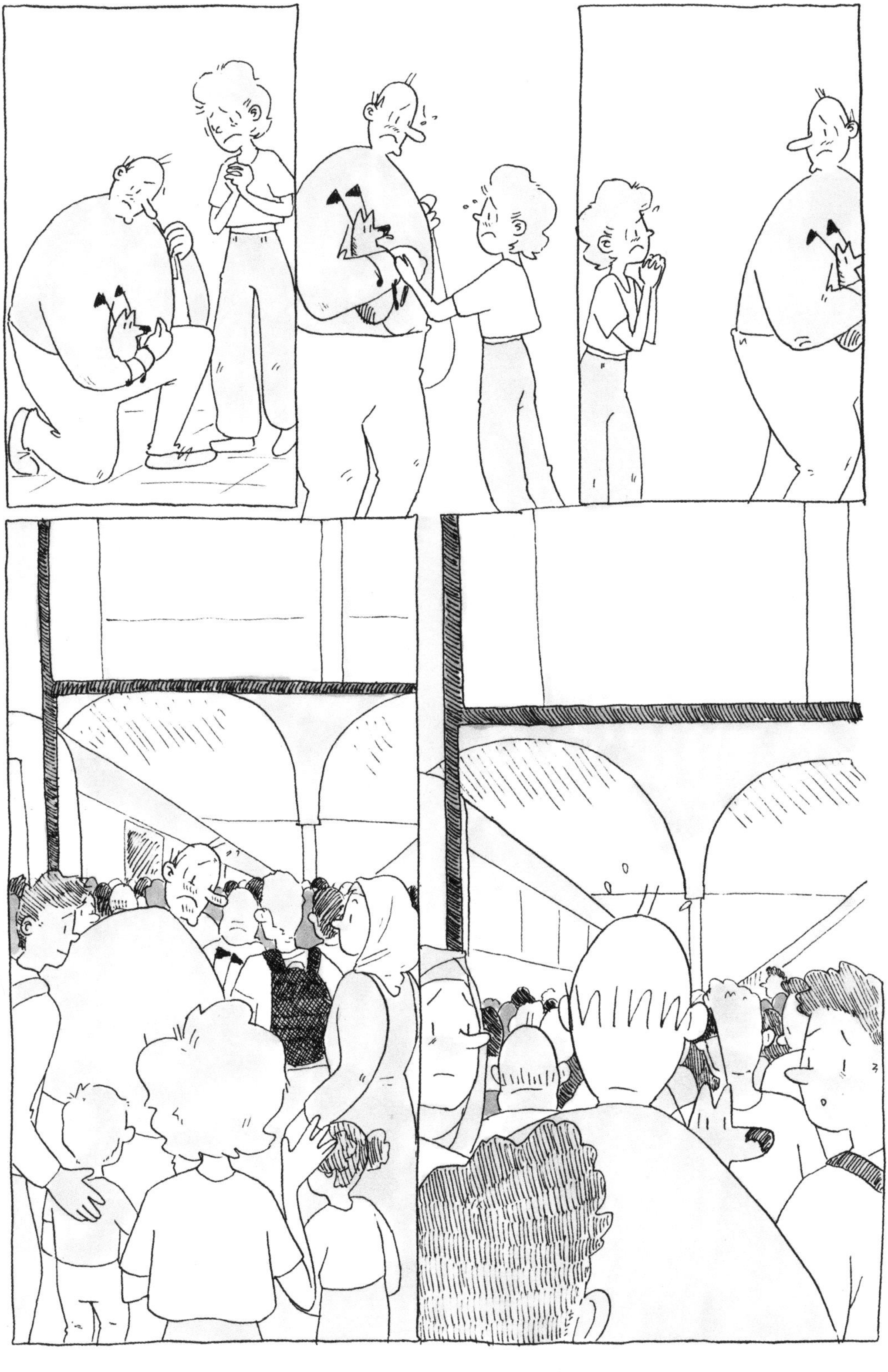

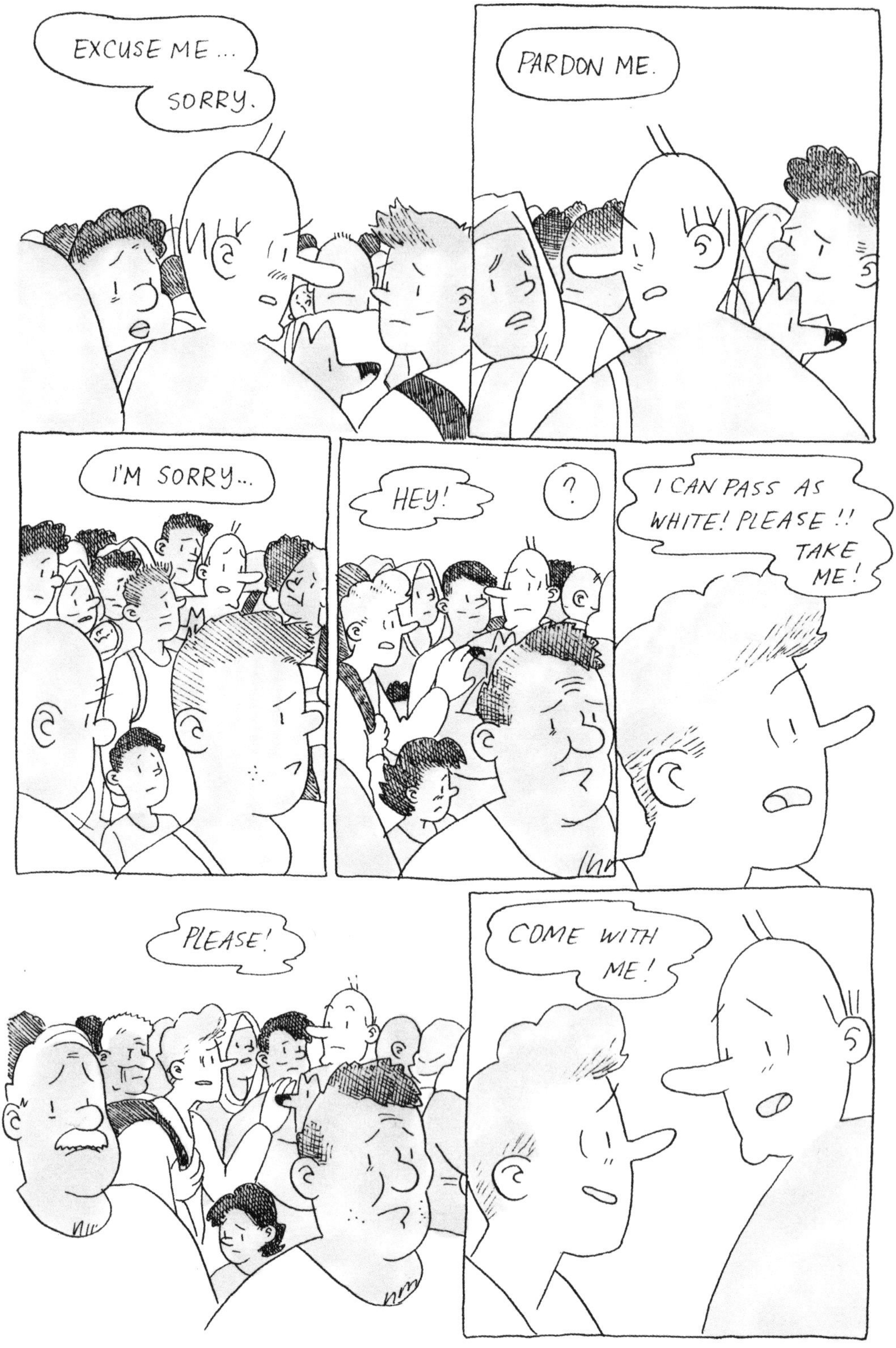
EXCUSE ME...
SORRY.
PARDON ME.
I'M SORRY...
HEY!
?
I CAN PASS AS WHITE! PLEASE!! TAKE ME!
PLEASE!
COME WITH ME!

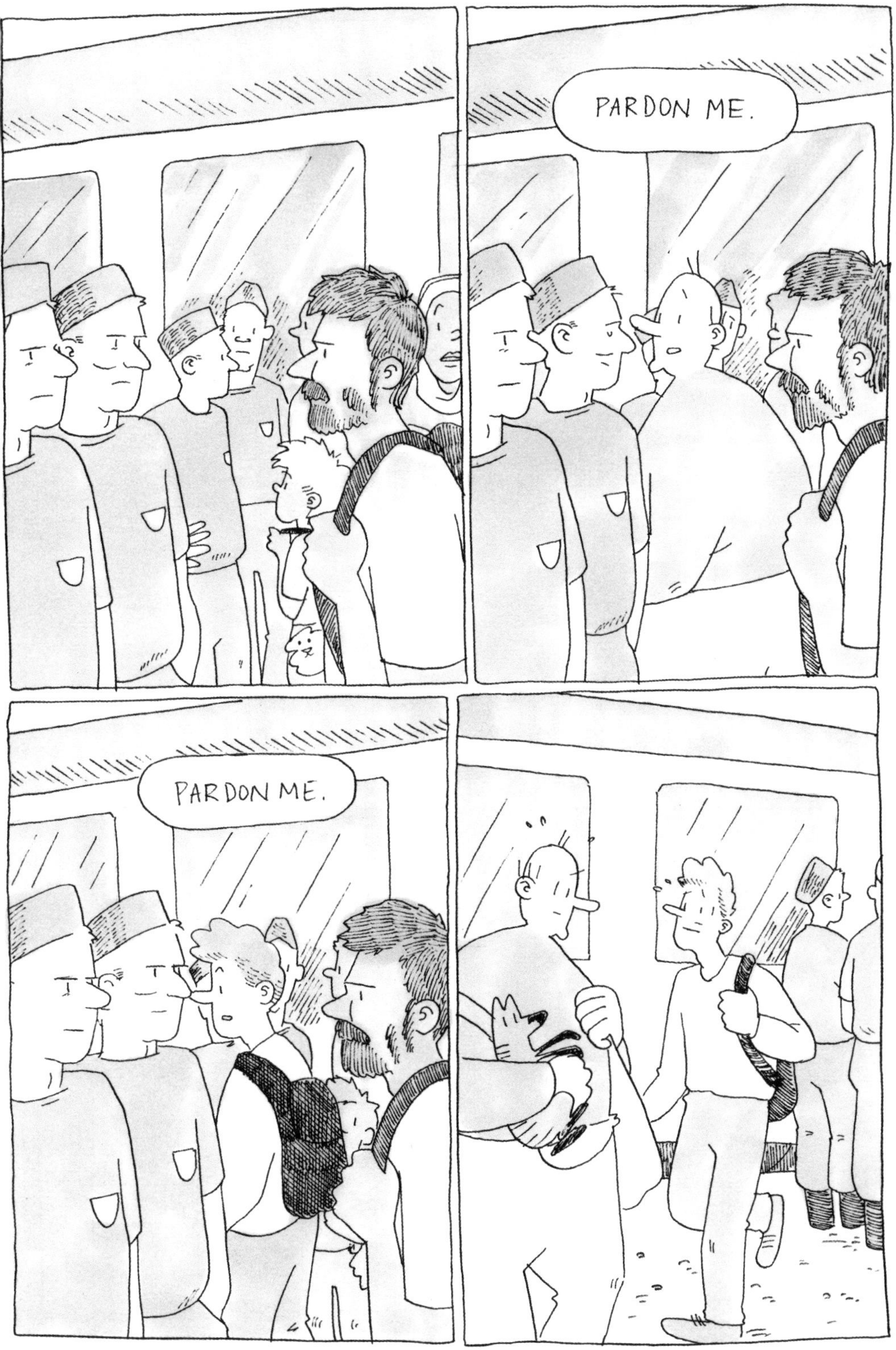
PARDON ME.
PARDON ME.

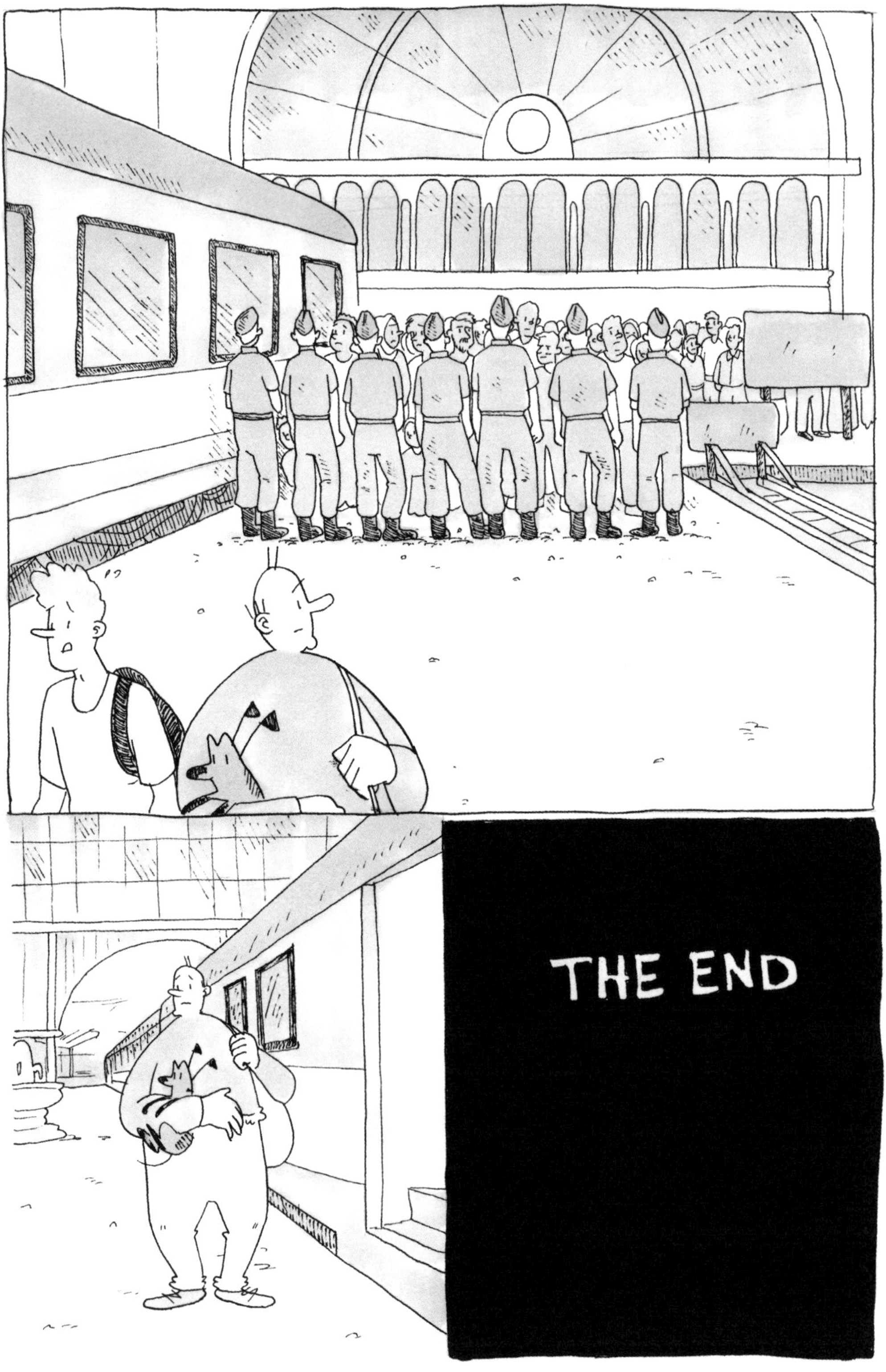
THE END

ACKNOWLEDGEMENTS

THANK YOU SO MUCH, ANDY BROWN
AND CONUNDRUM PRESS.
THANK YOU STEVEN SLIPP, SOL
UNDURRAGA AND JAN NIETFELD,
ANNA, ATTILA AND ABIGEL,
VERA SZABADKAI AND ALEXSANDAR
STOJANOVIC.